LEON TROTSKY

THE CHALLENGE OF THE LEFT OPPOSITION (1926-27)

Edited by Naomi Allen and George Saunders
with an Introduction by Naomi Allen

Pathfinder Press, New York

First Edition, 1980

Pathfinder Press
410 West Street
New York, N.Y. 10014

CONTENTS

Note About the Author   9
Preface   11
Introduction   15

Three Letters to Bukharin   35
Excerpts, Amendments to Rykov's Resolution:
    On the Economic Situation in the USSR   47
Notes on Economic Questions: The Law of
    Socialist Accumulation, the Planning
    Principle, the Rate of Industrialization,
    and—Lack of Principles   56
Party Bureaucratism and Party Democracy   61
Declaration of the Thirteen   73
For Equalization of Wages   93
Excerpts, The Elections to the Soviets   95
Questions and Answers about the Opposition   101
In Defense of the Opposition Bloc   109
Party Unity and the Danger of Split   112
Is Discussion Needed?   120
Statement of the Opposition   125
Speech to the Fifteenth Conference   130
Theses on Revolution and Counterrevolution   165
Speech to the Seventh (Enlarged) Plenum of
    the ECCI   173
Why the Opposition Will Vote Against the
    Resolution on Stalin's Report   190
Problems of the Comintern   195
For an Objective Assessment   205
National Aspects of Politics in Kazakhstan   210
Excerpts, Letter on the German "Lefts"   214
Stalin, the Peasant, and the Gramophone   222
Declaration of the Eighty-four   224
Letter to Krupskaya   240
The Party Crisis Deepens   244
Excerpts, Resolution of the All-Russia
    Metal Workers Union   249
"Defeatism" and Clemenceau   252

To a Member of the "Buffer Group" 254
Thermidor 258
The Opposition's "Insurrectionism":
A Statement on Molotov's Speech 265
Speech to the Joint Plenum of the CC and the CCC 270
Statement of the Thirteen 291
Protest on Abridgement of the Statement
of the Thirteen 296
Letter on the Tactics of the Opposition 298
Platform of the Opposition: The Party Crisis
and How to Overcome It 301
1. Introduction 302
2. The Situation of the Working Class
and the Trade Unions 311
3. The Peasantry—the Agrarian Question
and Socialist Construction 322
4. State Industry and the Building of
Socialism 330
5. The Soviets 340
6. The National Question 344
7. The Party 349
8. The Communist League of Youth 362
9. Our International Situation
and the War Danger 365
10. The Red Army and Navy 382
11. On the Real Issues in Dispute,
and the Artificial Ones 383
12. Against Opportunism—For the Unity
of the Party 388
The Clemenceau Thesis and the Party Regime 395
Excerpts, Speech to the Presidium of the ECCI 405
The Opposition and the Wrangel Officer 415
Excerpts, The Seven-Hour Day 428
Excerpts, Recognition of the Tsarist Debts 433
The Fear of Our Platform 437
How They Corrupt the Communist League of Youth:
A Letter to a Party Member in the League 449
Our Tone in the Discussion 452
Excerpts, Countertheses on the Five-Year Plan 455
Summing Up the Tenth Anniversary Events 463
For an Inquiry into the Attacks on
Oppositionists 467
In Memory of A. A. Joffe 470
The Opposition "Statement" and the Situation
in the Party 473
The Statement of the 121 481

Two Statements to the Fifteenth Congress 485
   I—The Zinovievist Statement 485
   II—The Trotskyist Statement 486
At a New Stage 488

Glossary 511
Further Reading 529
Index 533

LEON TROTSKY was born Lev Davidovich Bronstein in 1879 in the Ukraine. His first arrest for revolutionary activity was in 1898. He was exiled to Siberia, but escaped to collaborate with Lenin on *Iskra* in London in 1902. He broke with Lenin the following year at the time of the split between Bolsheviks and Mensheviks, was briefly aligned with the Mensheviks, but in 1904 broke with them and began a decade-long effort to reunite the Russian Social Democratic Labor Party. During the 1905 revolution he was the leader of the St. Petersburg Soviet and developed his theory of permanent revolution. He was again exiled to Siberia and again escaped. He was part of the tiny minority in the socialist movement who refused to support their governments in World War I. When the February revolution broke out in 1917 he was in New York, but he arrived back in Russia in May, joined the Bolshevik Party, was elected to its Central Committee, and in October was the leader of the Petrograd Soviet and the chief organizer of the Bolshevik insurrection. As the first commissar of foreign affairs, he headed the Soviet delegation to negotiate a peace with Germany at Brest-Litovsk. As commissar of war (1918-25) he created the Red Army and led it to victory through three years of civil war and imperialist intervention. He was a member of the Politburo of the Russian Communist Party from its formation until 1926, and of the Executive Committee of the Communist International from 1920 to 1927. He formed the Left Opposition in 1923 to fight for the preservation of Leninist internationalism and proletarian democracy. Defeated by the Stalin faction, he was expelled from the party in 1927, exiled first to Siberia in 1928 and then to Turkey in 1929. In 1933 he abandoned his efforts to reform the Communist International and called for the creation of a new International. He viewed his work on behalf of the Fourth International, founded in 1938, as the most important work of his life. In his final exile he was hounded from country to country by both the Stalinists and the fascists. He lived in Turkey until 1933, France until 1935, Norway until 1936, and Mexico until his death in August 1940 at the hands of a Stalinist assassin.

PREFACE

This is the second volume in a series of Trotsky's writings presenting the ideas of the Soviet Left Opposition on the main issues in dispute between its founding in 1923 and 1929, when Trotsky was deported from the Soviet Union. The present volume covers the years 1926 and 1927, during which the most important events were the formation of the United Opposition bloc with Zinoviev and Kamenev; the defeats of the British General Strike and the Chinese revolution; the debates over socialism in one country, industrial and agricultural policy, bureaucratism, Thermidor, and the first five-year plan; the threat of a new war by the capitalist powers against the Soviet Union, and the "Clemenceau thesis"; the Fifteenth Congress of the All-Union Communist Party; the expulsion of the Opposition from the party and from the Comintern; and the break-up of the Opposition bloc.

Unlike the first volume of this series, this one contains several documents that were written collectively by the leaders of the Opposition bloc, including the Platform of the Opposition. In cases where differences of opinion existed over political questions that had to be dealt with, the final version therefore represented some degree of compromise, rather than Trotsky's own position. This is particularly noticeable whenever the Chinese events are mentioned, but it is also evident on other questions. These joint productions have been included in a volume devoted primarily to the views of Trotsky and his closest cothinkers because they constitute the major documents of the struggle; because they have no other currency in English; and because in the last several years comprehensive and authoritative collections of Trotsky's writings on Britain and China have appeared, making indisputably clear what Trotsky's political assessments of these developments were and how his views differed from those of his associates in the Opposition bloc.* Moreover, Trotsky can be

---

Leon Trotsky on Britain (New York: Monad Press, 1973), 334 pages, and *Leon Trotsky on China* (Monad Press, 1976), 688 pages, are both

considered the main author of these collaborative efforts.

Considerations of space led us to omit Trotsky's key pronouncements on Britain and China. Readers whose chief interest is in the British and Chinese events of those years should go to the aforementioned books for Trotsky's writings on them. Here we have limited ourselves to mere outlines of the events in the introduction and references in the appropriate places. Other important documents of this period have been omitted because they are available in Trotsky's *Stalin School of Falsification* (Pathfinder, 1972).

In 1940, while writing his biography of Stalin, shortly before Trotsky sold his archives to Harvard University, he had occasion to look back over the Oppositionist writings of 1926-27 which he had brought out of the Soviet Union with him. In June or July 1940, he made a selection from those writings, apparently in consultation with leaders of the Socialist Workers Party, his cothinkers in the United States. The intention seems to have been that his American cothinkers would translate and publish this selection. And a start was made, for some of them appeared in the *Fouth International* magazine in 1941. But U.S. entry into World War II, and then the Cold War and McCarthyism, intervened, so that the project never saw completion. This 1940 selection, now housed in the Library of Social History in New York, was generously made available to the editors. The choice of what to include in this book is partly based on that selection.

A glossary and a list of Trotsky's other writings of this period are in the back of this book. Some of the pieces collected here were published in English in the 1920s or 30s but have been out of print for decades. Most of them were written not for publication but for the leadership bodies of the party. But even of those that were written for publication, almost all were banned from the Soviet press and are translated from the Russian and published here for the first time in any language. Some were written for Oppositionists and were circulated privately. An editorial note preceding each selection explains its source and gives other information about the events mentioned in it. To assist the reader, an account of the major events of these two years has been included in the editorial notes before each selection.

All translations are by George Saunders from the original Russian, unless otherwise indicated. Wherever possible, we have replaced Trotsky's citations of Russian texts with references to the standard English translation: in the case of Lenin's works, all references are to the English edition of the *Collected Works* (Moscow: Progress Publishers, 1960-69).

Of great help in compiling this volume was Louis Sinclair's *Leon Trotsky: A Bibliography* (Hoover Institution Press, 1972). This project could not have been successful without the kind permission of the Harvard College Library and the Library of Social History to examine, translate, and publish material in their collections.

The Editors

INTRODUCTION

The first volume in this series ended with the Fourteenth Party Congress in December 1925. This was the nadir in Trotsky's struggle to win the Soviet Communist Party back to Lenin's revolutionary internationalist program. He was alone and isolated, the target of a virulent slander campaign, and with no apparent avenues to continue the struggle.

However, the Fourteenth Congress—where the Russian Communist Party was renamed the All-Union Communist Party (AUCP)—had widened the split in the ruling Stalin-Zinoviev-Kamenev triumvirate. Feeling the pressure of the unrest and anxiety in the proletariat of Leningrad, Zinoviev and Kamenev had openly assailed Stalin's rejection of Leninist internationalism masked by the false theory of "socialism in one country," his policies in support of the rich peasants and the top layer of the petty bourgeoisie in general, and his resistance to a program for industrialization of the country. This split, which Trotsky underestimated at first, laid the basis for a realignment of forces in the leadership of the Soviet CP: Stalin, the apparatus man, turned to the right to Bukharin, Rykov, and Tomsky for a bloc that could give him a majority on the Politburo; while Trotsky and the Zinovievists were eventually able to cement an alliance that would make possible a new challenge to the bureaucracy, this time by a greatly expanded Leninist opposition with better prospects. The years 1926-27 witnessed the decisive struggle between the Opposition, with its new reinforcements from Leningrad, and the bureaucracy.

The United Opposition—composed of the veterans of the 1923-25 Opposition led by Trotsky, which had continued the fight that Lenin had organized at the end of his active life against the course of the bureaucracy, and the Leningrad followers of Zinoviev and Kamenev—was formed in April 1926, following a plenum (full meeting) of the CP Central Committee. It lasted until the Opposition was expelled from the party at the Fifteenth Party

---

Notes to the Introduction begin on p. 33.

Congress in December 1927, whereupon the Zinovievist leaders at once capitulated. The new bloc was not a homogeneous political grouping. It encompassed important political differences on such critical questions as Communist policy in the Chinese revolution and the character of the participation in the Anglo-Russian Trade Union Unity Committee; nor was there always agreement at key junctures on tactics in the inner-party struggle. Especially when the heavy hand of Stalinist repression was brought to bear, the Zinovievists vacillated or panicked and tended to prefer a conciliatory policy to one that was politically uncompromising. Moreover, they were sensitive to the Stalinist charge that they had capitulated to "Trotskyism." Zinoviev did not agree with the theory of permanent revolution, which Trotsky had elaborated twenty years earlier as a guide to action in prerevolutionary Russia, and the Stalinists were eager to drive a wedge between the allies by hammering away at their differences.

In addition to the Trotskyists and the Zinoviev-Kamenev group, there were other currents in the United Opposition. For a time at least, it included some former members of earlier syndicalist and ultraleft groups—the Democratic Centralists, Workers Opposition, and others. And there were also differences among those who were generally viewed as Trotsky's cothinkers, which would become more important after the Opposition's expulsion at the end of 1927. Nevertheless, the United Opposition was the instrument that Trotsky used to try to unite and mobilize the party veterans and arouse the proletarian core of the party to defeat Stalin on the central questions—the need to return to a revolutionary internationalist policy, the lack of party democracy, the political and economic concessions to the rich peasant at the expense of the worker, the need for a greatly stepped-up program of industrialization—all of which weakened the Soviet Union in the face of imperialism abroad and of the forces promoting capitalist restoration within.

Moreover, the formation of the Opposition bloc forced Zinoviev and Kamenev to publicly acknowledge the correctness of the 1923 Opposition and exposed the campaign against "Trotskyism" as an invention of the apparatus. By joining forces with Trotsky they broke the illusion that the party leadership was divided between Old Bolsheviks (who were, by implication, orthodox Leninists) and latecomers like Trotsky (who supposedly were not). And thousands of revolutionary workers who followed the Zinovievists came over firmly and for good to the Left Opposition, staying with it even after the Zinovievist leaders capitulated.

Under the pressure of the Opposition's criticisms Stalin and Bukharin were forced to retreat from the most blatant measures favoring the expansion of private capitalism and to adopt features of the Opposition's program. The Opposition could claim responsibility for forcing Stalin to back down on plans to dismantle the state monopoly of foreign trade; to continue resisting industrialization; to favor the wealthy peasants with tax breaks at the expense of the poor and middle peasants, agricultural laborers, and workers. It was at the Opposition's insistence that drafts for a comprehensive long-term economic plan were finally issued.

In an article written after the expulsion of the Opposition at the Fifteenth Congress, Trotsky said that its main task, despite all adversity, was to ensure the continuance of a genuinely Bolshevik party.[1] That meant to keep alive the history, traditions, and program of Bolshevism by preserving a cadre of educated and devoted revolutionists who could put their program into action when the opportunity arose. That was probably the chief contribution of the Opposition, a contribution that has had lasting effects despite organizational defeat and expulsion, the capitulations of many of its members, and Stalin's attempt to physically annihilate all traces of Bolshevism. And it was the Opposition's tireless theoretical and educational work during these years of semi-legality (1926-27) as well as in exile and deportation (from 1928 on) that provided the foundation for the International Left Opposition and Opposition groups around the world. Some of the questions that were explored in the discussions within the Opposition were: the social causes of the bureaucracy's rise and consolidation; Thermidor—what it was and how far, if at all, it had triumphed in the USSR;* the

---

*Trotsky's main ideas about Thermidor at this time are in his summer 1927 article by that title in this volume (p. 258). Before 1935, Trotsky used the term to mean capitalist counterrevolution. (The term was taken by analogy from a shift of power in the French revolution in Thermidor (July) 1794, when the radical Jacobins led by Robespierre were overthrown by a right wing in the revolutionary camp. The flaw in the analogy was that the French Thermidor, while opening up a period of reaction, did not go so far as to restore the feudal system.) In 1935 Trotsky modified his theory (see "The Workers' State, Thermidor and Bonapartism," in *Writings of Leon Trotsky [1934-35]*). From then on he used the term to mean a reactionary development, which jeopardized the course of the revolution, but which occurred "on the social foundation of the revolution" and which therefore did not alter the class character of the

meaning of the theory of socialism in one country; the applicability of the theory of permanent revolution to the colonial revolution in general; the relation of Lenin's concept of "democratic dictatorship" to the dictatorship of the proletariat; how a revolution in a technologically underdeveloped country, with a vast majority of peasants, can survive a protracted lull in the world revolution. The products of many of these discussions and others still enrich our understanding of major changes in the world since the October Revolution.

About the organizational side of the Opposition's struggle to return the party to the road of Leninism, very little emerges in Trotsky's archives. In part this is no doubt because it was necessary to observe the strictest secrecy in the face of the Stalinists' ruthless suppression of dissent. From the outset Oppositionists were plagued by GPU spying, disciplinary reprisals, including discharge from their jobs—which often meant extreme hardship for their families—expulsion from the party, physical abuse, and "transfers" to remote parts of the country. Later, when the pressure was increased, even being suspected of Opposition sympathies meant almost certain loss of employment, imprisonment, or exile. The Opposition therefore was condemned to semi-clandestinity in its organizational measures even before its formal expulsion from the party. The little that is known about its internal life comes mostly from its enemies and from scattered and not always reliable memoirs. Stalin claimed in 1927 that the Opposition had received 6,000 votes (against 725,000 who voted for the majority) and that perhaps 20,000 others had sympathized with the Opposition but did not vote.[2] Ten years later Trotsky estimated that in 1927 the Opposition had had 20,000 or 30,000 active members in Moscow alone.[3] According to the proceedings of the Fifteenth Congress, the Opposition published a daily bulletin right up until the congress.[4] The Opposition had a leadership which met, exchanged ideas, and negotiated the formulations that would be used in common declarations. Hundreds, perhaps thousands, of rank-and-file party members met secretly to discuss the Opposition's Platform

---

state. By these criteria, it became apparent to Trotsky in 1935 that the Russian Thermidor had triumphed in 1924-25, when the Stalinist bureaucracy took control of the state and the party. From then on he included the Stalinists among the Thermidorians instead of considering them centrists who merely gave objective aid to the Thermidorian forces.

and other documents and to debate the crucial questions of party life. But virtually no record of these meetings exists. As a result of the semi-clandestine existence of the Opposition and its paramount need for secrecy, much of its history is still obscure, and will be until the archives of the Soviet CP and secret police are opened. To make matters worse, although Trotsky maintained a personal archive from 1917 on, he did not begin systematically keeping every political document he wrote or acquired until 1928. This means that historians of the period have to surmise much about the actual course of the struggle, based on what is known about the class forces, the political events, and the individuals who figured in them.

In Soviet Russia's diplomatic relations with the imperialist world, this volume opens at the twilight of the relatively stable period that followed the conclusion of the civil war. The Locarno pact (October 1925), a military security pact between Great Britain, France, Italy, Germany, Poland, and Czechoslovakia, was widely regarded as a menacing anti-Soviet alliance. The spring of 1926 saw new war clouds gathering on the horizon which refused to disperse. The increasingly ominous threats of war would find an echo in the inner-party conflicts as both sides offered different proposals on how to cope with the war danger.

Two international events above all are central to the development of the struggle between the Leninist Left Opposition and the Soviet bureaucracy during these years: the defeats of the British General Strike and of the revolutionary upsurge in China. Neither of these is discussed at length in this volume because other books by Trotsky have been devoted to both. There is no substitute for reading those books, but some exposition of the events is necessary for an understanding of the development of the United Opposition and the inner-party struggle.

The Anglo-Russian Trade Union Unity Committee (ARC) was established in May 1925. It was an alliance between the trade union movements of England and the Soviet Union to promote trade union unity and to oppose capitalist reaction and the danger of new wars. The reformist British union officials wanted to use the alliance to bolster their credentials as "left-wingers" with the radicalizing ranks of the British working class. The Stalin-Bukharin group wanted to use it as a diplomatic tool, fostered illusions in the British union leaders, and promoted the pact as an alternative to the weak, inexperienced British CP. The alliance was invested with magical properties: it would allegedly

extend the influence of British communism and weaken the grasp
of the reformist leaders on the masses.
Trotsky supported the formation of the ARC and a temporary
bloc with the British union leaders. But when the General Strike
broke out in May 1926, and the reformist leaders strangled it in a
matter of days, he insisted that the Communists had to break
with them. Instead of advancing a revolutionary confrontation,
the ARC was now providing the labor bureaucracy with a mantle
of Soviet authority in crushing the workers. And the British
Communists, to avoid embarrassing the ARC, refrained from
sharply criticizing the reformist leaders. Trotsky called for the
Soviet unions to withdraw from the alliance, but the Stalinists
clung to it even after the ARC failed to condemn the British
bombardment of Nanking in March 1927. It remained for the
British reformists to rupture relations when it served their
purposes, and they did so in September 1927, when the imperialist offensive against China was under way, and shortly after
their government had broken off relations with the Soviet government.

In June 1928, Trotsky wrote that the weakness of the ARC was
that it had been viewed not as an episodic bloc with the reformist
leadership—which would have to be broken when the mass
movement turned in a revolutionary direction—but as a permanent alliance standing above the needs of the class struggle. Not
only Stalin, Bukharin, Tomsky, etc., but also—at least in the
beginning—Zinoviev, hoped to appease British imperialism
through the ARC and thus refused to use it as an instrument of
the class struggle in England.

Trotsky feared that Soviet policy in Britain was suffering from
the effects of the isolationist trend in Soviet foreign policy. Stalin
and Bukharin were using the alliance between the two trade
union federations to mollify the British bourgeoisie. They were
doing it at the expense of the workers' movement in England; and
an opportunity that could have posed a mortal threat to British
capitalism—or at least could have been used to build the British
CP and assure its future—instead was passed up for purely
diplomatic considerations.

Developments in China revealed similar tendencies by the
Stalinists. Just as Stalin put his confidence in the reformist union
leaders in Britain, he put his confidence in Chiang Kai-shek and
his Kuomintang (Nationalist Party) in China.

The Chinese Communists had been instructed by the Comintern to join the bourgeois Kuomintang in 1923. CCP leaders tried

to convince Moscow that they should sever their ties with the KMT, but in vain. Neither Stalin nor Bukharin believed in the future of Chinese communism and both wanted to keep the alliance with the KMT for diplomatic reasons. They were prepared to sacrifice the growth of Communist influence, if necessary, to maintain that alliance. To justify their position, Stalin and Bukharin insisted that the Chinese revolution was bourgeois; that the bourgeoisie in the KMT was revolutionary; that the CP had to maintain unity with it and not antagonize it. And they invoked Lenin to give the aura of orthodoxy to their theory: in 1905 he had urged socialists in Russia to aim at a "democratic dictatorship of the workers and peasants," on the road to a proletarian dictatorship. They neglected to mention that Lenin had emphasized that the bourgeois revolution could win in Russia only under the leadership of the workers, against the liberal bourgeoisie; and they also omitted the fact that in 1917 Lenin and Trotsky agreed that a situation of dual power appeared with the February overthrow of the tsar, and that the task was for the workers through their soviets to take power and, in alliance with the peasantry, establish the dictatorship of the proletariat and carry out socialist measures.

Early in 1926 the Comintern admitted Chiang as an honorary member of its Executive Committee and the Kuomintang as an associate party. A few weeks later, in late March, Chiang carried out his first anti-Communist coup, banning Communists from posts in the KMT and demanding a list of CCP members in the KMT. Stalin and Bukharin sent instructions that the CCP was to accede to all demands. The Moscow newspapers were silent.

Trotsky promptly protested the admission of the KMT to the Comintern and the adherence of CCP members to the KMT. But even Zinoviev and Kamenev, who had broken with Stalin and were on the verge of forming the United Opposition with Trotsky, defended the official position. In July, Chiang began the Northern Expedition, and city after city, under the influence of the Communists, fell to his army. Inspired by the urban victories, peasants rose against the landlords. Chiang became fearful of the revolutionary wave, forbidding strikes, suppressing trade unions, dispatching punitive expeditions to subdue the peasants. Again the CCP leadership asked permission to withdraw from the KMT, and again Moscow refused. Bukharin insisted, at the Fifteenth Party Conference in October 1926, that the Communists' main objective was to safeguard the unity of all anti-imperialist forces and to repulse threats to KMT unity.

In the spring of 1927, the workers of Shanghai, led by the Communists, seized control of the city. When the Comintern demanded that they lay down their arms to Chiang, the CCP obeyed. On April 12 Chiang ordered a massacre that claimed the lives of tens of thousands of workers and Communists. But even this debacle did not produce a rectification of Stalin's line in China: he directed the CCP to cooperate with the KMT "left wing" leader, Wang Ching-wei. In July, Wang too turned on the Communists. In desperation, to try to save the day and avoid the exposure of his disastrous policy, Stalin ordered an insurrection in Canton in December. It was crushed, and along with it the hopes for a Chinese Soviet government for many years to come.

It was during the workers' insurrection in Shanghai, and before Chiang's bloody massacre, that the Opposition made China a central question in its fight with the Stalin-Bukharin leadership. That they waited so long is not surprising. In the phase of the struggle for leadership of the Soviet party and Comintern that began in the spring of 1926, the principal issues were party democracy, the rate of industrialization, the policy toward the wealthy peasant, and the Anglo-Russian Committee. Trotsky initially favored an alliance with the KMT, but he wanted an alliance of two parties, in which the Communists would retain their independence and maintain a class policy that would go as far as possible toward consolidating the interests of the proletariat in China. But his allies in the United Opposition did not share his full position on China. Even in September 1927, after both the right (Chiang Kai-shek) and the left (Wang Ching-wei) wings of the KMT had savagely turned on the Communists, the United Opposition, in its keynote Platform, coauthored by Zinovievists and Trotskyists, did not call for withdrawal of the CCP from the KMT.

The events of 1926-27 marked a transition in Trotsky's thinking on the subject of the theory of permanent revolution. He had originally put it forward as a theory for the revolution in Russia only. The Second Congress of the Communist International adopted, in a report by Lenin, the view that soviets and a soviet revolution could appear in all countries after the experience of the Russian Revolution. Under fire by the Stalinists, Trotsky in 1923-25 had been willing to relegate permanent revolution to the archives to avoid letting it become an issue in the inner-party struggle. It was the impact of the Chinese revolution that convinced him that his theory of permanent revolution could be correctly applied to China. In the spring and summer of 1927, under the influence of the events in China, Trotsky reached the conclusion that the Chinese working class could follow the example of the Russian workers and take power, with the support of worker and peasant soviets, despite the absence of the material prerequisites for an industrial planned economy, as had been envisaged for the colonial countries in general in Lenin's report to the Second Congress of the Comintern in 1920. But by this time he was in a bloc with people who were not in complete agreement with him on the Chinese question. This limited his ability to express his views fully. The third volume of this series will follow the development of Trotsky's thinking on the revolutionary strategy in the colonial countries and thus the generalization of the theory of permanent revolution, to where, after the break-up of the bloc, in exile, he fought out the issue in a new way with members of his own group, like Radek, who disagreed with it.

Trotsky hoped that the bloc with Zinoviev and Kamenev would defeat the Stalinists on the questions of Soviet economic policy and international Communist strategy, and he subordinated to that bloc the part of his program that was unacceptable to his allies. Although he was not able to say as much as he would have liked, his statements are clearly a correct counter political line to the positions of Stalin and Bukharin. The recent collection *Leon Trotsky on China* makes it possible for the first time to differentiate Trotsky's own views on the events in China from those of the United Opposition, which he presented publicly. It also reveals Trotsky's actual battles in the leadership bodies of the Soviet CP on the China question, news of which was suppressed by the Stalinist apparatus and prevented from reaching the ranks of the party.

The defeat of the British General Strike in the spring of 1926 gave courage to the British ruling class, which at once stepped up efforts to form an anti-Soviet bloc of European powers under British leadership. Pilsudski's coup d'état in Poland, also in the spring of 1926, heightened fears of imperialist intervention from an outpost right on Soviet Russia's border; this was followed at the end of 1926 by a similar coup in Lithuania. The major fear in Soviet circles was that Germany, which was being courted by all sides, would be drawn into an anti-Soviet bloc. The ink was hardly dry on a Soviet-German pact of April 1926 when Germany was admitted to the League of Nations, which caused some alarm in Moscow; in 1926 this predecessor of the United Nations was still understood by the Kremlin to be an instrument of imperialist policy. In November-December 1926, Soviet-German relations were jeopardized by a scandal over the secret production of arms in a Soviet factory using German technology and advisers, in violation of provisions of the Versailles pact.

In the spring and summer of 1927, anxiety over the war preparations of the European imperialists reached a fever pitch when Britain—after raids on Soviet offices in Peking and London—broke off relations with the Soviet Union in May. The Chinese revolution was suffering defeat after defeat, and there were fears of a commercial and financial blockade of the USSR. In June the Soviet representative in Warsaw, Voikov, was assassinated by a Russian emigré. In October, the French government expelled Soviet Ambassador Rakovsky—the pretext was his signature on an Opposition declaration calling upon workers in capitalist countries to work for their own governments' defeat in any war with the Soviet Union.

There is no doubt that much of the alarm felt in Moscow about the war danger was genuine. After the defeat of the German revolution in 1923-24, the Soviet Union entered a prolonged period of political isolation, deepened by the setbacks in England and in China, which emphasized its vulnerability. The Red Army was known to be in poor shape. As the domestic economic crisis persisted, morale declined both in the countryside and in the cities. Nevertheless, a certain portion of the frenzy over the war danger was produced cold-bloodedly by the party leadership, which used the atmosphere of panic to stifle internal dissent and to intimidate the Opposition with charges of a "united front from Chamberlain to Trotsky." As will be seen, the Opposition refused to be silenced. It reaffirmed its loyalty to the Soviet state; and at the same time insisted that the best defense against the danger of war was to abandon the policies that were producing defeat after defeat in revolutions abroad, general disorientation over political goals, and an aggravation of the economic crisis at home.

The theoretical source for many of the crimes and errors the Stalinists committed—or to put it more correctly, the theoretical construct erected to support their new policies—was the theory of socialism in one country. In December 1924, Stalin revised the long-held Bolshevik position to endorse the notion that in Russia an adequate basis existed for building socialism whether or not revolutions triumphed in the more industrially developed countries.[5] Stalin now stated that socialism could be established in the USSR and only "the complete victory" of socialism was impossible without revolutions in other countries. This theory found a certain receptive mood: discouragement and demoralization due to the defeats of the European workers' movements; a growing national conservatism; a retreat from the international revolution into the comforting illusion of national self-sufficiency.

Neither Trotsky nor anyone else seems at first to have taken on the responsibility of refuting Stalin's idea. In part, he probably ignored it because it was so elementary an error that, given the internationalist traditions of Bolshevism, he could have had little doubt that it would be rejected by the party. Even when Zinoviev and Kamenev, breaking with Stalin, attacked the theory of socialism in one country at the Fourteenth Congress in December 1925, Trotsky remained silent.

Stalin took the offensive in January 1926, by publishing another essay on the subject, this time explaining that the Soviet Union had sufficient resources, human and material, to be self-reliant, and to create a "full" socialist society.[6] For this, all that was needed was to resolve the contradictions between the workers and the peasants. The victory of the revolution in other countries was not necessary. Once again he included the reservation: the threat of intervention precluded the "complete, final victory of socialism in one country," and to eliminate that, revolutions were necessary. But in the meantime, it was possible for the Soviet workers to build a socialist society.

Although Trotsky evidently had it on his mind,[7] he did not directly address himself to this theory and expose the spurious nature of the Stalinist claims concerning its orthodox antecedents for several more months. Perhaps he was reluctant to allow himself to be distracted by a debate over what was obviously a transparent, if cynical, maneuver. (While in Berlin in the spring of 1926, Trotsky met with Eugene Varga, the leading Comintern economist, who admitted that socialism in one country was worthless as a theory but was useful to inspire the Soviet masses.)[8] Nevertheless, Trotsky attacked the implications of the theory: the notion that Soviet Russia didn't need ties with the world market; that it could build socialism "at a snail's pace," by relying on the peasantry; that it could "abstract from the international factor"; that diplomatic connections with bourgeois or petty-bourgeois forces could replace active participation in the class struggle as a means of defending the Soviet Union against interventionist schemes by imperialist countries.

By the time of the Fifteenth Party Conference in November 1926, Stalin's theory had become a weapon in the inner-party struggle, and it was at that time that Trotsky first took it up in exhaustive detail in public and answered it, point by point.

Thereafter he returned to the subject with great frequency, not only during the struggle in the AUCP but for the rest of his life. The theory of socialism in one country had an immediate and pernicious effect on the debate over domestic economic problems. The chief economic controversy of this period, underlying every other dispute over economic priorities, was whether industrialization could be achieved as a result of subordinating economic policy to the development of a large layer of rich peasants, or whether it required an aggressive policy of initial investments by the state, at least partially financed by a tax on the wealthy peasants. The party majority favored the former view, encouraging the growth of private farming on which the NEP was based and hoping that the wealthy peasants, who would be the most productive, would sell their grain and provide the surplus that the Soviet state could use to develop its industrial base.

The Opposition had opposed the policy of concessions to the wealthy peasantry since 1923, arguing that the Soviet economy needed above all an accelerated pace of industrialization, financed by a tax on the wealthy peasants, that could be the basis of expanded international trade. This would support the growth of heavy industry, which would lessen the gap between the Soviet economy and that of the industrialized capitalist world and preserve the bond with the peasantry (the so-called *smychka*) that made socialist construction possible under conditions of a vast peasant majority. At first glance, the need for rapid industrialization appears to contradict the need to stimulate agriculture to produce more efficiently and abundantly, and it was this superficial contradiction that the Stalinists exploited, accusing the Opposition of wanting to "rob" the peasantry for the sake of industrialization. But Trotsky's point was that to have an incentive to sell their grain—or even to plant next year's crop—the peasants had to know that the price they would receive for it could be used to purchase manufactured goods of all kinds, including improved tools and implements. Faced, as they were, with a "goods famine," or shortage of consumer goods, they would plant smaller crops or use more of the harvest for the distillation of alcohol and for their own consumption, with the result that the cities would starve and there would be no surplus for export, which would in turn mean a cutback in needed imports. As Trotsky wrote in December 1925, the Stalinist slogan "Face to the countryside" was meaningless if the "face" shown to the countryside were not the industrialized face of the Soviet economy: the peasants had no use for the face that showed them shelves empty of consumer goods and tools, and they would withhold their grain.[9]

The policies favoring concessions to the wealthy peasant at the expense of the poor peasants and workers became explicit in 1924. The argument that was advanced was that individual peasant holdings could produce more for the market if they were cultivated under favorable conditions, if the proprietors felt secure in their future and were given incentives to increase their efficiency. This led to a dramatic increase in the class differentiation in the countryside because it freed the wealthy peasants, or kulaks, from the restrictions of the workers' state and allowed them to use capitalist measures to concentrate greater wealth in their hands.

The harvest of 1924 demonstrated, for those who wanted to see, that such policies would be at the expense of the workers and their state. The well-to-do peasants hoarded their grain in expectation of a rise in the price, and private traders bought it at prices higher than the state was offering. The call "Face to the countryside!" dates from this time, under the chief sponsorship of Zinoviev; if Zinoviev was anxious about the wisdom of this policy he kept his worries to himself in the interests of maintaining unity in the overriding struggle against Trotsky.

The pro-kulak policies were stepped up at the Fourteenth Party Conference in April 1925, when many of the restrictions on private property in the countryside were lifted, including the bans on leasing land and on hiring labor. The chief theoretician and spokesman of the course toward the kulak by this time was Bukharin, under the slogan "Enrich yourselves!" But the "wager on the kulak," as this came to be known, was greeted with indignation in large sections of the party; and while the slogans remained on the books, something of a reversal was inflicted on the pro-kulak policy during the summer, by which time further open concessions to the kulak were viewed as unacceptable.

The 1925 harvest was the largest since the revolution; but once again the wealthy peasants, who produced the overwhelming bulk of the surplus, refused to market it. They had learned that the price of grain, which was fixed by the state in the fall, would skyrocket in the spring. The hopes held by the party leadership, that industry could be financed out of the proceeds of a prosperous peasant economy, were shown to be illusory.

By the Fourteenth Congress, alarm over the rising strength and boldness of the wealthy peasant had become manifest in the party. The congress, while reaffirming the decisions of the

Fourteenth Conference on the agrarian question, paid lip service to the dangers of estranging the poor peasant and to the need to accelerate industrial development. Nevertheless, the central question remained unsolved: would the burden of industrialization fall on the workers in the cities or would it be borne by the wealthy peasants? Trotsky insisted that industry was lagging behind agriculture and had to be promoted by long-term credits, an increase in state planning, and a tax on agricultural surpluses, which would also reduce the class differentiation in the countryside, a source of oppression to the poor and middle peasant and a growing threat to the workers' state. The party majority evaded this question. During the two years covered by this volume, it passed resolutions deploring the growing political and economic strength and self-confidence of the kulak and the tendency of party and state organs to ignore the needs of the workers and poor peasants; but it continued to capitulate to the political and economic demands of the kulak and failed to prescribe measures that would reverse the tide in favor of socialist industry and the worker. The majority hoped, as late as the autumn of 1927, to finance industrialization chiefly through the "regime of economy," which meant trying to cut costs as far as possible, so as to avoid a confrontation with the kulak. In practice, this meant cutting back on the working conditions, benefits, housing, etc., of the urban workers.

By the fall of 1927, the policy of official optimism accompanied by refusal to see the growing shortages in the cities and the growing boldness of the kulak, was beginning to break down. The unexpectedly large harvest in 1926 and the success in getting the peasant to part with it were invoked to drown out the Opposition when it pointed to the growth in the role of the private trader at the expense of the state, and the larger-than-ever proportion of the harvest realized by the kulak at the expense of the poor and middle peasant. Because of severe withholding of grain, it was the 1927 harvest, also a postwar record, that marked the end of official complacency and the opening of a belated campaign of "forced pressure" against the kulak in October 1927, largely under the blows of Opposition criticism. But by this time rectifying the matter was not so easy.

Years later, when Trotsky looked back at the events of this period, the political terms of the struggle were clearer and more obviously dominant. At the time, however, the battles were joined on the particular issues that happened to arise. So great was the Stalinist deluge of falsification and slander that Trotsky could easily have spent all his time denying rumors, refuting allegations, disproving slanders. He did in fact spend considerable time doing that, although only a representative sample appears in this volume. On the persistent economic questions, Trotsky often came up against what seemed to be a Stalinist wall of ignorance, narrow-mindedness, timidity, lack of foresight, bureaucratic bungling, and indifference. But the years 1926 and 1927 saw the gradual clarification of the political issues that were at stake. By this time Trotsky could write with confidence that the bureaucracy represented the encroachments of nonproletarian class forces upon the party and the state; that these forces were fed by the growth of capitalism in the city and in the countryside and by the defeat of the revolution in Europe; and that their influence in turn nourished the tendencies that increasingly threatened the foundations of the dictatorship of the proletariat. This made it easier, for example, to understand the stubborn resistance of the ruling circles to acknowledging and acting upon the need for rapid industrialization: at the root of their resistance was not an inability to understand the economic and political repercussions of failure to industrialize for the future of the workers' state, but pressures from an increasingly strong and self-confident nascent bourgeoisie, making themselves felt even in the ruling party.

Despite the advantages of hindsight, it was clearly possible even in 1926-27—for those relatively few persons who were able to hear both sides—to see the class basis of the disagreements. Cataclysmic events repeatedly put the Stalinist course to the test and verified the Opposition's criticisms. That is why it is insufficient to view this historic controversy as merely an intellectual debate in which the soundest, most convincing arguments should have won the day, if not at once then at least after the benefit of experience and testing had clarified the issues.

The arguments were the expression of social forces that were at work within the Soviet Union, not least of all within the AUCP itself, altering the very terms of the controversy and the conditions under which it took place.

Moreover, while the party is a "subjective" factor, acting upon the material conditions with a conscious goal in mind, it is also unconsciously acted upon by them. The party that celebrated the tenth anniversary of the October Revolution was not the same as the party that had led the October Revolution in practically any measurable respect: it differed in class composition, size, outlook, and experience. On paper, its program was the same, but only on paper. The major elements of proletarian revolutionary strategy and internal democracy that had characterized the party under Lenin, and enabled it to resolve earlier thorny questions of policy, were being explicitly and implicitly undercut and disavowed by 1927. (In "Speech to the Joint Plenum of the CC and the CCC," August 6, 1927, Trotsky demonstrates how incongruous the historic internationalist program appeared when held up against the character of the Communist League of Youth in 1927.)

By the time he became general secretary in 1922, Stalin had begun his work of organizationally mastering the Bolshevik Party by creating an apparatus of party secretaries at all levels answerable only to him. This could not have been accomplished without the infusion into the party ranks of careerists and opportunists, eager to please and to win a secure position but without any knowledge of the history and traditions of Bolshevism or interest in them. In many cases, these newcomers to Bolshevism were former members of the Menshevik or Social Revolutionary parties, or even of bourgeois parties that had opposed the October Revolution. After the introduction of the NEP, the party began to feel the influence of the wealthy peasant and the private trader, the economic specialist and the bourgeois intellectual. Under the prevailing social conditions, these people gained ascendancy in the party in direct proportion to the success of Stalin's work in suppressing inner-party democracy and stifling dissent. The "Lenin levy," which Stalin initiated after Lenin's death (1924), resulted in a vast influx of new members into the party, most of them not revolutionary-minded; and by early 1927, the party's own statistics demonstrated that only one-third of its members were workers in the factories, the rest being peasants, office workers, and "others." Throughout this period, demoralization over international events and discouragement over the course of the party, as well as the hardships of everyday life, were draining the party of its proletarian membership and replacing it with better-off peasants, bourgeois intellectuals, and administrators from the economic management agencies, who must have felt that the tide was turning in their favor. In mid-1927, Stalin initiated a "sifting" process to re-examine the party registration of the entire membership, which resulted in a further loss of some 80,000 members, most of them workers. In October of that year, the party gates were once again opened wide for the recruitment of workers. This "October enrollment" did not alter the class composition of the party dramatically, but it again flooded the party with new recruits to whom the traditions and principles of Leninism were unfamiliar.

In the Platform of the Opposition, Trotsky analyzed the two major anti-Leninist tendencies in the leadership of the party. The first, under the tutelage of Rykov, favored the policy of concessions to the rich peasants; it was influenced by the bourgeois restorationist politicians like Ustryalov. This group was reinforced by the leaders of the Soviet trade unions, among them Tomsky, who sought closer ties with the Social Democratic-led Amsterdam International but supported the Rykov group in its effort to turn the course of the party to the right, domestically and internationally. The second tendency Trotsky identified as centrist. Its leader was Stalin, and it was tied to the first tendency through Bukharin. (In later years Trotsky came to view Bukharin as the central leader of the right wing.) The Stalinists controlled the apparatus and attached themselves to others for a political program that would assist their struggle to keep a monopoly of political power. Trotsky repeatedly stressed that the two tendencies were united by their common hostility to the Opposition; removal of the Opposition would inevitably—and did—lead to a new conflict and to a split between the erstwhile allies.

Prior to 1921, the Bolshevik Party had a rich history of internal debates over a wide spectrum of subjects. This was viewed as the normal and most effective way for a party to find the right course. Democracy in the party included the right of members, including leaders, to form groupings and factions, and to issue platforms in defense of what they considered the correct program. This right persisted throughout the years of reaction, revolution, and civil war, and was curtailed only in 1921, and then only as a temporary measure against factionalism to meet an extreme emergency in the country. Factionalism threatened to tear apart the party—and in the extremely harsh and difficult conditions following the civil war, this could lead to an overthrow of the workers' state itself. And even then the party had taken steps to safeguard the functioning of party democracy. The overcoming of the emergency coincided with Lenin's final illness and the Stalinization of the party and state. The bureaucratized apparatus inherited the temporary ban on factions, which the Stalinists did not hesitate to turn into its opposite—a tool to permanently strangle any real debate—to help them subdue the party and tie it hand and foot.

In 1923-25, Trotsky evidently decided to try to prevent the question of factions—an organizational question—from obscuring the political debates, and so he did not challenge the ban on factions. Nevertheless, he did place the blame for the emergence of factions and groupings on the leadership, for stifling party democracy and forcing loyal members into clandestinity because there were no guidelines for the permissible expression of political differences.

It should be remembered that all this time the Stalinists had themselves constituted a secret faction in the Politburo that they used to manipulate the selection of personnel and eliminate dissent throughout the party. In April 1926, after they had broken with Stalin, Zinoviev and Kamenev revealed the extent to which this secret faction had maneuvered to gain control of the party and to prevent a democratic discussion.

After that, Trotsky answered charges of factionalism by pointing out how the ruling circles were deliberately destroying the democratic rights of the party members and the right of the leadership bodies and then the party itself to hear all sides of an unresolved dispute, make a decision, and act accordingly. He explained that it was the illegal repression and restrictions imposed by the Stalinists in violation of party statutes that forced members to use surreptitious means to carry out acts that should have been the guaranteed right of every member.

One of the most persistent accusations against the Opposition was that it was working for the formation of a separate party from the Communist Party. There was no truth whatever in this charge. When Trotsky objected to the charge, it was not only for tactical reasons but also because he thought attempts to build an alternative party would be harmful to the revolutionary objectives of the Left Opposition. In his eyes the Russian CP possessed decades of invaluable experience and traditions, and by and large, even despite the expulsions, "levies," and "siftings" of the twenties, it provided the major concentration of revolutionary-minded workers in the USSR, as well as the Old Guard generation that had led the revolution, who had to be reached and educated, or reawakened, if the revolutionary Bolshevik traditions were to survive. That is why Trotsky did not call for the formation of a new party until 1933, when he decided that the Soviet CP was dead—unreformable—for the purposes of revolutionary action.

Trotsky had been relieved of his post as commissar of war and head of the Military Revolutionary Committee in January 1925. That May, he was offered, and accepted, a position on the Supreme Council of the National Economy (Vesenkha). Thanks to that assignment, he developed a detailed familiarity with the workings of the economy. Most of his time was taken up by studying, writing, and speaking on educational, cultural, and other subjects. He held this position until the July 1926 CC plenum, when he was evidently dismissed. His intervention into the April 1926 CC plenum marked his first active participation in the inner-party struggle in nearly two years. But, from that moment on, even when layer after layer of the Opposition wavered, panicked, or capitulated, Trotsky became stronger in his determination to conduct the fight for a return to Leninism to the end.

The next and last volume will follow Trotsky into exile at Alma-Ata, where he spent a year before his deportation to Turkey. From Alma-Ata Trotsky appealed his expulsion to the Comintern; assessed Stalin's "left course"; criticized the Sixth Congress of the Comintern; evaluated the new wave of capitulations to Stalin; and kept up an enormous volume of correspondence with cothinkers banished to remote corners of the USSR.

Naomi Allen
April 1980

1. "At a New Stage," late December 1927, p. 501 of this volume.
2. Cited in E.H. Carr, *Foundations of a Planned Economy 1926-1929*, vol. 2 (New York: Macmillan, 1971), pp. 41n-42n.
3. L. Trotsky, *The Case of Leon Trotsky* (New York: Merit, 1969), p. 330.
4. Cited in Carr, Op. cit., p. 35n. No trace of such a bulletin survives.
5. "The October Revolution and the Tactics of the Russian Communists," in J. Stalin, *Works* (Moscow: Foreign Languages Publishing House), vol. 6 (1953), pp. 374-420.
6. J. Stalin, *Problems of Leninism* (New York: International Publishers, 1934).
7. See his "Notes on Economic Questions," May 2, 1926, p. 56 of this volume.
8. Cited in I. Deutscher, *The Prophet Unarmed* (New York: Vintage, 1959), p. 266n.
9. See *The Challenge of the Left Opposition (1923-25)*, ed. N. Allen (New York: Pathfinder, 1975), p. 392.

THREE LETTERS TO BUKHARIN

January-March 1926

NOTE: The Fourteenth Congress in December 1925 saw the breakup of the ruling triumvirate of Stalin-Zinoviev-Kamenev and the decisive defeat of the Leningrad Opposition. During the following few months, members of the 1923 Opposition discussed among themselves whether to bloc with Stalin or Zinoviev-Kamenev or neither. Stalin feared a bloc between the Oppositions of 1923 and 1925 and made veiled overtures to Trotsky. It was probably at Stalin's prompting that Bukharin started the correspondence of January-March 1926. There is evidence in Trotsky's own writings of this period that he was still weighing the pros and cons of the different positions taken at the Fourteenth Congress. It was Zinoviev and Kamenev's break with the pro-kulak policy that was decisive to Trotsky in making this bloc, because their break was a reflection of class pressure from the workers.

After the Fourteenth Congress, the Central Committee met to take steps against the Leningraders. Stalin called for reprisals designed to break the hold of the Zinovievists on the Leningrad party apparatus. Trotsky opposed such measures, although he was not seeking a bloc with Zinoviev and Kamenev. At one point, Bukharin seconded Stalin's proposal and Kamenev protested: Why was Bukharin, who had opposed drastic reprisals against the Trotskyists, now calling for extreme measures against the Leningraders? Trotsky called out: "He has acquired the taste."

Following this episode Bukharin wrote to Trotsky, seeking to persuade him not to bloc with Zinoviev and not to try to extend inner-party democracy. Trotsky's reply of January 9 shows clearly that it was precisely party democracy that he insisted on. To Bukharin and his supporters this response was obviously unsatisfactory. There is no record that Bukharin wrote to Trotsky again. Instead, a campaign was begun against Trotsky to prevent him from addressing party gatherings in working class districts. This campaign was in the hands of Uglanov, who had

35

*replaced Kamenev as head of the Moscow party organization,
and who capitalized on Trotsky's assignment to three technical
commissions of the Supreme Council of the National Economy to
spread the rumor that he preferred speaking to bourgeois scien-
tists and intellectuals over speaking to workers. On March 4
Trotsky wrote to Bukharin again, pointing out the re-emergence
of anti-Semitism, which was now a tool of the bureaucratic
reaction, as it had formerly been a tool of the tsarist reaction, and
which reflected the Stalinists' appeal to Russian national chauvinism. Two weeks later Trotsky raised the charge of anti-Semitism
in the Politburo, where he met only indifference and contempt.*

*Excerpts from the January 9 letter, and the full text of the
March 9 letter, appeared in* Fourth International, *October 1941, in
a translation by John G. Wright, a leader of the American
Socialist Workers Party who translated many of Trotsky's
articles in the thirties and after. The remainder of the text has
been translated and the earlier translation partly revised by L.
Hall and George Saunders. The March 19 letter appears here for
the first time, by permission of the Harvard College Library.*

I
January 9, 1926

Dear Nikolai Ivanovich:

I am thankful for your note, since it gives us an opportunity—
after a long interval—to exchange views on the most urgent
questions of party life. And since, by the will of fate and the party
congress, you and I are serving on the same Politburo, an honest
attempt at such a comradely clarification of the issues can, at
any rate, do no harm.

Kamenev reproached you at a meeting [right after the Fourteenth Congress] with the fact that previously you had objected to
measures of extreme administrative pressure in relation to the
"Opposition" (apparently referring to 1923-24) but now you
support the most drastic steps in relation to Leningrad. My
thought, expressed out loud, was essentially this: "He has
acquired the taste." Taking up this remark of mine, you write:
"You think that I have 'acquired the taste,' but this 'taste' makes
me tremble from head to foot." By no means did I intend, by this
accidentally voiced observation, to suggest that you take *pleasure*
in extreme repressive measures by the apparatus. My thought

was rather that you have *accommodated yourself* to such measures, *grown used* to them, and are not inclined to notice their impact and effect outside the circles of the dominant elements of the apparatus.

In your note you charge that "out of formal considerations about democracy," I don't want to see the real state of affairs. But what do you yourself see as the "real state of affairs"? You write: "(1) The Leningrad apparatus is hardened to the core; the upper echelons are welded into one; they have been in power without any changes for eight years—they are welded together in their daily lives. (2) The secondary leadership is hand-picked; it is impossible to change all their minds (the top brass)—that is utopian. (3) What they seek to play upon, their main theme, is that the economic privileges of the industrial workers will be taken away (credits, factories, etc.); this is unconscionable demagogy." From this you conclude that "it is necessary to win people over *from below,* while crushing resistance from above."

It is by no means my purpose to polemicize with you or to recall the past. That is pointless. But in order to get at the essence of the problem, I must nevertheless say that you have produced a formulation which *counterposes the party apparatus to the rank and file* in the sharpest, harshest, and most glaring way. Your "construction" is as follows: There is a tightly knit, or as you put it, thoroughly "hardened" group at the top, and a secondary leadership hand-picked from above; then there is the party rank and file, deceived and corrupted by the demagogy of this apparatus; and beyond that, the mass of nonparty workers. Of course, in a private note you may express yourself in stronger terms than in an article. But even making allowance for that, the result is an absolutely devastating picture. Every thinking member of the party will wonder: If a conflict hadn't arisen between Zinoviev and the CC majority, would the top brass in Leningrad have continued to maintain for a ninth and a tenth year the kind of regime it established during the past eight years?

The "real state of affairs" is not at all as you see it. Actually it is this—the impermissible character of the Leningrad regime was revealed only because a conflict arose between it and *the top brass in Moscow,* certainly not because the *Leningrad ranks* made a protest, expressed dissatisfaction, etc. Can it be that this doesn't hit you right in the eye? If Leningrad, i.e., the most cultured proletarian center, is ruled by a "hardened" clique, "welded together in their daily lives," and a hand-picked secondary leadership, how is it that the party organization has failed to notice this? Are there really no vital, honest, and energetic party members in the Leningrad organization to raise the voice of protest and win over the majority of the organization to their side—even if their protest meets with no response from the CC? After all, we aren't talking about Chita or Kherson (although there too of course we can and should expect that a Bolshevik party organization would not, over a period of years, tolerate barbarities by the upper echelons). We are talking about Leningrad, where unquestionably the most proletarian and the most highly skilled vanguard of our party is concentrated. Do you really not see that it is precisely in this and in nothing else that the "real state of affairs" consists? And now, when you give some thought, as you should, to this state of affairs, you must conclude: Leningrad is by no means a world unto itself. In Leningrad one finds only a sharper and more deformed expression of the negative characteristics which are typical of the party as a whole. Is this really not clear?

To you it seems that "because of formal considerations about democracy" I fail to see the realities in Leningrad. You are mistaken. I have never proclaimed democracy to be "sacred," as one of my former friends once did [that is, Bukharin].

You will perhaps recall that two years ago, during a session of the Politburo at my home, I said that the ranks of the Leningrad party were muzzled more than was the case elsewhere. This expression (I confess, a very strong one) was used by me in an intimate circle, just as you used in your personal note the words "unconscionable demagogy."

To be sure, this did not prevent my remark concerning the muzzling of the party ranks by the Leningrad party apparatus from being broadcast through meetings and through the press. (That is another matter, however, and—I hope—not a precedent.) But doesn't this mean *I did see* the real state of affairs? Moreover, unlike some comrades, I saw it a year and a half and two and three years ago. At that time, during the same session, I remarked that everything in Leningrad goes splendidly (100 percent) five minutes before things get very bad. This is possible only under a super-apparatus regime. Why then do you say that I did not see the real state of affairs? True, I did not consider Leningrad to be separated from the rest of the country by an impenetrable barrier. The theory of a "sick Leningrad" and a "healthy country," which was held in high respect under Kerensky, was never my theory. I said and I repeat now that the traits of apparatus bureaucratism, characteristic of the *whole* party, have been brought to their extreme expression in the regime of the Leningrad party. I must, however, add that in these two and a half years (i.e., since the autumn of 1923) the apparatus-bureaucratic tendencies have grown in the extreme not only in Leningrad but throughout the entire party.

Consider for a moment this fact: Moscow and Leningrad, the two main proletarian centers, adopt *simultaneously* and furthermore *unanimously* (think of it: *unanimously!*) at their district party conferences two resolutions aimed against each other. And consider also this, that official party opinion, represented by the press, does not even dwell on this truly shocking fact.

How could this have happened? What social trends are concealed beneath this? Is it conceivable that in the party of Lenin, when there is such an exceptionally serious clash of tendencies, no attempt has been made to define their social, i.e., class, character? I am not talking about the "moods" of Sokolnikov or Kamenev or Zinoviev but about the fact that the two main proletarian centers, without which there would be no Soviet Union, turned out to be "unanimously" opposed to one another. How? Why? In what way? What are the special (?) social (?!) conditions in Leningrad and Moscow which permit such drastic and "unanimous" polar opposites? No one looks for them, no one wonders about them. What then is the explanation? Simply this, that everyone says inwardly, in silence—*the hundred percent counterposition of Leningrad and Moscow is the work of the apparatus.* That, Nikolai Ivanovich, is the real state of affairs. And I consider it in the highest degree alarming. Please try to grasp *that!!*

You allude to the way the Leningrad top echelons are welded together "in their daily lives" and you think that in my "formalism" I don't see that. But just by chance several days ago a comrade reminded me of a conversation he and I had had more than two years ago. At that time I proposed approximately the following line of thought: Given the extremely apparatus-heavy character of the Leningrad regime, given the apparatus arrogance of the ruling clique, the development of a special "mutual protection" system in the upper ranks of the organization is inevitable, and that in turn will inevitably lead to very negative consequences in the outlook of the less stable elements in the party and state apparatuses. Thus, for example, I regarded as extremely dangerous the special kind of "insurance" through the party apparatus for the positions of military, economic, and other officials. Through their "loyalty" to the secretary of the province committee they won the right, within the sphere of official work, to violate orders or decrees in force on a statewide basis. In the sphere of "daily life" they lived with the confidence that they would not be held accountable for any of their "shortcomings" in that sphere as long as they remained loyal to the secretary of the province committee. Moreover, they had no doubt that anyone who tried to bring objections of a moral or work-related kind against them would find themselves categorized as Oppositionists, with all the ensuing consequences. Thus you are greatly mistaken to think that "because of formal considerations about democracy" I have failed to note the reality, in particular the reality of "daily life." Only I did not have to wait until the conflict between Zinoviev and the CC majority to see this unattractive reality and the dangerous tendencies inherent in its further development.

But even in regard to "daily life" Leningrad does not stand alone. In the past year we had on the one hand the Chita business, and on the other that in Kherson. Naturally you and I understand that the Chita and Kherson abominations are exceptions precisely because of their excesses. But these exceptions are *symptomatic*. Could the things that happened in Chita have occurred had there not been among the upper echelons in Chita a special, closed-in, mutual-protection system, with independence from the rank and file as its basis? Did you read the report of Shlichter's investigating committee on the Kherson business? The document is instructive to the highest degree—not only because it characterizes some of the Kherson personnel, but also because it characterizes certain aspects of the party regime as a whole. To the question, "Why did all the local Communists, who had known of the crimes of the responsible workers, keep quiet, apparently for a period of two or three years?" Shlichter received the answer: "Just try to speak up—you'll lose your job, you'll get sent to the countryside, etc., etc." I quote, of course, from memory, but this is the gist of it. And Shlichter exclaims apropos of this: "What! Up to now only Oppositionists have told us that for this or that opinion they have *allegedly* (?!) been removed from posts, sent to the countryside, etc., etc. But now we hear from party members that they do not protest against *criminal actions* of leading comrades for fear of being fired, sent to the countryside, expelled from the party, etc." I cite again from memory.

I must in all honesty say that Shlichter's pathetic exclamation (not at a public meeting but in a report at the Central Committee!) surprised me no less than the facts he investigated in

Kherson. It goes without saying that the system of apparatus terror cannot stop with so-called ideological deviations, real or invented, but must inevitably extend to the life and activity of the organization as a whole. If the rank-and-file Communists are afraid to express any opinion that diverges or threatens to diverge from the opinion of the secretary of the bureau, province committee, district committee, county committee, etc., the same rank-and-file Communists will be still more afraid to raise their voices against impermissible and even criminal actions by officials in the central leadership. The one follows inseparably from the other. Especially because a morally tarnished official, in defending his post or his power or his influence, inevitably attributes any reference to his "tarnish" to the latest deviation, whatever it is. In such phenomena bureaucratism finds its most flagrant expression.

Today you condemn the Leningrad regime, exaggerating its apparatus character in the process, i.e., portraying the situation as though there were *no ideological bond of any kind between the upper echelons and the rank and file.* Here you fall into exactly the opposite error of the one you fell into when, politically and organizationally, you followed in Leningrad's wake—and that was not so very long ago. Proceeding from this error, you wish to drive one wedge out with another, so that in the struggle against the Leningrad apparatchiks you want—to tighten all the screws of the apparatus tighter than ever. In the resolution of December 5, 1923, you and I jointly wrote that the *bureaucratic tendencies in the party apparatus inevitably give rise, by way of a reaction, to factional groupings* [see *Challenge of The Left Opposition (1923-25)*, pp. 404-13]. And since that time we have had enough instances of this to see that *the apparatus struggle against factional groupings* [only] *deepens the bureaucratic tendencies in the apparatus.*

The purely administrative struggle against earlier "Oppositions"—a struggle which did not shrink from the use of any organizational or ideological means whatever—resulted in all decisions being adopted by party organizations in no other way than by unanimous vote. You yourself have praised this unanimous voting more than once in *Pravda* and, following Zinoviev's lead, have described it as the product of ideological unity of mind. But then it turned out that Leningrad "unanimously" opposed itself to Moscow, and you pronounce this the result of the criminal demagogy of the hardened Leningrad apparatus. No, the problem lies deeper. You have before you the ultimate dialectics of the apparatus principle: *unanimity is suddenly transformed into its opposite.* Now you have opened up exactly the same kind of struggle, using the same old stereotypes, against the *new* Opposition. *The ideological range of the dominant echelons of the party is constricted still more. Their ideological authority is inevitably reduced.* The need for an intensification of apparatus regimentation follows from this. This need has dragged you into the process as well. A year or two ago, in Kamenev's words, you "objected." But now you take the initiative, although in your own words it makes you "tremble from head to foot." I venture to say that in this instance you personally represent a fairly accurate and sensitive barometer of the degree of bureaucratization in the party regime over the last two or three years.

I know that certain comrades, possibly you among them, have until recent times been carrying out a plan somewhat as follows: give the workers in the cells the opportunity to criticize things on the workshop, factory, or district level, and at the same time, crack down resolutely on every "opposition" emanating from the upper ranks of the party. In this way, the apparatus regime as a whole was to be preserved by providing it with a broader base. *But this experiment was not at all successful.* The methods and habits of the apparatus regime inevitably trickle down from the top. If every criticism of the Central Committee and even criticism inside the Central Committee is equated, under all conditions, with a factional struggle for power, with all the ensuing consequences, then the Leningrad Committee will carry out the very same policy in relation to those who criticize it in the sphere of its absolute powers. And under the Leningrad Committee there are districts and subdistricts. After that come the working groups and collectives. The size of the organization doesn't change the basic trend. Criticizing a "red director"—if he enjoys the support of the cell secretary—means the same for the members of a factory workforce as criticizing the CC would mean for a CC member, a secretary of a province committee, or a delegate to a congress. Any criticism, if it is concerned with *vital* questions, is bound to infringe on someone, and the critic will invariably be accused of a "deviation," "squabbling," or simply personal insult. That is why it is necessary to begin all resolutions on party and trade union democracy over and over again with the words: "In spite of all the resolutions, decrees, and educational instructions, in the local areas, such and such goes on," etc. But in fact what goes on in the local areas is only what goes on at the top. By using apparatus methods to suppress the apparatus regime in Leningrad you will only arrive at an even worse Leningrad regime.

This cannot be doubted for a moment. It is no accident that the pressure has been put on in Leningrad more strongly than anywhere else. In the rural provinces with their scattered party cells, largely lacking in culture, the role of the party-secretary apparatus will loom quite large simply because of the objective conditions. And this must be accounted as an *inevitable* and—within limits that are nevertheless not excessive—a *progressive* fact. But in Leningrad, with the high political and cultural level of its industrial workers, matters are different. Here an *apparatus* regime can maintain itself only by *greater tightening of the screws,* on the one hand, and by demagogy, on the other. By smashing one apparatus with another, before the ranks of the Leningrad party—or the party as a whole—have understood anything whatsoever, you are forced to supplement this work with counterdemagogy which is very similar to the demagogy [you complain of].

I have taken up only the question you raised in your note. But major social questions show through the question of the party regime. I cannot dwell on them in detail in this already overly long letter, and anyway there is no time for that. But I would like to hope that you will grasp my meaning from the following few words.

When in 1923 the Opposition arose in Moscow (without the aid of the local apparatus, and against its resistance) the central and local apparatus brought the bludgeon down on Moscow's skull under the slogan: "Shut up! You do not recognize the peasantry." In the same apparatus-way you are now bludgeoning the Leningrad organization and crying: "Shut up! You do not recognize the middle peasant." You are thus terrorizing the thinking habits of the best proletarian elements in the two main centers of the proletarian dictatorship, teaching them not to give voice to their own views, whether correct or erroneous, not even to their anxieties concerning the general questions of the revolution and of socialism. And meanwhile in the rural areas, elements of [bourgeois] democracy are unquestionably being strengthened and entrenched. Can't you see all the dangers that flow from this?

I say once again that I have touched on only one aspect of the colossal question of the future destiny of our party and revolution. I am personally grateful to you that your note gave me occasion to express these thoughts to you. Why have I written? To what end? Well, you see, I think it is possible, as well as necessary and indispensable, to make a transition from the present party regime to a more healthy one—without convulsions, without new debates, without a struggle for power, without "triumvirates," "quadrumvirates" or "novumvirates"—through normal and full-bodied work by all the party organizations, beginning at the very top, the Politburo. That, Nikolai Ivanovich, is why I wrote this long letter. I am totally willing to continue our clarification of the issues and would like to hope that it will not hamper but at least in part will help smooth the road toward truly collective work in the Politburo and the Central Committee, without which there will not be collective work in any of the lower bodies of the party. It goes without saying that this letter is not in any way and not in the slightest degree an official party document. It is my private and personal letter to you in reply to your note. It was typed only because it was dictated to a stenographer, a comrade whose absolute party loyalty and discretion are beyond all question.

Regards!
Yours,
L. Trotsky

II
March 4, 1926

N. Ivanovich:

I am writing this letter in longhand (although I have gotten out of the habit), since it is embarrassing to dictate to a stenographer what I have to say.

You are of course aware that in accordance with the Uglanov line there is being conducted against me in Moscow a half-concealed struggle with all sorts of tricks and insinuations, which I refrain from characterizing here as they deserve.

By all sorts of machinations—which are generally unworthy of and degrading to our organization—I am not permitted to speak at workers' meetings. At the same time rumors are being spread systematically through the workers' cells that I give lectures "for the bourgeoisie" and refuse to speak to workers. Now just listen to what thrives on this soil, and this, once again, not at all accidentally. I cite verbatim from a letter of a worker-party member.

"In our cell the question has been raised, Why do you arrange to give lectures only for pay? The admission prices to these lectures are very high and the workers cannot afford them. Consequently only the bourgeoisie attends. The secretary of our cell has explained in conversations with us that you take a fee, a percentage for your own use, from these lectures. He tells us that for every one of your articles and for your by-line you also take a fee, that you have a big family and, he says, you run short of funds. Does a member of the Politburo really have to sell his by-line?"

You will ask: Isn't this silly nonsense? No, unfortunately for us, it is not nonsense. I have verified it. At first several members of this cell wanted to write a letter to the Central Control Commission (or Central Committee), but then they decided not to, saying: "They will kick us out of the factory, and we have families."

Thus, a working class party member has developed the fear that if he tries to verify even the most infamous slander against a member of the Politburo, he may be fired from his job, although as a party member he was following party procedure. And you know, if he were to ask me, I could not in good conscience say that this would not happen. The same secretary of the same cell also said—and again *not at all accidentally*—"The Yids on the Politburo are kicking up a fuss." And again no one dared report this to any quarter—for the very same openly stated reason: they will kick us out of the factory.

Another item. The author of the letter which I cited above is a Jewish worker. He, too, did not dare to write a report about such phrases as "the Yids who agitate against Leninism." His motive was this: "If the others, the non-Jews, keep quiet, it would be awkward for me . . ." And this worker—who wrote me to ask whether it is true that I sell my speeches and my by-line to the bourgeoisie—now expects at any hour to be fired from his factory job. This is a fact. It is also a fact that I am not at all sure that this won't happen—if not immediately, then a month from now. There are plenty of pretexts. And everybody in the cell knows "that's how it was, that's how it will be"—and they hang their heads.

In other words: *members of the Communist Party are afraid to report to the party institutions about Black Hundred agitation, thinking that it is they who will be kicked out, not the Black Hundred gangster.*

You will say: This is an exaggeration! I, too, would like to think so. Therefore I have a proposal to make: *Let us take a trip to the cell together and check into the matter.* I think that you and I— two members of the Politburo—have after all a few things in common, enough to calmly and conscientiously verify: (1) whether it is possible that *in our party, in Moscow, in a workers' cell,* propaganda is being conducted with impunity which is vile and slanderous, on the one hand, and anti-Semitic, on the other; and (2) whether honest workers are afraid to question or verify or try to refute any stupidity, lest they be driven into the street with their families. Of course you can refer me to the "proper bodies." But this would signify only *closing the vicious circle.*

I want to hope that you will not do this; and it is precisely that hope which prompts this letter.

Yours,
L. Trotsky

III
March 19, 1926

N.I.:

Although from yesterday's meeting of the Politburo it has become absolutely clear to me that the Politburo has firmly decided on a line of further pressure tactics—with all the consequences for the party that flow from that line—still, I do not want to refrain from one more attempt at clarification, especially since you yourself suggested to me that we talk over the situation that has arisen. Today I will wait for your call all day—until 7 p.m. After 7:00 I have a meeting of the Central Concessions Committee.

L.T.

AMENDMENTS TO
RYKOV'S RESOLUTION
On the Economic Situation
in the USSR

April 12, 1926

NOTE: These amendments by Trotsky to Rykov's draft resolution were submitted to the April 1926 joint plenum of the CC and the Central Control Commission. Rykov was a leader of the right wing in the Politburo and head of the Supreme Council of the National Economy.

In his speech to the plenum, Trotsky explained that he had been responsible for the proposal that the Politburo draft a resolution on the economic situation for the April plenum and that, in the light of the decisions of the Fourteenth Congress of December 1925, his proposal had been accepted unanimously. However, the CC draft resolution had deliberately been submitted to members of the Politburo on the very eve of the plenum, hindering the preparation of amendments or a counterresolution. When Trotsky had announced that he would not vote under the circumstances, the voting was postponed for two days.

His amendments cannot be called a counterresolution because he deliberately omitted several points that he considered to have been adequately formulated in Rykov's resolution. They contain a clear statement of Trotsky's economic program at this stage in the development of the Soviet economy, above all the need for more rapid industrialization, financed by a tax on the wealthy peasants (kulaks) and designed to lessen the gap between the Soviet economy and that of the industrialized capitalist world and to preserve the bond with the peasantry (the smychka).

Trotsky's proposals took the form of calling for the implementation of the decisions of the Fourteenth Congress. In an unpublished memorandum of March 27, he itemized the positive work of the congress, which, on paper at least, recognized the leading role

*of state industry, the need for consistent inner-party democracy,
and the incompatibility of the policy of concessions to the
wealthy peasant with a policy of rapid industrialization. He
ended the memorandum with the observation: "The question
comes down to how it is interpreted and how it is actually
implemented. Of enormous importance, in this respect, is sure to
be the economic resolution to be submitted for approval to the
April (1926) Central Committee plenum."*

*A factional atmosphere prevailed at the plenum. In answer to
several captious and argumentative objections that were raised in
the discussion, Trotsky said: "When such serious questions of
economics and general policy hang in the balance, it would be
miraculous if within the party there did not arise practical and
general disagreements, which should not be treated merely in an
exaggerated way and artificially blown up out of all proportion.
How else can the party exist and move forward? Otherwise . . .
on any pretext, charges of semi-Trotskyism will fly from right to
left and from left to right. Why are the accusers so easily
transformed into the accused? Because every question among us
is placed on the sharp edge of the apparatus razor and any
deviation from that sharp, thin line by one thousandth of a
millimeter is proclaimed—by means of apparatus myth-making—
to be a monstrous deviation. The specter of Trotskyism is
necessary to prop up the apparatus regime. . . ."*

*And he took up the criticisms of his statement, in the amend-
ments and elsewhere, that a good harvest, instead of accelerating
the economic development toward socialism, could disorganize
the economy and further strain relations between city and
countryside (see the Introduction, p. 26). "I repeat again that
on the basis of a [good] harvest two different kinds of economic
expansion are conceivable: toward capitalism or toward socialism. A good locomotive is an excellent thing, and the faster it
goes, the better. But if the switch isn't thrown in time, there is a
danger of a crash, and the faster the engine is going, the worse
the crash. A harvest is a fast-moving locomotive; if the industrial
switch is not in the right position, the danger of a crash is great."*

*The CC draft resolution was adopted by the plenum. It once
again paid lip service to the need for industrialization, but it left
unresolved the major questions of how industrialization was to be
financed and at what rate it should proceed. Trotsky's amendments were defeated, but not before Kamenev had supported
Trotsky's call for increased taxation of the kulak and his warning
that even a good harvest might have bad consequences. Finally,*

Trotsky announced that he would vote for Kamenev's amendment urging the plenum to take note of the increasing class differentiation among the peasantry even though Kamenev had not made clear the relationship between class differentiation and the rate of industrialization. The basis was laid for what was to become the United Opposition.

From Bulletin Communiste, *October-November 1927. Translated from the French by David Keil and corrected against the Russian original by George Saunders. The text has been abridged here to avoid repetition. Quotations from the March 27 memorandum and from Trotsky's plenum speech are by permission of the Harvard College Library.*

I. The Disproportion Between Industry and Agriculture and Problems of Economic Policy

The fundamental and at the same time most urgent aim of the NEP—after reviving the peasant's material interest in developing his own farm—was to ensure the progress of the productive forces in general in the countryside and, on this basis, to accomplish the task of developing industry in close connection with agriculture. In accordance with the market forms taken by this link between industry and agriculture, the slogans "Learn how to trade" and "Save every extra penny for industry" became part of the New Economic Policy. At the same time the party proposed a plan for large-scale electrification.

The problem of the *smychka,* the bond between proletariat and peasantry, determined the fundamental *economic* content of this policy. The aim of the state's economic policies as a whole is to ensure, on the basis of the growth of the productive forces, a dynamic equilibrium between industry and agriculture, with the socialist elements gaining increased predominance over the capitalist elements.

It is quite obvious that disruption of this equilibrium could occur under two main conditions: if the state, by its fiscal, budgetary, industrial, commercial, or other policies were to take from the economy and transfer to industry a *disproportionately large* share of the annual product and of our resources in general, as a result of which industry would run too far ahead, would become detached from the national economic base, especially the agricultural base, and would run into the roadblock of insufficient purchasing power; on the other hand, if the state, through all the levers it controls, took an *insufficient* share of the economy's resources and their annual increases, the result would be that the supply of industrial products would lag behind the effective demand. A disruption of the *smychka* is evident in either case. If industry's development is excessively forced, that imposes an insupportable burden on the peasant and thereby weakens agriculture. But the peasant would suffer just as great a loss if industry could not sufficiently meet the demand arising from the peasants' sale of the harvest, resulting in a "scissors" between wholesale and retail prices.

The Fourteenth Party Congress decided on the industrialization of the country as its cardinal directive. The means, methods, and pace at which this directive is carried out are *decisive* not only for our future progress toward socialism but also for the political rule of the working class in the Soviet Union.

The main contradiction in our present economic situation, and likewise in the relations between city and countryside, is that state industry lags behind the development of agriculture. Industrial production does not satisfy effective demand: this hinders the realization and export of the marketable portion of agricultural production and keeps imports in very narrow limits, hinders the expansion of industry and could even lead to a *worsening* of the fundamental disproportion. All our data confirm that the 1926 harvest will find our industry without any reserves of manufactured goods. That could mean *a repetition of the present difficulties on a larger scale.* Under those conditions, a good harvest, i.e., a potentially increased quantity of marketable surpluses in agriculture, could become a factor that would not accelerate economic development toward socialism but would on the contrary disorganize the economy and further strain relations between city and countryside and, within the city itself, strain relations between consumers and the state.

Practically speaking, a good harvest—in the absence of industrial goods—could mean greater utilization of grain for clandestine distillation of alcohol and longer lines in front of shops in the cities. Politically, this would signify a struggle by the peasant against the monopoly of foreign trade, i.e., against socialist industry. Underestimating such a danger could have serious consequences, if not in the near future, at least in the later development of that correlation of economic factors which tends to preserve the disproportion between industry and agriculture or to eliminate it too slowly. The way out is to ensure the correct line in economic policy, really conforming to the policy of industrialization adopted by the Fourteenth Congress. . . .

. . . . The fundamental economic difficulties, consequently, result from the fact that *the volume of industry is too small* both in relation to agriculture (personal and productive needs of the peasants) and in relation to the growing needs of the working class. This disproportion should be overcome not by slowing down the growth either of agriculture or of the needs of the working class, but by developing industry at a rate that would make it possible to eliminate this disproportion in a relatively small span of years.

This task is all the more imperative in that industry—in its present state—can no longer solve other vital problems, starting with the production of the means of production for industry itself, maintenance and development of the transportation system, and defense of the country.

In view of the above, the Central Committee instructs the Political Bureau:

—to draw up a concrete program of industrial development and new industrial construction for the coming economic period (five to eight years) in close relation to the perspectives of the growth of agriculture;

—to draw up a directive concerning the preparation of all programs and plans for 1926-27 that will ensure the possibility that substantial progress will be made in 1926-27 itself toward liquidating the internal disproportions of our economy.

The *long-term* plan should base itself on a working hypothesis—e.g., that the fundamental disproportion could be overcome over a period of five years (or by some other date)—in order to make a provisional determination of what the relative equilibrium will be in 1931 between the supply and demand of industrial products, under conditions of a policy of steadily lowering prices. Such a projection, naturally without pretending to be exact and definitive, would nevertheless be the compass for our whole economic policy.

*   *   *

With these aims, the programs and plans for the year 1926-27 should flow from the following considerations:

1. Agricultural taxation, with the appropriate burden being imposed on the upper strata in the villages, should be one of the most important levers for correctly distributing the wealth accumulated by the economy. . . .

2. A rise in the retail prices should not be permitted. On the contrary, there should be a struggle to reduce them by every

possible means. As for wholesale prices, a more flexible policy, adapted in a more specialized way to the various branches of industry, should be introduced, with the calculation that a larger share of the retail mark-up than before would end up in the hands of the state and the cooperatives.

3. The 1926-27 budget should be drawn up in such a way that a sufficiently large sum will be allocated to industry over and above the funds which are really only a redistribution, through the state budget, of industry's own resources. The net balance cleared by industry should not in any case be less than 150 to 200 million, and all efforts should be bent toward increasing this net balance.

This must be achieved by strictly holding down all nonproductive expenses, or at least refusing to increase them in the near future, keeping in mind that we have not yet left the stage of primitive socialist accumulation.

4. It is necessary to re-examine the question of vodka, basing ourselves on the experience we have acquired, which shows that the sale of vodka by the state plays a very insignificant role in the flow of resources from the village to heavy industry (which was the aim) and that at the same time if takes a big bite out of the workers' wages.

5. The possibility for substantial growth in long-term credits for new industrial construction will have to be assured, beginning in 1926-27. . . .

6. The system of amortization deductions should be organized in such a way that industry automatically has the means for maintaining its productive capacity at the existing level, using all additional resources for further expansion.

7. The export and import plan for 1926-27 should be drawn up in such a way as to assure the growth of productive capacity in industry and substantial technical reequipment of industry, including the construction of new factories.

8. Our whole economic policy should be fashioned in such a way as to assure the possibility that in the year 1926-27 a program of capital construction will be carried out at a level of no less than one billion rubles, as compared with 820 million in 1925-26 (i.e., an increase of at least 20 percent).

9. The resources of the Industrial Bank should be reinforced in order to strengthen the central industrial reserve fund, which provides for the steady expansion of working capital in industry.

10. It is necessary to draw up and begin today to make practical preparations for a system of measures capable of

ensuring realization of the next harvest—first of all, by the supplementary import of primary materials (cotton, wool, rubber, leather, metals) so as to increase our stocks of goods destined for the peasants in the autumn; second of all, by preparation for intervention in the world market, which may become inevitable—an intervention based on the principle of foreign credit proportional to our internal trade volume and strictly corresponding to the interests and possibilities of state industry.

11. It is necessary to ensure that the electrification plan for the country will be carried out at as energetic a pace as possible.

II. Problems of the Rate of Development

The expropriation of the nonproductive classes (the aristocracy, the bourgeoisie, the clergy, and the privileged bureaucracy), the nationalization of the land, the abolition of rent, and the concentration of the assets of industry, transportation, and the whole credit system in the hands of the state have assured, as the experience of past years has proven incontestably, an indubitable preponderance of the socialist elements over the capitalist elements in our economy.

But precisely the tremendous successes of our economy, which have more and more linked it to the chain of the world market, have by the same token placed our future successes and, first of all, our rate of industrialization, under the relative control of the world capitalist economy. It would be radically false to believe that socialism, within capitalist encirclement, could progress at an arbitrary pace. The advance toward socialism can only be assured if the distance separating our industry from advanced capitalist industry—in volume of production, cost-price, and quality—diminishes in a palpable and evident way, rather than increases. Only on this condition can our armed forces be given the technical base capable of protecting the socialist development of the country.

III. The Leading Role of Industry, and Agriculture

The resolution of the Fourteenth Congress clearly and categorically indicated the *leading* role of state industry in the economy as a whole. The duty of the party is to clearly grasp the full significance of this directive and to draw all the appropriate practical conclusions from it. . . .

Furthermore, since agriculture has neared the prewar level on the old basis of primitive technology, any serious advance in the rural economy in the future will be possible only through gradual industrialization, that is, a major growth in the manufacture of agricultural machinery, synthetic fertilizers, electrification, etc. The most effective form of state aid to peasant agriculture would be a substantial flow of the necessary agricultural tools produced by state industry at advantageous credit terms. This in turn presupposes a major growth in the manufacture of agricultural machinery, closely coordinated with the particularities of the main agricultural regions.

IV. The Plan: Its New Tasks and Methods

The importance of the planning principle has been demonstrated not only in our tremendous successes in economic construction but also in our failures and miscalculations. It would be a crude error to see these as an argument *against* the planning principle. On the contrary, the very possibility of discovering them in time and correcting them in one way or another is provided by the centralized system of economic administration. This system is inconceivable without the coordination of all the factors essential to it, both administrative and market-related.

The growth of our economy not only requires a general strengthening of the planning principle but also creates qualitatively new problems in this area. Until now planning consisted mainly in the attempt to foresee the movement of the essential economic elements for the year to come and to coordinate them by various maneuvers; that is, planning was limited to the functions described in the resolution of the Twelfth Congress. This kind of planning based on maneuverability within an ongoing operational framework might have been adequate during the so-called reconstruction period, when industry was developing on the technical bases inherited from the past. Now that this period is ending, the need to renew and expand the fixed capital of industry and transportation places entirely new problems before the party and the state, parallel to the old ones, in the area of planned management.

Until recently, industry—with considerable reserves of underutilized equipment at its disposal—could rapidly raise its output above the projections of the plan, in accordance with the needs of the market. But from now on its possibilities in this direction will be determined by the capital outlays industry will be able to make annually. The volume and application of these capital expenditures will have to be planned as thoughtfully and rigorously as possible by the state. The construction of new factories, power plants, and railways, the reclamation of huge areas, the training of suitably skilled workers in all categories, and the task of coordinating all this new construction with the existing economic conditions and with the plans for industry and for the economy as a whole—all that cannot be accomplished in a single business year. We are talking about the planning of very large units and projects which are expected to take a number of years and whose economic consequences will be felt for an additional period of years after that. The annual plan must be viewed as an individual part of an overall five-year plan. On the other hand, the five-year plan should be corrected annually to take account of the changes made in the current operating plan.

V. Wages

Economic difficulties do not allow us at present to chart a course toward a substantial rise in wages. The party should recognize, however, that the present wage level is inadequate and should set itself the following tasks in this area:

a. not to allow a decrease in real wages in the near future;

b. to create the material conditions for a future increase in wages, i.e., a sufficient increase in the volume of industrial production in 1926-27 for money wages to be appropriately supplemented in kind (40 to 45 percent of the worker's budget is now paid for in industrial products); a stubborn and systematic technical reequipment of industry, the only thing that can ensure a systematic and uninterrupted rise in the workers' standard of living. . . .

NOTES ON ECONOMIC QUESTIONS
The Law of Socialist Accumulation, the Planning Principle, the Rate of Industrialization, and—Lack of Principles

May 2, 1926

NOTE: Trotsky wrote these notes, apparently for his own use, or for his cothinkers, about how the economic issues raised by the Fourteenth Congress—in particular the interrelationship between the world and Soviet economies and the role of planning—were handled by the April plenum.

A controversy that took place in economic planning circles in the late winter and spring of 1926 was the source of Trotsky's apprehension, expressed in these notes, that Preobrazhensky's analysis might be exploited by the proponents of socialism in one country. Preobrazhensky, an economist and an Oppositionist, stressed that the conflict between the two laws of the Soviet economy—the law of value, rooted in the NEP, and the law of socialist accumulation, rooted in state industry—could only be resolved through the success of long-range planned accumulation, chiefly at the expense of the peasantry. Trotsky did not entirely share these views. Moreover, he feared that they might provide fuel to the charge that the Opposition wanted to break the bond with the peasantry, or that they might backhandedly be used to support the theory of socialism in one country by appearing to call for primitive socialist accumulation by the Soviet Union alone, without reference to the world market or the international revolution. (A good summary of Preobrazhensky's and Trotsky's views on this question is in the second volume of Isaac Deutscher's biography of Trotsky, The Prophet Unarmed, *pp. 234-39). In any case, Trotsky's differences with Preobrazhensky were still incidental at this stage; he is chiefly concerned in these notes with the increasing tendency of the Stalin-Bukharin majority to play down the importance of rapid industrialization and to ignore the tool of planning in industrial expansion.*

Socialism in one country flagrantly contradicted the entire internationalist tradition of Marxism. Yet it could not be promoted as a revision of basic party doctrine: it had to have a genealogy. The Stalinists combed the works of Lenin for support and emerged with two quotations that, if taken out of context and read in isolation from all of Lenin's other work, could be made to sound as though they endorsed the notion: one, referred to here as a "wrongly understood quotation from Lenin," was a statement from 1915, asserting that Russia had "all that was necessary and sufficient" to build socialism; the other was an unfinished passage from "On Cooperation," written shortly before Lenin's death and left in uncorrected form. These two quotations became the family tree for the theory of socialism in one country. Trotsky takes them up in detail and explains their actual place in Lenin's thinking in his speech to the Fifteenth Conference, November 1, 1926 (see p. 130).

By permission of the Harvard College Library.

1. The analysis of our economy from the point of view of the interaction (both conflicting and harmonizing) between the law of value and the law of socialist accumulation is in principle an extremely fruitful approach—more accurately, the only correct one. Such analysis must begin within the framework of the closed-in Soviet economy. But now there is a growing danger that this methodological approach will be turned into a finished economic perspective envisaging the "development of socialism in one country." There is reason to expect, and fear, that the supporters of this philosophy, who have based themselves up to now on a wrongly understood quotation from Lenin, will try to adapt Preobrazhensky's analysis by turning a methodological approach into a generalization for a quasi-autonomous process. It is essential, at all costs, to head off this kind of plagiarism and falsification. The interaction between the law of value and the law of socialist accumulation must be placed in the context of the world economy. Then it will become clear that the law of value that operates within the limited framework of the NEP is complemented by the growing external pressure from the law of

value that dominates the world market and is becoming ever more powerful.

2. In this connection the question of our rate of economic development takes on decisive importance, and above all, our rate of industrialization. The monopoly of foreign trade is a powerful factor in the service of socialist accumulation—powerful but not all-powerful. The monopoly of foreign trade can only moderate and regulate the external pressure of the law of value to the extent that the value of Soviet products, from year to year, comes closer to the value of the products on the world market. In calculating the value of Soviet products one should of course take into account the overhead expenses of social legislation. But in the context of the world competition between economic systems, the requirement mentioned above remains in full force—that is, the rate of Soviet industrialization must be such as to assure that Soviet products approximate those on the world market in a way perceptible to our workers and peasants.

3. The Fourteenth Congress resolution asserts that the limits of industrialization are the purchasing power of the market and the currently available financial resources of the state. These limits are not the only ones or the main ones; they only serve as empirical expressions, in market and money terms, of other limits. Within this larger framework, the lag of industry behind the development of our economy as a whole finds its expression in the goods famine and the wholesale-retail price scissors. In reply to these assertions, Gusev and others raise two objections, which have no connection but, in fact, contradict one another; moreover, both are indefensible to an equal degree. These objections are (a) that those who demand an end to industry's lagging behind and who urge that it take a leading role are "superindustrializers," and (b) that those who place limits on the extent to which industry can develop in terms of the market are allegedly afraid of the peasantry and have forgotten that production of the means of production cannot be geared to the level of the market.

4. Thus, people who, on questions involving the renewal of fixed capital, have now run into the problem of socialist accumulation and the planning principle counterpose these discoveries of theirs to the industrializers, who, for this special purpose, are transformed from "superindustrializers" into "agrarians" who capitulate to the peasant market.

5. This in no way prevents these newcomers to the question of socialist accumulation from remaining on their old ground on the

question of planning, i.e., an essentially market-oriented position. In recent years planning has consisted primarily, if not exclusively, in the regulation of the way the elements of the economy are combined on the basis of the market and within the framework of the current year. The question of the complex, constructive tasks of planning has now become absolutely unavoidable in relation to the need to renew and expand fixed capital. In this area, the socialist approach to the question ought now to find its most clear-cut expression. But the amendments answering to this need were rejected.

6. The question of the interaction between the Soviet and world economies is becoming more and more crucially important from every point of view. This was indicated above in regard to the laws of accumulation and value, as well as to economic growth rates. Of no less importance to the question of the so-called economic independence of the Soviet Union is foreign trade. This question needs to be discussed from every angle, and, as far as possible, on the basis of an analysis of the main elements of our import and export trade. *Approximate projections for the next five years need to be worked out along these lines.* The dialectic by which the growth of economic ties and interdependence paves the way for industrial "independence" needs to be demonstrated.

7. The question of the distribution and redistribution of agricultural and industrial, private and state accumulation must be linked with the refutation of the legend that the village is treated like a "colony."

8. At the plenum the question of the connection between the economy and the party regime was left completely untouched. However, the importance of this tie is immeasurable.

The question of economizing was posed sharply enough at the congress and in the congress resolution. But what was not dealt with at all was the question of why, since the time of the Twelfth Congress, when the question of economizing was posed as sharply as possible (payments exacted from economic enterprises by local party, soviet, and trade union organizations, senseless advertisements, etc.), the necessary success has not been achieved. It is quite obvious that success is impossible without the active participation and supervision of public opinion in the country, above all that of the party.

The selection of personnel for economic work should be dictated by considerations of the job to be done. Managers and directors must feel the eye of public opinion, of the workers, the party, etc., upon them.

It is characteristic of the bureaucratic regime that managers feel they are responsible only to the apparatus, above all to the party secretaries. This kind of situation is equally harmful from the point of view of the proper selection of managers and from that of the establishment of proper economic functioning, especially of the strictest economizing.

PARTY BUREAUCRATISM
AND PARTY DEMOCRACY

June 6, 1926

NOTE: Trotsky spent several weeks in Germany for medical treatment. While he was there, two important political events occurred. In Poland, Marshal Pilsudski, supported by the Communist Party, carried out a coup d'état and became dictator. And the British coalminers' strike led to a general strike, exposing the weakness of the Anglo-Russian Committee (see Introduction, pp. 19-20). On his return to Russia Trotsky argued that the Polish Communists had supported Pilsudski's coup because the Comintern had instructed them to strive for the "democratic dictatorship of the workers and peasants," which Lenin had called for in 1905, instead of the dictatorship of the proletariat. Zinoviev and Kamenev demurred on this. Their support to Lenin's 1905 slogan, despite Lenin's own disavowal of it during 1917, was inflexible. Trotsky called for the dissolution of the Anglo-Russian Committee; Zinoviev had helped to sponsor the committee and would not oppose it so absolutely. Thus, even in the initial days of the United Opposition, even as Trotsky, Zinoviev, and Kamenev began to merge their factions, the seeds of differences were already finding fertile soil in the day-to-day developments.

It was on the issue of party democracy that Trotsky reopened his struggle with Stalin. The growth of bureaucracy and the deterioration of inner-party democracy were central problems to which Trotsky would return again and again in his attempt to awaken the party to the need to counter these trends.

His reference to the debate about the dictatorship of the class versus the dictatorship of the party (p. 70) is a polemic against Stalin. In a speech to party secretaries on June 17, 1924, "The Results of the Thirteenth Congress of the RCP(B)," Stalin had described the dictatorship of the party as "sheer nonsense" (Works [Moscow: Foreign Languages Publishing House], vol. 6 [1953], p. 270). He was downgrading the party as a way of

achieving the apparatus's independence from it and unlimited
power over it: and thus over the working class as a whole.
By permission of the Harvard College Library.

To the Politburo:

I call your attention to the following circumstance:

On June 2 Comrade Uglanov gave a report to the enlarged
plenum of the party committee of the Zamoskvorechye district [in
Moscow]. Without going into any other aspects of this report, and
basing my comments on the account in *Pravda,* I find it
necessary to dwell at some length here on the way Comrade
Uglanov, the head of the Moscow party organization, conceives
of and defines *party democracy.*

What Is "Democracy"?

Let me cite the relevant passage word for word (from *Pravda,*
no. 127, June 4, 1926): "What is the essence of party democracy?
Comrade Uglanov gives a clear and concise answer: It is to
present the basic tasks facing the party and the country to the
party organization in a correct and timely way so that it can
resolve them; to draw the broad mass of party members into the
discussion and resolution of these problems; to explain the
fundamental problems of socialist construction to the proletariat
in a correct and timely way; to check the correctness of our
policies against the moods of the working class and its individual
detachments; and to rectify our line on the basis of such checking."

It is quite obvious that this definition, which the *Pravda*
account with full justification terms "clear and concise," has a
finished and programmatic quality to it. As a matter of fact, what
we have here is a theoretical formulation of *party bureaucratism*
as a system, in which the party per se functions only as raw
material in the hands of the apparatus. It is not hard, in fact, to
demonstrate that in the sum total of activities and relationships
which Comrade Uglanov calls party democracy, the role of
initiator of action is relegated exclusively to the party apparatus,
which at every given moment decides the forms in which and
limits within which it is to "exert its influence" upon the mass of
the party as a whole.

Let us analyze this definition point by point.

(a) It is democracy "to present . . . tasks . . . to the party . . .

in a timely and correct way." To the speaker it was totally self-evident and a foregone conclusion that tasks are presented to the party by the apparatus and only by the apparatus, and if it presents them "in a timely and correct way," the timeliness and correctness being decided by the apparatus itself, that is "party democracy."

(b) It is democracy, futhermore, "to draw the broad mass of party members into the discussion and resolution of these problems." The very phrase "draw into" is enough to fully characterize the direction of thinking here. The party is portrayed as an inert mass that tends to resist and must be *"drawn into"* the discussion of tasks that are *presented* to it by that very same party apparatus. And so, if the apparatus does its *presenting* in a timely and correct way and does its *drawing in* in a timely and correct way, that, then, is "party democracy."

(c) Going further, we learn that it is democracy "to explain the fundamental problems of socialist construction to the proletariat in a correct and timely way," i.e., the same questions which the apparatus has presented to the party, and into the discussion of which it has drawn the party. Here the one-sided, bureaucratic relationship between the apparatus and the party is extended to the class.

(d) It is democracy "to check the correctness of our policies against the moods of the working class and its individual detachments." The same apparatus that presents the tasks, that draws the party into the discussion of them, and that explains these tasks to the proletariat—this same apparatus checks its policies against the "moods" of the working class in order "to rectify the line on the basis of such checking." Thus, the line is rectified by the very ones who initiate it—the apparatus. It presents the tasks "in a timely and correct way," that is, those tasks it finds necessary and at such times as it finds necessary. It draws in the ranks of the party to discuss these tasks—within those confines and limits which it finds correct and timely. It explains what it finds necessary through the party to the working class. It, the apparatus, checks the results of this work against the "moods" of the working class. And it, the apparatus, on the basis of such checking, such an estimate of moods, rectifies its own line "in a timely way."

No other features of party democracy are indicated by Comrade Uglanov. The *Pravda* account, as we have seen, calls his definition of democracy "clear and concise." This definition, I repeat, has a finished and programmatic quality. It represents a

new word in the development of the party regime and party
ideology. Before June 2, 1926, the party many times gave its
definition of the kind of regime it meant by the term *party
democracy*. The most outstanding stages in the development of
party thought on this question were the resolution of the Tenth
Congress (1921) and the unanimous Central Committee resolution of December 5, 1923, subsequently confirmed by the Thirteenth Party Congress. The resolution of the last party congress,
the fourteenth, refers only to the necessity of remaining "on the
path of consistent party democracy." The concept of party
democracy is not spelled out in the Fourteenth Congress resolution precisely because this had already been done with the
necessary thoroughness at previous party congresses. The Fourteenth Congress proceeded on the assumption that there was no
question of a new, programmatic definition of party democracy
but that the task was to realize the existing one in practice. A
different approach is taken by Comrade Uglanov, head of the
Moscow organization. He raises the question, "What is the
essence of party democracy?" Having posed this programmatic
question, Comrade Uglanov fails to refer back to the definitions
of democracy given by the party earlier. He gives his own, new
definition, the one we have just examined.

In defining the "essence" of democracy, Comrade Uglanov has
actually counterposed his programmatic definition to the one
which the party has given until now and which was thought to be
beyond dispute. Thus the Tenth Congress resolution declared one
of the basic features of democracy to be "constant control on the
part of the public opinion of the party over the work of the
leading bodies." The unanimous resolution of December 5, 1923,
states: "Workers' democracy means the liberty of frank discussion of the most important questions of party life by all members,
and the freedom to have organized discussions on these questions, and the election of all leading party functionaries and
commissions from the bottom up" [*The Challenge of the Left
Opposition (1923-25)*, p. 408, where the translation used is slightly
different]. These three features: (a) *free discussion* by all party
members of all the most important questions, (b) constant *control
by the party* over its leading bodies, and (c) the *election* of
responsible individuals and collective bodies, from the bottom
up—all three of these features are left completely out of the
Uglanovist definition of the "essence" of party democracy. For
Uglanov, the apparatus checks up on the party, but not a word is
said about the party's control over the apparatus. In his version

the apparatus presents questions in a timely way and "draws" the party into the discussion of questions it considers timely. Of free discussion by the party on *all* questions, there is no mention whatsoever. And finally, in his version, the question of responsible and leading individuals being subject to election is totally excluded from the essence of party democracy.

The resolution of December 5, 1923, states: "The interests of the party, both for its successful struggle against influences generated by the NEP and to enhance its fighting capacity in all areas of work, demand a serious change in the party's course in the sense of an active and systematic implementation of the principles of workers' democracy" [*The Challenge of the Left Opposition (1923-25)*, p. 408]. The Thirteenth Congress approved this way of posing the question. The Fourteenth Congress again referred to the need to carry out the change in the party's course unanimously proclaimed by the Central Committee in December 1923. Various leading comrades have acknowledged a number of times that there exists a difference between the resolutions on party democracy and the practical reality, a difference that to some has seemed a crying contradiction and to others a temporary disparity. All, however, have taken as their starting point, at least programmatically, at least in words, at least formally, the assumption that practical reality should gradually draw closer to the definition of democracy existing in principle, that is, a party regime whose essence is defined above all by freedom of discussion on all questions, constant control by the general body of opinion in the party over party institutions, and the election of all responsible individuals and collective bodies.

Comrade Uglanov for the first time has made an open attempt to overcome the contradiction between the programmatic definition of democracy and the actual regime by bringing the program down, drastically, to the level of what has existed in practice. As the essence of democracy he proclaims the unlimited domination of the party apparatus, which presents, draws in, checks, and rectifies. On June 2, 1926, the party was given a fully perfected definition of a regime based on the absolute authority of the apparatus. Attempting to define the essence of democracy, Comrade Uglanov has defined the essence of bureaucracy. To be sure, in Comrade Uglanov's definition this bureaucracy does not simply command, but presents questions to the masses, draws them in, and rectifies the line. But that only means that Comrade Uglanov has given the definition of "enlightened" bureaucracy. There is not even a hint of democracy here.

Of course, it goes without saying that the party is first of all an action organization. The regime in its entirety should ensure the possibility of timely and single-minded action by the party as a whole. From this there follows both the necessity for genuine party democracy and real limitations upon it in the concrete historical conditions of any given period. We all know this. The party cannot be turned into a discussion club. The party has never lost sight of this fact, not at the Tenth Congress and not since then. But precisely in order to ensure the *capacity* of the party to carry on with the proletarian dictatorship under new, more complex conditions, the party has constantly, since 1921, advanced and repeated the idea that as the proletarian elements in the party grow stronger, as the cultural and political level of the party as a whole grows higher, the party regime must undergo uninterrupted change in the direction of overcoming bureaucratism and apparatus habits through the methods of free discussion, collective decision-making, control over the apparatus, and the election of the apparatus from the bottom up.

Since the time of the transition from war communism to NEP, from the civil war to economic and cultural construction, more than five years have passed. The announcement of the course toward party democracy followed naturally from the conditions of the transition from the civil war to extensive socialist construction. Since the end of 1923, when the need for "a serious change of the party's course" was proclaimed by the Central Committee itself, two and a half years have passed. During this five-year period, especially the second half, we have not had to be involved in war. Our economy has grown. The proletariat has been reviving. The party, in its basic composition, has become proletarian. The party has raised its level and grown in experience. It would seem that all these conditions would create a tenfold increase in the need for "a serious change of the party's course" toward democracy. That change, however, has not taken place. On the contrary, never before has the party regime been so permeated by the practice of appointments from above, habits of command, suspicion, and administrative pressure, i.e., by an all-embracing principle of apparatus rule. The contradiction, and it is a crying one, between the programmatic definition of party democracy, the oft-proclaimed and oft-confirmed need for charting a course toward party democracy, on the one hand, and the actual regime, on the other, is everywhere apparent. This contradiction is becoming increasingly thorny, painful, and simply unendurable for the party's consciousness. Nothing weighs so heavily upon a revolutionary party as two-facedness, a disparity between word and deed. Beyond certain boundaries such duality passes over into plain and simple falsehood. Yet Comrade Uglanov takes the initiative, on his own authority, of *revising the principles of the party's orientation* on the question of the party regime and workers' democracy in general. Comrade Uglanov boldly raises the question of the "essence" of democracy and reveals this essence to be—the timely and correct functioning of enlightened bureaucracy. If there were no other manifestations, this symptom alone would be grounds enough for saying: "We are standing at a crossroads in the development of the party." The duality of the present cannot be maintained. Either a serious change in the party regime must begin to be made, in full accordance with the decisions of past congresses' or the party will have to change its orientation, which means to pass from the Leninist standpoint to that of Uglanov.

The Source of Bureaucratism in the Relations Between Classes

The party regime does not have a self-contained, self-sufficient nature. On the one hand it is dependent on all of its surroundings; on the other, the general trend of politics is expressed through it. How could it happen that, despite the favorable change in economic circumstances and the cultural rise of the proletariat, the party regime has steadily shifted in the recent past in the direction of bureaucratization?

To explain this only by the country's lack of culture and by the fact that our party is a ruling party leads nowhere; first, because the uncultured character of the country is on the wane while party bureaucratism is on the rise; second, because if the party's role as a ruling party inevitably entailed its increased bureaucratization, that would imply the destruction of the party. But there can be no question of such a perspective. Lack of culture in and of itself, in the form of illiteracy and the absence of the simplest necessary skills, leads mostly to bureaucratism in the state apparatus. But the party, after all, counts among its members the most cultured and energetic of the vanguard of the toiling masses, and above all of the industrial proletariat. This vanguard is growing quantitatively and qualitatively. Consequently, as far as the regime within the party is concerned, it ought to be steadily becoming more democratic. But in fact it is growing more bureaucratic. It is clear that mere reference to lack of culture explains nothing and above all fails to take into account the trends or dynamics of historical development. Yet all the while, bureaucratization has gone so far that it seeks to be crowned theoretically. That is the central meaning of Comrade Uglanov's venture.

The fundamental cause of bureaucratization must be sought in the relations between classes. One cannot close one's eyes to the fact that, parallel to a certain increase in Soviet democracy in the village, we have had extreme pressure tactics applied in Moscow and Leningrad. Democracy is not a self-sufficing factor. What matters are the policies of the proletarian dictatorship in the arenas of the economy, culture, etc.; these policies should be such that the proletarian vanguard, the vehicle of these policies, can carry them out, to an ever increasing extent, through free discussion, with control over the apparatus, and with the right to elect it. It is plainly evident that if industry, that is, the base on which the socialist dictatorship rests, lags behind the develop- ment of the economy as a whole; if value accumulated in the economy is not distributed along lines that will assure the further ascendancy of socialist tendencies over capitalist ones; if the difficulties resulting from this are placed first and foremost on the backs of the working class; if wage increases for the workers are delayed, in the midst of a general advance of the economy; if such exceptional fiscal devices as the vodka monopoly become a growing burden on the workers—under such conditions the party apparatus is less and less able to carry out its policies by means of party democracy. The bureaucratization of the party in this case is an expression of the disrupted social equilibrium, which has been and is being tipped to the disadvantage of the proletar- iat. This disruption of the equilibrium is transmitted to the party and weighs upon the proletarian vanguard in the party. Hence the increased application of pressure tactics in the most powerful centers of the proletariat, in the main base areas of the party. Having thrown out free discussion, the collective resolution of tasks, control over the apparatus, and the election of it, Comrade Uglanov reduces the problem to one of checking party policies against the "moods" of the proletariat, i.e., feeling and probing by empirical apparatus methods to determine how much adminis- trative pressure the working class and its vanguard is willing and able to endure, pressure resulting from the entire economic and social orientation of the party leadership. From this it also follows that the methods of democracy are replaced by the methods of enlightened bureaucracy.

The Weakening of the Ideological Center as an Additional Cause of the Crackdown Within the Party

Any regime develops its own internal logic, and a bureaucratic regime develops it more rapidly than any other. It is quite natural for the major industrial and cultural centers of the country to become seats of resistance to incorrect economic policies and to the incorrect party regime that supplements those policies. It is natural for this resistance to find expression within the upper layers of the leadership as well. And again, it is quite logical, under conditions of domination by an apparatus regime, that there emerges a tendency for any and all differences to be transformed into a struggle between factional groupings. That a ruling party, under conditions of revolutionary dictatorship, cannot accept a regime of contending factions is absolutely unquestionable. One need only add that it is absolutely inevitable for an apparatus regime to breed factions from its own midst. Moreover, under a closed-off apparatus regime, which only gives orders but permits no control over itself, the formation of groupings is generally the only possible way to make corrections in apparatus policy.

The resolution of December 5, 1923, also spoke very distinctly about this, condemning a bureaucratic regime precisely because it considers "every criticism a manifestation of factionalism." Since that resolution was adopted unanimously, two and a half years have gone by, during which the apparatus regime has been deepened and intensified, and consequently the tendency for factional groupings to be produced by the apparatus regime has also deepened. The result of this has been the fragmentation of the party cadres, the removal from the party leadership of valuable elements representing a significant portion of its accumulated experience, and the systematic narrowing down and ideological impoverishment of the leadership core. That precisely this process is going on before our eyes, and with growing rapidity, and that it has not yet completed its destructive work—of that no serious Communist can have any doubt. The concentration of the all-powerful party apparatus in the hands of an ever more restricted leadership core gives rise to a new and extremely acute contradiction—between the growing might of the apparatus and the ideological enfeeblement of the leading center. Under these conditions fear of deviations is bound to grow progressively, with inevitable consequences in the form of so-called organizational measures, which narrow down still further the range of those called upon to be part of the leadership and which push them even further down the road of bureaucratization of the party regime.

At every stage in this process of fragmentation of the leading cadres, the apparatus leadership surrounds itself with illusory promises: If we can only deal with this one new obstacle, after that we can again, without interference, "present questions," "draw in the masses," "check," and "rectify." But in reality, under the conditions of the bureaucratic shift in party leadership, each new apparatus campaign to crush an opposition automatically produces new fissures and new dangers. That the process did not end with the Leningrad group is absolutely and completely clear. The fissures that exist in the central leadership core will not develop openly as long as the apparatus is still involved in its fight against the old (1923) Opposition and the new one of 1925. At a certain stage, and one that is not so far off, a new section of the apparatus will inevitably be thrown into opposition by the course of events—with all the ensuing consequences. Only the blind can fail to see that.

Dictatorship of the Party or Dictatorship of the Class?

At the last plenum a dispute was brought up again—only in passing, to be sure—over the dictatorship of the proletariat versus the dictatorship of the party. Abstractly posed, such a dispute can easily founder in scholasticism. Of course, the foundation of our regime is the dictatorship of the class. But this in turn assumes that it is the class not only "in itself" but also "for itself," that is, that it is a class that has come to self-consciousness through its vanguard, which is to say, through the party. Without this, the dictatorship could not exist. To present matters as though the party were only the teacher, while the class puts the dictatorship into effect, is to prettify the truth of the matter. Dictatorship is the most highly concentrated function of a class, and therefore the basic instrument of a dictatorship is a party. In the most fundamental respects a class realizes its dictatorship through a party. That is why Lenin spoke not only of the class dictatorship but also of the dictatorship of the party and, *in a certain sense,* made them identical.

Is it correct to make such an identification? That depends on the actual development of the process itself. If the dictatorship develops in such a way as to permit and encourage the advance of democratic methods in the party and working class organizations, with the maintenance of the proper "proportions" between workers' democracy and peasant democracy, the identification of the dictatorship of the class with that of the party is fully and completely justified historically and politically. But if a disproportion is found between the peasantry, or the private sector of the economy in general, and industry; if this disproportion finds political expression in the development of peasant democracy at the expense, to a certain extent, of workers' democracy—then the dictatorship inevitably falls into a bureaucratic-apparatus deviation. Under these conditions the apparatus is in a position of command over and above the party and tries, through it, to take command over the class. The above-cited formula of Comrade Uglanov's gives a finished expression to this kind of regime. Whoever says that the dictatorship of the class is not the dictatorship of the party should, it would seem, first understand that the dictatorship of the class is not the dictatorship of the party apparatus. The dictatorship of the party does not contradict the dictatorship of the class either theoretically or practically, but is the expression of it, if the regime of workers' democracy is constantly developed more and more. On the other hand, increasing coercion by the apparatus, in itself the result of the pressure of opposing class tendencies, inevitably confronts the party with a growing danger of shifts away from the class line. This danger is disguised by the apparatus regime to the extent that it tries to identify itself with the dictatorship of the class. The party serves the apparatus only as a means of probing the "moods" of the working class, so that, "on the basis of such checking," it can "rectify the line." Between Uglanov's definition of the essence of party democracy and the denial of the dictatorship of the party there is, then, a profound inner connection. The bureaucratic regime aspires to theoretical formulation. Bureaucratic theory has always been known for its poverty. Bureaucratism has always been drawn to the formula "L'état, c'est moi." "I am the state; I am the party" [says the bureaucrat]. Uglanov's way of posing the question essentially liquidates the party, dissolves it into the "moods" of the working class and replaces it by the centralized, self-sufficient party apparatus. Stalin's way of putting the question of the dictatorship of the class, counterposing it to the dictatorship of the party, leads inevitably to the dictatorship of the apparatus, because a class with a disorganized vanguard (and the lack of free discussion, of control over the apparatus, and of election rights means a disorganized vanguard) cannot help but become a mere object in the hands of the leadership of a centralized apparatus, which in turn removes itself further and further from the party and is more and more bound to come under the pressure of hostile class forces.

Conclusions

In sketching out this tendency we of course do not suppose for a moment that it will become a reality. In the working class, in the party, and in the party apparatus itself there are powerful forces opposing this historical trend, which inevitably flows from bureaucratism. The sooner and more completely the party realizes the threatening trend, and the more openly and daringly the best elements in the party apparatus help the party to become aware of the danger and turn the wheel—the fewer upheavals there will be and the smoother and less injurious the change of the party regime will be. From everything we have said above it is absolutely clear that a change of regime in the direction of workers' democracy is inseparable from a change in economic policy in the direction of genuine industrialization and a rectification of the line of the party leadership toward genuine internationalism.

The further development of the bureaucratic regime leads fatally toward one-man rule, with an equally fatal reduction in the ideological quality of the leadership. Democratization of the party regime not only permits but requires the reestablishment of collective leadership on a higher political and cultural level. The course toward industrialization, the course toward assuring the proletariat its rightful place in the economy and cultural life of the country, the course toward workers' democracy and, above all, party democracy, and finally, the course toward collective leadership of the party thus all merge together into a single task.

DECLARATION OF THE THIRTEEN
For the July 1926 Plenum
of the CC and CCC of the AUCP(B)

July 1926

NOTE: The party Central Committee convened on July 14, 1926, and met for ten days. The Declaration of the Thirteen, which marked the first intervention by the United Opposition, was probably submitted early in the plenum; the supplementary declaration was written after the July 20 events described in it.

The main debate was over a resolution submitted by the Stalin-Bukharin majority on the "Affair of Lashevich and Others, and Party Unity." The "affair" of Lashevich and others stemmed from an Opposition meeting held in June in a forest near Moscow. At the meeting, organized by G. Belenky, Lashevich, the deputy commissar of war and a candidate member of the CC, spoke. On June 20 both Belenky and Lashevich were severely reprimanded by the presidium of the Central Control Commission, which also called for Lashevich's removal from his post and his expulsion from the CC. During the July plenum, the scandal was extended to include Zinoviev, the president of the Comintern, implicated through association with Belenky, an official of the Comintern Executive Committee. Zinoviev was expelled from the Politburo and Lashevich removed from his post as deputy commissar of war.

"The Declaration of the Thirteen" refers for the first time to the "regime of economy" introduced by the Central Committee in the spring of 1926. This was an attempt to eliminate wastefulness and to reduce the costs of production in industry so as to lower the prices of industrial goods and increase industrial profits. In practice, this meant putting increased pressure on the workers by tying wage increases to higher labor productivity, worsening conditions on the job, raising quotas ("work norms"), imposing penalties for absenteeism and lateness, and wiping out the social

gains that had been guaranteed by the Labor Code enacted after the revolution. This campaign reached a peak in June and July 1926, but after sharp criticism by the Opposition at the July plenum, the party majority retreated, and in August issued statements condemning the "excesses" of the regime of economy and proposing wage increases.

References in point 5 to "influential voices" advocating transfer of the leadership of the agricultural cooperatives to the strong middle peasant and to forcing the poor peasants to sell their tools to get out of debt are to remind the plenum that the head of the agricultural cooperatives (G. Kaminsky) and the commissar of agriculture in the Russian Republic (A. Smirnov) proposed these measures, which would sharply undermine the position of the party and the workers' state in the countryside.

This declaration was signed by both Trotskyists and Zinovievists, including N.K. Krupskaya, Lenin's widow, a supporter of Zinoviev.

By permission of the Harvard College Library.

To All CC and CCC Members: A Declaration

The plainly threatening phenomena which have become more and more discernible in the recent period in the life of the party require careful and conscientious evaluation. Despite the attempts inspired from the top to isolate a certain section of the party from the mass of the workers and to force it astray from the correct party path, we believe unalterably in the preservation of party unity. It is precisely for this reason that we wish to present, with the fullest possible directness, clarity, and even sharpness, our view of the basic causes of the harmful phenomena threatening the party, without leaving anything unsaid and without blurring over or softening anything.

1. Bureaucratism as the Source of Factionalism

The immediate cause of the increasingly severe crises in the party is *bureaucratism,* which has grown appallingly in the period since Lenin's death and continues to grow.

The Central Committee of the ruling party disposes not only of ideological and organizational means for influencing the party, i.e., not only party means, but also governmental and economic means. Lenin always took into account the danger that the concentration of administrative power in the hands of the party apparatus could lead to bureaucratic pressures on the party. It was precisely for this reason that Vladimir Ilyich conceived the idea of organizing a Control Commission, which, while not having administrative power in its hands, would have all the power necessary to combat bureaucratism, to uphold the right of party members to freely express their opinions and vote according to their consciences, without any fear of punitive consequences.

An especially important task of the Control Commission at the present moment, said the resolution of the January 1924 party conference, is to struggle against bureaucratic distortions in the party apparatus and in party practice and to call to account those responsible party personnel who have prevented the principle of workers' democracy from being put into practice in the life of the party organizations (pressure against the free expression of opinions at party meetings, limits not provided for by the party rules on the principle of election from below, etc.).

However, in fact—and this must be said first of all—the Central Control Commission itself has become a purely administrative organ, which assists other bureaucratic agencies in applying pressure, carrying out the most punitive aspects of the work for them, persecuting all independent thinking in the party, every voice of criticism, every outspoken expression of concern for the fate of the party, and any critical comments about particular leaders of the party.

"By workers' democracy within the party," says the resolution of the Tenth Party Congress, "is meant the kind of organizational form which, along with the implementation of Communist Party policies, assures every member of the party, up to and including the most backward ones, an active role in the life of the party, in discussing all problems that come before it, in resolving these problems, and likewise an active role in building the party. The forms of workers' democracy rule out any systematic practices of appointment from above and are best expressed in the broadly based election of all institutions from the bottom up, accountability, control, etc."

Only a party regime totally imbued with these principles can in practice protect the party against factionalism, which is incompatible with the vital interests of the dictatorship of the proletariat. To separate the struggle against factionalism from the question of the party regime is to avoid the essence of the matter, to nourish bureaucratic distortions, and consequently to promote factionalism itself.

The resolution of December 5, 1923, which was adopted unanimously, points directly to the fact that bureaucratism, in suppressing freedom of opinion and stifling criticism, inevitably *drives honest party members down the road of secretiveness and factionalism.* The correctness of this assertion is fully confirmed by the events of the recent past, especially by the "affair" of Lashevich, Belenky, and others. It would be criminal blindness to depict this affair as the result of the ill will of a particular person or a distinct group. In fact we have before us an obvious and unquestionable consequence of the prevailing trend, in which all discussion is from the top down and the ranks below merely listen, thinking for themselves only in isolated cases and on the sly.

Those who are dissatisfied, have doubts, or are in disagreement are afraid to raise their voices at party meetings. The party masses hear only the speeches of the party authorities, all reading from the same schematic study outline. Ties are weakened and confidence in the leadership declines. At party meetings officiousness reigns and, along with it, the inevitable apathy associated with it. Often by the time issues come to a vote there is only an insignificant minority still present: the others are quick to leave so as not to be forced to vote for decisions that have been dictated in advance. Resolutions are universally adopted "unanimously," never any other way. All this is reflected in the internal life of party organizations. Party members are afraid to openly express their most cherished thoughts, hopes, and needs. These are the real reasons behind the "affair" of Lashevich and others.

2. The Cause of the Growth of Bureaucratism

It is quite clear that it is more and more difficult for the leadership to carry out its policies by methods of party democracy, the less the vanguard of the working class perceives these policies as its own. The divergence in direction between economic policies and the thoughts and feelings of the proletarian vanguard inevitably strengthens the need for high-pressure methods and imparts an administrative-bureaucratic character to all politics. All other explanations for the growth of bureaucratism are of a secondary nature and do not grapple with the heart of the problem. The lag of industry behind the economic development of the country as a whole means the lowering of the specific weight of the proletariat in society, despite its numerical growth. The lag in the exertion of influence on agriculture by industry and the rapid growth of the kulaks diminishes the social weight of the poor peasants and agricultural workers and lowers their confidence in the government and in themselves. The lag in the rise of wages behind the higher living standards of the nonproletarian elements in the cities and the upper strata in the villages inevitably means a reduction in the workers' political and cultural consciousness of themselves as the ruling class. This in particular is the reason for the markedly less active participation by the workers and village poor in elections for the soviets, which constitutes a warning to our party of the most serious kind.

3. Wage Problems

During the last few months the label of "demagogy" has been attached to the idea that we should by all ways and means assure the stability of real wages at a time of economic difficulties and that at the first improvement in the situation we should undertake to raise them higher. However, that approach to the problem is the most elementary and obligatory one for a workers' state. The proletarian masses, or their decisive central core, are mature enough to understand what is possible and what unattainable. But when they hear day in and day out that we are growing economically, that our industry is booming, that all assertions as to an inadequate rate of industrial growth are false, that the development of socialism is assured in advance, that all criticism of our economic leadership is based on pessimism, lack of confidence, etc.; and when, on the other hand, they are lectured to at the same time and told that the demand to maintain real wages at the existing level and the perspective of raising the level of real wages in the future—that those are demagogy—then workers cannot understand how the official optimism in regard to general perspectives ties in with the pessimism in regard to wages. Such speeches inevitably strike the masses as false, undermine their confidence in the official sources, and give rise to undercurrents of unrest. Out of distrust toward the official meetings, reports, and votes, even completely disciplined party members feel an urge to find out—by going around and outside the party apparatus—what is really on the minds of the rank-and-file workers. This holds a danger of the most serious kind. And we have to strike not at the symptoms of the illness but at its root causes, in particular at the bureaucratic attitude toward the question of wages.

The rejection of the motion at the April plenum for the maintenance of the existing level of real wages, an absolutely valid and necessary proposal, was a glaring and obvious error leading to an actual reduction in the wage level. The imposition of an agricultural tax on a certain portion of total wages made matters even worse.

The impact of these developments on the everyday existence and mood of the workers was intensified even more by the incorrect way of introducing the "regime of economy." The struggle for a more correct, more conscientious, more thrifty way of dealing with state resources, which is absolutely necessary in and of itself, has led—as a result of an incorrect approach; above all, as a result of not looking at the problem with the eye of the worker and of the peasant—to mechanical pressure tactics from the top down; in the last analysis, to pressure on the workers, and on the least protected and most poorly paid layers and groups at that. This threefold error—in wages, the agricultural tax, and the "regime of economy"—must be corrected decisively and without any procrastination. We must begin right now to lay the groundwork for a certain increase in wages in the fall, beginning with those categories that are the farthest behind in this respect. This is entirely possible given the present dimensions of our economy and budget, in spite of the difficulties that still exist and that are to come. In fact, precisely in order to overcome these difficulties, we must increase the active material interest of the mass of workers in heightening the productive power of state industry. Any other policy would be the most colossal short-sightedness, not only political but economic as well. One cannot help but regard it as a colossal error, therefore, for the present July plenum to refuse to take under consideration the general question of the *conditions of the workers,* as well as its refusal to give clear directives on the exceptionally important question of *the construction of workers' housing.*

4. The Question of Industrialization

The year just past has shown with full clarity that state industry is lagging behind the economic development of the country as a whole. The new harvest again catches us short of reserves of industrial goods. But progress toward socialism can be assured only if the rate of industrial development, instead of lagging behind the overall movement of the economy, draws the rest of the economy along after it, systematically bringing the country closer to the technological level of the advanced capitalist countries. Everything should be subordinated to this goal, which is equally vital for both the proletariat and the peasantry. Only on the condition of a satisfactorily powerful development of industry can both higher wages for the workers and cheaper goods for the village be assured. It would be senseless to base any calculations for the future to any great degree on foreign concessions, to which we cannot assign even an important overall role in our economy, let alone a leading one, without undermining the socialist character of our industry. Our task, then, is to make use of a correct policy of taxes, prices, credit, etc., to try to achieve such a distribution of accumulation in both town and country that the disproportion between industry and agriculture would be overcome as rapidly as possible.

If the upper layers in the village were able to hold back last year's harvest until this spring, thereby cutting into both exports and imports, increasing unemployment, and causing retail prices to rise, that means that the economic and tax policies that gave the kulaks the chance to pursue such a course against the workers' and peasants' interests were in error. Under these conditions, correct tax policies, along with correct price policies, are an essential part of socialist management of the economy. Several hundred million rubles accumulated and concentrated in the hands of the upper strata of the villages even now go to promote the debt bondage of the rural poor to the loan sharks and usurers. The merchants, middlemen, and speculators have already piled up many hundreds of millions of rubles, which have long since been parlayed into billions. It is necessary to apply the tax screws more energetically in order to extract a significant portion of these resources to nourish industry, to strengthen the system of agricultural credit, and to provide the lowest strata in the villages with support in the form of machinery and equipment on advantageous terms. The question of the *smychka* between agriculture and industry under present circumstances is above all a question of industrialization. But all the while the party sees with alarm that the Fourteenth Congress resolution on industrialization is in fact being set aside more and more the same way all the resolutions on party democracy have been reduced to nothing. In this crucial question, on which the life and death of the October Revolution depend, the party does not wish to live by the official study outlines, which are often dictated not by the interests of the cause but by those of factional struggle. The party wishes to know about things, to think them over, to test them out, and to decide upon them itself. The present regime prevents it from doing that. It is precisely from this situation that the secret circulation of party documents, the Lashevich "affair," and other problems arise.

5. Policy in the Countryside

In questions of agricultural policy, the danger of a *shift toward the upper strata in the village* has become more and more plainly delineated. Influential voices are already heard openly advocating the transfer of the actual leadership of agricultural cooperatives into the hands of the "strong" middle peasant; they argue also that the kulaks' contribution can remain veiled in total secrecy; and that careless or inefficient debtors, i.e., poor peasants, should be made to sell the implements they need the most; and so on. The alliance with the middle peasant is more and more transformed into an orientation toward the "well-to-do" middle peasant, who more often than not proves to be a junior edition of the kulak. One of the primary tasks of the socialist state is, through the formation of cooperatives, to bring the poor peasants out of their dead-end situation. The inadequate resources of the socialist state itself deny it the possibility of carrying out any dramatic changes immediately. But this does not give people the right to shut their eyes to the real state of affairs, to fill the poor peasants' ears with lectures about overcoming their dependent psychology, and at the same time to be excessively indulgent toward the kulak. This kind of approach, which is met with more and more often in our party, threatens to dig a deep chasm between us and our main base of support in the village—the poor. But it is only through an unbreakable link between the proletariat and the village poor that a properly established alliance in general between them and the middle peasantry will be possible, i.e., an alliance in which the leadership belongs to the working class. Meanwhile, the fact is that the decisions of last October's plenum on organizing the village poor have to this day found no application in the work of our local organizations. And the fact is that even at the upper levels of administration there is a noticeable desire to push back as much as possible the Communist or poor peasant layer of cadres in the agricultural cooperatives or to replace them with "strong" middle peasants. And the fact is that under the pretext of an alliance of the poor with the middle peasants we everywhere observe the political subordination of the poor to the middle peasants and through them to the kulaks.

6. Bureaucratic Deformations in the Workers' State

The number of workers in state industry in our country has not yet reached two million; if those in transportation are added, the figure is less than three million. Government personnel, professional people, those working in the cooperative network, and all other office workers by no means constitute a smaller figure. This statistical comparison, by itself, testifies to the colossal political and economic role of the bureaucracy. It is quite obvious that the state apparatus in its social composition and standard of living is bourgeois or petty bourgeois to a great extent, and is drawn away from the proletariat and poor peasantry toward, on the one hand, the comfortably fixed intellectual and, on the other, the merchant, the renter of land, the kulak, and the new bourgeois.

How many times Lenin referred to the bureaucratic deformations in the state apparatus and to the need for the trade unions, on frequent occasions, to defend the workers from the Soviet state. But it is precisely in this area that the party bureaucrat is infected with delusions and self-deception of the most dangerous kind. This was most vividly expressed in Molotov's speech at the fourteenth Moscow province party conference (*Pravda,* December 13, 1925). "Our state," he said, "is a workers' state. . . . But we are being offered a formula according to which it would be more correct to say that the working class must be drawn still closer to our state. . . . What is this? We are supposed to set ourselves the task of drawing the workers closer to our state. But this state of ours—whose is it, if not the workers'? Is it not a state of the proletariat? How are they to be drawn closer to the state, i.e., how are the workers themselves to be drawn closer to the working class, which is in power and is controlling the state?"

These astonishing words deny the very task of a struggle by the proletarian vanguard for the genuine ideological and political subordination to itself of the state apparatus. What a colossal distance separates this point of view from that of Lenin, who in one of his last articles wrote that our state apparatus "has only been slightly touched up on the surface, but in all other respects it is a most typical relic of our old state machine" [*Collected Works,* vol. 33, p. 481]. It is natural that any real serious, and not sham, struggle against bureaucratism is now perceived as nothing but interference, querulousness, and factionalism.

7. Bureaucratic Deformations in the Party Apparatus

In 1920, the party conference, under Lenin's leadership, felt obliged to declare it inadmissible for party bodies or individual comrades, in mobilizing party members, to be guided by any considerations other than those of the business at hand. *"Any acts of repression whatsoever against comrades because they are dissidents on one question or another are inadmissible by decision of the party."* The practical functioning of the party today contradicts that resolution at every turn. Genuine discipline is shaken and weakened and is replaced by subordination to influential figures in the apparatus. Cadres upon whom the party could rely in the most difficult times are being driven from the ranks in ever greater numbers; they are being reassigned, exiled, persecuted, and replaced everywhere by incidental figures who have never been tested but who make up for it by displaying the quality of unquestioning obedience. These severe bureaucratic defects in the party regime are what have made defendants out of Comrades Lashevich and Belenky, whom the party has known for more than two decades as devoted and disciplined members. The indictment against them is an indictment of the bureaucratic deformations in the party apparatus.

The importance of a tightly knit centralized apparatus in the Bolshevik Party needs no explanation. Without that solid backbone of the party the proletarian revolution would have been impossible. The party apparatus for the most part consists of devoted and self-sacrificing party members, people who have no motives other than to fight for the interests of the working class. Under a properly functioning regime and with the appropriate disposition of party forces these same party workers would successfully help to realize party democracy.

8. Bureaucratism and the Everyday Life of Rank-and-File Workers

Bureaucratism strikes heavily at the worker in all spheres—in the party, economy, domestic life, and culture. The social composition of the party has unquestionably improved over the last few years, but at the same time it has become quite clear that increasing the number of workers in the party, even the number directly from the bench, does not by itself secure the party from bureaucratic deformations and other dangers. In fact, the relative weight of the rank-and-file party member under the present regime is extremely low, often virtually nil.

The most unfortunate result of the bureaucratic regime is the way it affects the life of working class and peasant youth. Under NEP conditions, the youth, having no experience of the class struggle of former times, can rise to the level of Bolshevism only through the independent exercise of its capacity to think, be critical, and test things out in practice. We were warned many times by Vladimir Ilyich about the need to be especially careful and attentive in dealing with ideological processes among the youth. But bureaucratism does the opposite: it clamps the development of the youth in a vise, drives their doubts and questions back within them, cuts off criticism, and sows lack of confidence and discouragement on one side and careerism on the other.

In the upper circles of the Communist League of Youth careerism has developed to an extraordinary extent in the past period, pushing up many a new bureaucrat from the ranks of the young and the green. For this reason there is more and more a tendency for the proletarians, poor peasants, or agricultural workers to be pushed out of the Communist League of Youth leadership by intellectuals and philistines, who adapt themselves more easily to the demands of hierarchical leadership but who stand at a greater distance from the workers and the lower strata of the peasant masses. In order to guarantee the appropriate proletarian line in the Communist League of Youth, no less than in the party, the wheel must be turned toward democratization, i.e., the creation of conditions in which the youth can work, think, criticize, make decisions, and rise to revolutionary maturity under the watchful guidance of the party.

The bureaucratic regime penetrates like rust into the life of every factory and workshop. If party members are in fact denied the right to criticize their district committee, province committee, or the Central Committee, in the factories they are denied the chance to voice criticisms of their immediate superiors. Party people are intimidated. An administrator who is able to assure himself the support of the secretary of a higher party organization, because he is a "loyal man," thereby insures himself against criticism from below and often even from responsibility for mismanagement or outright petty tyranny.

In a socialist economy under construction a basic condition for the economical expenditure of national resources is vigilant control by the masses, above all by the workers in the factories and shops. As long as they cannot openly criticize and oppose irregularities and abuses, exposing those responsible by name, without fear of being called Oppositionists, "discontented elements," or troublemakers, or of being expelled from the party cell or even from the factory—as long as they cannot do that, the struggle for a "regime of economy" or for higher productivity will inevitably travel down the bureaucratic path, i.e., more often than not will strike at the vital interests of the workers. This is precisely what we see happening now. Inefficiency and sloppiness in setting pay rates and work norms, which make life hard for the workers, are nine times out of ten the direct result of bureaucratic indifference to the most elementary interests of the workers and of production itself. These can also be considered the source of nonpunctual payment of wages, i.e., the relegation to the background of what should be the foremost concern.

The question of so-called *excesses* by those at the top is totally bound up with the suppression of criticism. Many memoranda have been written against excesses. Quite a few "cases" have been brought by the control commissions. But the masses show an attitude of mistrust toward this kind of officeholders' struggle against excesses. Here too there is only one way out: the masses must not be afraid to say what they think. Where are all these urgent questions discussed? Not at the official party meetings, but off to the side, out of the way, on the sly, and always with caution. It was from these intolerable conditions that the affair of Comrade Lashevich et al. arose. The basic solution to this case must necessarily be to change the conditions.

9. The Struggle for Peace

The development of the world revolutionary movement based on the fraternal solidarity of all working people is the main way of guaranteeing the inviolability of the Soviet Union and the opportunity for peaceful socialist construction. It would, however, be a disastrous error to directly or indirectly build up hopes among the working masses that the Social Democrats or Amsterdamites, especially the British General Council, with such leaders as Thomas and Purcell, are willing or able to conduct a struggle against imperialism, military intervention, etc.

The British compromiser leaders, who so vilely betrayed their own workers during the General Strike and who are now completing their work of treachery in relation to the coalminers' strike, will betray the British proletariat even more outrageously—and with them the Soviet Union and the cause of peace—the moment a war threatens. In his remarkable instructions to our delegation at The Hague [December 4, 1922], Lenin explained that only a merciless exposure of the opportunists in the eyes of the masses can prevent the bourgeoisie from catching the workers off guard when it once again tries to provoke a war. "The most important thing would be to refute the opinion that the delegates at the Conference are opponents of war," wrote Lenin about the Amsterdam "pacifists" at The Hague, "that they understand how war may and will come upon them at the most unexpected moment, that they to any extent understand what method should be adopted to combat war, that they are to any extent in a position to adopt reasonable and effective measures to combat war" [*Collected Works*, vol. 33, p. 449].

Lenin called the attention of the party especially to the fact that on "the question of combating war," even the speeches of many Communists contain "monstrously incorrect and monstrously thoughtless statements on this subject. I think," he wrote, "these declarations, particularly if they have been made since the [First World] war, must be subjected to determined and ruthless criticism, and the name of each person who made them should be mentioned. Opinion concerning these speakers may be expressed in the mildest terms, particularly if circumstances require it, but not a single case of this kind should be passed over in silence, for thoughtlessness on this question is an evil that outweighs all others and cannot be treated lightly" [*Collected Works*, vol. 33, p. 450].

These words of Lenin's must be revived in our party's consciousness and in that of the entire world proletariat. It must be stated for all to hear that the Thomases, MacDonalds, and Purcells are as little able to prevent an imperialist attack as the Tseretellis, Dans, and Kerenskys were able to stop the imperialist slaughter.

A most powerful factor for defending the Soviet Union, and thus for preserving peace as well, is the inseparable connection between the Red Army, which is growing ever stronger, and the toiling masses of our country and of the whole world. All economic, political, and cultural measures that increase the role of the working class in the state, and strengthen its ties with the agricultural workers and poor peasants, by the same token strengthen the Red Army, make the land of soviets more secure against attack, and strengthen the cause of peace.

10. The Comintern

The rectification of the class line of the party means the rectification of its international line. All dubious theoretical innovations must be thrown out if they portray matters as though the victory of socialist construction in our country were not inseparably connected with the progress and outcome of the struggle for power by the European and world proletariat. The colonial peoples are fighting for independence. We are all fighting on the same front. Each unit at each sector of the front must do the maximum within its power without waiting for the initiatives of the others. Socialism will be victorious in our country in inseparable connection with the revolutions of the European and world proletariat and with the struggle of the East against the imperialist yoke. The question of the Comintern and the direction of its policies is indissolubly linked with its internal regime, and in turn with the regime in our party, which has been and remains the leading party of the Comintern. Any shift in our party is unavoidably transmitted to the parties of the International. It is more incumbent on us than ever, then, to have a genuinely Bolshevik testing of our line from the international angle. The Fourteenth Congress recognized the need for more independent participation by the foreign parties in the leadership work of the Comintern. However, this resolution, like so many others, remains only on paper. And not by chance. Sharply disputed questions in the Comintern can only be solved in a normal political and organizational way if a normal regime exists in our own party. Settling disputed questions in a mechanical way threatens more and more to weaken the inner solidarity of the Communist parties and their close ties with one another. In the Comintern arena, we need a decisive turn toward the path laid out by Lenin and proven correct under his leadership.

11. On Factionalism

During the two years before the Fourteenth Congress there existed a factional "Septemvirate" consisting of the six members of the Politburo and the chairman of the Central Control Commission (CCC), Comrade Kuibyshev. This factional clique at the top decided in advance, without the knowledge of the party, every question on the agenda of the Politburo and Central Committee, and unilaterally decided a number of questions that were never brought before the Politburo at all. It made party assignments in a factional manner, and its members were bound by internal faction discipline. Taking part in the work of the Septemvirate, along with Kuibyshev, were those very leaders of the CCC, such as Yaroslavsky, Yanson, etc., who are conducting a ruthless struggle against "factions" and "groupings." A similar factional grouping at the top has no doubt existed since the Fourteenth Congress as well. In Moscow, Leningrad, Kharkov, and other major centers, secret meetings are held, organized by only part of the top brass of the party apparatus, even though they have control of the entire official apparatus. These secret meetings of a select list of people are purely factional in character. Secret documents are read at them, and anyone not belonging to the faction who simply passes on such documents is expelled from the party. The claim that a "majority" cannot be a faction is obviously absurd. Discussion and adoption of resolutions is supposed to occur within the framework of the normal party bodies and not by having all matters decided in advance by a ruling faction behind the backs of the proper institutions. The ruling faction has its own minority, which places faction discipline above that of the party.

The purpose of all this factional machinery is to deny the party the chance to use the normal means, provided by the party rules, to make changes in the personnel and policies of the party apparatus. With every passing day this factional organization threatens the unity of the party more and more.

The deepgoing dissatisfaction with the party regime established after Lenin's death, and the still greater dissatisfaction over the shifts in policy, inevitably produce oppositional outbursts and give rise to heated disputes. But the leading group, instead of learning from the new and ever more striking facts that appear, and instead of rectifying its political line, systematically deepens the errors of bureaucratism. Now, as the evolution of the present ruling faction has shown, there can no longer be any doubt that the basic core of the 1923 Opposition correctly warned about the dangers of a shift away from the proletarian line and about the growing threat of the apparatus regime. Nevertheless, dozens and hundreds of leaders of the 1923 Opposition, including many old worker-Bolsheviks, steeled in the struggle, alien to careerism and obsequiousness, in spite of all the restraint and discipline they have shown, continue to this day to be kept away from party work. The repressive measures taken toward the basic cadre of the Leningrad Opposition after the

Fourteenth Congress could not help but arouse the greatest alarm among the best layer of workers belonging to our party, who are accustomed to regard the Leningrad worker-Communists as the most experienced proletarian vanguard. At a time when the need to repel the growing kulak danger had already matured completely, the leading group took action against the vanguard of the Leningrad workers, who were guilty only of warning against that danger. Hundreds of the best workers were expelled from Leningrad. Thousands of worker-Communists, who constituted the best and most active elements of the Leningrad organization, have in one way or another been removed from party work. The political correctness of these Leningrad workers in the main is now quite clear to every honest party member.

The wound opened in the Leningrad organization can be healed only through a radical change in the inner-party regime. If, however, things continue the way they are now going, there can be no doubt that ever new pressure campaigns, purges, and exilings will be needed not only in Moscow and Leningrad but in other political regions and centers as well, such as the Donbas, Baku, the Urals. They too will be decimated by repressions.

The deviation from Lenin expresses itself in nothing so glaringly as in the desire to get away from a Bolshevik assessment of the dangers in the present course of the party by using the catchword *Menshevism*. It is precisely the ideologically most ossified section of the "leaders" that excels in this approach. Menshevism, certain of the inevitable capitalist degeneration of the Soviet Union, bases all its calculations on a break between the working class and the Soviet state, just as the Social Revolutionaries (SRs) count on the "strong" peasant breaking with the Soviet state. In actuality Menshevism, as an agency of the bourgeoisie, could hope to emerge from insignificance for a while only if the fissure between the working class and the Soviet state should begin to grow. To keep this from happening it is necessary first of all to see this fissure the moment it appears and not to close one's eyes to it, as the bureaucrats do, denying the very need to work at the problem of drawing the Soviet state closer to the working class and the village poor. Prettifying reality; official optimism on general questions of the economy and pessimism on the question of wages; the wish not to see the kulak and at the same time the favoring of the kulak; insufficient attention to the poor peasantry; the especially crude pressure tactics in the working class centers; and the refusal to grasp the lesson of the recent Soviet elections—*all this signifies a real and immediate, not just verbal, paving of the way for Menshevik and SR influences.*

It is a crude self-deception to think that by mechanically taking reprisals against the so-called Opposition it will be possible subsequently to expand the framework of party democracy. On the basis of its entire experience the party cannot place any more faith in this consoling legend. New cracks and fissures are in the making as a result of the techniques of mechanical repression, new dismissals of people from their posts, new expulsions from the party, and new pressure tactics applied to the party as a whole. This system will inevitably narrow down the ruling clique at the top, lessen the authority of the leadership, and thereby force it to replace ideological authority with doubled and tripled application of pressure. The party must stop this destructive process at all costs. Lenin's example has shown that providing firm leadership for the party does not mean strangling it.

12. For Unity

There cannot be the slightest doubt that the party is fully capable of coping with all its difficulties. It would be the most arrant nonsense to think that the party could not find a way out on the road of unity. Moreover, it is *only* on the path of unity that a way out can be found. But for this an attentive and honest Bolshevik attitude toward questions that come up is necessary. We are against "perennial" discussion; we are against "the fever for discussions." Such discussions, imposed on the party from above, cost it far too dearly. For the most part, they *deafen* the party and do very little to enlighten or improve it.

We hereby propose to the CC plenum—let us, through our joint efforts, restore a regime in the party that will permit all disputed questions to be solved in full accordance with all party traditions and the feelings and thoughts of the proletarian vanguard.

Only on this basis is party democracy possible.

Only on the basis of party democracy is healthy collective leadership possible. There is no other way. In the struggle and the work along this only correct path, our unconditional support is guaranteed to the CC entirely and in full.

SUPPLEMENTARY DECLARATION

The question of the so-called Lashevich affair, placed on the agenda of the present plenum by decision of the Politburo on

June 24, was suddenly transformed, at the very last minute, by the decree of the CCC presidium on July 20, into the "affair" of Comrade Zinoviev. We consider it necessary first of all to state that in the draft resolution of the CCC presidium there is not one fact, not one report, not one suspicion voiced that was not already known six weeks ago, when the CCC presidium handed down its decision on the "affair" of Lashevich and others. In that document the name of Comrade Zinoviev was not mentioned. However in the latest draft resolution it is stated quite categorically that "all the threads" lead to Comrade Zinoviev as the president of the Comintern. This question, as is quite obvious to everyone, was decided not by the CCC presidium but by the factional group whose leader is Comrade Stalin.

We have before us a new stage in the implementation of a plan that was projected a long time ago and has been consistently carried out. As early as the immediate aftermath of the Fourteenth Congress, persistent discussions went on rather widely in relatively well-informed circles of party cadres—the inspiration for which came from the CC Secretariat—on the need to reorganize the Politburo by ousting a number of comrades who had taken part in the work of leadership under Lenin and replacing them with new elements who would constitute a reliable base of support for the leading role of Comrade Stalin. This plan met with support from the close-knit group immediately around Comrade Stalin, but encountered resistance from other elements who by no means belonged to an "Opposition." It is this that undoubtedly explains the decision of the leading group to carry out the plan bit by bit, making use of every appropriate opportunity for this purpose at each stage of the game. The enlargement of the Politburo, with the simultaneous transfer of Comrade Kamenev to candidate membership, was the first stage in this premeditated plan to radically reorganize the party leadership. The aim of leaving Comrades Zinoviev and Trotsky on the enlarged Politburo, and keeping Kamenev as a candidate member, was to give the party the impression that the old basic core was being preserved, and thus to soothe any feelings of alarm as to the competence and qualifications of the central leadership. As early as a month and a half or two months after the congress, together with the continuation of the struggle against the "new Opposition," a new chapter in the struggle against Comrade Trotsky was opened up simultaneously in various localities, above all in Moscow and Kharkov, as though at one signal. At the time the leaders of the Moscow organization said openly at a number of meetings of activists that the next blow should be struck against Comrade Trotsky. Certain members of the Politburo and CC, who by no means belonged to the "Opposition," expressed disapproval of the Moscow organization leaders, it being no secret to anyone that behind the backs of the Moscow leaders stood the CC Secretariat. At this time the question of the forthcoming removal of Comrade Trotsky from the Politburo was discussed rather widely in party circles, not only in Moscow but in a number of other places as well.

The case brought against Comrade Lashevich did not introduce anything essentially new into the basic plan for reorganizing the party leadership, but it prompted the Stalin group to make a few changes in the way the plan was carried out. Until quite recently the plan had been to strike the first blow at Comrade Trotsky, and to postpone the question of Zinoviev until the next stage, in order to gradually get the party used to its new leadership, presenting it at each new stage of partial change with an accomplished fact; however, the "affair" of Lashevich, Belenky, and others, because of their close ties with Comrade Zinoviev, prompted the leading group to switch the order and aim the next blow at Comrade Zinoviev. The fact that they did not come to this change of plans without wavering and resistance is apparent from the fact that, as we have said already, the initial CCC decision on the Lashevich "affair" did not raise the question of Comrade Zinoviev at all, although all the elements of the "case" recited in the new draft resolution of the CCC presidium were present from the moment proceedings were first brought against Comrade Lashevich. The proposal put forward at the very last moment—to remove Comrade Zinoviev from the Politburo—was dictated by the central Stalin group as a step along the way to replacing the old Leninist party leadership with a new—Stalinist—leadership.

As before, the plan is implemented bit by bit. Comrade Trotsky remains for the time being on the Politburo, in order, first of all, to make it possible for the party to think that Comrade Zinoviev was really removed in connection with the Lashevich affair and, secondly, not to arouse excessive alarm in the party by taking too abrupt measures. There can be no doubt, however, that the question of Comrade Trotsky, and of Comrade Kamenev, has been settled in advance in the minds of the Stalin nucleus, in the sense that they are to be removed from the leadership, and that the fulfillment of this part of the plan remains only a matter of organizational technique and suitable pretexts, real or invented. What is involved is a radical change in the party leadership. The political meaning of this change is evaluated in full in our basic declaration, which was written before the "affair" of Comrade Lashevich was transformed into that of Comrade Zinoviev.

At this point it remains only to add that the plainly discernible shift away from the Leninist line would have had an incomparably more energetic opportunist development if the reorganization of the leadership, projected by the Stalin group, had been carried out in practice. Together with Lenin, who clearly and precisely formulated his thinking in the document known as his Testament, we are most profoundly convinced, on the basis of the experience of the past few years, that the organizational policies of Stalin and his group threaten the party with the further grinding down of its basic cadres and with further shifts away from the class line. The issue at hand is the leadership of the party, the fate of the party. In view of what has been said above, we categorically reject the factional and profoundly harmful proposal of the CCC presidium.

M. Bakaev	Yu. Pyatakov
G. Lizdin	I. Avdeev
M. Lashevich	G. Zinoviev
N. Muralov	N. Krupskaya
A. Peterson	L. Trotsky
K. Solovyov	L. Kamenev
G. Yevdokimov	

FOR EQUALIZATION OF WAGES

July 11, 1926

NOTE: The demand for wage equalization—a principle taken for granted by the original Bolshevik regime—became a supreme "Trotskyist" sin under Stalin in the thirties. The Soviet press continues to agitate against uravnilovka *(wage "leveling"), although in the post-Stalin era there has been a trend toward raising some lower wage levels.*

This is Trotsky's comment on the significance of the party majority's refusal to act on the question of wage increases.

By permission of the Library of Social History.

Just before NEP was introduced, the Central Committee, under Lenin's leadership, emphasized the "necessity, again and again, of directing the attention of the party toward the struggle *to introduce greater equality:* first, within the party; second, within the proletariat and among the masses of working people as a whole; and third and last, among various government offices and groups of personnel, especially 'spetses' [specialists] and top personnel, as compared with the masses" [from a resolution of the September 1920 All-Russian Conference of the RCP; an incomplete copy of Lenin's "Draft Resolution on the Immediate Tasks of Party Development" is in *Collected Works,* vol. 42, pp. 212-13].

Of course the introduction of NEP brought big changes not only in the economy but in everyday life, and gave rise to conditions that run counter to equality. This does not mean, however, that the party can bow in silence before the bourgeois tendencies of NEP, either in this area or in others.

It is a highly alarming symptom, therefore, that in late 1925— five years after the introduction of NEP—when an attempt was made to place the question of greater equality on the agenda, it was met by quite a hostile attitude on the part of a number of leading party functionaries. Meanwhile, among the mass of the people, in the heart of the working class, and within the party

93

itself, the question of greater equality has not been abandoned as a topic of discussion and cannot be removed from the agenda.

An inattentive and even hostile attitude toward the unskilled or semiskilled sections of the working class, as some "gray mass" which has not come up to the "high" level of our bureaucrats and therefore dreams of equality, has become more and more widespread (especially incorrect on this point have been the speeches of Comrade Uglanov). Such an attitude toward the poorly paid sections of the working class is a typical sign of opportunism and of a retreat from the masses—and so, too, is the reluctance to take up in a practical way the question of systematically introducing greater equality despite the circumstances of NEP.

THE ELECTIONS TO THE SOVIETS

July 1926

NOTE: Village and urban soviets (councils) had sprung up during the revolution as representative bodies of the insurgent workers and peasants. Because the soviets were originally intended as a means of mobilizing wage workers, poor peasants, and their allies among the poor and oppressed sectors of the population to carry out the tasks of the revolution, the Russian constitution and the constitutions of the other republics had explicitly disenfranchised employers of hired labor or persons living on interest from capital. When the orientation toward the well-to-do peasant gained momentum, it was reflected in changes in electoral policy as well as agrarian policy: in the course of 1924 electoral rights were restored to kulaks who employed labor and rented out land. The soviet elections held in the winter of 1925-26 had been marked by aggressive participation by the petty-bourgeois elements of town and countryside, including bribery, threats, and physical violence, in an attempt to gain control of the soviets.

The party plenum of July 1926 examined the 1925-26 elections through a resolution introduced by Molotov and Kaganovich, which condemned the extension of the franchise to the kulaks and other petty-bourgeois elements but issued no substantial criticism of party policy in the previous period.

The reference to the Amsterdam International on p. 100 throws light on another Stalinist measure taken to try to discredit the Opposition. Ever since 1923, feelers had been extended between the Profintern (Red International of Labor Unions, based in Moscow) and the IFTU (International Federation of Trade Unions, based in Amsterdam) on the subject of trade union unity. When it became obvious that the IFTU would not consider a merger, the Soviet trade unions, through their All-Union Central Council of Trade Unions, began negotiations to enter the Amsterdam International.

*Trotsky viewed these developments with alarm, for they ap-
peared to be an extension of the line the Comintern was following
in Britain, of seeking an alternative to the hard road of party-
building through the inviting prospects of the large, Social
Democratic-led trade unions. The negotiations were protracted
throughout 1924 and 1925, and only came to an end when the
IFTU refused unequivocally to entertain them any longer.*

*Despite Trotsky's open opposition to the negotiations and to
any talk of affiliating the Soviet trade unions to the IFTU, Stalin
systematically spread the rumor that the Opposition advocated a
bloc with Amsterdam (possibly on the basis that Zinoviev, like
virtually every other majority leader, had been involved in one
stage of the negotiations in 1924). In similar fashion, on the eve
of World War II, Stalin would accuse his opponents of collusion
with Hitler—moments before signing the Hitler-Stalin pact.*

*By permission of the Harvard College Library. The text has
been slightly abridged to avoid repetition.*

To the Plenum of the CC and the CCC:

We are voting against the resolution, introduced by Comrade
Molotov in the name of the majority of the Politburo, because its
political conclusions are totally at variance with those facts of
great importance which the resolution itself acknowledges,
though in glossed-over fashion.

There is no doubt that the moods of the middle peasants and of
the urban petty bourgeoisie have become incomparably more
favorable than they were, not only under war communism but
also in the first years of NEP. However, it would be impermissible
to underestimate the dangers to the proletarian revolution that
the petty-bourgeios element conceals within itself. The lag of
industry behind the development of the economy as a whole,
accelerating the social differentiation within the village and
nourishing the private trader, heightens the economic role and
the political self-confidence of the petty bourgeoisie. Less than
ever, under such conditions, is it permissible to expand the voting
rights of the small property-owner, to bend the policies of the
cooperatives toward the upper strata in the villages, or to
minimize the dangers hidden within these trends.

The essential facts about the elections, according to Comrade
Molotov's resolution itself, are the following:

(a) "The rise in the political activity of the agricultural workers and poor peasants has not kept pace with the increased activity of other layers in the village." But it is precisely the agricultural workers and poor peasants who constitute the social base of the party and the workers' state in the village.

(b) In the town, as the resolution states, "there has been a noticeable increase in the proportional representation of the petty bourgeoisie in the soviets." This means a relative weakening of the representation in the soviets of the proletariat, i.e., of the ruling class.

(c) [There have been] violations of the Soviet constitution, in the form of [electoral] instructions favoring the petty-bourgeois elements.

It is fundamentally wrong, however, to try to portray these essential facts as the result of accidental circumstances and individual errors. The worst kind of policy is to make a partial acknowledgment of certain dangers, in order to get past them and go on to the immediate tasks of the day, that is, to continue the policies which gave rise to the dangers in the first place. We consider correct, although phrased with exaggerated caution, the conclusion drawn by the party's central newspaper: "The results of the election campaign are to a certain extent in contradiction with the line laid down by our party congress" (*Pravda*, July 7, lead article entitled "Lessons of the Elections to the Soviets").

Without understanding the contradiction referred to by *Pravda*, one cannot arrive at the proper conclusions. The contradiction is that our general political directives declare that the main danger is excessive pressure from the industrial workers, farmhands, and poor peasants upon the kulaks and the petty bourgeoisie as a whole—when in fact the main danger has shown itself to be the pressure from the kulaks and petty bourgeoisie.

The party's fire was directed not against the real danger, but against those who warned against this danger ahead of time.

It is wrong to dump the blame for the passivity of the agricultural workers solely on their "lack of culture." It was by relying above all on these elements in the countryside that the working class and its party fought and won a colossal peasant war. Over the past few years the cultural level of the lower strata in the villages has risen, not fallen. If nevertheless their political activism has lagged behind that of the other layers, a significant share of the blame for this lies with the incorrectness of the party's policies. . . .

We emphatically and categorically reject these tendencies, which have not been evaluated properly in Comrade Molotov's resolution. The agricultural cooperatives are among the most powerful instruments in the hands of the party and state for placing agriculture on the road to socialism. To put this instrument in the hands of the upper strata in the villages would be to transform the cooperatives from instruments of socialism into instruments of capitalism.

A prerequisite for raising the level of political activism among industrial workers, farmhands, and poor peasants, given the existing level of culture, is that the class content of the policies of the party, and of all state and public organizations, must go to meet such activism more than halfway, encourage it, and nourish it. The course charted toward the strong middle peasant inevitably dampens the activism of the farm laborers and poor peasants. The elections have merely made this fact plain. From what we have said the erroneousness of Comrade Kaganovich's motion must be quite obvious. It proposes to condemn that section of the CC and CCC which warned in advance against the dangerous deviations reflecting the pressure of the petty-bourgeois element and which pointed in a timely way toward a more energetic policy of industrialization, a firmer and more correct policy toward the kulak, and above all, the creation of the conditions for greater activism by the proletarian vanguard. Every party member must realize that we cannot rectify the party line, in the sense of a more clear-cut proletarian policy, if blows are aimed at those who defend and uphold this policy.

The bourgeoisie and the Mensheviks now place their hopes primarily on the degeneration of the soviets, just as during war communism they placed their hopes on military intervention. The hopes of the bourgeoisie and Mensheviks rest on the capitalist tendencies in our country's development, on the disproportion [between high prices for industrial goods charged to the peasants by state industry and the relatively low prices paid by the state for agricultural products], on the scissors, on the growth of the kulaks, the growth of private trader elements, and the increasing influence of the kulaks. Our policies are aimed at ensuring the preponderance of the socialist elements in our economy and preventing the slightest shift of real power from the hands of the proletariat and the rural poor, in close alliance with the middle peasant, into the hands of the petty-bourgeois elements who are trying to draw the middle peasants and poor peasants along after themselves, and who are in part succeeding. Especially in the current period, when the economic disproportion between town and country is intensifying, we must take a vigilant attitude toward any and all signs of a reduction in the political weight of the proletariat within the Soviet system.

We must continually engage in criticism of our own mistakes even though our enemies are watching. They will inevitably snap up every word of self-criticism. However, those who seek to suppress self-criticism by referring to the bourgeois enemy render the best service to that very enemy. It is not criticism but the glossing over of mistakes that can truly weaken us and aid our enemies.

We categorically reject the charge that we have used inaccurate statistics as the basis for our criticism of the line of the Politburo majority. The fundamental political processes and trends revealed in the soviet elections are beyond all question, regardless of the accuracy of one or another particular set of figures, all of which we took from the statistics of the Commissariat of the Interior or of the Central Committee itself.

On the contrary, we consider profoundly mistaken every attempt to play with figures in order to gloss over the fundamental political processes, on whose development in one direction or another the fate of the proletarian dictatorship depends.

An impermissible experiment in juggling statistics was made last autumn in regard to the fodder and grain question, with the aim of camouflaging the stratification of the village and minimizing the economic growth of the kulak. Everything that has happened in the area of economic policy since that time (the dumping of grain on the market in the spring, on the one hand, and the elections to the local soviets, on the other) constitutes a most emphatic warning against any and all attempts to bend statistics to fit preconceived political notions.

We reject the attempt to portray our ideological struggle against certain errors and deviations and for a definite line as the struggle of a factional group dictated by certain petty motives.

Such insinuations are insulting to the party as a whole and discredit those who resort to them.

Equally we reject any and all attempts to attribute to us certain ideas and inclinations with which we have nothing in common and which are, if anything, much closer to the views we are combating—and to do this instead of direct and open criticism of our actual views, which we have formulated clearly and precisely.

Only disrespect for the opinions of the party as a whole can explain the attempt made in a certain satirical article in *Pravda* and in several speeches at the plenum to attribute to us by hints, insinuations, and patchwork combinations—a sympathetic or tolerant attitude toward such proposals as the handing over of the bulk of state industry, or its leading elements, to foreign capital in the form of concessions; affiliation to the Amsterdam trade union international; indiscriminate and unworthy attacks on the Comintern; the counterposing of state industry to ruralism, etc., etc. We do not have the slightest affinity with such ideas, nor have we had in the past, nor could we—considering our fundamental positions. Only ideological poverty and lack of discrimination in the choice of tactics could dictate the use of such methods to fight us.

We are obliged to state, at the same time, that while attributing to us views that have nothing in common with those we really hold, the proponents of the leading group absolutely do not fight against similar mistakes, or even more glaring ones, when they are made by supporters of their own faction. We do not doubt for a minute that the party will separate the ideological core of the dispute from the mound of trash heaped upon it and that the party will have the final word both in the essence of the matter and in regard to the impermissible methods used in the debate.

In conclusion we declare that the incorrect positions of the leadership, which we have made clear, and the political errors flowing from them, do not in any way, or from any point of view, diminish the tremendous work that the party has carried out in educating and consolidating the ranks of the working masses in the city and the countryside, in all areas of public life, especially in the realm of Soviet construction.

Timely and clear-cut correction of errors will provide the opportunity to expand this positive work even more fully and to link it even more closely with the proletariat and the rural poor.

N. Muralov	G. Zinoviev
N. K. Krupskaya	M. Lashevich
L. Kamenev	Peterson
Yu. Pyatakov	L. Trotsky

QUESTIONS AND ANSWERS
ABOUT THE OPPOSITION

September 1926

NOTE: In September 1926, the Opposition leaders apparently decided to take their program directly to the rank and file in order to begin a discussion in preparation for the forthcoming Fifteenth Conference. Trotsky prepared several memorandums and articles for circulation under the heading "Toward the Fifteenth Conference." This item, and the following three pieces—none of which have specific dates—are from this period of late September and early October 1926.

The Medvedev letter mentioned in point 8 was the focus of a scandal around the time of the July plenum, when the officialdom tried to smear the Opposition because it included former members of the Workers Opposition, a syndicalist group that had been condemned by Lenin and other leaders. A former leader of the Workers Opposition, Medvedev, had written a letter in early 1924 to a party comrade in Baku, attacking the New Economic Policy as a sacrifice of the worker to the petty bourgeoisie, demanding a concentration of resources on heavy industry, and entertaining the idea of concessions to international capitalists if foreign aid could be obtained for industrial development. At a secret meeting of all Politburo members except Trotsky in August 1924, before the break-up of the triumvirate, Zinoviev had been asked to draft an official reply. Then the matter was entirely forgotten for nearly two years, until, a few days before the opening of the July 1926 plenum, Pravda opened a crushing attack on the Medvedev letter as an example of the right danger in the party. At the plenum, Zinoviev was censured for failing to carry out the 1924 decision to reply to the letter: he retorted that the decision had been made by an illegal faction and that, anyway, no one had thought about it for two years. No formal decision was made on the Medvedev case, but it laid the basis for one of the rumors that

101

persistently circulated against the Opposition. It was also part of Stalin's practice of muddying the theoretical waters by trying to throw all the Opposition currents into one bag and make each responsible for the others' programs, a practice he developed to an extreme during the Moscow trials a decade later.

From New International, *May 1938. Translated from the Russian by John G. Wright.*

1. *Is it true that the Opposition desires to transform the party into a conglomeration of factions, groupings, etc.?*

Answer: It is a nonsensical lie. The Opposition stands for reinforcing the proletarian dictatorship, which is being weakened by shifts toward petty-bourgeois elements. The dictatorship of the proletariat can be realized only through a party that is unified and capable of fighting. Various assertions to the effect that the Opposition is in favor of factions and groupings are lies spread for factional purposes.

2. *Is it true that factionalism is growing and assuming threatening proportions in the party?*

Answer: It is true. The case of Comrade Lashevich and others is only a manifestation of the growing danger. The difference between the Opposition and the ruling faction by no means consists in the fact that the Opposition is either reconciled to factionalism or considers it a normal condition for the party. But the Opposition cannot concede that factions appear and grow due to the ill will of isolated individuals. The Opposition holds that the cause of factionalism is the bureaucratic regime in the party.

3. *Is it possible to put an immediate end to bureaucratism?*

Answer: Naturally, that is impossible. In this sphere the Opposition does not at all demand some kind of miracle. But the point is that bureaucratism is not diminishing but on the contrary growing monstrously. Every serious attempt in the party to check bureaucratism calls forth reprisals from above and drives people to factionalism and division. The more bureaucratism struggles against factions, the more it breeds and nourishes them.

Ideological near-sightedness is always bound up with bureaucratism. The leaders of the ruling faction, who are isolating themselves to an ever greater extent, prove incapable of assessing the situation as a whole, foreseeing the future, and issuing broad directives to the party. The policy becomes small-minded or tail-endist. Attempts on anyone's part to generalize the difficulties, grasp their connection, and look ahead into the future arouse alarm in the conservative bureaucratic mind and call forth accusations of factionalism. The more difficulties in economics and politics the regime accumulates, the more intolerant it becomes.

4. *What is the basic cause of bureaucratism and small-mindedness?*

Answer: The basic cause for it is backsliding from the proletarian class line. The bulk of the party is composed of workers. The party's traditions are revolutionary and proletarian. The backsliding from the class line engenders the need to force policies through by bureaucratic apparatus methods.

5. *Does this imply that a split or the formation of two parties is inevitable or indispensable?*

Answer: By no means. The attempt to attribute such views to the Opposition is the most unconscionable and envenomed weapon in the struggle. It is necessary to conduct a struggle against the shift from the class line by inner-party means. We can and must straighten out the deviation within the framework of a single party.

6. *In what does this shift from the proletarian line find its expression?*

Answer: In the following:

a. The inability to understand the dangers that lurk in the lag of industry behind the development of the national economy as a whole;

b. The bureaucratic attitude toward such questions as wages, the "regime of economy," unemployment, housing construction, etc.;

c. The underestimation of the differentiation in the village and glossing over the growing role of the kulak;

d. The attempt on the part of the Commissariat of Agriculture, rural cooperatives, and other organizations, to steer a course toward the productively powerful middle peasant, i.e., in reality the kulak;

e. The underestimation of, or the inability to understand, the dangers flowing from the fact that the political activity of the urban and rural petty bourgeoisie is growing more rapidly than the activity of workers, agricultural laborers, and poor peasants;

f. The extension of the electoral decree and the actual elections, favoring the petty bourgeoisie;

g. The prettifying of the Soviet state as it exists and the denial of the need to draw it closer to the workers;

h. The prettifying of the NEP and the glossing over or playing down of its contradictions, minimizing the specific weight of capitalist tendencies;

i. The centrist deviation on questions of the world labor movement (the Anglo-Russian Committee, the Kuomintang, etc.);

j. The support given to grossly mistaken and dangerous hopes in the bloc with opportunist and treacherous leaders which is alleged to help secure the USSR against war;

k. The urge to break with the Profintern and join the Amsterdam International (making corresponding changes in the statutes of the Red trade unions);

l. The systematic struggle not against the right deviation but against those who warn against it;

m. Categorizing as ultralefts not only the real ultralefts but all those who are fighting to rectify the proletarian line.

7. *Is it true that the policy of the Opposition threatens to disrupt the "smychka" between the proletariat and the peasantry?*

Answer: This charge is utterly false. The *smychka* is now being endangered on the one hand by the lag in industry, and on the other by the growth of the kulak. The shortage of industrial goods is driving a wedge between the country and the city. The kulak is beginning to subordinate the middle and poor peasants to himself economically and politically and to oppose them to the proletariat. This process is still in its inception. But the threat to the *smychka* flows precisely from this source. The underestimation of the lag of industry and of the growth of the kulak acts to violate the correct Leninist leadership of the bond between the two classes which is the foundation of the dictatorship in the conditions in our country.

8. *Is it true that the Opposition maintains that state industry must be ceded to foreigners as a concession?*

Answer: Such an assertion is a revolting slander. The use of such methods is made possible only because the party has been strangled by bureaucratism.

Pravda asserts that Comrade Medvedev, in a letter written in

January 1924, came out in favor of giving up a great section of our state industry as a foreign concession. This letter of Comrade Medvedev's, written some two and a half years ago, has never been published anywhere. No one knows anything about it and no one can judge whether *Pravda* correctly cites its contents. But what possible connection is there between this letter, which is unknown to anybody, and the 1923 Opposition and the Leningrad Opposition (1925)?

The Opposition considers the question of the rate of the development of state industry to be decisive for the fate of socialism. To this end it demands a change in the system of taxation and price policy and a redrafting of the budget. Concessions can and must occupy only a rigidly restricted and subordinate position in our economy. Every attempt to extend the framework of concessions beyond specific limits, i.e., to offer foreign capital a dominant influence in our economy, or even a considerable one, would be tantamount to an outright betrayal of the cause of socialism.

9. *Is it true that the Opposition is in a bloc with the Amsterdam deviation?*

Answer: This assertion is as absurd as the previous one and it is based on the very same mysterious letter of Comrade Medvedev's. If Comrade Medvedev or any other member of our party were to come out against the Profintern and for Amsterdam, the Opposition would once again categorically and mercilessly condemn such an opportunist deviation, just as it has already done with regard to certain leading members of the All-Union Central Council of Trade Unions who effected behind the backs of the party an alteration in the statutes of almost all our trade unions by deleting "Profintern" and replacing it with "the international alliance of trade unions," which can signify nothing else but a removal of obstacles for an entry into Amsterdam.

Generally speaking, the attempt on the part of *Pravda* to place the blame at the door of the Opposition is made possible only by the monstrous suppression of the freedom of criticism and of the open functioning of thought in the party.

10. *Is it true that the Opposition denies the possibility of building socialism in our country?*

Answer: This accusation is false and it is based upon an erroneous formulation of the question itself. Decades are required to build socialism solely with our own forces in our backward

country. To presuppose that in the course of such a long period of
time capitalism will be maintained and will continue to develop
in other countries while we are in the meantime building socialism is to deny the ties of the world economy and world politics
and to fall into crude national narrow-mindedness. The building
of socialism in our country is an integral part of the world
proletarian revolution. The success of socialist construction in our
country is inseparable from the success of the revolutionary
movement in the entire world. The Opposition is profoundly
convinced of the victory of socialism in our country not because
our country can be torn free of the world economy and of world
revolution but because the victory of the proletarian revolution is
guaranteed the world over.

The shift from the proletarian line inevitably leads to national
narrow-mindedness, to an underestimation of our dependence on
the world economy and the crude prettification of the NEP.

11. *Is it true that the Opposition is a faction?*

Answer: It is impossible to deny the danger of the transformation of the Opposition into a faction. This danger is being created
and aggravated by the policies and organizational measures of
the ruling faction, which is becoming less and less tolerant of
criticism, collective discussion, and of a freely elected and
collective leadership.

12. *Can a "majority" constitute a faction?*

Answer: It can. The present majority is a faction. A majority is
not some sort of perpetual body of one and the same composition.
In a party that thrives on the basis of internal democracy, as new
questions arise they give birth to new groupings and shifts. The
faction of the majority has as its task the transformation of the
present majority into a permanent majority, independently of its
political line and of the changing tasks or the changed views of
the real majority of the party. The faction of the majority is
bound by its own secret discipline and this alone defrauds and
perverts the genuine will of the party. The faction of the majority
uses the party machine to prevent the party from determining by
democratic means where the real majority and minority are. The
most pernicious form of factionalism is the factionalism of the
ruling majority which speaks for the party as a whole.

The factionalism of the minority flows inevitably from the
factionalism of the majority.

13. *Is it true that the Opposition endangers the unity of the party?*

Answer: The unity of the party is threatened by the existence of a hardened faction of the majority, which is shifting the party policy from the proletarian line and is driving into the Opposition all those who struggle for the proletarian line and for the rehabilitation of the party regime.

What the leaders of the ruling faction understand by the unity of the party is the following: "Don't you dare criticize our policy; don't dare pose any new tasks and new questions without our permission; don't dare to seriously pose the question of a struggle against bureaucratism, the questions of industrialization, wages, the poor peasants, etc." From the standpoint of the leaders of the ruling faction, party unity is endangered by every word and every action that is directed against the mistakes of the leading group. But this only means that the leading group refuses to reconcile itself to a regime of party democracy.

14. *Is it true that the Opposition has moved away from the Leninist views on party leadership?*

Answer: No, that is not true. Just the contrary is true. It is the present leading group that directs all of its efforts toward smashing the old leading nucleus which was formed in collaboration with Lenin. During Lenin's illness and now after his death, the party was many times told of the importance of preserving the succession and continuity of the leadership. The chief slogan was: Long live the Leninist Old Guard! It was explained to the party that the experience of leadership is acquired in the course of many years and that in our party the leadership is most closely bound up with the experience of the two revolutions through which the party passed under Lenin's leadership.

At the present time the Stalinist group is making an abrupt turn on this question, by opposing to the Old Guard new forces, "practical workers," who developed on the basis of the work of reconstruction, etc. Such a counterposition is by itself a step toward renouncing the revolutionary traditions of the party, a step toward small-mindedness and opportunism. This deviation is being covered up by thoroughly reactionary speeches against "emigrés" and in favor of people rooted in the "native soil." The theory of socialism in one country is best adapted to this narrow, nationalistic, horse-trader's formulation of the question of party leadership.

15. *Is it true that by "smashing" the Opposition it is possible to secure the unity of the party and the unanimity of the leadership?*

Answer: No, this is a gross fallacy. The bureaucratic suppression of the party is pregnant with ever greater divisions. The ruling faction is by no means homogeneous. It contains a right deviation toward the kulak, the petty bourgeoisie, and middle class elements in general. It contains a trade unionist deviation which is marching hand in hand with the deviation toward the petty proprietor but which frequently comes into hostile conflict with the latter. It contains purely machine elements who are without a definite political line but who shield the right deviation from the criticism of the Opposition. Finally, it contains numerous elements who have completely preserved their revolutionary spirit but who have not yet come to grips with the shifts in party policy and party regime. At the present time the leaders of the majority faction are able to fuse it together by machine methods in the struggle against the Opposition. If we imagine for the moment that the Opposition were to be "smashed," then the majority faction, backsliding to the right, would immediately begin to split up into new factional groupings, with all the ensuing consequences. Within the factional group at the top there are already sharp frictions, which are being suppressed only by factional discipline. It is possible to prevent the development of this friction into new factional struggles not by smashing the present Opposition but on the contrary by assuming an attentive attitude toward its criticism, by effecting a genuine rectification of the party line, and by reestablishing party democracy and collective leadership in the party.

IN DEFENSE OF THE OPPOSITION BLOC

September 1926

NOTE: In this memorandum Trotsky defended the United Opposition against attempts to sow discord between the Zinovievists and the Trotskyists, and he defended himself, as he would again and again, against the renewed reminders of his old differences with Lenin.

From Mitteilungsblatt *[Information Bulletin], a publication of the Left Opposition in the German CP, ed. Hugo Urbahns, Berlin, no. 2, mid-January 1927. Translated from the German by David Keil.*

The Stalinist faction bases its policy of splitting the party on the counterposition of "Trotskyism" to Leninism and the assertion that the 1925 (Leningrad) Opposition has gone over from the position of Leninism to that of "Trotskyism." It is quite obvious to every thinking member of the party that the objective of such agitation is to turn attention away from the actual political differences—caused by the obvious backsliding of the Stalin faction from the class line—and toward the old political differences, which have either been completely overcome, have lost their sharp meaning, or have proven imaginary.

The allegation that the 1925 Opposition had given up and gone the way of the 1923 Opposition is untrue and is dictated by rude and disloyal political considerations. Since 1923 the party has accumulated enormous experience, and the only elements who have not learned from this experience are those who have slipped unconsciously into the petty-bourgeois swamp. The Leningrad Opposition sounded a timely alarm concerning the covering up of class differentiation in the village, the growth of the kulaks, and the expansion of their influence not only on the basic functioning of the economy but also on the policies of the Soviet government; over the fact that in the ranks of our own party and under the protection of Bukharin, a whole theoretical school of thought had taken shape clearly reflecting the pressure of the petty-bourgeois element in our economic life. The Leningrad Opposition took an energetic stand against the theory of socialism in one country as the justification of national narrow-mindedness. All these questions, which are of the greatest theoretical importance, were included in the joint declaration of the United Opposition ["Declaration of the Thirteen," p. 73]. In their declaration, both groups formulated the basic economic and party-political tasks:

1. The need to accelerate the rate of industrialization and change the approach to wage questions;

2. The need to counteract the pressure from the kulak, and from the petty bourgeoisie in general, upon the soviets and the cooperative societies; and the need to arrive at an understanding with the village population, especially the middle peasants, not through the kulaks but from below, through the agricultural workers and poor peasants. (On the question of the relations between proletariat and peasantry we stand completely on the ground of the theoretical and tactical teachings of Lenin based on the experience of the revolutions of 1905 and 1917, as well as the experience in socialist construction, all of which he summarized in the term *smychka*);

3. The need for a radical struggle against the tendencies toward petty-bourgeois degeneration in the ranks of our own party;

4. Finally, the need to ensure a maximum proletarian membership in the party and a decisive influence by the proletarian centers, districts, and cells on the policies of the party; and in conjunction with that, the need to return the party regime to the Leninist road of internal democracy.

We proceed from the fact that, as experience has irrefutably shown, on all more or less fundamental questions over which any of us differed with Lenin, *Vladimir Ilyich was entirely right*. We have united in the defense of Leninism against its falsifiers, with everyone's unconditional acknowledgment of all advice concerning each of us in Lenin's Testament (because the profound import of this advice has been completely confirmed in practice); on the basis of unconditionally putting the Testament into practice in life, not only the point about *the removal of Stalin* from the post of general secretary, but also the point about preserving the entire leadership team that was built under Lenin, and by *preventing the degeneration of the party leadership from Leninism to Stalinism*. Only due to the joint experience of both currents (the Opposition of 1923 and the Opposition of 1925) have all basic questions—the economy, the party regime, the policy of the Comintern—been given a correct and complete solution.

Each and every attempt to use old articles or theses by representatives of either current with the aim of sowing mutual distrust based on old ideological struggles constitutes an attack with defective weapons. *The Stalinist attempt at "discrediting leaderships"* will not succeed. In revolutionary politics what is decisive is not memories, no matter how maliciously distorted, but the revolutionary tasks facing the party. The United Opposition pointed out in April and July, and will point out again in October, that the unity of its views is only strengthened by all the rude and disloyal baiting. The party will come to understand that only on the basis of the views of the United Opposition is there a way out of the present severe crisis.

PARTY UNITY
AND THE DANGER OF SPLIT

Early October 1926

NOTE: In this memorandum, Trotsky describes the corrosive effect on the party of the apparatus manipulations against the Opposition and accurately predicts the result of the ouster of the present Opposition: "the transformation of the old group in the Central Committee into an opposition. A new discussion would be placed on the agenda," in which the Stalinists would turn on the Bukharinists, using Bukharin's own young intellectual protegés, while themselves being accused of hindering a speedy backsliding toward capitalism. This is an early statement of Trotsky's conviction that the Stalinists and the Bukharin-Rykov tendency were bound together only by their common hostility to the Opposition, and that their triumph over the Opposition would result in the suppressed antagonisms coming to the fore. That conviction is also expressed in "Questions and Answers About the Opposition," September 1926, and "At a New Stage," December 1927, and elsewhere.

On October 1, 1926, Radek, Pyatakov, Zinoviev, and Trotsky spoke at a party meeting at the Aviapribor factory in Moscow. The next day the Moscow party committee, under Uglanov's leadership, passed a resolution condemning the Aviapribor "demonstration" as "a crime against the party," charged the Opposition with trying to "fasten a discussion on the party," and urged the CC to call the Opposition to account. (The text of the resolution was published in Pravda, *October 3.) In this memorandum, which is probably a jointly authored document, it may have been Zinoviev's influence that produced the acknowledgment that "under a normal party regime" it is a crime to criticize decisions that are already made. Trotsky was evidently bothered by this formulation and wanted to modify it. (In one of three versions, he inserted, then crossed out, that this is correct "generally speak-*

*ing.") Zinoviev, on the other hand, was a very harsh centralist,
and his subsequent record shows his inclination to capitulate to
the apparatus no matter how unreasonable, even brutal, its
demands.*

By permission of the Harvard College Library.

This is the chief issue in the discussion. It is the main and, in
fact, the only slogan of the ruling faction. The Opposition is
accused of violating, or of threatening to violate, party unity.
This is the main accusation against the Opposition. The importance of party unity under the conditions of revolutionary
dictatorship is understood by every party member and every nonparty worker who is at all politically developed. This is the source
of the tremendous significance of the question of party unity and
the no less tremendous danger of an incorrect approach to this
question.

It must be said loud and clear: *The slogan of party unity, in the
hands of the ruling faction, is more and more becoming an
instrument of ideological terror (intimidation and bullying)
against the overwhelming majority of the party.*

The party is above all an action organization. The entire body
of its members should be capable of mobilization for combat at
any moment, under the leadership of the Central Committee.
Such combat-readiness is inconceivable without the unanimity of
the party. But it would be the crudest kind of error to think that
unanimity can be created by nothing else but official handbook
clichés handed down from above. Unanimity is produced by the
party as a whole through the constant renewal and accumulation
of collective experience, through a collective effort of thought, on
the basis of the party's program, rules, traditions, and past
experience. This process is inconceivable without differences,
criticism, and the clash of ideas. If revolutionary combat-
readiness requires a powerful centralism, then the maintenance,
development, and strengthening of ideological unity in a party
with over a million members requires a no less powerful party
democracy. Without centralism, party democracy is the organizational path to Menshevism. Without democracy, centralism is the
apparatus road to the bureaucratic degeneration of the party.

The organizational policy of the ruling faction has the same
kind of "scissors" as are found in all the rest of its policies: in
words, the recognition of party democracy; in deeds, the ever
increasing suppression of every manifestation of thought or
criticism outside the framework of the closed-in ruling faction at

the top. This is what constitutes the chief danger threatening the unity of the party.

The leading factional clique uses the entire apparatus of the party and state to defend its factional positions, including its factional errors. The concentration of the full complement of power in the hands of the Central Committee is an iron necessity. The concentration of all power in the hands of a closed-in secret faction is a terrible danger. Even a Central Committee, even the very best, can make mistakes. But the party, which lives a collective life, has the possibility, on the basis of its own experience, of correcting its Central Committee. But the situation changes radically when the resources of the party and the state are concentrated in the hands of a sealed-off faction, or of its tiny leading group (some "Septemvirate" or "Decemvirate"), which is bound by internal faction discipline, regarded as higher than the discipline of the party. The official institutions of the party, its conferences, and even congresses, are put in a position in which they have no choice but to assent, after the fact, to decisions already made or to accomplished facts. During the Fourteenth Congress, decisions of exceptional importance, radically altering the composition of the leading institutions of the party and the direction of its policies, were brought crashing down as complete surprises upon the heads of an unsuspecting party. The July plenum was confronted at the very last moment with a new, radical change in the party leadership, made behind the back of the party (the replacement of Comrade Zinoviev on the Politburo by Comrade Rudzutak, the revised listing of Comrade Kamenev as the eighth candidate member, and the introduction of new candidate members who in fact are members of the ruling faction's central leadership). Even congress delegates and ordinary members of the CC and CCC are each time caught unaware by the ruling faction at the top and placed in the position of having either to accede in silence to a decision already made or to go over to the "Opposition." But since any opposition, or even criticism, is declared a threat to party unity and is punished by the severest apparatus methods, the majority of congress delegates or CC and CCC members are left with no choice but to accede in silence to the measures taken by the factional ruling group.

The criticism of decisions already made is declared a crime. Under a normal party regime that would be correct. Criticism is much more timely during a discussion in preparation for a decision. But the whole crux of the present regime is to drop ready-made decisions on the party's head, decisions that have been discussed and arrived at in gatherings of the ruling faction which are kept secret from the party and at which the disposition of forces is decided in advance, the formal majority is assured in advance, etc. Thus, before the decision is made, the party knows nothing about it, no matter how important it may be. And after the decision has been brought down on the party's head as a total surprise, one is forbidden to discuss it on pain of being accused of violating discipline. Only by such methods, which are profoundly harmful and thoroughly against the party's interests, is the regime of unquestioned domination by a factional grouping maintained. Let them point to even one example of criticism in the party that has not immediately been proclaimed "opposition." Let them point to one example of opposition that has not immediately been proclaimed, from on high, to be a "faction." No one can point to such an example, and that alone is enough to give a complete characterization of the present party regime. Political retrogression from the class line inevitably drives them down the road of bureaucratic apparatus pressure on the party. Such a course inevitably leads to a closed-in factional grouping at the top and to a rigid selection of the entire apparatus by such a faction. In turn the concentration of power in the hands of a faction kept secret from the party inevitably encourages the tendency toward one-man rule. Collective leadership is inseparably connected with a regime of party democracy. *A bureaucratized apparatus, imposing its will on the party, inevitably seeks a single will at the top.* Under these conditions any independent expression of party thinking inevitably takes on a sharp oppositional character. The ruling faction suppresses any criticism, any opposition, with the slogan of party unity. The essence of the matter is that the factional group at the top, under the pretext of party unity, defends its monopoly on the leadership of the party by factional means.

But the whole problem is that the more violently the ruling faction defends "party unity," the more it endangers it. Discussions, even if distorted and one-sided, become more and more frequent, more and more heated; organizational consequences become more and more severe and painful. The tendency toward one-man rule in the party leadership becomes crudely and harshly apparent. As a result of all this the party has at present been artificially divided into three rather sharply marked-off parts: (1) the ruling faction, which constitutes the backbone of the apparatus selected from above; (2) the Opposition elements, fighting for a rectification of the party line and a restoration of normality in the party regime; and (3) the broad mass of the party in between, atomized, disoriented, and in effect deprived of any chance to actively affect the fate of the party. This fundamentally unhealthy situation in the party is the real and undeniable source of every kind of danger, above all the danger of a split.

One may be reconciled to any regime as long as it accomplishes some purpose. But the present regime is not bringing the party closer to unity; instead it is carrying it farther away. Since Lenin retired from active work we have had the 1923 discussion, the 1924 discussion, the 1925 discussion (with the Leningrad Opposition), the new apparatus discussion against "Trotskyism" (spring 1926), the new sharp discussion against the Leningrad Opposition, formally geared to the Lashevich "affair" (June-July 1926), and now a newly unfolding discussion against "Trotskyism" in general and against the Leningrad Opposition, which is accused of "Trotskyism," in particular. The character and methods of the present discussion are known to all and need no explanation. What until recently was clear only to the better informed circles is becoming clearer and clearer to the whole party, namely, that the aim of all these discussions and organizational measures is the complete defeat of the nucleus which until recently was called the Leninist Old Guard, and its replacement by the one-man rule of Stalin, relying on a group of comrades who always agree with him.

Only a dullard or a hopeless bureaucrat could think that the Stalinist struggle for "party unity" is capable of really achieving unity, even at the price of smashing the old leadership group and the entire present-day Opposition as a whole. From everything that has been said it is clear that the closer Stalin seems to come to his goal, the farther he is from it in fact. One-man rule in the administration of the party, which Stalin and his most intimate circle call "party unity," requires not only the defeat, removal, and ouster of the present United Opposition but also the gradual removal of *all authoritative and influential figures in the present ruling faction.* It is quite obvious that neither Tomsky, nor Rykov, nor Bukharin—because of their past, their authority, etc.—is capable of playing the role under Stalin that Uglanov, Kaganovich, Petrovsky, et al. play under him. The ouster of the present Opposition would in fact mean the inevitable transformation of the old group in the Central Committee into an opposition. A new discussion would be placed on the agenda, in which

Kaganovich would expose Rykov, Uglanov would expose Tomsky, and Slepkov, Sten, and Company would deglorify Bukharin.* Only a hopeless dullard could fail to see the inevitability of this prospect. But at the same time the more openly opportunist elements in the party would open fire against Stalin as one too much infected with "leftist" prejudices, one who hindered a more rapid and unconcealed retrogression.

*   *   *

Lenin wrote that a split in the party would become inevitable only if a split between the classes—the proletariat and the peasantry—proved to be inevitable [*Collected Works,* vol. 36, p. 594]. Can we say that that moment has come? Not at all. In spite of the mistaken shifts in economic, soviet, and other policies, the party still has the full capability of correcting these errors, straightening out the course of economic policy, and thus assuring *a new consolidation of the "smychka" on a higher economic and political basis.*

The question of the party regime and the party leadership is in a more perilous state. The party is the basic instrument of the revolution. If this instrument is blunted, that has a disastrous effect on all the tasks of the revolution and on its entire destiny. In order to achieve the correction of the economic errors and the rectification of the party line, the party must not only *want* this but also *have the opportunity* of putting its will into effect. That is why changing the party regime is the question of questions.

But is there not a danger that the very struggle to change the party regime could lead to a split? To deny this danger would be hypocritical. The source of this danger, however, is not the struggle against the disease but the disease itself, that is, above all, the policies of the Stalinist group. To refuse to try to cure the disease in time would mean only that it would develop further unhindered, which in the future could place the party in the position where it was too late for a cure.

To put it more simply: Can the party regime be changed without convulsions and above all without a disaster? We have no doubt that it can. At any rate, we are bending all our efforts in that direction. The bureaucratization of the party is far advanced

---

*Slepkov, as an individual, remained loyal to Bukharin throughout prison and exile. Uglanov became a Right Oppositionist in 1929 and was dropped from the CC in 1930.—Eds.

but by no means so far as to have paralyzed the will of the party and especially of its proletarian vanguard. In practice the task boils down to giving party members a chance to make use of their rights and express their will—within the framework of the party rules and in the spirit of unity.

But this in turn means that the Stalin faction, *which constitutes a faction within the ruling faction*, must be prevented, no matter what, from convulsing the party any further with one-sided discussions and disorganizing it with organizational measures paving the way for a ruinous regime of one-man rule in the party.

If the Central Committee and the Central Control Commission could find in themselves the strength to put an end to this destructive work, to abolish management of the party by a secret faction, and to restore collective leadership, the Opposition would support this initiative wholeheartedly and the entire party would greet such a courageous step with a burst of enthusiasm. However, after the experience of the April plenum and, especially, the July plenum, very little hope can remain for a unifying initiative by the CC or CCC. Both in April and in July the Opposition loyally submitted its proposals to the highest body of the party. The most important of these proposals were rejected without consideration, and were even deleted from the record of the proceedings. The Opposition was obliged to remain silent, but representatives of the majority, despite the silence of the Opposition, began a vicious slander campaign against it, presenting the party with monstrously distorted versions of the views and proposals of the Opposition. This more and more one-sided discussion has been and is being conducted only to prepare the party for even more unhealthy organizational measures. Never before have the methods of intimidation, terrorizing, smearing, and expulsion been used so unrestrainedly as now. The most responsible assignments (to Vesenkha, the Commissariat of Trade, diplomatic work, etc.) are made exclusively from the point of view of factional selection, to the detriment of our most vital interests in the economic and political spheres. The Stalin group wants to finish matters off organizationally as quickly as possible. They seek to subordinate the coming October plenum and the Fifteenth Party Conference to this aim. They again want to confront the party with accomplished, irreversible facts, after which the Fifteenth Congress will have no choice but to sanction the split carried out by the Stalin group.

It is entirely within the party's power to prevent these plans from being realized. To do so, the party members must simply make use of their party rights. What is needed is for a few members, or even just one member, in every party cell, in spite of all the grotesque pressure tactics applied from the top down, to take the floor at the crucial moment and say: "If the CC and the CCC are incapable of sparing the party new torments, they must at least stop preventing the party from receiving full information and having an open discussion of the differences which until now have been kept within the bounds of the ruling institutions of the party. We declare in advance that any attempt to decide fundamental questions of party life and party leadership behind the backs of the party and to confront the coming Fifteenth Party Congress with an accomplished fact is an antiparty and criminal act."

That is the path of *genuine* struggle for party unity.

IS DISCUSSION NEEDED?

Early October 1926

NOTE: In this memorandum, which was probably written shortly after Uglanov's party organization accused the Opposition of trying to fasten a discussion on the party, Trotsky tackles the accusation and demonstrates how it reveals Stalin's distrust of the party and his determination to deprive the rank and file of all political power.

By permission of the Harvard College Library.

Today a furious campaign is being waged in the party, from above, against discussion in general. *Pravda* runs articles arguing that discussion is harmful and dangerous. But no one indicates how else disputed questions are to be resolved.

What is a discussion? It is the formal consideration by the party of the questions which stand before it on which there are differences. Can the party decide these matters without discussing them? It cannot. And if the party is not to decide these questions, who is to decide them for it? This is essentially what it all comes down to—whether someone can decide disputed questions for the party, in place of the party, and behind the back of the party.

Pravda and those who speak against discussion say, "All these questions have already been decided by the party—by the Fourteenth Congress, the Central Committee plenums, etc." But the point is that ten months have already passed since the Fourteenth Congress. At the congress there were disputes over whether the influence of the kulak was growing in the village, or whether that of the party, the proletariat, and the poor peasantry was. At the April plenum there were disputes over whether industry was rushing too far ahead or lagging behind, and whether wage increases were keeping pace with the overall rise in the standard of living in the country, or whether, on the contrary, they were lagging behind.

At the July plenum there were disputes over whether the influence of the proletariat in the soviets was increasing or whether, as a result of the growing power of the kulak and as a result of the lag in industry, the influence of petty-bourgeois and kulak elements was on the rise in the soviets, at the expense of the influence of the proletariat, the agricultural worker, the poor peasant, and the Communist.

It is quite obvious that on such questions there cannot be one set answer, once and for all. Disputes are tested against the living reality. It is necessary to take stock of the facts that have accumulated over the course of the past year, so that the party can, on the basis of mature deliberation, arrive at its own decision on all disputed and undecided questions.

Who else is to decide these questions if not the party? We are talking about questions upon which the fate of the proletarian dictatorship depends. It is necessary to review the whole experience at every new stage. Who other than the party can review this experience? If serious and deep-going differences arise within the party, who can decide them if not the party congress? And how can the congress decide such questions if the party does not talk them over and deliberate on them from every angle before the congress? And deliberating on questions from every angle is precisely what a formal party discussion is.

Of course a discussion has its negative aspects. Time and energy must be spent on a discussion. To a certain extent the practical work suffers as a result. But what is involved, after all, is *the line to be followed* in all our practical work. We need the kind of practical activity that will lead to the political and economic strengthening of the proletariat and that will assure the preponderance of the socialist elements in our economy over the capitalist ones. If differences arise over these fundamental questions, it is absurd to say, "Stick to the practical work, and don't discuss what line is to be followed in that work."

What are the basic questions that cannot be disregarded by any member of the party? They are questions like the following:

1. During the past year the entire economy took a step forward. There was an upturn in industry. The overall standard of living in the country improved. At the same time, real wages, by comparison with the autumn of last year, declined. How and why did that happen? Isn't there a danger that the overall standard of living will continue to rise faster than wages? That would mean that the influence of the working class in society at large would decline. Is it necessary to discuss this question or isn't it?

2. The goods famine in our country means that industry is not providing the necessary quantity of goods to exchange for the surplus produced by peasant agriculture. This is the source of the so-called disproportion, the disparity between the peasant demand and the available quantity of industrial goods. Before the Fourteenth Congress and at the April plenum, there were disputes over whether this disproportion was diminishing or, on the contrary, increasing. The evidence of this autumn has made it plain to everyone that the disparity has grown worse. This means that industry, even though it has moved ahead, still lags behind the overall growth of the economy. This means that the relative weight of state industry in the economy did not grow greater but decreased. This specifically explains the fact that real wages fell rather than rose during the year. Has the party deliberated on this question? No, it has not. Can one explain this by referring to the fact that the question has already been settled? No, one cannot. To be sure, the Fourteenth Congress and the April plenum gave answers to these questions—answers that were binding upon the entire party. But what of decisions that the party arrives at itself and that are tested against the living reality? The party takes the results of such testing into consideration. If there are differences in the party or its Central Committee, the party discusses these differences and arrives at its own decision, which is binding upon everyone. The same is true of all other questions as well. They are linked together in one general chain. Industry lags behind the overall growth of the economy; socialist accumulation lags behind accumulation in the economy as a whole; wages lag behind the generally higher level of the economy. This means that the economic role of the proletariat is not growing rapidly enough and is even shrinking in relative terms. And this cannot help but have political repercussions. The latest soviet elections showed a certain decline in the relative political weight of the proletariat and its closest support in the village, the poor peasant. Can it be said that these questions have been decided once and for all? No, we have before us new facts of exceptional importance. In the assessment of these facts there are differences, including in the Central Committee. Who can arrive at a decision on this question? The party, in the form of its congress.

One may argue that the minority in the Central Committee must subordinate itself to the majority. That is absolutely beyond question. One may make the claim that certain Central Committee members have violated discipline. For this they can be penalized. But that does not eliminate the question of the party congress. The problem is that the party must be given the opportunity to review its old decisions in the light of the new facts and experiences. Is it true that the danger is not from the kulak but from those who warn against the kulak danger? Is it true that the party should direct its fire against the left, that is, against that section of the party which has sounded the alarm about the lag in industry, about the decline in the relative weight of the proletariat in Soviet society, the weakened influence of the poor peasant in the village, and so on? The problem before us is that of the general line of party policy. The present year has provided us with an enormous number of facts against which to test that line. How can this test be made, and by whom? How can the Fifteenth Congress arrive at its own decision, if the party does not give a hearing to all the points of view in dispute and make its own decision?

The whole difficulty is that certain comrades, the editors of *Pravda* in particular, are presenting arguments to the effect that it is possible for someone to arrive at decisions without the party. Discussion, they say, is harmful and dangerous. But that simply means, after all, that it is harmful and dangerous for the party to talk over controversial questions. What to do, then, in the event of disagreements? To this question they offer no answer.

Is it true that discussion is dangerous? That depends on the kind of discussion. Is it dangerous for a workers' cell to talk over the question of why wages have fallen in the midst of a general upturn in the economy? Is it dangerous for a workers' cell to listen to the opinion of the Central Committee majority on this, and the opinion of the Opposition? No, in this there is no danger. All that is needed is for the differing opinions to be presented in strict accordance with party procedure, to be discussed in the proper tone, to be dealt with from all angles, and for the entire party to be provided with the necessary documents, so that no one is left in the dark. It is quite a different matter when you have an unceasing, furious, one-sided discussion being conducted in the press and at party meetings—a discussion that degenerates more and more into plain baiting and vilification of the Opposition, while the basic documents in which the Opposition has set forth its point of view are kept hidden from the party. That is the kind of discussion that is dangerous. It poisons the collective mind of the party. It saps the unity of the party.

Pravda states that discussion distracts comrades from practical work. But even so a discussion is being carried on, and moreover one that has not let up since the Fourteenth Congress. Speeches are made, articles are written, pamphlets published, resolutions passed—all aimed against the Opposition. The Opposition's real views and proposals all the while are monstrously distorted. It is not given the right to express itself. Now a discussion has been launched from above to the effect that discussion is not needed. Some sort of new theory is being created that disputed questions can be decided without the party talking them over. A violent, one-sided discussion on this theme is under way. The party is squandering an enormous amount of energy instead of talking about the essential questions—why wages are being reduced, why the purchasing power of the *chervonets* has fallen, why kulak influence has grown in the village, and why the standard of living in this country as a whole has risen faster than that of the working class. It is these *facts* that threaten the dictatorship, not the consideration of them by the party. All the necessary measures must be taken to ensure that a discussion can proceed along correct party lines. Whoever wishes to do without a discussion thereby shows that he wishes to do without the party.

No one can decide a question for the party. We need to discuss, not whether to hold a discussion, but the most fundamental and vital questions on which the fate of the proletariat and the building of socialism in our country depend.

STATEMENT OF THE OPPOSITION

October 16, 1926

NOTE: Official obstruction of the Opposition's attempts to reach the ranks of the party inspired the Zinovievists with despair. Moreover, the apparatus had begun to take administrative reprisals and was talking about expulsions. The Zinovievists wanted a ceasefire. They would promise to respect the ban on factions issued in 1921. They would demobilize the Opposition as a faction. They would dissociate themselves from those who called for a new party, including their supporters abroad, some of whom had already been expelled.

Trotsky was willing to go along with them in promising to demobilize the Opposition and dissociating themselves from the advocates of a new party. But they would also restate the Opposition's principles; and they would continue to speak out within the CC and other party bodies.

On October 4, the Opposition leaders proposed a truce to the Politburo. After a week of haggling over terms, compromise formulations were reached.

Trotsky hoped that the declaration would gain the Opposition some much-needed breathing space. In his autobiography, he explained that the October 16 declaration "was intended not for the apparatus but for the mass of the party. It was an expression of our desire to remain in the party and serve it further. Although the Stalinites began to break the truce the day after it was concluded, still we gained time. The winter of 1926-27 gave us a certain breathing spell which allowed us to carry out a more thorough theoretical examination of many questions" (My Life, p. 529). In return for his opponents' agreement to abstain from "factionalism," Stalin evidently was expected to call off the campaign of hounding and organizational reprisals and to refrain from further Opposition-baiting at the approaching Fifteenth Conference. Whether this part of the bargain was ever

*made explicit or not is unclear; in any event, it represented a vain
hope.*

One of the transgressions the Opposition was called upon to
repudiate was a reference made by N.K. Krupskaya in her speech
to the Fourteenth Congress. Krupskaya had argued that freedom
of discussion should have been permitted in preparation for the
congress. It was the job of the congress to try to find the right
line; but the truth, she said, did not automatically reside with the
majority. As an illustration, she recalled the Fourth Congress,
which had been held in Stockholm in 1906. At that congress, the
majority had been held by the Mensheviks; and the major
decisions of that congress had later been fully reversed.

Krupskaya did not make explicit the analogy that must have
sprung to every listener's mind: that the minority at the Fourteenth Congress, like the one at the Fourth Congress, was a
Bolshevik minority confronted with a Menshevik majority temporarily in control of the party. The Stalinists resented this
suggestion because it was important to them to appear to be the
legitimate successors to Lenin—despite the protests of his widow.

Stalin instructed the Opposition to disclaim association only
with the Maslow-Fischer-Urbahns group in the German Communist Party (KPD). This was no accident: Maslow-Fischer-
Urbahns, supporters of Zinoviev, were probably the closest to the
United Opposition in program of any of the Oppositionist
currents abroad. The Opposition disavowed their support, but it
also—probably under Zinoviev's influence—voluntarily took its
distance from various other tendencies in German and European
communism.

The factional struggle in Moscow, and particularly the formation of the United Opposition, had called forth corresponding
developments in the European sections of the Comintern, first
and foremost in Germany, where three distinct left factions
existed: a group around Karl Korsch, a sectarian opponent of the
united front who also had opposed the ratification of the Soviet-
German treaty of April 1926 and had been expelled for speaking
to that effect in the Reichstag and for starting an independent
monthly journal; the "Wedding Opposition," led by Hans Weber,
a member of the Central Committee with a sizable following in
the Berlin working class district of Wedding, who had protested
against the undemocratic regimes in both the German and the
Russian parties; and a group around Arkady Maslow, Ruth
Fischer, and Hugo Urbahns, who had been the primary leadership of the KPD following the dethroning of the Brandlerites and

who, except for Urbahns, had been expelled in August 1926 for refusing to come to Moscow to defend themselves against Comintern charges. On September 11, 1926, a printed "Declaration of the 700" was delivered to the KPD Central Committee containing the signatures of party members from all three dissident groups. The declaration stated their complete solidarity with the Leningrad Opposition in the Russian party. The news about this declaration no doubt inflamed passions in the Russian Politburo.

Boris Souvarine, also mentioned in the Opposition's "Statement" of October 16, had been expelled from the French party in July 1924, after being the lone voice in support of Trotsky at the Thirteenth Congress of the Russian CP. Amadeo Bordiga was now the leader of a small and isolated sectarian group in the Italian CP; he would escape organizational reprisals by the Comintern until 1930, but only because he was arrested by Mussolini's police at the end of 1926.

Finally, the Opposition leaders dissociated themselves from the views of former Workers Opposition leaders, including Ossovsky, who had published an article in Bolshevik *in July arguing for abolition of the single-party system (a view for which he had been expelled); Medvedev, whose 1924 call for additional concessions to foreign capital and for a retreat from NEP had recently been dredged up; and Shlyapnikov.*

From International Press Correspondence, *no. 68, October 21, 1926. The English text has been corrected against the Russian in* Izvestia, *October 17, 1926.*

At the Fourteenth Party Congress and afterwards, we disagreed with the majority of the congress and of the Central Committee on a number of questions of principle. Our views are laid down in official documents as well as in speeches delivered by us at the congress, at plenums of the Central Committee, and in the Politburo. We stand at present on the basis of these views. We categorically reject the theory and practice of "freedom of factions and groupings," and recognize that such theory and practice are contrary to Leninism and the decisions of the party. We consider it our duty to carry out the decisions of the party regarding the impermissibility of factional activity.

At the same time, we consider it to be our duty to admit openly before the party that we and our supporters, in putting forward our views on a number of occasions after the Fourteenth Congress, have committed acts which violated party discipline, and that we have followed a factional course which goes beyond the limits of ideological struggle within the party laid down by the party. In recognizing these acts as wrong, we declare that we emphatically renounce factional methods of propagating our views, as these methods endanger the unity of the party, and we call upon all comrades who share our views to do the same. We call for the immediate dissolution of all factional groupings which have been formed around the views of the "Opposition."

At the same time, we admit that by our appearances in Moscow and Leningrad in October, we violated the decision of the Central Committee on the impermissibility of a discussion, in that we opened such a discussion against the decisions of the Central Committee.

It was equally wrong to mention the Stockholm Congress at the Fourteenth Congress, for this remark could be regarded as a hint and a threat of a split, although this was in no way intended by Comrade N.K. Krupskaya. We unanimously repudiate such a prospect, which is harmful and has nothing in common with our standpoint.

We emphatically condemn any criticism of the Comintern or the policy of our party which goes over to incitement, which weakens the position of the Comintern as the fighting organization of the international proletariat, that of the Communist Party of the Soviet Union as the outpost of the Comintern, or that of the Soviet Union as the first state of the proletarian dictatorship. Not only the agitation of Korsch and his consorts, who have broken with communism, but anybody who goes beyond these limits will meet with energetic resistance on our part. We categorically reject the right of those who carry on agitation of any sort against the Comintern, the CP, or the Soviet Union, to lay claim to any solidarity with us.

While recognizing the right of every member of the Comintern to advocate his views within the limits of the statutes and decisions of the congresses of the Comintern and of the ECCI, we consider it absolutely impermissible to support either directly or indirectly the factionalism of any group in the various sections of the Comintern against the line of the Comintern, be it the Souvarine group in France, the Maslow-Fischer-Urbahns-Weber group in Germany, the Bordiga group in Italy, or any other group, no matter what their attitude may be toward our views. We consider particularly impermissible any support of the activity of persons such as Ruth Fischer and Maslow, who have already been expelled by the Comintern and the party.

The views of Ossovsky, which are expressed in his articles, and of Medvedev, which were analyzed in *Pravda* (the theory of "two parties," advocating the liquidation of the Comintern and the Profintern, attempts to unite with the Social Democrats, widening of the concessions policy beyond the limits laid down by Lenin, etc.), we considered and consider to be profoundly erroneous, anti-Leninist, and fundamentally opposed to our views. The assessment Lenin made of the platform of the "Workers Opposition," defended by Comrades Shlyapnikov and Medvedev, we shared and share completely.

We consider the decisions of the Fourteenth Congress, the party CC, and the CCC to be absolutely binding for ourselves, and we will unconditionally submit to them and carry them out in practice.

Moreover, that is precisely what we urge all comrades to do who share our views.

Each one of us pledges to defend his views only in the forms established by the statutes and decisions of the congresses and the CC, in the conviction that everything that is correct in our views will be adopted by the party in its subsequent work.

In the course of recent months, a number of comrades were expelled from the party for one or another violation of party discipline and for the use of factional methods of struggle for Opposition views. From all that has been said above, it is clear that the political responsibility for these activities rests with the undersigned. We express firm hope that a real cessation of factional struggle on the part of the Opposition will open the way for the expelled comrades, who have acknowledged their errors as regards the breach of party discipline and the interests of party unity, to return to the ranks of the party; and we pledge ourselves to render every possible assistance to the party in the liquidation of factional struggle and to combat new breaches of discipline.

G. Zinoviev	G. Sokolnikov
L. Kamenev	L. Trotsky
Yu. Pyatakov	G. Yevdokimov

SPEECH TO THE FIFTEENTH CONFERENCE

November 1, 1926

NOTE: The breathing space that the Opposition leaders had sought to purchase by signing the declaration of October 16, proved to be short-lived. Less than one week later, the Politburo voted to submit theses refuting the Opposition's ideas to the coming Fifteenth Party Conference. In an angry scene, Trotsky accused Stalin of becoming the "gravedigger of the revolution." On the 23rd the Central Committee adopted a resolution removing Zinoviev from all work in the Comintern (he was its president) and removing Trotsky and Kamenev from the Politburo. It also approved Stalin's theses on the Opposition, which were published on October 26, the first day of the conference (see Stalin's Works *vol. 8 [1954], pp. 225-44).*

The theses noted that the Opposition, despite its formal submission, had not renounced its "errors of principle" and described its views as a "Social Democratic deviation." When the conference opened, the Opposition leaders, still hoping to salvage something of the ceasefire by prudent behavior, refused to take the floor for six days, even during the debate on the ecomonic theses, which were presented by Rykov.

On the seventh day, November 1, Stalin presented his "theses" on the Opposition in a vitriolic outpouring that dredged up any scrap that might be used against the Opposition and its leaders. Zinoviev, Kamenev, and Trotsky all spoke in reply.

This was Trotsky's final major speech to a delegated party meeting. Despite the hostility of his audience, he was heard with respect and his time was repeatedly extended to enable him to finish. Trotsky alluded to several ongoing debates between the Opposition and the apparatus. Stalin had sought to discredit the Opposition by smearing the Zinovievists with the charge of capitulation to Trotskyism. They denied this charge, but it is likely that fear of the label of "Trotskyism" kept other Old

Bolsheviks away from the Opposition. As a gesture to mollify that sentiment, Trotsky disavowed the theory of permanent revolution, as he had done in 1923-24.

For the first time in public he attacked and thoroughly refuted the theory of socialism in one country, and he demonstrated through quotations and argument where Lenin had stood on that question.

In several instances he dealt with the theoretical distortions that were becoming a perennial symptom of the Stalinists' efforts to give a heritage of respectability and orthodoxy to socialism in one country, and to the narrow nationalist spirit that accompanied it. Stalin claimed that the law of uneven development applied only to the imperialist era, not to pre-imperialist capitalism, when it was supposedly unknown. By this he sought to explain away the lack of support for socialism in one country in the writings of Marx and Engels. In a later speech, to the seventh plenum of the ECCI, Trotsky would demonstrate that this law was known not only to Marx and Engels but also to their literate contemporaries. Here he limited himself to pointing out that pre-imperialist capitalism was characterized by a greater, not a lesser, unevenness of development.

Trotsky had been accused of pessimism for pointing to the onset of an equilibrium in the capitalist world after the defeat of the German revolution in 1923-24, even though he had anticipated that the equilibrium would be short-lived and none too stable. By the time the Comintern got around to recognizing the existence of this "stabilization," its underpinnings had largely begun to collapse, as evidenced by the fact that bourgeois England was clinging "not to Baldwin, not to Thomas"—representatives of the bourgeoisie and the right-wing trade union leadership—"but to Purcell," a left-wing labor leader.

The Fifteenth Conference was marked by defections from the Opposition: In his summation, Stalin announced that Krupskaya had broken off relations with the Opposition; and Shlyapnikov and Medvedev, having been disavowed by the Opposition leadership, were persuaded to sign recantations of their views, which were then broadcast by Stalin as signs of a "further collapse of the Opposition bloc."

Trotsky predicted that Stalin's theses, if they were adopted—and they were adopted unanimously—would inevitably lead to the expulsion of the Opposition leadership from the party.

From New International, *August, November, December 1942, where it was incorrectly identified, and where it was reprinted*

from International Press Correspondence, *November 25, 1926.*
The English text has been corrected against the Russian in VKP
XV Konferentsiia Stenograficheskii Otchet.

Comrades! The resolution accuses the Opposition, including
me, of a Social Democratic deviation. I have thought over all the
points of contention which have divided us, the minority of the
CC, from the majority during the period just past, that is, the
period in which the designation "Opposition bloc" has been in
use. I must place on record that the points of contention, and our
standpoint with respect to the points of contention, offer no basis
for the accusation of a "Social Democratic deviation."

The question upon which we have disagreed most, comrades, is
that which asks which danger threatens us during the present
epoch: the danger that our state industry is lagging behind, or·
that it rushes too hastily forward? The Opposition—in which I
am included—has argued that the real danger threatening us is
that our state industry is lagging behind the development of the
national economy as a whole. We have pointed out that the policy
being pursued in the distribution of national income involves the
further growth of the disproportion. For some reason or other this
has been termed *pessimism*. Comrades, arithmetic knows neither
pessimism nor optimism, neither lack of faith nor capitulation.
Figures are figures. If you examine the control figures of Gosplan,
you will find that these figures show the disproportion—or, more
exactly expressed, the shortage of industrial goods—to have
reached the amount of 380 million rubles last year, while this
year the figure will be 500 million, that is, the initial Gosplan
figures show the disproportion to have increased by 25 percent.
Comrade Rykov states in his theses that we might hope (merely
hope) that the disproportion will not increase this year. What was
the basis for this "hope"? The fact that the harvest is not so
favorable as we all expected. Were I to follow in the false tracks of
our critics, I might say that Comrade Rykov's theses welcome the
fact that the unfavorable conditions prevailing at harvest time
reduced the otherwise respectable yield; and he welcomes this
because, had the harvest been greater, the result would have been
a greater disproportion. [*Comrade Rykov: "I am of a different
opinion."*] The figures speak for themselves. [*A voice: "Why
didn't you speak in the discussion on Comrade Rykov's report?"*]
Comrade Kamenev has here told you why we did not. Because I
could not have added anything to this special economic report, in
the form of amendments or arguments, that we had not brought

forward at the April plenum. The amendments and other proposals submitted by me and other comrades to the April plenum
remain in full force today. But the economic experience gained
since April is obviously too small to give us room for hope that at
the present stage the comrades present at this conference will be
convinced. To bring up these points of contention again, before
the actual course of economic life has tested them, would create
unnecessary tensions. These questions will inevitably be more
acceptable to the party when they can be answered by the
statistics based on the latest experience; for objective economic
experience does not decide whether figures are optimistic or
pessimistic, but solely whether they are right or wrong. I believe
our standpoint on the disproportion has been right.

We have disagreed on the *rate of our industrialization,* and I
have been among those comrades who have pointed out that the
present rate is insufficient, and that precisely this insufficient
speed in industrialization imparts the greatest importance to the
differentiation process going on in the villages. To be sure, there
is not as yet anything disastrous in the fact that the kulak has
raised his head or—this is the other side of the same coin—that
the relative weight of the poor peasant in the village has declined.
These are some of the serious problems that accompany the
period of transition. They are unhealthy signs. There is no reason
to "panic" of course. But they are phenomena which must be
correctly assessed. And I have been among those comrades who
have maintained that the process of differentiation in the village
may assume a dangerous form if industry lags behind, that is, if
the disproportion increases. The Opposition maintains that it is
our duty to lessen the disproportion year by year. I see nothing
Social Democratic in this.

We have insisted that the differentiation in the village demands a more elastic taxation policy with respect to the various
strata of the peasantry, a reduction of taxation for the poorer
middle strata of the peasantry, increased taxation for the well-to-
do middle strata, and energetic pressure upon the kulak, especially in his relations to trading capital. We have proposed that
40 percent of the poor peasantry should be freed from taxation
altogether. Are we right or not? I believe that we are right; you
believe we are wrong. But what is "Social Democratic" about this
is a mystery to me. [*Laughter.*]

We have asserted that the increasing differentiation among the
peasantry, taking place under the conditions imposed by the
backwardness of our industry, brings with it the necessity for

double safeguards in the field of politics, that is, we cannot take a tolerant attitude toward the *extension of the franchise* with respect to the kulak, the employer, and the exploiter, even if they operate only on a small scale. We raised the alarm when the famous electoral instructions extended the voting rights of the petty bourgeoisie. Were we right or not? You consider that our alarm was "exaggerated." Well, even assuming that it was, there is nothing Social Democratic about it.

We demanded and proposed that the course being taken by the agricultural cooperatives toward the "highly productive middle peasant," under which name we generally find the kulak, should be severely condemned. We proposed that the "slight shift" (this term was used in the report to the Politburo) of the credit cooperatives toward the well-to-do peasantry should be condemned. I cannot comprehend, comrades, what you find "Social Democratic" in this.

There have been differences of opinion on the question of wages. In substance, these differences consist of our being of the opinion that at the present stage of development of our industry and economy, and at our present economic level, the wage question must not be settled on the assumption that the workers must first increase the productivity of labor, which will then raise the wages, but that the contrary must be the rule, that is, a rise in wages, however modest, must be the prerequisite for an increased productivity of labor. [*A voice: "Where will we get the means?"*] This may be right or it may not, but it is not "Social Democratic."

We have pointed out the connection between various well-known aspects of our inner-party life and the growth of bureaucratism. I believe there is nothing "Social Democratic" about this either.

We have further opposed an overestimation of the economic elements of the capitalist stabilization and the underestimation of its political elements. If we inquire, for instance: What does the economic stabilization consist of in England at the present time? then it appears that England is going to ruin, that its trade balance is adverse, that its foreign trade is shrinking, that its production is declining. This is the "economic stabilization" of England. But to whom is bourgeois England clinging? Not to Baldwin, not to Thomas, but to Purcell. Purcellism is the pseudonym of the present "stabilization" in England. We are therefore of the opinion that it is fundamentally wrong, in consideration of the working masses who carried out the general strike, to combine either directly or indirectly with Purcell. This is the reason that we have demanded the dissolution of the Anglo-Russian Committee. I see nothing "Social Democratic" in this.

We have insisted upon a fresh revision of our trade union statutes, upon which subject I reported to the CC: a revision of those statutes from which the word "Profintern" was struck out last year and replaced by the words "international alliance of trade unions," which cannot mean anything other than "Amsterdam." I am glad to say that this revision of last year's revision has been accomplished, and the word "Profintern" has been reinserted in our trade union statutes. But why was our uneasiness on the subject "Social Democratic?" That, comrades, is something which I entirely fail to understand. [*Laughter.*]

I should like, as briefly as possible, to enumerate the main points of difference which have arisen of late. Our standpoint on the questions concerned has been that we have observed the dangers likely to threaten the class line of the party and of the workers' state under the conditions imposed by a long continuance of the NEP, and our encirclement by international capitalism. But these differences, and the standpoint adopted by us in the defense of our opinions, cannot be construed into a "Social Democratic deviation" by the most complicated logical or even scholastic methods.

That is why it was found necessary to leave these actual and serious differences, engendered by the present epoch of our economic and political development, and to go back into the past in order to construe differences in the conception of the "character of our revolution" in general—not in the present period of our revolution, not with regard to the present concrete tasks, but with regard to the character of the revolution in general, or as expressed in the theses, the revolution "in itself," the revolution "in its substance." When a German speaks of a thing "in itself," he is using a metaphysical term placing the revolution outside of all connection with the real world around it; it is abstracted from yesterday and tomorrow, and regarded as an "essence" from which everything proceeds. Now, then, in regard to this "essence," I have been found guilty, in the ninth year of our revolution, of having denied the socialist character of our revolution! No more and no less! I discovered this for the first time in this resolution itself. If the comrades find it necessary for some reason to construct a resolution on quotations from my writings—and the main portion of the resolution, pushing into the foreground the theory of original sin ("Trotskyism"), is built upon quotations from my writings between 1917 and 1922—then it would at least be advisable to select the *essential* from everything I have written on the character of our revolution.

You will excuse me, comrades, but it is no pleasure to have to set aside the actual subject and to retail where and when I wrote this or that. But this resolution, in trying to support the accusation of a "Social Democratic" deviation, refers to passages from my writings, and I am obliged to give the information. In 1922 I was commissioned by the party to write the book *Terrorism and Communism* against Kautsky, against the characterization of our revolution by Kautsky as a nonproletarian and nonsocialist revolution. A large number of editions of this book were distributed both at home and abroad by the Comintern. The book met with no hostile reception from the comrades most closely involved, including Vladimir Ilyich. This book is not quoted in the resolution.

In 1922 I was commissioned by the Political Bureau to write the book entitled *Between Imperialism and Revolution* [published in English as *Between Red and White*]. In this book I utilized the special experience gained in Georgia, in the form of a refutation of the standpoint of those international Social Democrats who were using the Georgian uprising as material against us, for the purpose of subjecting to a fresh examination the main questions of the proletarian revolution, which has a right to tear down not only petty-bourgeois prejudices but also petty-bourgeois institutions. Again, this book is not quoted.

At the Third Congress of the Comintern I gave a report, on behalf of the CC, declaring in substance that we had entered an era of unstable balance. I polemicized against Comrade Bukharin, who at that time was of the opinion that we were going to go through an uninterrupted series of revolutions and crises until the victory of socialism throughout the world, and that there would not and could not be any "stabilization." At the time Comrade Bukharin accused me of a right deviation (perhaps Social Democratic too?). In full agreement with Lenin at the Third Congress I defended the theses which I had formulated. The import of the theses was that we, despite the slower speed of the revolution, would pass successfully through this period by developing the socialist elements in our economy [see *The First Five Years of the Communist International,* (New York: Monad Press, 1972), vol. 1, p. 174 ff].

At the Fourth World Congress in 1922 I was commissioned by the CC to follow Lenin with a report on the NEP [see *The First Five Years . . .* , vol. 2, p. 220 ff]. What was my theme? I argued that the NEP merely signifies a change in the forms and methods of socialist development. And now, instead of taking these works of mine, which may have been good or bad, but were at least *fundamental,* and in which, on behalf of the party, I defined the character of our revolution in the years between 1920 and 1923, you seize upon a few little passages, each only two or three lines, out of a preface and a postscript written at the same period.

I repeat that none of the passages quoted is from a fundamental work. These four little quotations (1917 to 1922) form the sole foundation for the accusation that I deny the socialist character of our revolution. The structure of the accusation thus being completed, every imaginable original sin is added to it, even the sin of the Opposition of 1925. The demand for a more rapid industrialization and the proposal to increase the taxation of the kulaks all arise from these four passages. [*A voice: "Don't form factions!"*]

Comrades, I regret having to take your time, but I must quote a few more passages—I could cite hundreds—to refute everything that the resolution ascribes to me. First of all I must draw your attention to the fact that the four quotations upon which the theory of my original sin is based have all been taken from writings of mine between 1917 and 1922. Everything that I have said since appears to have been swept away by the wind. Nobody knows whether I subsequently regarded our revolution as socialist or not. Today, at the end of 1926, the present standpoint of the so-called Opposition on the main questions of economics and politics is sought in passages from my personal writings between 1917 and 1922, and not even in passages from my chief works, but in works written for some quite chance occasion. I shall return to these quotations and respond on every one of them. But first permit me to cite some quotations of a more essential character, written at the same period.

For instance, the following is an excerpt from my speech at the conference of the Moscow Trade Union Council on October 28, 1921, after the introduction of the NEP: "We have reorganized our economic policy in anticipation of a slower development of our economy. We reckon with the possibility that the revolution in Europe, though developing and growing, is developing more slowly than we expected. The bourgeoisie has proved more tenacious. Even in our own country we are obliged to reckon with a slower transition to socialism, for we are surrounded by capitalist countries. We must concentrate our forces on the largest and best equipped undertakings. At the same time, we must not forget that the taxation in kind among the peasantry, and the increase of leased undertakings, form a basis for the development of commodity production, for the accumulation of capital, and for the rise of a new bourgeoisie. At the same time, the socialist economy will be built up on the narrower but firmer basis of big industry."

At a membership meeting of our party on November 10 of the same year, in the Moscow district of Sokolniki, I stated: "What do we have now? We now have the process of socialist revolution, in the first place within a single state and in the second place in a state which is very backward, both economically and culturally, and surrounded on all sides by capitalist countries."

What conclusion did I draw from this? Did I propose capitulation? I proposed the following:

"It is our task to make socialism prove its advantages. . . . The peasant will be the judge who pronounces on the advantages or drawbacks of the socialist state. We are competing with capitalism in the peasant market. . . .

"What is the present basis for our conviction that we shall be victorious? There are many reasons justifying our belief. These lie both in the international situation and in the development of the Communist Party; in the fact that we retain full power in our hands, and in the fact that we permit free trade solely within the limits which we deem necessary."

This, comrades, was said in 1921, and not in 1926!

In my report at the Fourth World Congress (directed against Otto Bauer, to whom my relationship has now been discovered) I spoke as follows: "Our most important weapon in the economic struggle occurring on the basis of the market is—state power. Reformist simpletons are the only ones who are incapable of grasping the significance of this weapon. The bourgeoisie understands it excellently. The whole history of the bourgeoisie proves it.

"Another weapon of the proletariat is that the country's most important productive forces are in its hands: the entire railway system, the entire mining industry, the overwhelming majority of enterprises servicing industry are under the direct economic management of the working class.

"The workers' state likewise owns the land, and the peasants annually contribute in return for using it hundreds of millions of poods [one pood equals 36 lbs.] in taxes in kind.

"The workers' power holds the state frontiers: foreign commodities, and foreign capital generally, can gain access to our country only within limits which are deemed desirable and legitimate by the workers' state.

"Such are the weapons and means of socialist construction" [*The First Five Years . . .* , vol. 2, p. 239].

In a booklet published by me in 1923 under the title *Problems of Everyday Life,* you may read on this subject: "Now, what has the working class actually gained and secured for itself as a result of the revolution?

"1. The dictatorship of the proletariat (represented by the workers' and peasants' government under the leadership of the Communist Party).

"2. The Red Army—a firm support of the dictatorship of the proletariat.

"3. The nationalization of the chief means of production, without which the dictatorship of the proletariat would have become a form void of substance.

"4. The monopoly of foreign trade, which is the necessary condition of socialist state structure in a capitalist environment.

"These four things, definitely won, form the steel frame of all our work; and *every success we achieve in economics or culture—* provided it is a real achievement and not a sham—*becomes in this framework a necessary part of the socialist structure"* [*Problems of Everyday Life: And Other Writings on Culture and Science* (New York: Monad Press, 1973), pp. 15-16; emphasis added by Trotsky].

This same booklet contains another and even more definite formulation: "The easier it was (comparatively, of course) for the Russian proletariat to pass through the revolutionary crisis, the harder its work of socialist construction now becomes. But, on the other hand, the framework of our new social structure, marked by the four characteristics mentioned above, gives an objectively socialist content to all conscientious and rationally directed efforts in the domain of economics and culture. Under the bourgeois regime the workman, with no desire or intention on his part, was continually enriching the bourgeoisie, and did it all the more, the better his work was. In the Soviet state a conscientious and good worker, whether he cares to do it or not (in case he is not in the party and keeps away from politics) achieves socialist results and increases the wealth of the working class. *This is the doing of the October Revolution,* and the NEP has not changed anything in this respect" [*Problems of Everyday Life,* p. 20; emphasis added by Trotsky].

I could prolong this chain of quotations indefinitely, for I never did and never could characterize our revolution differently. I shall confine myself, however, to one more passage, from a book quoted by Comrade Stalin (*Toward Capitalism or Socialism?*). This book was published for the first time in 1925 and was printed originally as a series in *Pravda.* The editors of our central paper have never drawn my attention to any heresies in this book with respect to the character of our revolution. This year the second edition of the book was issued. It has been translated into different languages by the Comintern and this is the first time I've heard that it gives a false idea of our economic development. Comrade Stalin has read you a few lines, picked out arbitrarily in order to show that this is "unclearly formulated." I am thus obliged to read a somewhat longer passage, in order to prove that the idea in question is quite clearly formulated. The following is stated in the introduction, devoted to a criticism of our bourgeois and Social Democratic critics, above all, Kautsky and Otto Bauer. Here you may read: "These judgments"—formed by the enemies of our economic methods—"are of two kinds. In the first place, we are told that we are ruining the country by our work of socialist construction; in the second place, we are told that our development of the productive forces is in reality carrying us toward capitalism.

"Criticism of the first type is characteristic of the mode of thought of the bourgeoisie. The second style of criticism is rather that of social democracy, i.e., bourgeois thought in a socialist disguise. It would be hard to draw a sharp line between the two styles of criticism, and frequently the two exchange their arsenal of arguments in a neighborly manner, without noticing it themselves, intoxicated as they are with the sacred war against communist barbarism.

"The present book, I hope, will prove to the unprejudiced reader that both camps are lying, not only the outright big bourgeoisie, but also the petty bourgeoisie who pretend to be socialist. They lie when they say that the Bolsheviks have ruined Russia. Indisputable facts prove that in Russia—disorganized by imperialist and civil wars—the productive forces in industry and agriculture are approaching the prewar level, which will be reached during the coming year. It is a falsehood to state that the evolution of the productive forces is proceeding in the direction of capitalism. In industry, transportation, communications, commerce, finance, and credit operations, the part played by the nationalized economy is not lessened with the growth of the productive forces; on the contrary, this role is assuming increasing importance in the total economy of the country. Facts and figures prove this beyond dispute.

"The matter is much more complicated in the field of agriculture. No Marxist will be surprised by this; the transition from scattered single peasant establishments to a socialist system of land cultivation is inconceivable except after passing through a number of stages in technology, economics, and culture. The fundamental condition for this transition is the retention of power in the hands of the class whose object is to lead society to socialism (and which is becoming ever more able to influence the peasant population by means of state industry and by raising agricultural technology to a higher level and thus creating the prerequisites for a collectivization of agriculture)" ["Toward Capitalism or Socialism?" in *The Challenge of the Left Opposition (1923-25)*, pp. 320-21].

The draft of the resolution on the Opposition states that Trotsky's standpoint closely approaches that of Otto Bauer, who has said, "In Russia, where the proletariat represents only a small minority of the nation, the proletariat can only maintain its rule temporarily, and is bound to lose it again *as soon as the peasant majority of the nation has become culturally mature enough to take over the rule itself.*"

In the first place, comrades, who could entertain the idea that so absurd a formulation could occur to any one of us? Whatever is to be understood by "as soon as the peasant majority of the nation has become culturally mature enough"? What does this mean? What are we to understand by "culture"? Under capitalist conditions the peasantry has no independent culture. As far as culture is concerned, the peasantry may mature under the influence of the proletariat or of the bourgeoisie. These are the only two possibilities existing for the cultural advance of the peasantry. To a Marxist, the idea that the "culturally matured" peasantry, having overthrown the proletariat, could take over power on its own account, is a wildly prejudiced absurdity. The experience of two revolutions has taught us that the peasantry, should it come into conflict with the proletariat and overthrow the proletarian power, simply forms a bridge—through Bonapartism—for the bourgeoisie. An independent peasant state founded on neither proletarian nor bourgeois culture is impossible. This whole construction of Otto Bauer's collapses into a lamentable petty-bourgeois absurdity.

We are told that we have no faith in the establishment of socialism. And at the same time we are accused of wanting to "rob" the peasantry (not the kulaks, but the peasantry!).

I think, comrades, that these are not words out of our diction-ary at all. The Communists cannot propose that the workers' state "rob" the *peasantry,* and it is precisely with the peasantry that we are concerned. A proposal to free 40 percent of the poor peasantry from all taxation, and to lay these taxes upon the kulak, may be right or it may be wrong, but it can never be interpreted as a proposal to "rob" the peasantry.

I ask you: If we have no faith in the establishment of socialism in our country, or if (as is said of me) we propose that the European revolution be passively awaited, then why do we propose to "rob" the peasantry? To what end? That is incompre-hensible. We are of the opinion that industrialization—the basis of socialism—is proceeding too slowly, and that this negatively affects the peasantry. If, let us say, the quantity of agricultural products put upon the market this year is 20 percent more than last—I take these figures with a reservation—and at the same time the grain price has sunk by 8 percent and the prices of various industrial products have risen by 16 percent, as has been the case, then the peasant gains less than when his crops are poorer and the retail prices for industrial products lower. The acceleration of industrialization, especially through increased taxation of the kulak, will result in the production of a larger quantity of goods, reducing the retail prices, to the advantage of the workers and of the greater part of the peasantry.

It is possible that you do not agree with this. But nobody can deny that it is a system of views on the development of our economy. How can you claim that we have no faith in the possibility of socialist development, and yet at the same time assert that we demand the robbing of the peasant? With what object? For what purpose? Nobody can explain this. I contend that it cannot be explained. There are things that are impossible to explain. For example, I have often asked myself why the dissolution of the Anglo-Russian Committee can be supposed to imply a call to leave the trade unions? And why does the nonentry into the Amsterdam International not constitute an appeal to the workers not to join the Amsterdam trade unions? [*A voice: "That will be explained to you!"*] I have never received an answer to this question, and never will. [*A voice: "You will get your answer."*] Neither shall I receive a reply to the question of how we contrive to disbelieve in the realization of socialism and yet endeavor to "rob" the peasantry.

The book of mine from which I last quoted speaks in detail of the importance of the correct distribution of our national income, since our economic development is proceeding amidst the struggle of two tendencies: the socialist and the capitalist ones. ". . . The outcome of the struggle depends on the speed of development of each of these tendencies. In other words: if state industry develops more *slowly* than agriculture; if the latter should proceed to produce with increasing speed the two extreme poles mentioned above (capitalist farmers above, proletarians below); this process *would,* of course, lead to a restoration of capitalism.

"But just let our enemies try to prove the inevitability of this prospect. Even if they approach this task more intelligently than poor Kautsky (or MacDonald), they will burn their fingers. On the other hand, is such a possibility entirely precluded? Theoretically, it is not. *If* the dominant party were guilty of one mistake after another, in politics as well as in economics; if it were thus to retard the growth of industry, which is now developing so promisingly; if it were to relinquish its control over the political and economic processes in the village; then, of course, the cause of socialism would be lost in our country. But we are not at all obliged to make any such assumptions in our prognosis.

"How power is lost, how the achievements of the proletariat may be surrendered, how one may work for capitalism—all this has been brilliantly demonstrated to the international proletariat by Kautsky and his friends, after November 9, 1918. Nothing needs to be added to this lesson.

"Our tasks, our goals, our methods, are different. We want to show how power, once achieved, may be retained and consolidated, and how the form of the proletarian state may be filled with the economic content of socialism" [*The Challenge of the Left Opposition (1923-25),* pp. 322-23; emphasis added by Trotsky].

The whole content of this book [*A voice: "There is nothing about the cooperatives in it!"*]—I shall come to the cooperatives— the whole content of this book is devoted to the subject of how the proletarian form of state is to be given the economic content of socialism. It may be said (insinuations have already been made in this direction): Yes, you believed that we were moving toward socialism so long as the process of reconstruction was going on, and so long as industry developed at a speed of 45 or 35 percent per year, but now that we have arrived at a crisis in regard to fixed capital and you see the difficulties of expanding our fixed capital, you have been seized with a so-called "panic."

I cannot quote the whole of the chapter on "Material Limits

and Possibilities of the Rate of Development." It points out the four elements characterizing the advantages of our system over capitalism and draws the following conclusion: "Considered together, these four advantages, if rightly utilized, will enable us in the next few years to increase the coefficient of our industrial expansion not only to twice the figure of 6 percent attained in the prewar period, but to three times that figure, and perhaps to even more" [*The Challenge of the Left Opposition (1923-25)*, p. 358].

If I am not mistaken, the coefficient of our industrial growth will amount, according to the plans, to 18 percent. In this there are, of course, still reconstruction elements. But in any case the extremely rough statistical prognosis which I made as an example eighteen months ago coincides fairly well with our actual speed this year.

You ask: What is the explanation of those frightful passages quoted in the resolution? I shall have to answer this question. I must first, however, repeat that not a single word has been quoted from the fundamental works which I wrote on the character of the revolution between 1917 and 1922, and complete silence is preserved on everything that I have written since 1922, even on that written last year and this year. Four passages are quoted. Comrade Stalin has dealt with them in detail, and they are referred to in the resolution, so you will permit me to devote some words to them as well.

"4. The working-class movement achieves victory in the *democratic* revolution. . . .

"5. The . . . bourgeoisie becomes . . . counterrevolutionary. . . Among the peasantry, the whole of the well-to-do section, and a fairly large part of the middle peasantry, also grow 'wiser,' quieten down and turn to the side of the counterrevolution in order to wrest power from the proletariat and the rural poor. . . .

"6. . . . This struggle would have been almost hopeless for the Russian proletariat alone and its defeat would have been . . . inevitable . . . *had the European socialist proletariat* not come to the assistance of the Russian proletariat" [*Collected Works*, vol. 10, pp. 91-92].

I am afraid, comrades, that if anyone told you that these lines represented a malicious product of Trotskyism, many comrades would believe it. But this passage is Lenin's. The fifth volume of the *Lenin Miscellany* contains a draft of a pamphlet which Lenin intended to write at the end of 1905. Here this possible situation is described: The workers are victorious in the democratic revolution, the well-to-do section of the peasantry goes over to counterrevolution. I should say that this passage is quoted in the latest issue of *Bolshevik,* on page 68, but unfortunately with a grave misrepresentation, although the excerpt is given in quotation marks: the words referring to the considerable section of the middle peasantry are simply left out. I call upon you to compare the fifth *Lenin Miscellany,* page 451, with the latest issue of *Bolshevik,* page 68.

I could quote dozens of such passages from Lenin's works: vol. 9, pp. 135-36; vol. 10, p. 191; vol. 12, pp. 106-07. (I don't have the time to read them, but anyone may look up the references for himself.) I shall quote only one passage, from vol. 10, p. 280:

"The Russian revolution"—he is referring to the democratic revolution—"can achieve victory by its own efforts, but it cannot possibly hold and consolidate its gains by its own strength. It cannot do this unless there is a socialist revolution in the West. Without this condition restoration is inevitable, whether we have municipalization, or nationalization, or division of the land: for under each and every form of property or ownership the small proprietor will always be a bulwark of restoration. After the complete victory of the democratic revolution the small proprietor will inevitably turn against the proletariat."

[*A voice: "We have introduced the NEP."*]

True, I shall refer to that presently.

Let us now turn to that passage which I wrote in 1922, in order that we may see how my standpoint on the revolution in the epoch of 1904-05 had developed.

I have no intention, comrades, of raising the question of the theory of permanent revolution. This theory—in respect both to what has been right in it and to what has been incomplete and wrong—has nothing whatever to do with our present contentions. In any case, this theory of permanent revolution, to which so much attention has been devoted recently, is not the responsibility in the slightest degree of either the Opposition of 1925 or the Opposition of 1923, and even I myself regard it as a question which has long been consigned to the archives.

But let us return to the passage quoted in the resolution. (This I wrote in 1922, but from the standpoint of 1905-06.) "The proletariat, once having power in its hands, . . . would enter into hostile conflict, not only with all those bourgeois groups which had supported it during the first stages of its revolutionary struggle, but also with the broad masses of the peasantry, with whose collaboration it—the proletariat—had come into power" [*1905* (New York: Vintage Books, 1972), p. vi].

Although this was written in 1922, it was put in the future
tense—the proletariat would come into conflict with the bourgeoisie, etc.—because prerevolutionary views were being described. I
ask you: Has Lenin's prognosis of 1905-06, that the middle
peasants would go over to counterrevolution to a great extent,
proved true? I maintained that it has proved true in part. [*Voices:*
"In part? When?" Disturbance.] Yes, under the leadership of the
party and above all under Lenin's leadership, the division
between us and the peasantry was bridged over by the New
Economic Policy. This is indisputable. [*Disturbance.*] If any of
you imagine, comrades, that in 1926 I do not grasp the meaning
of the New Economic Policy, you are mistaken. I grasp the
meaning of the New Economic Policy in 1926, perhaps not so well
as other comrades, but still I grasp it. But you must remember
that at that time, before there was any New Economic Policy,
before there had been a revolution of 1917, and we were sketching
the first outlines of possible developments, utilizing the experience won in previous revolutions—the Great French Revolution
and the revolution of 1848—at that time all Marxists, not
omitting Lenin (I have given quotations), were of the opinion that
after the democratic revolution was completed and the land given
to the peasantry, the proletariat would encounter opposition not
only from the big peasants, but from a considerable section of the
middle peasants, who would represent a hostile and even counterrevolutionary force.

Have there been signs among us of the truth of this prognosis?
Yes, there have been signs, and fairly distinct ones. For instance,
when the Makhno movement in the Ukraine helped the White
Guards to sweep away the Soviet power this was one proof of the
correctness of Lenin's prognosis. The Antonov rising, the rising
in Siberia, the rising on the Volga, the rising in the Urals, the
Kronstadt revolt, when the "middle peasants" conversed with
Soviet power in the language of twelve-inch naval guns—doesn't
all this prove that Lenin's forecast was correct *at a certain stage*
of development in the revolution? [*Comrade Moiseyenko: "And*
what did you propose?"] Is it not perfectly clear that the passage
written by me in 1922 on the division between us and the
peasantry was simply a statement of these facts?

We bridged over the schism between us and the peasantry by
means of the NEP. And were there differences between us during
the transition to the NEP? There were no differences during the
transition to the NEP. [*Disturbance.*] There were differences over
the trade union question *before* the transition to the NEP, when

the party was still seeking a way out of the blind alley. These differences were of serious importance. But on the question of the NEP, when Lenin submitted the NEP resolution to the Tenth Party Congress, we all voted unanimously for it. And when a new trade union resolution arose as a result of the New Economic Policy—a few months after the Tenth Party Congress—we again voted unanimously for this resolution in the CC. But during the period of transition—and the change wrought by it was no small one—the peasants, including the middle peasants, declared: "We are for the Bolsheviks, but against the Communists." What does this mean? It means a peculiarly Russian form of desertion from the proletarian revolution on the part of the middle peasantry at a given stage.

I am reproached with having said that it is "hopeless to think that revolutionary Russia would be able to maintain itself in the face of conservative Europe" ["The Program of Peace," in *Fourth International,* September 1944, p. 285]. This I wrote in May 1917, and I believe that it was perfectly right. Have we maintained ourselves against a *conservative* Europe? Let us consider the facts. At the moment when Germany was discussing a peace treaty with the Entente, the danger was especially great. Had the German revolution not broken out at this point—that German revolution which remained uncompleted, suffocated by the Social Democrats, yet still sufficing to overthrow the old regime and to demoralize the Hohenzollern army—I repeat, had the German revolution, such as it was, not broken out, then we should have been overthrown. It is not by accident that the passage contains the phrase "in opposition to a conservative Europe," and not "in opposition to a capitalist Europe." Against a conservative Europe, maintaining its whole apparatus, and in particular its armies. I ask you: Could we maintain ourselves under these circumstances, or could we not? [*A voice: "Are you talking to children?"*] That we still continue to exist is due to the fact that Europe has not remained what it was. Lenin wrote as follows on this subject: "We are living not merely in a state, but *in a system of states,* and it is inconceivable for the Soviet Republic to exist alongside of the imperialist states for any length of time. One or the other must triumph in the end" [*Collected Works,* vol. 29, p. 153].

When did Lenin say this? On March 18, 1919, that is two years after the October Revolution. My words of 1917 signified that if our revolution did not shake Europe, did not move it, then we were lost. Is this not in substance the same? I ask all the older comrades, who were politically conscious before and during 1917: What was your conception of the revolution and its consequences?

When I try to recollect this, I can find no other formulation than approximately the following:

"We thought: either the international revolution comes to our assistance, and in that case our victory will be fully assured, or we shall do our modest revolutionary work in the conviction that even in the event of defeat we shall have served the cause of the revolution and that our experience will benefit other revolutions. It was clear to us that without the support of the international world revolution the victory of the proletarian revolution was impossible. Before the revolution, and even after it, we thought: either revolution breaks out in other countries, in the capitalistically more developed countries, immediately, or at least very quickly, or we must perish" [*Collected Works,* vol. 32, pp. 479-80].

This was our conception of the fate of the revolution. Who said this? [*Comrade Moiseyenko: "Lenin!" A voice: "And what did he say later on?"*]

Lenin said this in 1921, while the passage quoted from me dates from 1917. I have thus a right to refer to what Lenin said in 1921. [*A voice: "And what did Lenin say later on?"*] Later on I too said something different. [*Laughter.*] Both before the revolution, and after it, we believed that: "Either revolution breaks out in the other countries, in the capitalistically more developed countries, immediately, or at least very quickly, or we must perish." But: "In spite of this conviction, we did all we possibly could to preserve the Soviet system under all circumstances, come what may, because we knew that we were not only working for ourselves, but also for the international revolution. We knew this, we repeatedly expressed this conviction before the October Revolution, immediately after it, and at the time we signed the Brest-Litovsk Peace Treaty. And, generally speaking, this was correct" [p. 480].

This passage goes on to say that our path has become more intricate and winding, but that in all essentials our prognosis was correct. As I have already said, we went over to the NEP unanimously, without any differences whatever. [*Comrade Moiseyenko: "To save us from utter ruin!"*]

True, just for that reason, to save us from utter ruin.

Comrades, I beg you to extend the time allotted for my speech. I should like to speak on the theory of socialism in one country. I ask for another half hour. [*Disturbance.*]

Comrades, on the question of the relations between the proletariat and the peasantry . . .

Chairman: Please wait till we have decided. I submit three proposals; firstly, to adhere to the original time allotted to Comrade Trotsky; secondly, an extension of half an hour; thirdly, an extension of a quarter of an hour. [*On a vote being taken there is a majority for the half-hour extension.*]

Trotsky: The next passage quoted from my writings has brought me the reproach that whereas Lenin said "ten to twenty years of correct relations with the peasantry, and our victory is assured on an international scale," Trotskyism, on the contrary, assumes that the proletariat cannot enter into any correct relations with the peasantry until the world revolution has been accomplished. First of all I must ask the actual meaning of the passage quoted. Lenin speaks of ten to twenty years of correct relations with the peasantry. This means that Lenin did not expect socialism to be established within ten to twenty years. Why? Because under socialism we must understand a state of society in which there is neither proletariat nor peasantry, nor any classes whatever. Socialism abolishes the opposition between town and country. Thus the term of twenty years is set before us, in the course of which we must pursue a political line leading to correct relations between the proletariat and the peasantry. That is the first point.

Further on, however, it is said that Trotskyism is of the opinion that there can be no correct relations between the proletariat and the peasantry until the world revolution has been accomplished. I am thus alleged to have laid down a law according to which *incorrect* relations must be maintained with the peasantry as far as possible, until the international revolution has been victorious. [*Laughter.*] Apparently it was not intended to express this idea here, as there is no sense in it whatever.

What was the NEP? The NEP has been a process of shunting onto a new track, precisely for the establishment of correct relations between the proletariat and the peasantry. Were there differences between us on this subject? No, there were none. What we are arguing about now is the taxation of the kulak, and the forms and methods to be adopted in allying the proletariat with the village poor. What is the actual matter at hand? The best method of establishing correct relations between the peasantry and the proletariat. You have the right to disagree with individual proposals of ours, but you must recognize that the whole

ideological struggle revolves around the question of what relations are correct at the present stage of development.

Were there differences between us in 1917 on the peasant
question? No. The peasant decree, the "Social Revolutionary"
peasant decree, was adopted unanimously by us as our basis. The
land decree, drawn up by Lenin, was accepted by us unanimously
and gave rise to no differences in our circles. Did the policy of
"de-kulakization" afford any cause for differences? No, there were
no differences on this. [*A voice: "And Brest?"*] Did the struggle
commenced by Lenin, for winning over the middle peasantry,
give rise to differences? No, it gave rise to none. I do not assert
that there were no differences whatever, but I definitely maintain
that however great the differences of opinion may have been in
various and even important questions, there were no differences
of opinion in the matter of the main line of policy to be pursued
with regard to the peasantry.

In 1919 there were rumors abroad of differences on this
question. And what did Lenin write on the subject? Let us look
back. I was asked at that time by the peasant Gulov: "What are
the differences of opinion between you and Ilyich?" and I replied
to this question both in *Pravda* and in *Izvestia*. Lenin wrote
as follows on the matter, both in *Pravda* and in *Izvestia*, in
February 1919:

"*Izvestia* of February 2 carried a letter from a peasant, G.
Gulov, who asks a question about the attitude of our workers'and
peasants' government to the middle peasantry, and tells of
rumors that Lenin and Trotsky are not getting on together, and
that there are big differences between them on this very question
of the middle peasant.

"Comrade Trotsky has already replied to that in his "Letter to
the Middle Peasants," which appeared in *Izvestia* of February 7.
In this letter Comrade Trotsky says that the rumors of differences
between him and myself are the most monstrous and shameless
lie, spread by the landowners and capitalists, or by their witting
and unwitting accomplices. For my part, I entirely confirm
Comrade Trotsky's statement. There are no differences between
us, and as regards the middle peasants there are no differences
either between Trotsky and myself, or in general in the Communist Party, of which we are both members.

"In his letter Comrade Trotsky has explained clearly and in
detail why the Communist Party and present workers' and
peasants' government, elected by the soviets and composed of
members of that party, do not consider the middle peasants to be

their enemies. I fully subscribe to what Comrade Trotsky has said" [a slightly different translation is in *Collected Works,* vol. 36, p. 500].

This was before the NEP. Then came the transition to the NEP. I repeat once more that the transition to the NEP gave rise to no differences. On the NEP question I gave a report before the Fourth World Congress, in the course of which I polemicized against Otto Bauer [see *The First Five Years of the Communist International,* vol. 2, p. 220 ff]. Later I wrote as follows: "The NEP is regarded by the bourgeoisie and the Mensheviks as a necessary (but of course 'insufficient') step toward freeing the productive forces from 'enslavement.' The Menshevik theoreticians of both the Kautsky and the Otto Bauer variety have welcomed the NEP as the dawn of capitalist restoration in Russia. They add: Either the NEP will destroy the Bolshevik dictatorship (favorable result) or the Bolshevik dictatorship will destroy the NEP (regrettable result)."

The whole of my report at the Fourth World Congress went to prove that the NEP will not destroy the Bolshevik dictatorship, but that the Bolshevik dictatorship, under the conditions given by the NEP, will secure the supremacy of the socialist elements in the economy over the capitalist ones.

Another passage from my works has been brought up against me—and here I come to the question of the possibility of the victory of socialism in one country—which reads as follows: "The contradictions between a workers' government and an overwhelming majority of peasants in a backward country could be resolved only on an international scale, in the arena of a world proletarian revolution" [*1905,* pp. vi-vii].

This was said in 1922. The accusing resolution makes the following statement: "The conference places on record that such views as these on the part of Comrade Trotsky and his followers, on the fundamental question of the character and prospects of our revolution, *have nothing in common* with the views of our party, with Leninism."

They might have said this was a shade off from the party's position—although I do not find it so even today—or that these views had not yet been precisely formulated (I do not find this to be so either). But it is stated quite flatly: These views "*have nothing in common* with the views of our party, with Leninism."

Here I must quote a few lines closely related to Leninism: "The complete victory of the socialist revolution in one country alone is inconceivable and demands the most active cooperation of at least several advanced countries, which do not include Russia" [*Collected Works*, vol. 28, p. 151].

It was not I who said this, but one greater than I. Lenin said this on November 8, 1918. Not before the October Revolution, but on November 8, 1918, one year after we had seized power. If he had said nothing else but this, we could easily infer what we liked from it by tearing one sentence or the other out of context. [*A voice: "He was speaking of the final victory!"*] No, pardon me, he said: "demands the most active cooperation." Here it is impossible to sidetrack from the main question to the question of "intervention," for it is plainly stated that the victory of socialism demands—not merely protection against intervention—but the cooperation of "*at least several advanced countries, which do not include Russia.*" [*Voices: "And what follows from that?"*] This is not the only passage in which we see that not merely intervention is meant. And thus the conclusion to be drawn is the fact that the standpoint which I have defended, to the effect that the internal contradictions arising out of the backwardness of our country must be solved by international revolution, is not my exclusive property, but that Lenin defended these same views, only incomparably more sharply and categorically.

We are told that this applied to the epoch in which the law of the uneven development of the capitalist countries is supposed to have been still unknown, that is, the epoch before imperialism. I cannot go thoroughly into this. But I must unfortunately place on record that Comrade Stalin commits a great theoretical and historical error here. The law of uneven development of capitalism is older than imperialism. Capitalism is developing very unevenly today in the various countries. But in the nineteenth century this unevenness was greater than in the twentieth. At that time England was lord of the world, while Japan on the other hand was a feudal state closely confined within its own limits. At the time when serfdom was abolished among us, Japan began to adapt itself to capitalist civilization. China was, however, still wrapped in the deepest slumber. And so forth. At that time the unevenness of capitalist development was greater than now. Those unevennesses were as well known to Marx and Engels as they are to us. Imperialism has developed a more "leveling tendency" than pre-imperialist capitalism, for the reason that finance capital is the most elastic form of capital. It is, however, indisputable that today, too, there are great unevennesses in development. But if it is maintained that in the nineteenth century, before imperialism, capitalism developed less unevenly, and the theory of the possibility of socialism in one country was therefore wrong at that time, while today, now that imperialism has increased the heterogeneity of development, the theory of socialism in one country has become correct, then this assertion contradicts all historical experience, and completely reverses fact. No, this will not do; other and more serious arguments must be sought.

Comrade Stalin has written [in *Problems of Leninism* (New York: International Publishers, 1934), p. 71] that those who deny the possibility of establishing socialism in one country must deny at the same time the justifiability of the October Revolution.

But in 1918 we heard from Lenin that the establishment of socialism requires the direct cooperation of *at least several advanced countries*, "which do not include Russia." Yet Lenin did not deny the justifiability of the October Revolution. And he wrote as follows regarding this in 1918: "I know that there are, of course, wiseacres with a high opinion of themselves and even calling themselves socialists"—this was written against the adherents of Kautsky and Sukhanov—"who assert that power should not have been taken until the revolution broke out in all countries. They do not realize that in saying this they are deserting the revolution and going over to the side of the bourgeoisie. To wait until the working classes carry out a revolution on an international scale means that everyone will remain frozen in a state of anticipation. This is senseless." . . . —I am sorry, but it goes on as follows—"This is senseless. Everyone knows the difficulties of a revolution. . . . Final victory is only possible on a world scale, and only by the joint efforts of the workers of all countries" [*Collected Works*, vol. 27, pp. 372-73].

Despite this, Lenin did not deny the "justifiability" of the October Revolution.

And further. In 1921—not in 1914, but in 1921—Lenin wrote: "Highly developed capitalist countries have a class of agricultural wage-workers that has taken shape over many decades. . . . Only in countries where this class is sufficiently developed is it possible to pass directly from capitalism to socialism. . . ." —here it is not a question of intervention but of the level of economic development and of the development of the class relations of the country—"We have stressed in a good many written works, in all our public utterances, and all our statements in the press, that this is not the case in Russia, for here industrial workers are a minority and small peasants are the vast majority. In such a country, the socialist revolution can triumph only *on two conditions.* First, if it is given *timely* support by a socialist revolution in one or several advanced countries. . . .

"The second condition is agreement between the proletariat, which is exercising its dictatorship, that is, holds state power, and the majority of the peasant population. . . .

"We know that so long as there is no revolution in other countries, only agreement with the peasantry can save the socialist revolution in Russia. And that is how it must be stated, frankly, at all meetings and in the entire press" [from a speech to the Tenth Congress of the Russian Communist Party, in *Collected Works*, vol. 32, pp. 214-15].

Lenin did not state that the understanding with the peasantry sufficed, enabling us to build up socialism independent of the fate of the international proletariat. No, this understanding is only *one* of the conditions. The other condition is the support to be given the revolution by other countries. He combines these two conditions with each other, emphasizing their special necessity for us as we live in a backward country.

And finally, it is brought up against me that I have stated that "a real advance of socialist economics in Russia is possible only after the victory of the proletariat in the most important countries of Europe." It is probable, comrades, that we have become inaccurate in the use of various terms. What do we mean by "socialist economics" in the strict sense of the term? We have great successes to record, and are naturally proud of these. I have endeavored to describe them in my booklet *Toward Socialism or Capitalism?* for the benefit of foreign comrades. But we must make a sober survey of the extent of these successes. Comrade Rykov's theses state that we are approaching the prewar level. But this is not quite accurate. Is our population the same as before the war? No, it is larger. And the average per capita consumption of industrial goods is considerably less than in 1913. The Supreme Council of the National Economy calculates that in this respect we shall not regain the prewar level until 1930. And then, what was the level of 1913? It was the level of misery, of backwardness, of barbarism. If we speak of socialist economics, and of a real advance in socialist economics, we mean: no antagonism between town and country, general content, prosperity, culture. *This* is what we mean by the real advance of socialist economics. And we are still far indeed from this goal. We have destitute children, we have unemployed, from the villages there come three million superfluous workers every year, half a million of whom seek work in the cities, where the industries cannot absorb more than 100,000 yearly. We have a right to be proud of what we have achieved, but we must not distort the historical perspective. What we have accomplished is not yet a real advance of socialist economics, but only the first serious steps on that long bridge leading from capitalism to socialism. Is this the same thing? By no means. The passage quoted against me stated the truth.

In 1922 Lenin wrote: "But we have not finished building even the foundations of socialist economy and the hostile powers of moribund capitalism can still deprive us of that. We must clearly appreciate this and frankly admit it; for there is nothing more dangerous than illusions (and vertigo, particularly at high altitudes). And there is absolutely nothing terrible, nothing that should give legitimate grounds for the slightest despondency, in admitting this bitter truth; for we have always urged and reiterated the elementary truth of Marxism—that *the joint efforts of the workers of several advanced countries are needed for the victory of socialism*" [*Collected Works,* vol. 33, p. 206; emphasis added by Trotsky].

The question here is therefore not of intervention, but of the joint efforts of several advanced countries for the establishment of socialism. Or was this written by Lenin before the epoch of imperialism, before the law of unequal development was known? No, he wrote this in 1922.

There is, however, another passage, in the article on cooperatives, one single passage, which is set up against everything else that Lenin wrote, or rather the attempt is made so to oppose it. [*A voice: "Accidentally!"*] Not by any means accidentally. I am in full agreement with the sentence. It must be understood properly. The passage is as follows: "Indeed, the power of the state over all large-scale means of production, political power in the hands of the proletariat, the alliance of this proletariat with the many millions of small and very small peasants, the assured proletarian leadership of the peasantry, etc.—is that not all that is necessary to build a complete socialist society out of cooperatives, out of cooperatives alone, which we formerly ridiculed as huckstering and which from a certain aspect we have the right to treat as such now, under NEP? Is this not all that is necessary to build a complete socialist society? It is still not the building of socialist society, but it is all that is necessary and sufficient for it" [*Collected Works,* vol. 33, p. 468].

[*A voice: "You read much too quickly." Laughter.*] Then you must give me a few minutes more, comrades. [*Laughter. A voice:*

"Right!"] Right? I am agreed. [*A voice: "That is just what we want."*]

What is the question here? What elements are here enumerated? In the first place, the possession of the means of production; in the second, the power of the proletariat; thirdly, the bond between the proletariat and the peasantry; fourthly, the proletarian leadership of the peasantry; and fifthly, the cooperatives. I ask you: does any one of you believe that socialism can be established in one single isolated country? Could perchance the proletariat in Bulgaria alone, if it had the peasantry behind it, seize power, build up the cooperatives and establish socialism? No, that would be impossible. Consequently further elements are required in addition to the above: the geographical situation, natural wealth, technology, culture. Lenin enumerates here the conditions of state power, property relations, and the organizational forms of the cooperatives. Nothing more. And he says that we, in order to establish socialism, need not proletarianize the peasantry, nor do we need any fresh revolutions, but that we are able, with power in our hands, in alliance with the peasantry, and with the aid of the cooperatives, to carry our task to completion through the agency of these state and social forms and methods.

But, comrades, we know another definition which Lenin gave of socialism. According to this definition, socialism is equal to Soviet power plus electrification. Is electrification canceled in the passage just quoted? No, it is not canceled. Everything which Lenin otherwise said about the establishment of socialism—and I have cited clear formulations above—is *supplemented* by this quotation, but not *canceled*. For electrification is not something to be carried out in a vacuum, but under certain conditions, under the conditions imposed by the world market and the world economy, which are very tangible facts. The world economy is not a mere theoretical generalization, but a definite and powerful reality, whose laws encompass us; a fact of which every year of our development convinces us.

Before dealing with this in detail, I should like to remind you of the following: Some of our comrades, before they created an entirely new theory, and in my opinion an entirely wrong one, based on a one-sided interpretation of Lenin's article on the cooperatives, held quite a different standpoint. In 1924 Comrade Stalin did not say the same as he does today. This was pointed out at the Fourteenth Party Congress, but the passage quoted did not disappear on that account, but remains fully even in 1926.

Let us read: "Can this task be fulfilled, can the final victory of socialism be attained in a single country without the joint efforts of the proletariat in several advanced countries? No, it cannot. In order to overthrow the bourgeoisie, the efforts of a single country are sufficient; this is proved by the history of our revolution. For the final victory of socialism, *for the organization of socialist production, the efforts of a single country, and particularly of such a peasant country as Russia, are inadequate; for that, the efforts of the proletariat of several advanced countries are required"* [from the first edition of *Foundations of Leninism,* quoted by Stalin in *Problems of Leninism,* p. 61; emphasis added by Trotsky].

This was written by Stalin in 1924, but the resolution quotes me only up to 1922. [*Laughter.*] Yes, this is what was said in 1924: For the organization of socialist production—not for protection against intervention, not as a guarantee against the restoration of the capitalist order, no, no—but for "the organization of socialist production," the efforts of one single country, especially such an agrarian country as Russia, do not suffice. Comrade Stalin has given up this standpoint. He has of course a right to do so.

In his book, *Problems of Leninism,* he says:

"What is the defect in this formulation?

"The defect is that it links up two different questions. First there is the question of the *possibility* of completely constructing socialism by the efforts of a single country, which must be answered in the affirmative. Then there is the question: can a country, in which the dictatorship of the proletariat has been established, consider itself *fully guaranteed* against foreign intervention, and consequently against the restoration of the old order, without the victory of the revolution in a number of other countries, a question which must be answered in the negative" [*Problems of Leninism,* p. 62].

But if you will allow me to say so, we do not find these two questions confused with one another in the first passage quoted, dating from 1924. Here it is not a question of intervention, but solely of the impossibility of the complete organization of completely socialized production by the unaided efforts of such a peasant country as Russia.

And truly, comrades, can the whole question be reduced to one of intervention? Can we simply imagine that we are establishing socialism here in this house, while the enemies outside in the street are throwing stones through the window panes? The matter is not so simple. Intervention is war, and war is a continuation of politics, but with other weapons. But politics are applied economics. Hence the whole question is one of the economic relations between the Soviet Union and the capitalist countries. These relations are not exhausted in that one form known as intervention. They possess a much more continuous and profound character. Comrade Bukharin has stated in so many words that the sole danger of intervention consists of the fact that in the event that no intervention comes, "we can work toward socialism even on this wretched technical basis;"—we can work toward it, that is true—"this growth of socialism will be much slower, and we shall move forward at a snail's pace; but all the same we shall work toward socialism, and we shall realize it" [at the Fourteenth Party Congress].

That we are working toward socialism is true. That we shall realize it hand in hand with the world proletariat is incontestable. [*Laughter.*] In my opinion it is out of place at a Communist conference to laugh when the realization of socialism hand in hand with the international proletariat is spoken of. [*Laughter. Voices: "No demagogy!" "You cannot catch us with that!"*] But I tell you that we shall never realize socialism at a *snail's pace,* for the world's markets keep too sharp a control over us. [*A voice: "You are quite alarmed!"*] How does Comrade Bukharin imagine this realization? In his last article in *Bolshevik,* which I must say is the most scholastic work which has ever issued from Bukharin's pen [*Laughter.*], he says: "The question is whether we can work toward socialism, and *establish* it, *if we abstract this from the international factors"* ["On the Nature of Our Revolution and the Possibility of Successful Socialist Construction in the USSR," *Bolshevik,* no. 19-20, 1926].

Just listen to this: "Whether we can work toward socialism, and establish it, if we abstract this question from the international factors." If we accomplish this "abstraction," then of course the rest is easy. But we *cannot.* That is the whole point. [*Laughter.*]

It is possible to walk naked in the streets of Moscow in January, if we can abstract ourselves from the weather and the police. [*Laughter.*] But I am afraid that this abstraction would fail, both with respect to weather and to police, were we to make the attempt. [*Laughter.*]

"We repeat once more: *it is a question of internal forces and not of the dangers connected with the outside world. It is therefore a question of the character of the revolution"* [Bukharin, in *Bolshevik,* no. 19-20, p. 54].

The character of our revolution, independent of international relations! Since when has this self-sufficing character of our revolution existed? I maintain that our revolution, as we know it, would not exist at all but for two international prerequisites: firstly, the factor of finance capital, which, in its greed, has fertilized our economic development; and secondly, Marxism, the theoretical quintessence of the international labor movement, which has fertilized our proletarian struggle. This means that the revolution was being prepared, before 1917, at those crossroads where the great forces of the world encounter one another. Out of this clash of forces arose the Great War, and out of this the October Revolution. And now we are told to abstract ourselves from the international situation and to construct our socialism at home for ourselves. That is a metaphysical method of thought. There is no possibility of abstraction from the world economy.

What is export? A domestic or an international affair? The goods to be exported must be produced at home, thus it is a domestic matter. But they must be exported abroad, hence it is an international transaction. And what is import? Import is international! The goods have to be purchased abroad. But they have to be brought into the country, so it is a domestic matter after all. [*Laughter.*] This example of import and export alone suffices to cause the collapse of Comrade Bukharin's whole theory, which proposes an "abstraction" from the international situation. The success of socialist construction depends on the speed of economic development, and this speed is now being determined directly and more sharply than ever by the imports of raw materials and machinery. To be sure, we can "abstract ourselves" from our shortage of foreign currency, and order more cotton and machines. But we can only do that once. A second time we shall not be able to accomplish this abstraction. [*Laughter.*] The whole of our constructive work is determined by international conditions.

If I am asked whether our state is proletarian, I can only reply that the question is out of place. If you do not wish to form your judgment on two or three words picked at random from an uncorrected stenographic report, but on what I have said and written in dozens of speeches and articles—and this is the only way in which we should form a judgment on one another's views—if we do not wish to trip one another up with an uncorrected sentence, but seek to understand one another's real opinions, then you must admit without hesitation that I join with you in regarding our state as a proletarian state. I have already replied by several quotations to the question of whether this state is building socialism. If you ask whether there are in this country sufficient forces and means to carry out completely the establishment of socialism within thirty or fifty years, *quite independent of what is going on in the world outside,* then I must answer that the question is put in an entirely wrong form. We have at our disposal adequate forces for the furtherance of the work of socialization, and thereby also to aid the international revolutionary proletariat, which has no less prospect of gaining power in ten, twenty, or thirty years than we have of establishing socialism; in no way less prospect, but much greater prospect.

I ask you, comrades—and this is the axis upon which the whole question turns—what will be going on in Europe while we are working at our socialization? You reply: We shall establish socialism in our country, independent of what is going on all over the world. Good.

How much time shall we require for the establishment of socialism? Lenin was of the opinion that we shall not have established socialism in twenty years, since our agrarian country is so backward. And in thirty years we shall not have established it either. Let us take thirty to fifty years as a minimum. What will be happening in Europe during all this time? I cannot make a prognosis for our country without including a prognosis for Europe. There may be some variations. If you say that the European proletariat will certainly have come to power within the next thirty to fifty years, then there is no longer any question in the matter. For if the European proletariat captures power in the next ten, twenty, or thirty years, then the position of socialism is secured, both in our country and internationally. But you are probably of the opinion that we must assume a future in which the European proletariat does not come to power. Otherwise why your whole prognosis? Therefore, I ask what you suppose will be happening in Europe in this time? From the purely theoretical standpoint, three variations are possible. Europe will either vacillate around about the prewar level, as at present, the proletariat and the bourgeoisie balancing to and fro and just maintaining an equilibrium. We must however designate this "equilibrium" as unstable, for it is extremely so. This situation cannot last for twenty, thirty, or forty years. It must be decided one way or the other.

Do you believe that capitalism will find a renewed dynamic equilibrium? Do you believe that capitalism can secure a fresh period of ascendancy, a new and extended reproduction of that process which took place before the imperialist war? If you believe that this is possible (I myself do not believe that capitalism has any such prospect before it), if you permit it even theoretically for one moment, this would mean that capitalism has not yet fulfilled its historic mission in Europe and the rest of the world, and that present-day capitalism is not an imperialist and decaying capitalism, but a capitalism still on the upgrade, creating economic and cultural progress. And this would mean that we have appeared too early on the scene.

Chairman: Comrade Trotsky has more than exceeded the time allotted him. He has been speaking for more than one and a half hours. He asks for a further five minutes. I shall take your vote. Who is in favor? Who is against? Does anybody demand that a fresh vote be taken?

Comrade Trotsky: I ask for a fresh vote.

Chairman: Who is in favor of Comrade Trotsky's being given five minutes more? Who is against? The majority is against.

Comrade Trotsky: I wished to utilize these five minutes for a brief summary of conclusions.

Chairman: I shall take the vote again. Who is in favor of Comrade Trotsky's time being extended by five minutes? Those in favor hold up their delegate's tickets. Who is against? The majority is in favor. It is better to extend the time than to count votes for five minutes. Comrade Trotsky will continue.

Comrade Trotsky: If it is assumed that during the next thirty to fifty years which we require for the establishment of socialism, European capitalism will be developing upward, then we must come to the conclusion that we shall certainly be strangled or crushed, for ascending capitalism will certainly possess, besides everything else, correspondingly improved military technology. We are, moreover, aware that a capitalism with a rapidly rising prosperity is well able to draw the masses into war, aided by the labor aristocracy which it is able to create. These gloomy prospects are, in my opinion, impossible of fulfillment; the international economic situation offers no basis. In any case we have no need to base the future of socialism in our country on this supposition.

There remains the second possibility of a declining and decaying capitalism. And this is precisely the basis upon which the European proletariat is learning, slowly but surely, the art of making revolution.

Is it possible to imagine that European capitalism will continue a process of decay for thirty to fifty years, and the proletariat will meanwhile remain incapable of accomplishing revolution? I ask

why I should accept this assumption, which can only be designated as the assumption of an unfounded and most profound
pessimism with respect to the European proletariat, and at the
same time of an uncritical optimism with respect to the establishment of socialism by the unaided forces of our country? In what
way can it be the theoretical or political duty of a Communist to
accept the premise that the European proletariat will not have
seized power within the next forty to fifty years? (Should it seize
power, then the point of dispute vanishes.) I maintain that I see
no theoretical or political reason why it is easier to believe that
we shall build socialism with the cooperation of the peasantry
than that the proletariat of Europe will seize power.

No. The European proletariat has the greater chances. And if
this is the case, then I ask you: Why are these two elements
opposed to one another, instead of being combined like the "two
conditions" of Lenin? Why is the theoretical recognition of the
establishment of socialism in one country demanded? What gave
rise to this standpoint? Why was this question never brought
forward by anyone before 1925? [*A voice: "It was!"*] That is not
the case, it was never brought forward. Even Comrade Stalin
wrote in 1924 that the efforts of an agrarian country were
insufficient for the establishment of socialism. I am today still
firm in my belief that the victory of socialism in our country is
only possible in conjunction with the victorious revolution of the
European proletariat. This does not mean that we are not
working toward the socialist state of society, or that we should
not continue this work with all possible energy. Just as the
German worker is preparing to seize power, we are preparing the
socialism of the future, and every success which we can record
facilitates the struggle of the German proletariat, just as its
struggle facilitates our socialist progress. This is the sole true
international view to be taken of our work for the realization of
the socialist state of society.

In conclusion I repeat the words which I spoke at the plenum of
the CC: If we did not believe that our state is a proletarian state,
though with bureaucratic deformations, that is, a state which
should be brought into much closer contact with the working
class, despite many wrong bureaucratic opinions to the contrary;
if we did not believe that our development is socialist; if we did
not believe that our country possesses adequate means for the
furtherance of socialist economics; if we were not convinced of
our complete and final victory; then, it need not be said, our place

would not be in the ranks of a Communist Party.

The Opposition can and must be assessed by these two criteria: it can have either one line or the other. Those who believe that our state is not a proletarian state, and that our development is not socialist, must lead the proletariat against such a state and must found another party.

But those who believe that our state is a proletarian state, but with bureaucratic deformations formed under the pressure of the petty-bourgeois elements and the capitalist encirclement; who believe that our development is socialist, but that our economic policy does not sufficiently secure the necessary redistribution of national income; these must use party methods and party means to combat that which they hold to be wrong, mistaken, or dangerous, but must share at the same time the full responsibility for the whole policy of the party and of the workers' state. [*The chairman rings.*] I am almost finished. A minute and a half more.

It is incontestable that the inner-party disputes have been characterized of late by extreme sharpness of form, and by a factional attitude. It is incontestable that this factional aggravation of the dispute on the part of the Opposition—no matter by what premises it was called forth—could be taken, and has been taken by a wide section of the party members, to mean that the differences had reached a point rendering joint work impossible, that is, that they could lead to a split. This means an obvious discrepancy between the means and the aims, that is, between those aims for which the Opposition has been anxious to fight, and the means which it has employed for one reason or another. It is for that reason we have recognized these means—the faction—as being faulty, and not for any reason arising out of momentary considerations. [*A voice: "Your forces were inadequate; you have been defeated!"*] We recognize this in consideration of the whole inner-party situation. The aim and object of the declaration of October 16 was to defend the views which we hold, but to do this under the observance of the confines set by our joint work and our joint responsibility for the whole policy of the party.

Comrades, what is the objective danger involved in the resolution on the Social Democratic deviation? The danger lies in the fact that it attributes to us views which would necessarily lead, not merely to a factional policy, but to a policy of two parties.

This resolution has the objective tendency of transforming both the declaration of October 16 and the communiqué of the CC into fragments of paper that . . . [*A voice: "Is that a threat?"*] No, comrades, that is no threat. It is my last thought to utter any threat. [*A voice: "Why raise that again?"*] You will hear in a moment. Only a few words more.

In our opinion the acceptance of this resolution will be detrimental, but insofar as I can judge of the attitude of the so-called Opposition, especially of the leading comrades, the acceptance of this resolution will not cause us to depart from the line of the declaration of October 16. We do not accept the views forced upon us. We have no intention of artificially enlarging the differences, or of aggravating them and of thus preparing for a relapse into the factional struggle. On the contrary, each one of us, without seeking to minimize the existing differences, will exert every effort to keep these differences within the confines of our continued work and our joint responsibility for the policy of the party.

THESES ON REVOLUTION AND COUNTERREVOLUTION

November 26, 1926

NOTE: In the wake of the condemnation of the Opposition at the Fifteenth Conference, official attacks on Oppositionists and the Opposition continued unabated in the press and at party meetings. Oppositionists were fired from their jobs and treated as pariahs. Zinoviev and Kamenev advised their followers to avoid being drawn into debate—if necessary, to deny association with the Opposition. In the context of the severe repressions, this led to widespread demoralization and defections. The Trotskyists, with the experience of 1923-24 behind them, were better prepared to stick to their guns.

In this memorandum Trotsky undertook to analyze the reasons for the apparatus's strength and the Opposition's weakness. He recognized that the cause of the corrosive bureaucratism lay only partly in the growing separation between the ruling circles and the rank-and-file workers, but also partly in the new, more conservative moods of the workers, and that the revolutionary program was somewhat out of phase with popular sentiment. He took up this question in greater detail again in "For an Objective Assessment," February 21, 1927.

Excerpts of this memorandum were published in Fourth International, *October 1941, in a translation by John G. Wright. They have been revised somewhat for readability and stylistic consistency. Points 6-20 and 28, as well as several sentences throughout the text that were omitted from the 1941 version, were translated from the Russian by George Saunders, by permission of the Library of Social History.*

1. Revolutions have always in history been followed by counterrevolutions. Counterrevolutions have always thrown society back, but never as far back as the starting point of the revolution. The succession of revolutions and counterrevolutions is the

product of certain fundamental features in the mechanics of class society, the only society in which revolutions and counterrevolutions are possible.

2. Revolution is impossible without the participation of the masses on a broad scale. This participation is in turn possible only if the oppressed masses connect their hopes for a better future with the idea of revolution. In this sense the hopes engendered by the revolution are always exaggerated. This is because of the class mechanism of society, the terrible plight of the overwhelming majority of the masses, the objective need of concentrating the greatest hopes and efforts in order to insure even the most modest progress, and so on.

3. But from these same conditions comes one of the most important—*and moreover, one of the most common*—elements of the counterrevolution. The conquests gained in the struggle do not correspond, and in the nature of things cannot *directly* correspond, with the expectations of the backward masses awakened in large numbers for the first time in the course of the revolution. The disillusionment of these masses, their return to routine and futility, is as much an integral part of the postrevolutionary period as is the passage into the camp of "law and order" of those "satisfied" classes or layers of classes that had participated in the revolution.

4. Closely bound up with these processes, parallel processes of a different and, to a large measure, of an opposite character take place in the camp of the ruling classes. The awakening of the broad backward masses dislodges the ruling classes from their accustomed equilibrium, deprives them not only of direct support but also of confidence, and thus enables the revolution to seize a great deal more than it is later able to hold.

5. The disillusionment of a considerable section of the oppressed masses in the immediate gains of the revolution and—directly connected with this—the decline of the political energy and activity of the revolutionary class engender a revival of confidence among counterrevolutionary classes—both among those overthrown by the revolution but not shattered completely and among those who aided the revolution at a certain phase, but were thrown back into the camp of reaction by the further development of the revolution.

6. Proceeding from the above schematic outline, which more or less reflects the mechanics of all preceding revolutions, let us try to examine how these questions apply more concretely to the

circumstances of the first victorious proletarian revolution, which is heading toward its tenth anniversary.

The effect of the imperialist war, on the one hand, and the combination of a petty-bourgeois agrarian revolution with the proletarian seizure of power, on the other, drew the masses into revolutionary struggle on a scale never before seen or heard and thereby imparted an unprecedented sweep to the revolution itself.

7. Owing to the scope of the revolution and its leadership, characterized by a resoluteness that is unique in history, the old ruling classes and institutions of both socioeconomic formations—the precapitalist and the capitalist (the monarchy with its bureaucracy, the nobility, and the bourgeoisie)—suffered a total political defeat, which proved to be more radical and lasting in its consequences than ever because of the fact that the old ruling classes, led by foreign imperialism, strove for several years to overthrow the dictatorship of the proletariat by armed force.

8. The thoroughness with which the old ruling classes were smashed is one of the guarantees against the dangers of restoration, but the power and importance of this guarantee can be correctly estimated only in conjunction with other no less important circumstances.

9. Against a monarchist-landlord restoration the most important guarantee is the direct material interest the majority of the peasantry have in keeping the former great estates as their own.

Milyukov's idea of a purely bourgeois-republican restoration has the aim of politically neutralizing the peasantry and winning over its upper layers (through a bloc with the SRs) to the side of restoration.

10. There is no question that during the 1918-20 period the proletariat managed to hold onto power—and with that retained the nationalization of the plants and factories—only because the peasantry was at that time fighting to hold onto the land seized from those same enemies. The struggle to keep the factories and plants nationalized is of much less direct concern to the peasants, who thus far have been supplied with industrial goods at higher prices than they enjoyed under the bourgeois regime.

11. It was on the basis of this very assessment that Lenin wrote in 1922: "We wound up the bourgeois-democratic revolution more thoroughly than had ever been done before anywhere in the world. That is a great gain, and no power on earth can deprive us of it. . . . We have created a Soviet type of state and by that we have ushered in a new era in world history, the era of the political

rule of the proletariat, which is to supersede the era of bourgeois rule. Nobody can deprive us of this, either, although the Soviet type of state will have the finishing touches put to it only with the aid of the practical experience of the working class of several countries.

"But we have not finished building even the foundations of socialist economy and the hostile powers of moribund capitalism can still deprive us of that" [*Collected Works,* vol. 33, p. 206].

12. The question of the peasantry—so long as our revolution remains isolated—will remain as before the central question for the proletariat at all stages. The victory of the revolution and scope of this victory were determined by the combination of a proletarian revolution with a "peasant war." The danger of restoration (counterrevolution) is governed by the possibility of the peasantry being separated from the proletariat because of its lack of a direct stake in preserving the socialist regime in industry, the cooperative regime in the realm of trade, etc. As has been said, the Milyukov bourgeois-republican restoration for this very reason strives to establish for itself a destiny separate from the monarchist-landlord type of restoration, to make it easier to separate the peasantry from the proletariat.

13. The peasantry is a precapitalist class (social estate). Under capitalism it is transformed into a small-scale commodity producer, an agrarian petty-bourgeoisie. War communism held the petty-bourgeois tendencies of the peasant economy in a stranglehold. The NEP revived the contradictory petty-bourgeois tendencies among the peasantry, with the consequent possibility of a capitalist restoration.

14. The relation between industrial and agricultural prices (the scissors) should prove to be the decisive factor in the question of the peasants' attitude toward capitalism and socialism. The export of agricultural goods subjects the domestic "scissors" to the checking influence of the world market.

15. The peasants, having revived their economic effort as private commodity-producers who buy and sell, inevitably re-created the elements of capitalist restoration. The economic basis for these elements is the peasant's material interest in high prices for grain and low prices for industrial goods.

The political elements of restoration are re-created through trading capital, which restores the connections among the dispersed and fragmented peasantry, on the one hand, and between country and town, on the other. With the upper layers of the village acting as intermediaries, the trader organizes a strike against the town. This applies first of all, naturally, to private trading capital, but to a significant extent it also applies to cooperative trading capital, with its personnel who have a long experience in trade and a natural leaning toward the kulaks.

16. The immediate economic and political significance of the bourgeois and landlord emigrés, from the point of view of restoration, is in and of itself hardly worth mentioning. Only if the internal economic and political processes that we have indicated reach counterrevolutionary "maturity" could a direct link-up with the emigrés occur, especially with the transformation of the emigrés into agents and stewards of foreign capital.*

17. Between economic processes and the political expression of those processes many years will often intervene. The coming years will be very difficult precisely because the successes of the reconstruction period have brought us into the world market system and by that very fact—and through the day-to-day economic experience of the peasant—have laid bare the extreme backwardness of our industry. We can get through this difficult period only on the condition of the greatest possible solidity within the proletariat, of its political activism, and of the capacity of the proletarian party to maneuver decisively, for which absolute concentration of the dictatorship in its hands is necessary.

18. The life of the working class now centers around the experience of the reconstruction period. The ranks of the proletariat have been revived and replenished. Its age level has risen substantially by comparison with the first five years of the revolution.

The new stage, visible only in rough outline, which threatens to increase the economic and political role of the nonproletarian elements in the society, has not yet penetrated the consciousness of the proletarian masses.

19. The most dangerous thing about the party regime is precisely that it ignores the class dangers, glosses over them, and combats any attempt to call attention to them. It thereby lulls the vigilance and lowers the combat-readiness of the proletariat.

---

*Note: Just the fact that one had analyzed the possibility or danger of restoration would be proof to the bureaucratic blockhead of "lack of faith." But then, the bureaucratic blockhead's whole reason for existing is to make the restorationists' job easier by preventing the revolutionary elements from correctly evaluating the restorationist drive and mobilizing the proletariat in time to repel the attack.

20. It would be wrong to ignore the fact that the proletariat today is considerably less receptive to revolutionary perspectives and to broad generalizations than it was during the October Revolution and in the ensuing few years. The revolutionary party cannot passively adapt itself to every shift in the moods of the masses. But it must not ignore alterations produced by profound historic causes either.

21. The October Revolution, to a greater extent than any other in history, aroused the greatest hopes and passions in the popular masses, above all the proletarian masses. After the immense sufferings of 1917-21, the proletarian masses have considerably improved their lot. They cherish this improvement, hopeful of its further development. But at the same time their experience has shown them the extreme gradualness of this improvement which has only now brought them back to the prewar standard of living. This experience is of incalculable significance to the masses, especially the older generation. They have grown more cautious, more skeptical, less directly responsive to revolutionary slogans, less inclined to place confidence in broad generalizations. These moods, which unfolded after the ordeals of the civil war and after the successes of economic reconstruction and have not yet been undone by the new shifts of class forces—these moods constitute the basic political background of party life. These are the moods which bureaucratism—as an element of "law and order" and "tranquillity"—relies on. The attempt of the Opposition to put the new problems before the party ran up against precisely these moods.

22. The older generation of the working class, which made two revolutions, or made the last one, beginning with 1917, is suffering from nervous exhaustion, and a substantial section of it fears any new upheavals, with their attendant prospects of war, havoc, epidemic, and so on.

A bogey is being made out of the theory of permanent revolution precisely for the purpose of exploiting the psychology of this substantial section of the workers, who are not at all careerists, but who have put on weight, acquired families. The version of the theory which is being utilized for this is of course in no way related to the old disputes, long relegated to the archives, but simply raises the phantom of new upheavals—heroic "invasions," the disruption of "law and order," a threat to the attainments of the reconstruction period, a new period of great efforts and sacrifices. Making a bogey out of the permanent revolution is, in essence, speculating on the moods of those in the working class, including party members, who have grown smug, fat, and semi-conservative.

23. The dispute over "stabilization" has exactly the same significance. What is involved is not so much a realistic evaluation of the changes in the curve of capitalist development as an attempt to frighten people with the prospect of new upheavals. Today permanent revolution and our alleged "denial" of stabilization represent two sides of the same coin. In the one case as well as in the other, what is involved is that amorphous philistine moods are being given an explicit conservative form, which is directed against all revolutionary perspectives.

24. The young generation, only now growing up, lacks experience in the class struggle and the necessary revolutionary tempering. It does not explore for itself, as did the previous generation, but falls immediately into an environment of the most powerful party and governmental institutions, party tradition, authority, discipline, etc. For the time being this renders it more difficult for the young generation to play an independent role. The question of the correct orientation of the young generation of the party and of the working class acquires a colossal importance.

25. Parallel with the above-indicated processes, there has been an extreme growth in the role played in the party and the state apparatus by a special category of Old Bolsheviks, who were members or worked actively in the party during the 1905 period; who then, in the period of reaction, left the party, adapted themselves to the bourgeois regime, and occupied a more or less prominent position within it; who were defensists, like the entire bourgeois intelligentsia; and who, together with the latter, were propelled forward in the February revolution (of which they did not even dream at the beginning of the war); who were staunch opponents of the Leninist program and of the October Revolution; but who returned to the party after victory was secured or after the stabilization of the new regime, about the time when the bourgeois intelligentsia stopped its sabotage. These elements, who more or less reconciled themselves to the tsarist regime after its counterrevolutionary coup of June 3, 1907, by their very nature cannot help but be elements of a conservative kind. They are in favor of stabilization in general and against opposition in general. The education of the party youth is largely in their hands.

Such is the combination of circumstances which in the recent period of party development has determined the reorganization of the party leadership and the shift of party policy to the right.

26. The official adoption of the theory of "socialism in one country" signifies the theoretical sanction of those shifts which have already taken place and the first open break with Marxist tradition.

27. The elements of bourgeois restoration lie in: (a) the situation of the peasantry, who do not want the return of the landlords but still have no material stake in socialism (hence the importance of our political ties with the poor peasants); (b) the moods of considerable layers of the working class, the lowering of revolutionary energy, the fatigue of the older generation, and the increased specific weight of the conservative elements.

28. The elements militating against any restoration are the following: (a) the muzhik's fear that the landlord would return with the capitalist, just as he fled with the capitalist; (b) the fact that power and the most important means of production actually remain in the hands of the workers' state, though with extreme deformations; (c) the fact that the leadership of the state actually remains in the hands of the Communist Party, though it refracts within itself the molecular shifting of class forces and the changing political moods.

From what has been said it follows that it would be a crude distortion of reality to speak of Thermidor as an accomplished fact. Things have gone no further than the holding of some rehearsals within the party and the laying of some theoretical groundwork. The material apparatus of power has not been surrendered to another class.

SPEECH TO THE SEVENTH (ENLARGED) PLENUM OF THE ECCI

December 9, 1926

NOTE: The seventh enlarged plenum of the Executive Committee of the Communist International (ECCI) convened on November 22, 1926. The removal of Zinoviev as president of the ECCI was confirmed and he was stripped of his other Comintern functions. On December 7, Stalin presented a report repeating his attack on Opposition leaders. Discussion on this question lasted a week and occupied ten sessions. After Stalin's report, a declaration was read on behalf of the Russian delegation, stating that an appearance by Zinoviev would amount to an appeal to the ECCI against the Russian party's decisions and calling such an appearance "inopportune." The declaration also noted that Trotsky had refused to speak at the Fifth World Congress in 1924. However, the chairman ruled that the Opposition had the right to decide whether to speak, and all three Opposition leaders did speak.

This version is based on the version in International Press Correspondence, *January 6, 1927, with minor changes for stylistic consistency and readability.*

Comrades, first I should like to ask you not to limit my time. The question on the agenda turns, as on an axis, around so-called Trotskyism. One of the younger comrades very fittingly made a list—and this list is not even complete—of those comrades in this hall who have spoken against so-called Trotskyism: Bukharin, Kuusinen, Treint, Pepper, Birch, Stern, Brandt, Remmele, to say nothing of the three-hour speech of Comrade Stalin.

This discussion, which is coming to a close here, is a rather peculiar discussion. Our Central Committee, in January of this year, addressed a circular to fraternal parties. In this circular it is stated: "The CC of the CPSU is unanimous in the view that the extension of the discussion on the Russian question into the ranks of the Comintern is not desirable." Consequently this international discussion did not take place officially; we, at least, did not participate in it. Yet they want to close this discussion, which was never officially opened, with a bill of indictment against "Trotskyism."

The theory of Trotskyism was artificially manufactured—against my will, against my convictions, against my real views. In order to prove that I am not politically responsible for the doctrine of Trotskyism ascribed to me, I will urge the gathering to grant me unrestricted time to speak (at least two hours).

[*Comrade Trotsky was granted one hour.*]

Comrades, I take the floor on this important question even though we have read in today's *Pravda,* in our central publication, that the mere fact that Comrade Zinoviev spoke here is to be characterized as an attempt at factional activity. I believe that this is not correct. The decision of the enlarged Executive, on the motion of Comrade Riese, to permit representatives of the Opposition of the CPSU to speak, was not conceived and adopted in this spirit. The speeches of Comrades Thälmann and Ercoli contained an entirely different tone, and the communication from our Central Committee which was read today did not say that by our appearance here we would violate our declaration of October 16. Nor is this so. Had the Central Committee said so, I should never have asked the presidium to grant the floor. To be sure, the Central Committee said that an appearance here might give an impetus to the renewal of the faction struggle, *but it left the decision on this to us.* In the communication of the CC, it is recalled that at the Fifth World Congress, despite an invitation, I declined to appear because the Thirteenth Congress of our party had already decided the questions then involved. Comrades, as against this, I must remind you that *the Fifth World Congress condemned me in a decision because I did not want to speak.* In this decision it was said that I was resorting to formal grounds to avoid appearing before the highest forum of the International and expressing my opinion here.

When Comrade Zinoviev and I maintain that our appearance does not constitute an appeal, this is of course intended only in the very particular sense that we, first, are not introducing any resolution, and, second, that insofar as it depends on our intentions and our actions, we will do everything we can so that the ideas we express will not arouse comrades in the International who sympathize with us to factional struggle, but on the contrary will restrain them from factionalism. The charge that our appearance in itself constitutes a violation of the declaration of October 16 is false, because the declaration of October 16 and the reply to it by the CC reserves for us the possibility of defending our ideas through the normal avenues provided for in the statutes.

Comrades, I have already stated that the axis of the discussion is so-called Trotskyism. Our honorable chairman interpreted me incorrectly when he put the question as if I pretended to stand personally in the center of the discussion. That is by no means the case. What is involved here is a political and not a personal question. But this political question, as I have already stated, has been bound up artificially with my person and my name—quite incorrectly and against my will—by the comrades who criticize our views and not by me.

Comrade Stalin's speech, at least the first half—for I have unfortunately been able to acquaint myself only with that part, which appeared in today's issue of *Pravda*—is nothing but *one long charge of "Trotskyism" leveled against the Opposition.* This charge rests on quotations taken from several decades of political and journalistic activity in an attempt to answer current questions, which arise out of the new stage in our economic and social life and in the whole International, by diversion and by all kinds of logical maneuvers with old differences that have been eliminated by developments themselves. And again, this whole artificially fabricated construction turns around the fact that in my political life, in my political activity, I stood for years outside of the Bolshevik Party, and in certain periods quite vigorously combated the Bolshevik Party and important ideas of Lenin. This was a mistake on my part! The fact that I entered the Bolshevik Party, and of course without setting any "conditions"—for the Bolshevik Party recognizes no conditions in its program, tactics, organization, and party membership—this naked fact was proof that everything which separated me from Bolshevism was discarded on the threshold of the party.

[*Interjection by Remmele: "How can such a thing be discarded on the threshold of the party!"*]

This, comrades, is of course not to be interpreted in the formal sense in which Comrade Remmele seems to understand it, but in the sense that the differences were overcome in the struggles and experiences of political life, for crossing the threshold of the party means precisely that what was non-Bolshevik in my activity had been eliminated by developments and by the ideological experiences that grew out of them. In any event, I gladly grant Comrade Remmele and everybody else the right to consider themselves better Bolsheviks, more revolutionary Communists, than my humble self. After all, that is not the issue. The responsibility for my career I alone must bear. The party knows me only as its member, and only in that capacity am I defending a certain set of ideas before this forum.

The differences of that time when I was outside of the Bolshevik Party were quite weighty. They concerned, broadly, the concrete appraisal of class relations within Russian society and the perspective resulting from that with regard to the next revolution. On the other hand, these differences concerned the methods and ways of party-building and the relationship to Menshevism. On both of these questions—and I declared this in writing when such a demand was put to me—in both of these questions by far not all of the comrades that are here were in the right as against me, but Comrade Lenin, his doctrine, and his party, were absolutely right as against me. In a reply to comrades who doubted this I wrote: "We proceed from the fact that, as experience has irrefutably shown, on all more or less fundamental questions over which any of us differed with Lenin, Vladimir Ilyich was entirely right" [see "In Defense of the Opposition Bloc," p. 109 of this volume].

And further: "On the question of the relations between proletariat and peasantry we stand completely on the ground of the theoretical and tactical teachings of Lenin based on the experience of the revolutions of 1905 and 1917, as well as the experience in socialist construction, all of which he summarized in the term *smychka*" [Ibid., p. 110].

The theory which is now dragged into the discussion (quite artificially and not in the interest of the cause)—the theory of permanent revolution—I have never considered (even at the time when I did not see the inadequacies of this theory)—never considered it to be a universal doctrine applicable generally to all revolutions, a "suprahistorical theory," to use a phrase from one of Marx's letters. The concept of permanent revolution was applied by me to a definite stage of development in the historical evolution of Russia. I know only a single literary product—and this came to my knowledge only a few weeks ago—in which an attempt was made to create from this theory a universal doctrine, and to present it as an improvement upon the theoretical conceptions of Lenin. I shall read this citation to you. I need not say that I have absolutely nothing in common with this interpretation:

"Russian Bolshevism, born in the nationally limited revolution of 1905-06, had to go through the purification ritual of liberation from all typical features of national peculiarity, in order to win full rights of citizenship in international ideology. Theoretically, this cleansing of Bolshevism from the national taint which clung to it was carried out in 1905 by Trotsky, who tried *in the idea of the permanent revolution* to bring the Russian revolution into connection with the whole international movement of the proletariat." This was not written by me; this was written in 1918 by a comrade by the name of Manuilsky.

[*Interjection by Manuilsky: "Well, I said a stupid thing, and you repeat it!"*]

A stupid thing? I agree—absolutely. [*Laughter.*] But you need not worry about Comrade Manuilsky. Of course it is a very painful story, for he himself calls it a stupid thing. But Comrade Manuilsky, who has here ascribed to me a quite undeserved magnificent heroic deed, will promptly ascribe to me two equally undeserved mistakes, and in this way he will balance his bookkeeping. [*Laughter.*]

Comrades, on another occasion in recent years, I have encountered the theory of permanent revolution in that caricatured form which is from time to time retrospectively ascribed to me. This was at the Third World Congress. Just recall the discussion that developed on my report on the international situation and the tasks of the Comintern. At that time I was accused of defending almost liquidationist tendencies—although I defended them in complete agreement with Lenin—against several comrades who maintained that the capitalist crisis would proceed permanently and that it would become sharper. My position, that we were confronted with possible stabilization and marked improvements, etc., and that from this the tactical consequences must be drawn, was branded by some of the ultraleftists as almost semi-Menshevik. In the front ranks of those who did this was Comrade Pepper, who, as I recall, was then making his maiden appearance upon the stage of the International.

[*Interjection by Pepper: "But you had to accept my proposals for the resolution."*]

So? Since Comrade Pepper, despite my restricted speaking time, interrupts me from the presidium, I must remind him that I know the three gospels of Comrade Pepper. The first gospel, at the Third World Congress, was that the Russian revolution required permanent, uninterrupted revolutionary activity in the West. Therefore he defended the false tactic of the March action (Germany, 1921).

Then Comrade Pepper went to America and on his return brought back these glad tidings: the International must support the bourgeois La Follette party because in America the revolution will be brought about not by the workers, but by the ruined farmers. That was his second gospel.

The third gospel we hear from him now: namely, that the Russian revolution requires neither the farmer revolution in America, nor the March action in Germany, but that it will, quite unaided, build up socialism in its own home. A sort of Monroe Doctrine for the building of socialism in Russia. This is the third gospel of Comrade Pepper. Despite my gray hairs I am ready to learn even from Comrade Pepper, but it is impossible for me to relearn so radically every two years.

Comrades, I do not believe that the biographical method can bring us to a decision in questions of principle. Of course, I have made mistakes on many questions, especially at the time of my struggle against Bolshevism. If from this it follows that political questions as such are not to be discussed according to their inner content, but according to biographies, then we should formulate a list of the biographies of all the delegates. I, personally, can refer to a rather significant precedent. There once lived in Germany a man named Franz Mehring, who after a long and energetic struggle against the Social Democracy (until the last few years we all called ourselves Social Democrats) entered that party as quite a mature man. Mehring first wrote a history of the German Social Democracy as its enemy—not as a lackey of capital, but as an ideological opponent—but then he rewrote it, producing an excellent work on German Social Democracy, as its loyal friend. On the other hand, there are Kautsky and Bernstein. Neither of them ever opposed Marx openly, and both of them had Frederick Engels as their taskmaster; Bernstein is also known as Engels's literary executor. Nevertheless, Franz Mehring went to his grave as a Marxist, as a Communist, whereas the other two still live as reformist lackeys of capitalism. So, while biography is important, it is not decisive.

Not one of us has a biography free from mistakes and short-comings. Lenin made the fewest mistakes. But even he was not altogether without mistakes. In our struggles with him we were always in the wrong when more important questions of principle were involved.

Comrade Stalin, who enumerates others' mistakes here, should not forget to count his own as well. If "permanent revolution," insofar as it differed from the Leninist conception, was wrong, nevertheless, much in it was correct, and that is what made it possible for me to come to Bolshevism. In particular, "permanent revolution" did not prevent me, after the experience of the struggle with Bolshevism—in which, as I said, I was wrong—it did not prevent me in America in 1917 from outlining, in principle, the same basic line as the one Lenin proposed to the party and carried out in practice. After the February revolution, Comrade Stalin put forward wrong tactics (in an article in *Pravda* and in a resolution calling for conditional support of the Provisional Government), a line which Lenin characterized as a Kautskyist deviation. On the national question, on the question of the foreign trade monopoly, on the question of the dictatorship of the party, and on other questions, Stalin also later made quite serious mistakes, but the most serious of all, which he is making now, is his theory of socialism in one country.

The history of this question has been superbly presented here by Comrade Zinoviev, and I am absolutely convinced that every comrade who takes the pains to study the question carefully—of course not formally, according to the citations, but in the spirit of the writings from which the citations are taken—must inevitably come to the conclusion that *the tradition of Marxism and Leninism is entirely on our side*. Of course, tradition alone does not decide. One might say: from a Marxist standpoint we are now duty-bound to subject to revision the former decisions on the possibility or impossibility of building socialism in one country. Let them come out and say so! But I do not see any grounds for such a revision. The old answer to this question retains its full weight. I believe that the further this theme is developed—it is a very important theme for the whole International and this very thing has moved me to take the floor here—the more this theme is developed, the more the heralds of this new theory come into contradiction not only with the fundamental basis of our teachings, but also with the political interests of our cause.

Comrades, the premise of the theory is the law of the *unevenness of imperialist development*. Comrade Stalin charges me with a refusal to recognize, or with insufficiently recognizing, this law. Nothing of the kind! The law of uneven development is not a law of imperialism, but a law of the whole history of humanity.

Capitalist development in its first epoch extraordinarily intensified the economic and cultural differences between various countries; imperialist development, i.e., the newest phase of capitalism, has not enlarged these differences of level but, on the contrary, has led to a rather extensive leveling. This leveling will never be complete. Again and again the varying rates of development will break through and thereby make impossible an imperialism stabilized upon a definite level.

On the whole, Lenin attributes unevenness to two things: firstly to *rate,* and secondly to the *level* of economic and cultural development of the various countries. With regard to the rate, imperialism has increased the unevenness to the highest degree; but with regard to the level of the various capitalist countries, it has called forth a leveling tendency precisely because of the variation of rate. Anyone who does not understand this does not understand the heart of the question. Take England and India. The capitalist development in certain parts of India is much more rapid than was the capitalist development in England in its beginnings. The difference, the economic distance between England and India—is this today greater or smaller than fifty years ago? It is smaller. Take Canada, South America, South Africa, on the one hand, and England on the other. The development of Canada, South America, South Africa, has proceeded during the last period with gigantic strides. The "development" of England is in stagnation, yes, even in decline. Therefore, the rate is uneven as never before in history, but the level of development of these countries has been more closely approximated than thirty or fifty years ago.

What conclusions are to be drawn from this? Very important ones! Precisely the fact that in certain backward countries in the recent period the rate of development has become more and more feverish, whereas in certain other old capitalist countries the development has slowed down or even retrogressed; precisely this fact makes impossible the Kautskyan hypothesis of a systematic organized superimperialism, because in the various countries which are approaching one another in level—without ever reaching evenness—jealousies, needs for markets and raw materials, are being developed identically. For this very reason, the danger of war is again becoming constantly sharper, and these wars must take on more and more gigantic forms. Precisely through this the international character of the proletarian revolution is assured and deepened.

The world economy is not an empty abstraction, comrades, but a reality which has become more and more consolidated during the last twenty to thirty years by the accelerated rate of development of backward countries and whole continents. That is a fact of fundamental importance, and *precisely for this reason it is fundamentally false to consider the economic and political destiny of any single country apart from its relationship to the economic whole.*

What was the imperialist world war? It was the revolt of the productive forces not only against capitalist property relations but also against the national boundaries of the capitalist states. The imperialist war was proof of the fact that these boundaries have grown too narrow for the productive forces.

We have always maintained that the capitalist state is not able to master the productive forces developed by it, and that only socialism can coordinate these productive forces, which have grown beyond the limits of the capitalist states into a higher and more powerful economic whole. There is no road leading back to the isolated state!

What was Russia before the revolution, before the war? Was it an isolated capitalist state? No, it was part of the capitalist world economy. This is the heart of the matter. Anyone who ignores this disregards the fundamentals of all social and political analysis. Why did Russia enter the World War, despite its economic backwardness? Because it had bound up its destiny with European capitalism through finance capital. It could not do otherwise. And I ask you, comrades, what was it that gave the working class of Russia the opportunity to seize power? Above all things, the agrarian revolution. Without the agrarian revolution, without the "peasant war"—and this is what Lenin in his genius predicted and elaborated theoretically—the seizure of political power would have been impossible for the proletariat in our country. But did peasant wars bring the proletariat to power in other revolutions? No, at best they brought in the bourgeoisie.

Why, then, did our bourgeoisie not seize power? Because it was an integral part of the world bourgeoisie, because with the whole imperialist bourgeoisie, it had started on the downgrade before it seized power, because capitalist Russia was a constituent part of world imperialism and because it was the weakest link in the imperialist chain. If the all-Russian state had been an isolated state, if Russia had stood apart from world development, from imperialism, apart from the movement of the international proletariat, if it had known neither the rule of finance capital in its industry, nor the ideological predominance of Marxism in the proletariat, then "by its own resources" it could not have reached the proletarian revolution so quickly. And anyone who believes that after the working class has seized power it can withdraw the country from the world economy as easily as one switches off an electric light has a basically false conception of things.

The precondition for socialism is heavy industry and machine-building. This is also the most important lever of socialism. How are things with respect to the technical equipment of our factories and workshops? According to the expert statistical estimates of Warzar we find that prior to the war, 63 percent of our technical equipment, our tools, our machines, were imported from abroad. Only one-third was of native production. But even this third consisted of the simplest machines; the more complicated, more important machines, were brought from abroad. Thus, when you review the technical equipment in our factories, you see with your own eyes the crystallized dependence of Russia, and of the Soviet Union, upon world industry. Anyone who refuses to notice this, who speaks on this matter without even touching the economic and technical basis of the question in its connections with world economy and world politics, inevitably remains the captive of bare abstractions and randomly selected quotations.

In the course of the last decade we have made practically no renewal of our industrial fixed capital. During the civil war, under war communism, we imported no machines from abroad. That gradually gave rise, apparently, to the idea that this industrial equipment belongs, so to speak, to the "natural resources" of our country and that upon the basis of this "natural" foundation, we might, isolated, be able to build up socialism to its completion.

But that is an illusion. We have reached the end of the so-called reconstruction period; we have now reached approximately the prewar level. *However, the end of the reconstruction period is simultaneously the beginning of the reestablishment of our material connections with world industry.* We must renew our fixed capital, which is now going through a crisis; and anyone who thinks that within the next few years we will be able to produce all our equipment, or a large part of this equipment, with our own forces is a dreamer. The industrialization of our country—which was placed on the agenda as one of the most important tasks of the party by our Fourteenth Party Congress, for the immediate rather extensive future—means not the lessening, but, on the contrary, the growth of our connections with the outside world, i.e., also our (of course mutual) dependence upon the world market, capitalism, its technology and industry, and at the same time the growth of the struggle against the international bourgeoisie. This means that we cannot separate the question of building socialism from the question of what is going to happen to the capitalist economy during that time. These two questions stand in the closest connection with one another.

If we are told: But, dear friends, surely you can build machines yourselves, we reply: Of course, if the whole capitalist world goes to the devil, we shall in a few decades be able to build far more machines than now. But if we "abstract" ourselves from the capitalist world—which, after all, does exist—if we intend to make with our own hands all machines, or at least the most important of them, even in the immediate future, i.e., if we attempt to ignore the division of labor in world industry, and jump over our economic past that has made our industry what it is now—in a word, if, according to the famous "socialist" Monroe Doctrine which is now being preached to us, we are to make everything ourselves, this will unavoidably mean an extreme slowing down of the rate of our economic development. For it is entirely clear that a refusal to exploit the world market to fill the gaps in our technology will very seriously slow down our own development. *But the rate of development is a decisive factor,* for we are not alone on the earth: the isolated socialist state for the time being exists only in the powerful imagination of the journalists and writers of resolutions. In reality, our socialist state is constantly—directly or indirectly—under the equalizing control of the world market. The rate of development is not an arbitrary matter. It is determined by world development as a whole, because in the last instance the world economy controls each of its sections even if the section in question is under the dictatorship of the proletariat and is building up a socialist industry.

In order to industrialize our country we must import machines from abroad, and the peasant must export grain. Without export, no imports! On the other hand, the domestic market cannot consume all the products of agriculture. Thus, through the requirements of the peasantry on the one hand, and of industry on the other, we have been integrated into the world economy, and our connections with it (and consequently also our struggle against it) will from month to month become constantly stronger. We are more and more emerging from the isolation of war communism, and we are more and more entering the system of world economic connections and dependencies. And whoever discusses the theory of socialism in one country while disregarding the fact of both "cooperation" and the struggle between our economy and the capitalist world economy is engaging in barren metaphysical speculation.

Comrades, the rather one-sided discussion that has thus far taken place on this question has in any event already had the good result of moving Comrade Stalin to express his ideas somewhat more clearly and sharply, thereby revealing their complete fallibility.

I take the most important sections from the first half of Comrade Stalin's speech, in which the fallibility of the whole theory stands before us, so to speak, in black and white.

Comrade Stalin asks: "Is the victory of socialism in the Soviet Union possible? . . . But what is meant by 'building socialism' if one translates this formula into the concrete language of classes? Building socialism in the USSR means overcoming our Soviet bourgeoisie in the course of the struggle with our own forces."— Just listen to these ideas!—"Therefore, when one speaks of whether it is possible to build socialism in the Soviet Union, one wants to say thereby: Is the proletariat of the Soviet Union able with its own forces to overcome the bourgeoisie of the Soviet Union? This, and only this, is the way to pose the question in trying to solve the problem of the building of socialism in our country. The party's reply to this question is in the affirmative" [Stalin's speech to the same ECCI plenum is in his *Works*, vol. 9 (1954), pp. 3-155].

Here the whole question is therefore reduced to that of whether we are able to overcome our *own* bourgeoisie, as if the whole solution of the building of socialism was contained in this. No, that is not the case! The building of socialism presupposes the disappearance of classes, the replacement of class society by the socialist organization of all production and distribution. What is involved here is overcoming the contradiction between town and country, which again demands a deepgoing industrialization of agriculture itself. And all this while we remain in capitalist encirclement. This question cannot be equated with the bare fact of victory over our *internal* bourgeoisie.

One must always bear in mind that in various cases the words "victory of socialism" have been understood differently. If we say, as Lenin did in 1915, that the proletariat of a single country can seize power, organize socialist production, and take up the struggle against the bourgeoisie of neighboring countries—what did he mean by the *organization of socialist production?* That which we already have accomplished in recent years: the factories and workshops were taken from the bourgeoisie, the necessary steps made for the assurance of production at state expense, so that the people can live and build and defend themselves against capitalist states, etc. This is of course also a victory of socialism; it is likewise an organization of socialist production; but it is obviously only the very beginning. From here to the building of a socialist society is still a very long way.

I repeat: when we speak of the building of socialism in the full sense of this word, this means the disappearance of classes, and furthermore the withering away of the state. Now, says Comrade Stalin, we will carry out socialist construction in the full sense of the word when we have overcome our bourgeoisie *at home*. But comrades, we really need the state and the army against the *foreign* foe. These things remain, comrades, as long as the world bourgeoisie exists. Can one believe, further, that on the basis of our own internal resources, economic as well as cultural, the classes of the proletariat and peasantry will dissolve into a uniform socialist planned economy, *even before the European proletariat captures power?* To accomplish this, as I have said, we would have to raise our technology to a very high level, which presupposes increased exports of grain and increased imports of machinery. But for the time being, the machines are in the hands of the world bourgeoisie and it is also the purchaser of our grain. For the time being it dictates our prices, and thus we fall into a certain dependence upon and struggle with it.

In order to overcome this dependence it is by no means sufficient to overcome our *own* bourgeoisie, for what is involved is not the political elimination of the bourgeoisie—we eliminated it politically in our country in 1917—what is involved is, despite the capitalist encirclement—i.e., the (economic, political, and military) struggle with the world bourgeoisie—to build up the isolated socialist state. This can be done only if the productive forces of this isolated and, for the time being, still very backward state become stronger and more powerful than those of capitalism. Insofar as this involves not a year, or ten years, or even two decades, but a whole series of decades that are necessary for the complete building of socialism, we can achieve this only if our productive forces show themselves more powerful than the productive forces of capitalism. The question, therefore, does not hinge upon the struggle of the proletariat against its own bourgeoisie but upon the decisive struggle of the isolated *new socialist society against the capitalist world system*. This is the only way we can put the question.

Now we hear further: "If this were false"—says Stalin—"if the party had no grounds for maintaining that the proletariat of the Soviet Union was in a position to build a socialist society despite the fact that our country is relatively backward, then the party would have no reason"—No reason!—"to remain in power; it would be compelled to surrender power and continue as an opposition party."

Then he repeats: "Either one or the other," says Comrade Stalin. "Either we are capable of building socialism, and completely building it, by overcoming our national bourgeoisie—and in that case the party must remain in power and in the name of the worldwide victory of socialism it must direct the work of socialist construction in this country. Or else we are not capable of overcoming our bourgeoisie by our own efforts, since we cannot count on immediate"—Why "immediate"?!—"aid from abroad by the victorious revolution in other countries, and in that case we must openly and honestly withdraw from the government and take a new direction toward organizing a new future revolution in the Soviet Union. Can a party lie"—Why "lie"?—"to its own class, and in this case to the working class? No, it cannot. Such a party deserves to be destroyed. Precisely because our party has no right to lie to the working class it must openly admit that the *lack of certainty*"—Not a defeat, but only the lack of certainty?!—"with regard to the possibility of building socialism in our country leads to the problem of power and the transformation of our party from a governing party to an opposition party."

All this is absolutely false. Now, comrades, what did Lenin say about this?

[*The chairman, Comrade Kolarov, calls the speaker's attention to the fact that his time has expired.*]

I was told that I would get an hour, just like Comrade Zinoviev. The hour of Comrade Zinoviev, however, lasted an hour and thirty-five minutes. [*Laughter.*] I hope that you will give me the same time.

I have hardly said half of what I wanted to say to you. Of course, you have the full opportunity to deprive me of the floor now. That depends upon you. But I am only just beginning on the most burning questions.

Now, comrades, we have always maintained that our revolution is a part of the proletarian world revolution, which, while it may develop more slowly, is certain of its victory—and with this also our victory. We have always stigmatized the patriotic opportunists who considered the destiny of socialism only in the isolated perspective of their particular state, regardless of whether they were still flirting with the revolutionary idea or, like most of them, had openly discarded this idea and accepted the reformist standpoint. We have always said that the proletariat of one single country had no right to wait for another country if it had any chance whatever to go forward, to seize power, to develop socialist construction or exert military pressure, or more exactly, both the one thing and the other, for only in this way does the world revolution develop. *That our party at the head of the proletariat seized power, that we are successfully building socialism, that thereby we have given the world proletariat a great example, that we are more and more consolidating our country economically and politically on the road to socialism—all this is self-evident. Is there any dispute about this?* But precisely because we are a section of the world proletariat, of the world revolution—and because we participate in its victorious development through our socialist construction—precisely for this reason we cannot demand any special guarantee that in our country we shall build up socialism *independent of the world revolution.* But here it would seem that we, if we had demanded this guarantee (from whom?) and had not received it, we must resign, precipitate a ministerial crisis, and go over into opposition to the Soviet state. Is this not a fundamentally false formulation of the question?

But it is hardly likely that Stalin himself thinks in the terms he formulated in his report. Otherwise he too would have resigned long ago. How did matters stand until very recently? Comrade Zinoviev has already read a citation by Stalin in 1924. Nevertheless I must repeat it, for, if things stand this way—that unless we get a guarantee in advance of the possibility of building socialism in a single country, we must resign from power—then I must ask: How about Comrade Stalin in 1924, not Before Christ, not before the imperialist epoch, in which the law of uneven development is supposed to have been still unknown, but only two years ago? I again remind you that Comrade Stalin at that time wrote the following:

"In order to overthrow the bourgeoisie, the efforts of a single country are sufficient; this is proved by the history of our revolution. For the final victory of socialism, for the organization of socialist production, however, the efforts of a single country, and particularly of such a peasant country as Russia, are inadequate; for that, the efforts of the proletariat of several advanced countries are required" [from the first edition of

Foundations of Leninism, quoted by Stalin in *Problems of Leninism,* p. 61].

Yes, but in 1924 we did not resign from power, we did not go over to opposition to the workers' state! Just give it some thought! If the tradition of our party, if Bolshevism, if Leninism really at all times demanded faith in the possibility of the final victory of socialism in a single country (and in a backward country at that) without a world revolution—if everyone who does not accept this is to be branded a Social Democrat, how does it happen that Comrade Stalin, who surely should know the traditions of our party from his own experience, could write these lines even as late as 1924? Please explain this to me!

And now another riddle. I show you here the program and statutes of our Leninist Communist League of Youth. If you wish I will lay this little booklet upon the presidium table. This program was adopted by our party in September 1921, as a guide to the training of our whole youth movement. In the fourth paragraph of the program for the workers' youth movement it is stated (please pay close attention, especially you comrades from the Young Communist International, because our Russian youth league is after all a part of the Young Communist International):

"In the Soviet Union state power is already in the hands of the working class. In three years of heroic struggle against world capitalism the working class has established and fortified its Soviet government. Although Russia possesses enormous natural resources, it is nevertheless an industrially backward country in which a petty-bourgeois population predominates. The country can arrive at socialism only through a proletarian world revolution, which epoch of development we have now entered."

What is that? Perhaps pessimism? Discouragement? Perhaps even Trotskyism? I am not at present in a position to judge. But this is found in the program of our youth organization, which contains more than two million young workers and peasants. And if in defense of the new theory of socialism in one country it is said: But surely we must give our youth a perspective—that is a favorite argument with Comrade Stalin—otherwise they might succumb to pessimism, to discouragement, or—God save us from this, especially at this late hour!—to Trotskyism, then I will ask: Why has this misfortune not already overtaken us if the youth has had such a Trotskyist program for the last five years!

[*The chairman, Comrade Kolarov, calls it to Comrade Trotsky's attention that his time is up by ringing the bell.*] They always interrupt me in the most interesting places. I beg the presidium and the plenum to grant me the thirty-five minutes that I have mentioned.

The Chairman: Your time has expired.

Comrade Trotsky: I am extremely sorry, but of course I can do nothing but submit to the resolution that you intend to pass. The important arguments that I wanted to present, however, though unexpressed, will nevertheless retain their objective validity.

For this is not the last meeting of our International. And although this resolution will be adopted here unanimously—of that we are quite certain—especially after today's speech by Comrade Smeral, who so expertly accuses us of Social Democratic deviations—the facts nevertheless remain in existence. The facts will demonstrate their power, and the power of these facts will lend new strength to our arguments. This question will come up again at the sessions of our International, and I am firmly convinced that if not I then someone else will present before the Communist International the arguments which you have today refused to permit me to elucidate and which nevertheless retain their validity on this extremely important question.

WHY THE OPPOSITION WILL VOTE
AGAINST THE RESOLUTION
ON STALIN'S REPORT

December 14, 1926

NOTE: Stalin's resolution, passed unanimously, described the Opposition as a "right danger within the AUCP(B), sometimes masked with left phrases," and emphasized its connections with other Oppositions, both in Russia and abroad. The ECCI approved the expulsion of Trotskyists and Zinovievists from foreign Communist parties on the basis that they denied the proletarian character of the Soviet state. Allegations that the Opposition did not support the united front policy, that it opposed work in the reformist trade unions, and that it "denied" the partial stabilization in the capitalist world were in answer to its attacks on the Anglo-Russian Committee.

From Bulletin Communiste, *April-June 1927. Translated from the French by David Keil, and corrected against the Russian text by George Saunders.*

To the Presidium of the Seventh Enlarged Plenum of the ECCI:
Dear Comrades:

Before passing to a vote on the resolution on Comrade Stalin's report, we request that you read the following statement on the reasons for our vote. We ask that this statement be published in *Pravda*, in *International Press Correspondence*, and in the stenographic record.

Explanation of Vote

In voting against the resolution on the report by Comrade Stalin, we consider it our duty to give the following reasons:

1. We once again reject, categorically, the accusation that our speeches were factional. We again state that whoever tries, directly or indirectly, to solidarize with us while at the same time

denying the proletarian character of our party and our state and the socialist character of construction in the Soviet Union will be ruthlessly opposed and rejected by us.

2. All our criticisms have been directed against errors and deviations from the proletarian line, and dictated by our desire to maintain, assure, and reinforce the revolutionary proletarian policy of our party and its inseparable ties with the international revolution, in accordance with the teachings of Lenin.

3. We resolutely and categorically reject, as completely contrary to the facts, the accusation that we do not believe in socialist construction in the USSR. In reality, we unshakably believe, as in the past, that the proletariat in the USSR, under the direction of the Communist Party, will overcome all difficulties and with the aid of the international proletariat will build socialism in the USSR. In stating that we are against the theory of socialism in one country, we are only continuing to defend the ideas Lenin defended, which are the basis of all the programmatic resolutions of the Comintern up to now.

4. We resolutely and categorically reject the totally unfounded accusations of pessimism and lack of faith:

(a) When we try to draw our party's attention to the increasing danger of the kulaks, it is not to capitulate to this danger, but to advise the party to base itself on the poor peasants and rural workers and permit them, with the help of the proletarian government, to more easily bring the middle peasant into the struggle against the kulaks. It is not true that we proposed to "pressure the peasant" in favor of industrialization. What we want is to maintain the alliance of the workers and peasants as our most cherished achievement. Without this alliance, the proletarian dictatorship in the USSR would be condemned to perish. But we say that our base of support in the village is the agricultural worker and the poor peasant; our *ally* in the village is the middle peasant; our *class enemy* in the village is the rich peasant (kulak);

(b) When we insist on and call the attention of our party to the growth of private capital, it is not to capitulate to it, but so that a complete system of vigilance measures can keep private capital in a strictly subordinate position;

(c) When we speak of the inevitable position of dependence of our socialist economy on the world capitalist economy in a period of reconstruction, it is not to capitulate to this but to insist on a more appropriate distribution of the national income in the interests of state industry, an acceleration of the rate of development by every means, a rise in the material standard of living of the working class, and its education in the spirit of a profound understanding of the inseparability of the fate of our socialist construction from that of the international proletarian revolution.

5. We reject any accusation that we doubt the class character of our state and the socialist character of the society we are building. We in the Opposition have up to now worked with other comrades and under the direction of the CC in all branches of socialist construction: in the development of state industry, in establishing a stable currency, in strengthening our economic plans, in attaining a predominance of socialist tendencies. We could name dozens of the best-known militants who are in the Opposition and at the same time have carried out, not without success, one or another state task. The same will be true in the future to the extent that the Central Committee entrusts us with work of one kind or another.

6. It is not true that we are opposed to the tactic of the united front. We are *for* it. But we are opposed to agreements with Thomas, Pugh, and Purcell when they despicably betray the British miners.

7. It is not true that we are opposed to work in the reformist trade unions. No, we are for the participation of Communists in the most reactionary unions, in accordance with the teachings of Lenin. Communists ought to be wherever there are organized workers.

8. It is not true that we looked indulgently on "ultraleft" views. We struggle and we will struggle against all ultraleft errors. But we demand, in regard to honest revolutionary activists, even "ultraleft" ones, that the Comintern take the attitude taught by Lenin. We demand, in accordance with the teachings of Lenin, that the Comintern expose and denounce the right-wing leaders, diplomats, and parliamentarists who skillfully disguise their right-wing actions and plans with fine-sounding phrases.

9. We remain enemies of the Social Democracy, as we were in Lenin's time. We consider the Social Democratic leaders to be the greatest enemies of the labor movement. It is not true that the Social Democracy has changed its attitude toward us, the Opposition. No, it continues to hate us as in the past (and even more) and to attack us as only the petty bourgeoisie is capable of attacking intransigent proletarian revolutionists. The bourgeois and Social Democratic press, viewing with irreconcilable hostility the *policy* we defend, sometimes tries to make use of our *criticisms*. It has always been that way.

10. It is not true that we deny the fact of a partial stabilization of capitalism. We recognize it. We wrote of it in a series of articles on the British strike. What we deny is that this stabilization is destined to last for decades. We leave this profession of faith to Otto Bauer and Company. We retain the viewpoint of Lenin, who considered our epoch to be one of world revolution.

11. Thus it is evident that we are not guilty of the slightest "Social Democratic deviation." We are profoundly convinced that the future will prove that such an assertion cannot withstand the least criticism.

12. It is not true that we defend "Trotskyism." Trotsky has stated to the International that on all the fundamental questions over which he had differences with Lenin, Lenin was right—in particular on the questions of permanent revolution and the peasantry. We defend *Leninism*. We struggle above all against any revision of Lenin's teachings on the *international* revolution.

13. It is not true that we accuse the majority of our party of representing a "right-wing deviation." We believe only that in the AUCP there are right-wing currents and groupings which now have a disproportionate influence, but which the party will be able to overcome.

14. We will carry out to the end the obligations we assumed in our statement of October 16, 1926. But we have full right to defend our principles. We stated this in this same October 16 document and no one contested this right. In the seven years of the Comintern's existence, all differences of opinion that existed in any party, including the AUCP, have always been given a hearing in the Comintern, and any minority whatsoever had the right to defend its point of view and its principles. If the expression of a point of view before a leading body of the world Communist Party is considered to be factionalism, then what other means exist to defend ideas within the limits of the general decisions of the Comintern? *We will defend the unity of the AUCP* and the Comintern. We will struggle against factionalism.

15. The continual attempts of our enemies to exploit the slightest difference of opinion in the party should not be a reason to cease all self-criticism. If the conferences and congresses were supposed to be based on unanimity assured in advance, there would be no point in convening them. The regime of the Comintern, and that of each individual party, should, in full accordance with our program and our statutes, assure real possibilities for self-criticism that will not develop into factional activity or disrupt unity of action.

16. In our opinion, the proposed resolution not only gives an incorrect and tendentious characterization of the opinions which we defend and which, we are unshakably convinced, are in complete accord with the traditions of Marxism and Leninism—but it also could worsen the situation within the Comintern, further limiting the already insufficient possibilities for criticism within the party. We have no doubt, moreover, that even while adopting this erroneous decision, the Comintern will remain, as in the past, the only organization capable of correcting the errors of its different sections, and its own errors, basing itself on the experience of the revolutionary struggle of the world proletariat.

17. This profound and unshakable confidence gives us the right and duty to submit entirely to the decision that you will make and to call upon all the comrades who consider themselves in agreement with us to do likewise.

G. Zinoviev, L. Kamenev, L. Trotsky

PROBLEMS OF THE COMINTERN

January 18, 1927

NOTE: The Russian manuscript in the Library of Social History gives two different dates: June 1926 and January 18, 1927. The text was apparently drafted after the February-March 1926 (sixth) ECCI plenum (which was preoccupied with maintaining a blackout about the "Russian question" and with exposing the dangers of ultraleftism—an appellation which by this time included bona fide left-wing currents), and was then added to after the November-December 1926 (seventh) ECCI plenum. It bears the notation "Top Secret." It is addressed to the Soviet delegation to the ECCI. A note in Trotsky's handwriting on the manuscript says that it was "also distributed to the delegates of the plenum semi-illegally."

The lengthy section about the problems of the French Communist Party (PCF) may have been occasioned by a session of the PCF's Central Committee that was held January 11-13, 1927, in which the problems of the Russian party were linked to the development of the French Left Opposition. Two days after the French CC meeting, several French Oppositionists issued a letter to party members and to the International entitled "For Workers' Democracy," which denounced the degeneration of the party. Trotsky could not have known about that letter when he wrote this memorandum, but he had been closely involved with French politics since 1915 and had had considerable influence on the development of the French revolutionary movement. (His contact with Rosmer and Monatte, who had been expelled in 1924, dated to the earliest days of World War I; they had later become leaders of the Communist Party and then of the opposition to Stalinism.)

Trotsky's proposal for a book on "where France is headed" is unrelated to the book he actually wrote in 1934-36, Whither France? *(in English in* Leon Trotsky on France*).*

By permission of the Library of Social History.

To the AUCP(B) Delegation:

Bureaucratism as a Source of Opportunism

1. One of the main features of opportunism, especially its centrist-diplomatic variety, is its readiness to adopt radical resolutions in relation to other countries. In this way, opportunism to some extent gratifies the revolutionary moods of the working masses, without itself assuming any responsibilities. The entire history of the working class movement is filled with expressions of this kind of duplicity, especially in Great Britain. In Marx's era the trade unionists used to adopt radical resolutions in regard to Poland, but put the question of Ireland and India quite differently. In our day, the Independent Labour Party raises the question of a merger between the Second and Third Internationals, while refusing to engage in joint action with the British Communist Party. The General Council of British Trades Unions concludes a bloc with the Soviet All-Union Central Council of Trade Unions with the aim of uniting the world trade union movement, but during the general strike in Great Britain refuses to accept financial aid from this same AUCCTU. Such examples, large and small, can be multiplied without end.

2. To the extent that opportunist tendencies make their appearance within the Comintern, they display the same characteristic, that is, a readiness to adopt radical decisions in regard to others, mercilessly denouncing "rightist deviations" in all countries, while being inclined at the same time to give way—especially at the critical moment—before bourgeois public opinion in their own country. It goes without saying that "radicalism" of this sort is the deadly enemy of Bolshevism. The job of the Comintern is to develop genuinely revolutionary parties, especially through uncompromising struggle against every manifestation of sham radicalism, political duplicity, etc. Everything depends upon the degree to which the Comintern regime encourages this struggle.

3. We absolutely must come to realize that one of the most important present sources of opportunism in the Comintern—hidden and disguised, but all the more virulent for that reason—is the bureaucratic apparatus regime in the Comintern itself and in the Comintern's leading member party. There can be no doubt, after the experience of 1923-26, that in the Soviet Union, bureaucratism is both an expression of, and a vehicle for, the pressure of nonproletarian classes upon the proletariat. To the extent that the European Communist parties—or most of their leaderships—

have organizationally paralleled the apparatus shifts and re-alignments in the AUCP, the bureaucratism within the foreign Communist parties has above all been a reflection and extension of the bureaucratism within the AUCP. It is precisely here that the roots of the duplicity mentioned above are to be found. The selection of leadership elements in the Communist parties pro-ceeded and still proceeds for the most part on the basis of their readiness to accept and approve the latest alignments in the AUCP apparatus. The more independent and responsible ele-ments in the leaderships of the foreign parties, who would not submit to reshufflings of a purely administrative sort, were either thrown out of the party altogether or were driven into the right wing (often only seemingly a right wing), or, last of all, found themselves in opposition from the left. Thus, the organic process of selection and consolidation of revolutionary cadres on the basis of the working class struggle was, under Comintern leadership, cut short, changed around, distorted, and sometimes openly replaced by bureaucratic administrative pressure from above, from Moscow. It was natural if it happened that those leading elements in the Communist parties who more willingly accepted ready-made decisions and endorsed any and all resolutions—if such elements often gained the advantage over more revolutionary elements, instilled with a full sense of revolu-tionary responsibility. Instead of a selection of tried and true revolutionaries, a selection of the bureaucratically adaptable resulted.

4. We have seen bureaucratic elements in the Communist movement (in Germany, France, England, America, Poland, etc.) carry out fantastically opportunist actions with total impunity, hiding behind the protective coloring of their positions on general questions in the Comintern and above all on the internal questions in the AUCP. On the other hand we have observed, and this to a growing extent, the phenomenon whereby political figures in the Comintern have publicly and officially taken one position, and secretly, under the table and behind the scenes, but the more strongly for that, held another position, directly opposed to the official one. The so-called "double bookkeeping" of the Maslow–Ruth Fischer group was emphatically condemned at the [December 1926] enlarged plenum of the ECCI. But it is quite obvious that a formal condemnation, however just it might be, not only does not resolve but does not even pose the fundamental problem: Why do the most responsible Communists, leaders of the largest parties, resort to this kind of double bookkeeping? The

answer should be stated as follows: In the event of differences with the AUCP CC, even temporary ones, the regime of apparatus omnipotence confronts any of the foreign leaders with three possibilities: to be immediately driven into the arms of the right wing of the party or even expelled from the party; to immediately throw themselves into opposition from the left; or to practice double bookkeeping for a time while preserving their position in the party.

5. It by no means follows from what has been said, of course, that the right or left groupings in the Comintern are expressing a correct line—in contrast to the official center. There is no question that Social Democratic tendencies are strong in the right-wing groupings and there is more than a little of the "infantile disorder" in the left wing. It would also be incorrect to assume that the official leading cadres consist of unthinking bureaucrats. In fact a feeling of responsibility for the fate of the Soviet Union keeps many true revolutionists within the confines of the dominant regime despite the growing indignation against it. It follows from that, however, that radical regroupments are necessary within the Comintern with the aim of emancipating the Comintern from apolitical, mechanical apparatus coercion, which in turn is a task bound up in the most intimate way with that of changing the regime in the AUCP.

The sooner, and the more widely and emphatically, this task is posed by all viable elements in the Comintern—independently of the present groupings, which to a great extent are artificial—the fewer the shocks and convulsions when it is carried out.

The USSR and the Comintern

1. The theoretical untenability and practical danger of the theory of socialism in one country is quite obvious, or at least is becoming more and more obvious, to every revolutionist who has at all assimilated the Marxist view of the fundamental problems of historical development. Politically speaking, this theory is a completely uncritical camouflaging of what exists in the USSR and of everything that is coming into being, in all its contradictions and in an elemental and chaotic way. In this sense the theory of socialism in one country weakens and blunts the vigilance and alertness of the party in regard to capitalist tendencies and forces in both domestic and world development. It nourishes a passive fatalistic optimism, beneath which bureaucratic indifference to the destinies of socialism and the interna-

tional revolution is able to hide more successfully than otherwise.

2. No less fatal a role would be played by this theory, if it is legitimized, in relation to the Comintern. If Soviet socialist construction is viewed as an inseparable component of the world revolution, as a process inconceivable apart from the world revolution, then the relative importance of the Communist parties, their role, their independent responsibility, would increase and come more to the fore. If on the contrary the same old point of view is upheld that Soviet power, resting on the alliance of workers and peasants, will build socialism absolutely independently of what occurs in all the rest of the world—on the one condition that the Soviet Republic be protected from military intervention—then the role and significance of the Communist parties is immediately moved to the background.

The assurance that socialism will be fully victorious in our country regardless of the course of the revolution in other countries means that the chief task of the European Communist parties in the immediate historical period—a task that will be adequate for the victory of socialism—is not to win power but to oppose the interventionist attempts of imperialism. For it is quite obvious that it would be enough to secure the victory of socialism in our country to thereby assure its further spread to the whole world. The whole perspective in this way is turned around.

The problem of taking the fullest possible advantage of every genuinely revolutionary situation is pushed into the background. A false and consoling theory is constructed according to which time, in and of itself, "works in our favor." However, we cannot forget that we are living in conditions where we have a chance to catch our breath and by no means in conditions where the victory of socialism "in one country" is automatically assured.

We must take advantage of the breathing spell as fully as possible. We must prolong it as long as possible. But to forget that what is involved is precisely a breathing spell—i.e., a more or less prolonged period between the 1917 revolution and the next revolution in one of the major capitalist countries—means to trample underfoot the worldwide laws of historical development; it means in fact to renounce communism.

3. The ultraleftists charge that the united front policy means a retreat by foreign parties from independent revolutionary positions to the line of *assisting* the Soviet state by building an imposing "left" wing within the working class in each country. The theory of socialism in one country meets the ultralefts' criticism half-way, nourishes it, and within certain limits justifies

it. The left deviations, without ceasing to be manifestations of "infantile disorders," receive new nourishment, for their leaders appear as defenders of the independent revolutionary role of the Communist parties and of the responsibility of those parties not only for the fate of their own country but also for that of the Soviet Union, against the bureaucratic optimism according to which the cause of socialism in the Soviet Union is assured in and of itself, if only nobody "interferes" with it. In this aspect, which will inevitably become a more and more prominent one, the struggle of the left groupings becomes a progressive factor and may accordingly transform the best elements among them.

On the Comintern Program

It follows from the above that we now have a new and decisive confirmation of the idea that a correct orientation, not only of the policies of the USSR and of those of each Communist Party separately but also of the Comintern as a whole, is only conceivable if it begins with the world economy, which, in spite of its contradictions and the barriers that divide it—in fact, to a significant extent, because of them—is a single worldwide unit.

The program of the Comintern cannot be designed on the model of an old socialist program giving an abstract analysis of the economic, social, and political development of individual capitalist countries. What is needed is a concrete analysis of the complex of world economic relations viewed as an internally coherent process, with an indication of the interrelated perspectives for Europe, America, Asia, etc. This is the only Marxist way to pose the question and would in passing strike a deathblow at the anti-Marxist theory of socialism in one country.

Problems of the French Working Class Movement

1. In France more than anywhere else the groupings in the party were formed not so much on the basis of the French working class movement as by way of reflection of the inner-party struggle in the AUCP. French political questions stemming from the struggle to win over the proletariat for the sake of taking power have been subordinated to questions flowing from the difficulties of socialist construction in the Soviet Republic.

2. In 1923, during the struggle against so-called "Trotskyism," the struggle within the AUCP was openly placed at the center of the formation of groupings in France. Now the Russian question

has been, as it were, removed from the agenda within the International. Nevertheless, the groupings in the foreign parties, especially the French, are again following the line of the discussion within the Russian party, but this time anonymously, mutedly, without an open ideological struggle, thus fully revealing what it means to be dependent solely on the apparatus.

3. All this was inevitably bound to provoke a desire, by way of a reaction, for greater independence from "Moscow" on the part of the foreign Communist parties. This desire will be, and already has been, expressed in the form of contradictory tendencies: (1) an opportunist deviation, which everywhere leads to a weakening of international ties; and (2) a proletarian revolutionary current, which has arrived at the clear conclusion, on the basis of experience, that it is a danger to have a bureaucratic regime in which the leaders of the national parties are shuffled around from above like so many officials in a hierarchy. There is no need to say that the struggle against bureaucratic centralism cannot and should not make any concessions to opportunist federalism. The increased independence of the national parties in the Comintern, based on their establishing more profound ties with the working class in each of their countries, will inevitably mean the decline of the old groupings, which to a significant extent were artificial and bureaucratic, and the regroupment of their elements along new, more organic, vital, and relevant lines.

4. The objective political situation in France (the growth of contradictions and the prospect of major upheavals) provides the basic criterion for the regroupment within the party—based on the tasks brought to the fore by the political developments in France—in close connection, of course, with the tasks of the Comintern as a whole. Each of the old groupings and each member of each old grouping that has not yet come to a realization of the necessity for, and inevitability of, a radical regroupment of forces in the party will inevitably be pushed aside by further developments.

5. The most elementary criterion for a progressive grouping in the party should be the desire for an honest recognition of what is, of the real strength of the party, its actual numerical size, the real ties of its members with the masses, the actual vitality of its factory cells (the basic units for the reorganization of the party), the real number of members of the unitary trade unions, their actual participation in strikes, the real circulation of the Communist press, etc. The fight against bureaucratism should begin with a concrete clarification of what really is. Only through the

ruthless exposure of all fictions, all self-deception, can a serious, i.e., a Bolshevik attitude toward problems of organization and an understanding of the importance of organization as an instrument of revolution be taught to the leading elements of the French party. A chart of France showing the political parties and trade unions must be drawn up, including all the data delineating the actual state of the workers' organizations and all branches of the working class movement. On the basis of this chart we must come to a clear realization of why we are strong in some regions and weak in others. Such a businesslike and critical approach will be one of the most important means for testing out our tactics, their revolutionary relevance, and their capacity for capturing the masses. Basing itself on such a chart, which must be regularly modified and supplemented with accurately gathered, up-to-date information, the party should set itself concrete tasks for winning leadership in the most important proletarian centers and districts by concentrating its best forces in those places and applying slogans and struggle methods to the concrete situation.

6. As important as it is for the party to attract the petty-bourgeois elements of town and country who are being ruined by the big bourgeoisie, it is quite obvious that if this task were undertaken by the party to the detriment of the basic struggle to win over the proletariat, that would, at a certain stage, create the threat of a degeneration in the class character of the party itself. It is more important for us to win over a hundred workers in the departement du Nord [one of France's chief industrial areas] than a thousand civil servants or small shopkeepers in Paris or Marseilles. This should in no way be understood as a desire to weaken our effort in the struggle to influence the petty-bourgeois masses driven to desperation. But it is necessary that this struggle be an auxiliary process in relation to the basic work of strengthening and consolidating the proletarian backbone of the party. At any rate, unless we have the proletariat, which is capable of conquering power and transforming society, we will sooner or later lose the impatient petty-bourgeois auxiliaries, who will go rushing off toward fascism.

7. The party's conservatism in the area of the trade union movement is of an absolutely ruinous kind. Bringing the trade unions closer to the party at the price of separating the unions from the working class can have no value whatsoever. The tendency toward making the unions into slightly enlarged editions of the party must be decisively rejected. The main

criterion in evaluating the trade unions is their ties with the mass movement, with strikes that are actually under way, etc. Only on this basis can the strengthening of the party within the trade unions be important and valuable.

8. In Germany and England the reformist trade unions embrace millions of workers. In France the reformist unions are as weak as ours. A serious struggle for a united front in France therefore means first of all extending the influence of the trade unions to the unorganized masses: careful consideration of every strike, practical study of the conditions of its rise and development, working to establish connections with episodic organizations having the leadership of the strike, etc., etc. The work of the trade unions should be based on a painstaking inventory of all the expressions of economic struggle by the working class, on a businesslike study of these, and on working out methods for leading the day-to-day struggle of the masses.

9. The inner-party slogan is the slogan "concentration of forces" on the basis of the revolutionary tasks of the French proletariat. In particular, a radical differentiation needs to be carried out within the 1923 Opposition, based on the revolutionary way of posing the tasks of the movement, genuinely casting aside opportunist elements and building bridges to the revolutionary elements in the other groupings.

10. It is necessary to take a correct position in relation to the Monatte-Rosmer grouping. The criminal expulsion of Monatte and Rosmer from the party has led to a backward evolution on their part toward syndicalism and has resulted in a new grouping of revolutionary syndicalist elements around them. Pure-and-simple criticism of syndicalism, all alone, without any change in the party's trade union work in practice, cannot accomplish anything. Regardless of the extent to which the return of Monatte and Rosmer (or Rosmer only) to the party in the near future is realizable or worthwhile, Monatte and his group should be made to understand that they will inevitably be on the same side of the barricades in the proletarian revolution as the Communist Party and that they should make their politics correspond to this fact. Only on the basis of such a general line can the precious worker-revolutionists who support Monatte be won over.

11. The rallying of the truly revolutionary elements must be supplemented by a process of selection among them based on living experience. A most important part in the formation of party cadres must be the testing and checking of how party members conduct themselves in strikes, in demonstrations, in

conflicts with police, in clashes with the fascists, etc. In the past it was often true that serious faults in such matters were overlooked for the sake of apparatus reliability. The greatest vigilance and irreconcilability in the attitudes of party members on such questions must be developed.

12. In the French party Marxism still remains to a considerable degree an imported commodity. The party lives on echoes, often distorted ones, of the theoretical and other struggles in the AUCP. The leading elements of the French party must be helped to learn how to apply Marxism to the clarification of the basic questions of economic and political development in France in the present period. In particular, collective work is needed on a book on "where France is headed."

13. It is necessary to win for the French party, as for every foreign party, the possibility and the right to arrive at its own completely free and independent judgment about the discussions in the AUCP. If the foreign Communist parties do not find it easy to arrive at their own correct opinion about the course and methods of the only proletarian party in power, one should by no means conclude from that, that the foreign Communist parties should not concern themselves with the Russian discussion. This would only lead to a situation in which, under a surface appearance of "neutrality," a muted apparatus selection of personnel, as we have said, would go on.

It was absolutely correct to refuse to place the Russian question before the enlarged ECCI plenum: a decision passed without serious acquaintance with the question, without its having been predigested in the parties, would have had a purely formal character, and would have brought nothing to the AUCP or the International. All the more important is it, then, to have a serious, rounded, well-documented discussion of the present situation in the AUCP.

FOR AN OBJECTIVE ASSESSMENT

February 21, 1927

NOTE: In this memorandum, presumably submitted to the February 1927 CC plenum, Trotsky returns to the issues he had considered in "Theses on Revolution and Counterrevolution." The memorandum appears to be an effort to counter the pervasive official optimism, the practice, even in inner-party discussions, of reporting only positive developments, ignoring the negative ones, and often passing off the latter as the former. Any attempt to call attention to danger signals was denounced as lack of faith in building socialism and playing into the hands of the enemies of Soviet Russia by publicizing its weaknesses.

The "October developments of last year" (1926) mentioned in point 14 are probably the efforts of Opposition leaders to bring their program to the rank and file, the official campaign to silence them, and the subsequent "truce" with the ruling faction. In point 5, the "subjectivists" who "draw absolutely worthless conclusions" about these developments were probably the remains of the Democratic Centralist group led by Sapronov and V.M. Smirnov, who circulated a memorandum around this time criticizing the Opposition leaders. Trotsky called them "subjectivists" because they imagined that the Opposition's chance for success depended entirely on its choice of tactics and discounted the actual shifts in class forces domestically and internationally.

The otzovists and ultimatists mentioned in point 6 were sectarian currents in the then Russian Social Democratic Labor Party who in 1907-08 demanded the recall of Social Democratic deputies from the Third Duma (parliament) and opposed work in legal mass organizations. They represented the other end of the spectrum from the Liquidators, who were reluctant to resume the underground struggle and wanted to "liquidate" the underground party organization, engaging only in activities permitted by the tsarist authorities.

By permission of the Library of Social History.

205

To the Members of the Central Committee:

The question of evaluating the political condition of the proletariat, in connection with the entire situation, both domestic and international, was raised during the debates on the question of the Soviet elections and provoked disagreements that have not been clarified. I consider it necessary to explain my views on this, a question of the highest importance, because I think that a calm discussion of the question will at least clear away the false issues.

1. The proletariat, as a class, is not always identical with itself. Even under approximately the same economic conditions it changes politically, subject to the influence of numerous factors, both national and international in character.

2. Ten years ago our proletariat was at a much lower cultural level than now. But at that time, owing to a unique conjunction of domestic and international circumstances, it reached a pitch of revolutionary intensity that no other class in the world has reached. It would be absurd to think that this intense revolutionary pitch could be maintained for many long years, even decades. Downturns and upturns, sometimes very sharp and deepgoing ones, are absolutely inevitable—depending on the entire set of circumstances, the course of world capitalist development as a whole, and the pace of socialist construction here.

3. The proletariat expected, just as we did, that the European revolution would follow immediately after 1917. In 1923 it looked forward to a revolution in Germany. In 1926, during the miners' strike, it expected events in England to develop in a revolutionary direction. The years 1918-26 were years of very big defeats for the European proletariat. It would simply be stupid cowardice to close one's eyes to this fact (and equally stupid to draw so-called pessimistic conclusions from this). Our working class was deeply affected by the experience of these events. This took the form, first, of tense, highly concentrated expectation, and then of deep discouragement. Isn't it really quite clear that this experience was bound to produce something new in our proletariat's attitude toward the development of the world revolution in general, great caution and reserve; among tired-out elements, great skepticism; in immature circles, outright distrust?

4. The course of development within the country could not fail to affect the proletariat as a whole along the same lines: in our tenth year we have barely reached the prewar standard of living. Naturally the workers went into the revolution with much higher hopes, and the overwhelming majority of them, with big illusions. Following from this, especially given the retarded pace of

development, it was inevitable that there should be a certain disillusionment with the revolution and its capacity for changing life and relationships profoundly in a short time. To say, in this regard, that the proletariat is disillusioned with revolution in general or is ready to turn its back on revolution would be idiocy, or renegacy. But not to see that the revolution does not, in the present period, hold the will and attention of the proletariat with the same intensity as before; that its will and attention have been diverted to a number of other problems; that everyday living problems, needs and wants on the job, in the local areas, etc., have not only devoured great amounts of attention but have also overshadowed in general revolutionary perspectives and general class perspectives—one would have to be blind not to see that.

5. In the early 1850s, Marx, taking into account the entire international situation, especially the economic situation, concluded that a temporary ebb in the revolution had begun. Marx did not fold up the revolutionary banner, but he did break with the subjectivists who did not want to take notice of the ebb. Marx was not afraid to call it by its name.

6. In 1907, Lenin concluded that there was a certain ebb in the revolution, and raised the demand for "bread," for participation in the Third Duma, etc. He broke ruthlessly not only with the Liquidators but also with the subjectivists who did not wish to see the change in the situation or the change in the moods of the working class itself (the otzovists, ultimatists, etc.).

7. We recognize that there has been a certain stabilization of European capitalism. We have acknowledged the fact that after the 1923 defeat in Germany the German Communist Party steadily lost influence among the masses, and we have noted that during the past year there has been a weakening of the French, Czechoslovak, Polish, Swedish, Norwegian, and other Communist parties. In this weakening of Communist Party influence political mistakes have played a big role. But at the root of this decline lies a more profound process, which has been going on among the proletarian masses since the 1918-23 period. Will this continue for a long time? Our epoch is one of abrupt turns. But this does not change our evaluation of the process going on at present. The miners' strike in England ran its course while the European working class in fact remained apathetic. The defeat of that strike could only delay a new upsurge. Such are the facts that we must take into account, and certain ways of fighting for the proletarian revolution in Europe follow from these facts, at least for now.

8. Or is someone going to say that this is all more or less true of Europe but has no bearing on our situation? That would be national narrow-mindedness indeed—and in its most blatant form. We sometimes look at events in Germany, England, China, etc., over the heads of our working class. This bad habit is expressed in our press, which offers the working class only bits and pieces of world developments, primarily those of a celebratory nature. Our working class has felt the experience of the German, English, and Chinese events very deeply and the deposits that remain in the workers' consciousness from those events cannot be overcome merely by empty sloganizing.

9. Comrade Molotov's objection—"But what has happened to the ten-years' work of the party?"—is bureaucratic through and through. The class, its experiences and conclusions, are not just the product of the work of party institutions. We all know what an important factor the party is in the life of the class. But it is not the only factor. The party *cannot neutralize* the effect of the entire world situation, the victories and defeats of the working class, or *the slowness of our economic growth*. The party can and must soften the impact of the downturn. The party can and must look openly at all the processes under way in the working class, explain these to the vanguard, and prepare it for a new change in the situation. But the policy of closing one's eyes to what is happening is not our policy.

10. Comrade Bukharin in his Leningrad report spoke of the fact that there are in our party certain Black Hundred elements. We will not exaggerate their numbers. But alongside them, there are also elements who take a tolerant attitude toward Black Hundredism. And next to them in turn is a layer of those who are not disposed toward an active struggle against Black Hundredism, and so on. Do you think that this is accidental? Isn't there a correlation between these phenomena and the decline of class activism, vigilance, and alertness within the proletariat itself? Of course, as a party we bear a large part of the blame for this, because we have not helped the proletariat orient itself correctly. This is where we must begin. But *how* to begin depends on the extent to which the proletariat responds or fails to respond to warning voices, appeals, etc.

11. The classes and groups hostile or semi-hostile to the working class sense the weakening of its pressure, which is expressed not only through the state apparatus but also in the economy and in everyday life. Hence the rising tide of self-confidence among the politically active layers of the petty bourgeoisie.

This confidence keeps mounting regardless of one or another attempt to suppress or stop it. The proletariat undoubtedly has not yet realized the impending danger. This, to a considerable extent, is our fault.

12. The increased activism of the nonproletarian classes inevitably will bring the proletariat to its feet. It will arise to defend itself and, when conditions become at all favorable, will go over to the offensive. Such is the perspective for the morrow. For this we must prepare ourselves and others.

13. All this is simply not understood by the present-day subjectivists, who think that party bureaucratism is the only factor. On this question, as on many others, the subjectivists converge happily with the bureaucrats. The difference between them is not so great. The bureaucrat says, "All is well with the proletariat, and I am the expression of that." The subjectivists say, "All is well with the proletariat, and I would be the expression of that if it weren't for the bureaucrat." Both are grossly mistaken.

14. Precisely because of the incorrectness of their whole orientation, the subjectivists draw absolutely worthless conclusions about the October developments of last year. Precisely for that reason we part ways with the subjectivists. At the root of our disagreement lies a different assessment of the relationship of political forces, a profound variance in our assessment of the proletariat's general state of being at present.

15. It might be said, "All this is more or less true, but it isn't 'tactful' to talk about it." Such an argument is absolutely false. Precisely in order to protect the party, especially its most far-sighted elements, from demoralization, it is necessary to say what is. Of course we must do this in such a way as to be understood correctly, that is, we must offer a perspective for overcoming on the morrow the negative features of today. This perspective must include both objective and subjective aspects. But to close our eyes to the basic features of the present situation—that is not our kind of politics.

NATIONAL ASPECTS OF POLITICS IN KAZAKHSTAN

March 11, 1927

NOTE: This document is one of the few cases in which Trotsky took up the national question in the USSR in the 1920s. It is curious that he addressed it to Sokolnikov, who apparently parted company with the Opposition sometime in late 1926 or early 1927. This document may indicate he was still an Oppositionist in March. Sokolnikov had headed a commission in 1920 to investigate and correct Russian chauvinism and "colonialist" abuses by Soviet authorities in Turkestan.

Kazakhstan, which became a constituent republic of the USSR in 1936, is second in size only to the Russian Republic. By "European" Communists Trotsky means Russians; Kazakhstan is part of Soviet Central Asia. The "resettlement policy" refers to the policy of sending large numbers of Russians to settle in the other regions of the Soviet Union. Like other non-Russian populations, the Kazakhs had suffered the effects of centuries of domination by the Russian tsars and settlers and were understandably sensitive to incidents of heavy-handedness by the new wave of Russian bureaucrats and technicians.

Beys were the native bourgeoisie.

By permission of the Harvard College Library.

To Comrade Sokolnikov:

Grigory Yakovlevich:

I am sending you some notes which are the result of my discussion with two Kazakh Communists. I do not know if you are familiar with relations in Kazakhstan. At any rate you can draw certain conclusions by analogy with Turkestan.

[copy not signed]

*   *   *

In a meeting to discuss matters in their area, the Kazakh comrades put forward the following considerations:

1. The borderlands are lagging behind. Their rate of development should be increased so that they come closer to the level of development in Moscow, not fall more and more behind Moscow. Here we have, then, the general problem of the rate of development refracted in a special way.

2. Capital investments in the backward parts of the Soviet Union give no promise of bearing fruit very quickly. Hence the passive, and sometimes even active, opposition of the central bureaus to such investments.

3. Kazakhstan's participation in the directing agencies of the Russian Republic "has no tangible effect at all." Apparently there is a tendency favoring separation and adoption of the statutes of an independent republic.

4. There are complaints against the resettlement policy of the central authorities: The Kazakh masses were attracted to Soviet power by the revolution on the land; "encroachment" on Kazakh lands causes immediate alarm. "We are not against the resettlement policy, but first of all, the land needs of the native population must be satisfied."

5. "When we raise the question of Kazakhstan's interests in regard to land and other matters, the answer we get is, 'What are you trying to do, get revenge for the tsarist policies?' They have little confidence that we, as Communists, are capable of approaching such questions from the viewpoint of the general interests of the state."

6. The point of view that prevails in the government offices is that of old-time specialists, who still go by the traditions of the past when deciding all economic and cultural questions in the borderlands.

7. A layer of national Communists has arisen, but the leaders sent from the center give them no opportunity for advancement. "They think we haven't grown up yet."

8. Between the European and Kazakh Communists there is a wall. They live totally apart. They do not even play chess together.

9. The European Communists carry out the general line of the center. Among them there are no disputes or clashes on grounds of principle; the explanation given for this is their "indifference."

10. Among the nationals, on the other hand, things are bubbling. There are various groupings among them. The existence of these different groupings is supported and even cultivated

by the leaders sent from the center. For what purpose? "First, to strengthen their own domination; and second, to use these internal differences to divert attention from the problems connected with the policies of the center."

11. Among the Kazakh Communists there are three groupings: one around Goloshchekin—people who are always and in all things obedient to orders from above; another—a "left" grouping, which also supports Goloshchekin but, as I understood it, remains somewhat independent of him; and a third—a "right" grouping, to which my visitors belonged. Moreover, members of the "left" grouping sometimes join the "right."

12. What are the differences? "They reproach us for supposedly being opponents of the poor peasants and protectors of the *beys,* but we are ready to carry out any intelligent measures against the *beys,* if the leadership would propose these clearly and precisely."

13. "Goloshchekin stated in one speech: 'A small-scale October must pass through Kazakhstan.' What does that mean? He did not explain; he did not propose any concrete measures. We do not see any differences of principle, or even practical disagreements, concerning internal policies in Kazakhstan. All this is artificially encouraged in order to mask the question of relations with the Russian Republic."

14. The second comrade said: "The center of gravity in this question consists in the different attitude of the Goloshchekin group toward the *aul* (Kazakh village) on the one hand and toward the Russian village on the other. Goloshchekin's opinion is that the Russian kulak has been weakened and put down sufficiently but that the *beys* have hardly been touched. For that reason a new October must pass through the *auls.* In other words, Goloshchekin preaches civil peace in the Russian village and civil war in the *aul.*"

15. "We are suffocated by bureaucratism, which assumes forms that are all the more repulsive because of the wall between the European and the Kazakh Communists. Fear, hypocrisy, and informing play a big role."

*   *   *

In this account of the situation there is much that is unclear. The reference to the Russian village and the *aul* is of course especially important. What is going on here? It seems that the "right" grouping is being accused of a pro-kulak deviation. Is that true? Couldn't it be that some administrators, denying the existence of a pro-kulak deviation in general, discover one all the more easily in the backward regions, thus patching up their "left" reputation and at the same time making their job of administration easier for themselves?

Vladimir Ilyich said that the Russian Communists in the borderlands should function as helpers. Some of these helpers won't let those they are "helping" utter even a peep.

In general it seems that because of the low level of social differentiation in the milieu itself, the ideological groupings among the Communists must inevitably be fluid and unstable in character. This makes it easier than ever to label someone a member of a "right" or "left" faction. However, the possibility is by no means excluded that in the process of fighting against the bureaucratism of the center, elements of national-bourgeois ideology may emerge locally.

It would be good to send young and capable nationals of the more backward populations abroad for a closer acquaintance with the class struggle. [With experience only] in our country, they almost immediately develop a governmental-administrative frame of mind.

LETTER ON THE GERMAN 'LEFTS'

April 2, 1927

NOTE: This memorandum was occasioned by the exchange of views that took place around the Essen Congress of the KPD, which convened on March 1, 1927, and a conference of Left Oppositionists held simultaneously in Essen. By now, all the left currents in the German party had been expelled, and the Maslow-Fischer-Urbahns group, having considerable organizational success, was in touch with Opposition leaders in Moscow. They thus came under bitter attack by the party leadership and were the victims of a deliberate campaign to identify them in the party mind with the ultralefts.

These problems were compounded by the repercussions of a scandal that had broken in Berlin in December 1926, when it was revealed that German engineers had secretly constructed three factories in the Soviet Union for the production of airplanes, artillery shells, and poison gas, some of which had been secretly shipped to Germany. The willingness of the Germans to cooperate in this project represented virtually the only source of European military technology for Soviet Russia; it also constituted a violation of the terms of the Versailles treaty prohibiting German rearmament, on the one hand, and a violation of the European embargo against Soviet arms development, on the other. At the height of the crisis Schwartz, a dissident Communist and a supporter of Karl Korsch, launched an attack on the KPD and the Soviet leaders in the Reichstag, angrily opposing any military alliance between the Soviet Union and any bourgeois state. This position was immediately disclaimed by a representative of the German Left Opposition, but that did not prevent the Soviet commentators from branding them with Schwartz's position. Also in March, German government spokesmen were quoted in a French newspaper as having said that Germany had agreed to the passage of French troops across Germany in case of need to come to the aid of neighboring Czechoslovakia or Poland. Trotsky sorted out these developments and what they represented in point 18 of the present memorandum.

By permission of the Harvard College Library. The text has been abridged to avoid repetition.

Dear Comrade:

I have now read for the first time one of the issues of the information bulletin of the Left Opposition in the German Communist Party [KPD], no. 5-6, March 1, 1927. This issue provides a fairly clear picture of the general features characterizing the group of Maslow, Fischer, Urbahns, et al.

1. One cannot fail to stress that the claim that this group is conducting a renegade struggle against the Soviet Union, declaring it to be a bourgeois state, is *untrue*. The opposite is the case. The group very sharply poses the question of the struggle against imperialist intervention, which threatens the Soviet Union. Its statement to the Eleventh Congress of the KPD says: "*We* on the other hand will surely stand with Soviet Russia with all our strength—quite unlike the 'friends' from the reformist camp."

In their open letter to the party congress they say: "In exactly the same way we reject the false, non-Communist views put forward on the Russian question by such figures as Katz, Korsch, or Schwartz.

"We see Soviet Russia as the first proletarian state in the world and reject as liquidationist any and all talk of the 'bourgeois' character of the Russian revolution (Korsch) or of preparations for a 'real proletarian revolution' in Russia (Schwartz). As always, we consider support for proletarian Russia against any imperialist attack and against the slander campaign of the Mensheviks to be the self-evident duty of every Communist."

The text gives a reference to the appropriate speeches by representatives of the left in the Reichstag, etc., sharply delineating themselves from the ultralefts. . . . They advance a number of proposals which have the purpose of placing the struggle against the dangers threatening the USSR on a more concrete basis. This fact seems to me the central one from the point of view of whether or not it is possible, now or later, to restore this group to its place in the Comintern.

2. Among the measures proposed by the lefts for the struggle against intervention (calling a conference of transport workers, sailors, workers in war industry, etc.) there is also this proposal:

"Immediate convening of the Anglo-Russian Committee, whose reformist members—it goes without saying—will undertake nothing against their 'own' imperialist bourgeoisie, which they support. In response, we should use this as a basis for exposing these traitors and thus retrieve what was lost during the British General Strike and open the eyes of the British proletariat to 'left' as well as right-wing reformism."

This proposal is completely correct and politically expedient. The entire Communist press, following the initiative of our press, has said quite a bit in the recent period about the danger of intervention. The Anglo-Russian Committee, which they tell us "is not a corpse," has been silent the whole time. There has been a sharp exchange of diplomatic notes between the British and Soviet governments. On England's part this is an open threat to peace. The Anglo-Russian Committee remains silent. British artillery has been bombarding Nanking. The Anglo-Russian Committee remains silent. If it exists, why does it hold its peace? And if it does not exist, why is its demise kept quiet? We see here a worse repetition of the policy which the Russian Opposition denounced after the derailment of the British General Strike and which it continued to denounce as long as the coalminers' strike went on, a strike that was being betrayed anew every day by the British members of the Anglo-Russian Committee. Whether we mean to or not, we are now providing cover for the British Mensheviks, who—as Lenin said—are far, far worse than their Russian counterparts.

3. In the article dealing with the Essen Congress of the KPD, which was then about to convene, the situation is characterized as follows: "The relative stabilization of capitalism in Germany is reflected in the consolidation of the reformists' influence on the proletariat. This is revealed not only in the parliamentary elections of the recent past but—far more important—in all the trade union elections."

Farther on in the same article we find a statement of exceptional importance, which sheds light on the special character of the "stabilization" in Germany.

"In reality the biggest mistake of the lefts at the party congress* was that *they were not hard and unrelenting enough in telling the party how severe the defeat in 1923 was. They did not draw the necessary conclusions, did not explain to the party soberly and straightforwardly the tendencies toward the relative stabilization of capitalism, and did not present a corresponding*

---

*The Frankfurt Congress in spring 1924, at which the lefts took control of the party from the Brandlerites.

program of struggle and slogans for the period immediately to come, although that would have been entirely possible, along with their completely correct and absolutely necessary sharp emphasis on programmatic issues" (emphasis mine—L.T.).

I think that this acknowledgment, correct in essence, is exceptionally valuable as an indication that the lefts have learned a great deal on this question. That the crucial phase of the revolutionary situation had been missed; that the ebbtide had already begun; that the tide would ebb with greater force from month to month—all this was clear enough even by November-December 1923. Brandler, one of those chiefly responsible for the policies leading to this extremely heavy defeat for the proletariat, did not wish to acknowledge the downturn. He said that the revolutionary situation was "developing." Klara Zetkin said the same. But the lefts, too, failed to assess the full depth of the defeat at that time and therefore failed to foresee the inevitability of an abrupt and deepgoing turn in the whole political situation. Moreover, in the heat of the moment they were ready to write off as "liquidators" those who pointed even then to the inevitability of this turn, who warned against policies that would have been absolutely correct and necessary in 1923, but which could become extremely dangerous and even disastrous in 1924, unquestionably the year of stabilization. The article I have quoted refers quite correctly to the fact that as a result of the defeat, on the one hand, and of an incorrect assessment of its meaning and consequences, on the other, there was found in the left camp—and in our opinion there predominated—"an absolutely false conception of what 'leftism' meant under the conditions of that time." Thus many lefts, as the article puts it—we would say, the left current as a whole—considered it then to be "impermissible in principle to speak of a slowing of the pace of the revolution."

This is very aptly put. Leftism consisted in a superficial impatience and lack of desire to "resign oneself" to the fact that at that time a revolutionary situation of exceptional importance had been let slip. On this issue the views of the left coincided oddly with those of Brandler, although of course each proceeded from different assumptions and inclinations. Brandler sought to conceal the dimensions of the defeat, accusing us of "overestimating" the revolutionary situation of 1923, and portrayed himself as an optimist looking to the future. The lefts continued to push an *immediate* revolutionary perspective and thus were forced to minimize the significance of the 1923 defeat and to view the political situation of 1924 not as the result of an abrupt turn but

as the direct continuation of what had gone before. At the Fifth
Comintern Congress Brandler sharply condemned the assessment of the situation made by Trotsky. Not one of the lefts
corrected him. On the contrary, on that point, agreement reigned.
At the time of the Fifth Congress, i.e., a year and a half after the
stabilization and the ebbing of the revolution had begun, Stalin
spoke of the masses turning *to the left* (!). Precisely from this
assessment flowed the incorrect general orientation, which led
the left leaders in Germany into a number of mistakes and
facilitated their rapid elimination. . . .

It is not true that the lefts (Maslow, R. Fischer, Urbahns, et al.)
deny the so-called stabilization. On the contrary, as we see from
the quoted passages, they explicitly recognize it—and in quite a
correct way—not as some automatic economic process but as a
change in the balance of class forces. They see absolutely
correctly that the main *political* symptom of the stabilization is
the strengthening of reformist influences on the proletariat. They
quite correctly see the cause of this to be the defeat of the
revolution in the fall of 1923, when the party did not know how to
take advantage of the unquestionably revolutionary situation
and lead the unquestionably revolutionary masses to the conquest of power. This colossal defeat, after colossal sufferings and
hopes, could have no result but a decline in the revolutionary
activism of the proletariat and consequently a shift in the
relationship of political forces in favor of the bourgeoisie. The
political strengthening of the bourgeoisie gave it the opportunity
to pursue policies aimed at strengthening its economic positions.
Hence the very possibility of a whole series of government
measures paving the way to economic "stabilization."

The charge of denying the *economic* stabilization, aimed at the
Russian Opposition, makes no sense. The economic chaos of 1923
(in Germany) could not have lasted long: the political strengthening of the bourgeoisie was bound to lead to a restoration of order
in the economic sphere, and this, in turn, to a further strengthening of the positions of the capitalists. But in a period of such
highly concentrated changes it is more necessary than ever to
understand economic and political phenomena clearly in their
dialectical interdependence. We have nothing in common with
the vulgar fatalism which says that the onset of stabilization
(how? from what? why?) interrupted the development of the
revolution in Germany. The revolution was interrupted not by
economic but by political factors—the incapacity of the Communist Party to cope with the situation. That test, and the party's

failure to meet it, took place before the eyes of the entire proletariat, the eyes of all the people. Hence the search for ways out of the hopeless crisis along other paths, with the leading role passing over to the bourgeoisie. Whoever has not understood that has understood nothing.

The lefts, as we see, have understood the abrupt change in the situation at the end of 1923. This by itself is a sign of growing political maturity. Our epoch, unlike the prewar period, is an *epoch of abrupt political turns.* One must know how to recognize and assess them in time. To say, a year and a half after the ebbtide has begun, that the masses are "moving to the left" means to head straight toward the most disastrous kinds of errors. The lefts have now understood this. The qualifications they place upon this assessment are of secondary importance and flow from their past. They have understood the most important thing—namely, that the methods and techniques that were correct in 1923 could have become ruinous in 1924-25. They have understood that it was not "impermissible in principle" (!) to speak of a slowdown in the pace of revolutionary developments. On the contrary, it is impermissible in principle to fail to take the facts into account, if you do not wish to break your neck.

Things are quite different when it comes to the German "ultralefts" (see their publication *Communist Policy* for March 1, 1927). They totally reject any acknowledgment of the relative stabilization. They regard as mere hypocrisy the statement that a new revolutionary situation will develop out of this stabilization as it unfolds. In what way, they ask, can a revolutionary situation grow out of stabilization, i.e., the consolidation of capitalism? They treat stabilization just as fatalistically as the opportunists do—but from the opposite direction. To them stabilization is a self-contained process of capitalist consolidation. To us it is first of all a process in the class struggle, with shifts and changes in the balance of forces in one direction or the other. Every new stage in the stabilization reproduces the contradictions between the classes and between the capitalist states in a new and higher form, with a permanent tendency toward the aggravation of those contradictions. Lodged within this very dialectic is the inevitability of both revolutionary and military convulsions. Only pathetic philistines could suppose that the Communist Party is only needed during an immediately revolutionary situation. It can be said with certainty that the present imperialist epoch will see to it that there is no shortage of revolutionary situations. The German Communist Party need only utilize the present stabilization period to make the appropriate preparations. Here Brandler has not had any success; the success of the lefts is undeniable. . . .

Of an entirely different nature is the question of possible agreement by a workers' state with capitalist states for the purpose of defending its existence. It is absolutely clear that the Soviet Union cannot put itself in a position of permanent or prolonged defensive or offensive alliance with any capitalist state, for their aims and policies are so opposed that a temporary coincidence of interests may arise only by way of exception, not as a rule. But exceptions are possible: for example, an agreement with bordering states to refuse permission for foreign troops to pass through for purposes of intervention. If such an agreement were possible, even if very costly, it would be entirely permissible, and under certain circumstances quite expedient and useful. A Communist Party in such a border state should speak in favor of such an agreement without tying its own hands in any way, of course, in regard to criticism of its own bourgeoisie. Here it would be a question not of supporting "one's own" oppressed bourgeoisie, but of a national war by an imperialist state, even though a weak one, and of utilizing the special circumstances in which the imperialist state finds itself, be it small or large, in order to facilitate the defense of the workers' state against attack by other imperialist powers.

The recent campaign over artillery shells, based on lies and slander, has been and is being waged as a preparation for intervention. But we are fully justified in posing the question on the level of principle: Is it permissible for a workers' state to conclude an agreement of a military and technical kind—for joint manufacture of ammunition, let us say—with an imperialist state which because of circumstances has an interest in doing this? If the workers' state in question were a backward one, if it did not have sufficient technical resources of its own, if it could, through such an agreement, strengthen its defense capacity, it would have the right and the duty to conclude such an agreement. Lenin long ago dealt with this question in a polemic with Bukharin [see *Collected Works,* vol. 27, pp. 36-39]. The occasion was that we did not refuse military and technical aid from French imperialism against the Hohenzollern offensive. Can't an honest person get a pistol from a bandit? Lenin asked, to point up the error of Bukharin's position in a popular way. Nothing is changed if the bandit is willing to supply the honest person with the pistol on the condition that he, the bandit, be allowed the chance to make a pistol for himself at the same time. It would be absurd, pathetic, shameful to deny a workers' state surrounded by powerful enemies the right to make episodic arrangements with even the worst of the imperialists, in order to strengthen the workers' state in military or economic respects. Every revolutionist in Germany—or simply every honest worker—will understand that without such agreements the workers' state would long ago have perished. Only pathetic and contemptible blowhards such as Korsch, Schwartz, and Company could see treason in something that is, on the contrary, the duty of the government of the proletarian dictatorship.

With that I conclude my comments on the issue of the information bulletin of the lefts that I received. My general conclusion has already been stated above: Brandler has learned nothing over these past few years; the lefts have learned a great deal. This is why I think they will win back their place in the International.

STALIN, THE PEASANT, AND THE GRAMOPHONE

April 14, 1927

*NOTE: As chairman of the Board of Electrotechnical Develop-
ment, Trotsky had become well acquainted with problems of
electrification. In early 1926 he urged the Politburo to initiate a
project to harness the rapids of the Dnepr River to produce
electricity. At the April 1926 plenum of the CC, Stalin compared
the proposal to build "Dneprostroi" (literally, the Dnepr Construction Project) to the situation of a peasant who, having saved a
few kopecks, instead of repairing the plow and renovating the
farm, bought a gramophone (or phonograph) and went bankrupt.
A few months later the Politburo was forced to make hasty plans
to start a Dneprostroi project after all, but without the benefit of
thought-out estimates and projections because of the waste of
time. At the plenum of April 1927, Stalin denied having compared
Dneprostroi to a gramophone and Trotsky quoted his words from
the stenographic record of the April 1926 plenum. Subsequently
Stalin suppressed his own remarks. This is the only extant
citation from the stenographic record.*

*To Trotsky, Dneprostroi symbolized the Stalinists' lack of
foresight and imagination, their timidity in using economic
planning, their empiricism, their failure to grasp the connection
between broad plans for industrialization and the needs of the
rural economy.*

By permission of the Library of Social History.

At the session of the plenum meeting on April 13 Comrade
Stalin permitted himself to say that it was "a lie" when I recalled
his words to the effect that the Dneprostroi project was equivalent to a muzhik buying a gramophone. Here is what Comrade
Stalin said, word for word, at the April plenum in 1926: "What we
are talking about . . . is making Dneprostroi pay for itself.
However, very large sums are needed for this, several hundred
million. How can we help but get ourselves in the situation of the

muzhik who, having saved a few kopecks, instead of repairing
the plow and renovating the farm, bought a gramophone and . . .
bankrupted himself? . . . [*Laughter.*] Can't we take into account
the decision of the congress that our industrial plans must
correspond to our resources? Nevertheless Comrade Trotsky
obviously has not taken this decision of the congress into
account" (Stenographic record of the plenum, p. 110).

Comrade Stalin attempts to explain his position on the question with the argument that in 1926 we were talking about
spending 500 million rubles over five years but now we are only
talking about 130 million. But even if this were the case, my words
did not constitute "a lie." In regard to the amounts under
discussion, however, here too Comrade Stalin is now introducing
absolute confusion, which shows that he still fails to understand
the question today, just as he failed to understand it last year.
The outlays for Dneprostroi were estimated a year ago at 110-120-
130 million and not at all at several hundred million. Since then
the estimates have undoubtedly been made more exact but they
remain within the framework of those figures. As for the new
factories, which would be the consumers of the power produced by
the Dnepr power plant, their cost is very roughly projected at 200-
300 million. However, these plants are not being built for
Dneprostroi. They are needed for their own sake. Dneprostroi is
being built in order to serve these necessary factories. Their cost
will probably be determined more exactly hereafter but essentially the difference cannot be very great. It is absolutely
nonsensical therefore to assert that at the plenum last year we
were talking about half a billion and not 110-130 million, as we
are now. Both then and now the amounts under discussion have
been on the same order.

It is hardly necessary to qualify those traits of Comrade
Stalin's character which enable him to throw the term "lie"
around so lightly.

DECLARATION OF THE EIGHTY-FOUR

May 1927

NOTE: The "Declaration of the Eighty-four" was drafted shortly after Chiang Kai-shek's anti-Communist coup and massacre of the Shanghai workers in mid-April 1927. Under the impact of that development the Opposition entered a period of renewed activity, an important part of which was the circulation of this declaration to obtain signatures of party members. It was circulating on the eve of the eighth plenum of the ECCI (May 18-30, 1927) and was submitted to the Politburo on May 25. The Opposition had until then failed to gain a hearing for its criticisms of the majority's policy on China—none of its statements or protests had been published, and the Politburo and the CC had refused to convene a special meeting, even off the record, to discuss the question. Trotsky finally forced a debate by formally appealing to the ECCI, which was his right within the statutes of the Comintern. (His speeches to the ECCI are in Leon Trotsky on China.*) Nevertheless, his appeal was denounced in* Pravda *as a breach of discipline and a disloyal act and his speeches were omitted from the unpublished stenographic record.*

Trotsky later defended the declaration as an effort which had "spread the burden of responsibility to many more shoulders and by that alone helped to soften the blow" (see "Letter on the Tactics of the Opposition," p. 298). It marked a change from the Opposition's October 1926 renunciation of factional activity and a new effort to win over the proletarian core of the party. Although it was written under the immediate influence of the disaster in China and the severing of relations with Britain, it dealt with a wide range of domestic issues and insisted upon the Opposition's democratic right to circulate its Platform in preparation for the coming Fifteenth Party Congress.

Some references in the declaration will be unfamiliar to readers. In the spring of 1927 the party CC announced a campaign to improve industrial efficiency through the "rationalization of production." By this was meant the effort to extend the division of labor, introduce the assembly line, use more machines, and standardize parts. Because of bureaucratic mismanagement, rationalization shortly came to be seen by the workers as a herald of layoffs that occurred when jobs were eliminated through mechanization.

The allusion in the postscript to the "arbitrary Martynovist line in Pravda*" stems from the role of Alexander Martynov, a former right-wing Menshevik who opposed the October Revolution and joined the ruling party only in 1923. He was the author of the theory of the "bloc of four classes" (bourgeoisie, petty bourgeoisie, peasantry, proletariat) in China, which was used to justify the policy of having the Chinese CP remain inside of and subordinate to the Kuomintang—on the basis that Communists had to work with the progressive bourgeoisie.*

"The 'new' school—the so-called 'youth'" (p. 238) refers to the younger generation of party intellectuals who were disciples of Bukharin but carried his theories farther and made them more explicit than Bukharin was willing to do. These were Maretsky, Stetsky, and other "Red Professors" who preached reliance on the "economically strong" peasant in the countryside and other neo-Narodnik ideas in the press, the universities, and the propaganda departments.

On p. 226, the declaration complains that the party press attributes to the Opposition the demand to break with the Kuomintang. Actually, Radek and Zinoviev did not agree with this demand and thus it was not a demand of the United Opposition but one of Trotsky and his cothinkers. Radek and the Zinovievists would not consent to this demand until mid-summer 1927, when the left Kuomintang began expelling Communists anyway. In 1931, Trotsky wrote that Radek's vote had put the Zinovievists in the majority in the Opposition center, and that as a result the Opposition had had an equivocal position on this question (see Leon Trotsky on China, *pp. 492-93).*

The question of the Anglo-Russian Committee had become intertwined with the question of the Chinese revolution when the General Council of the British Trades Unions supported British imperialism's role in the bombardment of Nanking in March 1927. Despite this, the Soviet leaders refused to withdraw from the ARC. In April representatives of the Soviet trade unions again met with representatives of the British unions in Berlin and renewed their support to the ARC, even though the ARC had refused to endorse a CP-backed proposal for a "Hands Off China" campaign. On May 12, British police raided the Soviet trade headquarters in London and opened an anti-Communist witch-hunt.

From Bulletin Communiste, *July-September 1927. Translated from the French by Jeff White and corrected against the Russian by George Saunders. Several of the names are slightly at variance with the signatures of the "Statement of the 121" (December 3, 1927) either in their spelling or in the dates given for party membership; this is probably because they were hastily typed from handwriting on copies of the declaration, which was originally known as the "Declaration of the Eighty-three." Later the number of signatories rose to five hundred, and still later to three thousand.*

To the Politburo of the Central Committee of the AUCP(B):
Comrades:

The big mistakes made or tolerated by the leadership on the Chinese revolution have contributed to a grave defeat. We can escape this situation only by following the road mapped out by Lenin. The extremely abnormal conditions in which we are discussing the questions related to the Chinese revolution create a great deal of tension in the party. The one-sided "discussion" carried out in *Pravda* and *Bolshevik* is a systematic distortion of the Opposition's views (thus they attribute to the Opposition the demand to break with the Kuomintang). This demonstrates the desire of the leading group of the Central Committee to hide its blunders behind a campaign against the Opposition. As a result, the attention of the party is oriented in the wrong direction.

Finally, and with respect to the erroneous line of the Central Committee on the essential questions of party policy, our Bolshevik-Leninist duty demands that we address ourselves, through this declaration, to the Central Committee.

1. It is not enough to say that we have undergone an enormous defeat in China; we must look at *how* and *why* it happened.

Although we already have in China a powerful working class; although the proletariat of Shanghai in a most difficult situation was able to rise up and take over the city; although the Chinese proletariat receives powerful support from the rebellious peasantry; in short, although there were all the conditions for the victory of a "Chinese 1905" (Lenin), the result is that the Chinese workers pulled the fat out of the fire for the bourgeoisie, in much the same way as the European workers were condemned to do in the revolutions of 1848.

All the conditions were there for arming the Chinese workers (above all in Shanghai and Hankow). Nevertheless, the heroic proletariat of Shanghai found itself disarmed and the workers of Hankow are just as disarmed at the present time, even though Hankow is in the hands of the "left" Kuomintang.

"The line" in China, *in fact*, translates as follows: We must not arm the workers, or organize revolutionary strikes, or incite the peasants against the landowners, or publish a Communist daily paper, or criticize the bourgeois gentlemen of the right wing of the Kuomintang, and the petty bourgeois of the "left" Kuomintang, or build Communist cells in Chiang Kai-shek's army, or call for the formation of soviets, so as not to "drive off" the bourgeoisie or "scare off" the petty bourgeoisie, or disturb the government of the "bloc of four classes."

By way of reply, and in order to thank us for such a policy, the Chinese national bourgeoisie, as might have been expected, waits for the right moment, then guns down the workers and appeals for aid from the imperialist powers of Japan today, America tomorrow, and England the day after.

The defeat in China has left the Communist parties of the whole world, and broad circles of the AUCP, in tremendous disarray. Only yesterday they were told that the national army in China was really the revolutionary Red Army, that Chiang Kai-shek was their revolutionary commander, and that China was today (or, at the very latest, tomorrow) taking the "noncapitalist" road of development. But now, in struggle against the real Leninist line of Bolshevism, lame articles and speeches are published saying that in China there is no industry at all, no railways, that China is almost at the early stages of feudalism, that the Chinese are illiterate, etc., that it is too early to put forward the program of the revolutionary-democratic dictatorship of the proletariat and the peasantry, or for the creation of soviets. Instead of correcting our mistakes, we compound them.

A defeat in China could have direct repercussions on the future of the USSR. If the imperialists unite for a long enough period of time to "pacify" China, they will then march against us, the USSR. The defeat of the Chinese revolution could bring war against the USSR much, much closer. At the present time the party is unable to examine the Chinese problem—a crucial one for it as the first party of the Communist International. A principled discussion of the problems of the Chinese revolution is forbidden. Meanwhile, a violent, unilateral "discussion" is already being conducted by the leading group. This discussion is more precisely a campaign against the Opposition, with the aim of hiding the incorrect line of the dominant wing of the Central Committee.

2. The General Strike of the past year in England, which was betrayed and sold out by the General Council, ended in defeat, as did the miners' strike. Despite a massive shift to the left by millions of workers, and despite the fact that the treachery and wrongness of reformism have never before been so exposed to the light, the organized revolutionary wing of the English workers' movement has gained very little influence.

The main cause of this was indecisive, halfhearted, and inconsistent leadership on our part. The financial aid given the English miners by the Russian workers was magnificent. But the tactic of the Central Committee with regard to the Anglo-Russian Committee was completely wrong.

We upheld the authority of the traitors of the General Council during the period that was most critical for them, the weeks and months of the General Strike and the miners' strike. We helped them stay in control. We ended up capitulating to them at the recent Berlin conference, by recognizing the General Council as the *only* representative of the English proletariat (and even as the sole representative of their point of view) and by endorsing the principle of nonintervention in the internal affairs of the English workers' movement.

Against the background of the events in China, the decisions of the recent conference of the Anglo-Russian Committee take on a sinister character. In the entire international press, Tomsky and the other representatives of the All-Union Central Council of Trade Unions (AUCCTU) have declared that the Berlin conference had a "cordial character," that all decisions were made "unanimously," and that these decisions represent a so-called "victory" for the world proletariat, etc.

This is a falsehood and a lie, and can only lead the English proletariat to new defeats.

The Berlin conference did not say a word about the bandit role played by British imperialism in China, and did not even demand the withdrawal of imperialist troops. At the very moment that a direct war was being launched against the Chinese revolution, the Committee maintained a criminal silence, or, to put it differently, did exactly what the British bourgeoisie needed.

Can anyone doubt for a minute that those who now openly betray the interests of the English proletariat before the eyes of the whole world, even on so serious a question as the freedom of the union movement in England, will tomorrow, in the event of war against the USSR, play the same base and treacherous role as these gentlemen did in 1914?

Between the wrong line followed in China and the wrong line on the question of the Anglo-Russian Committee there is the closest inner connection. The same line pervades all the policies of the Communist International. In Germany, hundreds of left proletarians, the vanguard, have been expelled, for the simple reason that they solidarized with the Russian Opposition. The right-wing elements have more and more influence in all our parties. The crudest right-wing errors (in Germany, Poland, France, and elsewhere) remain uncorrected; yet the slightest voice of criticism from the left meets with expulsion. Thus, the prestige of the AUCP and the October Revolution is used to shift the Communist parties to the right, away from the Leninist line. All this, taken as a whole, prevents the Comintern from preparing for and carrying out the struggle against war in the Leninist manner.

3. No Marxist can dispute that the wrong political line in China and on the Anglo-Russian Committee is no accident. It is an extension and completion of the wrong line in domestic policy.

The economy of the Soviet Union has in general completed its period of reconstruction. During this period, we have registered substantial economic gains. Industry, agriculture, and other branches of the economy are about to reach prewar levels, or have surpassed them. The cooperatives have also registered gains. These advances are the best proof of the correctness of Lenin's New Economic Policy, and the best reply to the enemies of the October Revolution.

The land of proletarian dictatorship has shown itself entirely capable of socialist construction; it has scored some preliminary successes in this sphere, thereby contributing, along with the proletariat of other countries, to the definitive victory of socialism throughout the world.

However, simultaneously with these solid successes, major difficulties have become evident as a product of the economic reconstruction period. These difficulties, which spring from the insufficient development of our productive forces, i.e., our general economic backwardness, are made worse by the fact that they are hidden from the ranks of the party as a whole. Instead of a Marxist analysis of the real position of the proletarian dictatorship, a false, petty-bourgeois theory is brought forward of "socialism in one country," which has absolutely nothing in common with Marxism-Leninism.

This crude reversal of Marxism makes it more difficult for the party to see the *class content* of the economic processes which are now taking place. And yet it is precisely the class shifts unfavorable to the proletariat and the difficult situation for the broad masses of the population that constitute the *negative features* of the stage of the revolution that we are now passing through.

The questions of *wages and unemployment* are taking on an increasingly sharp character.

Incorrect policies are hastening the growth of forces hostile to the proletarian dictatorship: kulaks, NEPmen, and bureaucrats. This makes it impossible to use the material resources of the country as much as we want to and should for industry and the public sector as a whole. The lagging of heavy industry behind the demands of the national economy (the goods famine, high prices, unemployment) and of the entire Soviet system (national defense) strengthens the capitalist elements in our economy— especially in the countryside.

Wages have stopped rising; there is even a tendency to lower them for certain groups of workers. Instead of the practice followed up to now of increasing wages in accordance with increases in *labor productivity,* it is now being asserted as a general rule that wages can rise only on condition that the *intensity of labor* goes up (see paragraph two of the resolution of the Congress of Soviets, based on Kuibyshev's report). This means that from now on workers in the USSR can improve their material situation not in proportion to our economic growth and technological improvements but only as a result of greater physical exertion, a greater expediture of muscle power. This is the *first time* the question has been posed this way. Meanwhile the intensity of labor has at present reached the prewar level on the whole and in some cases has even surpassed it. This policy violates the interests of the working class.

Unemployment is growing, at the expense not only of peasants who have come in from the countryside but also of the traditional layer of industrial workers. The actual unemployment is greater than that on the books. The expansion of the army of unemployed worsens the economic situation of the working class as a whole.

The housing conditions of the workers in many places continue to deteriorate in terms of overcrowding and the restriction of tenants' rights.

The reduction in the number of adolescents hired [under the *bronya* system of guaranteed employment for a certain percen-

tage of youth newly entering the labor force] and the introduction
of unpaid apprenticeships mean an abrupt worsening of conditions for working class youth.

The dangers flowing from all this are clear, because the
relationship between our party and the working class is decisive
for the future of the workers' state.

Lowering the prices of manufactured goods has been accomplished only to a very small degree. Despite the Opposition's
voting at the plenum in February of this year *in favor* of the
resolution to lower prices, all the official propaganda has been
geared to accusing the Opposition of *not wanting to lower prices*.
Such propaganda leads the party astray and distracts its attention from the fundamental issues in our economic policy. The
problem of lowering prices is not helped one bit by this kind of
thing. Meanwhile there is growing discontent and impatience
among consumers in city and countryside alike.

Differentiation among the peasantry is proceeding at an
increasing rate. From the slogan "Enrich yourselves" and the
call for the kulak to "grow over into socialism," the dominant core
of the Central Committee has arrived at the point where they
maintain complete silence about the differentiation among the
peasants and play down this process, on the one hand, and on the
other, they place their bets in practice on the "strong peasant."

On the tenth anniversary of the October Revolution we have a
situation in which more than three million agricultural workers
play an extremely restricted role in the soviets, the cooperatives,
and the Communist Party cells; and the poor peasants are still
given inadequate attention and assistance. The resolution of the
last Congress of Soviets on agriculture says not one word on the
differentiation in the countryside, and so is silent on the *essential
question* of the economic and political development of the countryside. All of this weakens our support in the countryside and
impedes the alliance of the working class and poor peasants with
the middle peasants.

This alliance can be developed and reinforced only by a
systematic struggle against the exploitative aspirations of the
kulaks. We tend to underestimate the growth and importance of
the kulak. Such a policy is fraught with dangers that are
accumulating and can suddenly explode. Nevertheless, the official apparatus of the party and the soviets strikes out at the *left*,
thus leaving the door wide open to the real danger, the class
danger from the *right*.

The proposal to exempt from the agricultural tax 50 percent of peasant households—that is, the poor and badly-off peasants—is bitterly attacked, although the political and economic conditions of the countryside justify the measure completely. A few tens of millions of rubles out of a budget of five billion is of altogether minimal importance, whereas to take this sum from the poorer peasant households is to accelerate the process of differentiation and weaken the position of the proletarian dictatorship in the countryside. "To come to an agreement with the middle peasant— while not for a moment renouncing the struggle against the kulak and at the same time firmly relying solely on the poor peasant" [*Collected Works,* vol. 28, p. 191]—that is what our policy in the countryside ought to be.

Last September we read an appeal signed by three comrades occupying extremely important posts (Rykov, Stalin, and Kuiby-shev) which said that the Opposition, that is, a part of our own party and a part of our Central Committee, wanted to "rob" the peasantry. Instead of that, the appeal promised to follow a "regime of economy" to reduce nonproductive expenditure by 300 to 400 million rubles a year. In reality this bureaucratically distorted struggle to economize has led to new blows against the workers and has shown no tangible positive results.

The *rationalization* of industry has not been carried out according to an overall, considered plan, and has meant that more and more new categories of workers are being driven into the ranks of the jobless, without any accompanying drop in production costs.

It is necessary to reverse all decisions of the last two years that have *worsened* the situation for the workers, and to emphasize forcefully that without a planned and systematic improvement— even if at first it is only a slow improvement—in the conditions of the working class, this "main productive force" (Marx), it is impossible, in the present situation, to salvage either the economy or the construction of socialism.

The fundamental prerequisite for solving the problems facing the party at present in the sphere of economic construction, with the highly complicated and confused class relations within the country and the mounting threat of a hostile attack upon the USSR from without, and with the delay of the international proletarian revolution, *is the revival of democracy within the party and reinforcement of the real, living, and effective links between the party and the working class.*

We need iron discipline in the party, as in Lenin's time. But we also need democracy in the party, as in Lenin's time. The whole party, from top to bottom, in Bolshevik fashion, must be ideologically and organizationally a strongly welded collectivity, with real, rather than official, participation as a united force in the solution of all the questions facing the party, the working class, and the whole country.

The internal regime established for the party in recent times has caused an immense decline in the activity of the party, this leading force of the proletarian revolution. For the broad layers of rank-and-file members the opportunities for discussing and helping to solve the essential problems of the revolution in a fully conscious way have been restricted and minimized in the extreme. This could not help but affect the attitude of the working class toward the party and the level of activism of the working class as a whole—and it has affected them in the most negative way.

The regime established in the party has been carried over in full into the unions. The Russian working class, having behind it the experience of three revolutions which it made under the leadership of the Bolshevik Party and of Lenin, a class which has cemented the foundations of Soviet power with the blood of its finest sons, which has accomplished miracles of heroism and organization, has all the requirements for putting its creative and organizational abilities to use in the broadest way. But at present the established regime obstructs the development of activism by the workers and prevents them from setting about the construction of socialism to the fullest extent.

The proletarian dictatorship is being weakened in its very class base. At the Eleventh Congress Lenin told the party that the principal task of our economic work is to know how to pick the right people; but the present line runs directly counter to his advice. In practice, in many cases, the most conscientious and most qualified party workers, who show initiative in economic questions, are being driven from the factories, and they are replaced almost always by elements who do not work for socialism but who make themselves the obedient servants of their immediate supervisors. The flagrantly incorrect aspects of the party's internal regime thus affect the most vital interests of the masses in all their millions.

4. *The international situation* is becoming more and more tense. The danger of war is increasing. The central task of the AUCP and the entire vanguard of the world proletariat is to *avert war (or at least put it off as long as possible), to support and defend at all costs the policy of peace, which only our party and*

the Soviet power are capable of carrying out in full.

The cause of the USSR is the cause of the world proletariat. To turn aside the danger of a new war threatening the USSR is the most important task of the international proletariat. But we cannot do that by participating in a bloc with the traitors of the General Council. No serious struggle to prevent war is possible in alliance with Purcell and Citrine. To make approaches toward the Social Democratic and unaffiliated *workers* and involve them in the struggle against war is possible only by going *over the heads* of their traitorous leaders, and by *struggling* against them.

We insist that the CC assist the coming plenum of the enlarged Executive of the Comintern to study seriously, in detail, without bias, and relying on documents, the recent events in China (and that they involve in this work the comrades who have defended our point of view). In addition, the ECCI must consider the questions of China and the Anglo-Russian Committee in their fullest aspects, and the press of our party and the international Communist press must provide the opportunity for these problems to be discussed fully and in detail (with all due observance, of course, of the necessary secrecy).

The strengthening of the USSR internationally requires the strengthening of the revolutionary proletarian line within the USSR. We are weakened by the delay in raising wages, the deterioration of the workers' housing conditions, and the growing unemployment. We are weakened by the incorrect policy toward the poor peasants. We are weakened by the errors in our economic policy. We are weakened by the defeat of the British workers and of the Chinese revolution. We are weakened by a bad internal administration within the party.

All of our party's policies suffer from the rightward direction they have been given. If the new blow being prepared against the left, against the Opposition, is carried out, it will give a completely free hand to the elements of the right, the nonproletarians and antiproletarian elements, which are partly inside our party but for the most part outside it. The blow to the left will have the inevitable consequence of the triumph of Ustryalovism. Ustryalov has long been calling for such a blow against the Opposition in the name of a "neo-NEP." Ustryalov is the most logical, most principled, and most uncompromising enemy of Bolshevism. The self-satisfied administrators, officials who are after their bosses' jobs, petty-bourgeois elements who have made their way into positions of authority and who look down on the masses—they all feel the ground growing firmer and firmer beneath their feet and they raise their heads higher and higher. These are all neo-NEP elements. Behind them stand the Ustryalovite specialists. And in the last row are the NEPman and the kulak, the latter under the shingle "strong peasant." This is where the real danger is coming from.

In domestic matters the class shifts have not become so plainly evident as in foreign policy, because the domestic processes have developed much more slowly than the General Strike in England or the revolution in China. But the essential trends of official policy are the same in both areas, and the slower the pace at which they develop domestically, the more seriously and strongly they may come to the fore.

Lenin defined the Soviet state as a workers' state with bureaucratic deformations in a country with a predominantly peasant population. He said this in early 1921. This definition is more appropriate today than ever before. During the years of NEP, the new bourgeoisie of the city and the countryside has grown into a real force. In this situation, to deliver a blow against the Opposition means nothing other than to try, under the cover of hypocritical cries for unity ("The initiators of a split always cry the loudest for unity," said Engels), to discredit and destroy *the proletarian, Leninist, left wing of our party*. Such destruction would mean the swift, inevitable reinforcement of the right wing of the AUCP and the equally inevitable prospect of the subordination of the proletariat's interests to those of other classes.

5. We always need party unity, especially in the present circumstances. In the school of Lenin we all learned that Bolsheviks must direct their efforts toward unity *on the basis of a revolutionary and proletarian political line*. During the most adverse historical conditions—throughout the years of illegality; then in 1917, when, in the midst of a world war, we fought for power; in 1918, when, in an unprecedentedly difficult situation, we examined the question of the treaty of Brest-Litovsk; and in the subsequent years under Lenin—the party openly discussed disputed issues and found the correct road to a real unity, not an artificial one. That saved us in situations that were much more serious than the present one.

The main danger is that the actual content of the differences is being hidden from the party and the working class. Every attempt to lay the disputed issues before the party is denounced as an attack on party unity. The wrong line is imposed from above by mechanical means. Thus artificial unity is officially created and "everything is fine." In reality, this state of affairs weakens the position of the party in the working class and the position of the working class in its struggle against class enemies. Such a situation, which creates tremendous obstacles to the political development of our party and to a correct Leninist leadership, must inevitably result in extremely serious dangers for our party at the first sharp turn, or at the first severe blow, whether domestically or internationally.

We see these dangers clearly and consider it our duty to forewarn the CC, precisely to rally the party ranks on the basis of a *Leninist policy* in both international and domestic questions.

*   *   *

How to eliminate the differences and rectify the class line, without in any way harming the unity of the party?

The way we always did in Lenin's time.

We propose that the CC decide as follows:

1. Call a plenum of the CC no later than three months before the Fifteenth Party Congress for a preliminary discussion of all the questions confronting the Fifteenth Congress.

2. This plenum must do its utmost to work out *unanimous* decisions, which will best assure maximum unity and a genuine elimination of the conflict within the party.

3. The plenum must instruct the delegation of the AUCP to the Comintern to take the initiative in carrying out a number of measures in the ECCI to readmit those expelled comrades who request it and who are still supporters of the Comintern's platform and to create *full* unity in the fraternal parties. (This would obviously not include such elements as Katz and Korsch.)

4. If nevertheless at this plenum some differences of principle come to light, they will have to be formulated and published in good time. Each comrade must have the opportunity to defend his point of view before the party, in the press and at meetings, as in Lenin's time.

5. The debate must be conducted in a strictly comradely and businesslike framework, without venom or exaggeration.

6. The draft theses of the CC, of local organizations, and of individual party members or groups of members must be published in *Pravda* (or in the supplement to *Pravda*) as well as in local party newspapers, beginning about two or three months before the congress.

7. The party publishing houses must guarantee the timely publication of pamphlets, books, collections of articles, etc., written by comrades who want to express their points of view to

the party, even if they are not those of the party majority.

8. The main slogan for the preparation of the congress must be *unity*—the genuine Leninist unity of the AUCP.

P.S.—Our declaration has naturally been delayed while we collected signatures, and we are obliged to submit it [to the CC] at a time when the leadership is waging a campaign against Zinoviev on the pretext that he spoke on May 9 at a so-called nonparty meeting. Those of us who heard Zinoviev's speech, or who have been able to read a transcript of it, are prepared to place our signatures, without hesitation, at the bottom of the speech. In a restrained way, with irreproachable adherence to party principles, he expressed the alarm felt by broad circles of the party over the arbitrary Martynovist line in *Pravda*. Zinoviev's speech of course was simply a pretext to start attacking him. As is evident from our entire document, the direct preparation for this campaign against the Opposition began with the first news of the defeat of the Chinese revolution.

As far as we can tell, the immediate aim of the campaign against Zinoviev is to remove him from the Central Committee, *before* the congress and *without* a congress, in order to get rid of one of the critics of the party's incorrect line during the period of preparations for the congress and at the congress. The same thing could be repeated tomorrow with other Opposition members of the CC. Such procedures can only hurt the party.

The measure taken under the pressure of the Political Bureau to forbid the participation of Zinoviev in the plenum of the Comintern has no precedent in the history of the Communist International. They have removed one of the founders of the Comintern, its *first president*—elected on the nomination of Lenin. This removal of Zinoviev, who is still a member of the Executive Committee, at a time when the most important problems of the international workers' movement were under examination, can only be explained by a *lack of political courage* on the part of those who prefer administrative measures to ideological debate.

Besides its political significance, this action is also a crude violation of the formal rights of Zinoviev, a member of the Executive Committee elected unanimously at the Fifth World Congress. The road of removal and slander of Leninists is not the road of unity for the Communist International.

It is highly probable that this declaration will serve as a pretext to accuse us of factional activity. Above all, the functionaries who are ready for anything and those "men of letters" of the "new" school—the so-called "youth"—will spare no effort. But this declaration is aimed directly at them, among others. Some of them will be the first to abandon the cause of the proletariat in time of danger. In issuing this declaration, we are doing our duty as revolutionaries and as party members as it has always been understood among the ranks of the real Bolshevik-Leninists.

*   *   *

Under this declaration we have collected in a very short time dozens of signatures of Old Bolsheviks. We do not doubt for a minute that other Old Bolsheviks who are widely dispersed in the USSR as well as abroad would have added their signatures to this declaration if they had known about it.

We do not doubt for a moment that the point of view expressed here is shared by a large section of our party, especially its working class section. Whoever knows the real mood among the working class party members fnows that this is true.

Aleksandrov, A.N. (party member since 1917); Avramson, A.B. (1914); Alsky, A.S. (1917); Arshavsky, Z. (1915); Beloborodov, A.G. (1907); Belyais, Yan Yanovich (1912); Budzinskaya, R.L. (1914); Babakhan, N. (1917); Visnevskaya (1905); Vorobev, V. (1914); Valentinov, G. (1915); Vilensky (Sibiryakov) (1903); Vujović (member of the ECCI; member of the Yugoslav party since 1912); Vrachev, I. Yak. (1917); Vasilev, Iv. (1904); Vardin, Il. (1907); Gertik, Artem (1902); Gertsberg (March 1917); Gessen, S.M. (member of the ECCI elected at the Fifth Congress; member of the AUCP since 1916); Guralsky; Gordon, Nik. (1903); Yemelyanov, N.A. (1899); Yelkovich, N.A. (1917); Yevdokimov, G. Yer. (1903; member of the CC); Yezhov, P.S. (March 1917); Zhuk, Aleks. Vas. (1904); Zinoviev, G.E.; Zorin, S. (May 1917); Zaks-Gladnev (1906); Ivanov, V.I. (1915); Kospersky, I. (March 1917); Katta, M. (1917); Kuklin (1903); Kanatchikova (1914); Kostritsky, I.; Kovalenko, P. (date illegible); Korolev, A. (1916); Kavtaradze (1903); Kozlova-Passek (September 1917); Lelevich, A.G. (1917); Lobashev, G. (1917); Lifshits, B. (1915); Lazko, M. (1905); Lizdin (1892; member of the CCC); Muralov, N.I. (1903; member of the CCC); Minichev (1911); Maleta, V. (1916); Maltsev, B. (1917); Maten, G. (May 1917); Naumov, I.K. (1913); Nazimov, A. Ye. (July 1917); Ostrovskaya, N. (1905); Peterson, A. (1917; member of the CCC); Pozdeeva (1917); Primakov, V. (1914); Pyatakov, Yu. L. (1910; member of the CC); Psalmopevnev (1916); Ravich, O.N. (1903); Radek, K. (1902); Rem. M.S.; Serebryakov, L.P. (1905); Smirnov, Iv. Nik. (1899); Sergeev, A.N. (1914); Sokolov, A.A. (1914); Safarov, G. (1908); Smilga, I.T. (1907; member of the CC); Samsonov, M. (1903); Sosnovsky, L. (1903); Sarkis (1917); Sadovskaya (September 1917); Ter-Vaganyan (1912); Tumanov (April 1917); Trotsky, L.D.; Fedorov, Gr. (1907); Fonbershtein (1917); Foshkin, F.P. (September

1917); Kharitonov, M.M. (1905); Tsaturov, A.A.; Sharov, Ya. (1904); Shurygin, A.S. (1914); Shepsheleva, M.I.; Shuster, A. (1912); Tsibulsky, Z.S. (1904); Eltsin, B. (1898).

LETTER TO KRUPSKAYA

May 17, 1927

NOTE: Nadezhda K. Krupskaya, Lenin's widow, had been one of the signers of the "Declaration of the Thirteen" in July 1926, but had separated from the Opposition by the time of the Fifteenth Conference in October-November of that year. In the period of renewed Opposition activity following Chiang's mid-April coup in China, Trotsky sent repeated protests to the Politburo over its China policy, but none of them were published or circulated. On May 9, Zinoviev spoke at a public meeting and protested Pravda's boycott of the Opposition's views. For this he was censured by the Moscow and Leningrad party committees and by the Central Committee.

Evidently, Krupskaya wrote to Zinoviev criticizing the Opposition for making a "fuss" over China. On May 20, Pravda published an undated letter to its editorial board that was apparently a compromise between Krupskaya and the CC. In it she explained her differences with the Opposition (it had gone too far in its criticisms, its criticism had become factional) and called for an objective and sober discussion of the disputed questions, saying that criticism in the party was of paramount importance.

By permission of the Harvard College Library.

Dear N.K.:

I am writing to you on a typewriter so that you won't have to bother deciphering my handwriting, which has not improved with the years.

I read your letter. Although it was addressed personally to G. E. [Zinoviev], its subject is, to be sure, far from personal, so I therefore permit myself to speak out about it.

Most of all, I am struck by the word "fuss." Kosior used this word at the last plenum in relation to our speeches on the crushing of the Chinese workers and our capitulation to British Menshevism. Who is right in these questions: we or Stalin? Or is there a third position? Can one really speak of a "fuss" without having answered, in accordance with Lenin, this essential question?! "Fuss"—this signifies a squabble of little or no importance. What is this—the crushing of the Chinese workers by our "ally" Chiang Kai-shek, whom we feed, clothe, shoe, and acclaim, while we order the Chinese Communists to subordinate themselves to him—is it a detail, a trifle, which we can pass over? Or again, that we declared before the whole world our *unity* with the thoroughly prostituted British Mensheviks while their dirty work in relation to the British workers, China, and ourselves is in full swing? What is this: a joke, a trifle? And our criticism—is this a "fuss"?!

Perhaps it is still possible to doubt the extent to which such facts as the electoral instructions, "enrich yourselves," and so forth, are symptomatic and alarming. But in the light of recent events, can there be even the slightest doubt that *Stalin and Bukharin are betraying Bolshevism at its very core*—proletarian revolutionary internationalism? In the question of our relations with the Chinese "national" bourgeoisie, surely *the entire history of Bolshevism, starting with 1904 when this question was first actually posed,* has been totally negated.

N.K., you don't say a word on this point: Is Stalin's position or ours correct concerning the question on which the whole course of the Chinese revolution and the whole course of the Comintern depend? You merely repeat the word that Kosior tossed off, "fuss."

You say that self-criticism is one thing and criticism from the outside is another. But aren't you a member of the Central Control Commission? So why don't you secure for party members the possibility of self-criticism? Haven't we asked the Politburo and presidium of the Central Control Commission to convene a closed session of the plenum, without taking minutes, in order to discuss the essence of the situation? Of course, we intend to make an all-out fight there for the basic principles of Bolshevism on the basic issues of world revolution. But they have denied us this request. Why indeed is there no "self-criticism"? Not so long ago we both said that self-criticism does not develop because we have *an unhealthly, rude, and disloyal regime.* Do you really think that the regime improved during the last half-year? Or are the questions that require self-criticism today too petty and insignificant? A "fuss"?

We, the revolutionary wing of the party, have suffered a defeat. That is indisputable. But we have suffered a defeat of the same sort that Bolshevism suffered in 1907-12. The defeat of the

German revolution in 1923; the defeats in Bulgaria, in Estonia; the defeat of the General Strike in Britain; the defeat of the Chinese revolution in April, have severely weakened international communism. This process has a twofold expression: on one hand, during these years the number of members of Communist parties and the number of votes they received were severely reduced; and, on the other hand, the opportunist wing was greatly strengthened. Are we really excluded from this worldwide process? The grave defeats of the world revolution and the slowness of our growth surely have an impact on our proletariat, too. The bureaucratic blockheads do not understand this. They think that the official "educational" circulars of Agitprop and not the worldwide social and political processes determine the outlook of the proletariat. The ebbing of the international revolutionary mood of our proletariat is a fact, which is reinforced by the party regime and the teaching of false doctrines ("socialism in one country," and so forth). Under these conditions, is it any wonder that the left, revolutionary, Leninist wing of the party has to swim against the stream? *The more our forecast is sustained by the facts, the more furiously they fulminate against us.* This proceeds entirely from social laws and is inevitable for the genuinely Marxist wing in a period of a temporary but deep dip in the revolutionary curve. But we, and only we, preserve the ideological succession of revolutionary Bolshevism, learning and teaching—without Lenin—to apply the Leninist method of analyzing what is being done, and of forecasting what is in the offing. Didn't we warn the party about the inevitable defeat of the unarmed proletariat by Chiang Kai-shek, whom we armed? Didn't we predict almost a year ago the shameful Berlin capitulation to the very principles that Vladimir Ilyich dedicated almost his entire life to struggling against? And were we wrong in stating that *the wrong line being followed in domestic policy could take forms that are a menace to us in case of war?* And now, while it is still not too late, aren't we obliged to raise an outcry about this with one-hundredfold force? Is this really a "fuss"? Can it possibly be a "fuss"?

Stalin has now decided to change the "war of attrition" that has been waged for the past half-year against the Opposition into a "war of annihilation." Why? Because Stalin has grown weaker. His bankruptcy on the Chinese and Anglo-Russian questions is obvious, as are the heavy consequences of this bankruptcy for our international situation. The growing right wing is bringing pressure on Stalin: why did you get involved in the General Strike or in China? Why did you excite Chamberlain, calling forth the danger of intervention? We will build socialism in one country. That is the *basic, fundamental, essential tendency of the present moment, which is "defeating" us now.* Precisely because Stalin has become immeasurably weaker under the blows of the muffled criticism from the right and our half-stifled criticism from the left, he must change his war of attrition into a war of annihilation. The question is one not of trifles and not of small modifications, but of the basic line of Bolshevism on basic questions. Whoever says "fuss" is proposing that we swim with the stream in conditions where the stream is flowing against Bolshevism.

No, N.K., that we will not do. We will swim against the stream, even if you repeat aloud after Kosior the word "fuss." And we never felt as deeply and unmistakably our ties with the entire tradition of Bolshevism as we do now, in these difficult days, when we and only we are preparing the future of the party and the Comintern.

From my soul I wish you good health.

THE PARTY CRISIS DEEPENS

June 27, 1927

NOTE: The submission of the "Declaration of the Eighty-four" and Trotsky's speech at the ECCI plenum brought things to a head. Stalin's rejoinder was to play up the dangers of war facing the Soviet Union and to speak ominously of a "united front from Chamberlain to Trotsky." News about the continuing debacle in China was suppressed so absolutely that at one point Zinoviev demanded that Bukharin, the editor of Pravda, *should face charges before a party court.*

The close of the ECCI plenum was followed by wholesale "tranfers" and reassignments of leading Oppositionists, in many cases out of the country, on the pretext that they were needed in various diplomatic positions. (Ten years later these assignments would be used to provide fodder for charges that Oppositionists had engaged in anti-Soviet espionage and collaboration with capitalist governments.) Rank-and-file Oppositionists were not treated so diplomatically: they were fired from their jobs and sent packing to remote areas on no pretext at all.

On June 9, Smilga left Moscow for a post on the Manchurian border. A large crowd gathered at the Yaroslavl station to see him off. The event developed into a public demonstration of sympathy for the Opposition. Both Zinoviev and Trotsky spoke briefly. Reprisals were immediate.

An article in Pravda *accused the Opposition of disloyalty to the Soviet state. Zinoviev and Trotsky were brought before a tribunal of the CCC by Yaroslavsky and Shkiryatov, who demanded their expulsion from the CC. They were charged with appealing from the Russian party to the ECCI and holding a "demonstration" at the Yaroslavl station. Stalin was determined to have the Opposition expelled by the time of the Fifteenth Congress to prevent an embarrassing discussion of the shocking events in China. On June 24, Ordzhonikidze presided over the hearings at the head of a panel of Stalinist stalwarts, including Yaroslavsky, who raised the charge that Trotsky had had Communists shot during the civil war.*

Trotsky made short shrift of the formal charges against him.

244

*He denied the right of the CCC to weigh his expulsion and
reiterated his right to appeal to the Comintern. Then he launched
a peroration on the analogy that had been raised by one of his
judges with the French revolution, accusing his judges of preparing to open the "second chapter" of the revolution—the Thermidorian one (this speech is in* The Stalin School of Falsification, *pp.
126-48). The panel deliberated for four months, under pressure
from Stalin to proceed with the expulsions, but could find no
evidence to support expulsion.*

*On June 27, Trotsky addressed the following memorandum to
the CC. He focused on the forthcoming Fifteenth Party Congress,
urging the CC to permit a free precongress debate on the issues
and to restore the banished Oppositionists to their rightful places.*

By permission of the Harvard College Library.

To All Members of the Central Committee of the AUCP(B):
Dear Comrades:

For over three years the party has been going through a crisis.
The differences around which the discussion turned in 1923 have
not been outlived in the slightest. On the contrary, they keep
growing wider and deeper. By 1925 the very group which until then
had played the leading role in the Politburo fell apart completely.
From that group there separated the Leningrad Opposition,
against which the remainder of the former group has waged just
as bitter a fight as against the 1923 Opposition. In 1926 the
oppositions of 1923 and 1925 merged. At the same time within the
new leading group differences are again making their appearance
and a new "schism" is possible. All this shows quite plainly that
the party finds itself in the worst crisis it has experienced since
the revolution. And now, more than ever, it must be resolved.

In direct conjunction with the recent setbacks in China, which
were brought about to a significant extent by incorrect leadership
of the Chinese revolution, the international situation has
abruptly worsened. The danger of war and intervention is
unquestionable. A war against the USSR, a state that is a
dictatorship of the proletariat, could not be an ordinary war
between states. It could only be a conflict between the world
bourgeoisie and the international proletariat. The struggle
against international imperialism, to the extent that it assumed
military form, would inevitably bring a sharp intensification of
the class struggle in the rear areas of each of the contending
sides, creating domestic battlefronts as well as foreign ones. A
decisive role in this confrontation would be played by our link

with the revolutionary movement of the world proletariat. It is superfluous to speak of the fact that in such a struggle, just as in the historic battles of the civil war, that section of the party which now stands in opposition, would not occupy the least important position. But the success of the class struggle of the proletariat, no matter what forms it takes, is only possible if a solid and active party closely tied to the working class stands at its head. This solidity and activity does not now exist. This must be said plainly—so that those things can be achieved.

The party crisis must be resolved.

The Central Committee is trying to resolve it by the mechanical suppression of the Opposition. One spate of "working the Opposition over" follows another; one campaign against the "outbursts of the Opposition" after another. Comrades who hold the viewpoint of the Opposition are removed from the Politburo, and preparations are now under way to exclude them from the ECCI and the CC as well—all a few months before the gathering of the party congress, where a new CC would be established by normal procedure. Toward rank-and-file party members sharing the views of the Opposition, the reprisals are even harsher, up to and including expulsion from the party, regardless of these comrades' revolutionary service records or the fact that they are workers at the bench. Reprisals have begun against those who signed the Declaration of the Eighty-four, which was addressed to the CC according to completely legal party procedures. Oppositionists have been brought up on charges in the party only because they expressed views at *party* meetings that did not agree with the standpoint of the CC. *Party members are thus being denied their most elementary party rights.* Party opinion is being openly prepared for the expulsion of the Opposition from the party.

And that is not all. In the struggle against the Opposition the CC is using *nonparty means of applying pressure,* at the same time building a "case" against Comrade Zinoviev for supposedly "appealing to nonparty people." "You'll be laughing at the labor exchange" [unemployment office], the Opposition was threatened quite recently at a party meeting in Kharkov by Comrade Postyshev, a member of the Politburo of the Communist Party of the Ukraine. "We'll fire you from your jobs," was the way Comrade Kotov, a secretary of the Moscow Committee, tried to intimidate the Opposition in Moscow. They wish to force the Opposition into silence with the threat of starvation. *The CC is openly turning to the state apparatus for assistance against party members.*

One must be blind not to see that to fight the Opposition by such methods is *to fight against the party*. The CC does not allow the lower ranks of the party a chance to sort out the differences for themselves. The party knows the views of the Opposition only from the distorted way they are relayed by CC supporters. The articles and speeches of comrades who hold the Opposition viewpoint are not published, and sometimes (as at the April plenum of the CC on the China question) they are not even recorded stenographically. Even the proceedings of the ECCI plenum, against all previous tradition, have not been published in the party press, and in the excerpt from these discussions issued recently for party members, Comrade Trotsky's speech is not printed—under the pretext that he did not correct the stenographic text in time. If the Oppositionists are not allowed to speak, that means the party ranks are not allowed to know what the dispute is about. It means there is a desire to force them to take the official reporters at their word.

At party meetings, party members vote for the CC (if they don't simply avoid voting) under *threat of repression*. A much vaunted "unanimity" is introduced, the appearance of unity, having nothing in common with real unity in the party. This appearance of unity is achieved by suppressing the active life of the party. *The road that the CC is taking is not the road of unity but the road of destruction of the party*. It is also a monstrous perversion of the Leninist methods of party leadership.

"What must be done to achieve the most rapid and reliable cure? *All* members of the party must begin to *study,* completely dispassionately and with utmost honesty, first the essence of the differences and second the course of the dispute in the party. . . . It is necessary to *study* both the one and the other, unfailingly demanding the most exact, printed documents, open to verification by all sides. Whoever believes things simply on someone else's say-so is a hopeless idiot, to be dismissed with a wave of the hand. If there are no documents, there must be a 'cross-examination of witnesses' on both or on the several sides, and it must be a 'real third degree' and be done 'in the presence of witnesses'" [from Lenin's article "The Party Crisis," written January 19, 1921. For another translation of this passage, see *Collected Works,* vol. 32, pp. 43-47].

That is how Lenin presented the question in 1921 and that is the only way it can be presented now. The ranks of the party and above all the working class ranks are the only judges with the right to decide, and only they can resolve the prolonged party crisis. To surgically remove, behind the backs of the party ranks, the Opposition section of the party, which includes hundreds and thousands of comrades who have passed through the fires of three revolutions, fought on the fronts of the civil war, led the revolutionary struggle of the proletariat and stood at the head of the proletarian dictatorship at the most difficult moments—that is not the way out of the situation. Only by the Leninist road can we restore to the party *genuine unity, which means above all maximum active participation by the entire mass of the party* and its readiness to accept all sacrifices for the sake of the victory of the proletarian revolution and socialism.

The mass of the party has the right to hear a precise and detailed account of the views on all the questions in dispute, and each of the sides has the obligation to present such an account. We are fulfilling our part of that duty with the enclosed document. And the CC should carry out its duty to the party.

It should bring to the knowledge of the party ranks all the documents, including ours, with which the party ranks can orient themselves in the present complex situation. It should print these documents and send them to all party organizations as material for the Fifteenth Congress (with only about four months remaining until the opening of the congress). The coming CC plenum should be devoted to a discussion of the congress agenda, the precongress campaign, and the materials to be presented to the congress. We are confident that we will be given the opportunity at the plenum to defend the views we have presented.

The Fifteenth Congress is being called after a two-year interval at a time of extremely severe party crisis. All the more reason, then, that its preparation should be under conditions ruling out any possibility of terrorization of the party, any attempts at administrative pressure. Elections to the congress should be carried out in full accordance with the party rules and Bolshevik traditions, on the basis of broad discussion by the entire party of all the most important questions before it. Only then will the decisions of the congress be correct and carry weight.

RESOLUTION OF THE
ALL-RUSSIA METAL WORKERS UNION

July 1, 1927

NOTE: While censuring Zinoviev for his May 9 speech at a public meeting and Trotsky for his speech at the Yaroslavl station, the CC majority continued to use nonparty means of exerting pressure on the Opposition. The latest and most blatant was the introduction of a resolution into the Central Committee of the Metal Workers Union which, among other things, introduced the charge that the Opposition advocated the defeat of Soviet Russia in a war with imperialism. This charge would presently gather broader currency and be used to inflame patriotic sentiments while Trotsky's replies were not permitted circulation.

By permission of the Library of Social History. The text has been abridged to avoid repetition.

To the Central Committee of the Metal Workers Union:
Dear Comrades:

At the seventh plenum of your Central Committee you adopted a resolution on the present situation based on the report by Comrade Lepse. This resolution contains such false and rudely slanderous assertions about the Opposition that we find it impossible—if for no other reason than respect for the Metal Workers Union—to pass over it in silence.

1. First of all, the fact should be noted that you brought questions that are in dispute within the party before the plenum of the CC, which is a nonparty institution. There are no precedents for such an action in the past work of your union or in the work of any of our unions in general. By appealing to nonparty people against the Opposition you apparently wish to force us to explain, not only to party members but to nonparty people as well, that our position has nothing in common with the slanderous assertions in your resolution.

2. Your resolution asserts that the Opposition is carrying on "destructive propaganda activity in favor of its *defeatist* ideology." What is meant by the term *defeatism*? In the whole past history of the party, *defeatism* was understood to mean *desiring*

the defeat of one's own government in a war with an external enemy and *contributing to such a defeat* by methods of internal revolutionary struggle. This referred of course to the attitude of the proletariat toward the capitalist state. But you carry the term *defeatist* over and apply it to the politics of the Opposition, i.e., an ideological tendency within the AUCP. By this you are saying that the Opposition wishes the defeat of the Soviet state in its struggle against external, i.e., capitalist, enemies, and that it wishes to contribute to such a defeat.

It is enough to simply define the term *defeatism* to make clear the vile absurdity of this imputation of a defeatist attitude on the part of the Opposition toward the Soviet state—in whose founding and preservation Oppositionists have played no less a role than anyone else in the party, both now and in the past.

3. By telling the masses of the people that hundreds of veteran party members, former underground revolutionaries, Lenin's closest collaborators, organizers of and participants in the October Revolution, the civil war, and socialist construction, have at present become defeatists—by so doing you introduce the greatest confusion into the minds of the masses, which will have absolutely unfathomable consequences. All informed and honest readers among the workers or peasants are bound to think to themselves that either you are lying in making such a monstrous assertion, or the Soviet state has changed so fundamentally that even the people most closely involved in building that state have become its mortal enemies. You are driving the masses toward such conclusions, starting with their vanguard section, the metal workers.

4. Your words about defeatism are bound to seem more monstrous than ever to our workers and to workers internationally in view of the fact that the most important diplomatic posts, i.e., positions where the interests of the workers' state are directly defended against the capitalist enemy, are held at the present almost entirely by Oppositionists: in Berlin, Krestinsky; in Paris, Rakovsky, Pyatakov, Preobrazhensky, and Vladimir Kosior; in Rome, Kamenev and Glebov-Avilov; in Prague, Antonov-Ovseenko and Kanatchikov; in Vienna, Ufimtsev and Semashko; in Stockholm, Kopp; in Persia, Mdivani; in Mexico, Kollontai; in Argentina, Kraevsky; and so on. All these comrades belong to the Opposition and the majority of them have already endorsed the so-called letter of the eighty-four, in which the Opposition defined its attitude toward the fundamental political questions. If the Oppositionists are "defeatists," how could the CC of our party

entrust to such "defeatists" the protection of the most vital interests of the workers' state under the enemy's direct blows? Your assertion is slander not only of the Opposition but also of the CC, which would be criminally guilty before the party and the workers' state if it assigned diplomatic posts to "defeatists," i.e., to advocates of "defeat" rather than victory for our state against the bourgeois world.

5. The problem is of course not limited to Oppositionist diplomats. By now more than three hundred comrades with records in the party from before October, including many with long experience in the underground, have signed the declaration of the Opposition. . . .

All these comrades, like the majority of other Old Bolsheviks who signed the declaration, are doing responsible work on assignment by the party. "Defeatists"—we repeat—are people who undermine the military power of the state or its economic might. Can defeatists be permitted in any serious work whatsoever? The direct responsibility for the defeatists in the eyes of the party and the workers' state would fall on the CC of the party in such a case.

6. You of course know that the CC is not guilty of the crime you ascribe to it. You would not dare to assert that the Oppositionists carry out the military, diplomatic, economic, or other work assigned to them more poorly than supporters of the majority. You yourselves know very well that the phrase about the "defeatism" of the Opposition is a poisonous lie and nothing more. You have put this lie into circulation for the purposes of factional struggle against an ideological tendency in the party to which we belong in common. In doing this you have stooped to compromising the party in a terrible way and are doing great harm to the workers' state. By attributing such monstrous views to the Opposition and circulating such views, you establish and legitimize a banner for genuine enemies of the Soviet state. In general it is hard to imagine any more disruptive or divisive action than that represented by your resolution.

7. We will not go into the other assertions made about the Opposition in your resolution. They are all on roughly the same level. Our elementary revolutionary duty to the party and the workers' state commands us to take all measures within our power to refute your malicious and slanderous assertions before the eyes of the party and nonparty masses.

CC members Yevdokimov, Zinoviev, and Trotsky

'DEFEATISM' AND CLEMENCEAU

July 11, 1927

NOTE: In this letter, Trotsky takes up the persistent accusation of defeatism and refutes it, using the example of Clemenceau in France in 1914 to demonstrate how an Opposition, in a period of war danger, served its class better by its vocal criticisms of a ruling majority than it would have by obedient silence.

To understand the response of the Stalinists it is necessary to realize that they did not have to conduct a debate with Trotsky: by utterly controlling the press, both within the party and outside it, they prevented him from answering charges and guaranteed themselves total impunity in their attacks on the Opposition. They flung at him charges that were distortions, lies, nonsense, even self-contradictions, but denied him a forum to reply. The Stalinists became more unrestrained in their accusations. On the basis of the "Clemenceau thesis"—explained in this letter to Ordzhonikidze—they accused Trotsky of seeking a coup d'état in the midst of a war, of hoping for an attack on the Soviet Union so that he would have a chance to seize power, of being a defeatist or a semi-defeatist.

This excerpt was published in the periodical Communist International, *October 15, 1927. The Russian text is quoted by Stalin in his* Sochineniya (Collected Works), *vol. 10, p. 52. The full text of the letter is evidently lost, except for the copy sent to Ordzhonikidze, which may still exist in the Soviet Union. The 1927 translation has been corrected against the Russian.*

. . . What is defeatism? It is a policy which aims at contributing to the defeat of "one's own" state, which is in the hands of the enemy class. Any other understanding and interpretation of defeatism would be a falsification. Thus, for instance, if someone says that the political line of the ignorant and dishonest hand-book-pushers should be swept out as so much rubbish in order to speed the victory of the proletarian state, he does not thereby by any means become a "defeatist." On the contrary, under the given concrete circumstances he would be the real spokesman for the policy of revolutionary defense of one's own country; ideological rubbish does not bring victory.

Quite instructive examples in this respect may be found in the history of other classes. I will cite only one of them. The French bourgeoisie at the outset of the imperialist war had at its head a government without rudder or sails. The Clemenceau group was in opposition to that government. In spite of the war and the military censorship, in spite even of the fact that the Germans were within eighty kilometers of Paris (Clemenceau said "precisely because of that") Clemenceau conducted a furious struggle against the weak-kneed and wavering petty-bourgeois policies, and for imperialist ferocity and ruthlessness. Clemenceau did not betray his class, the bourgeoisie; on the contrary, he served it more faithfully, more firmly, decisively, and wisely, than did Viviani, Painlevé, and Company. This was shown by the subsequent course of events. The Clemenceau group came to power, and by a more consistent, a more predatory imperialist policy, it secured the victory of the French bourgeoisie. Were there any commentators in France who put the label of "defeatists" on the Clemenceau group? No doubt there were: fools and gossips will be found among the camp followers of all classes. But they are not always given the opportunity to play an equally important part.

TO A MEMBER OF THE 'BUFFER GROUP'

July 13, 1927

NOTE: A "buffer group," which still believed in the possibility of reconciling the majority and the Opposition, circulated a statement in June-July 1927 and gathered forty signatures. A supporter of that position, a certain Golman, wrote to Trotsky. The Opposition leader's reply follows.

By permission of the Harvard College Library.

Dear Comrade:

I read your letter with interest. You call yourself a member of the "buffer group." That is apparently so, to judge from your letter. You raise a number of questions, which I will try to answer in brief.

1. You propose a theoretical debate on the question of the possibility of building socialism in one country. But immediately you say in advance, with regret, that our articles probably would not be printed and you add, "intolerance of honest self-criticism . . . has achieved the solidity of entrenched prejudice among virtually all the party editorial boards of our magazines." But our editorial boards don't make policy on their own, do they? The matter goes deeper. "Intolerance" is treated by you from rather a psychological than a political angle. When a policy line is incorrect, when the course of events and the development of class relations argue profoundly against this incorrect line, "intolerance" appears as a form of self-defense, i.e., the automatic elimination of any exchange of opinion whatsoever on fundamental questions of the revolution. The problem, then, is not the editorial boards and not intolerance but the basic political line.

2. You express your opposition to a splintered leadership (i.e., having only Stalin, Bukharin, and Rykov, on the one hand; or only Zinoviev, Trotsky, and Kamenev, on the other, as you put it). You assume that a united leadership would provide surer guarantees against mistakes. Least of all would I be inclined to object to

that idea, which, as far as I can tell, coincides completely with Lenin's recommendations for the future course of our party's leadership. Despite the profundity and sharpness of the differences, I am completely and entirely willing to support any step that might contribute to the restoration of the basic group of Lenin's leading center. But this does not exhaust the question. The personal composition of the leadership in the revolutionary party is a function of the line of the leadership. We now see the development of crass and shameless attitudes according to which criticism of the CC is viewed approximately the same way the monarchists used to view *lèse majesté*. Such attitudes have nothing in common with Bolshevism. CC membership is not a hereditary or even a lifetime position. The CC is an authoritative body but it is still a party body. The party can replace the CC. And in order to do that, the party must be able to judge the CC. Criticism of the CC, especially on major questions of principle and especially in a precongress period, is the most legitimate right of every party member. To infringe on that right is to turn the party into a helpless chorus for the apparatus, with no will of its own. What kind of perspective this would open up can be understood by anyone with even the slightest knowledge of the mechanics of class relations.

3. You admit that "the line of the CC on the *China question,* beginning in March, has been crudely mistaken and led to the defeat of the Chinese revolution." It is here, I think, that we must look for the key to the weakness in your "buffer" position. Revolution is politics and history in concentrated form. The test of revolution is a highly concentrated test. That is why the line on the "China question" cannot be regarded merely as an episode, even a "major" episode. In China, precisely because there was a revolution and because relations assumed a solidly tangible and massive form almost at once, it would have been the easiest thing in the world to avoid mistakes if the initial, fundamental positions had been at all correct. Just as there is no socialism for just one country, there is no revolutionary proletarian policy for one country. Policy in China is a continuation of policy inside the USSR. But the logical outcome of the continuation was demonstrated more vividly because of the turbulent pace of the events. . . .

5. Serf relations and semi-serf relations in the economy and social life of China are very strong. Partly their origins date back to feudal times. And partly this is new growth, i.e., the revival of old forms on the basis of the retarded development of the

productive forces, surplus agricultural population, the operations of merchants' and usurers' capital, etc. But what decides the question is the kind of relations that are *dominant* in China. Are they "feudal" relations (more precisely, serf relations, and precapitalist relations in general)? Or are they capitalist relations? Undeniably the latter. Only because of the indisputably dominant role of capitalist relations throughout the economy of China is it possible to speak of the perspective of proletarian hegemony in the national revolution.

The productive role of the Chinese proletariat is already very great. In the coming years it can only become greater. Its political role could be colossal, as events have shown. The line of the leadership was aimed entirely against the perspective of the proletariat actually winning the leading role in the revolution.

6. You ask whether such expressions as "the CC's policy of betrayal," "treason," etc., are permissible? Here you refer to the alleged fact that I allowed myself to make such an assessment. On what basis do you say this?

7. You express your apprehension over the possibility that the sharpening of the differences may lead to a split. I totally agree with you that a split would be a very great misfortune. The sharpening of the differences did not result from the ill will of the Opposition but from the sweep of events. The party regime will not allow the differences to be resolved through normal party channels. In turn, the abnormal character of the party regime is the inevitable result of the incorrect political line. This is the main source of danger. Only an open and audacious presentation of all the questions can give the party the incentive to approach them, not according to the official handbook clichés, but by dealing with the real issues. This is the only way to fight for unity on a revolutionary Bolshevik basis. Neither pathetic "buffer group" lamentations nor apparatus intimidation can preserve unity.

8. You ask, "What is the advantage of the ideological and organizational bloc with Fischer and Maslow?" To speak of an *organizational* bloc is absolutely incorrect. All assertions to that effect are fabrications. But ideological and political affinity undoubtedly exists, as far as I can judge from a number of publications of the group you mention. I think that this group has repudiated a lot and learned a good deal. To accuse it of counterrevolution, rengacy, etc., is absolutely incorrect and is no different from accusing the Opposition of "supporting" Chamberlain.

In conclusion allow me to thank you for sending me a copy of your book. I will not have a chance to acquaint myself with it right away—not before the plenum in any case. I hope that I can manage to read it after the plenum, at least the chapter you indicated.

L. Trotsky

THERMIDOR

Summer 1927

NOTE: Parallels with the French Revolution, in this case the danger of a "Thermidor," had occupied the thoughts of the Bolsheviks almost since the seizure of power. Trotsky had argued on this question at a session of the CCC on June 24. In July, Pravda published a series of articles by Maretsky, a student of Bukharin, entitled "The So-called 'Thermidor' and the Danger of Degeneration," denouncing Trotsky's use of the analogy as slander. This memorandum may have been stimulated by that series, or it may have been drawn up in connection with the joint plenum of the CC and CCC in late July–early August.

There were many opinions about the likelihood of a Soviet Thermidor—what Trotsky called counterrevolution on the installment plan—and a lively debate in the ranks of the Opposition would persist long after 1927. Even in 1927 some Oppositionists were of the opinion that Thermidor had already been accomplished, while Trotsky felt that it had not been, although the tendencies leading toward it were being strengthened by the party's right wing.

By permission of the Library of Social History in New York.

Can a Thermidor occur in our country? In *Pravda* they have proved with the aid of quotations that it cannot. Stalin said something about the ignorance of those who make references to Thermidor. But all of this is wrong; it misses the point.

To denounce the Opposition as a petty-bourgeois deviation, as a reflection of the growing petty-bourgeois element, and at the same time to deny the very possibility of a "Thermidorian" return of a bourgeois regime, is to fail to put two and two together. It means to make two mistakes: in assessing the Opposition and in assessing the dangers facing us in the process of our development.

Before the introduction of NEP and during its first phase, many of us had quite a few discussions with Lenin about

Thermidor. The word itself was in great currency among us. It never entered anyone's head to argue—with absurd pedantry or charlatanism—that Thermidor was "impossible" in general, in view of the socialist character of the revolution, etc., etc.

In speaking of the Kronstadt uprising Lenin said: "What does [this event] mean? It was an attempt to seize political power from the Bolsheviks by a motley crowd or alliance of ill-assorted elements, apparently just to the right of the Bolsheviks, or perhaps even to their 'left'. . . .

"The nonparty elements served here only as a *bridge,* a *stepping stone,* a *rung on a ladder,* on which the White Guards appeared. This is politically inevitable" [an inadequate translation of this passage is in *Collected Works,* vol. 32, p. 184; emphasis added by Trotsky].

What was involved in Kronstadt, as we know, was not just nonparty elements: many sailors who were party members took part in the revolt. Together with the nonparty people they shifted power so that it ceased to hew to the class line.

The Kronstadt form of Thermidor was an armed uprising. But under certain circumstances a Thermidor can creep up on us in a more peaceful way. If the Kronstadters, party and nonparty elements together, could backslide toward a bourgeois regime with the slogan of soviets and in the name of the soviets, it is also possible to backslide into Thermidorian positions even with the banner of communism in one's hands. Herein lies the diabolical trickiness of history.

What is Thermidor? A stepping down one rung on the ladder of revolution—a slight shift of power to the right—as the result of a certain crucial change or break in the psychology of the revolution. At the top, at the helm, there seem to be the very same people, the same speeches, the same banners. The day after Thermidor, the victorious participants were profoundly confident that nothing catastrophic had happened: they simply had dealt with a group of "ex-leaders" who had become confusionists, disrupters, and "objectively" accomplices of Pitt, the Chamberlain of that day. But down below, deepgoing rearrangements of the class forces had taken place.

The propertied elements had succeeded by that time in righting themselves, recovering their strength, and gathering their courage. Civil order was restored. The new property owners wanted more than anything not to be prevented from enjoying the fruits of their property. They pressured the state apparatus and the Jacobin clubs, many of whose members felt themselves also to be property owners, people of order, and the Jacobin party was forced to regroup itself, to put forward some elements more disposed toward swimming with the new stream, to link up with new elements, not of Jacobin origin—and to press back, cast out, incapacitate, and decapitate those elements who reflected the interests and passions of the urban lower classes, the sans-culottes. In turn, these lower strata no longer felt the same confidence in their power as before—feeling the pressure of the new propertied elements and the state apparatus that covered up for the people of property.

The first shift of power was expressed in the movement within the same old ruling party: some Jacobins forced out others. But that too was—to use Lenin's words—a stepping stone, a bridge, a rung on the ladder, on which later the big bourgeoisie, headed by Bonaparte, was to step into power.

Is there a danger of Thermidor in our country? This question means: (a) Is there a danger of bourgeois restoration in general? (b) Are there reasons to think that this restoration would *not* be carried out all at once, with one blow, but through successive shiftings, with the first shift occurring from the top down and to a large extent within one and the same party—a shift from the elements who represented the upward sweep of the revolution to elements adapting themselves to its downward turn?

To deny the danger of bourgeois restoration for the dictatorship of the proletariat in a backward country under capitalist encirclement is inconceivable. Only a Menshevik or a genuine capitulator who understands neither the international nor the internal resources of our revolution could speak of the *inevitability* of a Thermidor. But only a bureaucrat, a windbag, or a braggart could deny the *possibility* of Thermidor. We of course are talking only about the possibility, only about the danger—in the same sense that Lenin did when he said that no force in the world could take back the agrarian revolution but that our enemies could still take away the socialist revolution.

But bourgeois restoration, speaking in general, is only conceivable either in the form of a decisive and sharp overturn (with or without intervention) or in the form of several successive shifts. This is what Ustryalov calls "going downhill with the brakes on." Of course when you go downhill with the brakes on things don't always work out smoothly, without injuries, as the French Revolution itself showed. The Ninth of Thermidor was supplemented by the Eighteenth Brumaire.

Thus, as long as the European revolution has not conquered,

the possibilities of bourgeois restoration in our country cannot be denied. Which of the two possible paths is the more likely under our circumstances: the path of an abrupt counterrevolutionary overturn or the path of successive shiftings, with a bit of shake-up at every stage and a Thermidorian shift as the most imminent stage? This question can be answered, I think, only in an extremely conditional way. To the extent that the possibility of a bourgeois restoration in general cannot be denied, we must keep our eyes out for *either* of these variants—with the brakes on or without the brakes—to weigh the odds, and to note elements contributing toward either. In politics, as in economics, the same question continues to be posed: Who will prevail?

At the Eleventh Congress Lenin brilliantly sketched out the possible way a Thermidorian shift in power might take place. He took up the question on the cultural level, which of course is closely linked with both politics and economics:

"History knows all sorts of metamorphoses. Relying on firmness of convictions, loyalty, and other splendid moral qualities is anything but a serious attitude in politics. . . . We were told in our history lessons when we were children: sometimes one nation conquers another, and the nation that conquers is the conqueror and the nation that is vanquished is the conquered nation. This is simple and intelligible to all. But what happens to the culture of these nations? Here things are not so simple. If the conquering nation is more cultured than the vanquished nation, the former imposes its culture upon the latter; but if the opposite is the case, the vanquished nation imposes its culture upon the conqueror" [*Collected Works,* vol. 33, pp. 287-88].

Did Lenin think that such a degeneration of the administrators was *inevitable*? No. Did he think it *possible*? Undeniably. Did he consider it *probable*? Under certain historical circumstances, yes. Did this signify *pessimism*? No; the very question sounds foolish.

(It should be stated parenthetically at this point that one of the pillars of the party had a bad trick played on him by a friend, who showed him the excerpt I have quoted from Lenin's speech at the Eleventh Congress under the pretext that it was his own article. Our party "stalwart" did not recognize the real author and judged Lenin's speech as follows: "The ravings of an old man; it has the smell of the Opposition about it.")

Thus Lenin did not think the possibility was excluded that economic and cultural shifts in the direction of bourgeois degeneration could take place over a long period even with power remaining in Bolshevik hands; it could happen through an inconspicuous cultural-political assimilation between a certain layer of the Bolshevik Party and a certain layer of the rising new petty-bourgeois element. By this very position Lenin acknowledged the possibility of a Thermidorian breaking point and a shift of the power, although that does not in any way mean he considered the party Thermidorian or was simply cursing at the Thermidorians. It is necessary after all to understand the language of Marxism.

Are there processes taking place in the country which can produce a very real danger of Thermidor—given blindly bureaucratic policies on our part? Yes there are. I will not dwell on the kulak, the private trader, or the external pressure from imperialism. These are known to all. But let us take this example: At a certain factory the old cadre of revolutionary workers is being pushed aside or is simply driven into opposition by new elements, sometimes ones who did not even go through the civil war, and among these new elements there are quite a few who before the revolution were obedient to the bosses and in the first period of the revolution were hostile to the Bolsheviks—and now these elements, as party members, rail at the Opposition, with the same words they had used at another time against the Bolsheviks. Such "shifts" even in the factories are not rare exceptions. What do they mean? They do not constitute a counterrevolution, or an overturn, but a realignment of the elements within one and the same class, one and the same party—the kind of regrouping that brings to the top those elements who most easily adapt themselves. By the same token this lowers the revolutionary powers of resistance of the class. Is a realignment of elements on this pattern taking place among us on a broader scale? I contend that it is. The frenzied struggle against the Opposition is in fact a method that facilitates the indicated realignment of forces inside the party—under the pressure of the nonproletarian classes. This is what the most dangerous process consists of, a process that can greatly facilitate the aim of the Thermidorian elements in the country to strike at the party.

Against our admonitions as to the danger of Thermidor they argue that there is a different correlation of classes in our country than there was in France, etc., etc. But we too have some inkling of the fact that the base of the Bolsheviks is not the preproletariat of the eighteenth century but the industrial working class of the twentieth. And we have heard about the fact that the French Revolution had no apparent way out, for France was surrounded by more backward feudal countries. Our revolution, on the other hand, has a way out, for we are surrounded by more advanced capitalist countries. The counterrevolution in France was an absolute historical *inevitability*. In our case it is only a *possibility*—in the event of an exceptionally unfavorable combination of international circumstances in the future and exceptionally incorrect policies internally.

One of the present-day theoretical disarmers of the party has quoted Marx to the effect that there is no reason to clothe the proletarian revolution in a costume of the past and has drawn the silly and sugary conclusion from this that there is no reason to speak of Thermidor. One may wrap oneself in the toga of the past in order to hide from oneself and others the puniness of one's historical role. That should not be done. But one can and should seek analogies with the past and learn from past examples. In 1902 [actually 1904] Lenin wrote that a Social Democrat is a Jacobin who has linked his fate with the revolutionary movement of the working class [see *Collected Works*, vol. 7, p. 383]. At that time, twenty-five years ago, I myself took the occasion to argue against Lenin to the effect that the French Revolution was a petty-bourgeois revolution and ours is a proletarian revolution, that there was no need to return to the past, to the Jacobins, etc. In short, I expounded the same super-wisdom that is now being repeated, and added to considerably, by the critics of the Opposition. There is no need to point out that Lenin had no worse an understanding than we did of the difference between the eighteenth and twentieth centuries, between the sans-culottes and the industrial workers. Nevertheless he was completely right in following the thread of historical continuity from the Jacobins to Bolshevism.

The analogy with Thermidor makes the same kind of sense. It teaches a great deal. Thermidor is a special form of counterrevolution carried out on the installment plan through several installments, and making use, in the first stage, of elements of the same ruling party—by regrouping them and counterposing some to others.

Several wise observers have referred to the fact that Robespierre's group was still in power on the Ninth of Thermidor and not in opposition. It is completely laughable to make much of that. No one is talking about an exact identity of the two processes. If the Thermidorians had not guillotined the Robespierre group right away but had only stripped them of power gradually—let's say, had only "worked them over" at the start—the group would have ended up in opposition. And on the other hand, we have no shortage of already fully fledged Thermidorians who call for speeding up measures of physical retribution against the Opposition. What is involved here is technicalities, and not the political essence of the process.

I have not the slightest doubt that from these words of mine someone will draw the conclusion, and publish it widely, that our revolution is doomed, that before us lies only the road of Thermidor, that our party is Thermidorian, that socialist development is impossible, and so on and so forth. I view this method of "working people over" as one of the most malignant symptoms of the influence of Thermidorian tendencies on the apparatus of our own party. This is the spiritual disarming of the proletariat, the anesthetization of the party, the obliteration of the ideological and political boundaries between right and left, between revolutionaries and opportunists, between Social Democracy and Bolshevism. The theoretical disarming and political narcotization of the party facilitates the work of Thermidorian tendencies. Against such a disarming the Opposition has waged, and will continue to wage, an irreconcilable struggle—precisely because it does not in any way regard a Thermidor as inevitable.

THE OPPOSITION'S 'INSURRECTIONISM'
A Statement on Molotov's Speech

August 4, 1927

NOTE: The plenum lasted from July 29 until August 9. Trotsky's main speech, delivered August 1, is in The Stalin School of Falsification *(pp. 161-77). This letter, marked "Top Secret," was sent to the plenum in reply to allegations made by Molotov to the effect that the Opposition favored "conditional defense" of the USSR and that its policy aimed at "insurrection against the party and Soviet power."*

The Left Communists, referred to in this letter, opposed the acceptance of the terms demanded by Germany for signing a peace treaty in 1918 and advocated instead a revolutionary war by the Soviet Republic against Germany. When the Left Communists, led by Bukharin, were defeated in the CC, they resigned all their posts in the party and government to be free to carry on their agitation against the decision in the ranks of the party, and published an independent paper polemicizing against the CC majority. Trotsky's point was to contrast how a disloyal leadership (Stalin's), bent on a split, dealt with a loyal faction, on the one hand, and how a loyal leadership (Lenin's), determined to preserve party unity, dealt with a faction that had exceeded the normal bounds of party discipline.

By permission of the Harvard College Library.

To the Joint Plenum of the Central Committee and the CCC of the AUCP(B):

The speech of Comrade Molotov on Saturday gave us to understand what the narrow faction of Stalin aims at and where it is going. In answering the slander of *defeatism* or *conditional defensism* we have declared in the past, and we declare again here, that the Opposition does not pose conditions for defense to anybody, but struggles and will continue to struggle for the creation of the *conditions for victory*.

Comrade Molotov has declared here—and this was the sole purpose of his whole speech—that the line of the Opposition, like the line of the Left Social Revolutionaries in 1918, *leads to insurrectionism against the party and Soviet power.* These words characterize in an absolutely precise and clear manner the line, not of the Opposition, but of the central group of Stalin.

The Left SRs constituted a separate party, which was in a temporary bloc with our party. The Left SRs disagreed especially sharply with our party over the question of whether to fight the Germans or sign a peace treaty. Finding themselves a minority in the Congress of Soviets, the Left SRs rose in armed revolt against Soviet power. Fortunately for the revolution, we crushed them completely.

The Left Communists came out against the Brest-Litovsk treaty at the same time as the Left SRs did. They conducted their struggle with the harshest methods, methods that were often totally impermissible, talked themselves into a position of conditional defense in relation to the socialist homeland, and threatened the party with a split in the middle of civil war and external danger. Nevertheless, things not only never reached the point of "insurrectionism"; they did not even go as far as a split. There was not even a single expulsion from the party. The explanation for this is that the CC of our party under Lenin's leadership not only did not try to exacerbate differences but, despite the open insurrection of the Left SRs, with whom the Left Communists had a partial rapprochement (voting together several times)—our leadership never once permitted itself even slightly provocative or suspicious comments regarding "insurrectionism." In this alone the radical difference between Stalinism and the profound party spirit and methods of Leninism is evident.

Molotov's words about the "insurrectionism" of the present Opposition section of the united party are not accidental. They are part of a carefully elaborated plan arrived at a long time ago. Many of you comrades have already carried out bits or pieces of this plan, without seeing or knowing the plan as a whole. In July of last year we warned you about the first stage of this plan—a radical change in the leadership of the party (in the Supplementary Declaration to the Declaration of the Thirteen, July 1926 [see p. 89]). Today, with the first stage of this plan nearing completion, Molotov's speech confronts us with the second stage, the concluding phase. By using the term "insurrectionism" in reference to the Opposition, the core of the Stalin faction intends to accustom the party to the idea of the destruction of the Opposition.

We consider it necessary to warn the CC and the CCC about this as clearly as possible.

It is not true that the Opposition holds the viewpoint of "conditional defensism." On the other hand it is absolutely true that the Stalin faction is trying to drive a wedge, in the area of military defense as elsewhere, between the Opposition and the remainder of the party, in shipping off the most prominent party personnel in the military to Khabarovsk, Japan, Afghanistan, etc., in the midst of a growing threat of war, and in this way is weakening the defense of the country.

It is not true that the Opposition is making preparations to form a *second party*. On the other hand it is absolutely true that the Stalin faction wishes to subordinate the party to itself once and for all not only with measures of a party character but also by using the state apparatus.

It is not true that the Opposition believes that the revolution has entered a period of Thermidor or that our party is Thermidorian. The party has been stifled and its capacity for resistance has been weakened. And Thermidorian elements are present in the country and are sticking their noses into party business with impunity. When that extremely vicious enemy of communism, Ustryalov, insistently calls on Stalin to destroy the Opposition completely, that is the plain and unambiguous language of Thermidor. And when Stalin makes the crushing of the left wing of the party the main focus of his work, he thereby lends weight to Ustryalov and Company; whether he intends to or not, he strengthens them and weakens the positions of the proletariat.

It is not true that the path of the Opposition leads to *insurrection against the party and Soviet power*. On the contrary it is an incontestable fact that the Stalin faction has cold-bloodedly planned to carry out our physical destruction in order to attain its goals. On the part of the Opposition there is not even a hint of a threat of insurrectionism. But on the part of the Stalin faction there is a real threat of further usurpation of the sovereign rights of the party. Through the mouth of Molotov this threat has been pronounced openly. While *in fact* paving the way, step by step, for the destruction of the Opposition on the pretext of its "insurrectionism," the top Stalinist leaders *verbally* soothe the hesitating members of the CC and the CCC with assurances that matters will never go that far, that it is merely necessary to *frighten* the Opposition. In this way the Stalin group gradually draws broader circles into its orbit and accustoms them to a plan which in its pure form would inevitably frighten them away even today.

In view of this we consider it necessary to say here what should be self-evident already: *The Opposition is not going to be intimidated either by slander or by threats of physical destruction.* Vacillating individuals will leave the Opposition but dozens and hundreds of rank-and-file party members, convinced by events, are joining us. You cannot intimidate the Opposition with threats. You cannot break the Opposition with repression. What we consider correct we will fight for to the end. We have confidence in the proletarian core of the party. We know that events are working in favor of the Leninist line, that is, for the Opposition. We are confident that the line of the party can be corrected—in peacetime and in war time—not only without "insurrectionism" or "two parties" but also without upheavals or repression in general.

The Opposition cannot be intimidated. But the revolutionary unity of the party must be defended against the increasingly dangerous tendencies toward usurpationism. The Opposition reserves the right to patiently and insistently explain its views, basing itself on objective events. But against further tramplings upon the party rules, against usurpation of the rights of the party congress, against the seizure of all control over party discussion and the party press by an artificially selected faction of Stalinists, against the forced closing of the Opposition's mouth by the state apparatus, against the doctrine that the leading Stalinist nucleus is irreplaceable, against the theory and practice of usurpationism, the Opposition will fight uncompromisingly by all means consistent with the revolutionary unity of the party and the lasting stability of the dictatorship of the proletariat. The Opposition will not allow the fundamental questions of the proletarian revolution to be decided behind closed doors by the Stalin faction. The party must decide, and it will. We are thoroughly and completely for the revolutionary unity of the party and the Comintern.

At the same time we declare again that we are ready to accept every proposal that can ameliorate the internal relations, allay the internal struggle, facilitate for the party and the CC a more efficient utilization of all the forces—in any work—for the needs of the party and the Soviet state, so as to create ultimately the conditions that will assure a general examination of the real differences by the party and the elaboration of a correct line at the Fifteenth Party Congress.

Kamenev	Trotsky	Lizdin
Zinoviev	Bakaev	Solovyov
Pyatakov	Peterson	Avdeev
Smilga	Rakovsky	
Muralov	Yevdokimov	

SPEECH TO THE JOINT PLENUM OF THE CC AND THE CCC

August 6, 1927

NOTE: This speech was in reply to Ordzhonikidze's report, proposing the expulsion of Zinoviev and Trotsky from the Central Committee. Trotsky began by trying yet again to defend the historical record of Bolshevism on the question of socialism in one country, this time using as an example the program of the Communist League of Youth, which was perfectly explicit about the link between world revolution and the success of Soviet socialism. The Youth League program, moreover, had been drawn up in 1921 by a commission directed by Bukharin, and had been approved by the Central Committee, headed by Lenin.

Once again, in defending the tactics of the Oppositionists, Trotsky used an example that shed light on his real relations with Lenin on the eve of Lenin's death. This was the organizational bloc with Trotsky that Lenin proposed to defend the state monopoly of foreign trade against Stalin's attempt to weaken it. This example refuted the Stalinist myth that Lenin had been "against factions," a myth that Trotsky takes up more explicitly later on. And it debunked the myth of Stalin's "orthodoxy," which was already gaining currency. (The struggle to preserve the monopoly of foreign trade is described in Lenin's Fight Against Stalinism, *part V.)*

On p. 285 Trotsky alludes to a scandal that was caused by a note he submitted to the Politburo on the subject of the army. In an undated memorandum composed around this time, Trotsky explained that a group of military officials, stimulated by the approaching war danger, had exchanged views on the state of the armed forces. Among them were Muralov, Putna, Primakov, Mrachkovsky, and Bakaev. As a result of their discussion they drew up a document proposing certain changes needed to improve the fighting capacity of the army. Trotsky submitted this document to the Politburo explaining that he did not ask that it be read aloud at the joint plenum because he "did not want to give the Molotovs, Yaroslavskys, and Voroshilovs a pretext for transforming a most important and urgent question into material for

. . . thoroughly false, nonparty, non-Communist speeches on the 'offended dignity' of their uniforms. . . ." In the Stalinist mill this episode became transformed into rumors about a military conspiracy, which would be embroidered and enlarged upon later.

Trotsky refers to charges that were made against him on August 1, when Voroshilov repeated the accusation first made by Yaroslavsky at the session of the CCC that day—that Trotsky had had Communists shot during the civil war. (Trotsky's December 25, 1918, letter to the CC about the "threat" to have Communists shot is in The Trotsky Papers, *ed. Jan M. Meijer, vol. 1 [The Hague: Mouton, 1964], pp. 204-09.)*

During the Russian civil war the Tenth Army, under the influence of Stalin and Voroshilov, became the seat of the Military Opposition, which opposed the use of military specialists from the tsarist army, favored guerrilla tactics, and resisted the centralization of the Red Army under a unified command. The Eighth Party Congress in March 1919 reaffirmed the military policy that Trotsky, as head of the Red Army, had been implementing. More background information about this episode is in The Stalin School of Falsification, *pp. 40-46, 48-49.*

By permission of the Library of Social History.

Trotsky [reading his speech]: Comrade Stalin said yesterday that the Opposition stands under the banner of "Trotskyism." The primary and essential characteristic that he gives for "Trotskyism" is its denial of the theory that socialism can be built in one country. This question, comrades, is still up for discussion—in my opinion; and I don't think it will be withdrawn from the agenda in the period ahead. To invoke this or that resolution as having already dealt with this question, even if that were true, would only bring us back to the problem that such a resolution was obviously mistaken and would have to be revised. In fact, however, this has never been taken up as a separate question in its full dimensions, and no resolution that was the least bit definitive has ever been passed on this subject.

Voice from the floor: Maybe you'd answer the questions put to you yesterday?

Trotsky: Moreover, precisely on this question it is most glaringly evident how unserious is the attempt to misrepresent our approach to the question as "Trotskyist," rather than Marxist or Leninist. [*Shouts from the floor.*] As I understand it, what is under discussion is a political tendency which is condemned above all for its political line—its so-called "Trotskyism," which allegedly differs from Leninism. It is in regard to precisely this basic charge against us that I am now making clarifications for the joint plenum. I assert, comrades, that *this basic charge is fundamentally incorrect.* You can't, after all, just dismiss the fact that as late as 1924, i.e., even after the death of Vladimir Ilyich, Stalin formulated his opinion in a very clear and exact way that it is impossible to build socialism, that is, a socialist society, in one country. It turns out that only two years ago, even after Lenin's death, Stalin expounded a "Trotskyist" view on the question of building socialism in one country.

Kaganovich: You talk about yourself.

Voice: This has already been discussed.

Trotsky: You might say that Stalin made a mistake and then corrected himself. But how could he make *such* a mistake on *such* a question? If it were true that as far back as 1915 Lenin gave us the theory of building socialism in one country (which of course is totally untrue); if it were true that afterwards Lenin did nothing but substantiate and develop that point of view (which is totally untrue); how then, we must ask, could Stalin, while Lenin was still alive, in the last period of Lenin's life, have developed an opinion on such a highly important question of the kind that found expression in Stalin's quotation of 1924? It seems that on this fundamental question Stalin had simply always been a Trotskyist and only after 1924 did he stop being one.

Antipov: Answer the questions that were put to you. Talk about point four. There's no use trying to distract us.

Kaganovich: You tell us about the discussion of 1915.

Trotsky: It wouldn't be a bad thing if Comrade Stalin could find in his writings even one quotation showing that before 1925 he discussed the building of socialism in one country. He won't find any. And Bukharin? Here are three quotations, one from 1917 and the other two from 1923.* They all testify to the fact that we Oppositionists are at present, on this most important question, developing the point of view which was common to the party as a whole not only during Lenin's life but even two years ago or a year and a half ago, in other words, since Lenin died. Bukharin was discussing the proletariat in Russia and the fact that it was heading toward power, toward socialism. "However, this task which 'is placed on the agenda' in Russia, cannot be resolved 'within national boundaries.' Here the working class comes up against an insurmountable barrier which can be broken through

---

*A mistake for 1919.—Eds.

only by the battering ram of the *international workers' revolution*" [*Class Struggle and Revolution in Russia* (Moscow, 1917), pp. 3-4]. In 1919 Bukharin said even more than that: "The period of a rise in the productive forces can begin only with the victory of the proletariat in several major countries" [in the magazine *Kommunistichesky Internatsional*, no. 5, September 1919, p. 614]. Thus according to Bukharin, not just the building of socialism but even a rise in the productive forces can only begin after the victory of the proletariat in several major countries. The conclusion is that the fullest possible development of the world revolution is necessary.

Shouts from the floor: Talk to the point!

Trotsky: And finally, Bukharin also said that "the International . . ."

Shouts: This can't be allowed. Stick to the point. Why are you dodging direct questions? [*General commotion. The chair calls the session to order.*]

Trotsky: . . . Bukharin said that "the International will make possible the practice of mutual aid on the part of the proletariat of various countries and without economic and other types of mutual support the proletariat is in no position"—no position!— "to build the new society" [*Kommunistichesky Internatsional*, no. 8, May 1919, p. 94]. With this I am replying directly to the assertion Comrade Stalin made here, under the same agenda point which we are now taking up, the assertion that the alleged turn of the Opposition away from Leninism and onto the road of so-called "Trotskyism" took place above all around the question of socialism in one country. I would further remind you that the Communist League of Youth program, adopted in 1921 and still in force, has the same position, clearly formulated, as the one for which we are accused of "Trotskyism."

Shouts: Stick to the point. You don't have the nerve to answer the charges.

Trotsky: I ask you, comrades, does this mean that Bukharin in 1917, 1919, and 1921 was a Trotskyist on this question? No. At that time precisely on this question he was closer to Marx, Engels, and Lenin than on many other questions. And the Communist League of Youth program? It is true that Comrade Shatskin has made a rather naive attempt to take upon himself the full responsibility for drafting that program.

Shatskin: I wrote it.

Skrypnik: You drag Shatskin in, too?

Trotsky: It seems that in 1921 Shatskin arrived independently, through his own thinking, at the idea that the whole former tradition of Marxism was wrong and, coming to that conclusion, found it possible to introduce and embody in the Communist League of Youth program his own Trotskyist heresy. [*Commotion.*]

Shvernik: You'd do better to talk about the charges that have been brought against you.

Trotsky: Neither Bukharin nor Stalin, it turns out, noticed this. [*Shouts.*] I will get to the other charges brought against me after I have answered the charge which is most fundamental and involves basic principles. Neither Stalin nor Bukharin noticed this, i.e., they did not notice that the Communist League of Youth program had a point about the link between the building of socialism and the world revolution, which is formulated in exactly the same way that we, the Opposition, formulate it now. This also went unnoticed by Lenin, who knew how to notice a great deal. [*Commotion.*]

Petrovsky: Comrade chairman, you must make the speaker stay closer to the point under discussion.

Voroshilov: Right!

Kaganovich: Did you argue with Lenin in 1915 or didn't you?

Shout: Tell us about your article in 1915.

Trotsky: If I am not interrupted, I will tell you about Lenin's article of 1915, where Stalin's mistake is most obvious of all.

No one, it turns out, noticed that on a fundamental question, on the question of the link between socialist construction and the world revolution, there was a Trotskyist heresy in the Communist League of Youth program, which has been in existence for several years and which is still in existence.

Shout: And who set you straight? Didn't Lenin?

Trotsky: I ask again, were Bukharin's statements really accidental? [*Commotion. The chair calls for order.*] Is the Communist League of Youth program an accident? An accident? Everything that Marx, Engels, and Lenin wrote on this question is swept aside, except for one single quotation of 1915, distorted by Stalin, and Comrade Stalin referred to this very quotation under point four on the agenda, although I am now being interrupted for doing the same. I must now say a few words about this quotation.

Voices: You'd do better to answer about Thermidor, Clemenceau, and the question of two parties. Answer all the charges brought against you.

Shout: You don't have the nerve to answer the charges.

Voice: That's enough about that quotation!

Trotsky: I would like to point out that it was none other than Comrade Stalin—under this very point on the agenda—who said that the Opposition had departed from Leninism on the question of building socialism in one country, that that was our sin of sins, that that was the essential expression of "Trotskyism." And just as the chair did not stop Stalin from speaking on that question, I ask the chair to give me the opportunity to make the necessary clarifications on this basic question. [*Commotion. Shouts: This is a mockery! Enough!*] In the theses on war and peace . . . [*Uproar.*]

Rykov (the chairman): Earlier I received a great many complaints from members of the plenum about the problem that Comrade Zinoviev's speech did not deal with the agenda point that was up for discussion. [*Voices: Right!*] This led me to give several of the speakers who followed him the opportunity to touch on the same topics that Comrade Zinoviev did. But it seems to me that if we want to finish point four today, we will sooner or later have to get down to a discussion of it. [*Voices: Right!*] Therefore it would seem to me that these requests are quite pertinent and that we should devote the rest of our session to discussion of the matter raised in Comrade Ordzhonikidze's report—the proposal for the expulsion from the Central Committee of two of its members, Zinoviev and Trotsky. [*Voices: Right!*]

Trotsky: Comrades, if all the other speakers, in the limits of the time allowed them, were given the chance to speak about all the questions which in their opinion were involved under point four on the agenda, I would think that I, who am being charged before the joint plenum of the CC and CCC on this question, that I at any rate could not be denied the same right. In his report— and no one reproached him for this—Comrade Ordzhonikidze dealt with all, or nearly all, the questions that are the subject of differences . . .

Voices: Not so! Nothing of the kind!

Talberg: Speak to the point!

Trotsky: . . . even the question of how I assess the effect of a good or bad harvest on the Soviet economy. Now, comrades, it is your right to deny me the floor, but within the limits of the forty-five minutes allowed me, I can say only what I think is necessary about the charges brought against me. If the chair decides that that is wrong, the chair can of course deny me the floor, and then it would be up to the plenum to confirm this decision or not. I would have no choice but to comply. But as long as I am at the speaker's stand I can speak only about what I myself consider important and essential for the joint plenum to hear in regard to point four on the agenda.

Voice: You've said that twenty times already.

Voice: Tell us whether you're going to dissolve your faction or not. That's what you should tell us.

Voice: We'll listen to that.

Rykov (the chairman): I think I will be expressing the opinion of all the members of the plenum if I say that the plenum expects to hear something from Comrade Trotsky on the question that is now on the agenda [*Voices: Right!*], that the question of building socialism has already been discussed at congresses and conferences and has been voted on and the vote confirmed many times. [*Voices: Right!*] At any rate no one has placed that question on the agenda of this plenum.

Voroshilov (from the floor): This is the question you should speak on—Are you or are you not going to carry out . . .

Trotsky: If I am to understand the chair in the sense that I have the right to develop my thoughts further and to present the necessary conclusions from general considerations of principle, that fully agrees with the outline of the speech which I have here. [*Laughter. Noise.*]

Voice from the floor: That doesn't agree with the agenda.

Voice from the floor: Don't get into sophistries.

Kaganovich: Speak to the point.

Trotsky: If you mean to tell me that I don't have the right to speak on what I consider essential before this plenum in relation to the charges against me [*Commotion.*], if the plenum does not feel it is necessary to hear me out, it has the right to deny me the floor. I would comply with that; that is the plenum's right.

Kaganovich: You've been given forty-five minutes. Speak to the point. Don't just keep jawing away.

Trotsky: What I am saying is that everything depends on what you think the point is. If there were no differences, everything would be very simple. But in my view of what the central issue is, I totally disagree with Comrade Kaganovich. That does not prevent him from presenting his point of view. And I am trying to present mine.

Voice: Speak to the point. [*Commotion.*]

Trotsky: On the question of what is the essence of the problem I disagree with Kaganovich in the same way as I do, for example, on the question of Amsterdam. But it seems to me I have the right to present my point of view.

In his theses on war and peace (January 7, 1918), Lenin said that "for the success of socialism in Russia a certain amount of time, *several months at least,* will be necessary" [*Collected Works,* vol. 26, p. 443]. What exactly did these words mean when he said them? What specific economic and social content did he invest them with?

Voroshilov (from the floor): You can send all that off and have it printed. [*Commotion.*]

Trotsky: In early 1918 Lenin wrote the following in his article " 'Left-Wing' Childishness and the Petty-Bourgeois Mentality": "If in approximately six months' time state capitalism became established in our republic, this would be a great success and a sure guarantee that within a year socialism will have been permanently consolidated and will have become invincible in our country" [the translation in *Collected Works,* vol. 27, p. 335, is inadequate]. During the period of transition to NEP Vladimir Ilyich referred to this quotation quite a few times. He quoted it in his speech to the Fourth Comintern Congress, adding immediately: "Of course this was said at a time when we were more foolish than we are now, but not so foolish as to be unable to deal with such matters" [*Collected Works,* vol. 33, p. 419]. It is quite clear . . . [*Voice from the floor: We have to reconsider the time allowed him.*] It is quite clear that Lenin's ironic comment, "we were more foolish than we are now" referred to the low estimate of the length of time required, i.e., that "within a year socialism will have been permanently consolidated and will have become invincible in our country." [*Commotion.*]

Rudzutak: This has nothing to do with the ruling of the Central Control Commission.

Trotsky: But how could Lenin have made such a low estimate of the time required for the final consolidation of socialism? [*Commotion.*] What material-productive content did he put in these words? And what, on the other hand, was the meaning of Lenin's words, mitigating the irony of his remark, that we were "not so foolish [*Commotion.*] as to be unable to deal with such matters"? It is quite clear that when he spoke of the final consolidation of socialism Lenin did not mean the building of a socialist society in one year's time . . . [*Commotion.*]

Rudzutak: This isn't a speech but a reading of the complete collected works of Trotsky. . . .

Trotsky: . . . He did not mean the abolition of classes or the elimination of the antithesis between town and country in twelve months. What he meant primarily was the renewed operation of the plants and factories in the hands of the victorious proletariat.

That was the whole thing. [*Commotion.*] In order to understand
Lenin's approach to the question of building socialism you
cannot tear isolated remarks out of context and arbitrarily
reinterpret them, remarks spoken under various conditions, for
various reasons and—most important—for various practical
purposes. Lenin's thought must be grasped in its historical
development. Then we will find that what Lenin said about
building socialism, what he said in 1915, for example, i.e., more
than two years before the October Revolution, can be understood
correctly and without any possibility of disagreement only if we
study the development of Lenin's thought on the building of
socialism in the years following the October Revolution, when it
was no longer a matter of making a prognosis but of theoretically
clarifying the living experience.

In 1915 Lenin wrote: "Uneven economic and political development is an unconditional law of capitalism. Hence the victory of
socialism is possible at first in a few or even in one capitalist
country alone. The victorious proletariat of that country, having
expropriated the capitalists and organized socialist production at
home, would stand opposed to the rest of the world—the capitalist
world—drawing to its side the oppressed classes of the other
countries, inspiring rebellions against capitalism in those countries, and in necessary cases even using military force against the
exploiting classes and their state" [the translation in *Collected
Works,* vol. 21, p. 42, is inadequate]. These words, which are still
fairly general (it was only 1915!), nevertheless contain not only a
polemic against the so-called revolutionaries who held that the
revolution should begin simultaneously in all of Europe, if not
throughout the world, but also—against the future "left-wing"
Communists. First, Lenin was saying that the revolution could
and should begin in a single country. Where? Wherever conditions first became ripe for it. Second, he seems even then to have
been giving a warning that it is not enough just to seize power
and immediately declare a revolutionary war against the whole
capitalist world. [*Commotion in the hall.*]

Voice from the floor: Speak on point four; quit dragging things
out.

Trotsky: . . . First of all it is necessary to gain time (the
"breathing spell") and "to organize socialist production at
home." Only then will it become possible to actively oppose the
capitalist world [*Commotion.*] and encourage the oppressed
classes of other countries to rise up in rebellion. Isn't it obvious
that we have here exactly the same thought that Lenin developed

two and a half years later [*Commotion.*] in a much more concrete and rounded way in his polemic against the "left-wing" adherents of revolutionary war? Holding power by itself is not enough for waging war. In addition, production, once it is in the hands of the proletariat, must be organized properly to provide for the livelihood of the population, which means to ensure the very possibility of waging war. [*Commotion.*] And "several months at least" are needed for that. . . .

Thus, in the 1915 quotation Lenin was not discussing the building of socialist society but the initial organization of state production—in exactly the same sense that he discussed it later, in 1918, in his January theses on the Brest-Litovsk peace. In speaking of socialism, he had in mind the revived operations of the plants and factories after they had passed into the hands of the working class, the revival of regular ongoing production on new foundations, in order at least to feed the army that was fighting the war, in order to protect the socialist republic, and so that the international revolution could be extended. It was still possible to misunderstand Lenin in 1915. But how can we fail to understand him today, when he explained his old idea so exhaustively both in word and in deed!

We could cite hundreds of statements by Lenin from 1917 to 1923 against the "theory" of socialism in one country. Not one of them has been explained away or refuted by Stalin. It is ridiculous to counter all of that with one falsely interpreted quotation from 1915!

This question of building socialism in one country has become a matter of extraordinary importance today in connection with the imminent threat of war, and it confronts us in a very concrete and vital way. I accidentally came across a worker-correspondent's report—you know the kind of worker-correspondents I mean, the kind who write, not for the press, but for the special information of their editors. At the end of February this year, after the Moscow province committee conference, where the question of the war danger was sharply posed, I was leafing through a notebook of such correspondents' reports, not intended for publication, and found the following truly remarkable conversation among some workers.

Voices: Is this on point four?

Kaganovich: This is a swindle.

Rudzutak: When will you speak to the point on the agenda?

Shvernik: Come on, let's hear from you on point four.

Trotsky: This happened at the state-owned Red October confections plant. A woman worker of about twenty-five is quoted first: "We don't want a war, but if war is forced on us, we should stand up and defend our country."

A worker of about forty: "You sing a pretty tune, but when are you going to come down to earth? Who asked you to get involved in British affairs and send money over there? You're to blame yourself. It means you don't want peace if you do such things."

The woman worker of about twenty-five: "When we help the British proletariat, we know they won't return evil for good; but when a crisis comes, they'll be able to stop the bloody slaughter that British capitalism is getting ready to unleash."

A worker of about fifty . . . [*Commotion. Laughter.*]

Gerasimov: No comments from the cemetery?

Voice: Nothing from a seventy-year-old woman?

Trotsky: A worker of about fifty: "Isn't it better to live in peace and build for ourselves at home? The Communists have been painting slogans everywhere you look, that we can build socialism in one country. So why the hell go poking your nose into some other country, sending a couple of thousand to the British miners?"

The worker of about forty . . . [*Commotion. Laughter.*]

Rudzutak: This is just Trotsky's program.

Shvernik: Why is the age limit forty?

Trotsky: The worker of about forty: "Socialism can be built in one country and should be; if they themselves want to fight a war, let them—we don't want to," and so on.

This very eloquent report, not for publication, confirms that the theory of socialism in one country gives the workers a perspective. But it is a false perspective. It does not take in the international process as a whole and for that very reason the conclusions drawn from it are wrong. It weakens the understanding of the fact that in building socialism we are vitally, intimately, and directly linked with the destinies of the international revolution. And thus this perspective leads to nonrevolutionary and pacifist conclusions, as is amply demonstrated by the correspondent's report I just read you. This theory, if it becomes entrenched, will have an extremely negative effect on the development of the Communist International.

That is why the party must be given the chance to discuss this new theory, not according to ready-made textbook clichés . . .

Rudzutak: You're the one who's reciting textbook clichés.

Trotsky: . . . not textbook clichés but honest, open, and real discussion. The question should be placed before the Fifteenth

Congress in good time—not in a sudden way but in a way that allows for a rounded ideological preparation, verification, and discussion, and for this a collection of materials must be published in time, and a discussion must be opened up in time in the pages of *Bolshevik* or some other periodical especially devoted to the precongress discussion. The Opposition must be given the chance to publish its speeches and articles on this question in a separate collection or together with the speeches and articles of representatives of the CC majority.

Stepanov: Is this on point four?

Ukhanov: You'd do better to read something from Chekhov.

Trotsky: Comrade Yaroslavsky says that on the question of internal relations in the party, including those between the Central Committee and the party, . . .

Voice: And what do you think of the party, of which you are a member?

Trotsky: . . . the Opposition is said to hold the viewpoint of "Trotskyism." But what does this Trotskyism consist of? Comrade Yaroslavsky specified what he meant by this charge in his report to the active membership in Kiev, where he cited the fact that the Opposition had sunk so low in its factional activity that Comrades Muralov and Kharitonov had placed amendments to the theses of Comrades Kalinin and Kuibyshev before the party fraction at the congress of Soviets. Of course it is Comrade Yaroslavsky's right to judge these amendments. But that is not the problem. The very fact that they were brought before the fraction is what he calls factionalism and *Trotskyism!* Here are his exact words: "Why should the party fraction at the congress of Soviets discuss this question after the CC plenum approved the line of the CC? Can the fraction at the congress of Soviets be *higher* than the plenum? That is a *Trotskyist conception of our party*, that is, if you disagree with the CC plenum, you can appeal from a CC plenum to the fraction at a congress of Soviets."

Comrades, if this is your interpretation of Trotskyism, I assure you that the concept of Trotskyism would include every attempt by a party member to utilize his or her fully legitimate rights within the party. As for the particular question of appealing to the party fraction at a congress of Soviets, one could perhaps hold CC members to blame if they did that. But this did not involve CC members. Precisely on this question I have evidence of exceptional importance. Is it really true that appealing to the fraction at a congress of Soviets constitutes a violation of party rules, party traditions, party law? Is that really Trotskyism?

Voice: Comrade Trotsky, please finish up by speaking to the point.

Trotsky: On December 12, 1922, Comrade Lenin wrote to Frumkin and Stomonyakov, who were not CC members, at a time when he had a disagreement with the CC on the question of the monopoly of foreign trade. He wrote: "I will write Trotsky of my agreement with him and ask him to take upon himself, in view of my sickness, the defense of my position at the plenum. . . .

"I hope to write again today or tomorrow and send you my declaration on the essence of the given problem at the plenum of the Central Committee. At any rate, I think that this question is of such fundamental importance that in case I do not get the agreement of the plenum, I will have to carry it into the party congress and before that announce the existing disagreement in the fraction of our party at the coming congress of Soviets." [This letter is not in the *Collected Works*. The full text is in *The Stalin School of Falsification*, pp. 59-60.]

On December 13, Vladimir Ilyich wrote me: "I think that you and I are in maximum agreement, and I believe that the State Planning Commission question, as presented in this case, rules out . . . any discussion on whether the State Planning Commission needs to have any administrative rights."

Molotov: This is on the State Planning Commission. Not on Trotskyism.

Trotsky: No. The agreement was on the monopoly of foreign trade; the question of the State Planning Commission was secondary. But I think that the question of the monopoly of foreign trade is one of the cornerstones of Leninism—in a backward socialist country, surrounded by capitalist countries. That is precisely why Vladimir Ilyich intended to appeal to the party fraction. He continued: "in the event of our defeat on this question we must refer the question to a party congress. This will require a brief exposition of our differences before the party fraction of the forthcoming congress of Soviets. If I have time, I shall write this, and I would be very glad if you did the same" [*Collected Works,* vol. 45, pp. 601-02].

On December 15, Vladimir Ilyich wrote: "I am sure that if we are threatened with the danger of failure,"—at the Central Committee plenum—"it would be much better to fail before the party congress and at once to address ourselves to the party fraction at the congress [of Soviets], than to fail after the congress" [*Collected Works,* vol. 45, pp. 604-05].

Also on December 15, Vladimir Ilyich wrote to me: "If for some reason our decision should not be passed we shall address ourselves to the party fraction at the congress of Soviets and declare that we are referring the question to the party congress."

He continued: "If this question should be removed from the present plenum (which I do not expect and against which you should of course protest as strongly as you can on our common behalf), I think that we should address ourselves to the party fraction at the congress of Soviets anyway and demand that the question be referred to the party congress, because any further hesitation is absolutely intolerable" [*Collected Works*, vol. 45, p. 604].

Finally on December 21, when the plenum, on Comrade Zinoviev's initiative, reversed its previous, incorrect decision, Vladimir Ilyich wrote: "Comrade Trotsky. It looks as though it has been possible to take the position without a single shot, by a simple maneuver. I suggest that we should not stop and should continue the offensive . . ." Who was Vladimir Ilyich proposing to continue the offensive against?

Voice: Trotsky!

Trotsky: No. The offensive was against the Central Committee. Lenin continued: ". . . and for that purpose put through a motion to raise at the party congress the question of consolidating our foreign trade and the measures to improve its implementation. This should be announced to the party fraction at the congress of Soviets. I hope that you will not object to this and will not refuse to give a report to the fraction" [the translation in *Collected Works*, vol. 45, p. 606, is inadequate].

That is what "Trotskyism" looks like in practice!

Now, comrades, the charge has been raised against me here of not telling the truth on the question of articles in *Sotsialisti-chesky Vestnik*, on the question of which side *Sotsialistichesky Vestnik* took in the fundamental differences over the question of the Chinese revolution.

Voice: We've heard.

Trotsky: I handed in a written declaration on a point of personal privilege which was not more than a page and a half in length. My request to have this read to the plenum was denied. The chair ruled that it should be appended to the stenographic record of the proceedings.

Now, comrades, in connection with the sharp questions that divide us, an attempt has been made to deduce from my article "What Is This Leading To?" which was directed against one of Moscow Agitprop's clichéd texts . . .

Voice: You're repeating textbook clichés yourself.

Talberg: You're reading from a clichéd text.

Trotsky: . . . a text which was published in an edition of 5,000 by the printshop of the OGPU—an attempt has been made to deduce from this some terrible evidence of our insurrectionist intentions.

The Opposition is said to be preparing to fight for a different defense policy, following the example of the Clemenceau group in France during the war. And this supposedly points toward Left SR insurrectionism. But these things just don't fit together.

Voice: They fit together very well.

Trotsky: If you talk about the Left SR uprising, you can't talk about Clemenceau, and if you want to make evidence against the Opposition out of the Clemenceau matter, you can't talk about the Left SR uprising. The Opposition, we are told, wishes to seize power like the Clemenceau group. The Opposition thinks—and it does not hide this from either the CC or the party—that its removal from the leadership hurts the interests of the party. Every serious ideological current cannot fail to hold such a view. We think that the removal of the Opposition from the leadership has had especially serious effects recently in regard to the line of the leadership in the Chinese revolution.

Voice: You won't get back on the CC!

Trotsky: We think that similar mistakes of a principled nature can do especially great harm to the effort to defend the USSR precisely if there is a war. Therefore our view is that even in the case of a war, the party should preserve—or more exactly, should restore—a healthier, more flexible, and more correct internal regime, one that would permit timely criticism, timely warnings, and timely changes of policy. In what way does insurrectionism follow from this? If we return to the historical reference, which I drew from the political history of bourgeois parties in France to illustrate my idea, it will be seen that the Clemenceau opposition came to power not at all through insurrection, and not at all through the violation of the bourgeois legality they had there, but through their own bourgeois, capitalist legality, through the mechanics of French parliamentarism. The French parliament did not even change its composition. There were no new elections. On the basis of the experience of the war the French bourgeoisie, in the person of its ruling cliques, came to the conclusion that a ministry of Clemenceau, Tardieu, and Company would better correspond to its interests during the war than the ministry of

Painlevé, Briand, and Company. Why should this historical example inspire thoughts of insurrectionism?

The objection may be raised—and we too will raise the objection—that we don't have a parliamentary mechanism. Yes, fortunately we do not. But we have the mechanism of the party. The party must maintain control over all its institutions, in wartime as well as in peace time. The party decides all fundamental questions at its congresses, regular and special. It is entirely possible for the party to arrive at the conclusion that the removal of the Opposition from its policy-making bodies was a mistake, and the party can correct this mistake.

Talberg: This is a lawyer's speech.

Trotsky: Can the party, or can it not, correct what was done during the interval between two congresses? Can the party, or can it not, decide at a congress that in the interests of our defense, and our economy, in the interests of the Chinese revolution and the entire Comintern, that the leadership of the party should be organized on the same principles that Lenin outlined in his Testament? Can the party or can it not? I think it can. I am sure that the entire Opposition thinks it can. Here there is not even a hint of so-called insurrectionism—let alone the monstrous accusation concerning the policy of two parties, the policy of a split.

In order to reinforce the accusation of insurrectionism, so very ambiguously thrown out here, a rather unusual and peculiar business was organized in connection with the note I submitted to the Politburo on the military question.

Chubar: What fancy talk is this?

Trotsky: Such notes have been submitted dozens of times over the ten years of our revolution, by both CC members and nonmembers and by individual military personnel and groups of them. It never occurred to anyone that the sending of a letter to the CC by a party member calling attention to one or another irregularity in the organization of the armed forces or to an incorrect military policy in general constituted an antiparty step.

Chubar: And there never was a demonstration at the Yaroslavl station, right?

Trotsky: At the Eighth Congress, as has been described here already, there was a close-knit group called the Military Opposition, which in the sphere of military organization counterposed to the centralized proletarian line the line of decentralization and guerrilla methods. It never occurred to anyone to regard even that group as an antiparty tendency. Comrade Voroshilov claims that I didn't dare show myself at the Eighth Congress precisely because of this issue. On this point I have submitted a statement of personal objection with a specific quotation from the decision of the Politburo, which instructed me to depart for the front, in spite of the congress, in view of our reverses in the east, our retreat from the vicinity of Ufa. Unfortunately this statement has also not been read to the plenum. The chairman has promised to have it appended to the minutes of these proceedings.

I return now to the military document. In early 1924 at the VAK, formerly the Military Academic Courses, there was an incident involving a document—a memorandum to the Central Committee drafted with the participation of Comrades Dybenko, Fedko, Uritsky, Belov, and other comrades, on questions of military organization. Through Comrade Kakhanyan and others the signatures of party members in military work were gathered in support of this document, which was submitted to the CC. It is true that in that endeavor word was spread that no special risk would be run by signing, since the document was known to several members of the CC. The document circulated rather widely from hand to hand. It dealt with the same difficulties in military work that are dealt with in the memorandum I submitted, but it treated them from a different angle. All those who signed this statement not only were left untouched but some of the most active participants received rather significant promotions soon after the memorandum was submitted.

I believe that as a member of the CC I had the right to submit a memorandum written on the basis of information I obtained by conferring with several military personnel whom I directly named by name. But when I did that an absolutely monstrous outcry arose, with accusations and even threats. Since the last page was not completely written and this caused the submission of the statement to be postponed for half an hour, the entire mechanism of the plenum was set into motion around this question; Comrade Unshlicht appeared in the corridor of the White Palace of the Kremlin with a formal ruling by the plenum of the Central Committee. What was all this for? Even the term "military conspiracy" was heard. A military conspiracy expressed in the fact that a member of the CC submitted a memorandum of one copy to the CC and, in submitting it, named a few absolutely loyal and reliable party members by name with whom he had conferred on particular aspects of military work! What is all this done for? Everyone understands the reason. This was organized in order to store up material for possible future use in making a case against the Opposition on charges of insurrectionism. Of course, this kind of approach can in no case improve relations within the party, and cannot produce the more normal conditions of party life that we desire in the interests of the ideas we are defending, and desire no less than any other member of the party or any other member of the CC and CCC.

Here I must say that no matter how great our differences, no matter how sharp they may be, it is absolutely unheard of in relations among Communists, even in a heated dispute over an internal party matter, to accuse a party member of "having Communists shot." And such an accusation was bound to provoke an extremely sharp reply, which in other circumstances might have been impermissible. When Comrade Yaroslavsky allowed himself to make such a statement at the CCC presidium, Comrade Ordzhonikidze immediately stopped him . . .

Voice from the floor: At the CCC Secretariat.

Trotsky: Absolutely right, at the Secretariat. And of course, since Comrade Ordzhonikidze stopped him, I did not venture to make the kind of retort that I was compelled to make here and which, of course, is absolutely impermissible within the framework of a leadership institution or a party institution in general. [*Yaroslavsky: You called Communists Black Hundredists.*] But unfortunately Comrade Voroshilov was not stopped from making his statement. In response to Comrade Voroshilov's words, which of course no member of the party could let go unchallenged, to besmirch his reputation—anymore than I could—I submitted a written statement, which unfortunately has not been read to the plenum. In this written statement I established firmly something that should be clear to every one of us already, namely, that those who were shot under me, under my command, or on my direct orders, were deserters, traitors, and White Guards, and that Communists were never shot. Communists were shot by our class enemies, the White Guards. If a Communist happened to fall into the category of deserter or traitor, he of course was subject to being shot as a deserter . . . [*Radchenko: What about Bakaev and Zalutsky?*] I will read to the plenum all the documents about Comrades Bakaev and Zalutsky if you will give me five or ten minutes. It is not true that I ever called for the shooting of Zalutsky and Bakaev. This question was investigated by the Central Committee at my request at the time. The situation was this. The Military Revolutionary Council issued an order, with CC approval, which said that all commissars must know the whereabouts of the families of the commanders that were attached to them, so that no commander whose family was located in enemy territory would be on the fighting line or in important posts in general, for such commanders might wish to reach their families and to do that might betray us and bring ruin to our fighting front and to hundreds and thousands of Red Army soldiers and commanders. The wording of the order was very strict in the sense that it obliged all commissars to attend to this matter. When there was wavering in one of the divisions on the Eastern Front because of treason by a group on the commanding staff, resulting in serious consequences for the whole sector, I was on the Southern Front. I learned of this act of treason by telegram and sent an inquiry by telegram to Comrades Smilga and Lashevich, ordering that the families of the traitorous commanders be taken prisoner immediately and held as hostages and according to the law of the time to have those family members shot who might have been accessories, accomplices, etc. The answer I got was that nothing was known about the families. Not knowing who the commissars were or what kind of commissars they were—and at that time there were cases of highly unreliable commissars; it was a time when the selection of personnel as commissars was not very reliable—I sent a telegram in which I said that commissars who did not know the whereabouts of the families of their commanding personnel should be brought before a tribunal and shot. This was not an order to have them shot. This was the usual kind of pressure that was practiced then. I have here dozens of telegrams from Vladimir Ilyich of the same kind, and I will read them now if you wish. [*Voice: Don't bother.*] Lashevich and Smilga answered me: "Our commissars are so and so; they are excellent comrades; we will answer for them; and if you are displeased with us you can remove us." To this I replied word for word: "Comrades, don't be coy. You are top-notch commissars; there couldn't be any better. I only want to say that you must do twenty times, a hundred times, better in keeping an eye on the families of commanders who may turn up on the other side of the enemy's lines." Comrades Bakaev and Zalutsky, as you know, were not shot; between me and those commissars stood such comrades as Smilga and Lashevich. When I sent the telegram I knew they would do nothing unwarranted. This was a form of military pressure common at the time. The CC was notified about all this by me at the time.

In the CCC session I showed the blank sheet that Vladimir Ilyich gave me precisely when these rumors about the shooting of

Communists reached the Politburo. The question of Comrades Zalutsky and Bakaev is essentially a misunderstanding. But the regimental commissar Panteleev actually was shot during the battle of Kazan. In this case the commander and the commissar abandoned the front line—while we were surrounded—seized a steamer, and tried to steam upriver to Nizhny Novgorod. We stopped them, placed them on trial, and they were shot. We reported this matter to the Politburo. On this question the Politburo found our decision to be justified. Later on, when they told Lenin that Trotsky had had Communists shot, Lenin gave me, on his own initiative, a blank sheet expressing the highest form of confidence. I submitted this document to the Lenin Institute. The page is blank but at the bottom some words are written which you will also find in the stenographic record of the CCC session. "Comrades: Knowing the strict character of Comrade Trotsky's orders, I am so convinced, so absolutely convinced, of the correctness, expediency, and necessity, for the success of the cause, of the order given by Comrade Trotsky that I unreservedly endorse this order. V. Ulyanov (Lenin)."

When I asked what this was for, Vladimir Ilyich said: "This is in case of the revival of such rumors. You will have a ready-made blank sheet on which you can write whatever decision may be required by the circumstances." I never ventured to make use of this document; it remained in my possession as a historical document, which I have given to the Lenin Institute. It testifies to the fact that despite the differences that came up, Vladimir Ilyich trusted that I would not abuse his confidence, that I would not abuse my power to the detriment of the cause or to harm individual comrades—even in the most trying circumstances of civil war.

In connection with the question of . . . [*Kaganovich: Speak about the Yaroslavl station. Voices: On Clemenceau. On Thermidor.*] I am just now coming to that.

Comrade Ordzhonikidze has quoted here from the statement of last October 16. The main idea in that statement was the renunciation of factional activity. Was our October 16 statement sincere? You have sufficient information, comrades, indicating with how much energy the Oppositionist members of the CC pursued this obligation . . . [*Commotion. Voices: Oho, you pursued factional activity with energy. You're laughing at us. In what respect?*] . . . in respect to the fact that we called on Oppositionists not to withdraw into themselves, not to go off in a corner and whisper, not to hide from the party, but to openly present their views in the party organizations to which we all belong. It is true that every tendency must bear responsibility on the whole and in general for its supporters—not, of course, for each one individually but for all of them as a whole. However, something else is also true: the party regime bears some responsibility for the forms that criticism within the party takes. [*Voices: Aha!*]

On the question of the conditions formulated by Comrade Ordzhonikidze, I can only endorse wholeheartedly what Comrade Zinoviev has said here on this question. It would, of course, be wrong to regard these conditions as the terms under which this or that comrade would be kept on the Central Committee. That of course is not the issue. In the near future there will be a party congress, which, after a two-year interval, will decide—among other questions—the question of the composition of the party's Central Committee. Expulsion or nonexpulsion from the CC under these circumstances is merely an *external* symptom of a further shift in relations within the party in one or another direction, nothing more. [*Shouts: Oho!*] Precisely in the interests of the defense of the views we stand for in the party [*Voice: Which you defend at the station.*] our defense must be such that the party can test out these views on the basis of its experience of events and of the ideological struggle. The struggle within the party, with all its sharp polemics and their consequences, is not accidental. It has led to such incidents as the farewell gathering for a member of the CC at the Yaroslavl station. No one considers this normal. But no one can consider it normal that for months *Pravda* has treated members of the CC as enemies of the socialist republic. Both the one and the other are abnormal. And the two things are connected. You cannot separate or disconnect them. Despite the best intentions there will be no success unless a more normal and a healthier regime is created in the party. [*Voices: What a regime!*] We declare that we are ready to do everything we can to improve relations within the party before the Fifteenth Congress and through the Fifteenth Congress, despite our profound differences of principle [*Voice: Permanent discussion!*] and to make it easier for the CC to make use of Opposition forces for any work, civilian or military. Every Oppositionist, unless there is a hanger-on or someone in the Opposition by mistake— and of course there are such elements in the Opposition too— every Oppositionist will do this with a clear conscience.

Voices: Just words! Quit talking! It's Tomsky's turn.

Chairman: Comrade Tomsky has the floor. [*Applause.*]

STATEMENT OF THE THIRTEEN

August 8, 1927

NOTE: Faced with a motion to expel Zinoviev and Trotsky from the Central Committee, and with panic on the part of the Zinovievists, the Opposition submitted the present statement. The following translation is based on the text submitted by the thirteen Opposition leaders to the Central Committee and on the heavily revised text published in Pravda *on August 10 and 11. The material in square brackets was not in the original statement submitted by the Opposition, but was added under pressure from the Stalinists at the joint plenum (see Trotsky's remarks of August 9 on p. 296). The bracketed material appeared in the officially sanctioned* Pravda *version, which left out the entire second part of the statement (here set off by asterisks).*

According to the majority resolution adopted at the plenum ("On Violations of Discipline by Zinoviev and Trotsky"), the majority proposed not to expel the two Opposition leaders if they would accept certain terms:

"1. Renounce Trotsky's semi-defeatist theory in face of the threat of war (Trotsky's thesis on Clemenceau), take the road of absolute and unconditional defense of our socialist motherland against imperialism, and denounce the Opposition's slander that our party and Soviet leadership have degenerated into Thermidorianism;

"2. Renounce the policy of splitting the Comintern, denounce the party formed by Maslow and Fischer, who have been expelled from the Comintern, rupture all contacts with that anti-Leninist, divisive party, and carry out all the decisions of the Communist International;

"3. Renounce the policy of splitting the AUCP(B), denounce the attempt to form a second party, disband the faction, and pledge to carry out all the decisions of the AUCP(B) and its Central Committee." (This resolution is reprinted in Against Trotskyism *[Moscow, 1972].)*

The joint plenum then voted to "sternly reprimand and cau-

*tion" Zinoviev and Trotsky instead of expelling them outright,
although it still considered the statement of August 8 "insufficient" in that it was hedged with "reservations" and "repudiated" only some of the Opposition's "errors."*

*In looking back after his expulsion from the party, Trotsky
viewed the August 8 statement in the same light as the October
16, 1926, declaration. Many academic historians consider these
"documents of surrender" (for example, E. H. Carr,* Foundations
of a Planned Economy, *vol. 2, p. 32). To Trotsky these declarations "had the aim of showing the party masses once more that
the goal of the Opposition is not a second party or civil war"—as
the ruling circles were claiming—"but rectification of the line of
the party and the state by the methods of deepgoing reform" (see
"At a New Stage," p. 508).*

By permission of the Harvard College Library.

Without entering into the polemical form in which the questions have been put, we are answering them on the substance of
the issues.

To the first question: We are absolutely and unconditionally for
the defense of our socialist motherland against imperialism. Of
course, we are absolutely and unconditionally for the defense of
the USSR with the present Central Committee and the present
Executive Committee of the Comintern in power.

If, in Comrade Trotsky's letter [to Ordzhonikidze, July 11, 1927;
see p. 252], the passage referring to Clemenceau has given
any grounds for incorrect interpretation—as favoring a struggle
for power by taking advantage of the difficulties of war—we
categorically reject such an interpretation. At the same time we
maintain our conviction that, in time of war, the party cannot
renounce criticism or refrain from correcting the policy of the CC
should it prove incorrect.

Our draft resolution on the international question, among other
things, puts forward the following slogans:

For the defeat of all bourgeois states that go to war with the
USSR.

All honest workers in capitalist countries should actively
contribute to the defeat of "their own" governments.

Let all foreign soldiers who do not wish to play the game of
"their own" masters cross over to the side of the Red Army.

The USSR is the homeland of all workers.

We have been defensists since October 25, 1917.

Our "national war" will be a war "for the Soviet Republic as a detachment of the world army of socialism"; our "national" war will not "end in the bourgeois state but in the international socialist revolution"—Lenin.

Not to defend the USSR is without doubt to betray the international proletariat.

On the question of Thermidorianism we declare: Elements of Thermidorianism are increasing in this country, and they have a rather substantial social basis. [We do not doubt that the party and the proletariat, by following the Leninist line and through inner-party democracy, will overcome these forces.] What we demand is that the party leadership should more firmly and systematically oppose these tendencies and their influence on certain sections of the party. We reject the idea that our Bolshevik party [or its CC or CCC] have become Thermidorian.

To the second question: We acknowledge that the German Communist movement is threatened by an open split and the formation of two parties. [While submitting to the decision of the Comintern concerning the impermissibility of maintaining organizational ties with the expelled Urbahns-Maslow group, we insist and shall not cease to insist in the Comintern that the decree of expulsion be re-examined, in view of the fact that] there are, among the expelled, hundreds of old revolutionary workers closely connected with the working masses, devoted to the cause of Lenin, and sincere in their readiness to defend the USSR to the very last.

The setting up of a second party in Germany would create a very great danger. We think that all possible steps should be taken to prevent that. We propose that the CC of the AUCP(B), through the Executive Committee of the Comintern, pursue the following means to avert that danger. On the condition that the Urbahns group cease publication of its paper and subordinate itself to all decisions of the Comintern congress, all those expelled members who accept these conditions should be reinstated in the Comintern and be assured the opportunity of defending their views in the party press and in the ranks of the party and Comintern in general.

To the third question: We categorically condemn any attempt whatsoever to create a new party. We consider the road toward the creation of a second party in the USSR as absolutely ruinous for the revolution. We shall oppose with all our might and in every possible way any tendency toward two parties. We condemn just as absolutely and categorically any splitting orientation. We will carry out all decisions of the AUCP(B) and its CC.

We are prepared to do everything possible to eliminate the elements of factionalism that have been engendered by the fact that, faced with the distortion of the inner-party regime, we were compelled to fight to make known to the party our real views, which were incorrectly presented in the press read by the entire country.

*   *   *

Having answered the questions posed to us, we consider it necessary, in turn, to express to the joint plenum of the CC and CCC our profound conviction about the following matter.

Several measures are absolutely necessary to keep the attempt to establish peace in the party, and truly eliminate factionalism and closed-mindedness, from ending up with the same results as after October 16, 1926.

1. Immediately condemn, in the name of the joint plenum of the CC and CCC, the publication of such materials by our press as the pamphlet "On War and the War Danger," issued by the Agitational and Propaganda Department of the Moscow committee, the article in the Ivanovo-Voznesensk party newspaper declaring the Oppositionists to be counterrevolutionaries, and the article in *Leningradskaya Pravda* of August 5 of this year, which went so far as to write, while this plenum was being held, that "the declarations of the Opposition bloc are as popular a commodity in the war ministries of hostile powers as the stocks of highly profitable enterprises are on the capitalist stock exchange."

2. Put an end to expulsions from the party and other repressive measures against Oppositionists for dissenting from official policies and restore the expelled members to the party.

3. Guarantee that the methods of preparing for the Fifteenth Congress will be the same as they were under Lenin, when there also were serious differences in the party. In particular:

(a) Publish in the press the theses, articles, and platforms of every minority in the party two months before the congress;

(b) Make it possible for all members of the party to familiarize themselves with the most important documents on disputed questions and to arrive at a considered decision on the basis of a thorough discussion;

(c) Guarantee a comradely discussion of the questions in dispute—without exaggerations, accusations of a personal nature, etc.;

(d) Adopt as the main slogan in preparing for the Fifteenth Congress, "The Unity of the AUCP and the Comintern, Above All Else."

Avdeev	Lizdin	Smilga
Bakaev	Muralov	Solovyov
Yevdokimov	Peterson	Trotsky
Zinoviev	Pyatakov	
Kamenev	Rakovsky	

PROTEST ON ABRIDGMENT OF
THE STATEMENT OF THE THIRTEEN

August 9, 1927

NOTE: The day after the Opposition submitted its statement of August 8 to the joint plenum, Stalin addressed the plenum and denounced the statement as inadequate. He charged the Opposition with "holding weapons in reserve for a future attack on the party" (J. V. Stalin, On the Opposition (1921-27) *[Peking: Foreign Languages Press, 1974], pp. 843-49). On the same day, the plenum voted to "separate" the Opposition's answers to the deliberately provocative questions posed by the majority from its demands for reform and rectification. The latter were dropped altogether from the printed version that appeared in* Pravda *the following day. This is the text of Trotsky's speech at the plenum protesting that step.*

By permission of the Harvard College Library.

Trotsky: Comrade Ordzhonikidze has explained that there is a *direct order* by the plenum . . . [*Commotion in the hall.*] . . . that there is a direct order obliging us to separate the two parts of our statement.

If there is a direct *order,* then as in any such case, we will comply with the direct order.

Voice from the floor: There is a proposal by the plenum.

Trotsky: To the plenum's *proposal* we replied that it was unacceptable to us and explained why it was unacceptable. It is unacceptable because complete clarity and precision are necessary on these questions. To a *decision* voted by the plenum, which obliges us to separate the parts of the statement, we can only reply in the way we would to any decision of the plenum. But in so doing, we reserve not only our right but our duty, wherever we may be . . .

Voice from the floor: On every street corner.

Voice from the floor: At the Yaroslavl station.

Trotsky: . . . everywhere and anywhere permissible under the party rules, where normal conditions of party life allow it, to explain that the commitments made in the first part of our declaration, artificially separated from the second part by your decision, can only offer the hope of serious progress, even if not rapid progress, on the condition that our efforts not be one-sided; if no weapons are held in reserve for a future attack on us by the comrades who, to a far greater extent than the minority, i.e., the Opposition, are guiding the fate of our party. For if Comrade Stalin expressed the thought here that the majority has no reason to take the Opposition at its word, because the Opposition might hold a weapon in reserve for a future attack on the party, he is not the only one with the right to make such a statement. [*Uproar.*] The very fact of the struggle will leave its mark on the party for a prolonged period, and this legacy can be eliminated only through good will on both sides.

Voice from the floor: What is this, a contract?

Voice from the floor: What about the party? There is the party, remember!

Voice from the floor: There aren't two sides; there is the party.

Trotsky: —No, this is not a "contract"; we are talking about good will on both sides. [*Uproar.*]

It is absolutely correct that there is the party. But if the Opposition did not exist as a fact, and not as some "contracting party," all the questions we have been talking about would not exist and you would not have had to raise the question of the Opposition. The Opposition is not trying to negotiate a deal, but is responding to questions put to it and expressing its views. It is only within this context that I speak of the majority and minority sides.

And so, we absolutely and completely remain on the standpoint we expressed in our statement—that the two parts of our declaration are a single whole. When you asked us whether we agree to separating one part from the other we answered through Comrade Kamenev, "No, we cannot do that, because we do not want the party to have illusions and we do not want to lead the party astray." Despite the clear and precise character of our statement, you find it appropriate to pass a resolution obliging us to separate the two parts. In the face of the decision voted by the joint plenum, obliging us to make such a separation, we have no recourse but to submit to this decision. [*Uproar.*]

LETTER ON THE TACTICS
OF THE OPPOSITION

August 12, 1927

NOTE: The folder containing the typescript of this letter bore a note by Trotsky: "I think this letter was written to Krestinsky in Berlin (or to Antonov-Ovseenko?)," who was also at a diplomatic post (in Prague).

The "vulgar philistine philosophy" that Trotsky paraphrases on p. 299 was shared by some of the Oppositionists, particularly among the Zinovievists, who tended to put considerable stock in the conciliatory declarations and hope that trouble would blow over if they lay low. Both Krestinsky and Antonov-Ovseenko capitulated to Stalin shortly after the Fifteenth Congress.

By permission of the Harvard College Library.

Dear Friend:

Your letter surprised and saddened me, and the reports of comrades who visited you have done so—even more. Isolation never fails to take its toll.

You write that the Declaration of the Eighty-four should not have been submitted. In your opinion the timing was wrong, it created tensions, and so on and so forth. The comrades who proposed the idea of submitting a collectively signed declaration at first ran into objections here inside the country of approximately the same order that you raise. The number of those who objected was substantial. Today *not one* comrade remains who would deny that the collective declaration was timely, and to the highest degree; that it strengthened the Opposition enormously and in that way softened the blow the Stalin faction was preparing to level against it. This is confirmed not only by the implications of events that have occurred since then but also by first-hand information we have received from the other camp. Try to reevaluate this point and you will come to a reevaluation of a number of your other arguments.

Relations became highly strained, not because of one or

another "incautious" step, but because of the abrupt surfacing of very deep differences over the events of the Chinese revolution. On the day of Chiang Kai-shek's coup, which we predicted, we said, "Stalin will be forced to intensify his struggle against the Opposition tenfold." How could this have been avoided? Only in one way: by keeping quiet about the mistakes being made or minimizing them by not tracing them back to their point of origin—the purely Menshevik line. But that would have been the road of ideological betrayal. If one is to do one's duty and call things by their right name, the question of "tone" becomes secondary. Finally, even on the question of "tone" the truth is that we did not commit any excesses. It was precisely the depth and intensity of the differences over China and the Anglo-Russian Committee that led Stalin to the idea of crushing the top layer of the Opposition as quickly as he could. The collective declaration spread the burden of responsibility to many more shoulders and by that alone helped to soften the blow.

The key to internal party questions, in this case as in all cases, is the class line. If you had doubts about the Chinese question or the Anglo-Russian Committee, it would be a different matter. But I don't want to think, even for a moment, that you could have doubts on those two questions. In the entire history of Bolshevism one could hardly find an example in which events so rapidly revealed the 100 percent incorrectness of one line (the Stalinists') and the correctness of the other (ours).

Some comrades argue as follows: The internal party regime is definitely intolerable; as for other questions, we still have to discuss them. The internal regime is viewed as something separate unto itself. One wonders, Why is the regime bad? Is it because of Stalin's nasty personality? No, the party regime is a function of the political line. It was precisely because Stalin stakes everything on Chiang Kai-shek and Purcell, on the bureaucrat and the upper layers in the village, etc., that he feels compelled to carry out his policies, not by relying on the mind and will of the proletarian vanguard but by suppressing the vanguard with administrative-apparatus methods, thereby reflecting and refracting the pressure of other classes upon the proletariat. That is the explanation for the frenzied fight against the Opposition, because it resists and combats that hostile class pressure.

There is a vulgar philistine philosophy that says, if you don't "create tensions," don't rock the boat, but remain silent, stand aside, and wait, things will work out by themselves. This philosophy will get one exactly nowhere. The key thing is to maintain continuity in the development of the thinking of the revolutionary party, to train revolutionary cadres who will prove capable of applying policies as required by the circumstances that arise. Unless we do that, Stalin's errors and the break-up of his group could mean only a further slide to the right in the political life of the country. That is the road of Thermidor, i.e., a situation in which there is a class shift at the seat of power, not through the replacement of one party by another, but through a realignment of elements within one and the same party. This is the road of split and of disaster for the revolution. This outcome (which is not at all necessary or inevitable) cannot be opposed passively, with a wait-and-see attitude, but only by an uncompromising Marxist analysis of all the processes under way in the country and the party, by a ruthless critique of the backsliding policies of the leadership, and by the training of new cadres to maintain the continuity of Bolshevik tradition—in other words, precisely what the Opposition is now doing.

One cannot first decide the question of tone, or the sharpness and pace of the struggle, and then adapt the political line to these considerations. Of course the question of how sharply to speak at the ECCI or at a Central Committee plenum is very serious and important. But it only makes sense to argue about such questions if you have come to firm agreement about the basic line. The slightest glossing over of the depth of the differences on fundamental questions of domestic policy and Comintern policy would be a crime, would be sliding back toward the backsliders, would be liquidation of the party and preparation for a split in the future. At the same time it would prepare the way for the downfall of the October Revolution.

Further realignments within the party—and very profound ones at that—are absolutely inevitable. A number of harsh blows from the right will ensue. If the Opposition maintains a firm line, the differentiation within the ranks of the party will accelerate—with the proletarian elements shifting to the left. The proletarian elements of the party will be decisive. Only *that kind* of differentiation can ensure unity on a revolutionary basis. Any other way of fighting for the unity of the party would be illusory, wrong, and non-Bolshevik.

I am absolutely certain that if you came here for a week or two and acquainted yourself with the real situation in the party, you would see that the policy we are now following is the only policy possible.

THE PLATFORM OF THE OPPOSITION
The Party Crisis and How to Overcome It

September 1927

NOTE: The title page of the Russian typescript identified this as a "draft" Platform, submitted to the Politburo by thirteen members of the Central Committee and the CCC for the Fifteenth Congress of the AUCP. "They reserve for themselves the right to make specific revisions in this Platform up to the eve of the congress—after the exchange of opinions in print and at party meetings." In the upper right-hand corner was the warning: "For circulation only to members of the AUCP(B)." The signatories were Muralov, Yevdokimov, Rakovsky, Pyatakov, Smilga, Zinoviev, Trotsky, Kamenev, Peterson, Bakaev, Solovyov, Lizdin, Avdeev. But in "An Appeal to Party Members" (see New International, *November 1934), Trotsky wrote that two hundred party members had contributed to the Platform.*

*The Platform of the Opposition is the principal document of the years 1926-27. It was designed as a contribution to the pre-congress discussion; Trotsky and the other Oppositionists hoped that it would be distributed to party members, as party rules insisted it should be, and they used it to sum up virtually every criticism of the Stalinists' policy that they had made since the United Opposition bloc was formed. According to Victor Serge—a French Oppositionist born in Belgium who was in the Soviet Union at this time (later arrested and confined, he was allowed to leave the USSR only in 1936)—the chapters on agriculture and the International were drafted by Zinoviev and Kamenev, the one on industrialization by Trotsky; as each section was completed it was submitted to meetings of Oppositionists for discussion and reworking (*Memoirs of a Revolutionary, *p. 222). In* The Third International After Lenin *(p. 128), Trotsky says that the Chinese revolution is dealt with in the Platform very insufficiently, incompletely, and in part positively falsely by Zinoviev. The completed draft was delivered to the Politburo on September 3.*

This is a new translation by George Saunders. An earlier one, by Max Eastman, was published in The Real Situation in Russia (1928).

Chapter 1
Introduction

In his speech at the last party congress he attended [1922] Lenin said: "Well, we have lived through a year; the state is in our hands; but has it operated the New Economic Policy in the way we wanted in this past year? No. But we refuse to admit that it did not operate in the way we wanted. How did it operate? The machine refused to obey the hand that guided it. It was like a car that was going not in the direction the driver desired, but in the direction someone else desired; as if it were being driven by some mysterious, lawless hand, God knows whose, perhaps a profiteer's, or a private capitalist's, or both. Be that as it may, the car is not going quite in the direction the man at the wheel imagines, and often it goes in an altogether different direction" [*Collected Works,* vol. 33, p. 279].

Those words gave the criterion we ought to apply in discussing our fundamental political problems. In what direction is the machine—the government, the state power—traveling? In the direction that we Communists, expressing the interests and will of the workers and the enormous mass of the peasants, desire? Or not in that direction? Or "not quite" in that direction?

In the years since Lenin's death we have more than once tried to bring the attention of the central institutions of our party, and afterward the party as a whole, to the fact that thanks to incorrect leadership, the danger indicated by Lenin has greatly increased. The machine is not going in the direction required by the interests of the workers and peasants. On the eve of the new congress we consider it our duty, despite all the persecution we are suffering, to call the party's attention with redoubled energy to this fact. For we are sure that the situation is rectifiable, that the party itself can correct it.

When Lenin said that the car often goes in a direction desired by forces hostile to us, he called our attention to two facts of supreme importance. First, that there exist in our society these forces hostile to our cause—the kulak, the NEPman, the bureaucrat—which take advantage of our backwardness and our political mistakes and, in doing so, rely in fact upon the support of international capitalism. Second, the fact that these forces are so strong that they can push our governmental and economic machine in the wrong direction, and ultimately even attempt—at first in a concealed manner—to seize the wheel of the car.

Lenin's words impose certain obligations on all of us:

1. To pay close attention to the growth of these hostile forces—kulak, NEPman, and bureaucrat;

2. To remember that in proportion to the general revival of the country, these forces will strive to unite, introduce their own "amendments" into our plans, exercise an increasing pressure on our policy, and satisfy their interests through our apparatus;

3. To take all possible measures to weaken the growth, unity, and pressure of these hostile forces, preventing them from creating that actual, though concealed, *dual power system* toward which they aspire;

4. To tell the industrial workers and all working people the whole truth about these class processes under way in our society. This is the key to the question of the "Thermidorian" danger and the struggle against it.

Since Lenin uttered his warning, many things have improved with us, but many have also grown worse. The influence of the state apparatus is growing, and with it the bureaucratic deformation of the workers' state. The absolute and relative growth of capitalism in the countryside and its absolute growth in the cities are beginning to produce a political self-consciousness in the bourgeois elements of our country. These elements are trying—not always unsuccessfully—to corrupt that part of the Communists with whom they come in contact at work and in social intercourse. The slogan presented by Stalin at the Fourteenth Party Congress, "Fire Against the Left!" could not but promote this union of the right elements in the party with the bourgeois-Ustryalov elements in the country.

The question "Who will prevail?" will be decided in a continuous struggle of classes on all sectors of the economic, political, and cultural fronts—a struggle for a socialist or a capitalist course of development, for a distribution of the national income corresponding to one or the other of these two courses, for a solid political power of the proletariat or a division of this power with the new bourgeoisie. In a country with an overwhelming majority of small and very small peasants, and small proprietors in general, the most important processes of this struggle go on for a while in a fragmentary and underground manner, only to burst "unexpectedly" to the surface all at once.

The capitalist element finds its primary expression in the class differentiation in the countryside and in the increased numbers of private traders. The upper layers in the countryside and the bourgeois elements in the city are interweaving themselves more and more closely with the various components of our government and economic apparatus. And this apparatus not infrequently helps the new bourgeoisie to shroud in a statistical fog its successful effort to increase its share in the national income.

The trade apparatus—state, cooperative, and private—devours an enormous share of the national income, more than one-tenth of the gross national product. Furthermore, *private capital,* in its capacity as commercial middleman, has handled in recent years considerably more than a fifth of all trade—in absolute figures, more than five billion rubles a year. Up to now, most consumers have obtained more than 50 percent of the products they need from private traders. For the private capitalist this is the fundamental source of profit and accumulation. The "scissors" (disproportion) between agricultural and industrial prices, between wholesale and retail prices, the price "gaps" between different branches of agriculture, and from one region or season to another, and finally the "scissors" between domestic and world prices (contraband) are a constant source of private gain.

Private capital is collecting usurious interest on loans and is making money on government bonds.

The role of the private capitalist in industry is also very considerable. Even though it has decreased relatively in the recent period, still it has grown absolutely. *Registered* private capitalist industry shows a gross output of 400 million a year. Small, home, and handicraft industries show more than 1,800 million. Altogether, the production of the nonstate industries constitutes more than a fifth of the whole production of goods, and about 40 percent of the commodities in the general market. The overwhelming bulk of this industry is bound up one way or another with private capital. The various open or concealed forms of exploitation of the mass of handicraft workers by commercial and home-enterprise capital are an extremely important and, moreover, a growing source of accumulation for the new bourgeoisie.

Taxes, wages, prices, and credit are the chief instruments for distributing the national income, strengthening certain classes and weakening others.

The agricultural tax in the countryside is imposed, as a general rule, in an inverse progression: heavily on the poor, more lightly on the economically strong and on the kulaks. According to approximate calculations, 34 percent of the poor peasant households in the Soviet Union (even omitting provinces with a highly developed class differentiation, such as the Ukraine, Northern Caucasus, and Siberia) receive 18 percent of the net income. Exactly the same total income, 18 percent, is received by the highest group, constituting only 7.5 percent of peasant households. Yet both these groups pay approximately the same amount, 20 percent each of the total tax. It is evident from this that on each individual poor farm the tax lays a much heavier burden than on the kulak, or "economically strong" peasant household in general. Contrary to the fears of the leaders of the Fourteenth Congress, our tax policy by no means "strips" the kulak. It does not hinder him in the least from concentrating in his hands a continually greater accumulation in money and kind.

The role of indirect taxes in our budget is growing alarmingly at the expense of direct taxes. By that alone the tax burden automatically shifts from the wealthier to the poorer levels. The taxation of the workers in 1925-26 was twice as high as in the preceding year, while the taxation of the rest of the urban population diminished by 6 percent (*Vestnik Finansov*, 1927, no. 2, p. 52). The liquor tax falls, with more and more unbearable heaviness, precisely upon the industrial regions. The increase in per capita income for 1926 as compared with 1925—according to certain approximate calculations—constituted, for the peasants, 19 percent; for the workers, 26 percent; for the merchants and the industrialists, 46 percent. If you divide the "peasants" into the three main groups, it will be seen beyond a doubt that the income of the kulak increased incomparably more than that of the worker. The income of the merchants and industrialists, calculated on the basis of the tax data, is undoubtedly represented as less than it is. However, even these doctored figures clearly testify to a growth of class differences.

The "scissors" between agricultural and industrial prices have opened even more during the last year and a half. The peasant received for his produce not more than one and a quarter times the prewar price, and paid for industrial products not less than two and one-fifth times as much as before the war. This overpayment by the peasants, and again *predominantly* by the lower strata, amounted in the past year to about one billion rubles. This not only increases the conflict between agriculture and industry, but greatly intensifies the class differentiation in the countryside.

On the scissors between wholesale and retail prices, the state industry loses, and also the consumer, which means that there is a third party who gains. It is the private capitalist who gains, and consequently capitalism.

Real wages in 1927 stand, at the best, at the same level as in the autumn of 1925. Yet it is indubitable that during the two intervening years the country has grown richer, the total national income has increased, the topmost kulak layer in the countryside has increased its reserves with enormous rapidity, and the accumulated wealth of the private capitalist, the merchant, and the speculator has grown by leaps and bounds. It is clear that the share of the working class in the total income of the country has fallen, while the share of other classes has grown. This fact is of supreme importance in appraising our whole situation.

Only someone who believes at the bottom of his heart that our working class and our party are not able to cope with difficulties and dangers can say that a frank description of these contradictions in our development, and of the growth of these hostile forces, constitutes *panic* or *pessimism*. We do not accept this view. It is necessary to see the dangers clearly. We point them out accurately, precisely in order to struggle against them more effectively and to overcome them.

A certain growth of the hostile forces—the kulak, the NEPman, and the bureaucrat—is unavoidable under the New Economic Policy. You cannot destroy these forces by mere administrative order or by simple economic pressure. In introducing the NEP and carrying it through, we ourselves made some room for capitalist relations in our country, and for a considerable time to come we still have to accept them as inevitable. Lenin merely reminded us of a naked truth which the workers have to know, when he said: "As long as we live in a small-peasant country, there will be a firmer basis for capitalism in Russia than for communism. That must be borne in mind. . . . We have not torn up the roots of capitalism and we have not undermined the foundation, the basis, of the internal enemy" [*Collected Works,* vol. 31, p. 516].

The supremely important social fact here indicated by Lenin cannot, as we said, be simply eliminated. But we can fight against it and overcome it through a correct, planned, and systematic working class policy, relying on the poor peasant and an alliance with the middle peasant. This policy basically consists in an all-round strengthening of all the social positions of the proletariat, in the swiftest possible build-up and expansion of the commanding heights of socialism, in the closest possible connection with the preparation and development of the world proletarian revolution.

A correct Leninist policy also includes maneuvering. In struggling against the forces of capitalism, Lenin often employed a method of partial concession in order to outflank the enemy, temporary retreat in order afterwards to move forward more successfully. Maneuvering is also necessary now. But in dodging and maneuvering against an enemy that could not be overthrown by direct attack, Lenin invariably remained upon the line of the proletarian revolution. Under him the party always knew the reasons for each maneuver, its meaning, its limits, the line beyond which it ought not to go, and the position at which the proletarian advance should begin again. In those days, under Lenin, a retreat was called a retreat—a concession, a concession. Thanks to that, the maneuvering proletarian army always preserved its unity, its fighting spirit, its clear consciousness of the goal.

In the recent period there has been a decisive departure by the leadership from these Leninist ways. The Stalin group is leading the party blindfolded. Concealing the forces of the enemy, creating everywhere and in everything an *official appearance* of success, this group gives the proletariat no perspective—or, what is worse, a wrong perspective. It moves in zigzags, accommodating itself to and ingratiating itself with hostile elements. It weakens and confuses the forces of the proletarian army. It promotes the growth of passivity, distrust of the leadership, and lack of confidence in the strength of the revolution. It disguises, with references to Leninist maneuvering, an unprincipled tendency to rush off, first in one direction, then in another. These turns are always a surprise to the party. It does not understand them and is weakened by them. The only result is that the enemy, having gained time, moves forward. The "classical" examples of such maneuvers on the part of Stalin, Bukharin, and Rykov are their Chinese policy and their policy with the Anglo-Russian Committee, in the international arena, and within the country, their policy toward the kulak. On all these questions the party and the working class found out the truth, or a part of the truth, only after the heavy consequences of a policy that was false to the core had crashed over their heads.

At the end of these two years, in which the Stalin group has really determined the policies of the central institutions of our party, we may consider it fully proven that this group has been powerless to prevent: (1) an immoderate growth of those forces which desire to turn the development of our country in a capitalist direction; (2) a weakening of the position of the working class and the poorest peasants against the growing strength of the kulak, the NEPman, and the bureaucrat; (3) a weakening of the general position of the workers' state in the struggle against world capitalism, a worsening of the international position of the Soviet Union.

The Stalin group is directly to blame because instead of telling the party, the working class, and the peasants the whole truth about the situation, it has concealed the facts, played down the growth of the hostile forces, and silenced those who demanded the truth and laid it bare.

The concentration of *fire against the left,* at a time when the whole situation indicates danger on the right; the crudely mechanical suppression of all criticism expressing the legitimate alarm of the proletariat over the fate of the proletarian revolution; outright complicity with deviations to the right; the sapping of the influence of the proletarian and Old Bolshevik nucleus of the party—all these things are weakening and disarming the working class at a moment which demands above all activity by the proletariat, vigilance and unity of the party, and loyalty to the true legacy of Leninism.

The party leaders distort Lenin, improve upon him, explain him, supplement him, in accordance with their need to conceal each successive mistake. Since Lenin's death a whole series of new theories has been invented, whose meaning is only this: that they give theoretical justification to the Stalin group's backsliding from the policy of international proletarian revolution. The Mensheviks, the Smenovekhovites, and finally the capitalist press have seen and welcomed the policies and new theories of Stalin-Bukharin-Martynov as a movement "forward from Lenin" (Ustryalov), "statesmanlike wisdom," "realism," and renunciation of the "utopianism" of revolutionary Bolshevism. In the removal of a number of Bolsheviks—Lenin's comrades in arms—from the party leadership, they see and openly welcome a practical step toward changing the fundamental course of the party.

Meanwhile the elemental processes of the NEP, not restrained and directed by a firm class policy, are laying the basis for further dangerous shifts.

Twenty-five million small farms constitute the fundamental source of the capitalist tendencies in Russia. The kulak stratum, gradually emerging from this mass, is carrying out the process of primitive accumulation of capital, extensively undermining the socialist position. The fate of this process depends ultimately upon the relation between the growth of the state economy and the private. The lag in the development of our industry greatly increases the rate of class differentiation among the peasants and the political dangers arising from it.

Lenin wrote that the kulaks "in the history of other countries have time and again restored the power of landowners, tsars, priests, and capitalists," that such was the case "in all earlier European revolutions when, as a result of the weakness of the workers, the kulaks succeeded in turning back from a republic to a monarchy, from a working people's government to the despotism of the exploiters, the rich, and the parasites"; and finally, that "even if they have quarreled, the kulak can easily come to terms with the landowner, the tsar, and the priest, but with the working class *never*" [*Collected Works*, vol. 28, pp. 55-56].

Whoever fails to understand this, whoever believes in "the kulak's growing into socialism," is good for just one thing—to run the revolution aground.

There exist in this country two mutually exclusive *fundamental* positions. One, the position of the proletariat building socialism; the other, the position of the bourgeoisie aspiring to turn our development in a capitalist direction.

The camp of the bourgeoisie and those layers of the petty bourgeoisie who follow in its wake are placing all their hopes upon the private initiative and the personal interest of the commodity producer. This camp places its bets on the "economically strong" peasant, aiming to make the cooperatives, industry, and foreign trade serve this peasant's interest. This camp believes that socialist industry ought not to depend on the state budget, that its development ought not to be such as to interfere with accumulation by the farmer capitalist. The struggle for greater labor productivity means to the increasingly influential petty bourgeois putting pressure on the muscles and nerves of the workers. The struggle for lower prices means to him cutting down on accumulation by socialist industry for the benefit of commercial capital. The struggle against bureaucratism means to him the break-up and dispersal of industry, the weakening of the principle of planning. It means the pushing into the background of heavy industry—that is, again, an adjustment in favor of the economically strong peasant, with the near perspective of abandoning the monopoly of foreign trade. This is the course of the Ustryalovs. The name of this course is *capitalism on the install-*

ment plan. It is a strong tendency in our country, and exercises an influence upon certain circles of our party.

The proletarian course was described by Lenin in the following words: "The victory of socialism over capitalism and the consolidation of socialism may be regarded as ensured only when the proletarian state power, having completely suppressed all resistance by the exploiters and assured itself complete subordination and stability, has reorganized the whole of industry on the lines of large-scale collective production and on a modern technical basis (founded on the electrification of the entire economy). This alone will enable the cities to render such radical assistance, technical and social, to the backward and scattered rural population as will create the material basis necessary to boost the productivity of agricultural and of farm labor in general, thereby encouraging the small farmers by the force of example and in their own interests to adopt large-scale, collective and mechanized agriculture" [*Collected Works,* vol. 31, pp. 161-62].

The whole policy of our party ought to be based on this approach—budget, taxes, industry, agriculture, domestic and foreign trade, everything. That is the fundamental stand of the Opposition. *That is the road to socialism.*

Between those two positions—every day drawing nearer to the first—the Stalinists are tracing a line consisting of short zigzags to the left and deep ones to the right. The Leninist course is a socialist development of the productive forces in continual struggle against the capitalist element. The Ustryalov course is a development of the productive forces on a capitalist basis by way of a gradual erosion of the conquests of October. The Stalin course leads, in objective reality, to a delaying of the development of the productive forces, to a lowering of the relative weight of the socialist element, and thus paves the way for the victory of the Ustryalov line. The Stalin course is the more dangerous and ruinous in that it conceals its real backsliding behind a mask of familiar words and phrases. The completion of the economic restoration process has meant that all the crucial questions of our economic development are now posed pointblank. This has undermined the Stalinist political line, because it is totally inadequate for solving major problems—whether these involve the revolution in China or the reconstruction of basic capital in the Soviet Union.

Notwithstanding the tension of the situation, heightened in the extreme by the crude mistakes of the present leadership, matters can be corrected. But it is necessary to change the line of the party leadership, and change it sharply, in the direction indicated by Lenin.

Chapter 2
The Situation of the Working Class and the Trade Unions

The October Revolution, for the first time in history, made the proletariat the ruling class of an immense state. The nationalization of the means of production was a decisive step toward the socialist reorganization of the entire social system based on the exploitation of some by others. The introduction of the eight-hour day was a step toward a total change in all aspects of the material and cultural living conditions of the working class. In spite of the poverty of the country, our labor laws established for the workers—even the most backward, who were deprived in the past of any group defense—legal guarantees of a kind that the richest capitalist state never gave, and never will give. The trade unions, raised to the status of the most important social instrument in the hands of the ruling class, were given the opportunity, on the one hand, to organize masses that under other circumstances would have been completely inaccessible to them and, on the other, to directly influence the whole political course of the workers' state.

The task of the party is to guarantee the further development of these supreme historical conquests—that is, to fill them with a genuinely socialist content. Our success on this road will be determined by objective conditions, domestic and international, and also by the correctness of our line and the practical skill of our leadership.

The decisive factor in appraising the progress of our country along the road of socialist reconstruction must be the growth of our productive forces and the dominance of the socialist elements over the capitalist—*together with improvement in all the living conditions of the working class*. This improvement ought to be evident in the material sphere (number of workers employed in industry, level of real wages, the kind of budget appropriations for the workers' needs, housing conditions, medical services, etc.); in the political sphere (party, trade unions, soviets, the Communist youth organization); and finally in the cultural sphere (schools, books, newspapers, theaters). The attempt to push the vital interests of the worker into the background and, under the contemptuous epithet of "narrow craft professionalism," to counterpose them to the general historical interests of the working class, is theoretically wrong and politically dangerous.

The appropriation of surplus value by a workers' state is not, of course, exploitation. But in the first place, we have a workers' state with bureaucratic distortions. The swollen and privileged administrative apparatus devours a very considerable part of the surplus value. In the second place, the growing bourgeoisie, through trade and by taking advantage of the price scissors, appropriates part of the surplus value created by state industry.

In general during this period of economic reconstruction, the number of workers and their standard of living have risen, not only absolutely but also relatively—that is, in comparison with the growth of other classes. However, in the recent period a sharp change has occurred. The numerical growth of the working class and the improvement of its situation has almost stopped, while the growth of its enemies continues, and continues at an accelerated pace. This inevitably leads not only to a worsening of conditions in the factories but also to a lowering of the relative weight of the proletariat in Soviet society.

The Mensheviks, agents of the bourgeoisie among the workers, point with malicious pleasure to the material wretchedness of our workers, seeking to rouse the proletariat against the Soviet state, to induce our workers to accept the bourgeois-Menshevik slogan "Back to capitalism." The self-satisfied official who sees "Menshevism" in the Opposition's insistence upon improving the material conditions of the workers is performing the best possible service to Menshevism. He is driving the workers toward its yellow banner.

In order to deal with problems, we must know what they are. We must judge our successes and failures in a just and honest way in relation to the actual condition of the masses of workers.

The Conditions of the Workers

The period of economic reconstruction brought with it a sufficiently rapid increase in wages up to the autumn of 1925. But the substantial decline in real wages which began in 1926 was overcome only at the beginning of 1927. Monthly wages in the first two quarters of the fiscal year 1926-27 amounted on the average in large-scale industry, in Moscow rubles, to 30 rubles 67 kopeks, and 30 rubles 33 kopeks—as against 29 rubles 68 kopeks in the autumn of 1925. In the third quarter—according to preliminary calculations—the wages amounted to 31 rubles 62 kopeks. Thus real wages for the present year have stood still, approximately at the level of the autumn of 1925.

Of course the wages and the overall material level of particular categories of workers and particular regions—above all, Moscow and Leningrad—are undoubtedly higher than this average level. But on the other hand, the material level of other very broad layers of the working class is considerably below these average figures.

Moreover, all the data indicate that the growth of wages is lagging behind the growth of labor productivity. The intensity of labor is increasing—the bad conditions of labor remain the same.

The requirement that there be greater *intensity* of labor is more and more being made the condition for an increase in wages. This new tendency, inconsistent with a socialist policy, was affirmed by the Central Committee in its famous resolution on rationalization (*Pravda*, March 25, 1927). The Fourth Congress of the Soviets adopted this same resolution. Such a policy would mean that an increase in social wealth resulting from technological progress (increased productivity of labor) would not *in itself* lead to an increase in wages.

The small numerical growth of the working class means a reduction in the number of working members in each family. In real rubles, the *expense budget of the working class family* has decreased since 1924-25. The increase in the cost of living quarters forces working families to rent out part of their space. The unemployed, directly or indirectly, burden the budget of the worker. The swiftly growing consumption of alcoholic liquors also takes away from the working class budget. As a result there is an obvious lowering of living standards. *The rationalization of production* now being introduced will inevitably worsen the conditions of the working class even more, unless it is accompanied by an expansion of industry and transport sufficient to take in the discharged workers. In practice, "rationalization" often comes down to "throwing out" some workers and lowering the material conditions of others. This inevitably fills the masses of workers with a distrust of rationalization itself.

When labor's living standards are under pressure, it is always the weakest groups that suffer most: unskilled workers, seasonal workers, women, and adolescents.

In 1926 there was an obvious lowering of the wages of women

as compared with those of men, in almost all branches of industry. Among the unskilled in three different branches of industry, the earnings of women in March 1926 were 51.8 percent, 61.7 percent, and 83 percent of the earnings of men. Necessary measures have not been taken for improving the conditions of women's work in such branches as the peat industry, loading and unloading, etc. The average earnings of adolescents, in comparison with the earnings of workers as a whole, are steadily declining. In 1923 they were 47.1 percent, in 1924 45 percent, in 1925 43.4 percent, in 1926 40.5 percent, in 1927 39.5 percent (Review of the Economic Situation of Young People in 1924-25 and in 1925-26).

In March 1926 49.5 percent of adolescents earned less than 20 rubles (Central Bureau of Labor Statistics). The abolition of the regulation providing for the employment of a certain number of adolescents for every given number of workers in an industrial establishment has been a heavy blow to the working youth and to the working class family. The number of unemployed adolescents is greatly increasing.

Farm Labor

Of the approximately 3,500,000 wage workers in the country, 1,600,000 are farmhands, men and women. Only 20 percent of these farmhands are organized in unions. The registration of wage contracts, which often contain terms amounting to outright servitude, is barely beginning. The wages of farmhands are customarily below the legal minimum—and this often even on the state farms. Real wages on the average are not over 63 percent of the prewar level. The working day is rarely less than ten hours. In the majority of cases it is, as a matter of fact, unlimited. Wages are paid irregularly and after intolerable delays. The miserable situation of the hired laborer is not only a result of the difficulties of socialist construction in a backward, peasant country. It is also unquestionably a result of the false course which in practice—in the reality of life—gives predominant attention to the upper levels and not the lower levels of the village. We must have an all-sided, systematic defense of the hired laborer, not only against the kulak, but also against the so-called economically strong middle peasant.

The Housing Question

The normal dwelling space for the workers is, as a rule, considerably smaller than the average space for the urban population as a whole. The workers of the great industrial cities are in this respect the least favored part of the population. The distribution of dwelling space according to social groups, in a series of investigated cities, was as follows:

Per industrial worker, 5.6 square meters; per office worker, 6.9; per handicraftsman, 7.6; per professional, 10.9; and for the nonworking element, 7.1. The workers occupy the last place. Moreover, the size of the workers' living space is diminishing from year to year; that of the nonproletarian elements is increasing. The general situation in regard to housing construction threatens the further development of industry. Nevertheless, the five-year plan of the State Planning Commission puts forward a perspective in which the housing situation at the end of five years will be worse than it is now—this, according to the admission of the commission itself. From 11.3 square arshins [8.1 meters] at the end of 1926, the average norm will be lowered by the end of 1931, according to the five-year plan, to 10.6 arshins [7.6 meters].

Unemployment

The slow growth of industrialization nowhere reveals itself so unhealthily as in the unemployment which has attacked the basic ranks of the industrial proletariat. The official number of registered unemployed in April 1927 was 1,478,000 (*Trud*, August 27, 1927). The actual number of unemployed is about two million. The number of unemployed is growing incomparably faster than the total number of employed workers. The number of unemployed industrial workers is growing especially rapidly. According to the five-year plan of the State Planning Commission, industry will absorb slightly more than 400,000 steadily employed workers during the whole five years. This means that, with the continual influx of workers from the countryside, the number of unemployed will have grown by the end of 1931 to no less than three million. The consequence of this state of affairs will be an increase in the number of homeless children, beggars, and prostitutes. The small unemployment insurance paid to those who are out of work is causing justifiable resentment. The average benefit is 11.9 rubles—that is, about 5 prewar rubles. The trade union benefits average 6.5 to 7 rubles. And these benefits are paid, approximately, to only 20 percent of the unemployed members of the union.

The Code of Labor Laws has undergone so many interpretations that these exceed by many times the number of articles in the Code. And they actually annul many of its provisions. Legal protection for temporary and seasonal workers has especially broken down.

The recent collective-bargaining campaign was characterized by an almost universal worsening of legal guarantees and a downward pressure on standards and wage scales. Giving government economic agencies the right of compulsory arbitration has reduced to nothing the collective agreement itself, changing it from a two-sided act of agreement to an administrative order (*Trud,* August 4, 1927). The contributions by industry toward workers' compensation are wholly inadequate. In 1925-26, according to the data of the Commissariat of Labor, there were 97.6 accidents resulting in disability for every thousand workers in large-scale enterprises. Every tenth worker is injured every year.

Recent years have been characterized by a sharp increase in labor disputes, most of them being settled by compulsory rather than by conciliatory measures.

The regime within the factories has deteriorated. The factory administrative bodies are striving more and more to establish their unlimited authority. The hiring and discharge of workers is actually in the hands of the administration alone. Prerevolutionary relations between supervisors and workers are frequently found.

The production conferences are gradually being reduced to nothing. Most of the practical proposals adopted by the workers are never carried out. Among many workers, distaste for these production conferences is nourished by the fact that the improvements which they do succeed in introducing often result in a reduction in the number of workers. As a result the production conferences are scantily attended.

In the cultural sphere, it is necessary to emphasize the problem of the schools. It is becoming harder and harder for the worker to give his children even an elementary education, to say nothing of vocational training. In almost all the working class districts there is a continually increasing shortage of schools. The fees demanded of parents for school supplies are in practice destroying free education. The shortage of schools and the inadequate provision of kindergartens are driving a considerable number of workers' children onto the streets.

The Trade Unions and the Workers

"A certain conflict of interests on the question of working conditions in the factory," which was noted in a resolution of the Eleventh Congress of the party, has grown very considerably in recent years. Nevertheless, the entire practical work of the party in relation to the trade union movement in the past few years, including the work of the trade union leaders, has had such an effect on the unions that, as even the Fourteenth Congress admitted: "The trade unions have often been unable to handle their work, showing one-sidedness, at times pushing into the background their principal and most important task—to defend the economic interests of the masses organized by them and to raise in every possible way their material and spiritual level."

The situation after the Fourteenth Congress did not become better, but worse. The bureaucratization of the trade unions went another step further.

In the staff of the elected executive bodies of ten industrial unions, the percentage of workers from the bench and nonparty militant workers is extremely small (12 to 13 percent). The immense majority of delegates to the trade union conferences are people entirely dissociated from industry (*Pravda,* July 3, 1927). Never before have the trade unions and the rank-and-file workers stood so far from the management of socialist industry as now. The independent initiative of the mass of workers organized in the trade unions is being replaced by agreements between the secretary of the party group, the factory director, and the chairman of the factory committee (the "triangle"). The attitude of the workers to the factory and shop committees is one of distrust. Attendance at the general meetings is low.

The dissatisfaction of the worker, finding no outlet in the trade union, is driven inwards. "We mustn't be too active—if you want a bite of bread, don't talk so much." Such sayings are very common (see material of the Moscow Committee, reports on the General Workers' Conferences, *Informational Review,* p. 30, etc.). In these circumstances, attempts on the part of the workers to improve their situation by action outside the trade union organization inevitably become more frequent. This alone imperatively dictates a radical change in the present trade union regime.

The Most Important Practical Proposals

A. *In the Sphere of Material Conditions*

1. Cut off at the root every inclination to lengthen the eight-hour day. Permit overtime only when absolutely unavoidable. Allow no abuses in the employment of occasional workers; no treating of full-time workers as "seasonal." Cancel every lengthening of the workday in unhealthy trades where it has been introduced in violation of earlier rules.

2. The most immediate task is to raise wages at least to correspond to the achieved increase in the productivity of labor. The future course should be a systematic elevation of real wages to correspond to every rise in labor productivity. It is necessary to achieve an increasing equalization in the wages of different groups of workers, by way of a systematic raising of the lower-paid groups; in no case by a lowering of the higher-paid.

3. We must put an end to all bureaucratic abuse of rationalization measures. Rationalization ought to be closely linked with the appropriate development of industry, with a planned distribution of labor power, and with a struggle against any waste of the productive forces of the working class—particularly failure to utilize the cadre of skilled workers.

4. To relieve the evil effects of unemployment: (a) Unemployment benefits must be adjusted to actually correspond to the average wage in a given locality; (b) In view of the duration of unemployment, the benefit period must be extended from one year to one and a half; (c) No further reduction in payments to the social insurance fund can be tolerated; a real fight must be waged against the actual failure to make these payments; (d) The spending of insurance funds upon measures of general public health and sanitation must be stopped; (e) We must energetically combat the tendency to "economize in relation to insured persons"; (f) We must annul all regulations that under various pretexts deprive really unemployed workers of their right to benefits and to registration at employment offices; (g) We must chart our course toward an increase in benefits for the unemployed, beginning with the industrial workers. We must have broadly conceived and carefully worked-out plans for long-term public works upon which the unemployed can be used with the greatest advantage to the economic and cultural growth of the country.

5. A systematic improvement of housing conditions for the workers. Firm carrying out of a class policy in all housing questions. No betterment of the housing conditions of nonproletarian elements at the expense of the workers. No eviction of discharged workers and workers whose workweek and earnings have been cut.

Energetic measures must be taken for the healthier development of housing cooperatives. They must be made accessible to the lower-paid workers. The upper echelons of office workers must not be allowed to take over apartments intended for industrial workers.

The housing plan of the State Planning Commission must be rejected as one in flagrant contradiction to socialist policy. Business enterprises must be obliged to increase their housing expenditures and their budget allotments and credits for this purpose sufficiently so that the next five years will see a definite improvement in the question of housing for workers.

6. Collective agreements should be made after real and not fictitious discussion at workers' meetings. The coming party congress should annul the decision of the Fourteenth Congress giving factory managements the right of compulsory arbitration. The Labor Code must be looked upon as the minimum and not the maximum of what labor has a right to demand. Collective agreements must contain guarantees against cutting down the number of industrial and office workers for the duration of the agreements (permissible exceptions to be expressly provided for). Output norms must be calculated on the basis of the average, not the exceptional workers and for the whole duration of the wage contract. In any case, all changes in the collective agreements which worsen the conditions of the workers in comparison with previous agreements should be declared impermissible.

7. The Bureau of Wages and Standards must be brought under more effective control by the workers and the trade unions, and the constant changing of wages and work norms must be stopped.

8. Appropriations for safety equipment and better working conditions must be increased. Greater penalties must be imposed for failure to observe regulations for workers' safety.

9. All interpretations of the Labor Code must be reexamined and those which resulted in a worsening of the conditions of labor annulled.

10. For women workers, "Equal pay for equal work." Provision to be made for women workers to learn skilled trades.

11. Unpaid apprentice work shall be forbidden. Likewise the attempt to reduce the wages of adolescents. Measures must be taken to improve the conditions of their work.

12. The regime of economy must in no case be carried out at the expense of the standard of living of the worker. We must restore to the workers the "trifles" which have been taken away (nurseries, streetcar tickets, longer vacations, etc.).

13. The trade unions must pay increased attention to the problems of seasonal workers.

14. Medical care for the worker in the factory must be increased (dispensaries, clinics, etc.).

15. In working class districts the number of schools for workers' children must be increased.

16. A series of government measures must be taken to strengthen the workers' consumer cooperatives.

B. In the Trade Unions

1. The work of the trade unions should be judged primarily by the degree to which it protects the economic and cultural interests of the workers, within the existing economic limitations.

2. The party organizations, in discussing measures that affect the economic and cultural interests of the masses of workers, should first hear reports on these matters from the Communist fractions in the trade unions.

3. Real elections, publicity, accountability, and responsibility to the membership at all levels must be the foundation of trade union work.

4. All administrative bodies in industry should be formed in real and not fictitious agreement with the appropriate trade union organizations.

5. At every trade union congress (including the all-union congress) and in all the elective bodies of the trade unions (including the All-Union Central Council of Trade Unions), there must be a majority of workers directly engaged in industry. The percentage of nonparty workers in these bodies must be raised to at least one-third.

At regular intervals, a certain number of the officials of the trade union apparatus must be sent to work in industry.

More utilization of voluntary work in trade union activities, a broader application of the principle of voluntary work, more involvement of workers from the factories in such work.

6. The removal of elected Communist members of trade union

bodies because of inner-party disagreements shall not be permitted.

7. The absolute independence of the shop committees and local trade union committees from the management must be guaranteed. The hiring and discharge of workers and the transfer of workers from one kind of work to another, for periods exceeding two weeks—all this must be carried out only after the factory committee has been informed. The factory committee, in struggling against abuses in this sphere, shall employ its right of appeal from the decisions of the management to the corresponding trade union and to the grievance commissions.

8. Definite rights must be provided to workers' press correspondents, and those who persecute such correspondents for making exposés must be strictly punished.

An article should be introduced into the Criminal Code punishing as a serious crime against the state every direct or indirect, overt or concealed persecution of a worker for criticizing, for making independent proposals, and for voting.

9. The functions of the control commissions of the production councils must be extended to include checking on how the decisions of the councils are put into effect and making sure that the workers' interests are protected in the process.

10. On the question of strikes in state industries, the decision of the Eleventh Party Congress, proposed by Lenin, remains in force.

As far as strikes are concerned, the concession industries shall be regarded as private industries.

11. The whole system of labor statistics must be revised. In its present form it gives a false and obviously touched-up picture of the economic and cultural conditions of the working class, and thus greatly hinders any work in defense of its economic and cultural interests.

The hard situation of the working class on the tenth anniversary of the October Revolution is of course explained in the last analysis by the poverty of the country, the results of intervention and blockade, the unceasing struggle of the encircling capitalist system against the first proletarian state. That situation cannot be changed at a single blow. But it can and must be changed if a correct policy is followed. The task of Bolsheviks is not to paint glowing and self-satisfied pictures of our achievements—which of course are very real—but to raise firmly and clearly the question of what remains to be done, of what must be done, and what can be done, following a correct policy.

Chapter 3
The Peasantry—the Agrarian Question and Socialist Construction

"Small-scale production *engenders* capitalism and the bourgeoisie continuously, daily, hourly, spontaneously, and on a mass scale" [from "'Left-Wing' Communism—An Infantile Disorder," in *Lenin's Collected Works,* vol. 31, p. 24].

Either the proletarian state, relying on the high development and electrification of industry, will be able to overcome the technological backwardness of millions of small and very small farms, organizing them on the basis of large-scale production and collectivization, or capitalism, establishing a stronghold in the countryside, will undermine the foundations of socialism in the cities.

From the point of view of Leninism, the peasantry—that is, the fundamental peasant mass which does not exploit labor—is the key ally, and correct relations with this ally are crucial for the security of the proletarian dictatorship and, consequently, for the fate of the socialist revolution. For the stage we are passing through, Lenin most accurately formulated our task with regard to the peasants in the following words: "To come to an agreement with the middle peasant—while not for a moment renouncing the struggle against the kulak and at the same time firmly relying solely on the poor peasant" [*Collected Works,* vol. 28, p. 191].

A revision of Lenin on the peasant question is being carried out by the Stalin-Bukharin group along the following main lines:

1. Abandonment of one of the central tenets of Marxism, that only a powerful socialist industry can help the peasants transform agriculture along collectivist lines.

2. Underestimation of the farmhands and poor peasants as the social base of the proletarian dictatorship in the countryside.

3. In agricultural policy, placing our bets on the so-called "economically strong" peasant, i.e., in reality on the kulak.

4. Ignoring or directly denying the petty-bourgeois character of peasant property and peasant agriculture—a departure from the Marxist position in the direction of the theories of the Social Revolutionaries.

5. Underestimation of the capitalist elements in the present development of the countryside, and hushing up of the class differentiations that are taking place among the peasants.

6. The creation of consoling theories to the effect that "the kulak and kulak organizations will have no chance anyway, because the general framework of evolution in our country is predetermined by the structure of the proletarian dictatorship" (Bukharin, *The Road to Socialism and the Worker-Peasant Alliance*, p. 49).

7. The policy orientation that "kulak cooperative nuclei can be integrated into our system" (Ibid., p. 49). "The problem may be expressed thus: that it is necessary to set free the economic possibilities of the well-off peasant, the economic possibilities of the kulak" (*Pravda*, April 24, 1925).

8. Attempts to counterpose Lenin's "cooperative plan" to his plan of electrification. According to Lenin himself, only these two plans in combination could ensure a transition to socialism.

Relying on these revisionist tendencies in official policy, representatives of the new bourgeoisie have established connections with certain sectors of our state apparatus and are openly aspiring to switch our whole policy in the countryside onto the capitalist path. At the same time, the kulaks and their ideological defenders hide all their ambitions under a pretense of concern for the development of the productive forces, increasing the volume of commodity production "in general," etc. As a matter of fact, a kulak development of the productive forces, a kulak increase of commodity production, would repress and retard the development of the productive forces of the entire remaining mass of peasant farms.

In spite of the comparatively swift reconstruction process in agriculture, commodity production from peasant agriculture is very low. In 1925-26, the total volume of goods sent to market was only 64 percent of the prewar level, the volume exported only 24 percent of the export in 1913. The cause of this, aside from the increasing total consumption in the village itself,* lies in the scissors between agricultural and industrial prices and in the rapid accumulation of foodstuffs by the kulaks. Even the five-year plan is compelled to recognize that "the lack of industrial products, in general, places a definite limit on the equivalent

---

*Because of population growth and the splitting-up of peasant holdings; with the result that 38 percent of peasant households in the grain-producing region buy additional grain.

exchange of goods between town and country, lowering the possible volume of agricultural products brought to the market" (p. 117). Thus the lagging of industry retards the growth of agriculture and in particular the growth of agricultural commodity production. It undermines the bond (*smychka*) between town and countryside and leads to a swift class differentiation among the peasants.

The views of the Opposition on disputed questions of peasant policy have been confirmed wholly and absolutely. The partial corrections made in the "general line," under pressure of sharp criticism from the Opposition, have not checked the continuing deviation of the official policy in the direction of the "economically strong peasant." To prove this, it is sufficient to recall that the Fourth Congress of the Soviets, in the resolution on Kalinin's report, had not one single word to say about class differentiation in the countryside or the growth of the kulak.

There can be but one result of such a policy: we shall lose the poor peasants and fail to win the middle ones.

Class Differentiation Among the Peasants

In recent years the rural districts have gone far in the direction of capitalist differentiation.

The groups that tilled little or no land have diminished during the last four years by 35 to 45 percent. The group that tilled from six to ten desyatinas [17 to 28 acres] increased at the same time by 100 to 120 percent. The group that tilled ten desyatinas or more increased by 150 to 200 percent. The decline in the percentage of groups that tilled little or no land is due very largely to their ruin and dissolution. Thus, in Siberia, during one year, 15.8 percent of those tilling no land, and 3.8 percent of those tilling less than two desyatinas, disappeared. In the Northern Caucasus, 14.1 percent of those with no land disappeared, and 3.8 percent of those with less than two desyatinas.

The advancement of horseless and toolless peasant households into the lower stratum of the middle peasantry is proceeding extremely slowly. To this day in the Soviet Union as a whole, 30 to 40 percent of the peasant households continue to be horseless and toolless, and the bulk of these fall into the category of those who till very small amounts of land.

The distribution of the main instruments of production in the Northern Caucasus is as follows: To the weakest 50 percent of peasant households belongs 15 percent of the means of production. To the middle group, constituting 35 percent of peasant households, belongs 35 percent. And to the highest group, constituting 15 percent of peasant households, belongs 50 percent of the means of production. The same pattern in the distribution of the means of production is to be observed in other regions (Siberia, the Ukraine, etc.).

This record of inequality in the distribution of land and of means of production is reasserted in the unequal distribution of grain reserves among the different groups of peasant households. On April 1, 1926, 58 percent of all the surplus grain in the country was in the hands of 6 percent of the peasant households (*Statistical Review,* 1927, no. 4, p. 15).

The renting of land assumes larger and larger proportions every year. The renting proprietors are, in the majority of cases, the peasants who till a lot of land and who own means of production. In the immense majority of cases, the fact that the land is rented is concealed in order to avoid taxes. The peasants who till little land, lacking tools and animals, work for the most part with hired tools and hired animals. The conditions both of renting land and of hiring tools and animals amount almost to slavery. Side by side with extortion in kind, money usury is growing.

The continuous splitting up of peasant properties does not weaken but strengthens the process of class differentiation. Machinery and credit, instead of serving as levers for the socialization of agriculture, nearly always fall into the hands of the kulaks and the better-off peasants, and thus contribute to the exploitation of the farmhands, the poor peasants, and the weaker middle peasants.

Besides this concentration of land and means of production in the hands of the upper strata, the latter are employing hired labor to a steadily increasing degree.

On the other hand, a larger and larger number of laborers for hire are being sloughed off by the poor peasant households and, in part, by the middle peasants. This is the result either of the total ruin and dissolution of the household or the forced departure of individual members from peasant families. These surplus farmhands fall into servitude to the kulak or to the "strong" middle peasant, or go away to the towns, where, in considerable numbers, they find no employment whatever.

In spite of these processes, which have gone very far, and which lead to a reduction in the relative economic weight of the middle peasant, the middle peasant continues to be numerically the largest group in the countryside. To win the middle peasant over to a socialist policy in agriculture is one of the most important tasks of the proletarian dictatorship. Meanwhile, the "wager on the stronger peasant" means, in fact, placing our bets on the further disintegration of this middle layer.

Only by paying the necessary attention to the farmhand, only by orienting toward the poor peasant, in alliance with the middle peasant, only by firmly combating the kulak, only by charting a course toward industrialization and toward class cooperatives and a class credit system in the countryside, will we be able to draw the middle peasant into the work of the socialist transformation of agriculture.

Practical Proposals

In the class struggle now going on in the countryside the party must stand, not only in words but in deeds, at the head of the farmhands, the poor peasants, and the basic mass of the middle peasants, and organize them against the exploitative aims of the kulak.

To strengthen and reinforce the class position of the agricultural proletariat—which is part of the working class—the same series of measures must be taken which we indicated in the section on the conditions of the industrial workers.

Agricultural credit must cease to be for the most part a privilege of the better-off circles in the villages. We must put an end to the present situation, in which the funds for assistance to the poor peasants, insignificant enough already, often are not spent for their intended purpose, but go to serve the better-off and middle groups.

The growth of individual farming must be offset by a more rapid development of collective farming. It is necessary to appropriate funds systematically year after year to assist the poor peasants who have organized in collectives.

At the same time, we must give more systematic help to poor peasants who are not in the collectives, by freeing them entirely from taxation, by assigning them suitable plots of land and providing credit for agricultural implements, and by bringing them into the agricultural cooperatives. Instead of the slogan, "Create nonparty cadres of peasant activists by revitalizing the soviets" (Stalin-Molotov), a slogan which is devoid of all class content and which will in reality strengthen the dominant role of the upper strata in the villages, we must adopt the slogan, *Build a*

cadre of nonparty activists among the farmhands, poor peasants,
and middle peasants who are close to the poor.

We must have a real, planned, universal, and durable organization of the poor, centered upon vital political and economic
problems, such as elections, tax campaigns, a voice in the
distribution of credit, machinery, etc., land division and land
utilization, the creation of cooperatives, and the use of funds
allotted to the village poor for forming cooperatives.

The party ought to promote by all means the economic advancement of the *middle peasants*—by a wise policy of prices for
grain, by the organization of credits and cooperatives accessible
to them, and by the systematic and gradual introduction of this
most numerous peasant group to the benefits of large-scale,
mechanized, collective agriculture.

The task of the party in relation to the growing *kulak strata*
ought to consist in the all-sided limitation of their efforts at
exploitation. We must permit no departures from the articles of
our constitution depriving the exploiter elements of electoral
rights in the soviets. The following measures are necessary: a
steeply progressive tax system; legislative measures to protect
hired labor and regulate the wages of agricultural workers; a
correct class policy in regard to land division and utilization; the
same thing in regard to supplying tractors and other instruments
of production to the villages.

The growing system of land rental in the countryside, the
existing method of land utilization, according to which rural
societies—standing outside of all Soviet leadership and control
and falling more and more under the influence of the kulak—
dispose of the land, the resolution adopted by the Fourth Congress of the Soviets for "indemnification" at the time of land
redistribution—all this is undermining the foundations of the
nationalization of the land.

One of the most essential measures for reinforcing the nationalization of the land is the subordination of these rural societies to
the local institutions of the state and the establishment of firm
control by the local soviets, purified of kulak elements, over all
questions of the division and utilization of the land. The purpose
of this control should be a maximum defense of the interests of
the poor and the weak middle peasants against domination by
the kulaks. On the basis of our present experience we must work
out a series of supplementary measures to eliminate kulak
domination of the rural societies. It is necessary in particular that
the kulak, as a landlord, should be wholly and absolutely, not

only in words but in fact, subject to supervision and control by the institutions of Soviet power in the countryside.

The party must level a jarring blow against all those currents tending toward the annulment or undermining of the nationalization of the land—one of the foundation pillars of the dictatorship of the proletariat.

The existing system of *a single agricultural tax* ought to be changed in the direction of freeing the 40 to 50 percent of poorer and poorest peasant families from all taxation, without any additional tax being imposed upon the bulk of the middle peasants. The dates of tax collection should be accommodated to the interests of the lower groups of taxpayers.

A much larger sum ought to be appropriated for the creation of state and collective farms. Maximum advantages must be offered to the newly organized collective farms and other forms of collectivism. People deprived of electoral rights must not be allowed to be members of collective farms. All the work of the cooperatives ought to be inspired by the aim of transforming small-scale production into large-scale collective production. A firm class policy must be followed in supplying agricultural machinery, and a special struggle must be waged against fake societies for machinery supply.

Careful attention must be paid to land distribution; above all, land must be allotted to the collective farms and the poor peasant farms, with maximum protection of their interests.

The prices of grain and other agricultural products ought to guarantee to the poor and the basic mass of the middle peasants the possibility, at the very least, of maintaining their farms at the present level and gradually improving them. Measures should be taken to abolish the disparity between autumn and spring grain prices. For this disparity counts heavily against the rural poor and gives all the advantage to the upper layers.

It is necessary not only to considerably increase the appropriations for the poor peasants' fund, but also radically to change the whole direction of *agricultural credit* so as to provide the poor and the weak middle peasant with cheap, long-term credits, and to abolish the existing system of guarantees and references.

Cooperation

The task of socialist construction in the countryside is to transform agriculture along the lines of large-scale, mechanized collective production. For the bulk of the peasants the simplest road to this end is cooperation, as Lenin described it in his work "On Cooperation." This is the enormous advantage which the proletarian dictatorship and the Soviet system as a whole give to the peasant. Only a process of growing industrialization of agriculture can create the broad basis for such socialist cooperation (or collectivization). Without a technical revolution in production methods—that is to say, without agricultural machinery, without the rotation of crops, without artificial fertilizers, etc.—no successful and broad work in the direction of a real collectivization of agriculture is possible.

Cooperative buying and selling will be a road to socialism only in the event that: (1) this process takes place under the immediate economic and political influence of the socialist elements, especially of large-scale industry and the trade unions; and (2) this process of making the trade functions of agriculture cooperative gradually leads to the collectivization of agriculture itself. The class character of the agricultural cooperatives will be determined not only by the numerical weight of the different groups of the cooperating peasantry, but more particularly by their relative economic weight. The task of the party is to see that agricultural cooperation constitutes a real union of the poor and middle groups of the peasants, and is a weapon in the struggle of those elements against the growing economic power of the kulak. We must systematically and persistently involve the agricultural proletariat in the task of building the cooperatives.

A successful cooperative structure is conceivable only if the participants enjoy a maximum of independent initiative. Proper relations by the cooperatives with large-scale industry and the proletarian state presuppose a normal regime in the cooperative organizations, excluding bureaucratic methods of regulation.

In view of the obvious departure of the party leadership from the fundamental Bolshevik course in the countryside, its tendency to rely on the well-off peasant and the kulak; in view of the covering up of this policy by anti-proletarian speeches about "poor man's illusions," "sponging," and "do-nothingism," and about the alleged disinclination of the poor peasant to defend the Soviet Union—in view of these things, it is more than ever necessary to remember the words of our party program. While unequivocally asserting the decisive importance for us of the alliance with the middle peasant, our program clearly and succinctly states: "The All-Russia Communist Party in its work in the village, as formerly, looks for support to the proletarian and semiproletarian groups there, and in the first place organizes them into an independent force, creating party cells in the villages, organizations of the rural poor, special types of trade unions of village proletarians and semiproletarians, and so on, bringing them into closer contact with the urban proletariat, and freeing them from the influence of the rural bourgeoisie and the interests of the small property owners."

Chapter 4
State Industry and
the Building of Socialism
The Rate of Industrial Development

"A large-scale machine industry capable of reorganizing agriculture is the only material basis that is possible for socialism" [Lenin, *Collected Works,* vol. 32, p. 459].

The basic condition for our socialist development at the present preliminary stage and in the present historical situation—capitalist encirclement and a delay in the world revolution—is a rate of industrialization sufficiently rapid to ensure that, in the near future, at least the following problems would be solved:

1. The material positions of the proletariat within the country must be strengthened both absolutely and relatively (growth in the number of employed workers, reduction of the number of unemployed, improvement in the material level of the working class and, especially, increasing the amount of living space per capita to meet basic health standards).

2. Industry, transport, and power plants must increase operations in order at least to keep pace with the growing demands of the country as a whole and not to lag behind the growing economic potential.

3. It must be made possible for agriculture to attain a higher technical level, so that it can provide industry with an expanding supply of raw materials.

4. In regard to the development of the productive forces, technological progress, and higher living standards for the working class and the toiling masses, the Soviet Union must not fall further behind the capitalist countries in the years ahead, but must catch up with them.

5. Industrialization must be sufficient to ensure the defense of

the country and in particular the adequate growth of the war industries.

6. The socialist, state-owned, and cooperative elements must increase systematically, forcing out some and subordinating and transforming others of the presocialist economic elements (capitalist and precapitalist).

In spite of our considerable success in the spheres of industry, electrification, and transport, industrialization is far from having attained that development which is necessary and possible. The present rate of industrialization and the rate indicated for the coming years are obviously inadequate.

There is not, and of course cannot be, a policy which would permit us to solve all our difficulties at one stroke, or leap over a prolonged period of systematic elevation of our economic and cultural level. But our very cultural and economic backwardness requires a rational and timely mobilization of all our accumulated reserves, the correct utilization of all our resources for the fastest possible industrialization of the country. The chronic lagging of industry, as well as transport, electrification, and construction, behind the demands and needs of the population, the economy, and the social system as a whole, holds all economic circulation in the country in a terrible vise. It reduces the sale and export of the marketable part of our agricultural production. It restricts imports to extremely narrow limits, drives up prices and production costs, causes the instability of the *chervonets*, and retards the development of the productive forces. It delays all improvement in the material condition of the proletarian and peasant masses, causes the dangerous growth of unemployment and the deterioration of housing conditions. It undermines the bond between industry and agriculture and weakens the country's defense capability.

The inadequate tempo of industrial development leads in turn to a retardation of the growth of agriculture. Yet no industrialization is possible without decisively raising the level of the productive forces in agriculture and increasing agricultural production for the market.

Prices

The necessary acceleration of industrialization is impossible without a systematic and determined lowering of production costs and of wholesale and retail prices on industrial goods, bringing them closer to world prices. That would mean real progress, both in the sense of advancing our production to a higher technical level and in the sense of better satisfying the needs of the masses of working people.

It is time to put an end to the senselessness and indecent outcry about the Opposition's alleged desire to raise prices. The party is absolutely unanimous in the desire to lower prices. But the desire alone is not enough. Policies should be judged not by intention, but by result. The results of the present struggle to lower prices have more than once compelled even important members of the leadership to raise the question of whether large sums of money were not being lost through this policy. "Where did the billion rubles go?" Bukharin was inquiring in January of this year. "What becomes of the difference between wholesale and retail prices?" asked Rudzutak, speaking after him on the same theme (Politburo minutes, March 3, 1927, pp. 20-21). Given the chronic shortage of goods, the sweeping and clumsily bureaucratic lowering of wholesale prices, since it does not in the majority of cases reach down to the worker and the peasant, entails a loss to state industry of hundreds of millions of rubles. The consequent widening of the scissors between wholesale and retail prices, especially where the private trader is concerned, is so monstrous that it would be entirely possible, by following a correct policy, to keep part of this commercial mark-up in the hands of state industry. The irrefutable conclusion from the whole economic experience of the last few years is the need for the price disproportion to be overcome as quickly as possible, the volume of industrial goods to be increased, and the rate of industrial development to be accelerated. That is the main road to a real lowering of wholesale and retail prices and above all to a lowering of the cost of production, which in recent years has shown a tendency to rise rather than fall.

The Five-Year Plan of the State Planning Commission (1926-27 to 1930-31)

The question of a five-year plan of development of the national economy, on the agenda of the coming Fifteenth Party Congress, ought properly to occupy the center of the party's attention. The five-year plan is not yet an officially accepted document and hardly will be accepted in its present form. Nevertheless, it does provide the most systematic and finished expression of the main line of the present economic leadership.

Capital investments in industry will hardly grow at all from year to year, according to this plan (1,142 million next year, 1,205 million in 1931). And in proportion to the total sum invested in the national economy, they will fall from 36.4 percent to 27.8 percent. The net investments in industry from the state budget according to this program will fall during the same years approximately from 200 million to 90 million. *The annual increase in production* is fixed at from 4 to 9 percent each year over the year preceding—the rate of growth in capitalist countries during boom periods. The tremendous advantages resulting from the nationalization of the land, the means of production, and the banks, and from centralized management—that is, the advantages deriving from the socialist revolution—find almost no expression in the five-year plan.

The individual consumption of industrial goods, beggarly at the present time, is to grow by only 12 percent in all during the five-year period. The consumption of cotton fabrics in 1931, which is to be 97 percent of the prewar amount, will be one-fifth of that in the United States in 1923. The consumption of coal will be one-seventh of that in Germany in 1926, one-seventeenth of that in the United States in 1923. The consumption of pig iron will be something over one-quarter of that in Germany, one-eleventh of that in the United States. The production of electric power will be one-third of that in Germany, one-seventh of that in the United States. The consumption of paper at the end of the five years will be 83 percent of the prewar amount. All this, fifteen years after October! To propose such a parsimonious, thoroughly pessimistic plan on the tenth anniversary of the October Revolution really means to work against socialism. *The lowering of retail prices* by 17 percent, as projected by the five-year plan, even if it is realized, will hardly have any effect upon the relation between our prices and world prices, which are two and a half to three times lower than ours.

But even with this insignificant price reduction (and that, too, still only projected), the five-year plan anticipates a shortage of 400 million rubles worth of industrial goods each year in relation to effective demand within the country. If we assume that the present appalling wholesale prices will be lowered by 22 percent over the five-year period—a more than modest reduction—that alone would result in a shortage of goods amounting to a full billion rubles. The *disproportion* between supply and demand is thus preserved inviolate, a constant source of new increases in retail prices. The five-year plan promises the peasants by 1931 approximately the prewar volume of industrial goods at prices one and a half times higher. To the worker in large-scale industry it promises an increase of 33 percent in the money wage over five years, aside from the ill-founded hope for a reduction in prices. The disproportion between supply and demand is to be overcome, according to the scheme of the State Planning Commission, by increasing the rent presently paid by the workers by a factor of two or two and a half, i.e., by approximately 400 million rubles a year. Since well-to-do sections of the population have some excess purchasing power, the officials of the Planning Commission are going to correct that situation by cutting down the real wages of the workers. It is hard to believe that such a method of achieving market equilibrium is proposed by the responsible agencies of a workers' state. This entire wrong perspective forcibly impels the consumer to seek a way out through the disastrous method of abolishing the monopoly of foreign trade.

The construction of 6,000 to 7,000 versts [one verst = 3,500 feet] of *new railroad tracks* projected in the five-year plan—as against 14,000 constructed, for example, during the five years from 1895 to 1900—will be dangerously inadequate, not only from the point of view of socialist industrialization, but from that of the most elementary economic needs of the principal regions.

With allowance for slight adjustments in one direction or another, we have here the essential orientation of the government bodies in charge of our economy. This is how the political line of the present leadership looks in practice.

The Soviet Union and the World Capitalist Economy

In the long struggle between two irreconcilably hostile social systems—capitalism and socialism—the outcome will be determined *in the last analysis* by the relative productivity of labor under each system. And this, under market conditions, is measured by the relation between domestic prices and world prices. It was this fundamental fact that Lenin had in mind when in one of his last speeches he warned the party of the "test" that would be imposed "by the Russian and international market, to which we are subordinated, with which we are connected, and from which we cannot isolate ourselves" [*Collected Works,* vol. 33, pp. 276-77]. For that reason, Bukharin's notion that we proceed toward socialism at any pace, even a "snail's pace," is a banal and vapid petty-bourgeois fantasy.

We cannot escape from capitalist encirclement by retreating

into a nationally exclusive economy. Just because of its exclusiveness, such an economy would be compelled to advance at an extremely slow pace, and in consequence would encounter not weaker, but stronger pressure, not only from the capitalist armies and navies ("intervention"), but above all from cheap capitalist commodities.

The monopoly of foreign trade is a vitally necessary instrument for socialist construction, under the circumstances of a higher technological level in the capitalist countries. But the socialist economy now under construction can be defended by this monopoly only if it continually comes closer to the prevailing levels of technology, production costs, quality, and price in the world economy. The aim of economic management ought to be not a closed-off, self-sufficient economy, for which we would pay the price of an inevitably lower level and rate of advance, but just the opposite—an all-sided increase of our relative weight in the world economy, to be achieved by increasing our rate of development to the utmost.

For this it is necessary: (1) To understand the colossal importance of our export trade, now so dangerously lagging behind the development of our economy as a whole (the USSR's share of world trade fell from 4.2 percent in 1913 to 0.97 percent in 1926); (2) Above all, to change our policy toward the kulaks, a policy that makes it possible for them to undermine our socialist export by the usurious hoarding of produce; (3) To develop our ties with the world economy by speeding up industrialization in every way and strengthening the socialist element, as opposed to the capitalist element, in our own economy; (4) Not to fritter away our meager accumulated reserves in the period ahead, but gradually and with a deliberate plan to invest in new types of production— and above all mass production—of the most necessary and most easily obtained machinery; (5) To supplement and stimulate our own industry skillfully and prudently by systematically utilizing the achievements of world capitalist technology.

The orientation toward the isolated development of socialism and a rate of development independent of the world economy distorts the entire perspective, throws our planning efforts off the track, and fails to provide any guideline for correctly managing our relations with the world economy. As a result we have no way of deciding what to manufacture ourselves and what to bring in from outside. Firm rejection of the theory of an isolated socialist economy would mean, even in the next few years, an incomparably more rational use of our resources, a swifter industrialization, and an increasingly well-planned and powerful growth of our own machine industry. It would mean a swifter increase in the number of employed workers and a real lowering of prices—in a word, a genuine strengthening of the Soviet Union despite capitalist encirclement.

Won't the growth of our ties with world capitalism involve a danger in case of blockade and war? The answer to this question follows from everything that has been said above.

Preparations for war of course require the stockpiling of strategic foreign raw materials and the timely establishment of vitally necessary new industries—for example, the production of aluminum, etc. But the most important thing in the event of a prolonged and serious war is to have industry developed to the highest degree and capable both of mass production and of rapid switching from one kind of production to another. The recent past has shown that the highly industrialized country of Germany, bound up by thousands of threads with the world market, nevertheless revealed tremendous vitality and powers of resistance, even though war and blockade at one blow severed its ties with the entire world.

If with the incomparable advantages of our social system we can, during this "peaceful" period, utilize the world market in order to speed up our industrial development, we shall meet any blockade or intervention infinitely better prepared and better armed.

No domestic policy can by itself deliver us from the economic, political, and military dangers of the capitalist encirclement. The task at home is to move forward as far as possible on the road of socialist construction by strengthening ourselves with a proper class policy, by proper relations between the working class and the peasantry. The internal resources of the Soviet Union are enormous and make this entirely possible. While we make use of the world capitalist market for this purpose, our fundamental historical expectations continue to be linked with the further development of the world proletarian revolution. Its victory in the advanced countries will break the ring of capitalist encirclement, deliver us from our heavy military burden, enormously strengthen us technologically, accelerate our entire development—in town and countryside, in factory and school—and give us the possibility of really building socialism—that is, a classless society, based on the highest level of technology and real equality among all its members both at work and in the enjoyment of the fruits of their labor.

Where to Find the Means

To the question of where to find the means for a bolder and more revolutionary solution of the problem of real industrialization, and a swifter elevation of the culture of the masses—the two problems upon whose solution the fate of the socialist dictatorship depends—the Opposition answers as follows:

The fundamental source is the redistribution of the national income by means of a correct use of budget, credit, and prices. A supplementary source is a correct utilization of our ties with the world economy.

1. According to the five-year plan, the *budget,* both state and local, will increase in five years from 6 to 8.9 billion rubles, and will amount in 1931 to 16 percent of the national income. This will be a smaller share of the national income than the prewar tsarist budget, which was 18 percent. The budget of a workers' state not only may but should occupy a larger place in the national income than a bourgeois budget. This assumes, of course, that it will really be a socialist budget and, along with increased expenditures for popular education, will allot incomparably larger sums for the industrialization of the country. The net appropriations from the budget for the needs of industrialization can and should reach 500 to 1,000 million a year during the next five years.

2. The *tax system* is not keeping up with the growth of accumulation among the upper layers of the peasants and the new bourgeoisie in general. It is necessary: (a) to tax all kinds of excess profits from private enterprises to the extent of not less than 150 to 200 million rubles, instead of 5 million as at present; (b) in order to strengthen our export, to assure a collection from the well-to-do kulak strata, constituting approximately 10 percent of all peasant households, of not less than 150 million poods [2,700,000 tons] of grain. This should be collected in the form of a loan from those stores of grain which in 1926-27 amounted to 800 to 900 million poods [14,400,000 to 16,200,000 tons], and which are concentrated, for the most.part, in the hands of the upper strata of the peasantry.

3. A decisive policy of *systematic and steady lowering of wholesale and retail prices* and narrowing of the scissors between them must actually be put into effect. And this must be done in such a way that the lowering of prices primarily applies to consumer goods needed by the mass of the workers and peasants.

(In contrast to present practice, this must be done without the adulteration of quality, which is low enough already.) This lowering of prices should not deprive state industry of the accumulation it needs. It should be carried out chiefly by increasing the volume of goods produced, lowering the cost of production, reducing overhead costs, and cutting down the bureaucratic apparatus. A more elastic price-lowering policy, more adapted to the conditions of the market, and more individualized—that is, taking into greater consideration the market position of each kind of goods—would retain enormous sums in the hands of state industry which now nourish private capital and commercial parasitism in general.

4. The *regime of economy* which, according to last year's announcement by Stalin and Rykov, was supposed to yield 300 to 400 million rubles a year, has in fact brought completely insignificant results. A regime of economy is a question of class policy and can be realized only under direct pressure from the masses. The workers must *dare* to exercise this pressure. It is entirely possible to lower nonproductive expenditures by 400 million rubles a year.

5. The skillful use of such tools as the *monopoly of foreign trade*, foreign credit, concessions, contracts providing for technical aid, etc., can provide supplementary capital. More important, it could greatly increase the efficiency of our own expenditures, multiplying their effect through the latest technology and accelerating the whole course of our development, thus strengthening our real socialist independence despite capitalist encirclement.

6. The question of *choosing personnel*—from top to bottom—and of the proper relations among them is, to some extent, a financial question. The worse the personnel, the more funds are needed. The bureaucratic regime runs counter to proper selection of personnel and proper relations.

7. The "tail-endism" of our present economic leadership means in practice the loss of many tens of millions. That is the price we pay for lack of foresight, lack of coordination, petty-mindedness, and foot-dragging.

8. Tax receipts alone cannot cover the continually growing demands of our economy. *Credit* must become a more and more important lever for redistributing the national income to serve the aims of socialist construction. This assumes, above all, a stable currency and a healthy circulation of money.

9. A firmer class policy in our economy, narrowing the limits of

speculation and usury, would make it easier for government and credit institutions to *mobilize private savings*. It would make possible an incomparably broader financing of industry through long-term credits.

10. *The government sale of vodka* was originally introduced as an experiment, with the idea that the bulk of the income from it should go toward industrialization, primarily to build up the metal industry. In reality industrialization has only lost through the state sale of vodka. It is necessary to acknowledge that the experiment has proved completely unsuccessful. Under the Soviet system the state sale of vodka is a negative factor, not only from the standpoint of the individual's budget, as was true under tsarism—but also and chiefly from the standpoint of state industry. The increase of absenteeism, careless workmanship, waste, accidents, fires, fights, injuries, etc.—these things add up to hundreds of millions of rubles a year. State industry loses from vodka no less than the budget receives from vodka, and many times more than industry itself receives from the budget. The abolition of the state sale of vodka as soon as possible (within two to three years) will automatically increase the material and spiritual resources for industrialization.

Such is the answer to the question where to find the means. It is not true that the slow pace of industrialization is directly due to the absence of resources. The means are scanty, but they exist. What we need is the correct policy.

The five-year plan of the State Planning Commission should be categorically rejected and condemned as basically incompatible with the task of "transforming the Russia of the NEP into socialist Russia." We must carry out in practice a redistribution of the tax burden among the classes—placing a heavier load on the kulak and NEPman and relieving the workers and poor peasants.

We must reduce the relative importance of indirect taxes. We must in the near future abolish the state sale of vodka.

We must put in order the finances of the railway transport service.

We must put in order the finances of industry.

We must restore to health the neglected forestry industry, which can and must become the source of an immense income.

We must guarantee the unconditional stability of our basic unit of currency. The stabilization of the *chervonets* requires the lowering of prices, on the one hand, and a balanced budget, on the other. The issuing of paper currency to cover a budget deficit must not be permitted.

We must have a strictly purposeful budget, without deficits, harsh and intolerant of everything superflous or incidental.

In the budget of 1927-28 we must considerably increase the appropriation for defense (primarily for the war industries), for industry in general, for electrification, for transport, for housing construction, and for measures leading to the collectivization of agriculture.

We must emphatically reject all attempts to tamper with the monopoly of foreign trade.

We must chart a firm course toward industrialization, electrification, and rationalization, with the aim of building a technologically more powerful economy and improving the material conditions of the masses.

Chapter 5
The Soviets

The bureaucratic apparatus in every bourgeois state, regardless of the form of that state, stands over and above the population, binding the bureaucracy together through the system of mutual protection typical of any ruling caste, and systematically promoting among the workers fear and subservience toward the rulers. The October Revolution, replacing the old state machinery by the workers', peasants', and soldiers' soviets, dealt the heaviest blow in history to the old idol of the bureaucratic state.

Our party program says on this question:

"Waging the most determined struggle against bureaucratism, the Russian Communist Party fights for the following measures in order to overcome this evil completely:

"1. the obligatory involvement of every member of a soviet in the performance of a particular task in administering the state;

"2. regular rotation of such tasks, so that eventually all branches of administration are covered;

"3. gradual involvement of the entire working population, without exception, in the work of administering the state.

"Complete and thoroughgoing realization of all these measures—representing a further step along the trail blazed by the Paris Commune—and a simplification of all administrative functions, combined with a rise in the cultural level of all workers, will result in the elimination of the state."

The question of Soviet bureaucratism is not only a question of red tape and swollen staffs. At bottom it is a question of the class role played by the bureaucracy, of its social ties and sympathies, of its power and privileged position, its relation to the NEPman and the unskilled worker, to the intellectual and the illiterate, to the wife of a Soviet grandee and the most ignorant peasant women, etc., etc. Whose hand does the official grasp? That is the fundamental question which is daily being tested in life's experience by millions of working people.

On the eve of the October Revolution, Lenin, referring to Marx's analysis of the Paris Commune, strongly emphasized the idea that: "Under socialism officials will cease to be bureaucrats, to be 'chinovniks' [high officials in the old tsarist civil service]. They will cease *insofar as* elections are supplemented by the right of instant recall; when *besides this,* their pay is brought down to the level of the pay of the average workers; when *besides this,* parliamentary institutions are replaced by 'working bodies'—that is, by institutions which both pass laws and carry them into effect" [from *The State and Revolution;* the translation in *Collected Works,* vol. 25, p. 492 is inadequate].

In what direction has the apparatus of the Soviet state been developing in recent years? In the direction of simplification and lowering of costs? Of proletarianization? Drawing near to the toilers of the city and the village? Diminishing the gulf between the rulers and the ruled? How do things stand as to the introduction of greater *equality* in the conditions of life, in rights and obligations? Are we making progress in this sphere? It is quite obvious that you cannot give an affirmative answer to a single one of these questions.

It goes without saying, of course, that actual and full equality can be achieved only with the abolition of classes. In the epoch of NEP, the task of equalization is hindered and delayed but it is not abolished. For us, NEP is not a road to capitalism but a road to socialism. Therefore the *gradual involvement of the entire working population without exception in the work of state administration and the systematic struggle for greater equality* remain under NEP two of the most important tasks of the party. That struggle can be successful only on the basis of a growing industrialization of the country and an increase in the leading role of the proletariat in all branches of material and cultural construction. This struggle for greater equality does not exclude in the transition period, higher pay for skilled workers, increased remuneration for experts, better payment of teachers than in bourgeois countries, etc.

It is necessary to be fully aware that the army of officials has been growing in number in the last few years. It is consolidating itself, raising itself above the general population, and interlocking with the wealthier elements of town and country. The "instructions" of 1925, which gave electoral rights to numerous exploiting elements, were only one very clear expression of the fact that the bureaucratic apparatus, to its very top, has become responsive to the importunities of the upper strata, the wealthy, accumulating elements, those who have enriched themselves. The annulment of these instructions—which were, as a matter of fact, in violation of the Soviet constitution—was a result of criticism from the Opposition. But the first election under the new instructions had already revealed, in a number of localities, the tendency, encouraged from above, to reduce as much as possible the number of those in the better-off groups who are disenfranchised. But even that is not the heart of the problem. With the continual relative growth of the new bourgeoisie and the kulaks, and their drawing together with the bureaucracy, with the incorrect policy of our leadership in general, the kulak and the NEPman, even when deprived of electoral rights, remain able to influence the composition and the policy of at least the lower soviet institutions, although remaining behind the scenes.

The penetration of the soviets by the lower kulak and "semi-kulak" elements and the urban bourgeoisie, which began in 1925 and was partially stopped by the attacks of the Opposition, is the kind of profound political process which, if ignored or glossed over, could threaten the proletarian dictatorship with very dire consequences.

The urban soviets, the fundamental instruments for involving industrial workers and all working people, without exception, in the task of state administration, in recent years have been losing importance. This undoubtedly reflects a shift in the relation of class forces to the disadvantage of the proletariat. It is not possible to counter these phenomena by a mere administrative "revival" of the soviets. They can be countered only be a firm class policy, by a decisive rebuff to the new exploiters, by an increase in the activity and importance of the proletariat and the poor peasants in all the institutions and agencies of the Soviet state without exception.

The "theory" of Molotov that we cannot demand that the state come closer to the workers because our state is already, in and of itself, a workers' state (*Pravda,* December 13, 1925) is the most malignant imaginable formula of bureaucratism. It sanctions in advance all possible bureaucratic distortions. Any criticism of this anti-Leninist "theory"—which enjoys the open or silent sympathy of broad circles of Soviet officialdom—is characterized, under the present leadership, as a Social Democratic deviation. But a harsh condemnation of this, and of all similar "theories," is an indispensable condition for any real struggle against bureaucratic deformations. Such a struggle does not mean merely transforming a certain number of workers into officials. It means bringing the *whole* state apparatus in *all* of its daily work closer to the workers and the poorer peasants.

The present official struggle against bureaucratism—not basing itself on the class activity of the workers but trying to replace this with the efforts of the apparatus itself—is giving and can give no essential results. In many cases it even promotes and reinforces the existing bureaucratism.

In the recent past a number of obviously negative processes in the inner life of the soviets are also to be observed. The soviets have had less and less to do with the settling of fundamental political, economic, and cultural questions. They have become mere appendages to the executive committees and presidiums. The work of administration has been entirely concentrated in the hands of the latter. The discussion of problems at the plenary sessions of the soviets is merely for show. At the same time the period between elections to the soviet institutions is being lengthened, and the independence of soviet bodies from control by the mass of workers is increasing. All this greatly increases the influence of the officials upon the decision of all questions.

The administration of important branches of municipal affairs often lies in the hands of one or two Communists, who select their own experts and their own staff, and often become completely dependent upon them. There is no proper training of the members of the soviet. They are not drawn into the work from the bottom to the top. Hence the continual complaints about the lack of skilled workers in the soviet machinery. Hence a still further shifting of power to the officialdom.

The elected leaders in important spheres of soviet administration are removed at the first conflict with the chairman of the soviet. They are removed still more quickly in cases of conflict with the secretary of the regional committee of the party. In consequence of this the elective principle is being reduced to nothing, and responsibility to the electors is losing all meaning.

It is necessary:

1. To adopt a firm policy of struggle against *chinovnichestvo* [the virulent old Russian form of bureaucratism]—to wage this struggle as Lenin would, on the basis of a real fight to check the exploitative influence of the new bourgeoisie and the kulaks, by way of a consistent development of workers' democracy in the party, the trade unions, and the soviets.

2. To make it our watchword to draw the state nearer to the worker, the farmhand, the poor peasant, and the middle peasant—against the kulak—unconditionally subordinating the state apparatus to the essential interests of the toiling masses.

3. As the basis for reviving the soviets, to increase the class activity of the workers, farmhands, and poor and middle peasants.

4. To convert the urban soviets into real institutions of proletarian power and instruments for drawing the broad mass of the working people into the task of administering socialist construction—to realize, not in words but in deeds, control by the urban soviets over the work of the regional executive committees and the bodies subject to those committees.

5. To put a complete stop to the removal of elected soviet officials, except in case of real and absolute necessity, in which cases the causes should be made clear to the electors.

6. We must see that the most backward unskilled worker and the most ignorant peasant woman become convinced by experience that in any state institution whatsoever they will find attention, counsel, and all possible support.

Chapter 6
The National Question

The slowing up of the general rate of socialist development; the growth of the new bourgeoisie in town and countryside; the strengthening of the bourgeois intelligentsia; the increase of bureaucratism in the state institutions; the bad regime in the party; and bound up with all this the growth of great-power chauvinism and the spirit of nationalism in general—all this finds its most unhealthy expression in the national regions and republics. The difficulties are redoubled by the existence in some of the republics of remnants of precapitalist economic forms.

Under the New Economic Policy, the role of private capital has grown especially rapidly in the industrially backward areas remote from the center. Here the economic agencies often rely entirely upon the private capitalist. They fix prices without considering the real situation of the masses of poor and middle peasants. They artificially lower the wages of farmhands. They have expanded the system of private and bureaucratic mediation between industry and the peasants who supply raw material to an excessive degree. They have turned the cooperatives in the direction of greater service to the richer elements in the villages. They neglect the interests of the especially backward group, the cattle breeders and those partly engaged in cattle breeding. The vital task of carrying out a plan of industrial construction in the national areas—especially a plan for industrializing the processing of agricultural raw materials—is kept completely in the background.

Bureaucratism, sustained by the spirit of great-power chauvinism, has succeeded in transforming Soviet centralization into a source of quarrels as to the allotment of official positions among the nationalities (the Transcaucasian Federation). It has spoiled the relations between the center and the outlying areas. It has reduced to nothing, as a matter of actual fact, the significance of the Soviet of Nationalities. It has carried bureaucratic tutelage over the autonomous republics to the point of depriving the latter of the right to settle land disputes between the local and the Russian population. To the present day this great-power chauvinism, especially as it expresses itself through the state machinery, remains the chief enemy of integration and unity among workers of different nationalities.

Real support to the rural poor, bringing the bulk of the middle peasantry into closer relations with the poor and the farmhands, organizing the latter into an independent class force—all this is of special importance in the national regions and republics. Without real organization of the farm laborers, without the formation of cooperatives and associations of the rural poor, we run the risk of leaving the backward and rural eastern part of our country in its traditional condition of slavery, and depriving our party groups in that area of all genuine ties with the working people.

The task of Communists among the more backward, newly awakening nationalities should be to direct the process of national awakening along Soviet socialist channels. We should draw the working masses into the economic and cultural work of construction, particularly by promoting the development of the local language and schools, and by the "nationalization" of the Soviet machinery.

In regions where there is friction between nationalities or national minorities, nationalism accompanying the growth of the bourgeois elements often becomes sharply aggressive. In these circumstances "nationalization" of the local apparatus takes place at the expense of the national minorities. Boundary disputes become a source of national rancor. The atmosphere of party, soviet, and trade union work is poisoned with nationalism.

Ukrainization, Turkification, etc., can proceed properly only by overcoming bureaucratic and great-power habits in the institutions and agencies of the Soviet Union. That is one side of the problem. The other side is that it can proceed properly only if the leading role of the proletariat is preserved in the national republics, only if we base ourselves on the lower strata in the countryside and carry on a continuous and irreconcilable struggle against kulak and chauvinist elements.

These questions are especially important in such industrial centers as the Donbas or Baku, whose proletarian population is largely of a different nationality from that of the surrounding countryside. In these cases correct cultural and political relations between town and countryside demand: (1) an especially attentive and genuinely fraternal attitude on the part of the town toward the material and spiritual requirements of the countryside where the nationality is different; (2) a determined resistance to every bourgeois attempt to drive a wedge between the town and the countryside—whether by cultivating a bureaucratic arrogance toward the rural districts, or a reactionary kulak resentment of the town.

Our bureaucratic regime has entrusted the actual implementation of its superficial show of "nationalization" to bureaucrats, bourgeois specialists, and petty-bourgeois teachers, who are connected by countless social ties with the upper strata in both town and countryside. They adapt their policies to the interests of these upper strata. This repels the local poor from the party and from Soviet power and throws them into the arms of the commercial bourgeoisie, the usurers, the reactionary priests, and feudal-patriarchal elements. At the same time our bureaucratic regime pushes into the background the genuinely Communist elements of the nationality, often denouncing them as "deviators" and persecuting them in every possible manner. This happened, for example, to an important group of Old Bolsheviks in Georgia who incurred the displeasure of the Stalin group and were hotly defended by Lenin in the last period of his life.

The elevation of the working masses of the national republic and territories, made possible by the October Revolution, is the reason why these masses aspire to direct and independent participation in practical constructive work. Our bureaucratic regime is attempting to paralyze this aspiration by frightening the masses with the cry of local nationalism.

The Twelfth Congress of our party recognized the necessity of a struggle against "surviving elements of great-power chauvinism," against "economic and cultural inequality between nationalities within the Soviet Union," against "survivals of nationalism in a whole series of peoples who have endured the heavy yoke of national oppression." The fourth conference on nationality questions, with responsible leaders of the national republics and regions in attendance (1923), declared that "one of the basic tasks of the party is to nurture and develop Communist organizations among the proletarian and semiproletarian elements of the local population in the national republics and regions." The conference unanimously declared that Communists who go from the center to the backward republics and regions ought to play the role "not of pedagogues and nursemaids but of helpers" (Lenin). In recent years matters have developed in exactly the opposite direction. The heads of the national party apparatus, appointed by the Secretariat of the Central Committee, take upon themselves the actual decision of all party and soviet questions. They force out active workers from the non-Russian nationalities as some kind of second-rate Communists whom one brings into the work merely to fulfill a formal "representative function" (Crimea, Kazakhstan, Turkmenistan, Tartaria, the mountain area of Northern Caucasus, etc.). An artificial division from above of all local party workers into "right" and "left" is carried out as a system in order that the secretaries appointed by the center may arbitrarily command both groups.

In the sphere of our national policy, just as in other spheres, it is necessary to return to Leninist positions:

1. To carry out an incomparably more systematic, more consistent, more vigorous, effort to overcome national divisions among workers of different nationalities—especially by an attitude of consideration toward newly recruited "national" workers, training them in skilled trades and improving their living and cultural conditions; to firmly remember that the real lever for bringing the backward national countryside into the work of Soviet construc-

tion is the creation and development of proletarian cadres in the local population.

2. To reconsider the five-year economic plan with a view to increasing the rate of industrialization in the backward periphery, and to work out a fifteen-year plan which shall take into consideration the interests of the national republics and regions; to adapt our state purchasing policy to the development of special crops among the poor and middle peasants (cotton in Central Asia, tobacco in the Crimea, Abkhazia, etc.). The cooperative credit policy and also the policy of land improvement (in Central Asia, Transcaucasia, etc.) ought to be carried out strictly on class lines, in keeping with the fundamental tasks of socialist construction; to give greater attention to the development of cattle-raising cooperatives, to carry out industrialization in the processing of agricultural raw materials in a manner adapted to local conditions. To revise our policy of settling new inhabitants in more backward regions* to conform to the aim of a correct policy on the national question.

3. To carry out conscientiously the policy of nationalization of the soviet apparatus, as well as the party, trade union, and cooperative apparatuses, with genuine consideration for the relations between classes and between nationalities; to wage a real struggle against "colonialist" deviations in the activities of government, cooperative, and other agencies; to reduce bureaucratic mediation between the center and the periphery; to study the experience of the Transcaucasian Federation from the standpoint of its promoting or failing to promote the industrial and cultural development of the nationalities concerned.

4. Systematically to remove every obstacle to the fullest possible union and cooperation of the working people of different nationalities in the Soviet Union, on the basis of socialist construction and international revolution; to wage a determined struggle against the mechanical imposition upon the workers and peasants of other nationalities of the predominant national language. In this matter the laboring masses should have full freedom of choice. The real rights of every national minority within the boundaries of every national republic and region must be guaranteed. In all this work special attention must be given to those exceptional conditions arising between formerly oppressed nationalities and nationalities who were formerly their oppressors.

---

*This often meant encouraging Russians to settle on lands sparsely inhabited by non-Russians.—Eds.

5. A consistent implementation of inner-party democracy in all the national republics and regions; an absolute repudiation of the attitude of command toward non-Russians, of appointment and transfer from above; a repudiation of the policy of arbitrary division of non-Russian Communists into "rights" and "lefts"; a most attentive promotion and training of local proletarian, semiproletarian, agricultural proletarian and (anti-kulak) peasant activists.

6. A repudiation of the Ustryalov tendency, and of all kinds of great-power tendencies—especially in the central commissariats and in the state apparatus in general. An educational struggle against local nationalism upon the basis of a clear and consistent class policy on the national question.

7. Transformation of the Soviet of Nationalities into a really functioning institution bound up with the life of the national republics and regions, and really capable of defending their interests.

8. Adequate attention to the national problem in the work of the trade unions and to the task of forming national proletarian cadres. Business in these unions to be transacted in the local language; the interests of all nationalities and national minorities to be protected.

9. No franchise under any circumstances for exploiting elements.

10. A fifth conference on nationality questions to be called on a basis of real representation of the rank and file.

11. Publication in the press of Lenin's letter on the national question, which contains a criticism of Stalin's line on this question [see *Collected Works,* vol. 36, pp. 605-11].

Chapter 7
The Party

No party in world history ever won such tremendous victories as our party, which has stood for ten years now at the head of a proletariat which has put its dictatorship into effect. The Russian Communist Party is the fundamental instrument of the proletarian revolution. The Russian Communist Party is the leading party of the Comintern. No party has ever borne such worldwide historic responsibility as ours. But exactly for this reason, and because of the power it wields, our party must criticize its own mistakes fearlessly. It must not cover up the darker aspects of its own situation. It must see clearly the danger of an actual degeneration, in order to take timely measures to prevent it. It was always so in the time of Lenin, who warned us most of all against becoming a party of "swelled heads" [*Collected Works,* vol. 30, p. 528]. In giving the following picture of the present condition of our party, with all its darker aspects, we Oppositionists express the firm hope that with a correct Leninist line the party can conquer its weaknesses and rise to the height of its historic tasks.

1. The social composition of the party has deteriorated more and more in the past few years. On January 1, 1927, we had in the party, in round numbers:

Workers actually employed in industry and transport	430,000
Agricultural workers	15,700
Peasants (more than half of them now office workers)	303,000
Office workers (more than half of whom were formerly industrial workers)	462,000

Thus, on January 1, our party had only one-third workers in the factories (in fact, only 31 percent), and two-thirds peasants, office workers, former industrial workers, and "miscellaneous."

In the last year and a half our party has lost about 100,000 workers in the factories. "Automatic attrition" from the party for 1926 amounted to 25,000 rank-and-file Communists, among whom 76.5 percent were factory workers (*Izvestia,* nos. 24, 25). The recent so-called "sifting" process that accompanied the new registration of party members resulted, according to the official data (which unquestionably minimize the facts), in the removal from the party of about 80,000 members, the immense majority of them industrial workers. "In relative figures the registration embraced 93.5 percent of the party membership at the beginning of the present year" (Ibid.). Thus, by the simple process of a new registration, 6.5 percent of the whole party membership was "sifted out" (amounting to about 80,000 members). Among those "sifted out" about 50 percent were skilled, and more than a third semiskilled, workers. The attempt of the Central Committee apparatus to minimize these already sufficiently minimized data is obviously unsuccessful. In place of the Lenin levy we now have a Stalin "sifting."

On the other hand, 100,000 peasants have been admitted to the party since the Fourteenth Congress, the majority of them middle peasants. The percentage of agricultural workers is totally insignificant.

2. The social composition of the leadership bodies of the party has deteriorated still more. In the county committees, 29.5 percent are peasants (in origin); 24.4 percent are office workers, etc.; 81.6 percent of the members of these committees work for government agencies. The number of factory workers in the leading bodies of the party is next to nothing. In the regional committees, it is 13.2 percent; in the county committees, from 9.8 to 16.1 percent (see the *Review of the Statistical Department of the Central Committee,* June 10, 1927).

In the party itself about one-third of the members are workers in industry, and in the decision-making bodies of the party only one-tenth are workers in industry. This constitutes a grave danger to the party. The trade unions have traveled the same road [see Chapter 2, on the situation of the workers and the trade unions]. This shows what an enormous share of the power the "administrators" from petty-bourgeois circles have taken away from us—and also those from the "labor aristocracy." This is the surest road to the "deproletarianization" of the party.

3. The role of the former Social Revolutionaries (SRs) and Mensheviks in the party apparatus and in positions of leadership in general has increased. At the time of the Fourteenth Congress, 38 percent of those occupying responsible and directing positions in our press were persons who had come to us from other parties (Report of the Fourteenth Congress, p. 83). At present the situation is even worse. The actual direction of the Bolshevik press is either in the hands of the revisionist school of the "young" (Slepkov, Stetsky, Maretsky, and others) or of former Social Revolutionaries and Mensheviks. About a quarter of the higher cadres of the active elements in the party is composed of former Social Revolutionaries and Mensheviks.

4. Bureaucratism is growing in all spheres, but its growth is especially ruinous in the party. Today's "leading" party bureaucrat looks at things in the following manner: "We have members of the party who still inadequately understand the party itself, just what it is. They think that the party starts with the cell or local unit—the cell is the building block; then comes the district committee, and so on, higher and higher, until you arrive at the Central Committee. That is not right (!!!). Our party must be looked at from the top down. And this view must be adhered to in all practical relationships and in the entire work of the party"

(speech of the second secretary of the Northern Caucasus Regional Committee of the Russian Communist Party in *Molot,* May 27, 1927).

The definitions of inner-party democracy given us by comrades in top positions, such as Uglanov, Molotov, Kaganovich, etc., come essentially to the same thing (see *Pravda,* June 4, 1926).

This "new" conception is dangerous in the extreme. If we really acknowledged that our party "must be looked at from the top down," that would mean that the Leninist party, the party of the mass of the workers, no longer exists.

5. The last few years have seen a systematic abolition of inner-party democracy—in violation of the whole tradition of the Bolshevik Party, in violation of the direct decisions of a series of party congresses. The genuine election of officials in actual practice is dying out. The organizational principles of Bolshevism are being perverted at every step. The party constitution is being systematically changed, to increase the rights at the top and diminish the rights of the base party units. The mandates of the county, district, and regional committees have been extended by the Central Committee to a year, to two years, and more.

The leaderships of the regional committees, the regional executive committees, the regional trade union councils, etc., are, in actual fact, irremovable (for periods of from three to five years and longer). The right of each member of the party, of each group of party members, to "appeal its radical differences to the court of the whole party," is in actual fact annulled. Congresses and conferences are called without a preliminary free discussion (such as was always held under Lenin) of all questions by the whole party. The demand for such a discussion is treated as a violation of party discipline. The saying of Lenin is completely forgotten, that the Bolshevik "general staff" must "really be backed by the *good* and *conscious* will of an army that follows and at the same time *directs* its general staff" [*Collected Works,* vol. 7, p. 118].

Within the party there is taking place—as a natural accompaniment of the general course—an extremely significant process of pushing out the veteran party members, who lived through the underground period, or at least through the civil war, and are independent and capable of defending their views. They are being replaced by new elements, distinguished chiefly by their unquestioning obedience. This obedience, encouraged from above under the name of revolutionary discipline, has really nothing whatever to do with revolutionary discipline. Not infrequently new Communists, selected from among workers who were always distin-

guished by their subservience to the old prerevolutionary authorities, are now promoted to leading positions in the working class
cells and in the administration. They curry favor by a demonstra-
tive and abusive hostility toward the old worker-members, the
leaders of the working class in the hardest moments of the
revolution.

Similar changes have been made in a far uglier form in the
state apparatus, where it is no longer a rare thing to meet the
perfected figure of the "party" Soviet officials. On solemn
occasions he swears by October; he distinguishes himself by a
complete indifference to his task; he lives with all his roots in a
petty-bourgeois philistine milieu, abuses the leadership in private
life, and in party meetings gives the Opposition a "good going
over."

The real rights of one member of the party at the top (above all,
the secretary) are many times greater than the real rights of a
hundred members at the bottom. This growing substitution of the
apparatus for the party is promoted by a "theory" of Stalin's
which denies the Leninist principle, inviolable for every Bolshevik, that the dictatorship of the proletariat is and can be
realized only through the dictatorship of the party.

The dying out of inner-party democracy leads to a dying out of
workers' democracy in general—in the trade unions, and in all
other nonparty mass organizations.

Inner-party disagreements are distorted. A vicious polemic is
carried on for months and years on end against the views of
Bolsheviks who are denounced as "the Opposition," while these
Bolsheviks are not permitted to expound their real views in the
party press. Yesterday's Mensheviks, Social Revolutionaries,
Cadets, Bundists, Zionists, attack and denounce in the pages of
Pravda documents submitted to the Central Committee by certain
of its own members. They take isolated sentences from these
documents out of context and distort them. But the documents
themselves are never printed. Party units are compelled to vote
"denunciations" of documents that are totally unknown to them.

The party is compelled to judge our disagreements on the basis
of the universally despised official summaries, or study outlines,
and speeches "working over" the Opposition, almost all of which
are illiterate and full of lies. The saying of Lenin—"Whoever
believes things simply on someone else's say-so is a hopeless
idiot"—has been replaced by a new formula: "Whoever does not
believe the official say-so is an Oppositionist." Factory workers
who incline toward the Opposition are compelled to pay for their

opinions with unemployment. The rank-and-file party members cannot state their views out loud. Veteran party activists are deprived of the right to express themselves either in the press or at meetings.

Bolsheviks who defend the ideas of Lenin are slanderously accused of desiring to create "two parties." This accusation was deliberately invented in order to arouse the workers, who naturally passionately defend the unity of their party, against the Opposition. Every word of criticism against the crude Menshevik mistakes of Stalin (on the problems of the Chinese revolution, the Anglo-Russian Committee, etc.) is described as a "struggle against the party," although Stalin never asked the party in advance about his policy in China or about any other important problem. This accusation that the Opposition desires to create "two parties" is repeated every day by those whose own purpose is to force the Bolshevik-Leninists out of the party in order to have a free hand in carrying out an opportunist policy.

6. Almost all advanced educational work in the party and all elementary political education has now been reduced to a course in Opposition-baiting. The method of persuasion is not only replaced on an immense scale by the method of compulsion; it is also supplemented by the method of deceiving the party. Since party education has been reduced to mere official propaganda, the general tendency is to evade it. Attendance at meetings, party schools, and study groups, dedicated as they are to Opposition-baiting, has dropped enormously. The party is employing passive resistance against the present wrong course of its apparatus.

7. Not only have careerism, bureaucratism, and inequality grown in the party in recent years, but muddy streams from alien and hostile class sources are flowing into it—for example, anti-Semitism. The very self-preservation of the party demands a merciless struggle against such defilement.

8. In spite of these facts, the fire of repression is directed exclusively against the left. It has become quite common for Oppositionists to be expelled for speaking at cell meetings, for making sharp replies, for attempting to read the Testament of Lenin. In their level of political understanding and, what is more important, in their devotion to the cause of the party, the expelled frequently stand higher than those who expel them. Finding themselves outside the party—for "lack of faith" and "pessimism" in regard to Chiang Kai-shek, Purcell, or their own bureaucrats—these comrades continue to live the life of the party. They

serve it far more loyally than many party careerists and philistines.

9. The present hail of repressions and threats, visibly increasing with the approach of the Fifteenth Congress, is designed to frighten the party more than ever. This shows that the united faction of Stalin and Rykov, in order to cover up its political mistakes, is resorting to the most extreme measures, confronting the party with a fait accompli in every instance.

10. The political line of the Central Committee (which was formulated at the Fourteenth Congress in terms of the principle "solidarity with Stalin") is erroneous. Although wavering, the present nucleus of the Central Committee moves continually to the right.* The abolition of inner-party democracy is an inevitable result of the fact that the political line is radically wrong. Insofar as it reflects the pressure of petty-bourgeois elements, the influence of the non-proletarian layers which surround our party, it must inevitably be carried through by force from above.

In the theoretical sphere the so-called "younger school" has a monopoly. This is a school of revisionists, who are ready at any moment to carry out the literary commands of the apparatus. The best elements of the Bolshevik youth, inspired by the genuine traditions of the Bolshevik Party, are not only forced out but actually persecuted.

In the organizational sphere the actual subjection of the Politburo to the Secretariat, and the Secretariat to the general secretary, has long been an accomplished fact. The worst fear expressed by Lenin in his Testament—the fear that Stalin would not be sufficiently loyal, would not employ in a party manner the "unlimited power" which he had "concentrated in his hands"—has been justified [Lenin's letters of December 24, 1922, and January 4, 1923].

At the present time there are three fundamental tendencies in the Central Committee and in the leading organs of the party and state in general.

The first tendency is a frank and open drift to the right. This tendency, in turn, is composed of two groups. One of them, in its opportunism and pliability, to a great extent reflects the interests of the "economically strong" middle peasant, toward whom it steers its course and by whose ideals it is inspired. This is a group of Comrades Rykov, A.P. Smirnov, Kalinin, G. Petrovsky,

---

*This sentence was not in the typescript.—Eds.

Chubar, Kaminsky, and others. Around them and in their immediate vicinity work the "nonparty" politicians—the Kondratievs, Sadyrins, Chayanovs, and other "business agents" of the wealthy peasantry, more or less openly preaching the doctrines of Ustryalov. In every province, often in every county, are to be found the little Kondratievs and Sadyrins enjoying their bit of real power and influence. The other group in this first general tendency is composed of trade union leaders who represent the better-paid class of industrial and office workers. This group is particularly characterized by a desire for closer association with the Amsterdam International. Its leaders are Comrades Tomsky, Melnichansky, Dogadov, and others. Between these two groups there is a certain amount of friction, but they are at one in the desire to turn the course of the party and the Soviet state to the right, in both international and domestic policies. They are both distinguished by their contempt for the theories of Leninism and their inclination to renounce the orientation toward world revolution.

The second tendency is the "centrism" of the official apparatus. The leaders of this tendency are Comrades Stalin, Molotov, Uglanov, Kaganovich, Mikoyan, Kirov. It is, de facto, the present Politburo. Bukharin, wavering between one side and the other, "generalizes" the policies of this group. In itself this centrist-official group least of all expresses the attitude of any broad mass, but it is trying—not without success—to substitute itself for the party. The caste of "administrators"—in the party, the trade unions, the industrial agencies, the cooperatives, and the state apparatus—now numbers in the tens of thousands. Among these there is no small number of "worker" bureaucrats—former workers, that is, who have lost all connection with the masses of workers.

There is no need to add that in the agencies of administration and leadership, so enormously important to the fate of the revolution, there are to be found many thousands of sturdy revolutionists, workers who have not lost their ties with the masses but who give themselves heart and soul to the workers' cause. It is they who are doing the real work of communism in these institutions.

This does not alter the fact that the degeneration of our political course and our party regime is giving birth to an enormous caste of genuine bureaucrats.

The actual power of this caste is enormous. It is precisely this group of "administrators" that insists upon "tranquillity" and "attending to business"—and above all, "no discussion." It is this very group that complacently announces (and even sometimes sincerely believes) that we have already "nearly reached socialism," that "nine-tenths of the program" of the socialist revolution has already been fulfilled. It is this group that looks "from the top down" upon the whole party, and still more, from the top down upon the unskilled workers, the unemployed, and the farmhands. This group sees the principal enemy on the left—that is, among the revolutionary Leninists. This is the group that has issued the call for "Fire Against the Left."

For the time being these two tendencies, the right and the "center," are united by their common hostility to the Opposition. Removal of the Opposition would inevitably accelerate the conflict between them.

The third tendency is the so-called Opposition. It is the Leninist wing of the party. The pitiful attempts to pretend that it is an Opposition from the right (accusing it of a "Social Democratic deviation," etc.) arise from the desire of the ruling group to hide its own opportunism. The Opposition is for the unity of the party. Stalin propagates his own program—to ostracize the Opposition—under the false flag of the charge that the Opposition wants to create a "second party." The Opposition answers with its slogan: "Unity of the Leninist Russian Communist Party at all costs." The Platform of the Opposition is set forth in the present document. The working class sections of the party and all genuine Leninist Bolsheviks will be for it.

Personal desertions from the Opposition are unavoidable in the hard circumstances under which it is compelled to struggle for the cause of Lenin. Separate personal regroupings among the leaders of all these three tendencies will occur, but they will not alter the fundamental facts of the matter.

11. All the above facts taken together constitute a party crisis. The inner-party disagreements have deepened continually since the death of Lenin, embracing an ever broader range of increasingly crucial questions.

The basic mood in the party ranks is for unity. The present regime prevents the party from understanding where the threat to unity comes from. The machinations of Stalin are all designed to place this dilemma before the party membership, upon every sharp or important question that arises: either renounce your own opinion or find yourself accused of favoring a split.

Our task is to preserve the unity of the party at all costs, to resist firmly the policy of splits, ostracism, expulsions, etc.—but at the same time to guarantee to the party its right to a free discussion and decision of all disputed questions within the framework of this unity.

In exposing the mistakes and abnormalities of the present situation in the party, the Opposition is deeply convinced that the fundamental mass of the working class section of the party will prove able in spite of everything to bring the party back to the Leninist road. To help in that process is the essential task of the Opposition.

Practical Proposals

1. It is necessary to prepare for the Fifteenth Congress on the basis of real inner-party democracy, as was done in Lenin's time. "All members of the party," wrote Lenin, "must begin to *study*, completely dispassionately and with the utmost honesty, first the essence of the differences and second the course of the dispute in the party. . . . It is necessary to study both the one and the other, unfailingly demanding the most exact, printed documents, open to verification by all sides" [for another translation, see *Collected Works*, vol. 32, pp. 43-47]. The Central Committee should make it possible for every member of the party to study both the essence of the present inner-party disagreements and the course of the present dispute. It should do this by publishing, in the press and in special collections and pamphlets, all the documents which it has up to this time hidden from the party.

Every comrade and every group of comrades ought to have an opportunity to defend their point of view before the party in the press, at meetings, etc. The draft theses (the platform) of the Central Committee, of local organizations, of individual members of the party and groups of members, ought to be published in *Pravda* (or in supplements to *Pravda*) and also in local party papers, at least two months before the Fifteenth Congress.

The debate ought to be conducted in a businesslike and strictly comradely manner, without personalities and exaggerations. The chief slogan for the whole preparation of the Fifteenth Congress ought to be unity—not a pretended, but a genuine Leninist unity of the Russian Communist Party and the whole Communist International.

2. It is necessary to adopt immediately a series of measures for the improvement of the social composition of the party and of its leading bodies. To that end we must reaffirm the decision of the Thirteenth Congress, that "the vast majority of the party members in the near future ought to consist of workers directly

employed in industry." In the next two or three years, as a general rule, the party ought to admit only working men and women from the factories and hired men and women working on the farms. From other social groups we should accept members only upon a basis of strict personal selection: Red soldiers and sailors only if they are of working class, or rural proletarian, or poor peasant origin; poor and economically weak peasants, only after they have been tested in social-political work for a minimum of two years. The admission of members who come to us from other parties must be stopped.

We must carry out the decision of the Thirteenth Congress, in practice annulled by the Fourteenth Congress (against the will of the Opposition)—to the effect that no less than 50 percent of the district committees, the regional committees, etc., should be workers from the factories. In the industrial centers we must have a firm majority of workers from the factories (not less than three-fourths of the total). In the county committees, a similar majority of workers, farmhands, and poor peasants.

3. To confirm and carry out in practice the resolution on inner-party democracy adopted by the Tenth Party Congress, reaffirmed by the Central Committee and the Central Control Commission on December 5, 1923, and by the Twelfth and Thirteenth Congresses of the party.

We must affirm in the name of the whole party that—contrary to the new anti-Leninist definitions of inner-party democracy devised and circulated by Uglanov, Molotov, Kaganovich, Zhivov, and others—"Workers' democracy means the liberty of frank discussion of the most important questions of party life by all members, and the freedom to have organized discussions on these questions, and the election of all leading party functionaries and commissions from the bottom up" ["The New Course Resolution," December 5, 1923, in *The Challenge of the Left Opposition (1923-25)*, p. 408, where the translation is slightly different].

We must take punitive measures against everyone who violates in practice this fundamental right of every member of the party.

As a rule, the point of view of the party minority upon any question of principle ought to be brought to the attention of all the members through the party papers, etc. Exceptions should be permitted only when the matters under discussion are secret. It goes without saying that after the adoption of a decision it is to be carried out with iron Bolshevik discipline. The network of party discussion clubs should be broadened and a real criticism of the mistakes of the party leadership made possible in the party press (in discussion bulletins, printed symposia, etc.).

All those changes for the worse that have been introduced into the party rules since the Fourteenth Congress (articles 25, 33, 37, 42, 50, etc.) must be annulled.

4. We must adopt a firm course toward proletarianization of the party apparatus as a whole. Workers from the factories, advanced Communist workers who are popular with the mass of party and nonparty workers, should constitute a decisive majority of the whole party apparatus. The apparatus should by no means consist entirely of paid personnel, and it should be regularly replenished with working class members. The budget of the local organizations (not omitting the regional organizations) should consist mainly of membership dues. The local organizations should render an account of their income and expenses regularly, and in actual fact, to the mass membership of the party. The present swollen budget of the party ought to be cut down vigorously, as well as the size of the paid apparatus. A considerable portion of party work should be done gratis by members of the party giving time outside their industrial or other work. One measure for regularly revivifying the party apparatus should be the systematic sending down of a part of the comrades from the apparatus into industry and other rank-and-file work. We must struggle against the tendency of secretaries to make themselves irremovable. We must establish definite terms for the occupation of secretarial and other responsible posts. We must struggle ruthlessly against the actual corruption and decay of the uppermost groups, against patronage, "mutual protection," etc. (examples: Syzran, Kherson, Irkutsk, Chita, etc.).

5. As early as the Tenth Congress, under the leadership of Lenin, a series of resolutions were passed, emphasizing the need for greater equality within the party and among the masses of workers. As early as the Twelfth Congress the party noticed the danger, under the NEP, of a degeneration of that part of the party workers whose activities bring them into contact with the bourgeoisie. It is necessary to: "Work out completely adequate practical measures to eliminate inequality (in living conditions, wages, etc.) between the specialists and functionaries, on the one hand, and the masses of workers, on the other, insofar as this inequality destroys democracy and is a source of corruption of the party and lowering of the authority of Communists" (Resolution of the Tenth Party Conference, p. 18).

In view of the fact that inequality has grown at an extraordinarily swift pace in recent years, we must bring up this question again and solve it as revolutionists.

6. It is necessary to reorganize party education along the line of study of the works of Marx, Engels, and Lenin, driving out of circulation the false interpretations of Marxism and Leninism now being manufactured on a large scale.

7. It is necessary to restore the expelled Oppositionists to party membership immediately.

8. It is necessary to reconstruct the Central Control Commission in the real spirit of Lenin's advice. Members of the Central Control Commission must be: (a) closely associated with the masses; (b) independent of the apparatus; (c) possessed of authority in the party.

Only thus can real confidence in the Central Control Commission be restored and its authority raised to the necessary level.

9. In forming the Central Committee and the Central Control Commission and their agencies, we must be guided by the advice of Lenin, as given in his letters of December 25 and 26, 1922, and January 4, 1923 (the Testament). These letters ought to be published for the information of all members of the Central Committee.

As Lenin wrote in his letters of December 26, 1922: "The working class members of the CC must be mainly workers of a lower stratum than those promoted in the last five years to work in Soviet bodies; they must be people closer to being rank-and-file workers and peasants, who, however, do not fall into the category of direct or indirect exploiters."

Also: "In my opinion, the workers admitted to the Central Committee should come preferably not from among those who have had long service in Soviet bodies, . . . because those workers have already acquired the very traditions and the very prejudices which it is desirable to combat."

Those letters were written by Lenin in the period when he gave the party his last and most carefully weighed advice upon the fundamental questions of the revolution ["Better Fewer But Better," "How to Reorganize the Workers' and Peasants' Inspection," "On Cooperation"].

The Fifteenth Congress of our party ought to select its Central Committee precisely from the point of view of the above-quoted advice of Lenin.

Chapter 8
The Communist League of Youth

The wrong political line and organizational repression have been carried over with full force, sometimes with increased force, into the Communist League of Youth. The internationalist education of the young workers is more and more pushed into the background. All critical thinking is suppressed and persecuted. For positions of leadership in the Communist youth organization, the party apparatus demands first of all "obedience" and readiness to bait the Opposition. The proletarian element among rank-and-file activists, the fundamentally healthy elements, are denied any encouragement by this regime. Here, even more than in the party, the mistaken policy pursued at the top opens the road for petty-bourgeois influences.

In recent years the Communist League of Youth has grown rapidly in membership, but at the cost of a deterioration in its social composition. Since the Thirteenth Party Congress, the proletarian nucleus within this organization has fallen from 40.1 percent to 34.4 percent, and affiliation to the League by young workers employed in industry has dropped from 49.8 percent to 47 percent. The political activity of young workers in general has declined.

In these circumstances, a number of recent decisions add up to an exceeedingly crude mistake, capable only of widening the separation between the League and the mass of working class youth, because they worsen the position of young workers more than ever, and do so in violation of the Fourteenth Congress (reduction in the number of apprenticeship openings, the special wage-scale for apprentices, restriction of the number of apprentices in industrial schools—and here also belongs the attempt to introduce unpaid apprenticeship).

The Communist League of Youth in the countryside is more and more losing its proletarian and poor peasant base. Its cultural and economic work in the countryside tends to focus primarily on the development of individual farming. The relative weight of the poor is systematically falling everywhere—in the general composition of rural party cells, in the active membership, and in the nuclei of party members within the

League. Along with the continual diminishing of the influx of young urban workers, the League is filling up in the countryside with middle and well-to-do peasant youth.

Both in urban and in rural areas, the tendency of the petty-bourgeois elements to get hold of the leadership of the League is growing. The categories of office workers and "miscellaneous" are playing a more and more significant role, especially in the rural organizations.

Thirty-six percent of all new party members come from the ranks of the Communist League of Youth (*Pravda,* July 14, 1927). However, within the party nucleus of the League from one-fourth to one-third are nonproletarian. In the party nuclei of the rural youth organizations, the middle peasants are rapidly gaining at the expense of the farmhands and the poor peasants. (Twenty percent were middle peasants in 1925, 32.5 percent in 1927.) Thus the Communist League of Youth is turning into another source of dilution of the party by petty-bourgeois elements. In order to prevent a further undermining of the leading role of the proletarian nucleus and its relegation to the background by newcomers from the intelligentsia, clerical workers, and well-to-do strata in the countryside, inevitably entailing a petty-bourgeois degeneration of the League, the following measures are necessary:

1. To put an immediate stop to the gradual negation of our revolutionary conquests in the sphere of labor and education for young workers—to revoke all those recent measures which worsen conditions for them. That is one of the principal premises for the struggle against the unhealthy tendencies in the Communist League of Youth (drunkenness, delinquency, etc.).

2. As the general living standards of the working class rise, the material and cultural level of the young workers must be elevated systematically and resolutely, by means of higher wages, broadening of the network of industrial schools and trade courses, etc.

3. To carry out the decisions of previous party and Communist Youth congresses for enrolling in the League 100 percent of the young urban and rural proletarians over the next few years.

4. To intensify the work of attracting into the League the poor peasant youth, not just in words but in deeds.

5. To attract into the League the economically weak middle peasants, and from the rest of the middle peasants only those who have been tested in public work, especially the work of struggling against the kulak.

6. To increase the League's defense of the interests of the poor,

directing its work toward the creation of a new rural society, not through individual enrichment, but through cooperation and the collectivization of agriculture.

7. To improve the social composition of the party nucleus, permitting recruitment during the next two years only from workers, farmhands, and poor peasants.

8. To make the leadership bodies of the Communist youth essentially proletarian and to systematically and resolutely advance farmhands and the poor peasant youth to positions of leadership. To establish the rule that in the great proletarian centers the regional committees and district committees of the League, and the bureaus of these committees, should consist in an overwhelming majority of workers from the factories, and that the latter should be really drawn into the task of leadership.

9. To wage a serious struggle against bureaucratism. To cut down decisively the paid officialdom, reducing it to the absolutely necessary minimum. To accomplish at least a half, and in industrial centers three-quarters, of the work of the League through the unpaid efforts of its members. To attract more and more of the rank-and-file members to carry out the work of the League.

10. The cultural and educational work of the League should be closely bound up with an active daily participation by the League in the general political life (the soviets, the trade unions, and the cooperatives) and in the party.

11. Put an end to the rubber-stamp regime, the deadening regime of orders from above, the lying and ignorant "study outlines." Introduce instead the serious study of Marxism and Leninism, upon the basis of live discussion, comradely exchange of opinions, and a real, not a sham, acquisition of knowledge.

12. Introduce, in deeds and not words, a democratic regime. Do away with administrative pressure tactics. Stop the persecution and expulsion of those who hold independent opinions about party questions and League questions. Adhere strictly to the timetables provided in the constitution for calling conferences and congresses on the district, county, and province levels.

Chapter 9
Our International Situation
and the War Danger
The Position of the Soviet Union in the World Arena

War by the imperialists against the Soviet Union is not only probable but inevitable.

To postpone this danger, to gain as much time as possible for strengthening the Soviet Union and consolidating the international revolutionary proletariat, must be one of our foremost practical tasks. Only victorious proletarian revolutions in the decisive countries can eliminate this danger.

The danger of a world war is increasing for the following reasons:

1. The past several years of struggle on the part of capitalism to strengthen itself, and the partial success obtained in that struggle, have made the question of markets a burning question for all the leading capitalist states.

2. The imperialist bourgeoisie has been convinced beyond any question that the economic might of the Soviet Union is growing, and it sees that the proletarian dictatorship, protected by the monopoly of foreign trade, will never give the capitalists a "free" market in Russia.

3. The imperialist bourgeoisie is speculating on the inner-party difficulties in the Soviet Union.

4. The defeat of the revolution in China, following the defeat of the British General Strike, has inspired the imperialists with the hope that they may succeed in crushing the Soviet Union.

The break in diplomatic relations between Britain and the Soviet Union was prepared long ago, but the defeat of the Chinese revolution hastened it. In this sense it was a reward for the Central Committee's refusal to adopt a real Bolshevik policy in China. It would be a great mistake to imagine that this matter reduces itself to a mere change in the form of trade between Britain and us. ("We will trade as we trade with America.") It is perfectly clear now that imperialist Britain has a broader plan of action. It is preparing a war against the Soviet Union, with a "moral mandate" from the bourgeoisie of several other countries, and intends by one means or another to drag Poland, Rumania, and the Baltic states, and perhaps also Yugoslavia, Italy, and Hungary, into war against us.

Poland, it appears, would prefer to have a longer period of preparation for war against us. But it is not impossible that Britain will compel Poland to fight sooner than it likes.

In France, the British pressure for a united front against the Soviet Union is finding support from an influential part of the bourgeoisie. They are becoming more and more irreconcilable in their demands, and, of course, at a favorable moment they will not hesitate to break diplomatic relations.

The more German diplomacy has dithered about recently, the clearer it has become that its general "orientation" is toward the West. The German bourgeoisie is already saying openly that in a war against the Soviet Union, Germany would perhaps at the beginning remain "neutral" (in the manner of America in 1914) so as to profit as much as possible from the war, and later openly sell its neutrality to the Western imperialists at a good price. Nothing could be worse for the fundamental interests of the Soviet Union than to gloss over this shift by the German bourgeoisie to a Western orientation, because a blow from the German bourgeoisie that we did not expect could have decisive significance. Only a perfectly open "statement of things as they are," only an awakening of the vigilance of the workers of the Soviet Union and the workers of Germany, could protect us against such a blow, or at least make it difficult for the German bourgeoisie to deliver it.

The Japanese bourgeoisie is maneuvering no less skillfully than the German in relation to the Soviet Union. It is very cleverly covering up its tracks, and pretending to be "friendly." It has even delayed the seizure of the Chinese Eastern Railroad by Chang Tso-lin for a while. But it is secretly holding the reins in China and may soon take off its mask in relation to us.

In the Near East (Turkey and Persia), we have not, to say the least, achieved a situation which would guarantee a firm neutrality in case the imperialists attack us. We should expect, rather, that in such a case the governments of these states, under pressure from the imperialists, would be inclined to render them the services required.

In the event of an attack on us, America, having preserved her wholly irreconcilable attitude to the Soviet Union, would play the role of the imperialist "rear." The significance of this role would be the greater because this is precisely the country which can provide the financing for a war against the Soviet Union.

To sum up: Whereas the years 1923-25 were years of diplomatic recognition of the Soviet Union by a series of bourgeois states, the period beginning now will be a period of diplomatic breaks. The recognitions of the preceding period did not necessarily mean that peace was assured, that there was a solid and lasting breathing spell. The diplomatic breaks of the present period do not necessarily mean that war is inevitable in the immediate future. But that we have entered into a new period of extreme tension in the international situation, containing the possibility of attacks against the Soviet Union, is unquestionable.

The contradictions within the capitalist world are very great. It would be extremely difficult for the world bourgeoisie to maintain a united front against us for a long period. But a partial union of several bourgeois states against us, for a certain length of time, is entirely possible.

All this taken together ought to impel our party: (1) To recognize that the international situation is dangerous; (2) To again bring the problems of international politics to the attention of the broad masses of the population; (3) To carry on a most intense and all-sided preparation of the Soviet Union for defense in case of war.

The parties of the bourgeoisie, including official Social Democracy, will try in every way to deceive their people as to the real character of the war which imperialism is preparing against the Soviet Union. Our task is to explain now to the broadest masses of the peoples of the whole world that this will be a war of imperialists and slave-owners against the first proletarian state and dictatorship—a war of capitalism against socialism. In this war the imperialist bourgeoisie will be fighting essentially to preserve the whole system of capitalist wage slavery. The Soviet Union will be fighting for the interests of the international proletariat, the colonial and semicolonial and enslaved countries, for the international revolution and socialism.

Even now all of our work ought to proceed under these slogans: (1) Down with the war of the imperialists against the state of the proletarian dictatorship; (2) Turn the imperialist war into a civil war in all states attacking the Soviet Union; (3) Defeat all bourgeois states making war on the Soviet Union. All honest proletarians in the capitalist countries ought to actively work for the defeat of "their own" governments; (4) All foreign soldiers who do not wish to help the slave-owners of "their own" countries should go over to the Red Army. The Soviet Union is the fatherland of all workers; (5) The slogan "Defense of the Fatherland" would be a false disguise serving the interests of imperialism in all bourgeois countries, except colonial and semicolonial countries that are carrying on a national revolutionary war against the imperialists. In the Soviet Union the slogan "Defense of the Fatherland" is correct, because we are defending a *socialist* fatherland and the base of the world working class movement; (6) We have been defensists since October 25, 1917. Our patriotic war will be a war "for the Soviet Republic, as one of the units of the international army of socialism." Our "patriotic" war is not a step toward a bourgeois state, but a step to an international socialist revolution (Lenin). Our defense of the fatherland is defense of the proletarian dictatorship. Our war will be waged by the workers and farmhands with the support of the poor peasants and in alliance with the middle peasants against "our own" kulaks, new bourgeoisie, bureaucrats, specialists of the Ustryalov school, and White emigrés. Our war will be a truly just war. Whoever is not a defender of the Soviet Union is unquestionably a traitor to the international proletariat.

The Defeat of the Chinese Revolution and Its Causes

The defeat of the Chinese revolution has changed the real relation of forces to the advantage of imperialism—of course, only temporarily. New revolutionary conflicts, a new revolution in China, are inevitable. That is guaranteed by the whole situation.

The opportunist leaders are trying, after the event, to explain their own failure by the so-called "objective relationship of forces." They forget that only yesterday they were predicting a speedy socialist revolution in China upon the basis of this same relationship of forces.

The decisive cause of the unfavorable outcome of the Chinese revolution at the present stage was the fundamentally mistaken policy of the leadership of the Russian Communist Party and the whole International. The net result was that at the decisive period there existed in China, in actual fact, no real Bolshevik Party. To lay the blame now upon the Chinese Communists alone is superficial and contemptible.

We had in China a classic experiment in the application of the Menshevik tactic in the bourgeois-democratic revolution. That is why the Chinese proletariat not only did not reach its victorious "1905" (Lenin), but has played, so far, essentially the same role that the European proletariat played in the revolutions of 1848.

The peculiarity of the Chinese revolution in the present international situation is not that there exists in China a so-called "revolutionary" liberal bourgeoisie—upon which Stalin-Martynov-Bukharin rested the hopes of their entire policy. Its peculiarities are as follows:

1. The Chinese peasantry, more oppressed than the Russian under tsarism, groaning under the yoke not only of their own but also of foreign oppressors, could rise, and did rise, more powerfully than the Russian peasantry in the revolution of 1905.

2. The slogan of "soviets" proposed by Lenin for China as early as 1920 had every possible justification in the conditions existing in 1926-27. Soviets in China would have offered a form through which the forces of the peasantry could have been consolidated under the leadership of the proletariat. They would have been real institutions of the revolutionary-democratic dictatorship of the proletariat and the peasantry. And that means institutions of real resistance to the bourgeois Kuomintang, and to the Chinese Cavaignacs emerging from it.

The doctrine of Lenin, that a bourgeois-democratic revolution can be carried through only by a union of the working class and the peasants (under the leadership of the former) against the bourgeoisie, is not only applicable to China, and to similar colonial and semicolonial countries, but in fact indicates the only road to victory in those countries.

3. It follows from this that a revolutionary-democratic dictatorship of the proletariat and peasantry, taking the form of soviets in China, would have every chance, in the present age of imperialist wars and proletarian revolutions and given the existence of the USSR, of developing relatively rapidly into a socialist revolution.

Without that perspective the only alternative is the Menshevik road of alliance with the liberal bourgeoisie, which leads unavoidably to the defeat of the working class. And that is what happened in China in 1927.

All the decisions made in Lenin's time by the Second and Fourth Congresses of the Communist International—the decision on soviets in the Orient, on the full independence of workers' Communist parties in countries with a national-revolutionary movement, and on the union of the working class with the peasants against "their own" bourgeoisie and the foreign imperialists—all these decisions were completely forgotten.

The resolution of the seventh enlarged plenum of the Executive Committee of the Communist International (November 1926) not only did not give a true Leninist evaluation of the already powerfully developing events in China, but it wholly and completely went over to the Menshevik course advocated by Martynov. In the resolution, incredible as it may seem, not one word was said about the first counterrevolutionary coup d'état of Chiang Kai-shek in March 1926. Not one word about the shootings of workers and peasants and other repressive measures carried out by the Canton government in a whole series of provinces during the summer and autumn of 1926. Not one word about the measures of compulsory arbitration directed against the working class. Not one word about the putting down of working class strikes by the Canton government, about the protection given by the Canton government to the yellow company unions of the employers. Not one word about the efforts made by the Canton government to strangle the peasants' movement, spit upon it, prevent its spread and development. In the resolution of the seventh plenum, there is no demand for the arming of the workers, no summons to struggle against the counterrevolutionary General Staff. The troops of Chiang Kai-shek are described in this resolution as a revolutionary army. No call is given for the creation of a daily Communist press, and it is not even stated clearly and definitely that we must have a genuinely independent Chinese Communist Party. To complete it all, the seventh plenum urged the Communists to enter the national government, a step which under the existing circumstances could only bring the greatest conceivable disaster.

The resolution of the International says: "The apparatus of the national revolutionary government (that is, the government of Chiang Kai-shek) offers a very real road to solidarity with the peasants." In the same place it says (this was in November 1926) that "even certain strata of the big bourgeoisie (!) may still for a certain time march hand in hand with the revolution."

The resolution of the seventh plenum passed over in silence the fact that the Central Committee of the Chinese party, after March 1926, undertook not to criticize Sun Yat-senism, renounced its elementary rights as an independent workers' party, adopted a Cadet agrarian program, and, lastly, permitted the secretary of its Central Committee, Comrade Chen Tu-hsiu, in an open letter dated July 4, 1926, to recognize Sun Yat-senism as the "common faith" of the workers and the bourgeoisie in the national movement.

At approximately the same time the most responsible Russian comrades were giving advice to the effect that the development of a civil war in the country might weaken the fighting capacity of the Kuomintang. In other words, they officially forbade the development of an agrarian revolution.

On April 5, 1927, when the situation, it might seem, was already sufficiently clear, Comrade Stalin, at a meeting of the Moscow party organization in the Hall of Columns, announced that Chiang Kai-shek was a fighter against imperialism, that Chiang Kai-shek submitted to the discipline of the Kuomintang and was therefore our trusted ally. In the middle of May 1927, when the situation had become still more clear, Comrade Stalin announced that the Kuomintang in Wuhan was a "revolutionary Kuomintang," a "revolutionary center purged of rightist elements."

The eighth enlarged plenum of the Executive Committee of the Communist International (May 1927) could not find the strength to correct these Menshevik mistakes.

The Opposition introduced at this eighth plenum the following statement: "The plenum would do well to bury Bukharin's resolution replacing it with a resolution of a few lines:

"In the first place, peasants and workers should place no faith in the leaders of the left Kuomintang but should instead build their own soviets jointly with the soldiers. In the second place, the soviets should arm the workers and the advanced peasants. In the third place, the Communist Party must assure its complete independence, create a daily press, and assume the leadership in creating the soviets. Fourth, the land must be immediately taken away from the landlords. Fifth, the reactionary bureaucracy must be immediately dismissed. Sixth, perfidious generals and other counterrevolutionists must be summarily dealt with. And finally, the general course must be toward the establishment of a revolutionary dictatorship through the soviets of workers' and peasants' deputies" ["It Is Time to Understand, Time to Reconsider, and Time to Make a Change," in *Leon Trotsky on China*, pp. 241-42].

The attempt of the Opposition to warn the party that the Kuomintang in Wuhan was not by any means a revolutionary Kuomintang was denounced by Stalin and Bukharin as "a struggle against the party," an "attack upon the Chinese revolution," etc.

Dispatches stating the facts as to the real course of the revolution and the counterrevolution in China were concealed and falsified. Things went so far that the central publication of our party (*Pravda*, July 3, 1927) announced the disarmament of the workers by the Chinese generals under the headline "Fraternization of the Soldiers with the Workers." In mockery of Lenin's teaching, Stalin asserted that the slogan of soviets in China would mean the demand for an immediate formation of the proletarian dictatorship. As a matter of fact Lenin, as long ago as in the revolution of 1905, advanced the slogan of soviets as organs of the democratic dictatorship of the proletariat and the peasants. The slogan of soviets for China, proposed at the proper time by the Opposition, was met by Stalin and Bukharin with the accusation of "aiding and abetting the counterrevolution," etc. When the strongholds of the revolt of the workers and peasants were smashed by "our" generals, the "revolutionary" generals, Stalin and Bukharin, in order to cover up their own bankruptcy, suddenly advanced the slogan of soviets for China—and then forgot it again the next morning.

At first the Chinese Communist Party was declared to be "a model section of the International," and the slightest criticism of it from the Opposition—at a time when its mistakes might still have been corrected—was suppressed and denounced as a "spiteful attack" upon the Chinese party. Afterward, when the dismal failure of Martynov-Stalin-Bukharin became perfectly clear, they attempted to throw all the blame upon the young Chinese Communist Party.

At first they staked everything upon Chiang Kai-shek, then upon T'ang Sheng-chih, then upon Feng Yü-hsiang, then the "tried and true" Wang Ching-wei. One after the other every one of these hangmen of the workers and peasants was hailed as a "fighter against imperialism" and "our" ally.

This Menshevik policy is now being completed by the frank and open emasculation of the revolutionary teaching of Lenin. Stalin-Bukharin and the "young school" are now busy trying to "prove" that Lenin's teachings on the national-revolutionary movement amount in effect to the gospel of "alliance with the bourgeoisie."

In 1920, at the Second Congress of the Communist International, Lenin said: "There has been a certain rapprochement between the bourgeoisie of the exploiting countries and that of the colonies, so that very often—perhaps even in most cases—the bourgeoisie of the oppressed countries, while it does support the national movement, is in full accord with the imperialist bourgeoisie, i.e. joins forces with it against all revolutionary movements and revolutionary classes" [*Collected Works,* vol. 31, p. 242].

How Lenin would denounce these people who dare refer to him today for justification of their Menshevik policy of union with Chiang Kai-shek and Wang Ching-wei. Lenin himself spoke of this very thing in March 1917: "Ours is a bourgeois revolution; *therefore* the workers must support the bourgeoisie, say [the Liquidators], the Potresovs, Gvozdyovs, and Chkheidzes, as Plekhanov said yesterday.

"Ours is a bourgeois revolution, we Marxists say; *therefore* the workers must open the eyes of the people to the deception practiced by the bourgeois politicians, teach them to put no faith in words, to depend entirely on their *own* strength, their *own* organization, their *own* unity, and their own *weapons*" [*Collected Works,* vol. 23, p. 306].

There could be no greater crime against the international proletariat than this attempt to represent Lenin as the apostle of "alliance with the bourgeoisie." You will rarely find in the history of revolutionary struggle a case where Marxist predictions were confirmed so swiftly and so accurately as were the views of the Opposition on the problems of the Chinese revolution in 1926-27.

A study of the course of events in the Chinese revolution and the causes of its defeat is the urgent and immediate task of Communists throughout the world.

These questions will tomorrow become questions of life and death for the working class movement, not only in China but in India and other Eastern countries—and thus, for the entire international proletariat. In the debates on these questions, which touch the very foundations of the Marxist world outlook, the genuine Bolshevik cadres of the coming revolution will be formed.

The Partial Stabilization of Capitalism and the Tactics of the Communist International

One of the fundamental tenets of Bolshevism is that the epoch beginning with World War I and our revolution is the epoch of the socialist revolution. The Communist International was founded as a "party of world revolution." A recognition of this fact was recorded in the "twenty-one points." And it was primarily along this line that the Communists split with the Social Democrats, Independents, and Mensheviks of all sorts and kinds.

A recognition of the fact that the war and October opened an epoch of world revolution does not mean, of course, that at every given moment an immediately revolutionary situation is at hand. In certain periods, in individual countries, and in individual branches of production, "dying capitalism" (Lenin) is capable of a partial reestablishment of its economy and even a further development of the productive forces. The epoch of world revolution will have its periods of rise and fall. So much the greater will be the importance of the preparedness of the working class and its party, the degree of influence exercised by counterrevolutionary Social Democracy, and correct leadership of the Comintern. But this ebb and flow of the revolution will not change the fundamental Leninist evaluation of the present historical epoch taken as a whole. Only this evaluation can form the basis of the revolutionary strategy of the Communist International.

Nevertheless, as a result of a series of defeats of the international revolutionary movement and the pessimistic moods growing out of them, the Stalin group, without itself even noticing, has arrived at a completely "new" and essentially Social Democratic appraisal of the present epoch. The whole "theory" of socialism in one country derives fundamentally from the assumption that the "stabilization" of capitalism will last for a number of decades. This whole "theory" is essentially a product of the degenerate mood of the apostles of "stabilization." It is no accident that the "theory" of socialism in one country has been welcomed by the Social Revolutionaries, both right and left. Chernov himself has written on this theme about the "Communist Narodism" of Stalin and Bukharin. The publication of the Left Social Revolutionaries wrote: "Stalin and Bukharin affirm, exactly like Narodniks, that socialism can win in one country" (*Znamya Borby*, nos. 17-18, 1926). The Social Revolutionaries support this theory because they see in it a renunciation of the orientation toward world revolution.

In the resolution of the Fourteenth Party Congress, adopted on the report of Stalin, the following obviously incorrect statement is made: "In the sphere of international relations we have a reinforcement and lengthening of the 'breathing spell,' which is transforming itself into a whole period" (Report of the Fourteenth Congress, p. 957). At the seventh enlarged plenum of the Executive Committee of the Communist International (December 7, 1926), Stalin based the whole policy of the International upon the same radically incorrect evaluation of the world situation (verbatim report, p. 12). This evaluation has already proved quite obviously incorrect.

The resolution of the joint plenum of the Central Committee and the Central Control Commission (July-August 1927) refers without any reservations to the technical, economic, and political stabilization of capitalism. This brings the Stalinist evaluation of the world situation very much nearer to that of the leaders of the Second International (Otto Bauer, Hilferding, Kautsky, and others).

Since the Fourteenth Congress something over a year and a half has passed. During that time, taking only the most important events, we have had the General Strike in Britain, the gigantic events of the Chinese revolution, the workers' uprising in Vienna. These events, irreversibly lodged in the very conditions of the present "stabilization," show us how much explosive material has been accumulated by capitalism, how unstable its "stabilization" is. All these events hammer away at the "theory" of socialism in one country.

The reverse side of the "stabilization" of capitalism is the unemployed population of twenty million, the colossal underutilization of productive capacity, the insane growth of military preparations, the extreme shakiness of international economic relations. Nothing so surely reveals the futility of the hope for a long peaceful period as the present new danger of war that hangs over Europe. It is the petty bourgeois who dreams about stabilization for "decades," blinded as he is by the victory of capitalism over the workers, blinded by the technical, economic, and political successes of capitalism. But the real facts are developing in the direction of a war which will explode every "stabilization." Moreover, the working class and the oppressed colonial masses of the East have attempted time and time again to overthrow this "stabilization" by force. First in Britain, then in China, then in Vienna.

A General Strike in Britain—and only 5,000 members in the British Communist Party! A workers' insurrection in Vienna, with enough victims for a whole revolution—and only 6,000 members in the Austrian Communist Party! A military uprising of the masses of workers and peasants in China—and the Central Committee of the Chinese Communist Party turns out to be a mere appendage to the bourgeois leadership of the Kuomintang! This is the most crying contradiction of the present world situation. This is what supports and prolongs the "stabilization" of capitalism. Our biggest task is to help the Communist parties raise themselves to the height of the gigantic demands which the present epoch places upon them. But this assumes, in the first place, a correct understanding of the character of the world situation on the part of the Communist International itself.

Our international Communist Party (the Communist International) ought to apply itself to the task of rallying the whole international working class for the struggle to prevent war, to defend the Soviet Union, and to turn any imperialist war into a war for socialism. To this end the Communist worker ought above all to win over the revolutionary-minded worker who is non-Communist, nonparty, Social Democrat, syndicalist, anarchist, trade unionist, and also that honest worker who is still a member of a purely bourgeois organization. "By the united workers' front must be understood the unity of all the workers who desire to struggle against capitalism, and that includes the workers still following the anarcho-syndicalists, etc. In the Latin countries, the number of these workers is still considerable." This was the resolution of the Fourth Congress of the Communist International, in Lenin's time. It retains its full force and applicability today. The present activities of the leaders of the Second International and the Amsterdam Trade Union International make it perfectly clear that their conduct in a future war will exceed, in vileness and unscrupulous betrayal, the role they played in 1914-18. Paul-Boncour (France) has introduced a law surrendering the workers in advance to the bourgeois dictators in time of war. The General Council of the Trades Union Congress (Britain) is defending the murderers of Voikov and has approved the sending of troops to China. Kautsky (Germany) is advocating an armed insurrection against Soviet power in Russia, and the Central Committee of the German Social Democracy is organizing the "artillery shell campaign." The Social Democratic ministers of Finland and Latvia, and the leaders of the Polish Socialist Party, are "always at the ready" for a war against the Soviet Union. The leaders of the official American trade unions are speaking in the manner of the most venomous reactionaries, openly opposing recognition of the Soviet Union. The Balkan "socialists" are supporting the hangmen of "their own" workers and are always ready to support a campaign against that "alien power"—the Soviet Union. The Austrian Social Democratic leaders are "for the Soviet Union" in words, but people who have helped their own fascists drown the workers' insurrection of Vienna in blood will obviously, at the decisive moment, be on the side of the capitalists. The Russian Mensheviks and Social Revolutionaries are not advocating intervention against the Soviet Union only because there are not yet any strong interventionist powers. The leaders of the so-called "Left Social Democracy," who are covering up for the counterrevolutionary essence of

Social Democracy, are the chief danger, because they more than anybody else prevent the workers who are following the Social Democratic banner from decisively breaking with these agents of the bourgeoisie in the workers' movement. Former members of the Communist International (such as Katz, Schwartz, Korsch, Rosenberg) are playing an equally traitorous role, having broken with communism by way of ultraleftism.

Flirting with these Social Democratic leaders (absolutely antirevolutionary in all their shades, from the open rightists to the purported "leftists") becomes increasingly dangerous as war draws near. The tactic of the united front should under no conditions be interpreted as a bloc with the traitors of the General Council or as a rapprochement with Amsterdam. Such a policy weakens and confuses the working class, increases the prestige of those who are undeniably traitors, and prevents the maximum consolidation of our own forces. The incorrect Stalinist policy summed up in the slogan "Fire Against the Left" has had the result in the last year or two that the predominant role in the leadership of the most important sections of the International has passed, against the will of the Communist workers, into the hands of the right wing (in Germany, Poland, Czechoslovakia, France, Italy, and Britain).

The policy of these right-wing leadership groups, aimed at the surgical removal of the whole left wing of the Communist International, erodes the forces of the International and stores up tremendous dangers for us to face.

In particular the removal of the Urbahns group in Germany was dictated by this policy of getting rid of the whole left wing of the International. Unduly emphasizing certain sharply polemical phrases used by the left-wing partisans of Urbahns and Maslow, in response to those who slandered and baited them without conscience as "renegades," "counterrevolutionaries," "agents of Chamberlain," etc., the Stalin group is obstinately pushing the German left wing onto the road of a second party. The Stalin group is trying its best to bring about a split in the ranks of the German Communists as a fait accompli.

In reality, on all fundamental questions of the international working class movement, the Urbahns group holds Leninist views. It defends the USSR and, at the decisive hour, it will undoubtedly continue to defend it to the end. The group includes hundreds of veteran rank-and-file worker-Bolsheviks, who are closely linked with the broad masses of the proletariat. It has the sympathy of many thousands of working class Communists who have remained in the German Communist Party.

Readmission into the International of all these expelled comrades, who accept the decisions of the congresses of the International—and first among them the Urbahns group—is the first step toward correcting the moves made by Stalin toward a split in the International. In his *"Left-Wing" Communism,* Lenin exposed the mistakes of the real ultraleftists, but wrote that the chief enemy of Bolshevism within the workers' movement is and remains opportunism. "It still remains the principal enemy on an international scale" [*Collected Works,* vol. 31, p. 31]. At the Second Congress of the International, Lenin added to this the statement that "compared with this task, the rectification of the errors of the 'left' trend in communism will be an easy one" [Ibid., p. 231]. When he spoke of the "left," Lenin had in mind the ultraleftists; whereas when Stalin speaks of the struggle against ultraleftism, he has in mind the revolutionary Leninists.

A decisive struggle with the right opportunist movement as the chief enemy, and a correction of the mistakes of the "left" tendency—that was the slogan of Lenin. We, the Oppositionists, propose the same slogan.

The power of "socialist" opportunism is in the last analysis the power of capitalism. During the first years after the war crisis (1918-21), when capitalism was swiftly sliding into the abyss, the official Social Democracy was weakening and falling with it. The years of partial stabilization of capitalism have brought a temporary strengthening of the Social Democracy. The defeat of the Italian workers in 1920-21, of the German proletariat in 1921-23, the defeat of the great strike in Britain in 1926, and the defeat of the Chinese proletariat in 1927, whatever may have been their causes, have themselves become the cause of a temporary decline in the revolutionary mood among the upper layers of the proletariat. These events have for a certain period strengthened the Social Democracy at the expense of the Communist Party. And within the Communist Party they have given the right wing temporary dominance at the expense of the left. The role of the labor aristocracy, the labor bureaucracy, and its petty-bourgeois associates, becomes at such a period especially great and especially reactionary.

To a certain extent these processes must inevitably affect the Communist Party of the Soviet Union. The administrative "center" has opened fire exclusively against the left and by purely mechanical methods has created a new relationship of forces, still more disadvantageous to the left, Leninist wing. A situation has been created in which in fact the party never votes, but only the apparatus.

Such are the general causes of the weakening of the influence of the Leninist wing upon the policies of the Communist International, the Russian Communist Party, and the Soviet state. At the same time, right-wing semi–Social Democratic elements, who long after October were still in the ranks of the enemy, and were at last admitted into the Communist International more or less on probation (Martynov, Smeral, Rafes, D. Petrovsky, Pepper, and others), are speaking more and more frequently and more and more loudly in the name of the International. And to them must be added the names of outright adventurers like Heinz Neumann and others of the same kind. Among the masses, however, the elements of a new movement to the left, a new revolutionary upsurge, are already accumulating. The Opposition is preparing both theoretically and politically for that new day.

The Principal Conclusion

1. Within the circles of the ruling majority, under the impact of the break in Anglo-Soviet relations and other difficulties, both foreign and domestic, a "plan" approximately as follows has been germinating: (a) recognize the tsarist debts; (b) more or less abolish the monopoly of foreign trade; (c) withdraw from China, that is, withdraw "for a time" our support of the Chinese revolution and of the national-revolutionary movement in general; and (d) within the country, carry out a maneuver to the right, that is, expand the NEP a little more. By paying this price, they hope to eliminate the danger of war, improve the international position of the USSR, and put an end to (or at least mitigate) the domestic difficulties. The whole "plan" is based on the sole assumption that capitalism is assured for decades.

In reality this would not be a "maneuver" but in the present situation a full capitulation on the part of the Soviet power—through a "political NEP," a "neo-NEP," back to capitalism. The imperialists would accept all our concessions and proceed all the more swiftly to a new attack and even to war. The kulaks, the NEPmen, and the bureaucrats, taking cognizance of our concessions, would all the more persistently organize the anti-Soviet forces against our party. Such a "tactic" on our part would result in the closest possible union of our new bourgeoisie with the foreign bourgeoisie. The economic development of the Soviet Union would fall under the complete control of international capital—a penny of loan for a ruble of slavery. And the working class and the bulk of the peasants would begin to lose their faith in the might of the Soviet state, their faith that the Soviet state knows where it is leading the people.

We are bound to try to "buy ourselves out" of war, if that is possible. But for that very reason we must be strong and united, unwaveringly defend the orientation toward world revolution, and reinforce the International. Only in this way will we really have a chance of postponing war as long as possible, without paying a price that would undermine the foundations of our power, and at the same time, in case war proves inevitable, of gaining the support of the international proletariat and winning.

Lenin made certain economic concessions to the imperialists in order to buy us out of war or to attract international capital upon acceptable terms. But neither in these circumstances nor in the hardest moments of the revolution did Lenin consider even for a moment the idea of abolishing the monopoly of foreign trade, of offering political rights to the kulak, or of easing away from the orientation toward world revolution in general.

We must, first of all, wholly and without reserve affirm and reinforce our support to the international revolution. We must offer a firm resistance to all "stabilization" tendencies, to all this pseudo-statesmanship which expresses itself in the remarks that we had no business "butting in" in China, that we had better "get out of China as quick as we can," that if we behave "reasonably," they will "leave us alone," etc. The "theory" of socialism in one country is now playing a directly harmful and destructive role, clearly hindering the consolidation of the international forces of the proletariat around the Soviet Union. It is lulling the workers of other countries, dulling their awareness of the danger.

2. Another task, of equal importance, is to consolidate the ranks of our party, to put an end to the open speculation of the imperialist bourgeoisie and the leaders of the Social Democracy on a split or expulsion, or "removal," etc. All this has the most direct connection with the question of war, for at present the "probing" of the imperialists is being carried out chiefly along this moral-political line. All the agencies of the international bourgeoisie and the Social Democrats are now showing a quite unusual interest in our inner-party disputes. They are openly encouraging and spurring on the present majority of the Central Committee to expel the Opposition from the leading bodies of the party, and if possible from the party, and if possible, indeed, to put them out of the way altogether. Beginning with the richest

bourgeois newspaper, the *New York Times*, and ending with the slimiest paper of the Second International, the Vienna *Arbeiter Zeitung* (Otto Bauer), all the publications of the bourgeoisie and the Social Democrats are saluting the "government of Stalin" for its struggle against the Opposition. They are urging this government to prove still further its "statesmanlike intelligence" by decisively removing these Oppositional "propagandists of international revolution." Other things being equal, a war will come so much the later in proportion as these hopes of the enemy for the removal of the Opposition, etc., remain unrealized. Moreover, we can buy ourselves out of a war, if that is possible—and win the war, if we have to fight—only if we preserve complete unity: if we disappoint the hopes of the imperialists for a split or an expulsion. Such a thing would benefit only the capitalists.

3. It is necessary to rectify our class line in the international workers' movement, stop the struggle against the left wing in the International, restore to the International those expelled members who accept the decisions of its congresses, and once and for all put an end to the policy of an "entente cordiale" with the traitorous leaders of the British General Council. A break with the General Council will have the same significance in the present situation as in 1914 the break with the International Socialist Bureau of the Second International. Lenin demanded in an ultimatum that the break be made by every revolutionist. To remain in a bloc with such a General Council means now, as it did then, to help the counterrevolutionary leaders of the Second International.

4. We must decisively correct our line in the national-revolutionary movement—first of all in China, but also in a number of other countries. We must liquidate the policy of Martynov-Stalin-Bukharin and return to the course outlined by Lenin in the resolutions of the Second and Fourth Congresses of the Communist International. Otherwise, instead of being an accelerator we shall become a brake upon the national-revolutionary movement and inevitably lose the sympathy of the workers and peasants of the East. The Chinese Communist Party must dissolve all organizational and political dependence upon the Kuomintang. The Communist International must expel the Kuomintang from its ranks.

5. We must consistently, systematically, and stubbornly wage the struggle for peace. We must postpone war, "buy ourselves out of the danger of war." Everything possible and permissible must be done to this end (see point 1). At the same time we must get

ready for war immediately, not folding our arms for one instant. And our first duty is to put an end to the political and ideological confusion and disagreement on whether an immediate danger of war exists.

6. We must decisively correct our class line in domestic policy. If war is inevitable, only a strictly Bolshevik policy can win: *the worker and farmhand, with the support of the poor peasant, in alliance with the middle peasant, against the kulak, the NEP-man, and the bureaucrat.*

7. An all-sided preparation of our entire economy, budget, etc., for the event of war.

Capitalism is entering a new stage of upheaval. A war with the Soviet Union, like a war with China, will mean a series of catastrophes for international capitalism. The war of 1914-18 was a gigantic "accelerator" (Lenin) of the socialist revolution. New wars, and especially a war against the Soviet Union—in which with a correct policy on our part we should win the sympathy of the laboring masses of the entire world—could become an even greater "accelerator" of the downfall of world capitalism. *Socialist revolutions will develop without new wars. But new wars will inevitably lead to socialist revolutions.*

Chapter 10
The Red Army and Navy

The international situation is more and more bringing to the fore the question of the defense of the Soviet Union. The party, the working class, and the peasantry must again give great attention to the Red Army and Navy.

All aspects of economics, politics, and culture are combined in the problem of defense. The army is a copy in miniature of the whole social structure. It reflects, in the sharpest possible manner, not only the strong but the weak sides of the existing regime. Experience teaches that in this sphere least of all is it safe to rely upon appearances. Here especially it is better to err in the direction of checking ourselves in everything three times over and engaging in strict self-criticism than to err in the direction of easygoing trust and confidence.

The question of the relations between classes in our country, and a correct policy of our party in this sphere, has a decisive significance for the inner cohesion of the army and for the relations between the commanding staff and the mass of the soldiers. The question of industrialization has decisive significance for the technical resources of our defense. All the measures advocated in the present Platform—in the sphere of international politics and the international workers' movement, industry, agriculture, the Soviet system, the national question, the party, and the Communist League of Youth—all these questions are of prime importance in strengthening the Red Army and Navy.

Our practical proposals in this field have been presented to the Politburo.

Chapter 11
On the Real Issues in Dispute, and the Artificial Ones

Nothing testifies so much to the erroneous political course of the Stalin group as its constant effort to argue, not with our real opinions, but with artificially manufactured views that we do not hold and never did.

When the Bolsheviks argued against the Mensheviks, Social Revolutionaries, and other petty-bourgeois tendencies, the Bolsheviks explained to the workers the actual system of opinions held by their opponents. But when the Mensheviks or Social Revolutionaries argued against the Bolsheviks, instead of refuting their real opinions they would attribute to the Bolsheviks things they had never said. The Mensheviks and Social Revolutionaries could not present the real views of the Bolsheviks to the workers with even partial accuracy because in that case the workers would have supported the Bolsheviks. The whole mechanism of the class struggle compelled these petty-bourgeois groups to combat the Bolsheviks by calling them "conspirators," "allies of the counterrevolution," and later "agents of Kaiser Wilhelm." In the same way now, the petty-bourgeois deviation in our own party cannot struggle against our Leninist views in any way other than by attributing to us things which we never thought or said. The Stalin group knows perfectly well that if we could defend our true opinions with even a semblance of free speech, a huge majority of party members would support us.

The most elementary conditions for an honest inner-party debate are not observed. On the question of the Chinese revolution, a question of world importance, the Central Committee has not to this day printed a single word of what the Opposition says.

After bottling up all discussion in the party and cutting off Opposition access to the party press, the Stalin group has carried on a continual, one-sided debate against us, day after day attributing to us greater and greater stupidities and crimes. But the rank-and-file party member is less and less inclined to believe these accusations.

1. When we state that the present stabilization of capitalism is not a stabilization for decades, and that our epoch remains an epoch of imperialist wars and social revolutions (Lenin), the Stalin group attributes to us a denial of all elements of stabilization in capitalism.

2. When we say, in the words of Lenin, that for the construction of a socialist society in our country, a victory of the proletarian revolution is necessary in one or more of the advanced capitalist countries, that the final victory of socialism in one country, and above all a backward country, is impossible, as Marx, Engels, and Lenin all argued, the Stalin group makes the wholly false assertion that we "have no faith" in socialism and in socialist construction in the Soviet Union.

3. When, following Lenin, we point out the growing bureaucratic distortions of our proletarian state, the Stalin group attributes to us the opinion that our Soviet state is not proletarian at all. When we announce before the entire Communist International that "whoever tries, directly or indirectly, to solidarize with us while at the same time denying the proletarian character of our party and our state and the socialist character of construction in the Soviet Union will be ruthlessly opposed and rejected by us"—the Stalin group conceals our announcement and continues its slander against us [see the declaration by Zinoviev, Kamenev, and Trotsky, December 14, 1926, at the seventh enlarged plenum of the ECCI, paragraph 1, pp. 190-91].

4. When we point out that Thermidorian elements with a rather substantial social base are growing in our country; when we demand that the party leadership offer a more systematic, coordinated, and firm resistance to these phenomena and their influence upon certain sections of our party, the Stalin group accuses us of stating that the party is Thermidorian, and that the proletarian revolution has degenerated. When we announce to the entire International: "It is not true that we accuse the majority of our party of representing a 'right-wing deviation.' We believe only that in the Communist Party of the Soviet Union there are right-wing currents and groupings which now have a disproportionate influence, but which the party will be able to overcome"—

the Stalin group conceals our announcement and continues to slander us [Ibid., paragraph 13, p. 193].

5. When we point to the enormous growth of the kulak; when we, following Lenin, continue to assert that the kulak cannot peacefully "grow into socialism," that he is the most dangerous enemy of the proletarian revolution—the Stalin group accuses us of wishing to "rob the peasants."

6. When we draw the attention of our party to the reality of the strengthening position of private capital, the excessive increase in the accumulation of such capital and of its influence in the country, the Stalin group accuses us of attacking NEP and calling for the restoration of war communism.

7. When we point to the incorrectness of party policy in regard to the material condition of the workers, the inadequacy of the measures against unemployment and the housing shortage; and especially when we point out that the share of the nonproletarian elements in the national income has increased excessively—they say that we are guilty of a "narrow craft-oriented" deviation, and of "demagogy."

8. When we point to the systematic lagging of industry behind the need of the national economy, with all its inevitable consequences—the price disproportion, the goods famine, rupture of the bond between town and countryside—they call us "superindustrializers."

9. When we point to the incorrect price policy, which is not reducing the high cost of living but making possible frenzied profiteering by private traders, the Stalin group accuses us of advocating a policy of raising prices. When a year ago we announced to the entire International: "The Opposition never in any of its utterances demanded or proposed a raising of prices, but saw as the chief mistake of our economic policy precisely the fact that it does not lead with sufficient energy to a reduction of the goods famine with which the high retail prices are inevitably bound up"—our announcement was concealed from the party and the slander continued.

10. When we speak against the "entente cordiale" with the betrayers of the General Strike, the counterrevolutionists of the British General Council, who are openly playing the role of Chamberlain's agents, we are accused of being opposed to the work of Communists within the trade unions and against the tactic of a united front.

11. When we oppose the entry of the trade unions of the Soviet Union into the Amsterdam Trade Union International, or any

kind of flirting with the leaders of the Second International, we are accused of a "Social Democratic deviation."

12. When we oppose a policy based on the Chinese generals, when we oppose the subjection of the Chinese working class to the bourgeois Kuomintang, when we oppose the Menshevik tactics of Martynov, we are accused of being against "the agrarian revolution in China," of being "in cahoots with Chiang Kai-shek."

13. When, on the basis of our evaluation of the world situation, we come to the conclusion that war is approaching and warn the party of this in good time, the Stalinists bring forward against us the dishonest accusation that we "desire war."

14. When, true to the teaching of Lenin, we point out that the approach of war makes it all the more urgent that we have a firm, definite, and clear-cut class policy, the Stalinists shamelessly assert that we do not want to defend the Soviet Union, that we are "conditional defenders," semi-defeatists, etc.

15. When we point out the absolutely undeniable fact that the entire world press of the capitalists and Social Democrats is supporting Stalin's struggle against the Opposition in the Russian Communist Party, praising Stalin for his repression of the left wing, urging him to remove the Opposition, to expel it from the Central Committee and from the party, *Pravda* and the entire party and Soviet press day after day deceitfully pretend that the bourgeoisie and Social Democracy are "for the Opposition."

16. When we oppose the passing of leadership in the Communist International into the hands of the right wing, and the expulsion of hundreds and thousands of worker-Bolsheviks, the Stalinists accuse us of attempting to split the Communist International.

17. The present deformations of the party regime are such that when Oppositionists who are loyal party members attempt to inform the membership of their real opinions, they are thrown out of the Russian Communist Party. They are accused of "factionalism." They are "brought up on charges" for allegedly trying to split the party. The most important party questions, instead of being discussed, are buried under a heap of rubbish.

18. But the favorite accusation in recent years is that we supposedly believe in "Trotskyism." We announce to the whole Communist International: It is not true that we defend "Trotskyism." Trotsky has stated to the International that on all the fundamental questions over which he had differences with Lenin, Lenin was right—in particular on the questions of the permanent

revolution and the peasantry [see the declaration of Kamenev, Zinoviev, and Trotsky, December 14, 1926, paragraph 12, p. 193]. That announcement, made to the whole Communist International, the Stalin group refuses to print. It continues to accuse us of "Trotskyism." The above-quoted announcement relates, of course, only to those differences with Lenin which existed in fact and not to those unscrupulously invented by Stalin and Bukharin. The relation which they pretend to discover between our differences in the remote past and the practical disagreements which arose in the course of the October Revolution is imaginary. We note the use of unacceptable methods in the attempt of the Stalin group to distract attention from the views of the Opposition, as expounded in the present Platform, by references to earlier disagreements between the 1923 group and the 1925 group. These disagreements have now been resolved on the basis of Leninism. The mistakes and exaggerations committed by both groups of Bolsheviks in the disputes of 1923-24, as a result of a series of obscurities in the state of affairs in the party and in the country, have now been corrected, and do not constitute an obstacle to collaboration and joint struggle against opportunism and for Leninism.*

By tearing quotations out of context, by using a biased and one-sided selection of old polemical statements by Lenin in a rude and disloyal way, by hiding from the party other, far more recent statements of Lenin's, by openly falsifying party history and the events of the past, and even more important, by distorting all the questions at present in dispute, and by flagrantly substituting artificial issues for real ones, the group of Stalin and Bukharin, departing farther and farther from the principles of Lenin, is trying to deceive the party into believing that this is a struggle between Leninism and Trotskyism. The struggle is, in actual fact, between Leninism and Stalinist opportunism. In exactly the same way the revisionists, under the pretext of a struggle against "Blanquism," waged their battle against Marxism. Our collaboration and joint struggle against the Stalin course has been possible only because we are all completely united in the desire and determination to defend the real Leninist proletarian line.

The present Platform is the best answer to the accusation of

---

*According to Max Eastman, who translated and published the Platform under the title *The Real Situation in Russia (1928)*, this paragraph was inserted in the Platform at the insistence of Zinoviev and Kamenev.—Eds.

"Trotskyism." Everyone who reads it will see that every line, from beginning to end, is based on the teachings of Lenin and is inspired by the genuine spirit of Bolshevism.

Let the party find out our real opinions. Let the party familiarize itself with the original documents on the disputed issues, especially on that question of such great international importance, the Chinese revolution. Lenin taught us that when there are differences, we should not believe anything on somebody's say-so, but should demand documents, listen to both of the contending sides, and find out conscientiously what the real disagreements are, setting false issues aside. We, the Opposition, repeat this advice of Lenin's.

We must, once and for all, put an end to the very possibility of what happened at the Fourteenth Congress, when the differences came crashing down on the heads of the party membership two or three days before the congress. We must create the conditions for an honest debate and an honest resolution of the real issues in dispute, as was always done in Lenin's time.

Chapter 12
Against Opportunism—
For the Unity of the Party

We have frankly set forth our opinion of the serious mistakes committed by the majority of the Central Committee in all the fundamental areas of foreign and domestic policy. We have shown how these mistakes of the Central Committee have weakened our party, which is the fundamental instrument of the revolution. We have shown that, in spite of everything, our party can correct its policy from within. But in order to correct the policy, it is necessary clearly and candidly to define the character of the mistakes committed by the party leadership.

The mistakes made have been *opportunist* mistakes. Opportunism in its fully developed form—according to the classic definition of Lenin—is a bloc formed by the upper strata of the working class with the bourgeoisie and directed against the majority of the working class. In the conditions now existing in the Soviet Union, opportunism in such fully developed form would express the desire of the upper strata of the working class to compromise with the newly resurrected native bourgeoisie (kulaks and NEPmen) and with world capitalism, at the expense of the interests of the broad mass of the workers and poor peasants.

When we call attention to the existence of such tendencies in certain circles of our party—in some places just appearing and in others fully developed—it is absurd to accuse us, on those grounds, of slandering the party. It is precisely to the party that we are appealing against these tendencies which threaten it. It is equally absurd to claim that we are accusing this or that section of the party or the Central Committee of disloyalty to the revolution, of betraying the interest of the proletariat. A false political line can be dictated by the most sincere concern for the interests of the working class. Even the most extreme representatives of the right wing are convinced that the compromises they are prepared to make with the bourgeois elements are necessary in the interests of the workers and peasants and that such compromises are only maneuvers with the enemy of the kind that Lenin considered entirely permissible. Even the right-wing group, which represents an open tendency to abandon the proletarian revolution, does not consciously desire a Thermidor. And this is still more true of the "center," which is carrying out a typical policy of illusion, self-consolation, and self-deception.

Stalin and his closest adherents are convinced that, with their powerful apparatus, they can outwit all the forces of the bourgeoisie rather than having to overcome them through an open struggle. Stalin and the Stalinists undoubtedly believed in all sincerity that they could "toy with" the Chinese generals for a certain period of time and then toss them away like so many squeezed lemons after using them in the interests of the revolution. Stalin and the Stalinists undoubtedly believed in all sincerity that they were "toying with" the Purcells and not vice versa. Stalin and the Stalinists believe in all sincerity that they can "freely" make concessions to "their own" bourgeoisie, and afterward with equal freedom take these concessions back.

In their bureaucratic self-importance, the Stalinists think they can make such maneuvers "easier" for themselves by in effect removing the party from all participation in policy-making decisions, thus avoiding any resistance by the party. The Stalinist group at the top decides and acts, leaving it to the party to "study" its decisions. But this weakens, if it does not entirely paralyze, the very force which could make effective use of a correct political maneuver, if the maneuver were necessary and appropriate, or which could minimize or overcome the bad consequences of maneuvers by the leadership if they were obviously incorrect. Thus, the conciliationist tendencies of the right wing in the Central Committee and the maneuvers of the centrist group have cumulative results—results which, taken together, add up to a weakening of the international position of the USSR, a weakening of the position of the proletariat in relation to other classes within the Soviet Union, a relative deterioration of its material living conditions, a weakening of its bond with the poor peasants, thus threatening its alliance with the middle peasants, a weakening of its role in the state apparatus, and a slowing down of the tempo of industrialization. It was these consequences of the policies of the majority of the Central Committee, and not its intentions, that the Opposition had in mind when it raised the question of the danger of a Thermidor, that is, a shift from the path of proletarian revolution in a petty-bourgeois direction. The enormous difference between the history and character of our party and those of the parties of the Second International is clear to everybody. The Russian Communist Party has been tempered in the fires of three revolutions. It has seized and held power against a world of enemies. It has organized the Third International. Its fate is the fate of the first victorious proletarian revolution. The revolution determines the tempo of its inner life. All ideological processes within the party, taking place under intense class pressures, have a tendency to develop and come to a head swiftly. For this very reason it is especially necessary in our party that there be a timely and decisive struggle against every tendency to depart from the Leninist line.

The opportunist tendencies in the Russian Communist Party have, in the present circumstances, deep objective roots: (1) The international bourgeois encirclement and the temporary partial stabilization of capitalism give rise to "stabilizational" moods; (2) The New Economic Policy, undoubtedly necessary as a road toward socialism, by partially resurrecting capitalism, has also revived forces hostile to socialism; (3) The elemental social force of the petty bourgeoisie, in a country where the peasantry is in the vast majority, is bound to flow over not only into the soviets, but also into the party; (4) The fact that the party has a monopoly in the political field, something absolutely necessary for the revolution, creates a further series of special dangers. The Eleventh Congress of the party, in Lenin's time, pointed out bluntly and openly that there already existed in the party entire groups of people (from the well-to-do peasantry, the upper strata of office workers, and the intelligentsia) who would have been in the Social Revolutionary and Menshevik parties, if those parties had not been illegal; (5) The state apparatus, which is directed by the party, in turn feeds much that is bourgeois and petty bourgeois into the party, infecting it with opportunism; (6) Through the specialists and the upper strata of office workers and intellectuals, necessary as they are to our work of construction, a steady stream of nonproletarian influences flows into our state, economic, and party apparatuses.

That is why the Leninist Oppositional wing of the party sounds the alarm so insistently over the obvious and dangerous deviations of the Stalin group, which increase daily. It is criminal light-mindedness to assert that the great past of the party, and its old cadres of Bolsheviks, constitute a guarantee in all circumstances and for all time against the danger of opportunist degeneration. Such an idea has nothing whatever in common with Marxism.

Lenin did not teach such ideas. At the Eleventh Party Congress he said: "History knows all sorts of metamorphoses. Relying on firmness of convictions, loyalty, and other splendid moral qualities is anything but a serious attitude in politics" [*Collected Works,* vol. 33, p. 287].

The workers who constituted the immense majority of the socialist parties of the West before the imperialist war were undoubtedly opposed to opportunist deviations. But they did not overcome in time the opportunist mistakes of their leaders, which at first were not very great. They underestimated the significance of these mistakes. They did not understand that the first serious historical disturbance after that prolonged period of peaceful development which had given birth to so powerful a workers' bureaucracy and aristocracy, would compel not only the opportunists but the centrists as well to capitulate to the bourgeoisie, leaving the masses disarmed at that critical moment. If you can reproach the revolutionary Marxists, who constituted the left wing of the Second International before the war, with anything, it is not that they exaggerated the danger of opportunism when they called it national-liberal labor politics, but that they relied too much upon the working class composition of the Socialist parties of those days. They relied upon the revolutionary instincts of the proletariat and upon the sharpening of class contradictions. They underestimated the real danger and were not energetic enough in mobilizing the revolutionary rank and file against it. We are not going to repeat that mistake. We are going to correct, in good time, the course of the party leadership. By that very fact we answer the charge that we desire to split our party and form a new one. The dictatorship of the proletariat imperiously demands a single and united proletarian party as the leader of the working masses and the poor peasantry. Such unity, unweakened by factional strife, is unconditionally necessary to the proletariat in the fulfillment of its historic mission. This can be realized only on the basis of the teachings of Marx and Lenin, undiluted with personal interpretations and undistorted by revisionism.

In fighting for a certain rate of industrialization as the premise for socialist construction, in combating the growth of the kulak and his aspiration toward supremacy in the countryside, in fighting for a timely improvement in the living conditions of the workers and for democracy within the party, the trade unions, and the soviets—the Opposition is not advocating ideas which might bring about a separation of the working class from its party; on the contrary its effort is to reinforce the foundations of real unity in the All-Union Communist Party. Without correcting the opportunist mistakes, you can have nothing but a show of unity, which will weaken the party as it faces mounting pressures from the growing internal bourgeoisie, and which, in the event of war, will mean that the party will have to reorganize itself under fire and on the march. When they find out our **real** views and proposals, the proletarian nucleus of the party—of **this** we are sure—will accept them and fight for them, not **as** "factional" slogans but as the very banner of party unity.

Our party has not yet clearly recognized, and for that reason has not corrected, the mistakes of its leadership. The extraordinarily swift growth of our industry during the restoration period has been one of the fundamental sources of the opportunist illusions which the majority of the Central Committee has systematically encouraged in the party and the working class. The first rapid betterment in the conditions of the workers, by comparison with their conditions during the civil war, fostered hopes in wide layers of the working class for a swift and painless overcoming of the contradictions of NEP. This prevented the party from detecting soon enough the danger of an opportunist deviation.

The growth of the Leninist Opposition in the party has impelled the worst elements of the bureaucracy to resort to methods previously unheard of in the practice of Bolshevism. No longer able to prevent discussion of political questions in the party units by just issuing orders, a section of the bureaucracy is now resorting—on the eve of the Fifteenth Congress—to the creation of gangs whose job is to break up all discussions of party problems by means of shouting, whistling, turning off lights, etc.

This attempt to bring the methods of naked physical violence into the party will arouse the indignation of all honest proletarian elements and will inevitably boomerang on its own organizers. No machinations by the worst part of the party apparatus will succeed in separating the party mass from the Opposition. Behind the Opposition stand the Leninist traditions of our party, the experience of the whole international workers' movement, the contemporary state of international politics and of our economic work of construction as seen by the international proletariat. Class contradictions, inevitably growing sharper after the restoration period, will more and more confirm our views on the way out of the present crisis. They will more and more consolidate the vanguard of the proletariat in the struggle for Leninism.

The growing danger of war has already prompted working class party members to think more deeply about the fundamental problems of the revolution. In the same way they will inevitably be compelled to undertake more actively the work of correcting opportunist mistakes.

The working class section of our party has been largely forced out of the party leadership in recent years. It has been subjected to the devastating influence of a long campaign of slander, whose goal has been to prove that left is right and right is left. This working class section of the party will reawaken. It will find out what is really happening. It will take the fate of the party into its own hands. To help the vanguard of the workers in this process is the task of the Opposition. It is the task of this Platform.

The most important, the most urgent, question, and the one which troubles all the members of our party, is the question of party unity. And in truth it is upon this question that the further fate of the proletarian revolution depends. Innumerable class enemies of the proletariat are listening intently to our inner-party disputes and are waiting with unconcealed delight and impatience for a split in our ranks. A split in our party, the formation of two parties, would represent an enormous danger to the revolution.

We, the Opposition, unconditionally condemn any attempt whatsoever to create a second party. The slogan of two parties is the slogan of the Stalin group in its effort to force the Leninist Opposition out of the All-Union Communist Party. Our task is not to create a new party, but to correct the course of the All-Union Communist Party. Only with a united Bolshevik Party can the proletarian revolution be completely victorious. We are struggling within the Communist Party for our views, and we decisively condemn the "two parties" slogan as the slogan of adventurers. The call for "two parties" expresses, on the one hand, the desire of certain elements in the party apparatus for a split, and, on the other, a mood of despair and a failure to comprehend that the task of Leninists is to win a victory for Lenin's ideas within the party, notwithstanding all difficulties. Nobody who sincerely defends the line of Lenin can entertain the idea of "two parties" or play with the suggestion of a split. Only those who desire to replace Lenin's course with some other can advocate a split or a movement along the two-party road.

We will fight with all our power against the idea of two parties, because the dictatorship of the proletariat demands as its very core a single proletarian party. It demands a single party. It demands a proletarian party—that is, a party whose policy is determined by the interests of the proletariat and carried out by a proletarian nucleus. Correction of the line of our party, improvement of its social composition—this is not the two-party road, but the strengthening and guaranteeing of its unity as a revolutionary party of the proletariat.

On the tenth anniversary of the October Revolution, we express our profound conviction that the working class did not make countless sacrifices and overthrow capitalism in order to prove unequal now to the task of correcting the mistakes of its leadership, carrying the proletarian revolution forward with a firm hand, and defending the Soviet Union, which is the center of the world revolution.

Against opportunism! Against a split! For the unity of the Leninist party!

THE CLEMENCEAU THESIS
AND THE PARTY REGIME

September 24, 1927

NOTE: The response of the ruling circles to the Platform was swift and sharp. Stalin regarded the Platform as a breach of the truce that had been purchased by the statement of August 8. To give himself more time to reach his goal of expelling the Opposition before the Fifteenth Congress, he postponed the congress for another month. At the same time he stepped up the use of gangster methods to silence the Opposition: squads of thugs, ready to beat up anyone upon orders, were formed and provided with total immunity for their work. Oppositionists who tried to speak were whistled, heckled, and shouted down, if not physically assaulted. Often this went on with the direct complicity of the organizers of the meetings, who were Stalinists or Bukharinists. In the meantime, Oppositionists continued to be expelled, deported, and imprisoned on any pretext or on none.

On September 6, Trotsky and other Opposition leaders submitted this protest to the Politburo and Central Committee and again demanded that the Platform be printed and circulated.

From New International, *July 1934, in a translation by John G. Wright, where most of three paragraphs were omitted (those dealing with the danger of Bonapartist degeneration). They were translated from the Russian typescript, and the entire text corrected against it. It is important to remember when reading that section that Trotsky wrote about democracy in two different senses: bourgeois democracy, the parliamentary system, on the one hand; and on the other hand, workers' democracy, both in the party and in the country as a whole. The editors have made some bracketed insertions to facilitate distinguishing between them.*

The campaign around the so-called "Clemenceau thesis" was carried on under great pressure. But in its final results, this campaign succeeded in proving something altogether different from what it had been intended to prove. It is time for some preliminary summaries to be drawn from it.

To begin, let us see how the "Clemenceau question" is formulated by the Agitprop of the Central Committee and of the Moscow committee of the party in its *Materials for the Report on the Summaries of the Joint Plenum of the CC and CCC, AUCP (B) July 29–August 9, 1927.* True, the Agitprop of the Moscow committee has a rotten reputation. Its theses have been called—both in the plenum and in the press—unsuccessful, bad, and even foolish by the representatives of the majority. But in this instance the Agitprop of the CC came to the aid of the Agitprop of the Moscow committee. Consequently, we have before us a more authoritative propaganda document. But what do we find in it on the Clemenceau question?

"In its attacks on the party and the Comintern, the Opposition has advanced the following assertions: (a) at the present time the leadership of the AUCP is passing through a period of Thermidorian degeneration; (b) the replacement of this leadership is inevitable, *after the manner of Clemenceau's coup in France in 1914*" [Our italics—L.T.].

The key place in this quotation is occupied by the words "after the manner of Clemenceau's coup in France in 1914." However, the only thing that is correct in this statement is the fact that Clemenceau operated in France. No coup whatever was achieved by Clemenceau. But if by "coup" is implied the coming to power of the Clemenceau group, then this occurred not in 1914 but in 1917. But there was no coup in 1917 either. The bourgeois parliament entrusted power to the Clemenceau group, considering it to be more capable of solving the war tasks of the imperialist bourgeoisie. The parliament is the mechanism by means of which the bourgeoisie solves its state affairs under normal conditions. Why then does the joint Agitprop of the CC and Moscow committee speak about Clemenceau's coup? Because without speaking about a coup, it would be impossible to ascribe to the Opposition the intentions of following in Clemenceau's footsteps on this road. The formulation is strictly purposeful. But why was Clemenceau's coup assigned to 1914? What difference does it make—let us reply—to what year one assigns an event which is nonexistent in history? Only wily Oppositionists would make a point of such trifles.

The pupil cannot surpass his master. The most official theoretician of our party is Comrade Bukharin. In his report to the general membership of Leningrad, Bukharin said that the Opposition set as its task "the perpetration on its own hook of Clemenceau's coup in our country even in the event that the enemy were a distance of eighty kilometers away from the centers of our revolution." In another place during the same speech reference is made to "Clemenceau's little coup," and at the same time these words are set in quotation marks as if they are a quotation—from the materials of the Agitprop of the CC perhaps? Only instead of a coup, mention was made of "a little coup." This is altogether in the Bukharin manner: if one must serve up a fib, let it be in a diminutive form. Rykov would have said upon the occasion, "Clemenceau's terrific coup," thus demonstrating an indomitable state of mind. Bukharin speaks of a "little coup." The objective Agitprop confines itself to "coup." In nature, however—due to utter misunderstanding—there was neither the one nor the other, nor any third. But that is precisely the reason for the existence of a secret "study outline" against the Opposition: in order to correct the nature of things.

In such a case what could one demand from Yaroslavsky? His fundamental peculiarity as an orator and a writer lies in his inability to render without distortion a single complex idea of any sort—even if he has no immediate interest in distorting it. This ability of his (or this inability) has been developing terrifically, fostered by impunity. Out of the "Clemenceau thesis" Yaroslavsky makes the following indignant deduction: "The Opposition is not loath to draw examples for its tactics from the alien class." The accusation immediately acquires the form of a colossal historic generalization. It would be a waste of time to follow in Yaroslavsky's footsteps along this line. This Saul, anointed as a prophet, does not even suspect what role the examples of "alien classes" played in the formulation of the entire theory and policies of Marxism. Upon more than one occasion the revolutionists had to teach by taking even reaction as an example, in order to explain that the reactionaries, in contradistinction to liberals and conciliators, were "not eloquent babblers but men of action." And on the other hand, the overthrow of feudalism by the French bourgeoisie played, as is well known, no unimportant role as an "example" for the teachings about the dictatorship of the proletariat. In general it would be impossible to take a single step without the examples of the tactics of the alien classes. But one must utilize these examples correctly. And this precludes, first of all, the falsification of history.

The notorious N. Kuzmin,* utilizing the same "Clemenceau thesis" as the inexhaustible source of knowledge, develops the following idea in *Komsomolskaya Pravda.* Clemenceau, if you please, strove for power in order to force the French army to carry the war to the end by applying ruthless measures against the workers and peasants; the Opposition, lacking faith in the peasantry, wants to obtain power in order to make short shrift of the peasantry "in the manner of Clemenceau." Of course, you can't expect anything from Kuzmin—he can argue this position or its opposite. But it is no accident, it is not on his own initiative—and precisely in *Komsomolskaya Pravda* besides!— that Kuzmin spins these abominations of his, which reek of Thermidorianism a kilometer away.

Still, a Marxist would not refuse to utilize the "example of Clemenceau" in this question as well—only in correlation with the class line of the proletariat. Clemenceau led the *imperialist* war, and he really led it. The imperialist war was in fundamental contradiction with the interests of the proletariat and the lower strata of the peasantry. It was impossible to lead such a war successfully, especially in its fourth year, other than by means of ruthless measures against advanced workers and revolutionary peasants. Our war will be a *socialist* war. It can be led only by leaning for support upon the idealism of the proletariat and the lower strata of the peasantry, only by holding in a vise the bourgeois-kulak and the Thermidorian elements of the country. Clemenceau leaned for support on the chauvinist "idealism" of the bourgeois and the petty-bourgeois kulak youth, befuddling and poisoning the workers and peasants and crushing every sign of a critical attitude toward the war. We will lean for support upon the heroism and resoluteness of the proletariat and the poor peasants, sweeping behind them the mass of the middle peasantry. We will be able to sustain and strengthen their revolutionary idealism only by telling the workers the whole truth and only the truth about the real situation, their real friends and their real enemies. That is why, in particular, Thermidorian lying in the

---

*Among other things, Kuzmin is notorious for his ability to write one way or another—all depending upon the conjuncture. In his own time Kuzmin wrote almost inspired dithyrambs on the subject of my five-volume *How the Revolution Armed Itself* (see, for example, *Izvestia,* May 22, 1924). Now he writes just the opposite. My attitude to Kuzmin's writings and to the author himself—and I think that in this I am by no means alone—remains as it was, despite all the "dialectical," not to say chameleonlike, transformations of Kuzmin.

spirit of Kuzmin deals the greatest injury to the cause of defense because it instills in the workers and peasants false conceptions as to where their friends and enemies are.

We pass by the writings of the Vareikises, from Saratov and elsewhere. Let us turn to the paper of the Ivanovo-Voznesensk district committee, *Rabochy Kray* [Workers' Land], a newspaper circulating among the proletarian masses of one of the most important of our industrial centers. Still elucidating the same fatal Clemenceau thesis, *Rabochy Kray* writes in its August 12 issue:

"In his Clemenceau thesis, Comrade Trotsky advances an idea analogous to the idea of Clemenceau, who in 1871, when the German army was advancing on Paris, proclaimed that before giving battle to the external enemy—to the German army—it was necessary to put an end to the enemy within."

Is this news to you? Now you are informed! These remarkable words represent the most finished, and, so to speak, the most "principled" and, in any case, the most expedient interpretation of the Clemenceau thesis. The only trouble is that nothing ever existed resembling the historical reference of *Rabochy Kray*. But is that really so troublesome? If the Agitprop of the CC could mix up 1917 with 1914, why shouldn't *Rabochy Kray* confound 1917 with 1871? True, the so-called Trotsky thesis on Clemenceau speaks with absolute clarity about the imperialist war of 1914-18, naming the ministries of Painlevé, Briand, and so forth; true, there was no Clemenceau coup either in 1914 or in 1871; true, Clemenceau did not speak in any of these years about the necessity of overthrowing the internal enemy prior to defending Paris; true, there was nothing generally resembling these fictions and there couldn't have been—but if one must perforce twist history in accordance with the requirements of the secret "study outline," then one must decidedly give preference to the Ivanovo-Voznesensk variant, as the one that best meets its purpose— slandering the Opposition, that is.

One could multiply almost indefinitely the number of similar examples of reworking the Opposition to fit Clemenceau, with the preliminary reworking of Clemenceau himself to fit the secret outline, and this without having to pass beyond the limits of speeches and articles in the *leading* publications and of the functionaries locally and in the center. Everyone can gather for himself without much difficulty in what form these revelations are served in the districts, in the village districts, in the Ivanovo-Voznesensk factories or to the Saratov peasants. Generally speaking it is difficult to imagine a more systematic poisoning of consciousness. All this does not pass by without leaving a trace; all this continues to add up; all this is getting ready to "back-fire"—the force of which may strike not only the authors of secret study outlines, the pupils, apprentices, and past masters of persecution, but the party as a whole.

Yaroslavsky, following the example of Stalin and of others in his article "The Party and the Opposition," which we have cited, speaks about the unsuccessful pamphlet of the Moscow commit-tee Agitprop, *On War and the War Danger*. Others have called this unsuccessful pamphlet idiotic. It is filled with illiterate assertions of a Black Hundred tinge. How did it happen that the Agitprop of the proletarian capital, Moscow, could issue such a pamphlet—and not merely a pamphlet, but a guide to political education—upon so fundamental a problem as war and the war danger? Yes, how could such a thing have happened? Unfortu-nately one cannot even hoodwink oneself by passing it off as an "accident." The secret study outline of the same Moscow commit-tee Agitprop, on the question of the Anglo-Russian Committee, has an even more scandalous character, if that is possible. In it there is an assertion that the Anglo-Russian Committee will become the center of the struggle against the war danger, the chief weapon of the international mobilization of revolutionary forces, and so forth and so on. When in July 1926 the Opposition called attention to this document, which disgraces the party, it was the Opposition that was condemned, and not the Agitprop of the Moscow committee. This same Moscow committee Agitprop issued an instructive pamphlet on the question of the Chinese revolution, simultaneously with its pamphlet on war and the war danger, of precisely the same quality and standard. Finally, after all these experiments, and after their exposure, there was issued the pamphlet of the Agitprop of the CC and Moscow committee, in which the world is informed of the intentions of the Opposition to follow the "example of the Clemenceau coup in France in 1914."

What has made this possible? The answer is incontrovertible: *It has been made possible by the general regime in the party and by the selection of personnel bound up with the regime.* People write not what they know, not what they have mulled over, not what they want to say, but what is demanded of them at any given moment. Every writer knows beforehand that he bears no responsibility whatever, provided only that he direct his igno-rance and his narrow-minded stupidity against the Opposition.

Everyone who writes knows that it is pointless to burden himself with research or the study of a question because the Opposition won't be able to refute the lie anyway, and also because everyone who might wish to refute it or to reestablish the facts would be immediately classed with the Opposition. The regime of strangulation of inner-party criticism, the regime of the mutual oath within the closed apparatus, the hegemony of the secret study outline and of irresponsibility, tend fatally to lower the official theoretical level of the party rung by rung.

Concurrently, the entire campaign around the so-called "Clemenceau thesis" was inaugurated *not* because the enemy was camped eighty kilometers away from Moscow, and not because the Opposition was preparing to accomplish a coup in the manner of Clemenceau—who accomplished no coup—but in order to stifle inner-party thinking still further, and by this very thing to unbridle still further the irresponsibility of the apparatus.

The Clemenceau example, the example from the political experience of a class inimical to us, was used by me to illustrate a solitary and very simple idea: the ruling class, in the guise of its leading vanguard, must preserve its capacity to reform its ranks under the most difficult conditions—without internal convulsions, without catastrophic splitting of forces. The dictatorship of the proletariat in a country which is surrounded by capitalist states does not allow either the existence of two parties or the factional splitting of a united party. But this same dictatorship demands a regime in the united and only party of the proletariat such as would afford it the possibility—by those methods which are peculiar to it as the revolutionary party, by the methods of democratic centralism—to control even under the most difficult conditions all its institutions, that is, to direct their policies, check them in action, appoint them, and replace them.

The dictatorship is a very sharp instrument. One must manipulate this instrument correctly in order not to dull or chip it. The accusation against the Opposition that it has leanings toward [bourgeois] democracy is nonsense. To the extent that this is an honest accusation it stems from the failure to understand that, considered theoretically, the dictatorship of the proletariat faces a danger—given unfavorable conditions and incorrect policies—not only of slipping back into democracy but also of degenerating into Bonapartism. Historically the second variant is more immediately real than the first. The disruption of the balance between democracy and centralism [in the party], the change from democratic centralism to bureaucratic centralism, constitutes the precondition within the party for the rise of the Bonapartist danger.

We foresaw the possibility that when we called this danger by its name there would be an orgy of slanders and accusations. "It was the Mensheviks who talked about Bonapartist degeneration of the dictatorship!" Yes, they did. Menshevism proceeds from the argument that degeneration of the dictatorship into Bonapartism is *inevitable* if the dictatorship is not replaced in time by democracy. For us, however, both democracy and Bonapartism are only different roads leading back to capitalism. In our peasant country, with the traditions of our revolutions and civil wars, Bonapartism is a much more likely road for a return to bourgeois society than democracy. To deny the existence of this historical danger simply because the Mensheviks seek to reap what gains they can from it would be to march head on toward this danger with one's eyes shut tight.

Ustryalov dreams of a Bonapartist-fascist shift—by installments—onto the bourgeois rails. In contrast to Ustryalov, who is the (temporarily) conciliationist representative of the new bourgeoisie, the Mensheviks fear a Bonapartist regime, preferring a democracy which would give the petty bourgeoisie a chance to preserve some semblance of a political role. To Ustryalov's question "tactic or evolution?"* Lenin replied to the effect that it is *possible* for a tactic to develop into an evolution. The same is true of the party regime. Stalin is of the opinion that the stifling of all criticism, the substitution of an almighty secret study outline for collective ideological life, and interminable repressions are only temporary evils, necessary to maintain the equilibrium of the party. In reality, however, these measures disrupt more and more the necessary correlation between democracy and centralism and foster the all too real historical danger of the bureaucratic degeneration of the dictatorship.

It is self-evident that the roots of these processes are embedded not in inner-party relationships, isolated by themselves, but in the interrelations of classes, in the relations between the classes and the state, in the relations between the party and the classes, *and in the line of the party policies taken as a whole.* Only an honest bureaucratic numbskull or an unconscionable adventurer

---

*Ustryalov questioned whether the introduction of the NEP was merely a tactic by which the Bolsheviks would hold onto power or an unintended beginning of an evolution back to capitalism. Lenin discussed this possibility in his political report of March 27, 1922, to the Eleventh Party Congress (in *Collected Works,* vol. 33, pp. 286-87).—Eds.

who does not care at all about tomorrow, could deny the progressive deterioration of the inner-party regime from the day after Lenin's death until the present time. We have seen above the eloquent consequences of this deterioration in the sphere of the *ideological* life of the party: the foremost organization in the country, the one in Moscow, on the most important questions of party policies—the Anglo-Russian Committee, the Chinese revolution, the war danger, and inner-party relations—issues pamphlets with directives of a most debased character. And this fact, so terrible by its very nature, not only passes unpunished but is shielded by repressions addressed against those who point out the radically wrong policies of the leadership of the Moscow committee.

Stalin and Molotov and Uglanov and Kaganovich and other more outstanding representatives of the bureaucratic degeneration of the party leadership are, of course, not striving for bureaucratism; on the contrary, they would like to put their policies through with methods of party democracy, that is, they would like the party to approve their policies and to reelect those who are ready to put them through. But they run up against some sort of dull resistance in the party and they are forced more and more to impose their policies from above. The party congress is only an inevitable evil for them. In direct contradiction to the party statutes they postpone this evil for an additional year. Discussion they decree to be an absolute evil, a hindrance to practical work, but at the same time they do nothing else except convulse the party with interminable discussions, a small sample of which we viewed above, on the matter of the Clemenceau thesis. They correlate this one-sided discussion with interminable purges of party institutions, which affect practical work cruelly. Expulsions from the party fall like hail. For what? For spreading "secret" documents. In the meantime, the actual crime consists in the fact that articles and speeches which should be the property of the entire party have been decreed—yes, even two months before the congress—to be secret documents. Instead of realizing the inner-party democracy which had been proclaimed during all the recent congresses, it is necessary to resort to even more forceful methods of inner-party repression.

The preparation for the Fifteenth Party Congress was long ago put under the sign of the war danger. Discussion was declared to be doubly impermissible because we were surrounded by enemies. In order to befuddle the party, the malignant myth was created to the effect that the Opposition threatened a coup "in the manner of Clemenceau." By the very nature of things, all this is aimed to finish off the remnants of inner-party democracy, completely supplanting it by the autocracy of the apparatus. And this amounts to the prerequisite for the Bonapartist danger, under the corresponding class shifts in the country and under corresponding shifts of the policies of the party leadership.

The danger of war is not some accidental, episodic, or temporary phenomenon. World contradictions are becoming more concentrated. The possible mitigation of the relations between us and the capitalist states will be of a rather temporary character. The fundamental line runs toward the sharpening of antagonisms, the deepening of the war danger. According to the logic of the present regime this means that it is necessary to bid goodbye forever to ideas of inner-party democracy. The campaign on the score of the "Clemenceau coup," plus a number of other similar campaigns, as well as the entire present interminable discussion convulsing the party from above, must drive out completely any thoughts of the possibility of switching party life back onto the rails of democracy.

Precisely in this sense it is incontestable that of all the dangers the most terrible one is the inner-party regime. These words have also served as the cause of an unbridled and thoughtless campaign—in the press and at meetings. And yet they are absolutely incontestable. If I were threatened by an enemy and my eyes were blindfolded or my hands tied behind my back, I would say that the chief danger was—not the enemy but the handicaps restricting my movements. It is a lie that the war danger or even war itself excludes the independent activity of the party, which discusses and decides all questions and which directs and checks all its organizations from top to bottom. If as a result of our mistakes the enemy did appear within eighty kilometers of Moscow, then the party's independent activity would have to be ten times greater than under any other conditions. But the task right now is not to *permit* such a situation, to prevent it. This can be realized only by a living party, independently active and completely alive. The first thing that follows from this is that there must be a change in the party regime.

SPEECH TO THE PRESIDIUM
OF THE ECCI

September 27, 1927

NOTE: On September 27, the ECCI presidium held an all-night meeting to consider motions to expel from the ECCI Trotsky and, along with him, Rakovsky and Vujović, a young Yugoslavian supporter of Zinoviev. His audience included Ernst Thälmann, under whose leadership the German party would capitulate to Nazism a few years later. The motions were made and passed.

The Central Committee had rejected the Opposition's request to circulate the Platform, and restricted the Opposition to presenting countertheses to the official theses. The Opposition decided to circulate its Platform clandestinely. Victor Serge describes the scene in his Memoirs of a Revolutionary *(pp. 222-23): "Some of the comrades got three or four typewriters together in a little room in Moscow. Agents of the GPU besieged these premises quite openly. One of the Red Army leaders, Okhotnikov, came complete with the tabs on his collar and ordered this surveillance to be called off; we were able to save some of our stocks. . . . Meanwhile we collected signatures to the Platform. . . . Since the situation was taking a rapid turn for the worse, only a few hundred, the names of the men of the Bolshevik Old Guard, were sent to the Central Committee." An old Communist and printer, Fishelev, managed to produce several thousand copies: he was immediately arrested, convicted of misappropriating paper and equipment, and sent to a labor camp on the Solovetsky Islands near the Arctic Circle.*

The accusation that the Opposition was preparing a military conspiracy, which had found only embryonic expression earlier, was renewed once the Opposition had published its Platform. To support their case, the Stalinists planted a GPU agent in the Opposition and then "exposed" him as a former officer of Baron Pyotr Wrangel, a White Guard general who had fought against the Soviets in the civil war. This attempt to smear the Oppositionists as collaborators with counterrevolutionaries was shown to be

405

a frame-up, but the Oppositionists could not publicly refute the charges against them.

By permission of the Harvard College Library. Points 3-9 of this speech, which concern China, are in Leon Trotsky on China.

1. You accuse me of violating discipline. I have no doubt that your verdict is already prepared. Today there is not one organization that discusses and decides; they only *carry out orders.* Even the presidium of the Communist International is no exception.

2. What do you call *factional work?* Anything that is not authorized by the AUCP Secretariat. But the Secretariat tramples the rules underfoot, shatters the very foundations of party discipline, and imposes a ban on what is the inalienable right and primary duty of every party member. . . .

The Struggle Against War

10. Are things any better with regard to the second question on the agenda of the last ECCI plenum, the question of the struggle against war? Comrade Vujović and I placed the question of the Anglo-Russian Committee at the center of the discussion on war. Partial, tactical questions cannot be decided without a basic strategic orientation. In reply to us the argument was made that the Anglo-Russian Committee is the road of linking up with the masses. As though strikebreaking could be a road for linking up with strikers. Against us they argued that the Anglo-Russian Committee could improve the USSR's international position. As though agents of imperialism could protect the revolution against imperialism. This was a policy of rotten illusions. The Heinz Neumanns, Smerals, Martynovs, and Kuusinens said that we, the Opposition, did not hold the defense of the USSR dear to our hearts. Stalin, rude and disloyal as ever, spoke of a united front from Chamberlain to Trotsky.

In theses we submitted at the last ECCI plenum we said: "The more acute the international situation becomes, the more the Anglo-Russian Committee will be transformed into an instrument of British and international imperialism against us. After all that has happened, only he can fail to understand who does not want to understand. We have already wasted too much time. It would be a crime to lose even another day" [from "The Struggle for Peace and the Anglo-Russian Committee," May 16, 1927, in *Leon Trotsky on Britain* (New York: Monad Press, 1973), p. 278].

Now several months have passed—and the proof is before us. We did not break with the traitors and strikebreakers in full view of the masses in order thereby to clarify the situation and aid the General Strike, the miners' strike, and the Chinese revolution. Instead the strikebreakers of the General Council broke relations with us, in order thereby to help Chamberlain against us more effectively. We covered up for the General Council by blocking with it during the months that were most critical for the General Council, after May 1926. By our radically wrong policy we helped Thomas and Purcell maintain all their positions and to convene the recent trade union congress in Edinburgh.

The entire official policy toward the Anglo-Russian Committee was a rude defiance of Bolshevism by opportunism. The international proletariat has been given a great lesson by this example. It should absorb the lesson. But to do that, it must know about it. That is why we cannot remain silent. At issue here are the fundamental interests of the international proletariat. This is something higher and more compelling than the orders of the Secretariat, which has shamefully led the international proletarian vanguard astray and created more and more obstacles to its development.

Questions of Discipline and Organizational Rules

11. Discipline is a very important tool of the revolution. But it is not the only one. Discipline cannot substitute for the correct line or for working it out collectively. The attempt to maintain discipline by mechanical means alone is hopeless and reactionary. The more mistaken the line, the more repression is needed to maintain formal discipline. Bureaucratic discipline, on the basis of a wrong political line, is a tool not for consolidating the party but for disorganizing and destroying it. These words describe the Stalinist regime, which has now been transplanted in its entirety into the Comintern.

12. In a recent letter by the Central Committee of our party, and in a number of other documents, the assertion is made that in our statement of August 8 we "acknowledged a number of errors" and made a commitment not to engage in factional work. In fact there is no mention of any errors of ours in the statement. When we declared on August 8 that we were for the unconditional defense of the USSR, against a split, against the course toward two parties, and against a system of permanent factionalism, we were not talking about mistakes of ours but were referring to the

slander which had been and still is being systematically heaped upon us. We explained factionalism in terms of the bureaucratic regime, in full consistency with the resolution of December 5, 1923. Factionalism can be fought only by fighting bureaucratism. We are waging this fight and will continue to do so.

13. You try to pose the question of the Opposition on the plane of pure discipline. But in order to demand discipline, you yourselves must abide by the basic norms of party democracy and rules of the organization. But these norms are being trampled upon more and more coarsely and rudely.

14. Let us begin with the simplest examples. The stenographic record of the session which discussed the Opposition at the last ECCI plenum was published with extraordinary speed. My speech was left out of the record, with a note claiming that I had not corrected the text. But the text was delivered to me at the very time when the report as a whole was coming off the presses. I submitted a complaint to you about that. What steps have you taken against this disgraceful violation of elementary rights and actual deception of the party? No decisive ones.

15. Comrade Vujović is a member of the ECCI, elected by the last Comintern congress. The Orgburo of the AUCP Central Committee has ordered Comrade Vujović sent to the provinces to deny him the possibility of carrying out the functions entrusted to him by the world congress. What is this if not a flagrant infringement of the rules and of discipline? Did you intervene in behalf of the rights of this member of the ECCI? Not at all. Today you wish to remove Vujović from the ECCI in order to cover up, after the fact, for the Orgburo's order violating the rules.

16. Soon after the last ECCI plenum, the Central Control Commission of the AUCP brought me up on charges for my conduct on the ECCI. Again this was a flagrant violation of the rules and discipline of the organization. This is the same as if a provincial Control Commission were to try me for my conduct at a Central Committee plenum. The ECCI itself passed a judgment on this question. Even though the matter was absolutely clear-cut, the Central Control Commission of the AUCP found it possible to condemn me for my speeches at the plenum of the ECCI.

Whoever fights against Stalin's course within the European Communist parties is expelled. More and more Bolsheviks are being expelled, both in the European parties and in the AUCP, because they share the viewpoint of the Opposition in the AUCP. Those who are expelled are declared renegades, and then we are accused of solidarizing ourselves with renegades. The word "renegade" has thus been cheapened in its meaning.

Chiang Kai-shek until yesterday was proclaimed an ally; Wang Ching-wei a reliable revolutionary; Purcell a friend. By the same logic, revolutionaries expelled for defending Leninism are proclaimed renegades. This abuse discredits the accusers, not the accused.

17. The presidium as well as the Executive Committee as a whole derives its powers from the Comintern congress. According to the rules, Comintern congresses must be held annually. That means that the powers vested in the Executive Committee and its presidium are of only one year's duration. The arbitrary prolongation of these powers is a violation of the rules. Of course, if a war, blockade, or the like prevented a congress from being called, it would be absurd to make an issue of the formal aspect of the question. But it was precisely during wars and blockades that the world congresses were held relatively regularly. Now, when absolutely nothing interferes with the convening of a properly organized congress, you are only getting around to calling a new one four years after the Fifth Congress; that is, for three years and more you have assumed powers that do not belong to you.

On what basis? The Chinese revolution alone would have justified the calling of two emergency congresses during the past year. Congresses of the Second International and of the Amsterdam group have been held during this time. Only the Third International—in a period of tremendous worldwide upheavals and a growing danger of war—has not come together in a congress for four years. And whether it will be convened next year is not at all certain. Isn't this a flagrant violation of rules and discipline? Isn't this outright usurpation?

18. And the congress of the AUCP? It has not been called for two years. What has prevented the congress from being called normally? Nothing but the intention of the Stalin faction to deal with the Opposition behind the back of the party, before a congress, and without a congress. The same consideration has led to another postponement of the Sixth Comintern Congress. Above all other questions there stands the question of the organizational self-preservation of the Stalin group. One cannot speak about the Chinese revolution, the Anglo-Russian Committee, our policy in Persia, Mongolia, Afghanistan, the class differentiation in the countryside, industrialization, price policy, or even Dneprostroi—because on all these questions Stalin's activity has shown only mistakes, wavering, opportunist blun-

ders, and defeats. Today we cannot talk about matters of international politics, in particular the negotiations with France about recognition of the tsarist debts. On these questions no fewer mistakes have been made than on others. And these questions have been decided behind the back of the party and dumped on its head as faits accomplis. The party knew less about these things than the international bourgeoisie. The inability of the leadership to orient itself in the international situation, to correctly assess the relations between classes and between states, has led and continues to lead to policies that are inane and out of place. This will cost us dearly and already is doing so. And it is obvious that we are now about to pay even more dearly for our mistakes and delays than would have seemed possible—and that in exchange for highly dubious results. It is particularly forbidden to discuss the regime within the party, although here all the other mistakes, all the political backsliding, find their most vivid expression. The party is ordered to remain silent because the policies of Stalin are the policies of bankruptcy. But that is the very reason why the party must speak. And that is precisely why the Opposition will speak.

19. The preparations for the Fifteenth Congress are a link in the chain of high-handed abuse of the party. The Central Committee, which has pursued a radically wrong line on all fundamental questions, bans any criticism of itself on the eve of the congress. Party members have been granted the kind permission to present their countertheses after Stalin and Bukharin have written their theses. As if in fact the problem were the written theses of Stalin. The real problem is his policies as a whole over the past two years. These policies lead into a blind alley. These policies have produced a series of defeats and are paving the way for even bigger defeats to come. But no. No one may dare to speak of these real, actual policies put into practice over the past two years. The Platform of the Opposition provides a thorough assessment of these policies. Precisely for that reason the Platform is declared an illegal document. Party members are subjected to searches, expulsions, and all kinds of physical repressive measures for circulating a Platform which criticizes the Central Committee two months before the congress.

The arbitrary postponement of the congress for a year, the ban on discussion, the use of administrative measures by the state to pressure party members, depriving Leninists of their daily bread because they do not wish to become Stalinists—none of that constitutes a violation of discipline; all that is the normal course of events. And to protest against that, to fight against those infamies, is to violate discipline and persist in factional activity. No, you cannot frighten us with such miserable, contemptible bureaucratic threats.

20. The party regime is the greatest of all dangers—because it paralyzes the vanguard of the proletariat, the main force for resisting the enemy.

If a soldier's hands have been tied, the main danger is not the enemy but the rope which binds the soldier's hands. The present regime ties down the initiative and independent activity of the party. That is the most immediate and most serious danger because it weakens the party in the face of the enemy.

21. Party members are magnanimously given the right to present their countertheses. After they are submitted they will be printed in the discussion bulletin. In the best of cases this would be three to four weeks before the congress. Then the discussion bulletin will be sent where the Secretariat deems it advisable. Meanwhile, preparations for local conferences, which will decide the composition of the congress, are under way. The so-called "discussion" will be opened after the congress has actually been elected—consisting of secretaries appointed by Stalin. It is hard to imagine a more disgusting way of playing with the party! All these machinations are permeated through and through with the spirit of usurpationism. Whoever does not fight against them is not worthy of the name *Bolshevik*. We will fight them to the very end.

Yesterday Comrades Okhotnikov, Gutman, Dvores, Kaplinskaya, Karin, Maksimov, Vladimirov, Rabinovich, Gerdovsky, and Vorobev were expelled for reproducing and distributing the Platform of the Opposition. They are all outstanding party members; most of them were tempered in battle despite their youth; they are devoted revolutionaries. Not careerists looking out for their own skins, but genuine Bolsheviks. The majority of Oppositionists who have been expelled are far superior to those who expelled them. But these ten comrades were not only expelled from the party; a vile attempt was also made to slander them by dragging some unknown, nameless "Wrangel officer" into this affair—through the GPU.

Something further must be added on this point. Today, after Zinoviev, Smilga, and Peterson wrote a protest, which I did not sign only because I was away—after that Menzhinsky stated that the so-called Wrangel officer, this supposed counterrevolutionary, is in fact an agent of the GPU who helps uncover conspiracies. I do not know if our comrades encountered this man in their work or not, but if they did, they encountered a GPU agent, not a Wrangel officer.

Whoever knows history knows that every step on the road to usurpation has always been accompanied by such denunciatory frameups. Comrades Serebryakov, Preobrazhensky, and Sharov, in a letter to the Central Committee, have stated that they were the organizers of the printing of the Platform. A letter of the Politburo calls the statement by the three comrades "renegade." The authors of this abuse only discredit themselves. Serebryakov, Preobrazhensky, and Sharov stand two heads taller politically and morally than any of those who cover their own crimes with insults.

Pitiful, triply pitiful, are the political bankrupts who have to hide from the Platform of the Bolshevik-Leninists (Opposition) behind the backs of the Wrangel officer. This will do them no good. Neither threats nor repression nor Thermidorian slander nor Bonapartist frameups will prevent us from carrying on the work of preserving the revolutionary traditions of the party and ensuring its revolutionary future.

What Is the Way Out?

22. Stalin whispers a solution in your ear: expel Trotsky and Vujović from the ECCI. I think you will carry out this suggestion. But what will be changed by that? Nothing. Or almost nothing. The main questions are decided outside the Executive Committee and outside of the presidium anyway. You know this no less than I. Like any measure which is abused, expulsions have lost their bite. Just in the last few days Stalin and Bukharin demanded that the French CC expel Treint from its ranks only because Treint spoke some bitter words of truth about Stalin and Bukharin's China policy. And Comrade Nin, one of the best staff workers of the international proletarian vanguard, a central staff member of the trade union International, what are you going to do with him? He too has openly declared his full solidarity with the Opposition. What fate are you preparing for him? What measures are you going to adopt in his case? In the German party, Comrade Thälmann, as the appointed chief, retains his hold— despite all his frightful political helplessness—only because anyone who criticizes him is recalled from Germany or expelled. In fact, behind Thälmann's back stands the opportunist Ernst Meyer. Revolutionary leaders are not made by apparatus appoint-

ment. People who are agreeable to anything in advance never become real revolutionaries, much less revolutionary leaders. I do not mean any personal offense to Smeral, Pepper, Kuusinen, and others. But these are not comrades who can take initiative in the proletariat's struggle for power. The term *Bolshevik* applies not to people who subordinate themselves to every order from the Secretariat of the AUCP but to those who know how to fight for the *dictatorship of the proletariat.*

23. Expulsions will do no good. There are too many of them. There are getting to be more and more. The Stalin regime is convulsing the party with one-sided discussions, expulsions, and all kinds of repression generally. The party never manages to emerge from these feverish discussions imposed from above: the apparatus starts a new discussion every month, the apparatus sets the theme, feeds the debate with false materials, sums up the results, holds trials and takes reprisals, postpones the congress for a year, and now is preparing a congress made up of its own apparatus personnel, people appointed in advance who are sure to authorize the gang at the top to carry the same work further. The Stalin regime is becoming more and more costly for the party and for the international revolution.

24. You will say, Does this mean a break, a split? To that I reply, Stalin's entire policy is aimed at a split; or more precisely, at a series of successive slices which are intended to become more and more frequent and go deeper and deeper. These results can be prevented only by a party which has regained its own rights. In order to do this, it must understand the dangers threatening it. Our Platform is entirely subordinated to that aim. Everyone who distributes our Platform is serving the unity of the party on the revolutionary basis of Leninism. There is only one way out—an honest congress. The same goes for the Comintern. First, the publication of all the documents. Then a discussion. And then an international congress.

25. You will say, Does this mean the Opposition is seeking a break with Stalin and Bukharin? No. We are talking about the line of the party and not about Stalin, Bukharin, or other personalities.

The personal misfortune of Stalin, which more and more is becoming the misfortune of the party, consists in the colossal disproportion between Stalin's theoretical resources and the power the state apparatus has concentrated in his hands. In his Testament, weighing every word, Lenin gave his assessment of the leading elements of the party. With especially great care he warned the party about Stalin—about his rudeness and disloyalty and his abuse of power—and about Bukharin, his scholasticism and his inability to master Marxism. Lenin wrote this assessment at a time when he wrote other wise counsel to the party. There is no need to point out that Lenin's comments did not contain one ounce of bias, ill-will, or the like. In that document, more than ever, he was guided by political and party considerations—and nothing else. In his comments on Stalin and Bukharin, very mild in form but very harsh in content, Lenin had no intention at all of branding or isolating them. He wished only to warn the party in regard to the position they might hold in the collective leadership.

One central idea pervades the whole of Lenin's letter: that under existing conditions and with the existing forces the party leadership can only be collective. The bureaucratic regime unalterably leads to one-man rule. Collective leadership is conceivable only on the basis of party democracy. We believe that on the question of the leadership it is still not too late to return to the advice Lenin gave in his Testament. But however important this question is, another more important question stands above it: The party must be placed back on the track of Leninist policies and a Leninist regime. And the Comintern must be returned to that road as well.

All our efforts are devoted to this aim. We presented our views in the Platform, in the drafting of which no less than two hundred Old Bolshevik party members participated, in full or in part. No fewer than a thousand party members have already added their signatures to this Platform. And all of them, together with us, have made it their task to present this Platform for open discussion before the party and the Comintern. We will achieve this aim no matter what.

THE OPPOSITION
AND THE WRANGEL OFFICER

October 1, 1927

NOTE: Stalin was determined to prevent the circulation of the Platform and to create the conditions for the expulsion, imprisonment, and exiling of Oppositionists. To do this he prepared a frameup that would become a model for the Moscow trials of the next decade. On the night of September 12-13, GPU agents raided the Opposition's "printshop"—actually a room belonging to Oppositionist Shcherbakov, containing three or four typewriters and a duplicating machine—arrested several individuals, and announced to the CCC on September 13 that they had discovered a military conspiracy. The former Wrangel officer—whom Trotsky later identified as one Stroilov—and another GPU plant, Tverskoi, were the links between the Opposition and counterrevolutionary forces that the GPU needed to bolster its charge of military conspiracy.

Trotsky had left that day for the Caucasus, but Preobrazhensky, Mrachkovsky, and Serebryakov came forward to refute the charges against the Opposition and to claim responsibility for the "printshop." They were immediately expelled from the party and Mrachkovsky was imprisoned—the first time this was done to a prominent Opposition leader. On September 23, Zinoviev, Smilga, and Peterson requested the identity of the Wrangel officer: they were informed by the GPU that he was one of its agents. On September 29, the Control Commission confirmed the expulsions of the fourteen party members involved.

The Opposition had no difficulty in refuting the charges brought against it, as Trotsky shows in this letter. But the frameup and persecution had more than face value to the Stalinists: they ensnared the Opposition in a seemingly endless web of charges and denials, guilt by association, innuendo and slander that took up its time and energy, cost it dearly in terms of reprisals, and struck terror into the hearts of any ordinary worker who might have been contemplating open support to the Opposition.

In this letter, Trotsky demands the convening of a special commission to investigate "the entire matter" and to determine the truth.

From New International, *November 1934. The translation, by John G. Wright, has been revised somewhat for consistency of style.*

To the Political Bureau of the Central Committee, AUCP(B), and the Presidium of the Central Control Commission:

I. The Opposition Printshop and Its "Connection" with a Military Conspiracy

On the night of September 12-13, a number of party members' homes were raided by agents of the GPU.

On September 15, the Secretariat of the CCC met to hear Comrade Yaroslavsky's report "concerning the participation of members of the AUCP(B) together with nonparty people in the activities of an *illegal counterrevolutionary organization*"; and resolved to "approve the action of the GPU."

On September 22 a communication relating to the discovery of a printshop was issued in the name of the Political Bureau and the presidium of the CCC, and it was transmitted to all party organizations. This communication stated that "a number of the arrested nonparty people were found to be actually involved with certain individuals from military circles who were planning a military coup in the USSR modeled on Pilsudski's coup."

This assertion, which was repeated in the communication several times, was based on the September 13 communication of the GPU. We think it necessary to cite here the main section of the GPU communication.

"On September 12, 1927, the GPU learned that a former officer in Wrangel's army had been approached by a certain citizen, one Shcherbakov, son of a former manufacturer and a nonparty man, with the proposal that he obtain a duplicating machine; almost simultaneously, information was received that the same individual had been approached by one Tverskoi, a nonparty man and a civil employee, who turned out to be intimately connected with Shcherbakov and who had information concerning the organization of a military coup in the USSR in the near future. Acting upon the said information on that very night of the twelfth, the GPU raided Shcherbakov's apartment; and the search revealed an illegal printshop, which was publishing the antiparty documents of the Opposition prohibited by the party. The GPU deemed it its duty to confiscate this literature and, in view of the connections between Shcherbakov and Tverskoi, to arrest all nonparty men involved in this matter. In view of the extraordinary nature of the case (the organization of a military conspiracy) and the absolute urgency of tracking it down as fast as possible, the GPU was compelled to raid without delay the homes of those party members who, as the search revealed, were *directly connected with the illegal Shcherbakov-Tverskoi organization.* Of course none of the party men was arrested.

"Since a number of party members (Griunshtein, Gerdovsky, Mrachkovsky, Okhotnikov, and others) are involved in matters relating to the illegal Shcherbakov-Tverskoi organization, the GPU deems it its duty to transmit all the details, together with all the material pertaining to this case, to the CCC.

"In view of the fact that the testimony of the arrested nonparty men has confirmed the existence of a group which sets as its aim the organization of the above-mentioned military conspiracy, we are continuing our investigation of this case."

From this communication it may be gathered that Shcherbakov, who did actually participate in the work of the Opposition printshop, had applied to a Wrangel officer on a matter concerning a duplicating machine. This same Wrangel officer was also approached by Tverskoi, who had no connection whatever with the Opposition printing operation, but who had "information concerning the organization of a military coup in the USSR in the near future."

Thus, we have two cases before us: one case dealing with an Opposition printshop, and another case dealing with a military conspiracy. Through what or through whom are these two cases linked? They are linked through the person of the "Wrangel officer" whom Shcherbakov approached regarding a dublicating machine, and whom Tverskoi informed about an impending conspiracy.

On September 23, Comrades Zinoviev, Smilga, and Peterson addressed a letter to the party organizations in which they put the following questions: "Who is this Wrangel officer? What is his name? Why is it being covered up? Has he been arrested? Why was this particular Wrangel officer approached, and simultaneously at that, both for a duplicating machine and with information regarding a military coup in the USSR in the 'near future'? For what reason was this latter information supplied him? Who was supposed to carry out this military coup in the 'near future'?

What group? What organization? What individuals?"

In reply to the letter of Comrades Zinoviev, Smilga, and Peterson with the foregoing questions, the Political Bureau and the presidium of the CCC transmitted on September 27 a new communication to all organizations, this time a letter of the chairman of the GPU, Comrade Menzhinsky, to the Secretariat of the CC, AUCP(B). This letter reads:

"The Wrangel officer referred to in the GPU communication to the CCC dated September 27, 1927, was not arrested by the GPU because this citizen, whose name I can supply only upon the direct order of the CC of the AUCP(B), has assisted the GPU on more than one occasion in tracking down White Guard conspiracies. Thanks to information he supplied, for example, the stores of arms of the counterrevolutionary Savinkov organization were discovered. It was he who aided the GPU in catching the individuals implicated in the recent military conspiracy.

"The raids and arrests bound up with this case were made with the aim of discovering this military conspiracy. The discovery of an underground printshop was an incidental and unexpected consequence of the arrest of nonparty individuals connected with the group in the military conspiracy. The GPU did not hold and is not holding any inquiries into the matter of the illegal Opposition printshop, in which party members were involved, but has turned this case over to the CCC."

Thus, the GPU communication of September 13 established that between the Opposition printshop and the military conspirators there existed a link in the person of a Wrangel officer. However, the communication of the chairman of the GPU of September 27 admits that the Wrangel officer is no Wrangel officer but an agent of the GPU. Thus, according to the new interpretation of the chairman of the GPU himself, the so-called connection between the Opposition press and the military conspiracy is personified by an agent of the GPU. This and this alone is the connection. There is not a single word about any other connection either in the GPU communications or in any other documents.

It is obvious that an agent of the GPU cannot be considered a counterrevolutionist. According to the GPU, Shcherbakov applied to this GPU agent "with a proposal that he obtain a duplicating machine." These words must obviously be understood to mean that Shcherbakov attempted to obtain a duplicating machine through a citizen who in no way could be considered a participant in a counterrevolutionary military conspiracy, because this citizen happens to be a GPU agent. There is not to be obtained even the tiniest bridge between the press and the military conspiracy, unless the GPU agent is transformed into a Wrangel officer, precisely as was done in the first GPU communication.

As we already know, a certain Tverskoi also applied to this same GPU agent with information about the preparation of "a military conspiracy in the USSR in the near future." From the first GPU text, where the GPU agent is recommended only as a Wrangel officer, one might draw the conclusion that one Tverskoi, unconnected in any way whatever with the Oppositionist press, informed a Wrangel officer about a military conspiracy—evidently in order to involve this Wrangel officer in the alleged coup. The second GPU communication presents the matter in just the reverse manner.

Tverskoi approached the GPU agent "with information concerning the organization of a military coup" obviously in order to expose this coup in time. Where then is the connection between the Opposition press and the military organization? One must presume that the GPU agent transmitted to the proper channels the information Tverskoi gave him regarding the military conspiracy. One would also assume that this agent informed the proper authorities of his negotiations with Shcherbakov about a duplicating machine, independently of the question of who had initiated these negotiations. Thus, the sole "connection" between the Opposition press and a military conspiracy was an agent of the GPU, who was doing surveillance on both the White Guards and the Opposition. Even if we allow that the GPU agent had accidentally stumbled across the duplicating machine—this agent still remains the only "link" between the Opposition press and the military conspiracy, about which we know nothing.

It is true that the first GPU communication speaks in passing about an intimate connection between Tverskoi and Shcherbakov, without explaining whether it is a question of family, neighborhood, political, or organizational ties. It is true that this same first communication says that the party members, "as the search revealed, were directly connected with the illegal Shcherbakov-Tverskoi organization."

But we learn from neither the first nor the second GPU document—what sort of an illegal organization the illegal Shcherbakov-Tverskoi organization is. In the papers relating to the case of the printshop, nowhere is any mention made of "the illegal Shcherbakov-Tverskoi organization." Yet the same GPU communication informs us that Shcherbakov had some conversations with the GPU agent about a duplicating machine, whereas it was Tverskoi who gave the GPU agent information about the pending military coup. What then does the "illegal Shcherbakov-Tverskoi organization" refer to? To the Opposition press, perhaps? But Tverskoi had no connection whatever with this press. To the military conspiracy? But nowhere is a single word said about Shcherbakov's participation in the military conspiracy. What then did the Shcherbakov-Tverskoi "organization" consist of? The communication informs us only that they both applied to one and the same GPU agent, even though for entirely different reasons—one on a matter relating to a duplicating machine, the other with information about a conspiracy.

With respect to the first GPU communication only, the reference to the "illegal Shcherbakov-Tverskoi organization" could be indirectly based on the fact that they both applied, even though for different reasons, to one and the same Wrangel officer, that is to say, a White Guard. But this construction collapses completely in the face of the second GPU communication, which attests that he was not a Wrangel officer but a member of a government institution, fulfilling secret commissions in the interests of the Soviet state. Consequently there is no illegal Shcherbakov-Tverskoi organization. It was precisely in order to maintain a semblance of such an organization that the GPU was impelled in its first communication to depict its own agent as a Wrangel officer. That is the incontrovertible testimony of the facts.

On September 27-28 the case of the Communists participating in the Opposition press was heard by the Moscow Control Commission and on September 29 by the CCC. At these hearings absolutely nobody supported the accusation that the Communists were "directly connected with the illegal Shcherbakov-Tverskoi organization." To all the demands of the accused as well as those of four Central Committee members who were present during the CCC hearings—Yevdokimov, Zinoviev, Smilga, and Trotsky— that it be definitely and clearly stated what the illegal Shcherbakov-Tverskoi organization consisted of and what the connections between Communists and this organization were, the members of the Moscow Control Commission and the CCC indignantly replied by accusing the questioners of attempting to sidetrack the hearing to matters which had nothing at all to do with the case; that they, the accused, were seeking to befuddle the issues in order to escape giving an answer to the question of the press, and so forth and so on.

The indictment of the Moscow Control Commission and the

CCC in the so-called printshop case accuses the party members of "creating jointly with nonparty bourgeois intellectuals an underground anti-party organization possessing its own illegal printshop." We have heard more than once the Moscow Control Commission and the CCC label the Opposition as "an underground antiparty organization." But this is a question separate and apart. Fourteen party members were held accountable on the question of the Opposition press. Twelve of them were expelled. But what happened to the "counterrevolutionary Shcherbakov-Tverskoi organization"?

The first GPU communication read: "Since a number of party members (Griunshtein, Gerdovsky, Mrachkovsky, Okhotnikov, and others) are involved in matters relating to the illegal Shcherbakov-Tverskoi organization, the GPU deems it its duty to transmit all the details together with all material pertaining to this case to the CCC."

This is of course entirely correct. But what has happened to "all the details" and "all the material"? When the accused comrades, Gerdovsky, Mrachkovsky, Okhotnikov, and others, demanded that Tverskoi's report be made public, that is, the testimony of one of the two founders of that very same "illegal organization" to which the above-named Communists supposedly belonged, the presidium of the CCC refused them point-blank—on the grounds that Tverskoi and his testimony have no connection whatever with the matter under investigation, namely, the Opposition press. By so doing, the CCC presidium was declaring the fraudulence of the first GPU communication, which asserted that Gerdovsky, Mrachkovsky, Okhotnikov, and others were involved in the illegal Shcherbakov-Tverskoi organization. The CCC turned out to have no information, either detailed or abridged, and no material at all on this score. Why? Obviously because the GPU sent no such documents to the CCC for the reason that it had none itself. Had such documents existed, there would have been no need to pass off a GPU agent for a Wrangel officer, and on this masquerade to erect "the illegal Shcherbakov-Tverskoi organization," in which Communists were supposedly involved.

This, however, did not prevent the chairman of the GPU from concluding his second communication, which completely refutes the myth about the Wrangel officer, with the following words: "It is no fault of the GPU that the allies of the Opposition among nonparty intellectuals turned out to be connected one way (?) or another (?) with military men who were contemplating a military putsch."

What does this imply? What sort of connections "one way or another" are these? This implies that the chairman of the GPU—who under the pressure of the letter written by Comrades Zinoviev, Smilga, and Peterson was compelled to disclose that the White Guard Wrangel officer was not arrested because he was not a White Guard but an agent of the GPU—is nevertheless making an attempt to sustain at least a semblance of the accusation against the Communists which was based upon this very same purported White Guard.

In the meantime both the September 22 and the September 27 communications of the Political Bureau and the presidium of the CCC are making the rounds of all the organizations, down to the nethermost cells. Moreover, the second communication, which was written after the trick played on the party regarding the Wrangel officer was already exposed, concludes with the following words: "The CC and the CCC declare that they will cut down with an iron hand every attempt to involve in the internal affairs of the AUCP a bourgeois intellectual crew like the Shcherbakovs and the Tverskois and the military putschists who hang onto their coattails and strive to overthrow the regime of the proletarian dictatorship."

These words leave no room for any doubts: The Opposition is accused of seeking to involve not only bourgeois intellectuals but also the military conspirators who hang onto their coattails in the internal affairs of the AUCP. Consequently the Opposition is seeking to involve military conspirators in the internal affairs of the AUCP. This was written on September 27, in connection with the discovery of the Opposition press. But on September 29, this same presidium of the CCC, which had endorsed the foregoing words, announced to the accused Communists that Tverskoi and his testimony, as well as the case concerning the coup in general, had no connection whatever with the case relating to the Opposition press. If that is so, what is the meaning of the signature of the presidium of the CCC, which was appended to the communications transmitted to all the members and candidates of the CC and the CCC of the party and the presidium of the Executive Committee of the Comintern and all the province, region, and district committees and control commissions of the party?

From what has been said up to now, the following questions arise:

1. When Comrade Yaroslavsky reported (September 15) to the Secretariat of the CCC "concerning the participation of members

of the AUCP(B) in the activities of an illegal counter-revolutionary organization," did he or did he not at the time know that the Wrangel officer—this only "link" between the Opposition press and the military conspiracy—was an agent of the GPU?

2. If Comrade Yaroslavsky was not aware of this, it implies that the GPU had misled him. Then it is necessary to establish who were the guilty ones on the staff of the GPU, and to hand them over to prosecution.

3. If Comrade Yaroslavsky did know, why did he fail to inform the Secretariat, which in its decision found that "the GPU had acted correctly"? Did Comrade Yaroslavsky mislead the Secretariat or, as we have already said, was he himself misled by the GPU?

4. When did the Political Bureau and the presidium of the CCC first find out the truth about the "Wrangel officer"? Was it when the first communication was made public or when the second communication of the GPU was received in answer to the direct inquiry of comrades Zinoviev, Smilga, and Peterson?

The significance of these questions is self-evident. The communication of the CC and the CCC deceived the party on the question of the supposed connection between the Opposition and the military conspiracy. The party is not free from the influence of this deception even now. On the contrary, the widening circles of deceit are spreading further and further in the country, and becoming cruder and cruder. Who played the active and conscious role in perpetrating this trickery? Who was involved in it because of blind factionalism? Who acted out of carelessness or slovenliness? And finally, who is the actual organizer and instigator of the fraud? Complete and unconditional clarity is needed on these questions. Without this clarity it is impossible to have honest preparation for the Fifteenth Party Congress.

II. The Military Conspiracy Case

Inside the party and far beyond its bounds a vile myth has thus been set in circulation, in two editions—a first and a second—concerning the Opposition's alleged attempts to "involve in the internal affairs of the AUCP military putschists striving to overthrow the regime of the proletarian dictatorship."

Who are these putschists? What is this military conspiracy? During the session of the presidium of the CCC we were told that this military conspiracy has no connection whatever with the

Opposition press. We were told by the GPU that matters relating to the military conspiracy were still in process of investigation. Nothing is left us except to hope that the conspiracy will be exposed and those implicated fittingly punished.

However, even at this stage we cannot pass over the question of the military conspiracy in silence—and not only because an attempt was made to implicate Communists in this matter through the medium of a fictitious "illegal Shcherbakov-Tverskoi organization," which was built upon a single Wrangel officer who turned out to be an agent of the GPU. Above we dealt with this aspect of the case as briefly as possible, leaving aside many details, each of which deserves separate treatment. But there is another aspect to the "case" that is no less instructive, one which sheds some light upon the future.

We have already been told by the GPU that in addition to Shcherbakov, there was another participant in the illegal counterrevolutionary organization—one Tverskoi, the same individual who had informed the GPU agent about "the organization of a military coup in the USSR *in the near future*." The gravity of this information requires no comment. The same communication from the GPU of September 13 reads: "The testimony of the arrested nonparty men has confirmed the existence of a group which sets as its aim the organization of the above-mentioned military conspiracy."

Thus Tverskoi's information had been confirmed. What did Tverskoi's information consist of? It is available in documents which the GPU handed over to the CCC. It is true that the presidium of the CCC has refused to make this information public, since it has absolutely no connection with the case. But on the other hand, we were indeed told by the same presidium that those conspirators about whom Tverskoi had informed were being involved by the Opposition in internal party questions. From the GPU we have learned that involved in the Shcherbakov-Tverskoi organization are Griunshtein, Gerdovsky, Mrachkovsky, Okhotnikov, and others. All this sufficiently justifies our interest in Tverskoi's report. We append the main portion of Tverskoi's statement, putting initials in place of proper names in order to confine ourselves only to those names which are already given in the communications of the CC and the CCC. Here is what Tverskoi reported:

"Citizeness N. related to me under a vow of great secrecy a conversation she had had with M. M. told her that there was a movement in military circles headed by Comrades Trotsky and

Kamenev, obviously a military movement, and that this organization is active. No mention was made that this organization intended to carry out a coup, but that was understood. From my conversation with N., I concluded that the Opposition was involved here, but when I asked her about it, she said that this was not entirely the case, although Trotsky and Kamenev were participating. From this I concluded that the organization has its own independent character. No mention was made that M. himself belonged to the organization, but this was also clear from the entire conversation."

Such was Tverskoi's information on the question of the "organization of a military coup in the USSR in the near future." We shall not here bring in the testimony of Citizeness N. and Citizen M., inasmuch as this testimony adds nothing new except for Citizen M.'s reference to the fact that the information concerning the conspiracy was supplied him by an individual who happened to be very far away from Moscow. Neither Tverskoi nor N. nor M. knew anything about the conspiracy at first hand. Tverskoi gets his information from N., N. from M., and M. from the above-mentioned and absent witness. The most concrete picture of the conspiracy is given by Tverskoi, insofar, at any rate, as he says that at the head of this conspiracy are Trotsky and Kamenev. According to the categorical statement of the chairman of the GPU, Menzhinsky, with whom Comrades Yevdokimov, Zinoviev, Smilga, and Trotsky had a conversation on this subject, there is no other material available concerning this military conspiracy case as yet. It was this information and only this information that confirmed, in the GPU's opinion, not only the existence of a group whose aim is the aforementioned "military conspiracy," but also the participation in this group of "a number of party members" (Griunshtein, Gerdovsky, Mrachkovsky, Okhotnikov, and others).

Both Shcherbakov and Tverskoi were arrested on the night of September 12-13. The very next morning, on September 13, the GPU was already writing to the CCC about the preparation of "a military coup in the USSR in the near future"; about the "illegal Shcherbakov-Tverskoi organization"; and about party members who "as the search revealed were directly connected with the illegal Shcherbakov-Tverskoi organization." However, as it appears from the documents, the only party member implicated in the "organization of the military coup in the USSR in the near future," and indicated by name is—Comrade Trotsky.

To our inquiry directed to Comrade Menzhinsky as to why he,

who placed such extraordinary significance upon Tverskoi's report, had failed to inform Comrade Trotsky about it, Menzhinsky replied that he could "not recall" if Trotsky's name was mentioned in these reports. Let us recall that the first communication of the GPU came on September 13; the second on September 27, while the conversation took place on September 28. Comrade Yagoda, who was present during the conversation, explained that when an investigation points toward the implication of party members in a case, the related documents are transmitted to the CCC. This was done in this case too. As a matter of fact, as we already know, the statements of Tverskoi, Citizeness N., and Citizen M., concerning the military conspiracy, were included by the CCC in that very volume of documents which deals with the Opposition press. The CCC in its turn also failed to communicate in any way whatever with Comrade Trotsky. Comrade Yevdokimov accidentally became acquainted with these documents and then called them to the attention of Comrade Trotsky and other Opposition members of the CC.

What does all this mean? For the time being we refrain from making any political comments.

III. The Necessary Conclusions

We move that a joint session of the Political Bureau and the presidium of the CCC be immediately called in order to draw up a new and a third communication to the party which must refute the false assertion contained in the first two communications. In other words, we move that the party be informed and that a categorical explanation be made to the party, with the greatest possible clarity and precision, concerning the decision reached by the presidium of the CCC, in which it refused to make Tverskoi's report public—the decision that the case relating to the Opposition press and the case of the so-called military conspiracy have nothing in common.

We move that the entire party be informed that it was misled by the first two communications of the Political Bureau and the presidium of the CCC.

We move that a special commission of the CC and the CCC, in which Opposition members of these bodies participate, be established to investigate this entire matter from beginning to end, to establish the guilty parties and bring them to account as soon as possible.

Only the hope that the Political Bureau and the presidium of the CCC will satisfy our most lawful and elementary demands makes it possible for us not to give here the appropriate *political evaluation* of the facts and circumstances written down above.

We insistently urge that arrangements be made by phone to have such a session called today.

G. Yevdokimov	I. Bakaev
G. Zinoviev	L. Trotsky
I. Smilga	

THE SEVEN-HOUR DAY

October 10, 1927

NOTE: The Opposition Platform had complained of increased intensity of labor, and a tendency to lengthen the workday beyond the statutory eight hours. Fearful that the Opposition's demands would strike a responsive chord among the workers, the party leadership tried a maneuver. On October 12, in a speech to the Moscow provincial trade union congress, Bukharin spoke of a "slow but sure transition to a shorter working day," and specifically the seven-hour day and five-day week, at the same time calling for higher productivity of labor. Ironically, it was Bukharin who, at the Fifteenth Conference in October-November 1927, had sneered at the proposal for a seven-hour day, branding it demagogy worthy of Mensheviks or Social Democrats.

In any event, the slogan received little publicity until it was incorporated into the party manifesto for the tenth anniversary celebrations of the October Revolution. A draft of the manifesto was submitted to the party fraction of the Russian delegation to the Central Executive Committee of the USSR session on October 15. Evidently, in some industries, the reduction of working hours was at least partly intended to facilitate going over to three shifts, and thus to increase output and decrease unemployment. But the main purpose was certainly to outflank the Opposition; and to do it by surprise (although Trotsky had evidently found out about this proposal in advance). Trotsky and Zinoviev both protested to the CEC party fraction, but the draft was nevertheless submitted to the CEC, where it was carried unanimously and without discussion.

*According to Isaac Deutscher (*The Prophet Unarmed, *p. 363n), the seven-hour day, five-day week were nominally in effect for thirteen years, but they were not honored in practice. At the start of World War II, the workweek was returned to a "normal" six days, eight hours. These were obligatory for nearly twenty years. In 1958 a gradual return to the seven-hour day (but not five-day week) was initiated.*

By permission of the Harvard College Library. The text has been slightly abridged for reasons of space.

1. A few weeks before the celebration of the revolution's tenth anniversary, the party learned that the Politburo had decided to add to the already prepared manifesto a point "on shortening the workday in industry to seven hours."

Did anyone expect such a reform? Did the party think this over? Did the party hear even a hint of such a measure two weeks ago?

No. And once again policies take the form of surprises, unexpected developments which catch the party unaware. . . .

2. What in fact is the meaning of this measure proclaimed by the Politburo? If this is a temporary shortening of the workday for the purpose of combating the severe unemployment, if this reform is to be understood in that way, it is not an improvement in the position of the workers, but a case of spreading the burden of unemployment among the working class as a whole. Capitalist states have resorted to such measures more than once in the past, by introducing short workweeks and so on. The necessity to resort to such a serious and burdensome reorganization of the production process could be dictated only by a situation in which the growth of unemployment was unavoidable for an indefinitely long period. It is clear that a "reform" of this kind would be nothing to celebrate. But the decree of the Politburo says nothing like this. It has in mind not a temporary shortening of the workday, but a planned transition from the eight-hour day to the seven-hour day throughout industry.

3. An actual introduction of the seven-hour day "with no reduction in pay," as the Politburo resolution states, means an increase in pay rates for a given amount of work and in general a very substantial rise in wages, amounting to several hundred million. Yet only yesterday the Opposition's pointing to the necessity for a more systematic raising of wages was called demagogy and met with nothing but objections. "Where would we find the means?" All the proceedings of the Central Committee, all the "study outlines," all the writings of the Bukharin-Slepkov school have turned on this single argument: "Demagogy! Where would we get the resources?"

Now it seems that the resources exist for a transition to the seven-hour day "with no reduction in pay." This surprising fact constitutes a ruthless condemnation of the baiting campaign waged against the Opposition on the labor question. Every party member and every worker in general knows that such a surprising promise as the seven-hour day would never have appeared in any manifesto by any manner of means if the Opposition had not fought so stubbornly and insistently during the whole preceding period against the indifferent, careless, inattentive, and "unbusinesslike" attitude toward the needs and requirements of the working class.

4. Who in fact are the demagogues? The ones who uphold the idea that socialist construction presupposes the systematic improvement of the workers' conditions in all spheres, based on the fact that expenditures in this area are recovered not only politically but also in production? Or are the demagogues the ones who on "normal days" consider it acceptable to carry out the "regime of economy," rationalization, and industrialization at the expense of the workers—and on holidays and anniversary celebrations suddenly announce without the slightest preparation the introduction of the seven-hour day?

5. The Platform of the Bolshevik-Leninists (Opposition) demands the following: "Cut off at the root every inclination to lengthen the eight-hour day. Permit overtime only when absolutely unavoidable. Allow no abuses in the employment of occasional workers; no treating of full-time workers as 'seasonal.' Cancel every lengthening of the workday in unhealthy trades where it has been introduced in violation of earlier rules" [see p. 318].

At first glance this sounds much more modest than the great anniversary leap from the eight-hour to the seven-hour day. But party members will inevitably ask themselves: "How did it happen that the Labor Code kept getting worse over the past few years, especially in regard to the length of the workday, while suddenly today, without the slightest preparation, a leap is made over all the constantly worsening versions of the Labor Code, over all the lengthenings of the workday, over all the abuses in the employment of occasional workers, etc., etc., a leap across those things directly to the seven-hour day? Can this reform be taken seriously? Can we have any confidence in it at all?"

6. To this fundamental question an answer is contained in the following sentences in the Politburo resolution:

"In regard to industrial workers in production . . . it is necessary to ensure, during the coming years, a transition from the eight-hour day to the seven-hour day with no reduction in pay."

For this it is necessary "to begin no later than within a year the gradual implementation of this resolution in regard to certain categories of workers in accordance with the resources of the country, the pace of the reequipment and rationalization of the plants and factories, the growth of labor productivity, and the obsolescence of certain jobs."

Presented in this way, the announcement of the reform is only a vague promise on a holiday occasion—and nothing more. The ABCs of socialism say that a workers' state can make a transition from an eight-hour day, not to a nine-hour day, but to a seven- or a six-hour day, depending on the growth of technology and the productivity of labor. The anniversary promise says that such a transition (from the eight- to the seven-hour day) should be accomplished "during the coming years." What does that mean? During the next five years? Eight years? Ten years?

The State Planning Commission's five-year plan, like the five-year plan of the Supreme Council of the National Economy, and all the other long-term industrial plans so far, have absolutely never included in their calculations a shift from the eight-hour to the seven-hour day. The five-year plans show clearly that there never was any discussion anywhere until now of such a switchover. This means that the economic planning agencies until now have never once even thought about exactly how many years it would be before a switchover from the eight-hour to the seven-hour day was possible. On the contrary the thinking of the economic management agencies has moved in the direction of worsening the Labor Code, not making it better.

7. Thus under the title of "shortening the workday" we have nothing but vague platitudes which in essence amount to a purely adventuristic promise that leaps off the pages of the manifesto to surprise and shock in equal measure not only the workers but the trade union officials, economic managers, peasants, and consumers in general. The anniversary reform provokes great apprehension in the minds of consumers in regard to prices—especially because the entire press up until now has cried out in one voice that wages have held too large a place in production costs. The sudden reform arouses great expectations among the workers, but as events take their course, these expectations will be disappointed. The political result of this anniversary surprise will prove to be exactly the opposite of what the authors of the so-called reform intended. What they care about are not the tremendously important economic and cultural questions involved, but merely "barring the way" to the Opposition for a month and a half until the party congress. Thus the reform now being announced is a devastating comment on the whole line of the present leadership.

8. Does this mean that a shift from the eight-hour to the seven-hour day is impossible in the next few years? No, it does not. The general course we chart should be aimed precisely in that direction. But this should be an overall policy direction and not one of zigzags and adventures. The question of the possibility of a shift to the seven-hour day and the time needed for such a shift is a question involving all of our economic policies together, above all the rate of industrialization of the country. What is needed is not an anniversary "cheer" but a change in the entire policy of economic leadership, first and foremost on questions affecting the material conditions of the workers.

In order to guide the thinking of the party and the Soviet state in the proper direction on this question we must carry out with a firm hand those measures which are indicated in the Platform of the Opposition. Above all it is necessary on the tenth anniversary of the October Revolution to restore the October Code of Labor Laws, beginning with the genuine assurance of a genuine eight-hour day.

RECOGNITION OF
THE TSARIST DEBTS

October 12, 1927

NOTE: Relations with France had been deteriorating ever since May 1927, when Britain broke relations with Soviet Russia. Negotiations over French investment credits and the payment of tsarist debts had become less and less promising until, in June 1927, the French government firmly refused to reopen such negotiations. There was some fear that the French would follow the British example and sever relations.

The situation was complicated by the fact that Soviet Ambassador Rakovsky was an Oppositionist. When Rakovsky signed the Statement of the Thirteen on August 8, 1927, calling for workers and soldiers in the capitalist countries to defeat their own governments in any war with the Soviet Union, the French government raised a hue and cry and demanded Rakovsky's recall. The demand was intensified in September, and it was apparently in an effort to mollify the French that the Soviet government offered improved terms for a settlement on credits and debt payments. This offer was turned down, however, and Rakovsky returned to Moscow in mid-October.

By permission of the Harvard College Library. The text has been abridged for reasons of space.

. . . . 4. There can be no question of recognizing the debts of the tsarist monarchy in principle. The annulment of those debts was one of the most important conquests of the October Revolution. This annulment made it possible to reach the present level of economic development on the basis of our internal resources. Recognition of the debts would be a crushing blow to socialist construction and the proletarian dictatorship, since it would lead to an abrupt worsening of the material conditions of the industrial workers and of working people in general, an even greater delay in our already slow industrialization, and a menacing growth in the power of foreign capital within our economy. All of this would mean, given other difficulties, the strangulation of the socialist revolution in the near future and our country's enslavement to foreign capital. Economic defeat of the workers' state would become one of the most important factors in the stabilization of world capitalism.

5. Individual, practical agreements on the debts, based on the principle of mutual benefits, are permissible, however. Remaining completely on the basis of the decree of January 28, 1918, certain strictly limited portions of the old debts can be recognized on the condition that appropriate economic or political benefits are granted us in return, in the form of new credits, agreement not to participate in any military bloc against us, and so on and so forth.

However, since such partial agreements imply such great responsibility and are of such tremendous importance, it is necessary to analyze the circumstances and terms of each such agreement with total clarity.

In the spring and summer of last year (1926) negotiations were held on partial recognition of the debts on our part in exchange for the granting of new credits by France. Our position in these negotiations was rather favorable. France had not yet managed to deal with the consequences of its inflation. England was paralyzed by the miners' strike. In China the Northern March had begun. In expectation of a good harvest the Soviet Union had increased its pace of economic construction. Pressed by its contradictions with England and by the intensifying Serbo-Italian conflict over Albania, the French government wanted an agreement and urged us to make haste. If the Politburo had placed its bets on its French card, it could at that moment have gotten an agreement on terms highly favorable to us.

Not only was the occasion missed; everything possible was done to land us in the present exceptionally difficult situation. Our international policy during this period was a typically petty-bourgeois policy, that is, a series of vacillations between overconfidence—when the situation shaped up more favorably—and readiness to make impermissible concessions, when bourgeois pressure was intensified.

6. The first half of 1926 was an especially flourishing time for the petty-bourgeois theory of socialism in one country.

This theory, representing the distorted reflection in the minds of Stalin and Bukharin of the economic recovery period, played a fatal role not only in regard to economic plans and perspectives but also in our negotiations with France. Disregard for our world economic ties and our economy's dependence on the world market, the Bukharin theory of the snail's pace, the assurance that we were already nine-tenths of the way through building socialism, the baiting of the Opposition for its "pessimism" and "lack of faith"—all this blended into a typical melange of petty-bourgeois overconfidence, shot through with provincial narrow-mindedness: the "world market," they said, is irrelevant; we don't need credits; we'll get by on our own, etc., etc. In fact, if the main danger was that of "industry running too far ahead" and the "superindustrialism of the Opposition," why even bother to seek agreements, credit, and an inflow of technology from the rest of the world? Proceeding from this fundamentally wrong position, at the heart of which lies petty-bourgeois national narrow-mindedness, the Stalinist leadership in effect broke off negotiations with France at the moment most favorable for reaching an agreement. . . .

8. The defeat of the revolution in China, the weakening of the Comintern, the bankruptcy of the Anglo-Russian Committee, the break with Britain, and the immediate threat of war—that was the situation in 1927 when the Politburo undertook its super-hasty, exceptional measures to revive the negotiations with France. Under these conditions our hasty willingness to move toward concessions, in the eyes of the French bourgeoisie, appeared to be simply an expression of unsureness, shortsighted-ness, and weakness on the part of our leadership. The position of our delegation in the talks was bound to worsen abruptly. The heart of the matter is that France is now demanding our recognition of a very substantial portion of the tsarist debts in return for nothing more than maintaining diplomatic relations with us. The French government has separated the question of the debts from that of credits. The correlation between our debt obligations and possible credits now shapes up in immeasurably less favorable terms than were possible in 1926. Such a proposition is unacceptable to us. We must therefore say clearly, *"We are against this particular agreement."* . . .

12. In the event that it is necessary to accept one or another agreement, which will impose new sacrifices on the land of the Soviets, a question of tremendous importance arises: *Who will pay?*—that is, the question of our wage policy, our tax policy, and our overall policy course toward the kulak and poor peasant. Maneuverist concessions to the world bourgeoisie require not only a correct world policy but also a revolutionary class policy at home.

The possibility for maneuvering effectively presupposes an

active and cohesive party controlling its own institutions. We cannot "buy off" the bourgeoisie by paying millions and at the same time poison our own party with slander about the alleged ties of its left wing with a Wrangel officer and a military conspiracy. Such policies can only bring defeat. This is confirmed once again by the course of the negotiations with France. While rejecting untimely concessions, which can only lead to an intensification of pressure against us, we at the same time reject and condemn the policy that has led us to new international defeats.

G. Zinoviev, L. Trotsky, I. Smilga, G. Yevdokimov

THE FEAR OF OUR PLATFORM

October 23, 1927

NOTE: On October 17, during the same session of the Central Executive Committee that had approved the seven-hour day proposal, a demonstration was held in Leningrad to honor the CEC meeting. Whether intentionally or otherwise is not known, but the Opposition leaders found themselves on a separate reviewing stand from the other party leaders. The ranks of demonstrators, having passed the official reviewing stands, recognized the Opposition leaders and waved, gesticulated, and milled around, blocking traffic around the Oppositionists' stand and leaving only empty pavement around the officialdom. Amid these throngs, the usual police and gangster efforts proved useless. In the end, the officials moved over to the Oppositionists' platform.

The Zinovievists saw this spontaneous demonstration as a sign that the workers were with the Opposition. Trotsky viewed it more as a token of passive sympathy, and anticipated that it would goad the Stalinists into speeding up the destruction of the Opposition. In this he proved correct. At the meeting of the Central Committee of October 23, Stalin renewed his demand for the expulsion of Zinoviev and Trotsky, this time more insistently.

The meeting was marked by a level of violence that was unprecedented up to that time. Books and water glasses were thrown at Trotsky and his speech was interrupted by frenzied heckling 'among the jeers that may bewilder readers are the charges that he was mouthing the political line of Sotsialisti-chesky Vestnik, *a Menshevik emigré journal, or* Rul, *a Cadet emigré journal). Trotsky, undeterred, continued to read the prepared text of his speech. Unable to silence him, the meeting finally adjourned even as he was speaking. Afterwards, the CC unanimously approved a motion limiting the Opposition's rights to publishing countertheses to the official theses (thus effectively barring publication of the Platform) and a motion expelling Trotsky and Zinoviev from the CC.*

Trotsky later charged that the physical violence and heckling

*that characterized this meeting were intended as a model for
other party meetings to follow.*

*Fragments from the first half of this speech at the Central
Committee plenum were published in* Pravda *on November 2. The
full text, as prepared by Trotsky, was translated by Max Eastman and published in* The Real Situation in Russia. *The present
translation is by Naomi Allen, from the French version in the
Oppositionist journal* Contre le Courant, *November 20, 1927. It
has been corrected against the Russian. The editors have decided
to use the full text of the proceedings to the extent that it was
available, including the interruptions from the floor, because it
documents the crude and violent methods of the Stalinists better
than any description could.*

Trotsky: My motion to consider separately the question of the
Wrangel officer and the military conspiracy has been voted down.

Skvortsov-Stepanov: Again! Shame!

Trotsky: I raised the fundamental question why, how, and by
whom the party was deceived when it was told that Communists
of the Opposition participated in a counterrevolutionary organization. In order to show once more what you mean by a
discussion, you decreed that my short speech on the purported
Wrangel officer should be expunged from the record—that is,
hidden from the party. Bukharin has presented us here with the
philosophy of a Thermidorian amalgam on the basis of these
documents of the GPU, which have nothing whatever to do either
with the printshop or with the Opposition.

Skrypnik: And now, Shcherbakov. Not bad!

Trotsky: What we need is not Bukharin's cheap philosophy . . .

Unshlicht: But Trotsky's philosophy!

Trotsky: . . . but facts. There are no facts.

Skrypnik: And Shcherbakov?

Trotsky: Therefore the insertion of this whole question into the
discussion about the Opposition was a trick. Rudeness and
disloyalty have grown to the dimensions of criminal betrayal. All
the documents read by Menzhinsky speak unequivocally against
the present political course—it is only necessary to illumine them
with a Marxian analysis. But I have no time for that. I can only
raise the fundamental question: How and why the present ruling
faction [*Interruptions.*] . . . found it necessary to deceive the
party, passing off an agent of the GPU for a Wrangel officer and
disclosing these fragments of an unfinished investigation, in
order to alarm the party with a false communication about the

participation of Oppositionists in a counterrevolutionary organization. Where does this come from? Where does it lead? Only that question has political meaning. The rest is of second- and even tenth-rate importance.

Chubar: Of first-rate importance is the duplicating machine.

Trotsky: First, however, two words on so-called "Trotskyism." Every opportunist is trying to cover his nakedness with that word. The falsification factory is working night and day on three shifts to manufacture "Trotskyism." I wrote a letter on this theme not long ago to the Bureau of Party History, containing about fifty quotations and documents convicting the present ruling theoretical and historical school of fabrications, distortions, hiding of facts and documents, perversions of Lenin—all for the purpose of the so-called struggle against "Trotskyism."* I demanded that my letter be sent to members of the joint plenum. This was not done, although the letter consists almost entirely of documents and citations. I will send it to the *Discussion Bulletin* of *Pravda*. I think they too will hide it from the party, for the facts and documents I cite are too deadly to the Stalin school.

In our July declaration of last year, we predicted with complete accuracy all the stages through which the destruction of the Leninist leadership of the party would go, and its temporary replacement by a Stalinist leadership.

Skrypnik: In other words, you made plans for your leadership?

Trotsky: I say *temporary* replacement, because the more "victories" the present ruling group wins, the weaker it will be. We can now supplement our July prediction of last year with the following conclusion: the present organizational victory of Stalin precedes his political shipwreck. It is absolutely unavoidable, . . .

Chubar: That's straight from *Sotsialistichesky Vestnik*.

Trotsky: . . . and—given the Stalin regime—will begin at once. The basic task of the Opposition will be to see that the consequences of the ruinous policies of the present leadership bring as little loss as possible to the party and its links with the masses.

You want to expel us from the Central Committee. We recognize that this step is in full accord with the present policy at the present stage of its development, or, rather, of its degeneration. This ruling faction, which is expelling from the party hundreds and thousands of its best members, its unwavering worker-

---

*Trotsky's "Letter to the Bureau of Party History" is in *The Stalin School of Falsification*, p. 1.

Bolsheviks—this bureaucratic clique which dares to expel such Bolsheviks as Mrachkovsky, Serebryakov, Preobrazhensky, Sharov, Sarkis, and Vujović, comrades who could alone create a party Secretariat infinitely more authoritative, abler, infinitely more Leninist . . . [*Uproar in the hall.*]

Voroshilov: That's the Secretariat, your party.

Petrovsky: A Menshevik speech!

Trotsky: . . . than our present Secretariat [*Uproar.*]—this Stalin-Bukharin clique, which has locked up in the inner prison of the GPU devoted and admirable men like Nechaev, Shtikgold, Vasilev, Shmidt, Fishelev, and many other—this group of officials, holding its place on top of the party by violence, by strangulation of the party's thought, by disorganization of the proletarian vanguard not only in the USSR but throughout the world—this thoroughly opportunistic faction, at whose tail are marching in recent years the Chiang Kai-sheks, the Feng Yü-hsiangs, the Wang Ching-weis, the Purcells, Hicks, Ben Tilletts, Kuusinens, Smerals [*Uproar.*], Peppers, Heinz Neumans, Rafeses, Martynovs, Kondratievs, and Ustryalovs . . .

Petrovsky: A disgusting speech, a Menshevik speech—it's truly horrible!

Skrypnik: What infamies you are speaking, Trotsky!

Voroshilov: That is the amalgam.

Trotsky: —this faction cannot endure our presence in the Central Committee even one month before the party congress. We understand this.

Rudeness and disloyalty go hand in hand with cowardice. You have hidden our Platform—or, rather, you have tried to hide it. [*Uproar.*]

Babushkin: It's you that should be hidden.

Skrypnik: What good does it do to listen to him? It's just one long insult to the CC!

Goloshchekin: He's having a good time!

Trotsky: [*His words are lost in the uproar and among the shouts of protest.*] What does fear of a platform mean? Everybody knows: *fear of a platform is fear of the masses.*

We announced to you on September 8 that in spite of all decrees to the contrary, we would bring our Platform to the attention of the party. We have undertaken this, and we will carry the work through to the end. Comrades Mrachkovsky, Fishelev, and all the others who printed and distributed our Platform, have acted and are acting in full solidarity with us. As Oppositional members of the Central Committee and the Central Control Commission, we take full responsibility, both political and organizational, for their acts. [*Uproar.*]

Lomov: And Shcherbakov, is he also in solidarity with you?

Trotsky: The rudeness and disloyalty of which Lenin wrote are no longer mere personal characteristics. They have become the character of the ruling faction, both of its political policy and of its organizational regime. It is no longer a question of external manners. The fundamental character of our present leadership is its belief in the omnipotence of methods of violence—even in dealing with its own party. [*Uproar.*]

Babushkin: He reads *Sotsialistichesky Vestnik*. A petty bourgeois in the proletarian state!

Skrypnik: Another article from *Sotsialistichesky Vestnik!*

Trotsky: [*Exclamations: Menshevik!*] From the October Revolution our party inherited a mighty apparatus of compulsion, without which the dictatorship of the proletariat is unthinkable. The focal point of this dictatorship is the Central Committee of our party. [*Uproar.*] In Lenin's time—with a Leninist Central Committee—the organizational apparatus of the party was subordinate to a revolutionary class policy on an international scale. It is true that Stalin inspired Lenin with apprehension from the very day of his election as general secretary. "This cook will serve only spicy dishes"—thus Lenin spoke to his close comrades at the time of the Eleventh Congress. [*Uproar. Exclamations: Menshevik! That's enough!*] But with Lenin's leadership, with a Leninist staff in the Politburo, the General Secretariat played a completely subordinate role. [*Uproar.*] The situation began to change from the hour that Lenin fell sick. The selection of personnel through the Secretariat, the grouping of Stalinists in official positions, became an independent operation entirely unrelated to our political policy. That is why Lenin, weighing the prospect of his departure, gave the party his last counsel: Remove Stalin, who may carry the party to a split and to ruin. [*Uproar.*]

Skvortsov-Stepanov: An old slander!

Talberg: What a gossip; what a scandal-monger! [*Exclamations: Shame!*] And you have a correct political line, I suppose?

Skrypnik: Until his fall! What nerve!

Petrovsky: [*Exclamations: It's a lie!*] You are a contemptible Menshevik!

Kalinin: Petty-bourgeois radical!

Trotsky: [*His words are drowned out by the noise and shouting. A voice: Martov!*] The party did not know about this counsel in time. A selected apparatus concealed his letter. We can all now

see the full consequences. [*Uproar.*] The ruling faction thinks
that with the help of violence it can accomplish everything.

A voice: It's from *Sotsialistichesky Vestnik.*

Trotsky: That is a profound error. Violence can play an
enormous revolutionary role, but only under one condition—that
it is subordinated to a true class policy. [*Uproar.*] The violence of
the Bolsheviks against the bourgeoisie, against the Mensheviks,
against the Social Revolutionaries, employed under definite
historical conditions, gave gigantic results. The violence of
Kerensky and Tseretelli against the Bolsheviks only hastened the
defeat of the compromisers' regime. By banishing, and arresting,
and depriving of employment, the ruling faction is employing
both knife and bribe against its own party. [*Uproar.*]

Kris: Get down! What nerve! Menshevik! Traitor! We don't have
to listen to this! What a slander against the Central Committee!

Trotsky: The worker-member is afraid to say what he thinks in
his own cell. He is afraid to vote according to his conscience. A
dictatorship of the apparatus [*Uproar.*] is terrorizing our party,
which is supposed to be the highest expression of the proletarian
dictatorship. In terrorizing the party, the ruling faction . . .

Kris: Get down! Liar!

Lomov: Very cunning, but empty of substance. [*Uproar.*]

Trotsky: . . . is diminishing its ability to hold in fear the
enemies of the proletariat.

But an organizational regime does not live an independent life.
In the party regime, the whole political line of the party leadership finds its expression. This political line has swerved of late
years—its class core and momentum have swerved from left to
right, from the proletarian to the petty bourgeois, from the worker
to the specialist, from the rank-and-file party member to the
functionary, from the farmhand and the poor peasant to the
kulak, from the Shanghai worker to Chiang Kai-shek, from the
Chinese peasant to the bourgeois generals, from the English
proletarian to Purcell, Hicks, and the General Council, etc. In
that lies the essence of Stalinism.

Voroshilov: They say it better in *Rul,* old man.

Trotsky: At first glance it seems as if the Stalin course were
completely victorious. The Stalin faction seems to deal its blows
to the left (in Moscow and Leningrad) and to the right (in the
Northern Caucasus). But in reality the whole policy of this
centrist faction is itself going forward under the blows of two
whips—one from the right and one from the left. [*Uproar.*] This
bureaucratic centrist faction, lacking all class basis, staggers

between two class lines, . . . [*A voice: Liar! Get down!*] . . . systematically sliding away from the proletarian to the petty-bourgeois course. It does not slide away in a direct line, but in sharp zigzags.

Skrypnik: Menshevik! [*Uproar.*]

Trotsky: . . . We have had plenty of these zigzags in the past. Especially sharp and memorable was the broadening of electoral rights under pressure from the kulak (a blow of the whip from the right) [*Uproar.*] and then the annulment of these instructions under pressure from the Opposition (a blow from the left). [*Uproar.*] We have had plenty of these zigzags in the sphere of labor legislation, wage policy, tax policy, policy toward the private capitalist, etc., etc. But the general course has been steadily shifting to the right. The recent manifesto is an unquestionable zigzag to the left. But we are not going to shut our eyes for one minute to the fact that this is only a zigzag . . .

Yaroslavsky: And a funeral mass for the peace of Trotsky's soul!

A voice: A funeral dirge!

Trotsky: . . . which does not in the least change the general course of the policy, and that it will, as a matter of fact—and in the very near future—hasten the drift of the ruling center toward the right.

A voice: Scoundrel! Menshevik! [*Uproar.*]

Trotsky: Today's shouting about *"forced pressure" on the kulak*—that same kulak to whom yesterday they were shouting "Enrich yourselves!"—cannot change the general line. Anniversary celebration surprises, such as a seven-hour workday, cannot change it either. [*Shouts, whistling.*] The political line of the present leadership is not defined by these individual adventuristic gestures . . .

Chubar: There could be no greater adventurism than yours.

Skrypnik: Menshevik! Get out of the party!

Trotsky: . . . but by the social support which this leadership has gathered around itself in its struggle against the Opposition. Through the Stalin apparatus, through the Stalinist regime, the forces that are pressing down on the proletarian vanguard . . . [*The noise grows louder, until Trotsky's words are barely audible.*] . . . are the bureaucrat, including the workers' bureaucrat, . . . [*Louder shouting and whistling.*] . . . the industrial manager, the small proprietor, the new private capitalist, the privileged intelligentsia of the town and countryside . . .

Voroshilov: Zinoviev, listen to this disgrace!

Skrypnik: The CC podium is not the place for these abominations!

Skvortsov-Stepanov: It's Dan, making the rounds!

Trotsky: —all these elements who are beginning to point out the kulak to the worker and say, "Remember, this is not 1918!"

It is not the left gesture that is decisive, but the fundamental political course. The selection of your supporters is decisive. The personnel is decisive. Where your social support comes from is decisive. You cannot strangle the workers' cells and at the same time attack the kulak. The two things are incompatible. [*Uproar, renewed whistling. Voices: Gravedigger of the revolution! Shame! Get down, scum! Down with the renegade!*]

Trotsky: Your left anniversary zigzag, as soon as it begins to be carried out, will run into violent opposition in the ranks of your own majority. Today, "Enrich yourselves!" and tomorrow, "Down with the kulak!" . . .

Voroshilov: That's enough! Shame!

[*Renewed whistling. Tumultuous noise. Nothing can be heard. The chairman rings for order. Voices cry: "Get down from the podium!" The chairman adjourns the meeting. Comrade Trotsky continues reading, but not a single word can be understood. The members of the plenum leave their places and begin to disperse.*]

Trotsky: That is easy for Bukharin. He chooses with his pen, and is ready. He has nothing to lose. But the kulak, the manager, the powerful bureaucrat, the specialist—they see it differently. These people have no taste for sudden jumps at anniversaries. They will have their say.

Comrade Tomsky, who is caught in a worse situation than anybody else, rose in opposition to the present anniversary zigzag. Tomsky has a foreboding of what the workers will ask in the trade unions. He will be the one who has to answer. Tomorrow the workers are going to demand from Tomsky that he at least really stop the drift to the right, seeing that the manifesto announces a course to the left. This will make a struggle within the ruling bloc inevitable. In the right wing of our party there is a small proprietors' tendency and a trade unionist tendency. They work together for a time, as has often happened in the history of the workers' movement. But this anniversary zigzag to the left is driving a wedge between the small proprietors and the trade unionists. The professional bureaucrat, balancing between them, will lose his support.

This anniversary zigzag is, on the one hand, a most undeniable and solemn recognition of the correctness of the Opposition's views on all the fundamental problems of our life, both in the city and in the countryside. On the other hand, it is a political self-disavowal on the part of the ruling faction, a confession of its own bankruptcy. It is a confession in *words* from those impotent to show anything in *deeds*. This anniversary zigzag will not retard but hasten the political bankruptcy of the present course.

The party regime flows inevitably from the whole policy of the leadership. Behind the backs of the apparatus extremists stands the reawakening domestic bourgeoisie. Behind its back, the world bourgeoisie. All these forces press down on the proletarian vanguard, preventing it from lifting its head or opening its mouth. The more the policy of the Central Committee departs from the proletarian class line, the more necessary it becomes to force that policy upon the proletarian vanguard by methods of compulsion from above. That is the root cause of the present intolerable regime in the party.

When Martynov, Smeral, Rafes, and Pepper play the lead in the Chinese revolution, and Mrachkovsky, Serebryakov, Preobrazhensky, Sharov, and Sarkis are expelled from the party for printing and distributing a Bolshevik platform for the coming congress, these facts are not of a mere inner-party character. By no means. These facts are the expression of a changing relative influence of classes.

The *domestic* bourgeoisie brings its pressure to bear, of course, less impudently than the *world* bourgeoisie against the dictatorship of the proletariat and its proletarian vanguard. But these two pressures are closely united and are simultaneously brought to bear. Those elements of the working class and our party who first felt this advancing danger and first spoke of it—that is, the most revolutionary, most steadfast, most farsighted, most uncompromising representatives of the working class struggle—those elements now constitute the ranks of the Opposition. These ranks are growing both within our party and throughout the International.

Facts and events of enormous weight are confirming the position we took. Your repressions are strengthening our ranks, gathering to us the best of the party's "older generation," tempering the youth, and grouping around the Opposition the genuine Bolsheviks among the new generation. The Oppositionists you have expelled from the party are the *best members* of the party. Those who are expelling and arresting them—although still unconscious of it and uncomprehending—are the instruments through which other classes are pressing back the proletariat. In trying to tramp our Platform into the mud, the ruling faction is fulfilling the social command of Ustryalov—of the reviving petty and middle bourgeoisie. In contrast to the politicians of the dying, *old*, emigrant bourgeoisie, Ustryalov, the clever, far-seeing politician of the *new* bourgeoisie, does not aspire to counterrevolution or to any disturbance. He does not want to "jump over stages." The present stage for Ustryalov is the Stalin course. Ustryalov is openly placing his bets on Stalin. Ustryalov is demanding that Stalin put the Opposition out of the way. In expelling and arresting the Oppositionists, in advancing against us this perfectly Thermidorian accusation in regard to a Wrangel officer and a military conspiracy, Stalin is executing the social orders of Ustryalov.

The immediate task that Stalin has set for himself is to split the party, to cut off the Opposition, to accustom the party to the method of physical destruction. Fascist gangs of whistlers, physical violence, throwing of books and stones, the prison bars—here for a moment the Stalin regime has paused in its course. But the road is predestined. Why should the Yaroslavskys, Shverniks, Goloshchekins, and others argue with the Opposition about government statistics, when they can let fly a heavy volume of those statistics at the head of an Oppositionist?* Stalinism finds in this act its most unrestrained expression, going to the point of open gutter violence. And we repeat: These fascist methods are nothing but a blind and unconscious fulfillment of the social commands of other classes. The goal: to cut off the Opposition and physically destroy it.

Voices are already to be heard: "We will expel a thousand, and shoot a hundred, and have peace in the party." These are the voices of pitiable, frightened, and also rabid blind men. This is the voice of Thermidor. The worst elements, perverted with power, blinded with bureaucratic hatred, are preparing for the Thermidor with all their might. For this, they need two parties. But their violence will break to pieces against a correct political course. In devotion to that course the revolutionary courage of the

---

*Yaroslavsky threw a volume of the control figures for the five-year plan at Trotsky while Trotsky was arguing for placing a special point on the agenda about the "Wrangel officer" and the allegation of a military conspiracy, a speech that was deliberately deleted from the stenographic record of the joint plenum. Shvernik threw a book at him under a later point and Kubyak threw a water glass at him from the presiding committee table.

Opposition ranks is standing firm. Stalin will not create two parties. We openly say to the party: The dictatorship of the proletariat is in danger! And we firmly believe that the party, its proletarian nucleus, will hear, will understand, will meet this danger. The party is already deeply stirred. Tomorrow it will be stirred to the bottom.

Behind the few thousand members *in the actual ranks of the Opposition* come a second and a third layer of *those who are loyal to the Opposition,* and behind them a still broader layer of worker-members who have already begun to listen attentively to our voice and are moving to our side. This process cannot be turned back. The nonparty workers have not believed your lies and slanders against us. Their legitimate dissatisfaction at the growth of bureaucratism and repression was clearly expressed by the working class of Leningrad in its demonstration of October 17. The proletariat is for Soviet power, unwaveringly, but it wants a different policy. All these processes are irresistible. The apparatus is powerless against them. The more brutal your repressions become, the stronger will be the authority of the Opposition in the eyes of the rank-and-file party member and the working class in general. For every hundred Oppositionists expelled from the party, a thousand new Oppositionists will spring up within the party. The expelled Oppositionist feels himself a party member and remains one. You can tear the party card by violence out of the hands of the real Bolshevik-Leninist. You can deprive him for a time of his party rights. But he will never renounce his duties to the party. When Yanson asked Comrade Mrachkovsky, at the session of the Central Control Commission, what he would do when he was expelled from the party, Comrade Mrachkovsky answered, "I will pick up the pieces and carry on."

Every Oppositionist will say the same thing. No matter where he is expelled from, the Executive Committee of the Comintern, the Central Committee of the party, or the party. Every one of us is saying with Mrachkovsky, "I will pick up the pieces and carry on."

We stand at the helm of Bolshevism. You will not tear it away from us. We are going to hold it true. You will not cut us off from the party. You will not cut us off from the working class. We are familiar with repressions. We are accustomed to blows. We will not surrender the October Revolution to the politics of Stalin—the entire essence of which is contained in these few words: *Repression of the proletarian nucleus, fraternization with the comprom-*

isers of all countries, capitulation before the world bourgeoisie.

You expel us from the Central Committee one month before the party congress, which you have already converted into a narrow meeting of the Stalin faction! The Fifteenth Congress will appear to be the supreme triumph of your bureaucratic mechanics. In reality it will be the sign of your complete political shipwreck. The *victories* of the Stalin faction are the victories of alien class forces over the proletarian vanguard. The *defeats* of the party led by Stalin are defeats of the proletarian dictatorship. The party already feels this. We will help it to understand. *The Platform of the Opposition is before the party.* After the Fifteenth Congress the Opposition will become immeasurably stronger within the party than it is now. The calendar of the working class and the calendar of the party do not agree with Stalin's bureaucratic calendar. The proletariat thinks slowly, but surely. Our Platform will hasten this process. What is decisive in the last analysis is the political line, and not the bureaucrat's fist.

The Opposition is unconquerable. Expel us today from the Central Committee, as yesterday you expelled Serebryakov and Preobrazhensky from the party, as you arrested Fishelev and others. Our Platform will find its way. The workers of the whole world are already asking themselves in deep alarm: "For what reason, on the tenth anniversary of October, are they expelling and arresting the best fighters of the October Revolution? Whose hand is here? The hand of what class? The class that conquered in October? Or the class that is edging out and undermining the victory of October?"

Even the most backward workers of all countries, aroused by your repressions, will take our Platform in their hands, in order to test the truth of your vile slander about the Wrangel officer and the military conspiracy. Your persecutions, expulsions, arrests, will make our Platform the most popular and the most cherished document of the international workers' movement. Expel us. You will not stop the victory of the Opposition—the victory of the revolutionary unity of our party and the Communist International!

HOW THEY CORRUPT
THE COMMUNIST LEAGUE OF YOUTH
A Letter to a Party Member in the League

October 31, 1927

NOTE: Trotsky's contention that the Central Committee had been setting an example for the rest of the party in the brutality it had shown the Opposition was rapidly substantiated. Opposition speakers were whistled and shouted down at party meetings, prevented from taking the floor, and physically attacked.

The Oppositionists continued collecting signatures on the Platform and also began to turn to secret meetings of workers and students, usually held in workers' homes, to reach an audience the Stalinists were determined to prevent them from reaching. Frequently these meetings were broken up by Stalinist thugs as well. The gangsterism was readily extended to the Communist League of Youth. At a meeting of the Moscow youth organization on October 26, Kamenev and Rakovsky were hooted down when they tried to speak.

By permission of the Harvard College Library.

You belong to the official tendency, although apparently you are wavering on certain questions. You write me that "the Opposition is apparently right on some questions, but then it resorts to antiparty methods of struggle, such as illegal print-shops, etc."

What first catches my attention are your words that the Opposition is "apparently" right on a number of questions. How could you have found that out? From the articles of Bukharin, Slepkov, and Maretsky, who systematically distort the Opposition's views beyond all recognition? Obviously you have read some documents published by the Opposition itself. That is the only way you could have learned that the Opposition is correct on a number of questions. But do you have the right to accuse of us of publishing "illegally" if that is the only way you had a chance

449

to learn the views of the Opposition and to realize that these views are correct?

I accidentally overheard the speeches being broadcast at the anniversary meeting of the Moscow Communist League of Youth several days ago. I will not dwell on the greetings in official jargon and the obsequiously grateful responses. Here there was not one living thought! Comrade Ter-Vaganyan tried to make a few extremely modest and cautious observations in his speech. Pointing to the tremendous historic work accomplished by the League, Comrade Ter emphasized the insufficiency of the international aspect of education for the proletarian youth. He pointed in particular to the fact that *Komsomolskaya Pravda* devotes too little space to international topics. At these words they angrily began to interrupt him. Comrade Ter's attempts to continue were met with bitter obstruction. Even from the transmission by loudspeaker one could tell that the minority participating in this sabotage was not large. The majority at the meeting was simply intimidated by the jeerers and loudmouths. The person who was chairing, Comrade Kosarev it seems, stated afterwards that Comrade Ter had gone into things in his speech which he shouldn't have. "He'd do better to go off to one of the conspiratorial meetings of the Opposition."

Comrade Ter's speech, as I have said, was in the highest degree peaceful, soft-spoken, comradely, and calm. His critical observa· tions were filled with a spirit of profound commitment to the Communist League of Youth. Nevertheless, the apparatus could not restrain itself. Comrade Kosarev declared in effect that the shortcomings of *Komsomolskaya Pravda*—in particular the scarcity of articles on international topics—could be discussed only at a conspiratorial meeting. This approach of the young apparatchik constitutes a definitive explanation of why Oppositionists are compelled to gather at so-called "conspiratorial" meetings, i.e., at meetings where the whistle-blowers and thugs in general will not interrupt speeches with noise, commotion, whistling, banging, and stamping.

At the meeting of the Moscow active membership on October 26, the whistle-blowers were organized in strictly military fashion under the command of Spunde. The latter directed them sitting with his back to the speaker's platform. During the speeches of Comrades Kamenev and Rakovsky, the saboteurs raised a furious and obscene uproar. What was this? This is precisely the kind of regime which, according to the December 5, 1923, resolution, drives even the most conscientious and restrained party members onto the road of closed groupings and factionalism.

If you are to speak seriously about a discussion, it is necessary to ensure the most minimal rights for all participants in the discussion. Thugs who throw books and glasses, who whistle and create an uproar and in general deprive party members of the chance to exchange views on the fundamental questions of the revolution, must be called to order. Participants report that the two thousand party members at the Hall of Columns made strenuous efforts to hear what Comrades Kamenev and Rakovsky were saying; they stood up, cupped their hands to their ears, etc. But the disrupters were doggedly determined not to let the audience hear the speeches of Opposition representatives. Essentially the same thing was done with the Platform of the Opposition. Only those who fear the party are capable of banning the Platform or creating an uproar during speeches by Comrades Kamenev and Rakovsky; that is, those who fear that the party will listen and understand. If you have no arguments, you have to throw books and stir up an unbridled commotion. That is the most essential cause of factionalism and withdrawal into closed circles.

Every honest party member should help to isolate the fascists, thugs, and disrupters. This is a phenomenon alien to the proletarian party. An end must be put to this at all costs. If you will help to do this, you will thereby help the Opposition abandon factional methods of struggle.

> With Communist greetings,
> L. Trotsky

P.S.—I am including the text of my speech at the joint plenum ["The Fear of Our Platform"] with the request that it be printed in the *Discussion Bulletin*.

OUR TONE IN THE DISCUSSION

November 2, 1927

NOTE: Despite the escalating repression, the Opposition's activity reached a high pitch in the month of November. Collection of signatures on the Platform continued, along with the proscribed meetings. At the same time, Trotsky began to anticipate mass expulsions of Oppositionists from the party. He hoped that the shock of mass expulsions would arouse the party ranks sufficiently to stimulate a genuine debate, in which Opposition views would finally be able to be heard. The Stalinists and Bukharinists were still vacillating. Like the Oppositionists, they knew that there was a thin line between mass expulsions and mass imprisonment of Oppositionists, and there was no certainty that the ranks of the party would tolerate this second step. But the Zinovievists were vacillating too, inclined as they were to lie low after every fresh blow, and Trotsky probably wrote this memorandum to urge them to keep up the pressure and not adopt a conciliatory tone.

By permission of the Harvard College Library.

1. The overriding importance of the Platform is that it reduces the differences to their class foundations and views the party regime as the consequence of a class shift in politics, that is, the result of the party leadership's backsliding from the proletarian line to the petty-bourgeois line. The fight is being waged, consequently, over the class character of the party and the class character of the state.

2. Only this kind of open, clear, and distinct presentation of the basic questions can make clear to rank-and-file worker-members of the party why the dispute is so sharp, and only this can justify the dispute in their eyes. A purely formal presentation of questions of the "inner-party regime," "discipline," etc., without any connection to the revolutionary line, is fundamentally contradictory to Bolshevism. The apparatus, which violates the party rules at every turn, at the same time strives to place all questions on the plane of formal discipline, or, more precisely, of respect for

rank. The less the mass of the party understands the meaning and depth of the differences, the more the apparatus will succeed in this effort.

3. That is why any speech which blurs over and avoids the most sharply disputed differences can do the Opposition harm rather than help it. "Is it worth upsetting the party over second-rate disagreements?" party members will wonder, if they hear a speech whose tone and character are more like a self-justification than an indictment.

4. The apprehension voiced by some individual comrades to the effect that a sharp presentation of the questions could drive "buffer-minded" elements away from us is, in its way, a "classical" error of a kind that arises in any serious struggle within the party. This error is all the more unforgivable in this instance because it has already been tested by experience. We have several cases of "buffer" statements by party members who enjoy well-deserved respect. These buffer positions have gathered a minimal number of votes. On the other hand, the more openly, decisively, and distinctly the Opposition speaks out, the more votes it wins. Any toning down, any drawing toward the buffer group, would unavoidably weaken us and encourage the enemy to redouble the pressure of his onslaught.

5. The Stalin-Molotov faction is trying to "intimidate" the Opposition with the Fifteenth Congress, which is supposedly going to declare that acceptance of the Opposition Platform is incompatible with membership in the party.

Such a resolution would mean an attempt by organizational pressure tactics to bring about political self-denial, that is, renegacy. There is no need to say that not one serious and honest party member would agree to that. Even if we grant that the Stalinist party membership, in the name of the Fifteenth Congress, would support a decision so destructive to the party, it is not hard to foresee that the implementation of that decision would encounter enormous and constantly increasing difficulties, which—with a correct policy on our part—could and should strengthen the Opposition in the party.

6. Approximately a month and a half remains until the congress. The ranks of the Opposition—slowly, perhaps, but surely—are growing and becoming stronger. With a firm, decisive, aggressive political line on our part we will be strengthened significantly over the next month and a half. Every group of Oppositionists in a party cell is surrounded by the sympathy and semi-sympathy of a significant section of party members. Under

these conditions the attempt to expel Oppositionists in whole batches from party cells, especially working class cells, will inevitably provoke resistance and protest by a significant sector in each cell. Party members will want to know what the Oppositionists are being expelled for. The question of the Platform will confront the party with renewed sharpness after the Fifteenth Congress if the congress decides to take the road of expelling the Opposition. The discussion, stifled in the period before the Fifteenth Congress, could heat up after the congress. Everything must be done to turn this possibility into a reality.

7. Comrades expelled from the party, such as Mrachkovsky, Serebryakov, Preobrazhensky, Sharov, Sarkis, Griunshtein, etc., will not allow themselves to be torn away from the party. An attempt to expel several thousand Oppositionists would be ineffective as far as breaking our ties with the party is concerned, especially our ties with the proletarian section of the party.

8. Arrests of party members, again, cannot prevent those expelled from the party from carrying out their party duty. The expulsion of Oppositionists by the thousands would inevitably mean the arrests of thousands. The policies of Stalin and Molotov will drive the party down this road. The party will feel instinctively that this is the road of ruin for the proletarian dictatorship. Stalin and Molotov will try to reassure party members. They will say that things won't go that far, that the Opposition will "get frightened" and will submit to the arbitrariness of the apparatus faction, which has placed itself above the party. (It is precisely the arbitrariness of the apparatus toward the party that is now called party discipline.)

It is absolutely clear that every accidental toning down will be interpreted by the apparatchiks as a retreat by the Opposition and as a confirmation of the correctness of the Stalinist policy of an organizational onslaught.

Thus the line of a political offensive by us is not only the surest means of organizational self-defense and of promoting the growth of the Opposition; it is also the only means of safeguarding the unity of the party against the deliberate splitting line of Stalin.

COUNTERTHESES OF THE OPPOSITION ON THE FIVE-YEAR PLAN

November 1927

NOTE: In 1925 Gosplan (the State Planning Commission) assigned Krzhizhanovsky to prepare drafts of a five-year plan of the national economy. This was to be ready in time for the tenth anniversary celebrations. Krzhizhanovsky prepared two drafts by the spring of 1927; the third Gosplan draft came out in October.

On October 23, the Central Committee decided formally to limit the Opposition to the publication of countertheses to the official theses, which were submitted to the CC only hours before it met, giving the Opposition no time to prepare countertheses or amendments. The official theses, submitted by Rykov and Krzhizhanovsky, were issued on October 25.

Since the Opposition was officially prohibited from publishing its Platform, it used the countertheses as an opportunity to restate the basic principles that had already been expounded in the Platform. This is the only form in which those principles were published in the Soviet press. We have excerpted only those sections that deal with a new crisis that had begun to show itself: the crisis in grain collections. Always a barometer of economic well-being and state-peasant relations, the grain collections had fallen off, slowly in September and more sharply in October. The party leaders, preoccupied with the struggle against the Opposition, belittled the figures and even denied that they were accurate. Nevertheless, the draft theses prepared by the majority spoke of a "more decisive offensive against the kulak." This marked a change from the conciliatory position toward the wealthy peasant that had been condoned explicitly in 1924 and tacitly tolerated ever since. But there was no mention of why such a "more decisive offensive" should be necessary, no note of alarm at the encroachments of the kulak in the rural economy.

The last half of 1927 was marked by more serious attention to the problems of industrialization, partly under the pressure of the

Opposition's critique and partly because of the deteriorating international situation and the threat of war. The need to accelerate the rate of industrialization became clearer too as the "goods famine" remained severe. In October, Vesenkha produced the draft of a five-year plan proposing a considerable acceleration of the rate of industrialization.

However, the Stalin leadership aimed at breaking or expelling the Opposition leadership before adopting important features of its pro-industrialization policy. In the meantime, the theses on the five-year plan that had been approved by the October CC plenum showed a waning of enthusiasm for industrialization and a leaning toward laudable generalizations unsupported by statistics of any kind.

By the time the Opposition's countertheses appeared in Pravda, *delegates to the congress had been elected and its impact on the congress could only be slight.*

From International Press Correspondence, *December 12, 1927. Some obvious errors have been corrected against the Russian text that was printed in* Pravda's *"Discussion Bulletin" supplement on November 19, 1927, and some changes have been made for readability and stylistic consistency. The countertheses were signed by Bakaev, Kamenev, Rakovsky, Yevdokimov, Muralov, Smilga, Zinoviev, Peterson, and Trotsky.*

4. The "Starting Point"

The next defect of the CC theses consists of their complete failure to elucidate the present economic situation. Without a proper survey of the results of the economic management of the last two years, and without an analysis of the deficiencies of this management, no economic verification of planned economic activity is possible.

In the resolution passed by the July plenum in 1927 we read: "The overall economic results of the current year, so far as these can be judged from the provisional data, appear to be favorable, and on the whole economic activity has developed during the current year *without* crises. This demonstrates the considerable improvement that has taken place in planned economic management."

These assertions have been refuted by actual facts.

During the past year, the official press has unanimously asserted that the goods famine in our country has been considerably alleviated, if not altogether overcome.

This theory that the goods famine has been overcome was

necessary for the purpose of refuting the Opposition's theses on the failure of industry to keep pace with the growing economic needs of the population and of the national economy.

As a matter of fact there has been no alleviation of the goods famine; all that has been achieved is an apparent pacification of the goods market during the first half of the economic year 1926-27, brought about by measures *artificially limiting demand*. The result has been that in the second half of the year the goods famine revealed itself with full force.

The most striking proof of this goods famine is the lines to be seen outside the shops in the towns, and the entirely inadequate supply of industrial goods to the rural districts. The triumph of the People's Commissariat of Trade over the market, proclaimed by the bureaucratic optimists, has suffered complete shipwreck.

In 1925-26, 584.4 million poods of grain were bought by the state and cooperative grain supply organizations [one pood = 36 pounds]. Besides this the amount bought by private and small cooperative buyers was about 300 million poods. In 1926-27 these same supply organizations brought in less grain than in the previous year.

Although 1927-28 is the *third* year in a row with a good harvest, the situation in the grain market has begun to worsen since the end of September. The collections dropped and are at present 10 percent below last year's level. When we take into account that the number of private and small purchasers have also declined considerably in comparison with last year, the deficit in supply becomes even greater. The decline in the total collection of grain products is on the one hand a clear sign of the profound disturbances in the relations between town and countryside, and on the other a source of new and threatening dangers. The destruction of our export plans, and thus of our import plans, involving the slowing down of industrialization, is an obvious result of this state of affairs (in the fourth quarter of 1926-27 the amount of grain exported was only 23 percent of the amount for the corresponding quarter of the previous year). To this must be added the unexampled gap between the purchase and consumption prices.

"In 1927 the consumer pays for a pood of flour 1 ruble 14 kopeks more than the price paid to the peasant for a pood of rye. In the case of wheat the difference is 2 rubles 57 kopeks. This difference is two and a half times greater than that of prewar prices" (*Pravda*, July 1927). Do the present leaders of our economy understand the real meaning of this? No, they do not understand it. They say that in 1927 we began to "eat a great deal" (Rykov, in his report at the Profkhorovka factory); that the war danger has upset the economy (If that is the case, what will happen in time of war? But happily it is not so); and that the apparatus is bad (which is true enough). These explanations do not rise beyond the level of ideas of a conventional-minded farmer. Three facts alone serve to explain the difficulties in the grain market: the goods famine (backwardness of industry); the accumulation of reserves by the kulaks (differentiation in the countryside) and an imprudent policy in the sphere of money circulation (excessive issue of currency). If this is not grasped, the country will be plunged into an economic crisis. "*Practically* speaking, a *good* harvest—in the absence of industrial goods— could mean greater utilization of grain for clandestine *distillation of alcohol* and longer lines in front of shops in the cities. *Politically*, this would signify *a struggle by the peasant against the monopoly of foreign trade, i.e., against socialist industry*" ["Amendments to Rykov's Resolution: On the Economic Situation in the USSR," p. 50 of the present volume; emphasis added by Trotsky].

Subsequent events have fully confirmed the fears of the Opposition. Comrade Stalin attempted to misrepresent the purport of these warnings, and to sweep them aside with a cheap sneer. "Comrade Trotsky," said Comrade Stalin, "seems to believe that our industrialization will be realized, in a manner of speaking, by some sort of 'crop failure'" (Stenographic report of the Fifteenth National Conference of the AUCP, p. 459).

All these grave errors and miscalculations of our economic leaders have brought about a disorganization of the commodities and money markets, and threaten the stability of the *chervonets*. The demand for gold is growing among the peasantry, and the village shows an increasing distrust of the *chervonets*. As the peasant has no opportunity to exchange the *chervonets* for goods, he prefers to sell less, and this leads to the decline of the grain and raw material supplies, to increased prices, to the restriction of export, and to the disorganization of the whole economic system.

Is it possible to simply ignore such facts when assessing our economic situation, and when drawing up a five-year plan? To hide these facts from the party merely because they throw too glaring a light on the policy of the CC during the past few years would be more than an error—it would be a crime against the party. . . .

8. The Roots of Our Difficulties

The chief and general cause of our difficulties may be briefly formulated as follows: Industry has developed too slowly during the last few years, and fails to keep pace with the overall development of the national economy. The city cannot supply enough commodities in exchange for the products of the countryside. The incorrect political line that has been adopted, especially the incorrect taxation policy, makes it easy for the kulak to concentrate the great bulk of the grain and other reserves in his hands. This disproportion is a constant source of growth of parasitic elements, speculators, and gigantic profits of the capitalist strata.

At the same time there is a rapid growth of the capitalist elements among the small agricultural producers. Owing to this, *the dependence of the state economy on kulak and capitalist elements* is growing, as regards food, exports, and supplies of raw materials.

The kulak elements, relying on their improved economic position and on their growing reserves, join their capitalist allies in the city to sweep aside the economic plans of Soviet power, place restrictions on export—and thereby on capital investments and on the rate of industrialization—which actually retard the process of building socialism.

A further aspect of these basic phenomena is the weak development of export, the insufficient import of means of production, the lack of fresh capital for the construction of new factories and for the expansion and reequipment of the old ones, the continuous growth of unemployment in town and countryside. The result is that at the end of this decade we have not only economic success to record—as, for instance, the uninterrupted growth of production in state industry; the increase of capital investment and of building activity; the growth of commerce between town and countryside, accompanied by the absolute and relative growth of the cooperatives and of state industry; and the improvement of the material position of the middle peasantry—but we have at the same time to record an indubitable growth of difficulties of a social and class character.

The Opposition demanded a more rapid development of industry by a more powerful and systematic taxation pressure on the kulak and NEPman, and by cutting back the enormous bureaucratic apparatus. The majority of the CC accused the Opposition of "superindustrialization," and "panic" over the kulak. The majority drifted along without sail or rudder, trusting to chance. The present difficulties are the penalty for the procrastinating policy of the leaders.

At the beginning of the present year 800 to 900 million poods of agricultural products lay accumulated in the villages, mainly in the hands of the kulaks and better-off peasants. These reserves far exceed the security store required, are growing rapidly, and will increase by 200 to 300 million poods, reaching a billion by the end of the present agricultural year. This fact is a threatening symptom of the stagnation of commodity circulation in the village, and its end result is bound to present obstacles to increasing the area under cultivation.

Here we have a consequence of the inadequate development of industry, which is not in a position to provide an exchange fund for these stocks in the village. The slow development of industry retards the development of agriculture.

This accumulation of agricultural products in the village is closely connected with the question of our inadequate exports and the frustration of our export and import plans by the better-off peasants and kulaks. When Comrade Kamenev very correctly explained our failure to carry out our grain export plan in 1925 by referring to the fact that the kulak was holding back his grain, thereby thwarting the plan, he was overwhelmed with an avalanche of attacks and statistics intended to "refute" his statement. But the present accumulation of agricultural products in the village, inaccessible to government purchasers, has reached such a point that Comrade Kamenev's assertion has become a platitude recognized by every economist. And not only that: his successor, Comrade Mikoyan, will be faced this year by the frustration of the original grain export plan, and by the prospect of the failure of an import plan already considerably cut down. This second "miscalculation" is all the more unpardonable in that it has been made two years after the first, that is, under conditions when the consequences of the differentiation in the countryside have become more obvious to everyone. Comrade Mikoyan, in his article in no. 252 of *Pravda,* pointed out very rightly that "our foreign trade turnover is the boundary limiting the speed of our industrial development." But who establishes this boundary? The extent of our foreign trade is determined to a certain degree by the extent of our industrial export (35.8 percent in 1925-26), but chiefly by the extent of agricultural export, which comprised 64.2 percent of our total exports in 1925-26. And since our supplies of grain and raw material surpluses for export are chiefly obtained from the better-off peasants, while precisely these strata are most determined to hold back their grain, the result is that we are being "regulated" by the kulak and the well-to-do peasant.

Foreign trade is rightly designated as one of the key leading positions of our state economy. The growth of capitalism in the countryside results in a certain extremely important section of this key position (made important by the fact that ours is an agrarian country) passing into the hands of our class enemy. Here, the working class is confronted with one of the most dangerous results of the policy pursued by the CC since the Fourteenth Party Congress under the slogan of "Fire Against the Left." This devastating result is comprehensible to the simplest workers. It means: cutting down exports at a time when a billion poods of grain reserves are on hand; difficulties in importing the raw material necessary for the textile, wool, and leather industries and for producing articles of mass consumption; difficulties in importing the most necessary machinery; difficulties in settling credit obligations abroad; worsening of the goods famine in town and countryside.

The objective result of the economic policy of the CC during the last two years has been to protect the accelerated growth of capitalist elements, especially in agriculture, now reaching a point at which these elements exert a noticeable pressure on the economic plans of the Soviet state, and even thwart them. Even the blindest can see this (see the above-quoted declaration of Comrade Mikoyan, and other passages from the same article).

But only those who refuse to see can fail to observe that the above-named difficulties all tend in one direction—the *foreign trade monopoly.*

There are only two means of escape from the situation thus created, and the situation as it stands cannot last.

The first way is that proposed by the Opposition, a compulsory grain loan from the wealthiest 10 percent of kulak farms, totaling from 150 to 200 million poods. After the needs of the towns have been satisfied, the remainder of this grain is to be exported, raw materials and machinery bought with the proceeds, and in this way the additional volume of commodities required to meet the goods famine in the countryside and the lack of food supplies in the cities can be produced within the country itself.

Those who reject this way are left with the sole alternative of abandoning the foreign trade monopoly, of resorting to foreign capital for export and import, and of importing foreign goods for the villages in exchange for the export of the accumulated reserves of grain. The present majority of the CC, with its policy of marking time in one spot, is organically incapable of making a timely choice, either to the left or to the right. This irresoluteness leads to decisions being made at the last moment in panicky haste, and then inevitably in the direction of a right policy.

The Opposition has never at any time or place said that the CC has resolved to annul the foreign trade monopoly, to recognize old debts, etc. The idea of the annulment or modification of the foreign trade monopoly has never been officially suggested, either in meetings or in the press. But in the offices of various officials, or in narrower business circles, even among Communists, a "reform" of the foreign trade monopoly, a "modification," is being referred to with increasing frequency as a necessary prerequisite for the growth of agricultural export and the development of the productive forces of the country (it need not be said, on capitalist and not on socialist lines). The overall direction of the CC's policy and its objective consequences are stronger than all its assurances on paper. The Opposition warns the party against the impending turn to the right on the question of the foreign trade monopoly. . . .

SUMMING UP THE TENTH ANNIVERSARY EVENTS

November 8, 1927

NOTE: The Oppositionists decided to take part in the demonstrations celebrating the tenth anniversary of the revolution under their own slogans, to bring their ideas to the attention of the millions who were expected to participate. They would march as separate contingents carrying their own banners: "Strike Against the Kulak, the NEPman, and the Bureaucrat!" "Against Opportunism, Against a Split—For the Unity of Lenin's Party!" These were slogans that echoed the official proclamations; and it was the Opposition's intention to demonstrate its loyalty and discipline while protesting against the slide to the right on the part of the leadership.

Nevertheless, the Stalinists and Bukharinists were determined to suppress any such independent demonstration. They took brutal measures against Oppositionists caught carrying banners or pictures of Opposition leaders and later alleged that the peaceful demonstration was an attempted "insurrection." In both Leningrad and Moscow Oppositionists were physically attacked. In the light of these events, Trotsky concluded that while Thermidor had not yet been achieved, "the danger of Thermidor is at hand."

Once again, as at every critical juncture, the thinking of the Trotskyists and the Zinovievists diverged. Trotsky and his cothinkers felt that they had at least stated their views, including their support to party unity, although they had no illusions in the party machine and fully expected reprisals. Zinoviev and Kamenev felt the full pressure of the repression. They wondered what good would come of continuing the fight. They greatly feared a split and thought that by retreating they could avoid one.

By permission of the Library of Social History. Trotsky's title for this was "After a Verbal Zigzag to the Left, a Profound Shift to the Right."

1. The Stalin faction has carried on the entire "discussion," that is, the baiting of the Opposition, up until now under the slogan of "Party Unity." This slogan is now being torn out of the Stalinists' hands. Ever more numerous are the rank-and-file party members who interpret party unity to mean "Stop baiting the Opposition, stop mobilizing gangs of whistlers, stop expelling and arresting Communists."

2. On November 7, the Opposition raised the slogan "Against Opportunism, Against a Split—For the Unity of Lenin's Party." The Opposition placards bearing this slogan were destroyed under the direction of the Stalinist apparatus. Workers carrying these placards were beaten with cruel fury. And how could it have been otherwise? "Against Opportunism." That means against Stalin. "Against a Split." Who is that directed against if not Stalin? "For the Unity of Lenin's Party." That is an obvious blow at Stalin.

3. "For a Leninist Central Committee of the All-Union Communist Party." This too was rejected as a slogan for the demonstration by the Moscow apparatchiks. "For a Leninist Central Committee," they argued, "that will be interpreted to mean 'For a Central Committee constituted as it was in Lenin's time.'" Correct! The Stalinists need a Stalinist Central Committee, not a Leninist one.

4. The Opposition joined the demonstration with placards bearing the slogan "Let Us Turn Our Fire to the Right—Against Kulak, NEPman, and Bureaucrat." These placards were torn from the hands of their bearers and ripped to pieces. The workers who carried them were beaten up. This fact alone completely exposes the real line of the present party leadership. We Oppositionists are often asked: What makes you think there is a danger of Thermidor? Our answer is simple and clear. When Bolsheviks are beaten up because they call for turning our fire to the right, against kulak, NEPman, and bureaucrat, then the danger of Thermidor is at hand. Those who do the beating, those who organize the beatings, and those who regard them with indulgence are Thermidorians or connivers at Thermidor.

5. In the tenth anniversary manifesto and the speeches of the official orators there was reference to the need for intensifying the pressure on the kulak and NEPman. Two years ago, according to the Bukharins, the time was not ripe for that. And now, just at the tenth anniversary, it suddenly becomes time. But why is it, in that case, that on November 7, 1927, placards demanding that we turn our fire to the right, against kulak, NEPman, and

bureaucrat, were torn to pieces? It is enough to contrast these facts to thoroughly expose the policies of the present leadership. Stalin and Bukharin proclaim intensified pressure on the bourgeois elements in words only. The Opposition wants to apply that pressure in fact. Why, then, do Stalin and Bukharin put the pressure on the Opposition?

6. "Let Us Carry Out the Testament of Lenin." This is another of the hated Opposition placards snatched from the hands of those carrying it, torn from the walls with rakes, and ripped to pieces before the eyes of the crowd. The hatred for Lenin's Testament on the part of the apparatchiks becomes all the more furious, the clearer it becomes how profound and far-sighted that document's appraisal of Stalin was. At meetings and particularly in private conversations, the hate-filled Stalinists say openly that Lenin wrote his Testament at a time when he was ill. This is the latest argument of the apparatchiks in their struggle against Lenin. They simply forget that the Testament was written (December 23, 1922–January 4, 1923) at roughly the same time that he wrote such articles as "Better Fewer But Better" (March 2, 1923), "On Cooperation" ([published] May 26, 1923 [written January 4-6, 1923]), and "How We Should Reorganize the Workers' and Peasants' Inspection" (January 23, 1923). The whole party knows that these articles contain some of the most remarkable expressions of the power of Lenin's thought. Stalin and Bukharin seek, on the basis of a single, arbitrarily twisted sentence from the article "On Cooperation," to construct their petty-bourgeois theory of socialism in one country. This does not prevent them from vilifying Lenin's Testament as the product of a state of illness and virtually a counterrevolutionary document.

7. Portraits of the Opposition leaders have been strictly banned for a long time. It is almost impossible to obtain them in the stores. Displaying them is equivalent to a crime. Nevertheless, Oppositionists in many localities consciously took the risk and hung out portraits of the Opposition leaders from their windows or unfurled them on the streets. They were mercilessly beaten for their daring and the portraits were torn to pieces and ground into the dirt. However, this did not stop other Oppositionists from doing the same.

Stalin's portraits are not forbidden by anyone. On the contrary, displaying them is one of the avenues to a good career. Nevertheless, portraits of Stalin were not to be seen anywhere, neither in windows nor on demonstrators' placards. This fact by itself speaks more eloquently than any words. The immortal Broido, former chief of Gosizdat (the State Publishing House), has tried by coercion and extortion to foist Stalin's portraits upon the country as household items. But there are things that cannot be achieved by naked repression.

*   *   *

The policies of the Stalin leadership are a composite of brief zigzags to the left and profound zigzags to the right. That was stated in the Platform of the Bolshevik-Leninists (Opposition). In just the past few days the Stalinist leadership—under the lash of the Opposition—made a zigzag to the left. It proclaimed the seven-hour day, pressure on the kulak, insurance for the poor peasant, etc., etc. A few days passed, and in the wake of the verbal zigzag to the left came a decisive shift to the right. The rabid assault on the Opposition placards was dictated directly by the class interests of kulak, NEPman, and bureaucrat, who hasten to take revenge for the slight scare they were given by the anniversary manifesto. The attack on the Leninist slogans of the Opposition was carried out by the worst elements in the Stalin apparatus, in alliance with the very dregs of gutter philistinism. This is one of the most important lessons of November 7, 1927.

FOR AN INQUIRY INTO THE ATTACKS ON OPPOSITIONISTS

November 9, 1927

NOTE: The same day that Trotsky wrote this letter demanding an inquiry into the attacks on Oppositionists, the Moscow party committee announced that the Opposition's demonstration was proof that it sought to found a second party and strongly recommended the expulsion of Trotsky, Zinoviev, and Smilga from the party. No investigation of the attacks was held.

By permission of the Library of Social History. A note in Trotsky's handwriting on the folder containing the typescript read: "Written by me. Evidently signed collectively." The copy had no signatures.

To the Politburo and the Presidium of the CCC:

We formally demand an immediate and rigorous investigation, and the calling to account of the guilty, in connection with the numerous irregularities, brutalities, and pogromist actions committed during the anniversary demonstration of November 7, 1927.

1. We have already written to you about the fact that a group consisting primarily of military personnel—and not just rank-and-file Red Army men—burst into the apartment of a member of the Central Committee of the AUCP(B), Comrade Smilga, after breaking down the door, and forcibly removed a red banner with portraits of Lenin, Zinoviev, and Trotsky.

At the same time attempts were made from the roof, by using a rake, a plank, etc., to tear down a placard with the slogan "Carry Out the Testament of Lenin." Glass in the window was broken in the process.

Before the doors of the apartment were broken down, GPU agents and other individuals repeatedly knocked and demanded to be let in to take down the placards. The owner of the apartment, Comrade Smilga's wife, was forced to take her children to another apartment. The housebreakers stationed themselves at all the doorways and staircases, checked the papers of all people entering or leaving, and assumed authority over them. It would not be difficult to establish the identity of all those guilty of breaking into Comrade Smilga's apartment. One of the organizers of the assault, according to evidence in our possession, was a certain Lashuk, head of the military school of the CEC. We can indicate a large number of witnesses who saw, and could easily identify, the housebreakers, several of whose names are known even now.

2. A second attack was organized against the balcony of the Hotel Paris. Several comrades were standing on that balcony, including Smilga, Preobrazhensky, Griunshtein, and Alsky. Here the organizer of the fascist group was the not unknown Boris Volin, whose moral profile needs no commentary. After bombarding the balcony with potatoes, pieces of ice, etc., the attackers burst into the adjacent room, forced the above-named comrades off the balcony with blows and kicks, and then detained them, that is, held them in effect under arrest in one of the rooms of the Hotel Paris for several hours. A number of Oppositionists were beaten. Comrade Trotskaya was knocked down. The blows were accompanied by ugly swearing that was all the uglier because some of the attackers were drunk.

3. As the automobile carrying Comrades Kamenev, Muralov, and Trotsky was going down Semyonov Street, an enigmatic incident occurred which could be investigated without much effort if there were a will to do so. As the automobile passed the rows of demonstrators it was greeted by the shouts and applause of the majority, accompanied by whistles of insult from an insignificant minority. Coming toward that automobile, along the same path beside the demonstrators, was an automobile carrying Comrades Budenny, Tsikhon, and others. Quite obviously each of these automobiles had the same right to be there. After the automobile with Comrades Kamenev, Muralov, and Trotsky had left the column of demonstrators behind, four shots overtook it—they could be heard one after the other. Gunshots during the anniversary demonstration were so unexpected that those in the automobile supposed at first that these sounds had some other origin (blowouts, firecrackers, etc.). But several figures could be seen chasing after the automobile. The driver slowed down. Onto the running board on one side jumped a fireman (a chief) and on the other side, two suspicious types who immediately grabbed at the wheel. The fireman burst out swearing in gutter language. Several others came running to back him up,

and they tried to carry matters to the point of physical violence. Only the group of demonstrators who had by then reached the automobile restrained them. Between his teeth the fire chief had a whistle made of horn, the kind used by the gangs of fascist whistlers. The whistle was snatched away from the fireman by one of those in the automobile and can be presented as evidence in an investigation of the affair. In the crowd it was said that police had fired the shots. However, none of the police came over to the automobile, nor did they make any inquiries of us. There should be no difficulty in establishing the identity of those who fired and those who pursued the automobile (in plain sight of Budenny and Tsikhon).

4. In various parts of the processsion Oppositionists were jumped and beaten. Most often such attacks were accompanied by Black Hundredist shouts, more specifically, shouts of an anti-Semitic nature—regardless of the nationality of the person being beaten. In a point-by-point repetition of what was seen in July 1917, when Bolsheviks were beaten on the streets of Leningrad, the most energetic and determined behavior was shown by the most Black Hundredist elements. A large number of Communists who suffered such beatings are known to us. On the basis of their testimony and the testimony of witnesses it should be possible to identify the guilty parties without difficulty. There was nothing in these actions that had the slightest resemblance to violence on the part of the crowd. On the contrary, all these acts were committed behind the backs of the crowd, when there were only a few onlookers, and the forces used were small groups, the leading part being played by official or semiofficial persons who, as we have said, should not be hard to find.

We must ask, Do you intend to conduct a formal, open, and impartial investigation into these hoodlum attacks against Oppositionists or those suspected of being Oppositionists, some of which we have described, although there were many more we have not mentioned? There is no need to explain the importance of this question for our country's further internal development. In the event that we receive no reply from you we will take such measures to shed light on this whole affair as follow from the interests of our party, our revolution, and the international working class movement.

IN MEMORY OF A. A. JOFFE

November 19, 1927

NOTE: On November 14, the CC and the CCC convened a special session and expelled Trotsky and Zinoviev from the party for inciting counterrevolutionary demonstrations. Rakovsky, Kamenev, Avdeev, Smilga, Yevdokimov were expelled from the CC and six other Opposition leaders from the CCC. Hundreds of rank-and-file members were expelled. The split was accomplished, and in time to prevent the Opposition from speaking at the Fifteenth Congress.

Trotsky moved out of the Kremlin. The next day the other Opposition leaders were evicted unceremoniously. That night, Adolf Joffe, a leading Soviet diplomat, an Oppositionist, and an old personal friend of Trotsky, committed suicide. His immediate motivation was the refusal of the authorities to grant him permission to seek medical treatment abroad. In a note to Trotsky that he wrote right before his death he described his suicide as a protest against Trotsky's expulsion (the note is in Leon Trotsky: The Man and His Work *[Merit Publishers, 1969], p. 124).*

Joffe's funeral was held on November 19, an ordinary working day, but thousands of people attended the procession. The GPU tried to disperse the crowd before it entered the cemetery; it surged forward and moved to the grave site, where it listened to officials of the party and government and to Trotsky and Rakovsky. This was Trotsky's last public appearance in Moscow.

By permission of the Harvard College Library.

Comrades, Adolf Abramovich has become part of the history of the last decade above all as a diplomatic representative of the first workers' state in history. It has been said here—and in the press—that he was an outstanding diplomat. That is correct. He was a diplomat—that is, he served at the post to which he was assigned by the revolution and the workers' government. But he was a great diplomat because he was a revolutionist through and through.

By social origin, Adolf Abramovich was the product of a bourgeois environment—more precisely, of a wealthy bourgeois family. But as we know, there have been cases in history when the products of this sort of environment have made such a sharp break with their background—a break that goes to the very marrow of their bones—that from then on, there is no danger of their ever being won over to petty-bourgeois ideas. Adolf Abramovich was and remained a revolutionist to the end.

Speakers here today have referred—and rightly so—to the high level of his cultural attainments. As a diplomat he was forced to move in enemy circles, among cunning, sharp-eyed, and venomous foes. He knew this world, its customs and habits, and he assumed the ways of this world with subtlety and skill; but for him this was like putting on a uniform required by his post of duty. Adolf Abramovich never wore a uniform on his soul. It has been said here—and said correctly—that he was a stranger to routine or stereotyped attitudes on any question whatsoever. He approached every problem as a revolutionist. He held posts of responsibility but he was never a bureaucrat. Bureaucratism was alien to him. He looked at every problem from the point of view of the working class, which had raised itself from the depths of the underground to the heights of state power. He approached every problem from the point of view of the international proletariat and the international revolution. And this was the source of his strength, a strength he called on constantly to combat his own physical weakness. His strength of mind and his ability to exert its power remained with him to the very last moment, when the bullet left the dark stain that we can see here today upon his right temple.

Comrades, you might say that he withdrew from life by his own choice. And the revolution permits none of us to withdraw on our own initiative. But let no one presume to judge Adolf Abramovich. For he withdrew at a point when, in his own thinking, he had nothing left to give the revolution but his death. Then, firmly and courageously, as he had lived life, he left it.

Difficult times never frightened him. He remained on the same even keel in October 1917 when he was a member, and later chairman, of the Military Revolutionary Committee in Petrograd; the same on the battleground outside the city as the shells from Yudenich's cannon burst all around; and the same at the diplomatic table in Brest-Litovsk, and later in so many capitals of Europe and Asia. Difficulties did not distress him. What impelled him to abandon life was the consciousness that it was impossible for him to combat those difficulties.

Comrades, let me say this—and it is a consideration I believe corresponds in full to Adolf Abramovich's last thoughts and last testament—such an action, withdrawing from life by one's own decision, has a contagious power. Let no one presume to follow the example of this old fighter in his death. No. Follow him in his life.

Those of us who were his close friends, who not only fought side by side but lived side by side with him for decades, are forced now to tear ourselves away from the vivid image of this exceptional person and friend who remains in our hearts. There was a gentle and steady glow about Adolf Abramovich that gave warmth to all around him. He was a focal point around whom others gathered—in the emigré circles, in the penal colonies, and in prison. He came, as I have already said, from a well-to-do family, but the means at his disposal in his younger years were not just his own property. They became the resources of the revolution. He helped comrades with a generous hand, not waiting to be asked—as a brother, as a true friend.

Here in this coffin we bring the mortal remains of this exceptional person, at whose side it was so easy and pleasant for us to live and fight. Let us take our leave of him in the same spirit that he lived and fought: he took his stand under the banner of Marx and Lenin; under that banner he died. And we vow to you, Adolf Abramovich, we will carry your banner through to the end!

THE OPPOSITION 'STATEMENT' AND THE SITUATION IN THE PARTY

November 20, 1927

NOTE: On November 14, thirty Oppositionists sent a protest to the Central Control Commission against the expulsions, reaffirming their loyalty to the party and emphasizing their opposition to factionalism and to forming a new party. This protest was suppressed: neither the text nor the names of the signers was published, and there is no copy in the Trotsky archives at Harvard. However, Trotsky summarizes its contents in this memorandum, which he began on November 17 and completed three days later.

In the meantime, Stalin began circulating rumors that the Opposition had capitulated; and indeed, the Zinovievists felt that the time had come to surrender. They reasoned that the expulsions would inevitably lead to the formation of a second party, which they feared would undermine the Soviet state. Therefore, they reasoned, the Oppositionists had to do everything in their power to gain readmittance to the party. Trotsky urged the Oppositionists to continue to consider themselves part of the party. He felt that the repression might yet work in their favor by calling forth protests from the party ranks, particularly among those layers that agreed with the Opposition but had not yet found the courage to vote for it.

By permission of the Library of Social History.

1. What is the Opposition? The left, Leninist, proletarian wing of the party. The character of the Opposition is expressed in its Platform. The Opposition is a minority in the party. Its methods of work are determined by that. The Opposition is fighting for influence in the party, above all for influence upon the proletarian core of the party.

The Opposition's main method of struggle is propaganda, that is, explaining its views, applying them to specific questions, and defending them.

2. If conditions were such that the party regime was normal, the party could assimilate the basic content of the Opposition's views much more easily and quickly, and the Opposition would not be compelled to resort to ways of propagating its ideas that fall outside the party rules. The bureaucratic regime in the party, reflecting the pressure of the nonproletarian classes upon the proletarian vanguard, distorts all relations within the party and in particular the forms by which a minority can struggle to influence party opinion.

3. When the Opposition circulated its views through private meetings or through articles and speeches copied over on onion-skin paper it was, in this confined, truncated, and allegedly "illegal" form, carrying out the elementary duty of all party members to participate in working out party decisions collectively.

In this period the apparatus people said, "Why don't the Oppositionists speak out openly in the party cells?" But in order for people in the cells, which are far removed from one another, to really have gotten to know the views of the Opposition, those views would have had to be printed. That the apparatus refused to do, however. Hence the inevitably "factional" techniques of the Opposition. When the views of the Opposition had been disseminated so widely that they did appear in the cells, the apparatus began to expel people from the party for speaking out openly, seizing upon extraneous and incidental pretexts. Thus at this stage, too, the bureaucratic regime pushed people onto the road of factionalism.

4. The precongress period intensified and enlivened the ideological and political interests of the party, previously choked by the apparatus. The artificial isolation of the cells from one another and the impossibility of expressing one's views within them forced large layers of the party onto the road of private meetings, where at first twenty or thirty people would gather, then fifty or a hundred and even as many as two hundred. In Leningrad and Moscow many thousands of working class party members passed through such meetings, including not only people who were wavering but also supporters of the majority line. All of them knew that they ran a risk of repression by participating in these meetings. Not one of them would have gone to such meetings if the possibility of a normal exchange of views in the party had existed. Thus the so-called *smychki* (meetings not provided for by the rules) were also the product of the bureaucratic regime and of that alone.

5. The meeting in the Technical School grew out of the so-called *smychki* in response to pressure from the large number of party members who could not fit in the private apartments. It is obvious here too that the only thing involved was the propaganda of the ideas of the Opposition. The "eye-catching" forms of this propaganda, plainly abnormal in and of themselves, were caused by the flagrant abnormalities of the party regime.

6. The Opposition's participation in the November 7 demonstration with a number of placards was inspired by the need to counterpose the truth about the Opposition to the systematic lies and slanders with which both party members and nonparty people are being poisoned. What did the Opposition placards say in essence? It is not true that we want to rob the peasantry; we are for cracking down on the kulak. It is not true that we are for bourgeois democracy; we are for carrying out the Testament of Lenin. On these placards the Opposition defended itself against low-minded slander in the simplest, most nonpolemical, and genuinely party-spirited way, i.e., it did everything to keep from intensifying the dispute. Of course, the very fact that we carried our own placards is abnormal. But this abnormality was imposed upon us by the immeasurably more serious, dangerous, and unhealthy abnormalities of party life and the party regime.

7. The apparatus organized fighting squads, which took physical reprisals against Oppositionists. That it was not a matter of any particular placards is shown by the example of Leningrad, where the Opposition did not carry placards but was subjected to the same violence as in Moscow.

8. The Central Committee announced on November 11 that any further meetings by party members in private apartments would be broken up by force. The very fact that the Central Committee had to resort to such measures, in which one section of the party assumes police duties in relation to another, testifies to the very deepgoing deformations in the party regime. By this the apparatus has declared that it cannot tolerate any propagation of the views of the Opposition, even in the precongress discussion period—whether at open party meetings (whistling, commotion, rattles, fist-fighting, and beatings, not to mention tampering with the time limits for speakers) or at private gatherings.

9. The Central Committee resolution has created a new situation. To the Opposition the *smychki* (private meetings) were only a form of propaganda. The apparatus has decided to turn the *smychki* into a form of physical confrontation between two sections of the party. It is quite obvious that the Opposition never

in any way desired to take that road, and could not take it.

All the efforts of the apparatus in the recent past have been aimed at imposing the form of physical confrontation upon any propagation of Opposition views. On this basis it erects the poisonous lie of alleged anti-Soviet work, mobilization of gutter elements against Soviet power, preparation for civil war, and so on. The purpose of these machinations is to frighten the party and prevent it from trying to understand the theses, articles, and speeches of the Opposition, i.e., the aim is to obstruct the effort by the minority in the party to propagate its views.

10. It was precisely this situation that determined the aim and content of the Opposition statement of November 14.

The Opposition stated that it was discontinuing the so-called *smychki,* not wishing to assist Stalin in his effort to organize clashes such as had already been accompanied by pistol shots in Kharkov.

The Opposition reminded the party over and over again that it, the Opposition, does not forget for one moment that it is only a *minority* in the party and that its basic task is the propagation of its views with the aim of winning over party opinion, or at least the proletarian core.

The attribution to the Opposition of any other aims—of a putschist, adventurist, or insurrectionist kind—is a lie, similar to the business with the Wrangel officer, and flagrantly contradicts the Marxist, Leninist, and Bolshevik character of the Opposition.

11. Closely connected with this is the question of party unity. The apparatus tries to impose the form of civil war, though embryonic, upon the Opposition's effort to propagate its views. This inevitably implies the splitting of the party. The Opposition has nothing in common with such methods. Its road is the road of reform. It holds firmly to the perspective of rectifying the line of the party and of the workers' state by methods of an internal character within the party and within the working class—and without revolutionary convulsions.

12. This basic Opposition standpoint is determined by its attitude toward the nonparty workers. The attempt to attribute to the Opposition the intention of counterposing nonparty people to the party or of basing itself on nonparty people against the party is based on a lie—and a deliberate lie at that. The Opposition cannot, however, look on with passive indifference at the obvious estrangement the apparatus policies are causing between party and nonparty workers, i.e., within the class. In this growing estrangement are hidden very great dangers for the dictatorship.

The Opposition calls for party differences to be resolved by normal party means and, at the same time, demands that nonparty workers not be poisoned by lies about the Opposition. Our party leads the working class. The working class cannot passively follow the party without regard for the processes going on within the party. It wants to know about the differences and has a right to know about them. In past years nonparty workers always knew about the existence of differences in the party from the printed discussions in which the various sides expressed their views. Now only one side speaks, and tells lies about the other. This has been going on for several years. More and more the working class perceives this as impermissible violence against itself by the apparatus of the ruling majority. Such a situation cannot last. Before anything else the party must know the truth in order to straighten out the line. The nonparty workers should be given an accurate picture of the differences in order to help the party rectify its line.

13. As regards the Opposition statement of November 14, the ruling faction has two ready-made stories: (a) the declaration marks the capitulation of the Opposition; and (b) it is an attempt to deceive the party. Both these assessments are well known from past experience. Both are equally false. Neither can prevent the declaration from attaining its goal, i.e., informing the party of the Opposition's true intentions and methods of struggle.

14. Is it true that the Opposition capitulated? If by capitulation is meant the Opposition's abandonment of the *smychki* under the threat of physical reprisals against Communists gathering at private apartments for discussion, it must be said that the Opposition definitely has retreated in the face of this threat of violence. The task of the Opposition is to propagate its views in the party and not to get into brawls with hand-picked fighting squads. If by capitulation is meant abandonment of its Platform and views, or of the propagation and defense of these views in the party, the Opposition can only reply with a shrug of contempt. The ideological correctness of the Opposition was never so obvious as now. Never has the political bankruptcy of the CC been so undeniably apparent as in the present precongress discussion period. There has never been a case in history in which organizational machinations and repression have been able to prevent the correct line from winning through to the consciousness of the proletarian vanguard.

15. Is it true that the Opposition wishes to deceive the party? The Opposition does not and cannot have any interest in

deceiving the party, which is being fed deceptions all the time against the Opposition. The Opposition has no need to look better or worse than it is. The Opposition is a minority in the party. It wishes to fight for its Platform as a genuinely Bolshevik and Leninist platform, and it will fight for it. It is in the Opposition's vital interest that the party understand and reject the apparatus lies about its alleged anti-Soviet, insurrectionist, etc., intentions. The Opposition had recourse to ways of fighting to propagate its views that went outside the rules because the CC trampled the rules underfoot and continues to do so, denying party members their elementary rights. The Opposition is prepared to do everything in order to bring the propagation of its views back into the normal channels of inner-party life. But for that it is necessary to reconstitute those normal channels. The Opposition is ready to render any and all assistance to that end. Despite all the flagrant abnormalities in calling and preparing for the Fifteenth Congress, the Opposition is ready to support every measure of the Fifteenth Congress genuinely aimed at restoring normal party life.

16. There is no need to say that repressive measures will not frighten the Opposition. Such measures are expressions of the rude and disloyal abuse of power of which Lenin accused Stalin (see Lenin's Testament) and which now have become the standard method of the ruling Stalin faction. The Opposition is now more than ever confident of its correctness. For the AUCP and the Comintern there is no road other than the Opposition Platform. The knowledge that it is right gives the Opposition the strength not only to continue the struggle but also to practice self-discipline in the course of this struggle. Repression will not frighten the Opposition but neither will it drive the Opposition onto the road of two parties or other adventures, which the worst elements in the apparatus try to encourage the Opposition to do. More and more the party wishes to hear what the Opposition has to say and to understand it. The Opposition will do everything it can so that the party can learn its views and understand them. The line will be rectified and the unity of the party will be preserved.

17. The central aim of the Opposition statement was to inform the party, which is being deluded as to the true intentions of the Opposition, and thereby to help ease tensions and improve relations within the party. If we were to assume for the moment that the CC actually believes the charges of insurrectionism and other similar aims it attributes to the Opposition, the statement

of the thirty Oppositionists would show them that this was not so. In that case it would be up to the CC to state that the Opposition—under threat of physical confrontation—had abandoned the so-called *smychki*; and it would be the CC's duty to make the statement known to the party as soon as possible. But the CC did the opposite; it hid the statement from the party. At the same time stupid rumors are circulating in the apparatus about the alleged "capitulation" of the Opposition. The party is consciously and deliberately kept in a state of uncertainty and alarm: Did the Opposition capitulate? Or is it mobilizing to form a "second party," for "civil war," etc.? In fact there can be no question of a "second party" or of "civil war." The Opposition will continue to fight for its views with all its energy, renouncing those forms of struggle that would make Stalin's policy of forcing a split easier for him.

18. It is necessary for the CC to hide the Opposition statement—if only temporarily—in order to have a chance to wage as widespread a campaign of repression as possible before the congress. What else is left for the Stalin faction to do? The countertheses of the Opposition expose the ideological poverty of the CC theses too glaringly and convincingly. The Platform of the Opposition also continues to have its effect. The maneuver over the seven-hour day, etc., was exposed too clearly as politically motivated. The entire world bourgeois press sees the campaign against the Opposition as its own campaign. Under these circumstances the most important, if not the only, weapon of the Stalin faction is repression. To justify the repression the poisonous lie about the insurrectionist aims of the Opposition is necessary. The statement by thirty Oppositionists shatters that lie. That is precisely why it is kept hidden from the party. But since it cannot be hidden for long, the repression is given a hasty, massive, and crudely arbitrary character. They don't even look for formal pretexts now for expelling people: mere sympathy with the Opposition is enough.

19. "Will you comply with the decisions of the Fifteenth Congress?" we are asked by those who are organizing the Fifteenth Congress with flagrant violations of the party rules and accompanying the preparations for the congress with unremitting repression. In the crooked thinking of the Stalin faction the expulsion of many hundreds of the best party members, culminating in the expulsion of Comrades Zinoviev and Trotsky, is nothing but an attempt to force the Opposition into the position of advocating a second party. Isn't there the danger that the

artificially prepared Fifteenth Congress will approve this policy of the Stalin faction or at least reinforce it simply by failing to reverse it?

It is impossible to deny the existence of such a danger. Will the Opposition comply with a decision that means a further step in the direction of a split into two parties? No, the Opposition will not submit to such a decision. The Opposition will not allow itself to be torn away from the AUCP. And neither will it undertake to organize a second party. It will not let itself be pushed onto that road, even if such a push were to come from the artificially selected Fifteenth Congress. Whatever the decisions of this congress, the Opposition will regard itself as a component part of the AUCP and will act accordingly.

Through mass expulsions the Stalin faction could accomplish a split, if the Opposition were isolated within the party. But that is not at all the situation. Behind the Opposition there is already a semi-Opposition. Behind the semi-Opposition there are sympathizers, i.e., those who cannot bring themselves to vote for the Opposition but who express their disagreement with the party regime by not voting. There are many of these, and their number is growing. They are moving toward the Opposition. Repression against the Opposition will push this growing layer even closer. The expulsion of hundreds and even thousands of Oppositionists from the party will not break the ties these Oppositionists have with the party. The party will not let itself be split apart. The Opposition will not let itself be split away.

THE STATEMENT OF THE 121

December 3, 1927

NOTE: Despite the divergence in their thinking, the Trotskyists and the Zinovievists addressed a common statement to the Fifteenth Congress, which opened on December 2. The statement is evidently a compromise between the two groups, the former of which wanted to continue the struggle and the latter to capitulate. Stalin made the report on the Opposition, ending with the demand that the Opposition "renounce its anti-Bolshevik views" or leave the party—or be thrown out. In his summary, he rejected the statement of the one hundred twenty-one Oppositionists as an inadequate token of surrender.

The statement was published in Pravda *on December 20, 1927. It was published in English in* International Press Correspondence, *January 12, 1928, where the only signature was Kamenev's, to vouch "for the genuineness of the signatures." The list of names is from the Russian text in the stenographic record of the Fifteenth Congress (published 1961-62), which has also been used to correct obvious errors. Some additional changes have been made to improve readability and achieve stylistic consistency.*

To the Presidium of the Fifteenth Congress of the AUCP(B):

Comrades! The unity of the Communist Party is the highest principle in the epoch of the proletarian dictatorship. Without the unity of the party on the basis of Leninism, the dictatorship cannot be maintained, progress toward the establishment of socialism cannot be made, and the development of the world revolution cannot be promoted.

The unity of the party has, however, been openly endangered lately by the development of inner-party strife. If the further development of our struggle leads to a split, and then to a fight between two parties, it would mean the greatest possible danger to Lenin's cause.

We have no desire to deny our share of responsibility for the acuteness of the inner-party situation. In the struggle for our views, we have taken the path of factionalism, which at times took extremely sharp forms; and on several occasions we resorted to methods which go against party discipline. We were urged onto this path only by a profound conviction that our views were correct and Leninist; by our determination to bring these views to the attention of the masses of party members; by the obstacles we encountered on this path; and by the accusations that have been made against us, accusations that are intolerable to Bolsheviks.

There are no programmatic differences between us and the party. We have pointed out the presence and the growth of Thermidorian dangers in the country, and the insufficient measures being taken to guard against them; but we never thought and do not now think that our party or its CC have become Thermidorian, or that our state has ceased to be a workers' state. We stated this categorically in our Platform. We still maintain, and shall continue to maintain, that our party has been and is the embodiment of the proletarian vanguard, and that the Soviet state is the embodiment of the proletarian dictatorship. We allow no doubts or hesitations on the question of the defense of the Soviet Union, the first proletarian state in the world, the fatherland of all workers. We have never had and do not now have the intention of making nonparty people the judges of our inner-party conflicts. However, we are firmly convinced that in fundamental political questions the party has nothing to conceal from the nonparty working masses, who constitute the class basis of our party, and that those who are not party members must be kept informed about inner-party affairs by means of an objective outline of the different points of view within the party, as was the case under Lenin.

However, the inner-party struggle has become so acute that it threatens the unity of the party, and consequently the fundamental interests of the proletarian dictatorship. This cannot and must not continue. The struggle in this form must be liquidated. Before the eyes of the international bourgeoisie, which is speculating on a split in our party and is therefore preparing all the more feverishly for a war against the Soviet Union; before the eyes of the international proletariat, which correctly sees the unity of the AUCP as the most important guarantee for the success of its revolutionary struggles—we consider it our duty to do everything necessary to strengthen the fighting unity of our party.

We cannot renounce views which we are convinced are correct, and which we have submitted to the party in our Platform and our theses; but to preserve the unity of the party, to safeguard its full fighting capacity as the leader of the state and the world proletarian movement, we declare to the congress that we will cease all factional work, dissolve all factional organizations, and call upon all those sharing our way of thinking in the party and the Comintern to do the same. We consider it to be an unconditional duty of every party member to submit to the decisions of the party congress, and we shall fulfill this duty. We have worked for our party for years and for decades. We shall not agree either to a split or to the establishment of a second party. We categorically reject the idea of a second party. We consider any attempt in that direction to run counter to Lenin's teachings, and to be doomed to failure. We shall continue to work for our party and shall defend our views only within the limits imposed by the party rules and the formal decisions of the party. That is the right of every Bolshevik, as laid down in many basic congress decisions in Lenin's lifetime and since.

This declaration is the expression of our firm determination.

We are convinced that we express the views of all those who share our way of thinking who have been expelled from the party, and that, on the basis of this declaration, the party should take the first step toward restoring a normal party life, by readmitting those who have been expelled, releasing from prison those who have been arrested for Oppositional activities, and giving each of us the opportunity to demonstrate the firmness of our resolve by our work in the party.

We do not doubt that analogous measures in the Comintern toward those who share our views, in connection with their ceasing of factional activities, will also help to restore normal conditions in the other sections of the Comintern.

At the congress and during the party discussions before the congress we defended our views with firmness and determination. Now that we have decided to submit to the congress, we shall carry out this resolve with equal firmness and determination, as true soldiers of the Bolshevik proletarian army.

(1) Avdeev, Iv. (party member since 1901); (2) Aleksandrov, A. (1918); (3) Alekseev, G. (1916); (4) Alsky (1917); (5) Andreev, N. (1914); (6) Ausem (1901); (7) Beloborodov, A. (1907); (8) Belyais, Ya. (1912); (9) Babakhan, S. (1917); (10) Batashev, A. (1918); (11) Baranov, S. (1913); (12) Belenky, G. (1901); (13) Bakaev, Iv. (1906); (14) Budzinskaya (1914); (15) Boguslavsky, M.; (16) Vorobev, V. (1914); (17) Vardin, I. (1907); (18) Vrachev, I. (1917); (19) Vujović, V. (1912); (20) Gessen, S. (1915); (21) Greizha, P. (1917); (22) Gusev, V. I. (1917); (23) Gordon, N. (1903); (24) Gertik, Ar. (1902); (25) Ginsburg, L. (1919); (26) Guralsky, A. (1918); (27) Goryachev, V. (1909);

(28) Drobnis; (29) Dmitriev, T. (1915); (30) Yelkovich, Ya. (1917); (31) Yevdokimov, G. (1903); (32) Yezhov, P. (1917); (33) Yefretov, Ye. (1917); (34) Zhuk, A. (1904); (35) Zinoviev, Gr.; (36) Zorin, S. (1917); (37) Zalutsky, P. (1907); (38) Zverev, D. (1917); (39) Ishchenko, A. (1917); (40) Ivanov, A. (1913); (41) Ivanov, V. (1915); (42) Ilyin (1917); (43) Kamenev, L.; (44) Kavtaradze, S. (1903); (45) Kaspersky (1913); (46) Krasovskaya, M. (1912); (47) Kovalevsky (1905); (48) Kuklin, A. S. (1903); (49) Kasparova, V. (1904); (50) Kcrolev, A. (1916); (51) Krysin (1917); (52) Komandir (1912); (53) Kagalin (1917); (54) Kostritsky (1917); (55) Konkova, A. (1912); (56) Katalynov, I. N.; (57) Korshunov, Ye. (1919); (58) Lashevich, M. (1901); (59) Levin, V. (1917); (60) Lubin, G. (1917); (61) Lelozol, P. (1905); (62) Lizdin (1892); (63) Lobanov, G. (1918); (64) Muralov, N. (1901); (65) Malyuta, V. (1916); (66) Milner, Kh. (1918); (67) Minichev, A. (1911); (68) Makarov, P. (1917); (69) Naumov, Iv. (1913); (70) Nikolaev, N. (1914); (71) Nikolaev, A. (1913); (72) Nalivaiko (1917); (73) Natanson, M. Ya. (1917); (74) Preobrazhensky, Ye. (1903); (75) Pyatakov, Yu. (1910); (76) Ponomarev, V. (1917); (77) Pitashko (1918); (78) Peterson, A. (1917); (79) Paulson, I. (1918); (80) Reingold, I. (1917); (81) Ravich, O. (1903); (82) Radek, K.; (83) Rakovsky, Khr.; (84) Rotskan (1915); (85) Ryzhov (1918); (86) Rafail, R. (1910); (87) Rem, M. (1918); (88) Rumyantsev, V.; (89) Safarov, G. (1908); (90) Smilga, I. (1907); (91) Serebryakov, L. (1905); (92) Safronov, P. (1917); (93) Sarkis (1917); (94) Sokolov (1914); (95) Semenov, Iv. (1917); (96) Semenov, P. (1917); (97) Solovyov, M. (1915); (98) Sosnovsky, L. (1903); (99) Smirnov, I. N. (1899); (100) Semenov, S. G. (1919); (101) Senkov, Z. (1919); (102) Trotsky, L.; (103) Tuzhikov (1919); (104) Tarkhanov, O. (1917); (105) Tarasov, I. I.; (106) Tartakovskaya, F.; (107) Utkin, K. (1918); (108) Ukonen (1918); (109) Federov, Gr. (1907); (110) Furtichev, Iv. (1917); (111) Fortin, Iv. (1919); (112) Filippov, I. (1919); (113) Kharitonov, N. (1905); (114) Khachkov, D. (1917); (115) Chernov (1917); (116) Sharov, Ya. (1904); (117) Shepshelova, M. (1918); (118) Shurygin, A. (1914); (119) Eshba, Ye. (1914); (120) Yakovlev, M. (1916); (121) Lilina, Z. I. (1902).

On behalf of the above,
L. Kamenev

TWO STATEMENTS TO
THE FIFTEENTH CONGRESS

December 10, 1927

NOTE: The resolution adopted on Stalin's report by the Fifteenth Congress on December 7 formally made membership in the Opposition incompatible with membership in the party. This broke the will of the Zinovievists and fatally undermined the bloc of the United Opposition. On December 10, both parts of the Opposition submitted statements to the congress, the Zinovievists basically a document of surrender and the Trotskyists a recapitulation of their principled stand.

A note on the typescript refers to the two statements as "Without Zinoviev" and "Without Trotsky": evidently neither Trotsky nor Zinoviev signed the statements personally, probably because both had been expelled. The two statements were published in Pravda, *December 20, 1927.*

By permission of the Harvard College Library.

I. The Zinovievist Statement

The resolution of the congress on the Central Committee report declares that adherence to the Trotskyist Opposition and propagation of its views are incompatible with continued membership in the ranks of the Bolshevik Party. The Fifteenth Congress in this way has not only rejected our views but banned the propagation of those views. At the congress, in defending our principled positions, of whose correctness we are convinced, we at the same time emphasized in our statements to the congress that we considered it obligatory to abide by the decisions of the congress no matter how onerous they might be for us.

The question of a second party is posed by the entire situation. In principle we reject the road of a second party for ourselves under the conditions of the proletarian dictatorship. In view of that and in abiding by the resolution of the congress, we state the following:

1. The Opposition faction should cease to exist; and

2. The decision of the congress to ban the propagation of its views is accepted for implementation by all of us.

We urge all our cothinkers to draw the same conclusions for themselves from the decisions of the congress.

Each of us should remain at whatever post the party assigns us and carry out its decisions with full energy in everyday practical work, helping the party move toward the goals set by Lenin.

Comrades expelled from the party for Opposition activity have already appealed to the congress for reinstatement in the party. We second this appeal and support it, regarding as self-evident the absolute necessity for the release of comrades arrested in connection with their Oppositional activity.

II: The Trotskyist Statement

The resolution of the Fifteenth Party Congress that adherence to the Opposition is incompatible with continued membership in the party prompts us to make the following statement:

Abiding by the decision of the congress, we hereby discontinue all factional work, dissolve all factional organizations, and call upon our cothinkers to do likewise.

The road of a second party we reject categorically and we consider any attempt in this direction to be totally contradictory to the existence of the dictatorship of the proletariat and for that reason bound to end in disaster.

It clearly follows from this that, in accordance with the decisions of the congress, we assume the obligation not to engage in the propagation of our views by factional methods.

At the same time we believe that each of us may, in relation to the party and within the framework of the party rules, defend our views as set forth in our Platform and theses. To renounce the defense of our views within the party would be the equivalent politically of renouncing those views themselves. Such a renunciation would be obligatory for us if we were convinced that they were incorrect, i.e., did not correspond to the program of the AUCP(B) or were of little importance from the point of view of the fate of the party and the proletarian dictatorship. Otherwise, to renounce the defense of our views would in fact be to renounce the performance of our elementary duty toward the party and the working class.

We have no doubt that our cothinkers, including those expelled from the party, will prove their loyalty to the party of Lenin and will not waver in their commitment to the cause of safeguarding its unity as a necessary condition of the dictatorship of the proletariat.

We firmly believe that the party will find the road by which to restore to its ranks those who have been expelled and to release those arrested for Oppositional activity.

AT A NEW STAGE

Late December 1927

NOTE: On December 19, the last day of the Fifteenth Congress, Kamenev presented Rykov with a declaration signed by twenty-three expelled members of the Zinovievist wing of the Opposition recanting their views and begging for reinstatement in the party. The presidium refused to examine the document, instructing the CCC to examine only individual applications for readmission from former Oppositionists, and not to do even that for at least six months after they were received.

In a sweeping move, the congress expelled another seventy-five Oppositionists, including Kamenev, Pyatakov, Radek, Rakovsky, and Smilga. Immediately after the congress, hundreds of Oppositionists were expelled and hundreds more recanted. This is Trotsky's assessment of the Fifteenth Congress, probably written shortly after it ended, after the capitulations and expulsions but before the deportations began. Trotsky assesses the current political situation in the country and emphasizes the main tasks that lie ahead for the Opposition. The Opposition was in turmoil. There were new defections every day. Very soon the mass deportations would begin and Trotsky too would be on his way to Central Asia, charged under article 58 of the Soviet Constitution with counterrevolutionary activities.

From Die Fahne des Kommunismus, *December 21, 28, 1928. Translated from the German by Iain Fraser, and corrected against the Russian by George Saunders.*

The crisis in the party refracts the crisis of the revolution itself. The crisis of the revolution was produced by the shift in class relations. The fact that the Opposition is a minority in the party and finds itself constantly under attack reflects the pressure of the domestic and world bourgeoisie on the government apparatus; the pressure of the government apparatus on the party apparatus; and the pressure of the party apparatus on the left, proletarian wing of the party. Today the Opposition is the focus upon which the most powerful worldwide pressures against the revolution are concentrated.

I. The Danger of Thermidor

Proletarian dictatorship or Thermidor?

1. Bukharin puts it this way: If it is a proletarian dictatorship, then we must unconditionally support everything that is given that name. If it is Thermidor, then we must wage just as unconditional a struggle against everything. In fact, the elements of Thermidor—in conjunction with the whole international situation—have been growing in the country far more rapidly over the last few years than the elements of the dictatorship. Defending the dictatorship means fighting against the elements of Thermidor. Not only in the country as a whole but among influential layers of the party itself.

2. But even in a process of retrogression there must come a critical point at which quantity passes over into quality, i.e., when the state power changes its class character and becomes bourgeois. Hasn't such a point been reached already? An individual worker may come to the conclusion from his daily experiences that power is no longer in the hands of the working class: in the factory the "triangle" reigns supreme; criticism has been banned; in the party the apparatus is all-powerful; behind the backs of the soviet organizations high-ranking bureaucrats give all the orders; and so on. But it is sufficient to look at the question from the viewpoint of the bourgeois classes in town and countryside to see very clearly that power is not in their hands. What is taking place is the concentration of power in the hands of the bureaucratic agencies which rest on the working class, but which are pushing more and more in the direction of the petty-bourgeois upper layers in town and countryside, and partly intermeshing with them.

3. The struggle against the danger of Thermidor is a class struggle. The struggle aimed at tearing the power from the hands of another class is revolutionary. The struggle for changes (sometimes of a decisive character but still under the rule of the same class) is a reformist struggle. Power has not yet been torn from the hands of the proletariat. It is still possible to rectify our political course, remove the elements of dual power, and reinforce the dictatorship by measures of a reformist kind.

4. Predominance in the party, and therefore in the country too,

is in the hands of the Stalin faction, which has all the features of centrism—moreover, centrism in a period of retrogression, not upsurge. That means slight zigzags to the left, and deep zigzags to the right. There can be no doubt that the latest move to the left (the anniversary manifesto) will produce a need to placate the right wing and its real sources of support in the country—not in words but in deeds.

5. The zigzags to the left are not only expressed in half-baked anniversary manifestos. The Canton rising is unquestionably an adventurist zigzag by the Comintern to the left, after the disastrous consequences of the Menshevik policy in China have made themselves fully apparent. The Canton episode is a worse and more pernicious repetition of the Estonian putsch of 1924, after the revolutionary situation of 1923 in Germany had been missed. Menshevism plus bureaucratic adventurism have dealt a double blow to the Chinese revolution; we need not doubt that the revenge for Canton will be a new and much deeper zigzag to the right in the field of international politics, especially Chinese.

6. The objective task of a Thermidorian regime would be to place the most important political commanding heights in the hands of the left wing of the new possessing classes.

The most important (but not the only) condition for a victory of Thermidor would be to crush the Opposition so thoroughly that it no longer needed to be "feared." In the party and state apparatuses, the pure wheeler-dealers who have managed to interweave with the new bourgeoisie, using every possible thread, would gain predominance over the purely political figures, the centrists—that is, the Stalinist apparatchiks—who frighten the "practical workers" with the Opposition and thereby maintain their temporary independence. What would happen in this case with the centrists of the Stalinist type is a secondary question. Some of them might perhaps swing to the left. Others, in larger numbers, would simply drop out of the game. Still others would abandon their present pseudo "independence" (centrism) and enter into a new, purely Thermidorian combination. *And that would be how the first stage on the bourgeoisie's rise to power would look.*

7. What causes the backsliding? The pressure from the anti-proletarian class forces on the Soviet state could meet with organized resistance only from the ranks of the veteran party cadres and the proletarian part of the state apparatus and the party. Meanwhile, the proletarian part of the state apparatus, which was earlier sharply divided from the cadres of the old bourgeois intellectuals and did not trust them, in the last few

years has separated itself more and more from the working class and, in its style of life, has drawn closer to the bourgeois and petty-bourgeois intellectuals, and has become more susceptible to hostile class influences. On the other hand, after the terrible exertions of the revolution and in its present material conditions during the period of reconstruction, the main mass of the proletariat, which gave the bureaucratic apparatus its vanguard, has developed great political passivity. The series of defeats of the international revolution during the last few years has had no small influence in the same direction. Then there is also the effect of the party regime. The proletariat bears within itself a large inheritance from the capitalist past. The first years of the revolution raised up the most active revolutionary Bolshevik elements of the class. At the moment a selection of the servile and obedient is taking place. The "restless" elements are suppressed and persecuted. That weakens the party and the class as a whole, disarms the class in the face of the enemy. Thus the increasing pressure of the bourgeois forces on the workers' state has until very recently proceeded without active resistance from the main mass of the proletariat.

Such a situation cannot last forever. We have reason to suppose that the great interest which the nonparty masses of workers showed in the party discussion before the Fifteenth Congress, as well as the phenomena associated with the campaign for collective agreements, signify the awakening of interest of the broad mass of workers in the main political problems of our days and increasing anxiety about the fate of the proletarian dictatorship. The more the activity of the proletariat grows, the more demand there will be for the Opposition among the workers. During the years of its struggle against backsliding within the party (1923-27) the Opposition was able only to slow down this process. This process can be seriously restrained only by a widespread class struggle of the proletariat, directed against the new bourgeoisie, against the nonproletarian influence on the state, against world imperialism. The proletariat is in the habit of perceiving dangers and reacting to them through the party. The monopoly position of the party after 1917 has strengthened this role of the party still more. The whole acuteness of the situation consists in the fact that the party regime acts as a brake on and paralyzes the activity of the proletariat, while official party theory at the same time lulls the proletariat and puts it to sleep. Under these conditions the Opposition bears an even greater responsibility.

II. Ustryalovism and Menshevism

8. Bukharin likens the Opposition's standpoint to that of Ustryalov. What is the essence of this theoretical charlatanism? Ustryalov speaks openly of the *inevitability* of Thermidor as the saving stage in the national development of the Russian revolution. The Opposition speaks of the *dangers* of Thermidor and indicates the ways to struggle against the danger. Centrism, drifting to the right, is forced, with its eyes shut to the danger, to deny its very possibility theoretically. Thermidor can be rendered no greater service than denying the reality of the Thermidorian danger.

9. The attempt to liken the views of the Opposition on Thermidor to those of the Mensheviks is the same kind of charlatanism. The Mensheviks think that the main source of Bonapartist danger is the system of proletarian dictatorship itself, that it is a fundamental error to count on the international revolution, that a correct policy would necessarily be to abandon political and economic restrictions on the bourgeoisie, and that salvation from Thermidor and Bonapartism lies in democracy, i.e., in the bourgeois parliamentary system.

The Opposition, however, in no way denies the dangers of Thermidor; on the contrary, it strives to concentrate the whole attention of the proletarian vanguard on it; it holds that the greatest failing of the proletarian dictatorship is the insufficiently deep connection with the international revolution, the extraordinary softness toward the internal and external bourgeoisie. Parliamentary democracy for us is only one of the forms of capitalist rule.

10. Menshevism is Thermidorian through and through. Ustryalov is realistic in his Thermidorianism. Menshevism is utopian through and through. Is it actually likely that in the event of the defeat of the dictatorship, bourgeois democracy will replace it? No, that is the least likely of all possible variants. Revolutionary dictatorship has never in history been replaced by democracy. Thermidor is in its essence a transitional regime, a kind of Kerenskyism in reverse. Kerenskyism in 1917 was a screen over dual power, and in that situation it floundered around and, against its will, helped the proletariat to wrest power from the bourgeoisie. A Thermidorian regime would mean legalization once again of a dual power situation, this time with the bourgeoisie holding the upper hand, and once again, against its own will,

such a regime would help one class, the bourgeoisie, wrest power from the other, the proletariat. The Thermidorian regime would, by its essence, be of short duration; its objective role would be to cover the bourgeoisie's acquisition of power with a screen of Soviet forms, to which the workers are accustomed. But there would inevitably be resistance by the proletariat; it would attempt to hold on to its positions or win back those it had lost. To beat back these attempts and to consolidate their hold in a genuine way, the bourgeoisie would soon need, not a transitional, Thermidorian regime, but a more serious, solid, and decisive kind—in all probability, a Bonapartist or, in modern terms, a fascist regime.

The Mensheviks, as the left wing of bourgeois society, would fight under Bonapartism for legality. In doing this they would serve as a safety valve for the bourgeois regime. The Bolshevik-Leninists, however, would fight for the conquest of power in the form of the dictatorship of the proletariat.

III. The Question of "Timing"

11. The general question of the danger of Thermidor brings up more concrete questions: How near is this danger? Has Thermidor not already begun? What are the real indications of whether it has been carried through or not?

The question of the rate at which the various shifts are going on is of great importance for [our] tactics. *The pace of political realignments* within the classes and between the classes is much more difficult to determine than *the pace of the economic processes in the country*. In any case, those who expect that the backsliding process will continue at the present rate for a number of years may make a major error. That is the most improbable of all perspectives. In the process of decline, very precipitous shifts can and will occur under the pressure of domestic and external bourgeois forces. How long these shifts will take cannot be predicted. They could take a much shorter time than we think. Those who do not want to take this into account, who put this thought out of their minds, will inevitably be caught unprepared. There is no need to recall that the capitulation of Zinoviev and Kamenev has confronted them from the very first with the need to gloss over the situation, minimize the danger, and lull the left wing of the party to sleep.

Some comrades have connected the question of the pace of Thermidor with the question of the composition of the CC as the revolution's embodiment of authority and power. As long as Oppositionists were tolerated on the CC, they acted as an internal brake on the backsliders and the policy of the CC was, in the words of Comrade Tomsky, "neither fish nor fowl," i.e., the drift toward Thermidor encountered internal hindrances. The removal of the Oppositionists from the CC—such was the thinking of the comrades I have mentioned—would mean that the backsliders could no longer bear to collaborate with the representatives of the consistent proletarian internationalist line. It would mean, in effect, the official inauguration of Thermidor. Putting the question in such a way is, to say the least, incomplete, and for this reason could lead to incorrect conclusions.

The strength of the Opposition is that, equipped with the Marxist method, it can foresee the course of developments and warn of it. The "strength" of the Stalin faction consists in its abandonment of the Marxist orientation; the Stalin faction today is playing a role that can only be played by wearing blinders, by looking to neither side and by not looking ahead to future consequences. The Stalin faction regards the Marxist predictions of the Opposition as personal insults, slander, etc. In this the Stalinists reveal the typical characteristics of petty-bourgeois narrow-mindedness. And this is why they attack the Opposition with redoubled fury.

However, does the expulsion of Oppositionists and even the formal amputation of the Opposition as a whole mean that Thermidor is an accomplished fact? No, so far there has only been *preparation for Thermidor within the framework of the party.* The Stalin faction, by knocking over the left proletarian barrier, is, independently of its own wishes, making the bourgeoisie's progress toward power easier. But this process is yet to be consummated—in politics, in the economy, in culture, and in daily life. In order to assure the victory of Thermidor in fact, first of all, the monopoly of foreign trade must be removed (or limited), the electoral instructions must be revised, etc.

12. Within the party and in the immediate layers around the party we can see the reflection and get a foretaste, in a very sharp form, of much deeper processes inside the classes, which are maturing and must someday break through to the surface. A gigantic role in these processes falls to the party and its groupings, but the class will decide matters. As the real struggle between the classes for power intensifies, the very groupings within the classes will be more sharply defined. To the Opposition's advantage or disadvantage? That depends both on the

objective conditions, including international conditions, and on the work of the Opposition itself, again not only on a national but also on an international scale.

13. The strength of the Thermidorian onslaught and the strength of the proletarian resistance will only become apparent in the process of the actual class struggle. For that reason it is wrong to think that the expulsion of the Opposition from the party means that Thermidor has already been accomplished. Or, more exactly, such an evaluation could prove to be correct, if the further course of events showed that no more working class elements within the party would move toward the Opposition, that the working class had no more strength to resist the bourgeois offensive, and that accordingly the appearance of the numerically small Opposition was the last historical ripple of the October wave. But there is no basis for such an evaluation. There is no ground for supposing that the proletariat, despite the phenomena of passivity and apathy observed in the last few years, is incapable of defending the conquests of October against its own bourgeoisie, as well as against the external bourgeoisie; that would mean capitulating before the battle and without a battle. There can be no doubt that further pressure from the right will strengthen the influx of proletarian elements in the party into the ranks of the Opposition and reinforce the influence of the ideas of the Opposition on the working class as a whole. The question of the timing of Thermidor and the chances of its success or lack of success cannot at all be a question of abstract theoretical analysis or prognosis. What is involved is a *struggle of living forces*. The outcome will be determined by the struggle itself. The struggle within the party, despite all its intensity, is only the introduction to an epoch of class battles. Our job still lies wholly and entirely before us.

14. It is clear that it will be much easier for the Opposition to carry out its historical task if there is a more rapid and more favorable course of the revolutionary movement in West and East. But even with a slower course of the world revolution things are not at all hopeless. Of course the Opposition is not going to undertake to "build socialism in one country." If one starts from the assumption that imperialism will remain victorious for a number of decades in West and East, it would be extremely childish to think that the proletariat of the USSR could hold on to power and build socialism—over victorious world imperialism. But there is no basis for such a pessimistic international perspective. The contradictions of the world economy are not diminish-

ing, but sharpening. There will be no lack of great upheavals. The whole problem will be to use them in the interest of the victory of the proletariat. It is precisely this lesson that the Opposition is trying to teach based on the example of the Chinese events, the Anglo-Russian Committee, etc. Success on this path is possible only on condition that the continuity and activist character of genuine Bolshevism is preserved, even if for the moment only by a small minority.

15. But even if the whole course of the struggle in the immediate future turned out to be fundamentally unfavorable for the dictatorship of the proletariat in the USSR and resulted in its downfall, even in that case the work of the Opposition would retain all its significance. The completion of Thermidor would inevitably mean the splitting of the party. The Opposition would lead the revolutionary cadres of Bolshevism over to the struggle against the bourgeois state. Our left wing would then constitute not a "second" party, but the continuation of the historical party of the Bolsheviks. The [real] "second" party would arise out of the interpenetration of bureaucratic and property-owning elements, which even today have points of support in the right wing. This "second" party would only be a stepping stone for the real bourgeoisie, that is, the imperialist bourgeoisie, both domestic and foreign. The task of the Bolshevik Party—after a bourgeois overturn—would be the preparation of the second proletarian revolution.

Now, however, the task is to prevent such a turn of events—by means of the proletarian core of the AUCP and the working class as a whole.

IV. The Perspectives

16. Now, after the formal ouster of the Opposition, the non-proletarian classes will feel more confident. The pressure will increase still further. The forms and methods of this pressure will become more and more varied and comprehensive: from the pressure of the foreman in the shop up to the pressure of the American and European bourgeoisie on the question of the monopoly of foreign trade.

But even on the assumption that the pressure from the domestic and international bourgeoisie would end with its victory (which is not at all foreordained), it should still not be imagined that the process would go smoothly along the road of more rapid backsliding, without any obstacles, with no resistance from below, without any attempt at proletarian counterpressure from below. It is precisely the growing offensive by the nonproletarian classes that is bound to push ever wider layers of the proletariat onto the path of active defense. In order for this defensive struggle to have a political leadership, the proletarian core of the party and the proletariat as a whole have need of the Opposition even in the event of the most unfavorable course of developments. There is no need to explain that the proletarian core of the party and the working class will turn in even broader layers to the Opposition if the Opposition itself is able to show that its views truly correspond with the genuine interests of the proletariat on all questions of the life and struggle of the masses. This presupposes the activism of the Opposition itself, its continual intervention in all aspects of the economic, political, and cultural life of the working class.

17. The Stalin faction is threatened not only by increasing pressure from the right, but also by inevitable resistance from the left. The Stalinists persecute the Opposition, hoping that they themselves will succeed in controlling the inevitable resistance from the left against the forces encroaching from the right.

Elements in the right wing of the party, as well as Ustryalovist elements in the state apparatus, "understand" the need for a certain maneuver to the left, but they fear that this maneuver might go too far. The right-wing elements, both those belonging to the party and those who do not, but who nevertheless take part in all decisions of the party, are characterized by their organic connection with the new property-owners. They can only accept those maneuvers which signify a certain "sacrifice" to benefit the proletariat but at the same time do not reduce the material standard of living for the exploiting classes, nor challenge their growing political role. And it is precisely from this viewpoint that they look at the questions of the seven-hour day, wages, help to the poor peasants, etc. *The left maneuvers will not save Stalin's policy; the tail will hit the head.*

The growth of the right wing is directly expressed in the ever-increasing predominance of the state apparatus over the party apparatus. This process can be closely followed in the two-year period between the Fourteenth and Fifteenth congresses. The Fourteenth Congress was the apogee of the party apparatus and, along with it, of Stalin. The Fifteenth Congress revealed an already substantial rightward shift of forces. The proud declarations of the centrist apparatchiks that, in passing, they would also crush the right wing, never came about. The Politburo remained just as unstable as it was before the Fifteenth Congress. Several new figures came onto the new CC and CCC, based exclusively on their official "duties." The Fifteenth Party Congress rather clearly revealed a reduction in the relative weight of the party apparatus in the general system of the Soviet regime. The Stalin-Rykov conflict reflects to a significant extent the struggle between the two apparatuses, which in turn refracts the struggle of classes. The pressure from the nonproletarian classes is expressed much more broadly and directly through the state apparatus. This does not mean, however, that the conflict between Stalin, Rykov, and others has any directly corresponding class framework. No. If the policy of marking time and putting things off, the perennial wait-and-see policy, becomes impossible in the future, Stalin could succeed in changing horses, mounting the one on the right, and eliminating Rykov by simply taking his place. But even this question of personnel cannot be resolved without deepgoing new shifts and upheavals in the party.

18. Economic difficulties are approaching with irresistible force. The Opposition has proved to be right both in its understanding of the economic situation in the country and in its predictions on the further course of events. The sudden lack of success in grain procurement in the first half of the year [1927] shows a serious disturbance in the equilibrium of the whole economy of the USSR. The export plan has already suffered serious damage, and consequently the import plan too. The shortage of provisions has already caused such an important proletarian center as Leningrad, in practice, to go over to the ration card system. For 1927 and 1928 monetary inflation will be the specific cause of economic difficulties. Inflation is precisely what has so greatly intensified the difficulties that exist in our economy as a result of the lagging state of industry, the disproportion, etc. Inflation is the expression of the fact that, first, the real outlays of the state sector of the economy have proved to be much larger than the real earnings of that sector and, second, that such a situation in our country inevitably leads to a disruption of the *smychka,* the bond between town and countryside.

Real resources for a more rapid industrialization of the country can be obtained only by a substantial reallocation of the national income in favor of the socialist elements of our economy. Without that even the plan for capital outlays now being carried out has put too great a strain on our capacities for issuing solvent currency. The struggle now being waged against material shortages (the increased supply of industrial goods to the villages, while the markets in the towns are stripped bare) can lead to partial success in some areas—but only by creating new difficulties in other areas. The whole economic situation shows the bankruptcy of the present policy, which leads to case-by-case decisions with a false general line.

The Opposition's plan has been rejected; the Stalin group has no plan at all; the right is afraid for the moment of making its real intentions clear—that's how the economic leadership looks at the present moment. The most likely thing is that in the event of a further aggravation of the economic situation, the line taken by the right, which was foreseen quite correctly in the Platform of the Opposition, will triumph.

The roots of the present manifestations of severe crisis lie in the disproportion between industry and agriculture. This disproportion can be evened out in two ways: either by methods of planned regulation, through an appropriate policy on taxes, prices, credits, etc., or by the anarchic methods of the market, not only the domestic market—which would be inadequate for this purpose—but also the world market. The first way is that of a more correct distribution of the national income. The second is the way of abolition of the monopoly of foreign trade.

19. The key to the situation is the question of *the monopoly of foreign trade*. There is no doubt that the abolition of the monopoly of foreign trade or a substantial reduction in the monopoly would at first lead to a significant rise in the productive forces. Goods would become cheaper, wages higher, the purchasing power of the peasant's ruble would increase. But all this together would mean an accelerated shift of the economy onto the capitalist track and the growing economic and political subjugation of the Soviet Union to world capital. The dictatorship of the proletariat could then last only for a short time, a period to be measured not in years but in months. Renewed dependence on foreign capital would mean the direct or indirect division of Russia into spheres of influence, its incorporation into imperialist world politics, and military upheavals—with the prospect of ruin and decline after the pattern of China. Nevertheless, in the first phase the abolition of the monopoly of foreign trade undoubtedly would give an impetus to the development of the productive forces and give the masses a temporary improvement in living conditions. Both the kulaks, who withhold the grain, and the American

capitalists, who withhold credits, are pressing precisely in this direction.

One need not think that the slogan of the abolition of the foreign trade monopoly will immediately be raised by the right wing. There are more than a few partial and roundabout ways, as the history of the electoral instructions showed. At first the pressure will find expression through these roundabout ways. But the demand to abolish the foreign trade monopoly can soon enough be raised in its fullest form. The workers will be told, "Of course Lenin was for the monopoly. But everything depends on the circumstances of time and place. Our theory is not a dogma. The situation has changed. The development of the productive forces requires . . ." etc. There can be no doubt that if the present blind-alley policy continues, the slogan of the gradual abolition of the monopoly of foreign trade can draw a certain part of the working class behind it.

20. At the same time the pressure from the right will move along other lines as well. The revision of the electoral instructions will be placed on the agenda again. On matters of tax policy, the rights of factory administrators, credit policy, especially in the village, etc., etc., pressure will again be exerted from the right. The Stalin apparatus will run up against this pressure very soon and will reveal its impotence in the face of it. Rykov's people may be dismissed, the dismissal of Rykov himself may be prepared, but these bureaucratic tricks will not solve the problem. Refraction of the pressure from the right makes its way not only through the Rykov group; the pressure itself has roots far more profound than just the Rykov faction. The sources are the new property-owners and the bureaucrats connected with them. One must base oneself either on the new property-owners against the workers or on the workers against the new property-owners.

All this means that the formation of the right-wing faction will proceed at a faster pace, both inside the party and outside its boundaries. The class pressure cannot be contained by the barrelhoop of the bureaucratic apparatus alone. The logic of the situation is such that the Fifteenth Congress will, by all indications, signify the beginning of increased pressure on the party from the right, tending to break it into factions. The role of the left wing under these circumstances will be decisive for the fate of the party and the dictatorship. The critique of opportunism, correct class orientation, and correct slogans for the revolutionary education of the best elements of the party—this work is under all circumstances the most necessary and our greatest obligation.

The main task of the Opposition is to ensure the continuance of a genuinely Bolshevik party. For the present period, that means—to swim against the stream.

V. The Opposition and the Comintern

21. The resolution of the Fifteenth Congress says, according to the CC report: "At the present time in Europe the short-term ebb in the revolutionary wave (after the defeat of the German revolution in 1923) is being replaced by an upsurge, an increase in militant activity by the proletariat." There we have for the first time an official and open admission that after the defeat of the German revolution in 1923 an ebb in the European workers' movement commenced, and lasted, at least on the European continent, around four years. The beginning of this ebb could and should have been foreseen as early as November-December 1923. Precisely at that time the Opposition predicted the inevitable beginning of a certain "normalization," a certain "pacification" in the capitalist conditions, the inevitable increase of American intervention in Europe's politics and economy and consequently the inevitable increase of the influence of Social Democracy at the expense of communism. This Marxist prediction was at the time called liquidationist. The entire Fifth World Congress in 1924 was conducted on the basis that the revolutionary upsurge was continuing and the direct "organization of the revolution" was the task arising from that. The Estonian rising was one of the most glaring results of this false position. The so-called Bolshevization of the Comintern parties, proclaimed by the Fifth Congress, combined both the tendency to exclude the really worthless and rotten elements and the struggle against the correct Marxist analysis of the particular phases within the imperialist epoch, the ebbs and flows of the period, without which a revolutionary Bolshevik strategy in general is impossible. The incorrect orientation of the Fifth Congress inevitably nourished ultraleft errors and tendencies. When the new Comintern leadership, which is strong in wisdom *after* the fact, recognized the full depth of the ebb, it struck at the left elements of the party. The *system of leaders who serve as orderlies* in the Comintern has become even more firmly entrenched during the last two years.

The most important tasks of the Sixth Congress will be the correct evaluation of the main errors in the position of the Fifth Congress and the decisive *condemnation* of a leadership which, at each new sharp change in events, takes reprisals for its own

helplessness and tail-endism on the leaderships of the national
sections, thereby disorganizing them and giving them no chance
to form leadership cadres capable of orienting themselves correctly within the workers' movement as the periods of ebb and
flow shift back and forth.

22. In the European working class an unquestionable swing to
the left is apparent. This is shown in the growing strike movement and in the growth of Communist votes. But this is only the
first stage in a leftward shift. The number of Social Democratic
voters is growing, parallel to the number of Communist voters,
and is partly still overtaking it. If this process broadens and
deepens, the next stage, the swing from Social Democracy to
Communism, will begin. At the same time, the Communist
parties must consolidate themselves, which by all appearances
cannot yet be said to have happened. One of the greatest
hindrances to the growth and consolidation of the Communist
parties is the political course of the Comintern and its internal
regime. *The continued campaign against the left wing is creating
a new "scissors" between the right course of the party and the
leftward-moving working class.* The revolutionary situation can
arise at one of the next stages in the countries of Europe with
exactly the same strength and force as it did in Vienna. Everything will depend on the strength of the Comintern parties, on
their political line and their leadership. The recent events in
Canton—an adventuristic addendum to a Menshevik policy—
shows that it would be the greatest crime to entertain any
illusions about the leadership's present line on international
questions.

Only the Opposition, with systematic, constant, stubborn,
uninterrupted work, can help the Communist parties of the West
and East to come onto the Bolshevik road and prove themselves
equal to the challenge of the revolutionary situations, of which
there will be no shortage in the next few years. The Opposition in
the USSR can fulfill its tasks only as an international factor. All
the more scandalous, therefore, is Zinoviev and Kamenev's
abandonment of the Comintern left.

VI. The Question of Two Parties

23. The official struggle against the Opposition is being waged
with two main slogans: against "two parties" and against
"Trotskyism." The Stalinist pseudo-struggle against two parties
conceals the formation of dual power in the country and the

formation of a bourgeois party within the right wing of the AUCP, using its banner for camouflage. In a whole series of government agencies and in the offices of party secretaries, secret meetings between party apparatchiks and "specialists," i.e., Ustryalovist professors, are being held, to work out methods and slogans for the fight against the Opposition. That is the real formation of a second party, which is striving with all its might to subjugate the proletarian core of the party to itself—and partly succeeding in that, too—and to wipe out its left wing. The apparatus, while concealing the formation of this second party, accuses the Opposition of attempting to set up a second party— precisely because the Opposition is striving to wrest the proletarian core of the party from the growing pressure and influence of the bourgeoisie; if it is not wrested away, the unity of the Bolshevik Party is beyond salvation. The idea that the dictatorship of the proletariat can be maintained by mere verbal incantations about party unity is the purest illusion. The question of one or two parties in the material, class sense, not just in the words of official propaganda, is decided by whether and to what extent the forces of resistance within the party and within the proletariat can be awakened and mobilized. The Opposition can achieve this only provided that it is thoroughly imbued with an understanding of the whole depth of the developing class processes, if it does not allow itself to be frightened or intimidated by the bogey of two parties and the charlatan hogwash about "Trotskyism."

24. In Comrade Zinoviev's theses "The Results of the July Plenum," the following is said about two parties: "But Stalin is expelling whole batches of Oppositionists from the party, and tomorrow he may go on to even more massive expulsions from the ranks of the AUCP. Yes, that is so. Nevertheless the slogan of two parties by no means follows from that. Things have come to the point that under the Stalin regime the only way one can fight for the views of Lenin is at the risk of expulsion from the AUCP. That is indisputable. Those who have not yet solved this question for themselves, those who say, 'We are ready for anything— except expulsion from the party,' cannot under the present conditions be genuine fighters for Leninism, i.e., cannot be resolute Oppositionists. It is highly possible that substantial numbers of Oppositionists (including all the leading elements of the Opposition) will find themselves for a certain time outside the party. Their task, however, will be to continue pursuing their course, even if formally they are no longer members of the party, and not to deviate from Lenin's teachings one iota. Their task

will be, in the most difficult times, to maintain a course not toward the formation of a second party but toward return to the AUCP and the rectification of its line. There is no question that it would be extremely hard for Leninists to be outside the party. But that is absolutely necessary from the standpoint of our fundamental aims."

And further: "As the whole experience of the struggle has shown, the Opposition is unanimous in believing that the struggle for the unity of the party on a Leninist basis can in no case turn into groveling before the apparatus, playing down differences, reducing the sharpness of political expression. When fellow travelers of the Opposition diverge from it to go to the right, they usually do not attribute their departure to their own capitulation to Stalin's standpoint on the main questions of domestic and foreign policy; rather, they accuse the Opposition of steering toward a second party; in other words, they only repeat the Stalinist charges to cover up their own retreat" (pp. 14-15).

It is true that now it is not July but November,* but what was said in these lines still holds true today.

25. Once again: If the right wing in the party and outside the party merge, and in the immediate future subjugate a significant part of the proletarian core of the party to themselves, then two parties would be historically inevitable, which would mean, however, the downfall of the dictatorship and the consequent crushing of the workers who would raise their heads in revolt. That is the political road of triumphant Ustryalovism. An opposite road can be envisaged only through the isolation of the right wing by the struggle of the Opposition against apparatus centrism for influence over the proletarian core of the party. The dictatorship of the proletariat cannot long endure with ever new defeats being dealt to the left proletarian wing. On the contrary. The dictatorship is not only compatible with the isolation and political liquidation of the right wing, but energetically demands such liquidation. Capitulation to apparatus centrism in the name of party unity would therefore also be direct work for the two parties, i.e., for the downfall of the proletarian dictatorship.

VII. On the Capitulation of Zinoviev and Kamenev

26. If the Opposition at the congress had unanimously submitted a firm and loyal declaration—a single one, and not half a

---

*Possibly an error for December or a reference to when this work was first drafted.—Eds.

dozen—open and firm on all political questions, especially on the reasons for factional activity, our situation would [now] be incomparably more favorable. The vacillations in the ranks of the Opposition came not from below, but from above. The behavior of Comrades Zinoviev and Kamenev constitutes something unprecedented in the history of the revolutionary movement—one may even say, in the history of political struggle altogether. Formally, Zinoviev and Kamenev base themselves on party unity as the highest criterion. By this they are saying that the attainment of unity is conceivable not only by struggling for one's views, but by ideological renegacy. But that is the most merciless condemnation of the party that one can imagine. In reality, this kind of behavior does not contribute to the maintenance of party unity, but to demoralization. All double-dealing and careerist elements concerned with saving their own skins thus seem to gain ideological justification. Abandoning the defense of one's views means in particular justifying that broad layer of corrupted philistines in the party who sympathize with the Opposition but vote with the majority.

The renegacy of Zinoviev and Kamenev was fed by the false belief that one can get oneself out of any historical situation by a cunning maneuver, instead of by maintaining a principled political line. That is the worst caricature of Leninism. Characterizing Lenin's maneuvering policy, our Platform says: "Under him [Lenin] the party always knew the reasons for each maneuver, its meaning, its limits, the line beyond which it ought not to go, and the position at which the proletarian advance should begin again. . . . Thanks to that, the maneuvering proletarian army always preserved its unity, its fighting spirit, its clear consciousness of the goal" [see "The Platform of the Opposition," p. 307].

All these conditions for maneuvering in a Leninist way have been trampled on by Zinoviev and Kamenev in the most unprincipled manner.

The hope that after a few months the capitulation document would be "buried" by new events and a new struggle is a pathetic self-deception. Indifferent elements in the party and working class will of course overlook these documents, but the cadres of the Stalinist faction and of the Opposition will not forget them, and at a new turn they will remind the working class of them.

Politically, Zinoviev and Kamenev's renegacy means an attempt to go from a revolutionary position to a left-centrist one, as a counterweight to Stalin's right-centrist position. Centrism can maintain itself for a long time in the epoch of slow development

(Kautskyism before the war). Under the conditions of the present epoch, centrism rapidly surrenders its positions to the right or to the left. In a period of upsurge left centrism is quite often the bridge to a revolutionary position. In a period of decline, such as the present one, left centrism is only a little bridge from the Opposition to Stalin. The Zinoviev-Kamenev group will not play any independent role; their capitulation is a shift in forces at the top under the colossal national and international pressure on the revolutionary wing of the AUCP and the Comintern. Events will "bury" the capitulationist declaration of December 18, but only in the sense that they will roll right over Zinoviev and Kamenev.

VIII. On Trotskyism

27. Zinoviev and Kamenev, who in 1924-25 played a leading role in the creation of the legend of Trotskyism, said in the July 1926 declaration: "Now, as the evolution of the present ruling faction has shown, there can no longer be any doubt that the basic core of the 1923 Opposition correctly warned about the dangers of a shift away from the proletarian line and about the growing threat of the apparatus regime." It is quite clear that if the 1923 Opposition had warned two years earlier of dangers threatening the party and the proletarian dictatorship, then the accusation of so-called "Trotskyism" against the Opposition can be based only on the gravest misconception of the whole situation and of the task arising therefrom. Together with the leaders of the 1923 Opposition, Zinoviev and Kamenev worked out the most important documents of the Opposition, including the most important of all, the Platform. It is clear that the accusation of petty-bourgeois deviation, "Trotskyism," and so on, are thereby reduced to nought.

The belated attempt to renew the struggle against the "regurgitators" of "Trotskyism" constitutes nothing but a pathetic "regurgitation" of Zinoviev's and Kamenev's own errors of 1923, errors which aided the fateful shift of the party regime from the Leninist road to the road of decline into the swamp of centrism and opportunism.

IX. The Balance Sheet of the Bloc

28. The capitulation of Zinoviev and Kamenev again raises the question whether the bloc as a whole was not an error. The individual comrades who incline to this conclusion do not con-

sider the history of the bloc as a whole, but only the closing chapter of that history. The Opposition of 1923 was born in Moscow; the Opposition of 1925-26 in Leningrad. The right wing has its base of support in the Northern Caucasus, where the fight between the Stalinists and the Rykov people was played out most starkly and clearly. This local distribution of the political groups is not accidental, and it alone explains the bloc of Moscow and Leningrad, i.e., of the two most important proletarian centers of the Soviet Union. Irrespective of the various vacillations at the top, the bloc was nevertheless produced by deep class tendencies. Under these circumstances it is wretched jabbering to speak of the "unprincipled" nature of the bloc. The Leningrad Opposition, thanks to its highly skilled proletarian basis, also made a very valuable contribution in theoretical respects to the bloc. The coming together of the advanced workers of Moscow and Leningrad still persists on the basis of the Platform despite the renegacy of the leading elements of the Leningrad Opposition.

The same may also be said of the Opposition in the Comintern. The most revolutionary elements keep finding their way back to each other after some vacillations, which were mainly produced by the measures of the Fifth Congress. The best elements of the Oppositions of 1923 and 1925-26 are also uniting on an international scale. Zinoviev and Kamenev's capitulation will not stop the process.

X. Evaluation of the Opposition's Tactics

29. Three periods may be discerned in the history of the Opposition bloc: (a) from April 1926 to October 16, 1926; (b) from October 16, 1926, to August 8, 1927; and (c) from August 8, 1927, to the Fifteenth Party Congress. Each of these periods is characterized by a rise in Oppositional activity, mounting to a certain critical point, after which came an unwinding to a greater or lesser degree, accompanied by a declaration renouncing factional activity. This peculiar "cyclical pattern" in the Opposition's tactics suggests that certain general causes are present here. These are to be sought on the one hand in the general conditions of proletarian dictatorship in a peasant country, and on the other in the special conditions of the ebbing of the revolution and the general political backsliding.

In its struggle against the left wing, the apparatus is equipped with all the methods and resources of the dictatorship. The Opposition's weapon is propaganda. The distribution of speeches, work with individuals, the private meetings (*smychki*), and the carrying of placards on the street on November 7 are all only different forms of propaganda. The apparatus strives to transform these forms of propaganda into the initial forms first of a faction, then of a party, and finally of a civil war. The Opposition will not follow this path. Each time it has gone as far as the line at which the apparatus confronts it with the necessity of renouncing some types and methods of propaganda. All three declarations of the Opposition—October 16, August 8, and November-December—had the aim of showing the party masses once more that the goal of the Opposition is not a second party or civil war but rectification of the line of the party and the state by the methods of deepgoing reform.

The critics of the Opposition's tactics from outside, who point to its "zigzag" character, criticize it as though the Opposition could determine its tactics freely, as if there were no furious pressure from the hostile classes, as if there were no apparatus power, no political backsliding by the leadership, no relative passivity of the working class, etc. The Opposition's tactics, with their unavoidable internal contradictions, can only be understood if one does not forget for a moment that the Opposition is swimming against the stream, fighting against difficulties and obstacles unprecedented in history.

In the cases where critics do not confine themselves to individual, partial points, some just, some unjust, but attempt to counterpose to our tactics, which arose from real conditions, some other tactics, they usually end up hinting at capitulation.

As for the actual capitulators, they try to characterize the present tactics of the Opposition in such words as "Neither peace nor war." "Peace" they call capitulation, "war" two parties. But Zinoviev's own theses on the "Results of the July Plenum" are thoroughly permeated with the thought "Neither capitulation nor two parties." That was the whole line of the Opposition. But the capitulators must of course always spit upon their own past.

There are no textbooks telling how to set things right in a proletarian dictatorship that is being buffeted by the forces of Thermidor. The ways and means must be sought by starting with the real situation. These ways will be found if the fundamental orientation is correct.

Some Conclusions

1. Theoretical self-education is at the present moment the most important task of every Oppositionist, the only pledge of firmness which can be taken seriously. Study of the proceedings of the Fifteenth Party Congress in the light of the Opposition's counter-theses and the new facts of economic and political life must be the main work of every Oppositionist, especially after the dissolution of the faction.

2. Oppositionists, quite irrespective of whether they are inside the party or outside it, must set themselves the task of becoming actively involved in all proletarian organizations and all soviet organizations in general (the party, trade unions, soviets, clubs, etc.). Oppositionists can in no case restrict themselves to the role of critics; they must do constructive work and do it better and more conscientiously than the paid officials. Only on this basis will principled criticism reach the consciousness of the masses.

3. It is necessary to appeal to the Comintern, so that the question of the Opposition will be presented in its full dimensions at the Sixth Congress.

GLOSSARY

The persons, organizations, terms, and events in this glossary are Soviet, unless otherwise specified.

Amsterdam: Home of the International Federation of Trade Unions, the Social Democratic–dominated trade union federation.

Anglo-Russian Committee (ARC): Formed by the British Trades Union Congress and Soviet trade unions (May 1925); the Soviet unions remained in the ARC even while the British reformist leaders sabotaged the General Strike (May 1926); the British members walked out (September 1927).

Antonov-Ovseenko, V. (1884-1938): A leader of the Petrograd Soviet's Military Revolutionary Committee in October 1917; an early member of the Left Opposition; held various diplomatic posts and was in Prague in 1927; capitulated after the Fifteenth Congress (December 1927).

Arshin: 28 inches.

AUCCTU: All-Union Central Council of Trade Unions, the Soviet trade union federation.

AUCP(B): All-Union Communist Party (Bolsheviks), the name adopted by the Russian Communist Party (Bolsheviks) in 1925; founded in 1898 as the Russian Social Democratic Labor Party (RSDLP); split into Bolshevik (majority) and Menshevik (minority) wings in 1903; RSDLP(B) renamed Russian Communist Party (Bolsheviks) in 1918; name changed to Communist Party of the Soviet Union in 1952.

Bakaev, I. (1887-1936): Old Bolshevik, active in the October Revolution and civil war, where his name figured in charges that Trotsky was threatening to shoot Communists; a supporter of Zinoviev, he recanted Opposition views in February 1927 but was expelled by the Fifteenth Congress.

Baldwin, S. (1867-1947): British Conservative prime minister (1923, 1924-29, 1935-37).

Bauer, O. (1881-1938): Leader of the Austrian Social Democracy after World War I and chief theoretician of Austro-Marxism.

Belenky, G: Oppositionist; organized an Opposition meeting June 6, 1926, near Moscow, for which he was censured; recanted May 1927.

Bernstein, E. (1850-1932): Leading theoretician of the German Social Democracy and Engels's literary executor; from 1899 he predicted that capitalism would gradually be transformed into socialism and rejected the prospect of socialist revolution as a guide to practical politics.

Bey: One of the native bourgeoisie in Turkmenistan and Kazakhstan.

Black Hundreds: Violent right-wing and anti-Semitic gangs in Russia who led pogroms against Jews and left-wing workers and were supported by the tsarist government.

Blanquism: After Louis Auguste Blanqui (1805-1881); the theory of socialist revolution through insurrection by a small conspiratorial group.

Bolsheviks: Majority faction of Russian Social Democratic Labor Party after split with Mensheviks (1903); led by Lenin, became a separate party in 1912; led the October Revolution in 1917; became Russian CP(B) in 1918, AUCP(B) in 1925, CPSU in 1952.

Bordiga, A. (1889-1970): A leader of the Italian CP; imprisoned by Mussolini (1926-30); expelled from the Comintern in 1930.

Brandler, H. (1881-1967): Head of the German CP when it let the revolutionary crisis of 1923 slip; was made a scapegoat and removed from the leadership in 1924.

Brest-Litovsk treaty: Signed March 3, 1918, ending hostilities between Germany and Russia; the subject of a sharp struggle at the Seventh Congress between Lenin's faction, which felt Russia was too weak to continue fighting and had to sign; Bukharin's Left Communists, who repudiated the treaty and called for revolutionary war as a matter of principle; and Trotsky, who opposed continuing the war but urged signing the treaty only when there was no other choice; when Germany attacked, Trotsky voted with Lenin, giving him a majority.

Briand, A. (1862-1932): Former Socialist; French premier (1915-17); representative to the League of Nations (1925-32).

Bukharin, N. (1888-1938): Old Bolshevik; leader of the Left Communists opposing Brest-Litovsk treaty in 1918; after 1923 he became the major spokesman for the right-wing pro-kulak policies; editor of *Pravda* (1918-29); succeeded Zinoviev as president of the Comintern (1926-29); formed Right Opposition (1928); expelled (1929).

Bund (General Jewish Workers Union of Lithuania, Poland, and Russia): Part of the RSDLP until 1903, when it lost its demand for a federated party structure; allied with the Mensheviks in 1906; in 1920, a portion joined the Bolsheviks.

Cadets (Constitutional Democrats): Liberal bourgeois party founded 1905; led by Milyukov; initially favored a constitutional monarchy, then a republic; after the civil war, existed only in emigration.

Cavaignac, L. (1802-1857): Military officer who savagely crushed the Parisian workers in the June days of 1848.

Centrism: Trotsky's term for a tendency in the radical movement that stands or wavers between reformism and Marxism; since a centrist tendency has no independent social base, it must be evaluated in terms of its origins, internal dynamic, and the direction it is taking or being pushed toward by events; until 1935, Trotsky saw Stalinism as a special type of centrism: bureaucratic centrism.

Chamberlain, A. (1863-1937): British Conservative foreign secretary (1924-29).

Chang Tso-lin (1873-1928): Chinese warlord who controlled Manchuria with Japanese backing in the 1920s; captured Peking (1924).

Chayanov, A.: Former Social Revolutionary; head of the Scientific Research Institute of Agricultural Economics; an exponent of individual family farms.

Ch'en, Eugene (1878-1944): Elected to the Central Executive Committee of the Kuomintang (January 1926); became foreign minister in June; supported Wang Ching-wei in an April 1927 split with Chiang Kai-shek; fled to the USSR in July 1927, after Wuhan's break with the CCP.

Chen Tu-hsiu (1879-1942): A founder of the Chinese CP and its principal leader until 1927; after the defeat of the revolution he joined the Left Opposition; expelled from CCP (1929).

Chernov, M. (1891-1938): A leading Social Revolutionary; commissar of agriculture in the Provisional Government in 1917; sided with the counterrevolution in the civil war; emigrated in 1921.

Chervonets: Currency unit introduced in the monetary reform of 1922-24; equal to U.S.$5, or ten prerevolutionary gold rubles.

Chiang Kai-shek (1887-1975): Principal military leader of the KMT from March 1925; staged a coup in Canton (March 1926) and a bloody massacre of Shanghai workers and Communists (April 1927).

Chicherin, G. (1872-1936): Former tsarist diplomat and then Social Revolutionary; joined the Bolsheviks in 1918 and was commissar of foreign affairs (1918-30).

Chinese Eastern Railroad: Part of the Trans-Siberian Railroad that ran through Manchuria to Vladivostok.

Chinovnik: Bureaucrat of the tsarist civil service; after the revolution the term continued to be used to mean an arrogant bureaucrat.

Citrine, W. (1887-   ): General secretary of the British Trades Union Congress (1926-46) and an official of the Anglo-Russian Committee.

Clemenceau, G. (1841-1929): Became French premier and minister of war (1917); pursued a vigorous campaign against pacifists and defeatists.

Clemenceau thesis: An analogy, stated in 1927, that Trotsky used to explain why the Opposition should not renounce the struggle to change the line of the party in time of war. Clemenceau had sharply criticized the ineffectual policies of the French bourgeois government during World War I, becoming its leader when it became apparent that he was its best defender.

Comintern (Communist International): Founded 1919 under Lenin's leadership as the revolutionary successor to the Second International, which had supported bourgeois governments in World War I; the theses of its first four congresses (1919-22) were the programmatic cornerstone of the Left Opposition and later of the Fourth International; after Lenin's death and with the Stalinization of the AUCP(B), the Comintern became an instrument of Soviet foreign policy and was finally dissolved in 1943 as a gesture to Stalin's imperialist allies in World War II.

Communist League of Youth (Komsomol): Founded 1918; its 1921 program, written by Bukharin and approved by Lenin's Politburo, stressed internationalist principles.

Dan, F. (1871-1947): Menshevik leader and after 1922 editor of *Sotsialistichesky Vestnik* in Berlin.

Democratic Centralists: Dissident group of Bolsheviks who held semisyndicalist views and argued at the Ninth Congress (March 1920) that the party was run by a bureaucratic clique and that party elections were not democratically conducted; some of them adhered to the United Opposition in 1926 although Trotsky disclaimed their call for a new party.

Desyatina: Land area equal to 2.7 acres.

Disproportion: Expression used to mean any of several imbalances in the economy: between high prices for industrial goods (charged to the peasants by state industry) and low prices (paid by the state) for agricultural products; between high retail prices (charged consumers by private traders) and low wholesale prices (paid to state industry by the middlemen).

Dogadov, A.: Trade union functionary and an official of the AUCCTU.

ECCI: Executive Committee of the Communist International.

1848: A year of struggles for bourgeois democratic rights, national independence, and constitutional reforms throughout Europe, during which the industrial working class first appeared as a force in its own right.

18 Brumaire: The date in the French revolutionary calendar of Napoleon's 1799 coup d'état against the Directory (actually November 9-10).

Ercoli: Pseudonym of Palmiro Togliatti (1893-1964), the Stalinist leader of the Italian CP.

Farmer-Labor Party (U.S.): Founded 1920; in 1923 the CP, under Pepper's influence, captured it and for a short time used it to endorse La Follette's 1924 Progressive Party presidential campaign.

February Revolution (1917): Fed by the demands of workers' struggles and dissatisfaction with tsarist war policy; toppled the tsarist system and instituted the bourgeois Provisional Government.

Feng Yü-hsiang (1882-1948): Northern Chinese warlord; joined KMT in spring 1926; allied with Chiang Kai-shek in June 1927.

Fischer, R. (1895-1961): With Maslow, a central leader of the German CP after Brandler's disgrace in 1924; expelled in 1926 for supporting the Soviet United Opposition.

Fishelev: Oppositionist and printer; worked on publishing the Platform of the Opposition, for which he was arrested and exiled to the Solovetsky Islands.

Galliffet, G. (1830-1909): French military officer notorious for the ferocity of his suppression of the Paris Commune (1871).

General Council: Leadership body of the British Trades Union Congress; it called off the General Strike of May 1926 after nine days, abandoning the coalminers in their prolonged strike.

Glebov-Avilov, N. (1887-1942): Former secretary of the AUCCTU; an Oppositionist; assigned to a diplomatic post in Rome in 1927.

Goods famine: A shortage of manufactured goods.

Gosplan: See State Planning Commission.

GPU: Soviet secret police.

Hicks, G.: Member of the General Council during its betrayal of the General Strike.

Hilferding, R. (1887-1944): Economist and a spokesman of Austro-Marxism; finance minister in the German Social Democratic governments (1922-23, 1928-30).

Ho Lung (1896-): Chinese military leader who joined the CCP; a leader of the August 1, 1927, Nanchang uprising.

Izvestia (News): Official organ of the Soviet government.

Joffe, A. (1883-1927): CC member and diplomat; supported the Opposition and committed suicide when he was refused a foreign visa to obtain medical treatment.

Kaganovich, L. (1893-): CC member from 1924 and an undeviating Stalinist.

Kalinin, M. (1875-1946): President of the Soviet Central Executive Committee from 1919 and an ally of Rykov on the CC.

Kamenev, L. (1883-1936): Old Bolshevik CC member; initially opposed the October insurrection; after Lenin's death he blocked with Stalin against Trotsky until late 1925; in 1926 he and Zinoviev joined with Trotsky to form the United Opposition; appointed Soviet representative in Rome (January 1927); capitulated after his expulsion from the AUCP in December 1927.

Kaminsky, G.: Party member and spokesman of the agricultural collectives; Trotsky accused him of being responsible for the policy of transferring control of the cooperatives from the poor peasants to the "economically strong" middle peasants—a code name for kulaks.

Katz, I.: A leader of the KPD ultraleft in Hanover and a former delegate to the ECCI presidium; opposed the united front tactic; expelled January 1926.

Kautsky, K. (1854-1938): A leader of the German Social Democracy and a founder of the Second International; adopted a centrist and pacifist stand in World War I and opposed the Bolshevik revolution of 1917.

Kerensky, A. (1882-1970): Prime minister of the Provisional Government produced by the February 1917 revolution; deposed by the Bolsheviks in October.

Kirov, S. (1886-1934): CC member from 1923 and Stalinist Leningrad party secretary from 1926, when he replaced Zinoviev.

KMT: See Kuomintang.

Kolarov, V. (1877-1950): Former Socialist and founding leader of the Bulgarian Communist Party (1919); elected to the ECCI and its presidium

(1922); after the abortive September 1923 insurrection he fled to Russia and became a Comintern functionary.

Kollontai, A. (1872-1952): A former leader of the Workers Opposition tendency in the Bolshevik Party; the world's first woman ambassador, she filled diplomatic posts for twenty-five years and was in Mexico on a diplomatic mission in 1927.

Komsomol: See Communist League of Youth.

Kondratiev, N.: Former Social Revolutionary and professional economist; as an official of the Commissariat of Finance he suggested that the class differentiation in the countryside was not serious.

Korsch, K. (1886-1961): Member of the German CP until 1926, when he was expelled for opposing ratification of the Soviet-German treaty of April 1926; also opposed the united front tactic.

Kosarev, A. (1903-1937): A leader of the Communist League of Youth and a prominent Stalin supporter.

Kosior, V.: A former leader of the Democratic Centralists and a supporter of the United Opposition; he occupied a diplomatic post in Paris in 1927 and was expelled after the Fifteenth Congress.

KPD: German Communist Party.

Krestinsky, N. (1883-1938): Old Bolshevik and Soviet ambassador in Berlin (1921-27); renounced the Opposition immediately after the Fifteenth Congress.

Kronstadt mutiny: Uprising of sailors against the Bolshevik regime in 1921, crushed by the Bolsheviks; led to the concessions of the New Economic Policy.

Krupskaya, N. (1869-1939): Old Bolshevik and Lenin's widow; she briefly aligned herself with the United Opposition in 1926.

Krzhizhanovsky, G. (1872-1959): Old Bolshevik and Stalinist; head of the State Planning Commission (1921-30).

Kuibyshev, V. (1888-1935): Stalinist; became a member of the CC in 1922; head of the CCC (1923-26); member of the Politburo from 1927; chairman of the Supreme Council of the National Economy in 1926.

Kulak: Wealthy peasant who owned and rented out land or hired others to work it.

Kuomintang (KMT): Nationalist Party of China, a bourgeois party founded by Sun Yat-sen in 1912; in 1925 it began a campaign to defeat the warlords of North China; under Chiang Kai-shek it became the ruling bourgeois party in China.

Kuusinen, O. (1881-1964): Finnish Stalinist and Comintern secretary (1922-31).

Kuzmin, N. (1883-1939): Old Bolshevik, former commissar of the Baltic Fleet; he held military posts until 1930; a Stalinist ideologue.

La Follette party (Progressive Party, U.S.): In 1924, Robert La Follette (1855-1925), Republican senator from Wisconsin, ran for president on the Progressive ticket; the CP had captured a convention of the Farmer-Labor Party in 1923, and its leadership sought to link it to La Follette's third-party campaign for the presidency; the ECCI declared this policy opportunist and the CP pulled back from the La Follette candidacy.

Lashevich, M. (1884-1928): Old Bolshevik military leader, candidate CC member, and deputy commissar of war, positions he lost in July 1926 after he spoke at an Opposition meeting; he recanted and was made assistant to the president of the board of the Chinese Eastern Railroad.

Left Communists: Faction in the Bolshevik Party in 1918, headed by Bukharin and Radek, that opposed signing the Brest-Litovsk treaty and called for a revolutionary war; they controlled the Moscow party organization and issued their own periodicals assailing Lenin and the CC; it was rumored that when he failed to win a majority to his position, Bukharin spoke of "arresting" Lenin's government; the faction included Pyatakov, V. Smirnov, Krestinsky, Osinsky, Sapronov, Preobrazhensky, Yaroslavsky, I. Armand, Bela Kun, Kollontai, Muralov, Uritsky, S. Kosior, Kuibyshev.

Lenin, V.I.: (1870-1924): Founder of the Bolshevik faction, leader of the October Revolution, head of the first Soviet government, founder of the Comintern.

Lenin levy: Stalin's scheme, following Lenin's death in January 1924, to admit new members to the party without the usual selection process; the hundreds of thousands who joined between February and May, including careerists of all sorts, gave Stalin's machine complete independence from the party.

Lenin's Testament: Written in December 1922 and January 1923, it gave his final evaluation of the other Soviet leaders; since it called for the removal of Stalin from the post of general secretary it was suppressed in the Soviet Union until after Stalin's death; it is included now in volume 36 of Lenin's *Collected Works*.

Liquidators: Bolsheviks who were reluctant to resume the underground struggle against tsarism during the years of reaction (1907-14); they wanted to "liquidate" the underground organization and engage only in activities that were acceptable to the authorities.

Lozovsky, S. (1878-1952): Stalinist; head of the Red International of Labor Unions (1921-37); in 1922 he was a delegate to the Hague Congress called by the Amsterdam trade union international to discuss the struggle against war; also active in Comintern and diplomatic work.

Makhno, N. (1884-1934): Leader of small partisan bands of peasants in the Ukraine during the civil war; fought against Ukrainian reactionaries and German occupation forces; refused to integrate his forces into the Red Army and was finally routed by Soviet forces.

Manuilsky, D. (1883-1959): Former otzovist who became a CC member in 1923 and a Comintern functionary in 1922; from 1924 on he served as Comintern representative at KPD congresses and was in Berlin in the autumn of 1927; a member of the ECCI's Secretariat (1926-43).

March action (1921, Germany): Abortive insurrection crushed in two weeks because of lack of support; the Third Comintern Congress that year repudiated it and the ultraleft theories used to justify it and adopted the tactic of the working class united front.

Maretsky, G.: Disciple of Bukharin in the Institute of Red Professors; in summer 1927 he published an article in *Pravda* denouncing Trotsky's "slanderous accusations" about Thermidor.

Martov, J. (1873-1923): A founder of the Russian Social Democracy and a close associate of Lenin until 1903, when he became a leader of the Mensheviks; emigrated to Berlin (1920) and founded *Sotsialistichesky Vestnik*, an emigré Menshevik paper.

Martynov, A. (1865-1935): Right-wing Menshevik and opponent of the October Revolution; principal Menshevik theorist of "two-stage" revolution; joined Soviet CP in 1923 as a Stalin supporter; architect of the "bloc of four classes" in China; Comintern functionary.

Maslow, A. (1891-1941): One of the central leaders of the German CP after Brandler's demotion in 1924; a member of the ECCI; supported the United Opposition and was expelled in 1926.

Mdivani, P. (1877-1937): An Old Bolshevik and former premier of Soviet Georgia; sympathized with the United Opposition; sent to Paris on a diplomatic mission in 1927; expelled in 1928 for "Trotskyist activity."

Medvedev, S.: Former member of the Workers Opposition whose 1924 letter to a comrade in Baku became the subject of a scandal in 1926 designed to embarrass the United Opposition.

Mehring, F. (1846-1919): German Marxist historian and scholar; biographer of Marx; one of the leading theoreticians of the left wing of the German Social Democracy; just before his death he helped found the Communist Party.

Melnichansky, G. (1886-1937): Old Bolshevik and a trade union functionary aligned with Tomsky.

Mensheviks: Minority faction of the Russian Social Democratic Labor Party, after the split with the Bolsheviks (1903); led by Martov and Dan, they were moderate socialists who believed that the working class must combine with the liberal bourgeoisie to overthrow tsarism and establish a democratic bourgeois republic.

Menzhinsky, V. (1874-1934): Old Bolshevik; succeeded Dzerzhinsky as head of the GPU (1926-34).

Meyer, E.: Leader of a center group in the German CP in 1926; he was incorporated into the leadership in late 1926; he served on the ECCI as German delegate.

Mikoyan, A. (1895-1978): Old Bolshevik and Stalin supporter; a CC member from 1923 on; became commissar of trade in 1926.

Military Opposition: Led by Stalin and Voroshilov during the civil war; opposed the use of military specialists from the tsarist army and resisted centralization of the Red Army under a unified command; the CP's Eighth Congress (March 1919) reaffirmed the military policy that Trotsky, as head of the Red Army, had been carrying out; the faction included V. Smirnov, Safarov, Pyatakov, and Frunze.

Milyukov, P. (1859-1943): A leader of the bourgeois Cadet Party and minister of foreign affairs in the Provisional Government (March-May

1917); emigrated to Paris, where he edited *Poslednie Novosti.*

Molotov, V. (1890-   ): Old Bolshevik and Stalin supporter; member of the CC from 1920 and of the Politburo from 1926.

Monatte, P. (1881-1960): French syndicalist; became a leader of the CP, which he joined in 1923, only to leave a year later; in 1926 he founded the Syndicalist League.

Monroe Doctrine (1823): U.S. plan to ban European political and economic intervention in the Western hemisphere under the pretext of protecting Latin America against military domination by Europe.

Mrachkovsky, S. (1883-1936): Old Bolshevik and famous civil war commander; expelled from the party in 1927 and arrested by the GPU for helping to publish the Platform of the Opposition.

Murphy, J. (1888-1965); British Stalinist and member of the ECCI; in May 1927 he made the motion to expel Trotsky from the ECCI.

Muzhik: Middle peasant.

Narodniks (Populists): Movement of Russian intellectuals who saw the liberation of the peasantry as the key to the country's development; after a split in 1879, one wing led by Plekhanov became Marxist while another evolved into the Social Revolutionary Party.

NEP (New Economic Policy): Adopted at the Tenth Congress of the RCP in March 1921 as a temporary measure to replace war communism; allowed a limited growth of free trade inside the Soviet Union and foreign concessions alongside the nationalized and state-controlled sectors of the economy; the NEPmen—petty traders, merchants, and swindlers, who benefited from this policy—were viewed as a potential base for capitalist restoration.

Neumann, H. (1902-1937?): German Stalinist on the Comintern staff (1925); Stalin's representative in China (1927-28); chief organizer of the Canton Commune (December 1927).

Nin, A. (1892-1937): A founder of the Spanish CP; secretary of the RILU; expelled (1927) because of Opposition sympathies.

1905 revolution: Grew out of discontent over the Russo-Japanese war and lasted from January 9 (when police fired on workers marching peacefully to the tsar's palace) until the crushing of the December uprising in Moscow; severe repression followed this unsuccessful revolution.

October Revolution (1917): A revolutionary upsurge, led by the Bolsheviks, overthrew the bourgeois Provisional Government backed by the Mensheviks and SRs and instituted a workers' state with a government based on soviets (councils).

Okhotnikov: Oppositionist in the GPU who was instrumental in preventing the destruction of the clandestinely printed Platform of the Opposition, for which he was expelled.

Ordzhonikidze, G. (1886-1937): Old Bolshevik and organizer of the Stalin faction; later put in charge of heavy industry; became head of the CCC in the autumn of 1926.

Ossovsky, Ya.: Party dissident who advocated raising industrial prices as a way of extracting peasant surpluses and called for legalizing other political parties; expelled August 1926.

Otzovists (recallists): Dissident group of Bolsheviks after the 1905 revolution who advocated the recall or withdrawal of the Social Democratic deputies elected to the Duma (parliament) on the grounds of the Duma's extremely reactionary character.

Painlevé, P. (1863-1933): French premier during World War I, until he was replaced by Clemenceau in 1917.

Panteleev: Communist who had been political commissar of the Second Petrograd Regiment during the civil war when he deserted from Kazan and was shot along with nineteen other under a command Trotsky had issued covering the punishment of deserters at the front.

Paul-Boncour, J. (1873-1972): Right-wing French Socialist.

Pepper, J. (1886-1937): Member of Bela Kun's short-lived Hungarian Soviet Republic in 1919, which declared the outright nationalization of the land, alienating the peasantry and hastening the government's downfall; he went to the U.S. as Comintern representative to the American CP; in 1923 he masterminded the CP's takeover of the Federated Farmer-Labor Party and its endorsement of Progressive Republican Robert La Follette's presidential candidacy; he later returned to Moscow.

Petrovsky, D.: Former member of the Bund who sided with the Mensheviks in the split in the RSDLP; he joined the Bolshevik Party after the October Revolution and in the early 1920s joined the Comintern central apparatus as a specialist in British affairs.

Petrovsky, G. (1878-1958): Old Bolshevik and CC member (1921-39); candidate member of the Politburo (1926-38); became editor of *Leningradskaya Pravda* (1928); president of the Soviet Ukrainian Republic (1919-38).

Pilsudski, J. (1867-1935): Led the Polish army against Soviet forces in the Ukraine (1920); in May 1926 he led a coup that returned him to power and was dictator of Poland until his death.

Pitt, W. (1759-1806): British prime minister (1783-1801, 1803-06); in 1794 he raised forces among European reaction to fight the armies of the French revolution.

Plenum: Full meeting, generally of the membership of the Central Committee or of the combined CC and Central Control Commission.

Politburo: The ruling body of the AUCP, although it was ostensibly subordinated to the CC; Bukharin, Voroshilov, Zinoviev, Kalinin, Molotov, Rykov, Tomsky, and Trotsky were elected to it in January 1926, when Kamenev was moved from a full member to a candidate; during 1926 Zinoviev, Trotsky and Kamenev were removed; the Politburo elected after the Fifteenth Congress consisted of Bukharin, Voroshilov, Kalinin, Kuibyshev, Molotov, Rykov, Rudzutak, Stalin, and Tomsky.

Pood: 36 pounds.

Poslednie Novosti (Latest News): Journal of one of the factions of the Cadet Party in emigration, edited by Milyukov.

Postyshev, P. (1888-1940): Old Bolshevik, Stalinist, and secretary of the Ukrainian CP; became a Politburo member in 1926.

Pravda (Truth): Official organ of the CC of the AUCP.

Preobrazhensky, E. (1886-1937): Old Bolshevik and leading economist; author of *The New Economics* (1926); expelled in 1927 as an Oppositionist; capitulated in 1929.

Profintern (Red International of Labor Unions): Organized in 1920 as a Communist-led rival to reformist Amsterdam International.

Progressive Party: See La Follette party.

Provisional Government (1917): Set up by the February revolution; supported by the Mensheviks and SRs, it governed until the October Bolshevik Revolution.

Pugh, A. (1870-1955): Chairman of the General Council of the Trades Union Congress during the General Strike; one of the negotiators with Baldwin and the Tories.

Purcell, A. (1872-1935): British left Labourite and MP; a leader of the TUC General Council during the General Strike.

Pyatakov, Yu. (1890-1937): Old Bolshevik and an Oppositionist from 1923 to 1928; deputy chairman of Vesenkha; head of the Soviet trade delegation to France in 1927; expelled in 1927, he capitulated quickly and was reinstated in the party.

Radek, K. (1885-1939): Prominent revolutionist in the Polish, German, and Russian Social Democratic parties before 1917; supported the Left Communists in 1918; became secretary of the Comintern (March 1920) with particular responsibility for Germany and China; supported the Opposition in 1923 and was subsequently dropped from all leading CI bodies; expelled from the party at the Fifteenth Congress, he capitulated in 1929.

Rafail: Editor of *Leningradskaya Pravda* after Skvortsov-Stepanov and until 1928.

Rafes, M. (1883-1942): Member of the Bund Central Committee (1912-19); participated in the anti-Communist Petlyura government in the Ukraine (1917-18); joined the CP in 1919; worked in the Comintern directing the Chinese CP in the late twenties.

Rakovsky, Kh. (1873-1941): Leading revolutionary in the Balkans before World War I; prime minister of the Ukrainian government (1919-23); later Soviet ambassador to Paris (1925-27); an early leader of the Left Opposition; expelled from the AUCP in 1927 and capitulated in 1934.

Regime of economy: Based on an August 16, 1926, proclamation by Rykov, Stalin, Kuibyshev, which sought to subsidize industrialization through frugality in industry and government rather than through an agricultural tax; in practice it led to curtailment of the workers' living standards and benefits.

Remmele, H. (1886-1939): Stalinist and a leader of the German CP from 1921 to 1933; president of the KPD for a short time after Brandler; became a member of the ECCI presidium (March 1926) and its Secretariat (December 1926).

Riese, M.: Representative of the Wedding Opposition in the German CP; spoke at the seventh ECCI plenum (1926), calling for more revolutionary actions, denying the capitalist stabilization, and pointing to right dangers in the KPD.

RILU: See Profintern.

Rosenberg, A.: A leader of the German ultraleft at the KPD's Tenth Congress (July 1925).

Rosmer, A. (1877-1964): Revolutionary syndicalist who was a leader of the French CP and the Comintern until his expulsion as an Oppositionist in 1924.

RSDLP (Russian Social Democratic Labor Party): Founded 1898; split in 1903 between Lenin's Bolsheviks and Martov's Mensheviks led to separate parties in 1912; in 1918 the Bolsheviks renamed their party the Russian Communist Party (Bolsheviks); in 1925 the RCP(B) became the All-Union Communist Party (Bolsheviks).

Rudzutak, Ya. (1887-1938): Old Bolshevik, member of the CC from 1920 and of the Secretariat from 1923; a specialist on the trade union movement and later in the economic apparatus; commissar for communications (1924-30); a member of the Politburo after the Fifteenth Congress.

Rul (Rudder): Journal of one of the factions of the Cadet Party in emigration.

Rykov, A. (1881-1938): Old Bolshevik, succeeded Lenin as head of state (1924-30); head of Vesenkha; with Bukharin, ideological leader of the right wing in the party under NEP and until his capitulation to Stalin in 1929.

Sapronov, T. (1887-1939): A leader of the Democratic Centralists and a member of the United Opposition in 1926; expelled from AUCP in 1927; later developed state capitalist views.

Savinkov, B. (1879-1925): Social Revolutionary terrorist during the 1905 revolution; became a minister in Kerensky's Provisional Government but joined Kornilov's counterrevolutionary uprising; after October he led insurgents against the Soviet regime, was captured, and committed suicide in prison.

Schwartz, E.: Ultraleft member of the KPD who attacked the military alliance between Germany and the USSR in a public speech in the Reichstag.

Scissors: The term first used by Trotsky in 1923 to call attention to the simultaneous rise of industrial prices and fall of agricultural prices occurring when agriculture was being revived at the expense of industry; on a graph the price changes resembled a scissors opening; the crisis would be eliminated, Trotsky said, by closing the "blades," that is, chiefly by lowering the prices of industrial products.

Septemvirate: The six members of the Politburo after Lenin's final withdrawal (excluding Trotsky) plus Kuibyshev, who was chairman of the CCC; the six others were Zinoviev, Kamenev, Stalin, Bukharin, Rykov, and Tomsky; this secret faction met and made all the major decisions for the party without its knowledge or consent; it functioned from 1923 until the rift with the Leningrad Opposition in 1925.

Serebryakov, L. (1890-1937): Old Bolshevik and former member of the Secretariat (1919-20) and deputy commissar for communications in the mid-twenties; visited China and Japan to negotiate railroad agreements (1926); a supporter of the United Opposition; expelled in October 1927, recanted in 1929.

Shatskin, L.: Member of the "Young Stalinist Left," a group of anti-Bukharinist party and Communist League of Youth leaders.

Shcherbakov: Oppositionist who had a duplicating machine in his apartment used to produce copies of the Opposition Platform in September 1927.

Shlyapnikov, A. (1883-1937): Old Bolshevik and CC member from 1915 on; chairman of the Metal Workers Union and first Soviet commissar of labor; a leader of the Workers Opposition (1921-23); expelled, readmitted, and expelled again in 1927.

Shvernik, N. (1888-1970): Old Bolshevik; a Stalinist member of the CC from 1925 on; a former CC secretary and a former leader of the Urals party organization.

Skrypnik, N. (1872-1933): Old Bolshevik and leader of the Ukrainian CP; he promoted de-Russification and was at various times commissar for internal affairs and for education; committed suicide when faced with the prospect of a purge of the Ukrainian party.

Skvortsov-Stepanov, I. (1870-1928): Old Bolshevik and former editor of *Izvestia*; assistant editor of *Pravda* (1924); replaced a Zinovievist as editor of *Leningradskaya Pravda* (1925); director of the Lenin Institute (1926); translated Marx and wrote on political and economic topics.

Slepkov, A.: Young historian and protegé of Bukharin in the Institute of Red Professors; one of the foremost elaborators of Bukharin's ideas in the official press.

Smenovekhovites: Group of emigré Russian intellectuals in Prague from 1921 on who published the journal *Smena Vekh* (Changing Landmarks) expressing sympathy with the Soviet government to the extent that it departed from the ideals of Bolshevism and appeared to be moving toward capitalism.

Smeral, B. (1880-1941): Right-wing Social Democrat who became a leader of the Czechoslovak CP from its founding (1921); elected to the ECCI and its presidium (1922).

Smilga, I. (1892-1938): Old Bolshevik and a civil war hero; later a member of the Supreme Council of the National Economy and the State Planning Commission; CC member (1917-20, 1925-27); an Oppositionist leader, expelled in 1927, deported in 1928; capitulated in 1929.

Smirnov, A. (1877-1938): Old Bolshevik, deputy commissar for internal affairs and for food; a supporter of Rykov.

Smirnov, I. (1881-1936): Old Bolshevik and civil war hero; CC member from 1920 and commissar of posts and telegraph; an Oppositionist, expelled in 1927; capitulated in 1929.

Smirnov, V.: A leader of the Democratic Centralists and a member of the first Vesenkha staff; joined the United Opposition in 1926, although he called for a new party; expelled from AUCP December 1927.

Smychka: This Russian term has two meanings in this book: (1) the "bond" or link between the workers and the peasants that the workers' state had to maintain to be able to build socialism in a predominantly peasant country; (2) Trotsky also uses it to refer to the clandestine meetings of Oppositionists held in the autumn of 1927.

Social Revolutionaries (SRs): Major radical-intellectual and peasant current in Russia from 1900 until the revolution; in 1917 the party split and the left wing supported the Soviet government until it signed the Brest-Litovsk peace with Germany.

Sokolnikov, G. (1888-1939): Old Bolshevik and a CC member from 1917 on; played an important role in the civil war; commissar of finance (1922-26); before the formation of the Leningrad Opposition, of which he was a member, he was the leading spokesman for the financial policies of the majority, including its rejection of economic planning and its reliance on currency manipulation.

Sotsialistichesky Vestnik (Socialist Herald): The chief Menshevik emigré journal, published weekly in Berlin (1921-33).

Souvarine, B. (1893-   ): A founder of the French CP, expelled in 1924 as a Trotskyist; in 1929 he broke with Trotsky and shortly thereafter turned against Marxism.

"Spetses": From the abbreviation of the Russian word for "specialists," usually managers or technicians in economic, military, or industrial positions, who were not loyal to the Soviet regime but agreed to continue serving it in return for high salaries and privileges.

Stalin, J. (1879-1953): Old Bolshevik, CC member from 1912 on; became general secretary in 1922; in 1917 he favored a conciliatory attitude to the Provisional Government before Lenin returned and reoriented the Bolsheviks to winning power; Lenin called in 1923 for his removal from the post of general secretary because he was using it to bureaucratize the party and state apparatuses; after Lenin's death this process was intensified until Stalin became virtual dictator of the Soviet Union and the party.

State Planning Commission (Gosplan): Highest planning body in the USSR, established in 1921.

Sten, I.: Member of an anti-Bukharinist party youth group sometimes called the "Young Stalinist Left."

Stetsky, A.: Young Bukharin disciple and a member of the CCC; he also headed the Agitprop bureau of the Leningrad party organization and became a full CC member in 1927; he defected to Stalin in March 1929.

Stockholm Congress (1906): First joint congress of the Bolsheviks and Mensheviks since the split of the two factions in 1903; the majority was held by the Mensheviks in Stockholm; the unity was short-lived.

Sukhanov, N. (1882-193?): Menshevik-Internationalist during World War I; a well-known intellectual and historian of the Russian revolution; worked in the Soviet economic apparatus.

Sun Yat-sen (1866-1925): Bourgeois nationalist leader of the Chinese revolution of 1911 and founder of the Kuomintang.

Supreme Council of the National Economy (Vesenkha): Set up in December 1917, became the main instrument for centralizing and administering industry; in the early days of the revolution, it had the power to operate all branches of industry and commerce and to direct economic planning; gradually it became the chief organ of industrial planning.

T'ang Sheng-chih (1890-   ): Hunanese militarist who affiliated to the KMT in June 1926, participating in the Northern Expedition; helped take Wuhan for the KMT (August-October 1926); became military chief of the "left" KMT government at Wuhan after the split with Chiang Kai-shek (April 1927); led the military suppression of the Chinese CP in Wuhan (July 1927).

Tardieu, A. (1876-1945): A right-wing French politician who advocated the pillage of Germany after World War I.

Ter-Vaganyan, V. (1873-1936): An Old Bolshevik and a civil war veteran, wrote numerous works on the national question; a Left Oppositionist; expelled in 1927; capitulated in 1929.

Thälmann, E. (1886-1944): Elected to the ECCI in 1924; a faithful Stalinist, he became the unchallenged leader of the party after the expulsion of Maslow, Fischer, and Urbahns.

Thermidor: By analogy with the period of reaction in the French Revolution, Trotsky used this term to mean capitalist counterrevolution; the extent to which this was being accomplished was the subject of some debate in the Opposition and in the party as a whole (see Introduction, p. 17.).

Third Duma (1907-08): A reactionary parliament with only fourteen Social Democratic delegates out of some 300.

Thomas, J. (1874-1949): Member of the TUC General Council and one of the three negotiators with Baldwin in the 1926 General Strike.

Tomsky, M. (1880-1936): Old Bolshevik, head of the Soviet trade unions and a Politburo member; he was associated with Bukharin's right-wing policies.

Treint, A. (1889-1972): Formerly a central leader of the French CP, he supported the Russian Leningrad Opposition and was expelled in 1927.

"Triangle": Factory power caucus consisting of the party secretary, the factory director, and the chairman of the factory committee, who together wielded control over the factory and its trade union life.

Trades Union Congress (TUC): British trade union federation, headed by a General Council; during the civil war the TUC had spoken out vigorously against British intervention in Russia despite its reactionary leadership.

Tseretelli, I. (1882-1959): Russian Menshevik who held posts in the Provisional Government but emigrated in 1919.

Tverskoi: GPU agent who implicated the Opposition in allegations of a military conspiracy and a secret printing press in 1927.

"Twenty-one points": Conditions for membership in the Comintern, drafted by Lenin and adopted by its Second World Congress (1920) to prevent the affiliation of centrist parties that had not fully broken with reformism.

Uglanov, N. (1886-193?): Old Bolshevik and civil war veteran; secretary of the Moscow party organization and a member of the CC Secretariat from 1924; he supported Bukharin in 1928-29 and was eliminated from the leadership in 1930.

Ultimatists: Group of Bolsheviks who called in 1908 for an ultimatum to the Social Democratic deputies in the Third Duma, demanding that they obey the CC's instructions unconditionally.

"Unitary" French unionists: Members of the left-wing French labor federation (CGTU).

Unshlicht, J. (1879-1938): Old Bolshevik and Stalinist who held high positions in the security police and, after 1925, in the Red Army.

Urbahns, H. (1890-1946): A leader of the German CP after Brandler was demoted (1924); expelled with Maslow and Fischer in 1926 and helped found the Leninbund.

Ustryalov, N. (1890- ?): Member of the Cadet Party who fought on the White side in the civil war; after the victory of the Bolsheviks he went to work for the Soviet government as an economist because he believed it would inevitably be compelled to restore capitalism.

Vareikis, J.: Head of the press section of the CC; he took over the editorship of *Molodaya Gvardiya* in early 1925; his 1925 pamphlet "Is the Victory of Socialism in One Country Possible?" made him one of the leading exponents of Stalin's theory.

Verst: 3,500 feet.

Vesenkha: See Supreme Council of the National Economy.

Viviani, R. (1863-1925): Right-wing French statesman and former Socialist; premier at the outbreak of war (1914-15) and minister of justice under Briand (1915-17) and Clemenceau.

Voikov, P.: Soviet ambassador to Poland, whose assassination in June 1927 by a White emigré following the rupture in relations with Britain was widely feared to mean the escalation of hostilities with Western Europe.

Voroshilov, K. (1881-1969): Old Bolshevik and Stalin supporter; a leader of the Military Opposition (1919); member of the Politburo from 1926; commissar of war (1925-30).

Vujović, V. (1895- ?): Yugoslav Communist and a founder of the Communist Youth International (1919) and its general secretary (1922-26); elected to the ECCI as a youth representative (1924); a supporter of Zinoviev and a participant in the United Opposition; expelled from the Comintern (September 1927); capitulated in 1929.

Wang Ching-wei (1884-1944): Second-ranking member of the KMT executive from 1924; chairman of the Nationalist government formed at

Canton (July 1925); became a leader of the left wing of the KMT, favoring alliances with the CCP and the USSR; resigned after Chiang's March 1926 coup in Canton; followed Chiang's example in purging the CCP and the trade unions in Wuhan in July 1927; after autumn 1927, he headed a dissident faction in the KMT.

War communism: Harsh economic policies that prevailed during the civil war, including requisitioning needed supplies and nationalizations, required to win the military struggle; after the Kronstadt uprising in 1921, war communism was replaced by the NEP.

Weber, Hans: Dissident German CC member and head of the Wedding Opposition in the KPD.

Workers Opposition: Syndicalist group in the CP in the early twenties which opposed the NEP and called for transferring all control and leadership of the national economy to the trade unions; it was expelled at the Tenth Congress; some of its leaders joined the United Opposition in 1926 and were expelled and deported in 1927.

Wrangel, P. (1878-1928): White Guard general who was the last commander-in-chief of the counterrevolutionary forces in the civil war; in the autumn of 1920 he was defeated by the Red Army and fled abroad; the "Wrangel officer" was a GPU agent introduced into the Left Opposition at the end of 1927 in an attempt to discredit the Opposition through its alleged association with White forces; Trotsky later identified him as Stroilov (in *The Case of Leon Trotsky*, p. 362).

Yagoda, H. (1891-1938): Old Bolshevik and Stalinist; deputy chief of the GPU from 1924 to 1934, when he became its head.

Yanson, N.: Stalinist member of the CCC and an official of the Commissariat of Justice.

Yaroslavl station: Site of a public demonstration of sympathy for the Opposition when Oppositionist Smilga left Moscow for Khabarovsk, June 9, 1927; Zinoviev and Trotsky both addressed the crowd.

Yaroslavsky, E. (1878-1943): Old Bolshevik and Stalinist; member of the presidium of the CCC and coauthor of the official charges brought against Trotsky in July 1927.

Yeh T'ing (1897-1946): Joined the KMT in 1922 and the CCP in Moscow in 1925; a leader of the August 1, 1927, CCP putsch at Nanchang; commanded CCP troops in the Canton Commune (December 1927).

Yevdokimov, G. (1884-1936): A CC secretary, removed from the Secretariat in 1926 because he was a supporter of Zinoviev, and expelled from the CC in 1927.

Zalutsky, P. (1887-1937): Old Bolshevik and former member of the Petrograd Military Revolution Committee; active in the civil war, where he was named in connection with charges that Trotsky was threatening to shoot Communists; an Oppositionist, he recanted in March 1927 but rejoined the Opposition and was expelled in December 1927; recanted again in 1928.

Zetkin, K. (1857-1933): Veteran of the German labor movement and a founder, theoretician, and activist of the women's movement; a Communist deputy in the Reichstag from 1920; served as a member of the ECCI and lived in Russia after the left wing took over the German CP leadership in 1924; she took part in enlarged ECCI plenums in 1925, 1926, 1927.

   Zinoviev, G. (1883-1936): Old Bolshevik CC member; initially opposed the October insurrection; head of the Comintern (1919-26); after Lenin's death blocked with Stalin against Trotsky until late 1925; formed the Leningrad Opposition (1925); in 1926 he and Kamenev joined with Trotsky to form the United Opposition; expelled in 1927; recanted almost at once.

Further Reading

The following works contain articles or speeches by Trotsky during 1926-27, relating directly or indirectly to the Left Opposition's activities or positions (all are published or distributed by Pathfinder Press, unless otherwise indicated):

Leon Trotsky on Britain. 1973. Includes "Problems of the British Labor Movement" (Dec. 22, 1925–May 19, 1926); "On Tempos and Dates" (published Feb. 11); "Brailsford and Marxism" (March 10); "Once More on Pacifism and Revolution" (May 3); "The Future of the British Communist Party" (June 3); "Resolution on the General Strike in Britain" (July); "Amendments to the Resolution on the Situation in Britain" and "Resolution of the Opposition on the Anglo-Russian Committee" (Feb.-March? 1927); "The Struggle for Peace and the Anglo-Russian Committee" (May 16); "What We Gave and What We Got" (Sept. 23).

Problems of Everyday Life and Other Writings on Culture and Science. 1973. "Next Tasks for Worker Correspondents" (Jan. 13, 1926); "Culture and Socialism" (Feb. 3); "Radio, Science, Technology, and Society" (March 1).

Leon Trotsky on Literature and Art. 1970. "To the Memory of Sergei Essenin" (Jan. 19, 1926).

Europe and America. 1971. "Europe and America" (Feb. 15, 1926); "Introduction" (Feb. 25).

Writings of Leon Trotsky (1932). 1973. Speech to the Polish Commission of the Comintern (July 2, 1926), reproduced in "Pilsudskism, Fascism, and the Character of Our Epoch."

Leon Trotsky on China. 1976. "First Letter to Radek" (Aug. 30, 1926); "The Chinese Communist Party and the Kuomintang" (Sept. 27); "Second Letter to Radek" (March 4, 1927); "A Brief Note" (March 22); "Letter to Alsky" (March 29); "To the Politburo of the AUCP(B) Central Committee" (March 31); "Class Relations in the Chinese Revolution" (April 3); "On the Slogan of Soviets" (April 16); "The Friendly Exchange of Portraits Between Stalin and Chiang Kai-shek" (April 18); "The Chinese Revolution and the Theses of Comrade Stalin" (May 7); "The Communist Party and the Kuomintang" (May 10); "The Sure Road" (May 12); "A Protest to the Central Control Commission" (May 17); "Letter to the Secretariat of the Central Committee" (May 18); "Statement to the Plenum of the ECCI" (May); "It Is Time to Understand . . ." (May 27); "Hankow and Moscow" (May 28); "Is It Not Time to Understand?" (May 28); "Why Have We Not Called for Withdrawal from the Kuomintang Until Now?" (June 23); "For a Special Session of the Presidium of the ECCI" (July); "New Opportunities for the Chinese Revolution . . ." (Sept.).

The Stalin School of Falsification. 1971. Two speeches at a session of the Central Control Commission (June 24, 1927); "The War Danger—Defense Policy and the Opposition" (Aug. 1); "Letter to the Bureau of Party History" (Oct. 21); "Some Documents Relating to the Origin of the Legend of 'Trotskyism'" (Nov. 1927–Jan. 1928).

Among the works by Trotsky written after 1927 which contain important material about the 1926-27 Opposition are the following:

The Case of Leon Trotsky. 1969.
Diary in Exile 1935. Harvard University Press, 1976.
My Life. 1970.
The Permanent Revolution. 1969.
Portraits, Political and Personal. 1977.
The Revolution Betrayed. 1972.
Stalin: An Appraisal of the Man and His Influence. 2 vols. London: Panther, 1969.
The Third International After Lenin. 1972.
Writings of Leon Trotsky (1929-40). 12 vols. plus 2-part Supplement. 1969-79.

Among other works that were consulted in the preparation of this volume and/or that provide further information on the subject are the following:

Boukharine, N. *Le Socialisme Dans Un Seul Pays* (Socialism in One Country). Paris: Union Générale des Editions, 1974.

Broué, Pierre. *Le Parti Bolchevique: Histoire du P.C. de l'U.R.S.S.* Paris: Minuit, 1971.

Calhoun, Daniel F. *The United Front: The TUC and the Russians, 1923-1928.* Cambridge Univ. Press, 1976.

Carr, E. H. *A History of Soviet Russia.* 14 vols.: vols. 1-3, *The Bolshevik Revolution, 1917-1923*; vol. 4, *The Interregnum, 1923-1924*; vols. 5-8, *Socialism in One Country, 1924-1926*; vols. 9-14 (9-10 with R. W. Davies), *Foundations of a Planned Economy, 1926-1929.* London: Macmillan, 1951-1978.

Cohen, Stephen F. *Bukharin and the Bolshevik Revolution.* New York: Knopf, 1973.

Daniels, R. V. *The Conscience of the Revolution: Communist Opposition in Soviet Russia.* New York: Simon and Schuster, 1969.

Daniels, R. V. *A Documentary History of Communism.* New York: Random House, 1960.

Day, R. B. *Leon Trotsky and the Politics of Economic Isolation.* Cambridge Univ. Press, 1973.

Deutscher, Isaac. *The Prophet Armed (Trotsky: 1879-1921); The Prophet Unarmed (Trotsky: 1921-1929); The Prophet Outcast (Trotsky: 1929-1940).* Oxford Univ. Press (paperback eds.), 1980.

Haupt, Georges, and Jean-Jacques Marie. *Makers of the Russian Revolution: Biographies of Bolshevik Leaders.* Cornell Univ. Press, 1974.

Institute of Marxism-Leninism (Moscow). *Against Trotskyism.* Moscow: Progress Publishers, 1972.

Knei-Paz, Baruch. *The Social and Political Thought of Leon Trotsky.* Oxford: Clarendon Press, 1978.

Lenin, V. I. *Collected Works.* 45 vols. Moscow: Progress, 1960-69.

——, and Leon Trotsky. *Lenin's Fight Against Stalinism.* New York: Pathfinder, 1975.

Leon Trotsky, the Man and His Work: Reminiscences and Appraisals by Joseph Hansen, James P. Cannon, Natalia Sedova Trotsky, Jean van Heijenoort, Farrell Dobbs, and others. New York: Merit, 1969.

Lewin, Moshe. *Lenin's Last Struggle.* New York: Monthly Review Press, 1978.

——. *Political Undercurrents in Soviet Economic Debates.* Princeton Univ. Press, 1974.

Mandel, Ernest. *Trotsky: A Study in the Dynamic of His Thought.* London: New Left Books, 1979.

Medvedev, Roy. *Let History Judge: The Origins and Consequences of Stalinism.* New York: Knopf, 1972.

——. *On Stalin and Stalinism.* Oxford Univ. Press, 1979.

Meijer, Jan M., ed. *The Trotsky Papers, 1917-22.* 2 vols. The Hague: Mouton & Co., 1964.

Preobrazhensky, E. A. *The Crisis of Soviet Industrialization: Selected Essays.* White Plains, N.Y.: M. E. Sharpe, 1979.

——. *The New Economics.* Oxford: Clarendon Press, 1965.

Schapiro, Leonard. *The Communist Party of the Soviet Union.* New York: Vintage, 1960.

Serge, Victor. *Memoirs of a Revolutionary.* Oxford Univ. Press, 1967.

——, and Natalia Sedova Trotsky. *The Life and Death of Leon Trotsky.* New York: Basic Books, 1975.

Stalin, J. V. *Works.* 13 vols. Moscow: Foreign Language Publishing House, 1952-1955.

——. *Problems of Leninism.* New York: International Publishers, 1934.

Trotsky, L. *The First Five Years of the Communist International.* 2 vols. New York: Monad Press, 1973.

Tucker, Robert C. *Stalin as Revolutionary, 1879-1929.* New York: Norton, 1973.

See also the weekly *International Press Correspondence* during 1926, 1927, and early 1928.

BOOKS AND PAMPHLETS BY LEON TROTSKY*

Against Individual Terrorism
The Age of Permanent Revolution
The Basic Writings of Trotsky
Between Red and White
The Bolsheviki and World Peace
(War and the International)
The Case of Leon Trotsky
The Challenge of the Left Opposition (1923-25) (incl. The New Course, Lessons of October, Problems of Civil War, and Toward Socialism or Capitalism?)
The Challenge of the Left Opposition (1926-27) (incl. The Platform of the Opposition)
The Crisis of the French Section (1935-36)
Europe and America: Two Speeches on Imperialism
Fascism: What It Is and How to Fight It
The First Five Years of the Communist International (2 vols.)
The History of the Russian Revolution (3 vols.)
Kronstadt (with V. I. Lenin)
In Defense of Marxism
Lenin: Notes for a Biographer
Lenin's Fight Against Stalinism (with V. I. Lenin)
Leon Trotsky Speaks
Literature and Revolution
Marxism in Our Time
Military Writings
My Life
1905
On Black Nationalism and Self-Determination
On Britain (incl. Where is Britain Going?)
On China (incl. Problems of the Chinese Revolution)
On France (incl. Whither France?)

On the Jewish Question
On Literature and Art
On the Paris Commune
On the Trade Unions
Our Revolution
The Permanent Revolution and Results and Prospects
Portraits, Political and Personal
Problems of Everyday Life and Other Writings on Culture and Science
The Revolution Betrayed
The Spanish Revolution (1931-39)
Stalin
The Stalin School of Falsification
The Struggle Against Fascism in Germany
Terrorism and Communism
Their Morals and Ours (with essays by John Dewey and George Novack)
The Third International After Lenin
The Transitional Program for Socialist Revolution (incl. The Death Agony of Capitalism and the Tasks of the Fourth International)
Trotsky's Diary in Exile, 1935
The War Correspondence of Leon Trotsky: vol. 1 (The Balkan Wars)
Women and the Family
Writings of Leon Trotsky (1929-40) (12 vols. and a two-part supplement)
The Young Lenin

In preparation:
The Challenge of the Left Opposition (1928-29)
The War Correspondence of Leon Trotsky: vol. 2 (World War I)

---

*This list includes only books and pamphlets by Leon Trotsky published in the United States and in print as of 1980.

INDEX

(Page references in italics indicate glossary entries.)

Adolescents. *See* Youth

Afghanistan, 409

Agitprop, 242, 283, 294, 396-97, 399, 400

Agricultural workers, 314, 327, 329, 344, 345, 350-51; activism of, 98, 110, 121, 231, 345; and Soviet regime, 96-97, 191, 322, 325-26, 344, 345, 368, 382

Agriculture, 47-48, 80, 88, 95, 98-100, 103, 134, 231-32, 301, 322-30; mechanization of, 141, 322, 323, 327, 328-29, 330, 345. *See also* Kulaks; Peasantry; Tax policy

Albania, 434

Aleksandrov, A., 238, 483

Alekseev, G., 483

Alsky, A., 238, 468, 483

All-Union Central Council of Trade Unions. *See* AUCCTU

All-Union Communist Party. *See* AUCP

Amsterdam International (International Federation of Trade Unions—IFTU), 84-85, 95-96, 100, 104, 105, 135, 142, 246, 356, 376, 377, 385, 409, *511g*

Andreev, N., 483

Anglo-Russian Committee (Anglo-Russian Trade Union Unity Committee), 20, 61, 104, 135, 142, 190, 215-16, 234, 299, 385, 400, 403, 406-07, 409, 435, 496, *511g*; Berlin conference (April 1927), 225, 228, 242; and Chinese revolution, 20, 225, 228-29

Antipov, 272

Anti-Semitism, 36, 45-46, 469

Antonov-Ovseenko, V., 250, 298, *511g*

Apparatus pressure methods: in Comintern, 196-98, 237; in party, 36-37, 40-42, 44-46, 48, 68, 70, 76, 89, 103, 113-14, 118, 244, 256, 299, 308, 364, 453. *See also* Nonparty methods

Arbeiter Zeitung (Vienna), 381

Arshavsky, Z., 238

Arshin, *511g*

AUCCTU (All-Union Central Council of Trade Unions), 95, 104, 105, 196, 228, 320, 356, 385-86, *511g*

AUCP (All-Union Communist Party), 229, 292, 300, 340, 355-57, 388-91, 393-94, 491, *511g*; Bureau of Party History, 439; class changes in, 103-04, 108, 110, 193, 235, 349-62, 378, 452, 482; education in, 361, 450; expulsions from, 439-40, 445-46, 452, 453-54, 467, 470, 473, 480, 483, 485, 488, 494, 495, 503-04; gangsterism in, 392-93, 438, 439-42, 446-47, 449-51, 463-65, 467-69, 475; internal life stifled, 35-46, 113-19, 245-48, 267, 383, 386, 387, 401, 440; Orgburo, 408; Politburo, 86-87, 90-91, 114, 130, 222, 224, 289, 355, 498, *521g*; relations with workers, 231-33, 329-30, 392, 402, 476-77; Secretariat, 90, 355, 406, 407, 411, 440, 441; social composition of, 82-83, 350, 351, 353, 358-59, 360, 394; sympathy for Opposition in, 383, 437, 447, 453-54, 473, 478, 480,

495; tenth anniversary manifesto, 428, 429, 443-45, 463-66, 490; Fourth Congress (April-May 1906), 126, 128; Eighth Congress (March 1919), 271, 285-86; Ninth Conference (Sept. 1920), 82, 93; Tenth Congress (March 1921), 64, 66, 75, 147, 359, 360; Tenth Conference (May 1921), 360; Eleventh Congress (March-April 1922), 233, 261, 302, 317, 321, 390, 391, 402n, 441; Twelfth Congress (April 1923), 54, 59, 282-83, 347, 359, 360; Thirteenth Conference (Jan. 1924), 75; Thirteenth Congress (May 1924), 64, 65, 127, 174, 358-59, 362; Fourteenth Conference (April 1925), 27; Fourteenth Congress (Dec. 1925), 35, 64, 65, 86, 114, 120, 122, 124, 126, 127, 128, 129, 156, 303, 305, 317, 319, 351, 355, 359, 360, 362, 374, 388, 461, 497; Fourteenth Congress, resolution on industry, 27, 47-48, 50, 53, 56, 79, 182, 223; Fifteenth Conference (Oct.-Nov. 1926), 101, 118, 125, 130, 131, 165, 240, 428; Fifteenth Congress (Dec. 1927), 118, 119, 123, 224, 236, 244, 245, 246, 269, 281, 290, 294-95, 298, 319, 332, 355, 361, 392, 395, 409, 448, 453-54, 478, 479-80, 481, 485-86, 497-98, 500-01; Fifteenth Congress, precongress discussion for, 248, 301, 358, 403, 410, 411, 413, 423, 474, 475, 491. *See also* Apparatus pressure methods; Bureaucratism; Central Committee; Central Control Commission; Nonparty methods; Party apparatus; Party democracy; Party discipline; Party leadership; Party tasks; Party unity

Ausem, 483

Austria, 375, 376, 502

Avdeev, I., 92, 269, 295, 301, 470, 483

Aviapribor factory, 112

Avramson, A., 238

Babakhan, N., 238, 483

Babushkin, 440, 441

Bakaev, M., 92, 269, 270, 287-88, 289, 295, 301, 427, 456, 483, *511g*

Baku, 88, 346

Baldwin, S., 131, 134, *511g*

Baltic states, 366

Baranov, S., 483

Batashev, A., 483

Bauer, O., 138, 140, 141, 151, 193, 375, 381, *511g*

Belenky, G., 73, 76, 82, 91, 483, *511g*

Beloborodov, A., 238, 483

Belov, 286

Belyais, Ya., 238, 483

Bernstein, E., 178, *511g*

Beys, 210, 212, *512g*

Birch, 173

Black Hundreds, 45, 208, 287, 400, 469, *512g*

Blanquism, 387, *512g*

"Bloc of four classes," 225, 227. *See also* Martynov

Boguslavsky, M., 483

Bolshevik, 226, 281

Bolshevik Party, 175-76, 241, 262, 264, 383, *512g*; democracy in, 233, 235, 352, 355

Bolshevism, 373, 388, 407, 411, 413, 442, 496

Bonapartism, 141, 395, 401-02, 404, 492, 493

Bordiga, A., 127, 128, *512g*

Bourgeoisie, 172, 260-61, 303-05, 308, 309-10, 312, 323, 342, 344, 368, 388, 445, 490; and NEP, 98, 138, 151, 167-68, 234-35, 306. *See also* Kulaks; NEPmen; Ustryalov

Brandler, H., 217-18, 220, 221, *512g*

Brandt, 173

Brest-Litovsk treaty, 150, 235, 265, 266, 471, *512g*

Briand, A., 285, 399, *512g*

Britain, 96, 152, 180, 203, 206, 208; intervention in China, 216, 225,

228, 241, 376, 407; relations with USSR, 224, 225-26, 280, 365-66, 379, 433, 435. *See also* Anglo-Russian Committee; Coalminers' strike; General Council: General strike

Broido, 465-66
Budenny, S., 468, 469
Budget, 105, 309, 310, 311, 337, 340
Budzinskaya, R., 238, 483
Buffer groups, 254, 256, 453
Bukharin, N., 116-17, 117n, 136, 173, 220, 265, 332, 356, 410, 413-14, 444, *512g*; and China, 241, 244, 307, 369, 371, 372, 381, 412; on economic isolationism, 158-59, 374, 465; and party democracy, 35-46, 208, 387, 428, 438, 449; and peasants, 158, 307, 323, 334, 446; on Thermidor, 489, 492. *See also* Bukharin-Rykov tendency; Left Communists; Stalin-Bukharin faction
Bukharinists, 112, 225, 237, 351, 355, 372, 395, 429, 449, 452, 463
Bukharin-Rykov tendency, 112, 116-17, 377, 378, 384, 389, 390, 444, 498. *See also* Stalin-Bukharin faction
Bukharin "School of Red Professors," 112, 225, 237, 258, 351, 355, 372, 429, 449
Bulgaria, 242
Bund, 353, *512g*
Bureaucratism, 60, 102, 338; causes of, 68, 76-77, 103, 165, 256, 299, 390-91, 445, 452, 490; in Comintern, 193, 194, 196-98, 406-10, 413, 435; in industry, 83-84, 225, 316; in national republics, 210-13, 355-49; in party, 35-46, 61-72, 74-76, 79, 82, 88, 104, 113-17, 134, 169, 193, 209, 210-13, 235-36, 241, 255, 256, 268, 290, 299, 351-54, 378-79, 383, 386, 392-93, 400-04, 407, 408, 410-11, 413-14, 437-48, 452, 474, 475; in state, 81, 162-63, 172, 235,

303-04, 312, 340-44, 379, 384
Bureaucrats, 356-57, 443, 444, 464, 489; and Soviet power, 230, 302-03, 306, 307, 368, 379, 382

Cadets, 353, 370, 437, *512g*
Canada, 180
Canton Commune (China, 1927), 22, 490-502
Capitalism, growth of, 191, 303, 306, 308, 322, 323, 344-45, 385, 443, 459
Capitalist restoration. *See* Bourgeoisie
Central Committee (CC), 231, 246-47, 250-51, 255, 351, 355-57, 358, 361, 410, 455; plenums: Oct. 1925, 80; April 1926, 47-50, 56, 118, 120, 122, 133, 222-23; July 1926, 73, 89, 95, 101, 114, 118, 121; Oct. 1926, 118; Feb. 1927, 205, 231; April 1927, 222, 240, 247; July-Aug. 1927, 234, 258, 265, 270, 291, 294, 296, 374-75, 456; Oct. 1927, 437
Central Control Commission (CCC), 73, 75, 87, 90, 91, 118, 241, 244, 258, 277, 288, 361, 408, 415, 416-17, 420, 469, 473
Centrism, 104, 356-57, 378, 390, 442-43, 490, 497-98, 504, 506, *512g*. *See also* Stalinists
Chamberlain, A., 243, 244, 256, 259, 385, *513g*
Chang Tso-lin, 366, *513g*
Chayanov, A., 356, *513g*
Chen Tu-hsiu, 370, *513g*
Chernov, M., 374, 484, *513g*
Chervonets, 124, 331, 339-401, 458, *513g*
Chiang Kai-shek, 224, 227, 240-41, 242, 299, 354, 386, 409, 440, 442, *513g*
Chinese Eastern Railroad, 366, *513g*
Chinese revolution, 152, 207, 224, 229, 234, 240-41, 242, 244, 245, 301, 365, 378, 379, 400, 403, 409,

434, 496; and British intervention, 216, 225, 228, 241, 376, 407;
and campaign against Opposition, 226-27, 237, 299, 383-84, 386,
388, 435; class relations in, 241,
255-56, 368-73; soviets in, 227,
369, 371-72; Stalinist policy in,
368-70, 371, 372, 386, 490, 502
Chinovniks, 341, 344, *513g*
Chkheidze, N., 373
Chubar, V., 285, 356, 439, 443
Citrine, W., 234, *513g*
Civil war, Russian, 66, 170, 182,
244, 246, 262, 271, 352, 392
Class differentiation in village,
103, 109, 303-04, 305, 323, 409,
458; and industry's lag, 49, 96,
104, 121, 133, 143, 231, 309, 324,
326
Clemenceau, G., *513g*
Clemenceau thesis, 252-53, 274,
284-85, 289, 291, 292, 395-404,
513g
Coalminers' strike (Britain, 1926),
84, 192, 206, 207, 216, 238, 407,
434
Collective farming, 326, 328, 329.
See also Cooperatives
Comintern (Communist, or Third,
International), 61, 100, 111, 136,
140, 189, 191-204, 245, 280, 301,
358, 373-76, 377, 379, 501-02, 509,
513g; bureaucracy in, 86, 193,
194, 196-98, 406-10, 413, 435; on
China, 224, 229, 234, 381; opportunist elements in, 104, 196-97,
219, 242, 378, 407; Oppositionists
in, 125-28, 195-204, 214-21, 224,
229, 236, 237, 242, 291, 293, 378,
381, 386, 405, 408-12, 483, 507;
"21 points," 373, *526g*; ultralefts
in, 192, 198, 199-200, 377; Congresses: Second (1920), 369, 372,
377, 381; Third (1921), 136, 177-
78; Fourth (1922), 136-37, 138,
151, 277, 369, 376, 381; Fifth
(1924), 173, 174, 218, 237, 409,
501, 507; Sixth (1928), 409, 501-
02, 509. *See also* ECCI
Commissariat of Agriculture, 74,
103
Commissariat of Labor, 316
Commissariat of Trade, 118, 457
Communist League of Youth, 83,
188, 270, 273-74, 311, 362-64, 449-
51, *514g*
Communist parties: Austria, 375;
Britain, 196, 197, 375; China, 225,
226, 227, 368, 370, 372, 381;
Czechoslovakia, 207; France,
127, 195, 200-04, 207, 412; Germany (KPD), 126-27, 128, 197,
207, 214-21, 291, 293, 377-78;
Italy, 127, 128; Norway, 207;
Poland, 61, 207; Sweden, 207;
USSR, *see* AUCP. *See also* Co-
mintern
Concessions (to foreign capital-
ists), 79, 100, 104-05, 127, 129, 338
"Conditional defense," 265, 266,
267
Cooperatives, 74, 80, 96, 97-98, 103,
110, 134, 143, 156, 229, 231, 304,
309, 326-27, 328, 331; Lenin on,
155, 323, 329
Credit, 304, 326, 327, 328, 337, 338
Crimea, 347
Criticism, 99, 193-94, 240, 241, 255,
292, 308, 349-50, 359-60, 410, 489
Czechoslovakia, 207, 214, 377

Dan, F., 85, 444, *514g*
Defeatism, 249-51, 252-53, 266, 291,
292, 386
Defense preparations, 270-71, 285,
330, 331, 340, 366-68, 376-77, 380-
82, 382-83. *See also* War danger
Defensism, 215, 291, 292-93, 368,
406, 407
Democracy: bourgeois, 71, 395, 401-
02, 492-93; workers', 40-43, 45, 70,
72, 75, 81, 344, 353, 395. *See also*
Party democracy

Democratic centralism, 113, 401-02
Democratic Centralists, 205, *514g*
Democratic dictatorship of the proletariat and peasantry, 369, 372
Desyatina, *514g*
Dictatorship of the party vs. dictatorship of the class, 61, 70-71, 179, 353
Dictatorship of the proletariat, 61, 323, 328, 353, 401, 441, 482; 492, 493, 499, 503, 504
Discipline. *See* Party discipline
Disproportion, *514g*; between agricultural and industrial prices, 51, 71, 78-79, 98, 122, 132-33, 304, 332, 385, 499; between supply and demand, 333-34. *See also* Scissors
Dmitrev, T., 484
Dneprostroi, 222-23, 409
Dogadov, A., 356, *514g*
Donbas, 88, 346
"Double bookkeeping," 197-98
Drobnis, Ya., 484
Dual power, 303, 489, 492, 502-03
Dvores, 411
Dybenko, P., 286

ECCI, 293, 405, 412, *514g;* plenums: sixth (May 1926), 195; seventh (November 1926), 173, 174, 190, 195, 197, 369-70, 374, 384; eighth (May 1927), 224, 234, 244, 247, 371, 406, 408. *See also* Comintern
Education, 316, 320, 363
1848 revolutions, 146, 226, 369, *514g*
18 Brumaire (Nov. 9-10, 1799), 260, *514g*
Eight-hour day, 311, 318, 420, 430. *See also* Seven-hour day
Electoral rights, 95, 97, 104, 134, 241, 327, 342, 349, 443, 499. *See also* Soviet elections
Electrification, 156, 310, 323, 331, 340

Eltsin, B., 239
Engels, F., 131, 152, 178, 235, 273, 274, 361, 384
Equality, 93-94, 341-42, 353, 354, 360-61
Ercoli, 174, *514g*
Eshba, Ye., 484
Estonia, 242, 490, 501

Factionalism, 174, 281, 474; of majority, 86-87, 99, 106-07, 114-17, 251; of Opposition, 99, 106-07, 128-29, 163, 174-75, 190, 193, 224, 289-90, 386, 406, 407-08, 451, 482; causes of, 69, 75-76, 102, 106, 127-28, 294
Farmer-Labor Party (U.S.), 178, *514g*
Farmhands. *See* Agricultural workers
February revolution (1917), 171, 179, *514g*
Fedko, 286
Fedorov, G., 238, 484
Feng Yü-hsiang, 372, 440, *514g*
Filippov, I., 484
Finland, 376
"Fire Against the Left," 123, 231, 303, 308, 357, 377, 378, 461
Fischer, R., 126-27, 128, 197, 214, 215, 218, 256, 291, *514g*
Fishelev, 405, 440, 448, *514g*
Five-year plan, 348, 455, 458; Gosplan draft, 315, 319, 323, 332-34, 339, 431, 455; Vesenkha draft, 431, 456. *See also* Planning
Fonbershtein, 238
Foreign trade monopoly, 50, 58, 138-39, 309-10, 334-35, 338, 340, 365, 461, 496; Lenin on, 270, 282-83, 380, 500; Stalinists on, 179, 270, 282-83, 379, 461-62, 499-500
Fortin, I., 484
Foshkin, F., 238
France, 127, 128, 195, 197, 200-04,

207, 229, 252-53, 262-63, 284-85, 366, 376, 377; and tsarist debts, 379, 410, 433-36; Oppositionists in, 195, 200-04

French Revolution (1789), 17-18n, 146, 245, 258, 259-60, 263

Frumkin, M., 282

Gangster methods of Stalin-Bukharin faction, 392-93, 395, 437-38, 439-42, 446-47, 449, 463-65, 467-69, 475

General Council (British Trades Union Congress), 84-85, 196, 225, 228, 234, 376, 377, 381, 385, 407, 442, *515g*

General strike (Britain, 1926), 19, 20, 23, 61, 84-85, 134, 196, 216, 228, 235, 242, 365, 375, 378, 385, 407

Georgia, 136, 347, 349

Gerasimov, 280

Gerdovsky, 411, 417, 421, 424, 425

Germany, 203, 208, 265, 333, 336, 366; 1918 revolution, 143, 147; March action (1921), 178, *517g;* 1923 revolution, 131, 207, 217-18, 242, 378, 490, 501; Oppositionists in, 126-27, 128, 197, 214-21, 229, 291, 293, 377, 378

Gertik, A., 238, 483

Gertsberg, 238

Gessen, S., 238, 483

Ginsburg, L., 483

Glebor-Avilov, N., 250, *515g*

Golman, 254

Goloshchekin, 212, 440, 446

"Goods famine," 58, 122, 132, 230, 332, 333, 385, 456-58, 461, 499, *515g*

Gordon, N., 238, 483

Goryachev, V., 483

Gosizdat (State Publishers), 466

Gosplan, *See* State Planning Commission

GPU, 405, 467, 470, *515g*; and

Wrangel officer, 405, 411-12, 415-27, 438

Grain crisis (1927-28), 455, 457, 458, 460, 498

Great-power chauvinism, 344, 345, 349. *See also* National question

Greizha, P., 483

Griunshtein, 417, 421, 424, 425, 454, 468

Gulov, 150

Guralsky, 238, 483

Gusev, V., 58, 483

Gutman, 411

Gvozdyov, 373

Hankow (China), 227

Harvest, 275, 468; of 1924, 27; of 1925, 27, 79, 457; of 1926, 28, 48, 50, 78, 79, 132, 434, 457; of 1927, 28, 457

Hicks, G., 440, 442, *515g*

Hilferding, R., 375, *515g*

Hohenzollern, 147, 220

Housing problem, 78, 103, 230, 234, 311, 315, 319, 330, 331, 385

Hungary, 366

IFTU. *See* Amsterdam International

Ilyin, 484

Independent Labour Party (Britain), 196

India, 180, 196

Industrialization controversy, 47-55, 58, 76, 78-79, 103, 105, 110, 120, 122, 132, 137, 142, 182-83, 230, 315, 330-40, 385, 390, 392, 409, 430, 433, 435, 455-62, 498-99; and class differentiation, 49, 96, 104, 121, 133, 143, 231, 309, 324, 326. *See also* Superindustrializers

Insurrectionism, 265, 284-85, 301, 463, 476, 478-79. *See also* Clemenceau thesis

Intelligentsia, bourgeois, 344, 391

Intensity of labor, 313, 428
Internationalism, 86, 160-62, 180, 186-87, 191, 192, 199, 241, 245-46, 272-74, 280, 308, 356, 380, 491, 495-96
International situation, 19, 23-24, 84-85, 308, 365-80, 382, 386, 390, 406, 410, 433-36
Ireland, 196
Irkutsk, 360
Ishchenko, A., 484
Italy, 366, 377, 378
Ivanov, A., 484
Ivanov, V., 238, 484
Izvestia (News), 150, *515g*

Jacobins, 259-60, 263
Japan, 151, 366
Joffe, A., 470-72, *515g*
July Days (1917), 469

Kagalin, 484
Kaganovich, L., 95, 98, 116-17, 272, 274, 276, 279, 289, 352, 356, 359, 403, *515g*
Kakhanyan, 286
Kalinin, M., 281, 324, 355, 441, *515g*
Kamenev, L., 35-36, 39, 48-49, 93, 100, 129, 194, 250, 269, 295, 297, 301, 425, 449-51, 456, 460, 468, 484, *515g*; vacillates, 165, 463; removed from leadership, 90-91, 114, 130, 254, 470; capitulates to Stalin, 488, 493, 502, 504-07
Kaminsky, G., 74, 356, *515g*
Kanatchikov, 250
Kanatchikova, 238
Kaplinskaya, 411
Karin, 411
Kaspersky, 484
Katalynov, I., 484
Katta, M., 238
Katz, I., 215, 236, 377, *515g*
Kautsky, K., 136, 140, 143, 151, 153, 178, 179, 180, 375, 376, *515g*
Kavtaradze, S., 238, 484

Kazakhstan, 210-13, 347
Kerensky, A., 85, 442, 492, *515g*
Khachkov, D., 484
Kharitonov, M., 239
Kharitonov, N., 281, 484
Kirov, S., 356, *515g*
KMT. *See* Kuomintang
Kolarov, V., 173, 175, 186, 188, 189, *515-16g*
Kollontai, A., 250, *516g*
Komandir, 484
Komsomol. *See* Communist League of Youth
Kondratiev, N., 356, 440, *516g*
Konkova, A., 484
Kopp, 250
Korolev, A., 238, 484
Korsch, K., 126, 128, 214, 215, 221, 236, 377, *516g*
Korshunov, Ye., 484
Kosarev, A., 450, *516g*
Kosior, V., 250, *516g*
Kospersky, I., 238
Kostritsky, I., 238, 484
Kotov, 246
Kovalenko, P., 238
Kovalevsky, 484
Kozlova-Passek, 238
KPD. *See* Communist parties: Germany
Kraevsky, 250
Krasovskaya, M., 484
Krestinsky, N., 250, 298, *516g*
Kris, 442
Kronstadt mutiny, 146, 259, *516g*
Krupskaya, N., 74, 93, 100, 126, 128, 131, 240, *516g*
Krysin, 484
Krzhizhanovsky, G. 455, *516g*
Kubyak, 446n
Kuibyshev, V., 86-87, 230, 232, 281, *516g*
Kuklin, 238, 484
Kulaks, 47-48, 80, 103, 110, 123, 388, *516g*; enfranchised, 95-100, 104, 134, 327, 342, 349, 443, 449;

favored by state, 79, 80, 88, 134, 169, 304-05, 314, 322-23, 335, 435; increasing influence of, 76, 104, 109, 121, 124, 133, 191, 230, 231, 232, 262, 303, 308, 324-29, 337, 339, 342, 344, 385, 392, 459-61; pressure on, 28, 443-44, 455, 464; and Soviet power, 302-03, 306, 368, 379, 382

Kuomintang, 20-22, 104, 225, 227, 369, 371, 375, 381, 386, *516g*

Kuusinen, O., 173, 406, 413, 440, *516g*

Kuzmin, N., 398, 398n, 399n *516g*

Labor Code, 74, 311, 316, 319, 430, 431, 432

Labor productivity, 310, 313, 318, 334

La Follette, R., 178, *516-17g*

Land rental, 325, 327

Lashevich, M., 73, 76, 82, 84, 90, 91, 92, 100, 102, 116, 288, 484, *517g*

Lashuk, 468

Latvia, 376

Law of socialist accumulation, 56, 57-59

Law of uneven development, 131, 152-53, 155, 179-80, 187, 278

Law of value, 56, 57-59

Lazko, M., 238

Left Communists (1918), 265, 266, 278-79, *517g*

Left-Wing Communism (Lenin), 378

Lelevich, A., 238

Lelozol, P., 484

Lenin, V.I., 84, 86, 101, 129, 136, 147, 176, 177, 178, 180, 192, 193, 207, 216, 220, 241, 311, 321, 334, 341, 344, 372-73, 376, 380, 381, 392, *517g*; on Bukharin, 414; on cooperatives, 155, 323, 329; on dictatorship of party, 70, 353; on electrification, 156, 310, 323; on equality, 93, 341, 360; on foreign trade monopoly, 270, 282-83, 380, 500; illness and death of, 31, 74, 107, 116, 270, 272, 308, 403, 441; on international revolution, 147-48, 193, 380, 384; on Kronstadt, 259, 260; maneuvering by, 307, 389, 505; on national question, 213, 347-49; on NEP, 302-03, 306, 402, 402n; on opportunism, 378, 389; on party democracy, 82, 232-33, 236, 247, 270, 294, 350, 352, 353, 358, 388, 482, 483; on party leadership, 89, 92, 107, 110, 117, 233, 247-48, 255, 265, 266, 285, 361, 441; on peasantry, 143-44, 146, 149, 150-51, 154, 181, 232, 260, 309, 322, 380, 384; relations with Trotsky, 281-83, 288-89; on *smychka*, 104, 110, 176, 322; on socialism, 155-56, 310, 323, 330; on socialism in one country, 57, 131, 151-55, 160, 184, 186, 191, 272, 273, 274, 276-79, 384; on Stalin, 110, 179, 347, 349, 355, 413-14, 441, 465; on state, 81, 167-68, 235, 341; Testament of, 92, 110, 285, 354, 355, 361, 413-14, 441-42, 465, 478, *517g*; on Thermidor, 258-59, 261-62, 263, 391; on war, 85, 382, 386

Leningrad Opposition (1925), 15, 35-44, 70, 87, 88, 90, 105, 110-11, 116, 127, 137, 145, 245, 387, 507. *See also* Zinovievists

Lenin levy (1924), 30, 350, *517g*

Lepse, 249

Levin, V., 484

Lifshits, B., 238

Lilina, Z., 484

Liquidators, 205, 207, 217, 373, *517g*

Lithuania, 23

Lizdin, G., 92, 238, 269, 295, 301, 484

Lobanov, G., 484

Lobashev, G., 238

Locarno pact (October 1925), 19

Lomov, 442

Lozovsky, S., *517g*

Lubin, G., 484

MacDonald, R., 85, 143
Makarov, P., 484
Makhno, N., 146, *517g*
Maksimov, 411
Maleta, V., 238
Maltser, B., 238
Malyuta, V., 484
Maneuvering, 307, 379, 389-90, 435-36, 505
Manuilsky, D., 177, *517g*
Maretsky, G., 225, 258, 351, 449, *518g*
Martov, J., 441, *518g*
Martynov, A., 225, 237, 308, 369, 370, 372-73, 379, 381, 406, 440, 445, *518g*
Marx, K., 131, 152, 176, 178, 196, 207, 232, 263, 273, 274, 341, 361, 384
Maslow, A., 126-27, 128, 197, 215, 218, 256, 291, 293, *518g*
Maslow-Fischer-Urbahns group (Germany), 126-27, 128, 214, 215
Maten, G., 238
Mdivani, P., 250, *518g*
Medvedev, S., 101, 104-05, 127, 129, 131, *518g*
Mehring, F., 178, *518g*
Melnichansky, G., 356, *518g*
Mensheviks, 113, 126, 176, 177, 260, 299, 373, 383, 428, 437, *518g*; join RCP, 30, 33, 225, 351, 353, 359, 379; and counterrevolution, 88-89, 98, 151, 308, 312, 373, 376, 402, 492, 493; in Britain, 216, 240-41; in China, 368-70, 371, 372, 386, 490, 502
Menzhinsky, V., 411, 418, 422, 425-26, 438, *518g*
Metal Workers Union, 249
Meyer, E., 412, *518g*
Mikoyan, A., 356, 460, *518g*
"Military conspiracy," 271, 286-87, 405, 415-27, 438, 446, 448
Military Opposition (1919), 271, 285-86, *518g*

Military problems, 270-71, 285
Military Revolutionary Council, 33, 287
Milner, Kh., 484
Milyukov, P., 167, 168, *518-19g*
Minichev, A., 238, 484
Moiseyenko, 146, 148
Molotov, V., 81, 95, 96, 97, 207, 265-66, 267, 271, 281, 326, 342-43, 352, 359, 403, 453, 454, *519g*
Monatte, P., 195, 203, *519g*
Mongolia, 409
Monopoly of foreign trade. *See* Foreign trade monopoly
Monroe Doctrine, 178, 183, *519g*
Mrachkovsky, S., 270, 415, 417, 421, 424, 425, 440, 445, 447, 454, *519g*
Muralov, N., 92, 100, 238, 269, 271, 280, 295, 301, 456, 468, 484
Mussolini, B., 127

Nalivaiko, 484
Natanson, M., 484
National question, 179, 210-13, 344-49
Naumov, I., 238, 484
Nazimov, A., 238
Nechaev, 440
NEP (New Economic Policy), 49, 56, 106, 127, 229, 277, 379, 392, *519g*; and bourgeoisie, 98, 101, 104, 138, 151, 167-68, 234-35, 258, 302, 306, 344-45, 385, 390; and bureaucratism, 66, 83, 93-94, 341; discussion in party over, 136-37, 146-47, 148, 149, 151
NEPmen, 230, 235, 262, 302-03, 306, 307, 339, 341, 342, 379, 382, 388, ·459, 464, *519g*
Neumann, H., 379, 406, 440, *519g*
"New Course" resolution (December 5, 1923), 41, 64, 65, 69, 76, 408, 450
New York Times, 381
Nikolaev, A., 484
Nikolaev, N., 484
Nin, A., 412, *519g*

1905 revolution, *519g*
1923 Opposition, 43, 70, 87, 105, 109, 110, 115, 203, 245, 506-07; and peasants, 26, 387
Nonparty methods of bureaucracy, 40-41, 74-75, 114, 165, 246-47, 249, 387, 392-93, 410, 440, 442
Northern Caucasus, 324, 347, 352, 442, 507
Northern March (China), 434
Norway, 207

October Revolution (1917), 153, 167, 170, 171, 229, 278, 311, 340, 347, 373, 387, 433, 471, *519g*
Okhotnikov, 405, 411, 417, 421, 424, 425, *519g*
Old Bolsheviks (Old Guard), 107, 116, 131, 171, 238, 251, 308, 352, 391, 405
Opportunism: in Comintern, 104, 196-97, 219, 242, 378, 407; in party, 357, 387, 388-94, 439
Opposition. *See* United Opposition
Ordzhonikidze, G., 244, 252, 270, 275, 287, 289-90, 296, *519g*
Ossovsky, Ya., 127, 128-29, *520g*
Ostrovskaya, N., 238
Otzovists, 205, 207, *520g*

Painlevé, P., 253, 285, 399, *520g*
Panteleev, 289, *520g*
Paris Commune (1871), 340, 341
Party: apparatus, 37, 82, 87, 115, 171, 231, 246-48, 264, 353, 354, 356, 357, 360, 379, 389, 393, 404, 413, 489, 497-98; democracy, 61-72, 75, 79, 89, 108, 110, 113, 120-24, 232-33, 255, 293, 349, 355, 358-59, 392, 403-04, 408; discipline, 122-23, 224, 265, 359, 406, 407-12, 452, 454, 483; leadership, 89, 107-08, 110, 115, 117, 119, 254-55, 351, 361, 412-13, 414, 439, 440, 464; tasks, 29, 61, 66, 70-71, 113, 117, 120-24, 170, 285, 311, 321, 327-28, 341, 394, 400, 491, 496; unity, 89,

102, 107, 108, 112-19, 193, 235-37, 247, 248, 268, 295, 354, 357-58, 381, 388-94, 464, 476, 481-82, 503-04. *See also* AUCP; Bureaucratism in party; Central Committee; Press
Paul-Boncour, J., 376, *520g*
Paulson, I., 484
Peasantry, 26, 141-42, 144-46, 149-50, 154, 167-68, 172, 181, 191, 304-05, 322-30, 350, 351, 368, 382, 390; poor, 110, 121, 191, 231-32, 234, 304-05, 322, 324-28, 339, 344, 345, 368, 382, 435; middle, 80, 96, 98, 110, 134, 144, 146-47, 150, 191, 231, 232, 322, 325-26, 327, 328, 329, 344, 345, 355, 363. *See also* Agricultural workers; Agriculture; Class differentiation in village; Kulaks
Pepper, J., 173, 177-78, 379, 413, 440, 445, *520g*
Permanent revolution, 131, 145, 170-71, 176-77, 179, 193, 386-87
Persia, 366, 409
Personnel, 59, 338, 400, 441, 498
"Pessimism," 131, 132, 141-42, 162, 191, 206, 261, 306, 354, 435
Peterson, A., 92, 100, 238, 269, 295, 301, 411, 415, 417-18, 420, 422, 425, 456, 484
Petrovsky, D., 379, *520g*
Petrovsky, G., 116, 274, 356, 440, 441, *520g*
Petty bourgeoisie, 96-97, 103-04, 110, 134, 208-09, 262, 362-63, 390
Pilsudski, J., *520g*
Pitashko, 484
Pitt, W., 259, *520g*
Planning, 51, 54-55, 56, 59. *See also* Five-year plan
Platform of the Opposition. *See* United Opposition, platform of
Plekhanov, G., 373
Poland, 23, 61, 196, 197, 207, 229, 365-66, 377
Ponomarev, V., 484

Pood, *520g*
Poslednie Novosti (Latest News), *521g*
Postyshev, P., 246, *521g*
Potresov, 373
Pozdeeva, 238
Pravda (Truth), 120, 123-24, 174, 175, 224, 225, 236, 237, 258, 371-72; suppresses Opposition documents, 240, 244, 247, 254, 268, 281, 290, 291, 294, 353, 358, 386-87, 439, 474. *See also* Press
Preobrazhensky, E., 56, 57, 250, 412, 415, 440, 445, 448, 454, 468, 484, *521g*
Press, 351, 400; suppresses China news, 371-72, 384; suppresses Opposition documents, 124, 244, 247, 254, 268, 281, 290, 291, 294, 353, 358, 386-87, 439, 474. *See also Pravda*
Price policy, 79, 105, 304, 312, 337, 385, 409; for grain, 142, 327, 328; for industrial goods, 51-52, 142, 230, 231, 331-32, 337-38; domestic vs. world prices, 331, 333, 334
Primakov, V., 238, 270
Primitive accumulation of capital, 138, 309. *See also* Capitalism, growth of
Problems of Leninism (Stalin), 153, 157, 188
Productivity of labor. *See* Labor productivity
Profintern (Red International of Labor Unions—RILU), 95, 104, 105, 129, 155, 412, *521g*
Provisional Government (1917), 179, *521g*
Psalmopevnev, 238
Pugh, A., 192, *521g*
Purcell, A., 84, 85, 131, 134, 192, 234, 299, 354, 389, 407, 409, 440, 442, *521g*
Putna, 270
Pyatakov, Ya., 92, 100, 112, 129, 238, 250, 269, 295, 484, 488, *521g*

Radchenko, 287
Radek, K., 112, 225, 238, 484, 488, *521g*
Rafail, *521g*
Rafail, R., 484
Rafes, M., 379, 440, 445, *521g*
Rakovsky, Kh., 250, 269, 295, 301, 405, 433, 449, 450, 451, 456, 470, 484, 488, *521g*
"Rationalization of production," 224-25, 232, 313, 318, 340, 430
Ravich, O., 238, 484
Rem, M., 238, 484
Red Army, 270-71, 285, 287-88, 382-83
"Regime of economy," 59, 73-74, 78, 84, 103, 232, 320, 338, 430, *521g*
Reingold, I., 484
Remmele, H., 173, 175-76, *521-22g*
"Resettlement policy," 210, 211
Restoration tendencies: bourgeois-republican, 167, 168; monarchist-landlord, 168. *See also* Bourgeoisie
Riese, M., 174, *522g*
Right, shift to, 193, 231, 234, 235, 242-43, 302-03, 308, 355-56, 384, 442-43, 444-48, 464, 496, 497-98, 499, 500, 504, 507. *See also* Bukharin-Rykov tendency
RILU. *See* Profintern
Robespierre, M., 17-18n, 263
Rosenberg, A., 377, *522g*
Rosmer, A., 195, 203, *522g*
Rotskan, 484
RSDLP (Russian Social Democratic Labor Party), 205, *522g*
Rudzutak, Ya., 114, 277, 279, 280, 332, *522g*
Rul (Rudder), 437, 442, *522g*
Rumania, 365
Rumyantsev, V., 484
Rykov, A., 116-17, 232, 275, 276, 307, 338, 355, 397, 488, 498, *522g*; economic theses of, 47, 130, 132, 154, 455, 458; as leader of right wing, 47, 254, 355-56, 500. *See*

also Bukharin-Rykov tendency

Rykov group, 498, 500

Ryzhov, 484

Sadovskaya, 238

Sadyrin, 356

Safarov, G., 238, 484

Safronov, P., 484

Samsonov, M., 238

Sapronov, T., 205, *522g*

Sarkis, 238, 440, 445, 454, 484

Savinkov, B., 418, *522g*

Schwartz, E., 214, 215, 221, 377, *522g*

Scissors: between domestic and world prices, 304; between industrial and agricultural prices, 168, 304, 323, *522g;* between wholesale and retail prices, 50, 58, 98, 304, 305-06, 312, 332, 337-38. *See also* Disproportion

Second International, 196, 375, 376, 381, 386, 390, 391, 409. *See also* Social Democracy

Semashko, 250

Semenov, P., 484

Semenov, S., 484

Senkov, Z., 484

"Septemvirate," 86-87, 114, *522-23g*

Serebryakov, L., 238, 412, 415, 440, 445, 448, 454, 484, *523g*

Serge, V., 301, 405

Sergeev, A., 238

Seven-hour day, 428-32, 437, 443, 479. *See also* Eight-hour day

Shanghai massacre (China, April 12, 1927), 21-22, 224, 225, 226

Sharov, Ya., 239, 484, 412, 440, 445, 454

Shatskin, L., 273-74, *523g*

Shcherbakov, 415-27, 438, 441, *523g*

Shepsheleva, M., 238, 484

Shkiryatov, 244

Shlyapnikov, A., 127, 129, 131, *523g*

Shmidt, 440

Shtikhgold, 440

Shurygin, A., 239, 484

Shuster, A., 239

Shvernik, N., 274, 279, 280, 446, 446n, *523g*

Skrypnik, N., 273, 438, 439, 440, 441, 442, 443, 444, *523g*

Skvortsov-Stepanov, I., 438, 441, 444, 448, *523g*

Slepkov, A., 117, 117n, 351, 429, 449, *523g*

Smenovekhovites, 308, *523g*

Smeral, B., 189, 379, 406, 413, 440, 445, *523g*

Smilga, I., 238, 244, 269, 288, 295, 301, 411, 415, 417-18, 420, 422, 427, 436, 456, 467, 468, 470, 484, 488, *523g*

Smirnov, A., 74, 355, *523g*

Smirnov, I., 238, 484, *523-24g*

Smirnov, V., 205, *524g*

Smychka, 26, 47, 49-50, 79, 80, 104, 110, 117, 191, 199, 324, 331, 385, 390, 498, *524g*

Social Democracy, 140, 147, 192, 264, 367, 373, 374, 376-78, 380-81, 386, 428, 501, 502. *See also* Amsterdam International; Second International

"Social Democratic deviation," 130, 132, 133, 134, 135, 136, 188, 189, 193, 343, 357, 386

Socialism in one country, 56, 86, 105-06, 110, 151-63, 172, 179-88, 229, 242-43, 254, 270, 335-36, 375, 380, 434-35, 465; Lenin on, 57, 131, 151-55, 160, 184, 186, 191, 272, 273, 274, 276-79, 384; Stalin on, 24-25, 153, 156-57, 162, 179, 184-88, 271-80

Social Revolutionaries, 30, 33, 88-89, 167, 322, 374, 376, 383, 391, *524g;* Lefts, 266, 284, 374; join RCP, 351, 353, 359

Sokolnikov, G., 39, 129, 210, *524g*

Sokolov, A., 238, 484

Solovyov, K., 92, 269, 295, 301

Solovyov, M., 484

Sosnovsky, L., 238, 484

Sotsialichesky Vestnik (Socialist

Herald), 283, 437, 439, 441, 442, *524g*

South Africa, 180

South America, 180

Souvarine, B., 127, 128, *524g*

Soviet democracy. *See* Workers' democracy

Soviet economy, 47-55, 56-60, 106, 169, 229, 275, 338-40, 455-62, 498-99; and world economy, 25, 56, 57-59, 156-59, 181-84, 191, 200, 332, 334-46, 435, 457-62, 498. *See also* Industrialization controversy

Soviet elections, 77, 95-100, 104, 122, 206. *See also* Electoral rights

Soviets, 311, 327, 340-44, 392; pressure of petty bourgeoisie on, 110, 121, 231, 259, 390; and "revitalization campaign," 326, 342; Soviet of Nationalities, 345, 349; in China, 227, 369, 371-72

Soviet state, 302, 303, 304, 322, 340, 341, 342-42; apparatus of, 81, 109, 171, 172, 231, 302, 303, 304, 312, 323, 341-43, 344, 353, 356, 391, 497-98; bureaucratic deformations in, 162-63, 172, 235, 303-04, 312, 343, 344-46, 378-79, 384, 490; class character of, 135-43, 158-60, 162-63, 190-91, 192, 235, 384, 452, 482; relation of, to workers, 88, 104, 344, 490-91; and treaties with capitalists, 214, 220

Specialists (spetses), 93, 271, 346, 368, 391, 442, 444, *524g*

Spunde, 450

Stabilization of capitalism, 131, 134, 136, 160-61, 171, 177, 190, 192, 207, 216-19, 373-82, 384, 390

Stalin, J., 102, 130, 140, 144, 179, 184-86, 190, 218, 232, 254, 258, 338, 355, 356, 389, 400, 403, 465; *524g;* on China, 20-22, 240, 241, 354, 369, 371, 372, 389; on Dneprostroi, 222-23; on foreign trade monopoly, 179, 270, 282-83; Lenin on, 110, 179, 347, 349, 355, 413-14,

441, 465; on party leadership, 116-17, 265, 266, 268; plan of, to eliminate Opposition, 35, 90-93, 118, 125, 126, 242-43, 244-45, 266-68, 296-97, 299-300, 357, 377-78, 387, 395, 409-10, 413, 415, 479, 480; on uneven development, 131, 152-53, 187. *See also* Dictatorship of party; Military Opposition; Socialism in one country; Stalin-Bukharin faction

Stalin-Bukharin faction, 57, 374, 380-81, 490, 499; on Britain, 228, 307, 381, 389, 400, 403; on China, 226-27, 241, 245, 255-56, 284, 307, 368-73, 379-80, 381, 389, 400, 403; frictions in, 70, 107-08, 116-17, 245, 355, 357, 444, 498, 500; leads party to right, 308, 310, 322-23, 329-30, 442-43, 444-48, 463, 489-90, 497-98; plan of, to eliminate Opposition, 90-92, 113-19, 377-78, 383-88, 409-10, 413, 497. *See also* Apparatus pressure methods; Gangster methods

Stalinists ("center group"), 109, 117, 252, 291, 298, 300, 377-78, 395, 442, 446, 447-48, 479; as tendency within ruling faction, 30-31, 112, 116, 118, 356-57, 389, 390, 391, 442, 498; try to force split, 393-94, 446-47, 452-54, 463-64, 466, 479, 480. *See also* Centrism

State Planning Commission (Gosplan), 282, 315, 319, 332, 334, 339, 431, 455, *524g*

Sten, I., 117, *524g*

Stepanov, 281

Stern, 173

Stetsky, A., 225, 351, *524g*

Stockholm Congress (1906), 126, 128, *524g*

Stomonyakov, 282

Stroilov. *See* Wrangel officer

Sukhanov, N., 153, *525g*

Sun Yat-sen, 370, *525g*

"Superimperialism," 180

"Superindustrializers," 58, 385, 435, 460
Supreme Council of the National Economy (Vesenkha), 36, 118, 154, 222, 431, 456, *525g*
Sweden, 207

Talberg, 275, 284, 285, 441
T'ang Sheng-chih, 372, *525g*
Tarasov, I., 484
Tardieu, A., 284, *525g*
Tarkhanov, O., 484
Tartakovskaya, F., 484
Tartaria, 347
Tax policy, 17, 26, 27, 47, 48, 51, 78, 79, 105, 133, 137, 142, 231-32, 304-05, 310, 327, 328, 337, 339, 435, 459, 500
Ter-Vaganyan, V., 238, 450, *525g*
Thälmann, E., 174, 405, 412, *525g*
Thermidor, 17, 17-18n, 172, 245, 258-64, 274, 289, 291, 293, 300, 303, 384, 389-90, 391, 396, 438, 446, 463, 464, 482, 489-509, *525g*
Third Duma (1907-08), 205, 207, *525g*
Thomas, J., 84, 85, 131, 134, 192, 407, *525g*
Tillett, B., 440
Tomsky, M., 15, 30, 116-17, 228, 290, 356, 444, 494, *525g*
Traders, private, 168-69, 304, 332, 385
Trade unions (Soviet), 317-21, 351, 356, 385; regime in, 233, 317, 320-21, 344, 392; role of, 81, 95-96; statutes of, 135; dispute over (1920), 146-47. *See also* AUCCTU
Transcaucasian Federation, 345
Treint, A., 173, 412, *525g*
"Triangle," 317, 489, *525g*
Trades Union Congress (Britain), *525g. See also* General Council
Triumvirate, 15, 31, 35, 101
Trotsky, L., 33, 92, 100, 129, 194, 238, 251, 269, 295, 301, 420, 427, 428, 436, 456, 484; accusations

against, 135-37, 141, 244, 271, 287, 291, 424-25; expelled from Central Committee, 244, 254, 291-92, 437, 439-40, 448; expelled from ECCI, 405, 412; expelled from party, 467, 470, 479; pre-Bolshevik period, 175-76, 178, 179; relations with Lenin, 109, 110-11, 150-51, 281-83, 288-89, 386-87
"Trotskyism," 109, 116, 117, 130-31, 135-36, 149, 173-75, 188, 193, 200, 271-73, 275, 280-81, 283, 386-88, 439, 502-03, 506
Tsarist debts, 379, 410, 433-36
Tsaturov, A., 238
Tseretelli, I., 85, 442, *525g*
Tsibulsky, Z., 25, 239
Tsikhon, 468, 469
Tumanov, 238
Turkestan, 210
Turkey, 366
Turkmenistan, 210, 346, 347
Tuzhikov, 484
Tverskoi, 415-27, *526g*
"Twenty-one points," *526g*
"Two parties," 103, 125, 127, 129, 163, 268, 271, 285, 291, 293-94, 354, 377, 390-92, 393-94, 446, 467, 473, 479-80, 483, 485, 486, 496, 502-03, 504

United Opposition, 89, 103, 163, 240-41, 473-80, 485; accusations against, 101-08, 112, 118, 120, 124, 132, 135, 141-42, 231, 232, 244, 249-51, 256, 265-69, 271, 280, 284, 332, 354, 357, 383-88, 389, 401, 405, 406, 415-17, 435, 436, 438, 467, 476; in Comintern, 125-28, 195-204, 214-21, 224, 229, 236, 237, 242, 291, 293, 378, 381, 386, 405, 412; countertheses of, 455-62, 509; defections from, 131, 165, 240, 357, 488; differences in, 61, 109-11, 225, 387; expulsion of,

112, 116-17, 294, 488, 496; formation of, 49, 245; platform of, 301, 357, 395, 405, 410-12, 413, 414, 428, 430, 437, 440-41, 445, 448, 449, 451-52, 453, 455; printshop, 415-27, 438, 449-50; private meetings, 449-50, 474-75, 476, 477, 508; reprisals against, 87-89, 244, 246-48, 267, 386, 395, 415, 439-40, 445-46, 463-66, 567-69, 475; sympathy for, in party, 383, 437, 447, 453-54, 473, 478, 480; tactics of, 16, 298-99, 452-54, 507-08; tasks of, 16, 17, 163, 357-58, 391-94, 412, 488, 494-501, 503-04, 509; "Declaration of the Thirteen" (July 1926), 73, 110, 111, 240, 439, 506; Declaration of October 16 (1926), 163-64, 174, 175, 193, 224, 288, 292, 507-08. "Declaration of the 84" (May 1927), 224, 244, 246, 250, 298; Statement of August 8, 1927, 291-92, 296-97, 407, 507-08; Statement of November 14, 1927, 473, 476, 477, 479, 507-08; "Statement of the 121" (December 3, 1927), 481-84

Ufimtsev, 250

Uglanov, N., 35-36, 44, 62-71, 94, 112, 116-17, 117n, 120, 352, 359, 403, *526g*

Ukhanov, 281

Ukonen, 484

Ukraine, 146, 346

Ultimatists, 205, 207, *526g*

Ultraleftism, 104, 192, 198, 199-200, 215, 219, 316, 318

Unemployment, 103, 154-55, 230, 232, 234, 313, 315-16, 318, 330, 331, 385, 429

United front policy, 190, 192, 199, 203, 376-77, 385

United States, 197, 333, 365, 366, 376

Unshlicht, J., 286, 438, *526g*

Urals, 88

Urbahns, H., 126-27, 128, 214, 215, 218, 293, 377-78, *526g*

Uritsky, 286

Ustryalov, N., 30, 234-35, 260, 267, 303, 308-10, 349, 356, 368, 402, 402n, 440, 446, 492, 497, 503, 504, *526g*

Utkin, K., 484

Valentinov, G., 238

Vardin, I., 238, 483

Vareikis, J., 399, *526g*

Vasilev, I., 238, 440

Versailles pact, 214

Vesenkha. *See* Supreme Council of the National Economy

Vienna, 375, 502

Vilensky (Sibiryakov), 238

Visnevskaya, 238

Viviani, R., 253, *526g*

Vladimirov, 411

Vodka monopoly, 52, 68, 313, 339

Voikov, P., 23-34, 376, *526g*

Volin, 468

Vorobev, V., 238, 414, 483

Voroshilov, K., 271, 274, 276, 277, 286, 287, 440, 442, 443, *526g*

Vrachev, I., 238, 483

Vujović, V., 238, 405, 406, 408, 412, 440, 483, *526g*

Weber, H., 126, 128, *527g*

Wedding Opposition (Germany), 126

White Guards, 146, 368, 376

Women, 313-14, 319

Workers': conditions, 28, 55, 68, 73-74, 76, 78, 84, 93-94, 103, 121, 230, 232, 234, 311-21, 330, 339, 385, 390, 392, 428-32, 433; democracy, 40-43, 45, 70, 72, 75, 81, 344, 353, 395; moods, 165-72, 206-07, 242, 491, 495; relation with AUCP, 231, 232-33, 368, 382; social weight, 98, 122, 124, 202, 208-09, 312, 390. *See also* Housing problem; "Regime of economy"; Unemployment; Wages

Workers Opposition, 101, 127, 129, *527g*

Work norms, 319

World War I, 181, 373-74, 391

Wrangel, P., Wrangel officer, 405-06, 411-12, 415-27, 436, 438, 446, 476, *527g*

Yagoda, H., 426

Yakovlev, M., 484

Yanson, N., 87, 447, *527g*

Yaroslavl station "demonstration," 244, 249, 285, 289, 290, 296, *527g*

Yaroslavsky, E., 87, 244, 271, 280, 287, 397, 408, 416, 422-23, 443, 446, 446n, *527g*

Yefretov, Ye., 484

Yelkovich, N., 238

Yelkovich, Ya., 484

Yemelyanov, N., 238

Yevdokimov, G., 92, 129, 238, 251, 269, 295, 301, 420, 425, 427, 436, 456, 470, 484, *527g*

Yezhov, P., 238, 484

Young Communist International, 188

Youth, 83, 171, 188, 230-31, 313-14, 320, 362-64; Bukharinist, 225, 227, 258, 351, 355, 372, 429, 449

Yudenich, 471

Yugoslavia, 366

Zaks-Gladnev, 238

Zalutsky, P., 287-88, 289, 484, *527g*

Zetkin, Klara, 217, *527-28g*

Zhirov, 359

Zhuk, A., 238, 484

Zinoviev, G., 93, 96, 100, 101, 112-13, 129, 194, 238, 244, 246, 249, 251, 269, 275, 283, 290, 295, 301, 427, 428, 436, 456, 484, *528g*; capitulates, 485-86, 493, 502, 504-07; on China, 226, 240, 244, 301; expelled from party, 467, 470, 479; removed from leadership, 73, 90-91, 114, 130, 173, 237, 244, 254, 270, 275, 291-92, 437, 439-40, 448; at seventh ECCI (November 1926), 173, 174, 179, 186; vacillates, 165, 463; and Wrangel officer affair, 411, 415, 417-18, 420, 423, 425

Zinovievists, 125, 126, 437; acknowledge 1923 Opposition was right, 86-87, 506; capitulate, 485-86, 488, 493, 502, 504-07; and "Trotskyism," 22-23, 116, 130-31; vacillate, 165, 291, 298-99, 452, 463, 473. *See also* Leningrad Opposition

Zionists, 353

Zorin, 238, 484

Zverev, D., 484